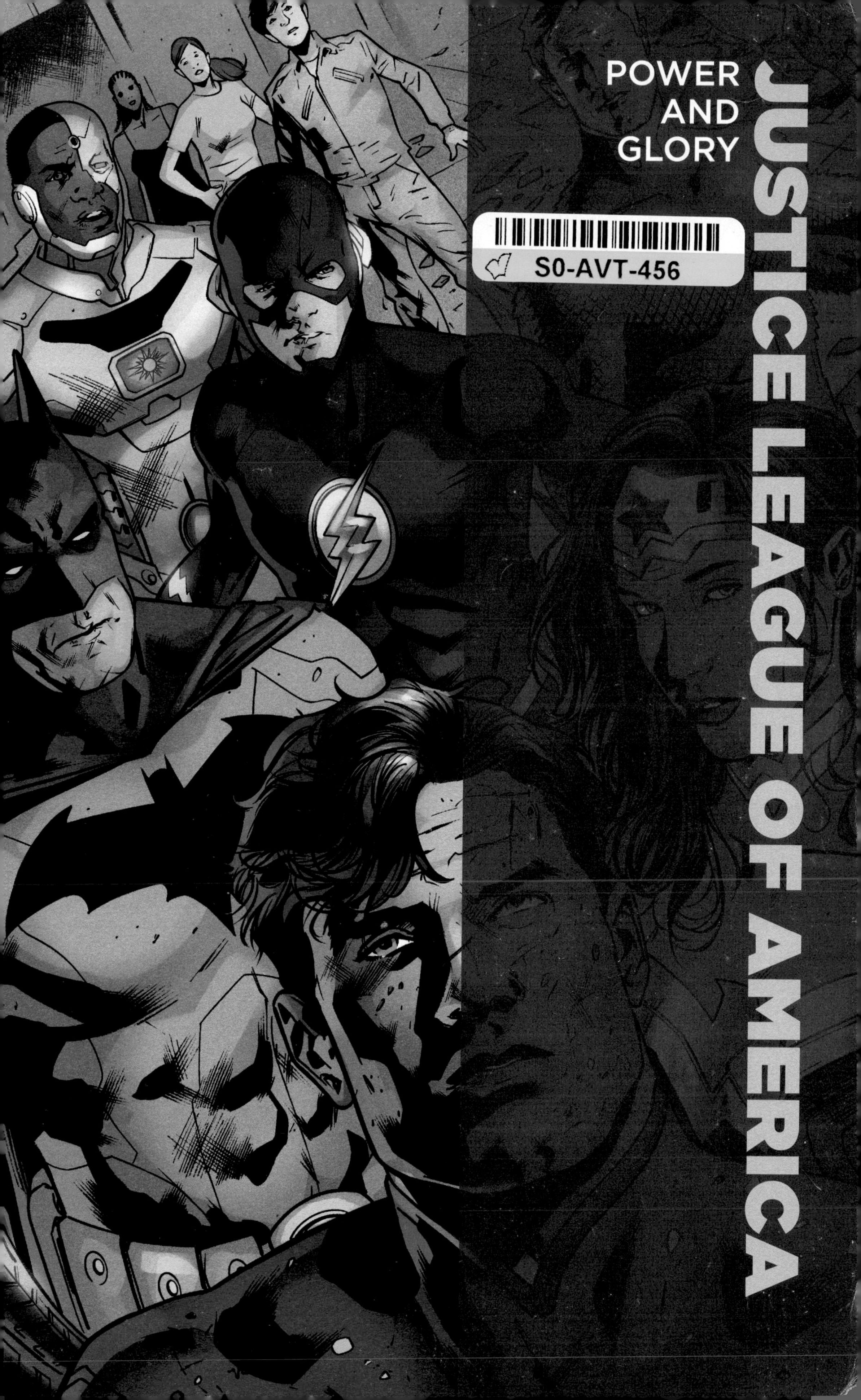
POWER
AND
GLORY
JUSTICE LEAGUE OF AMERICA

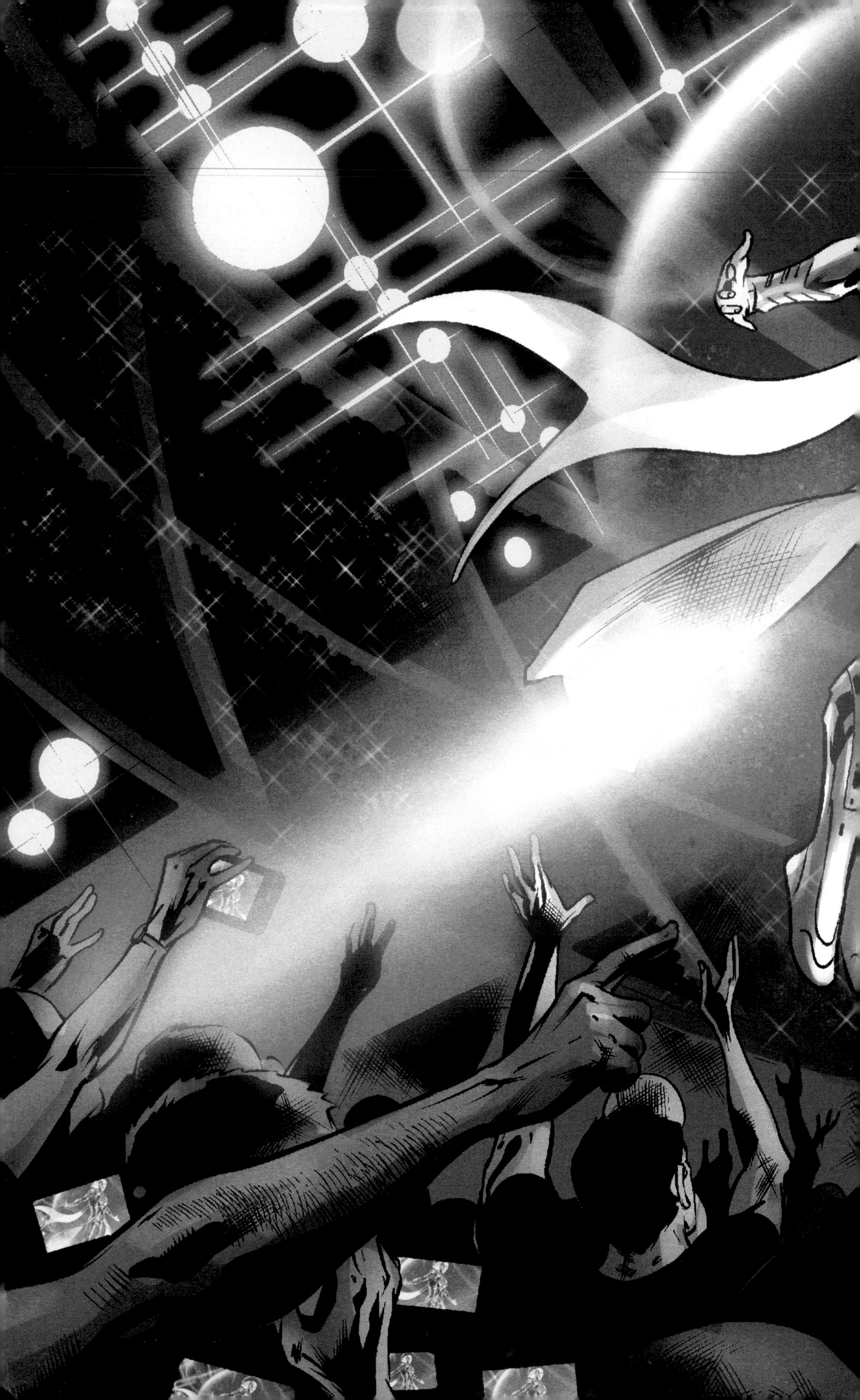

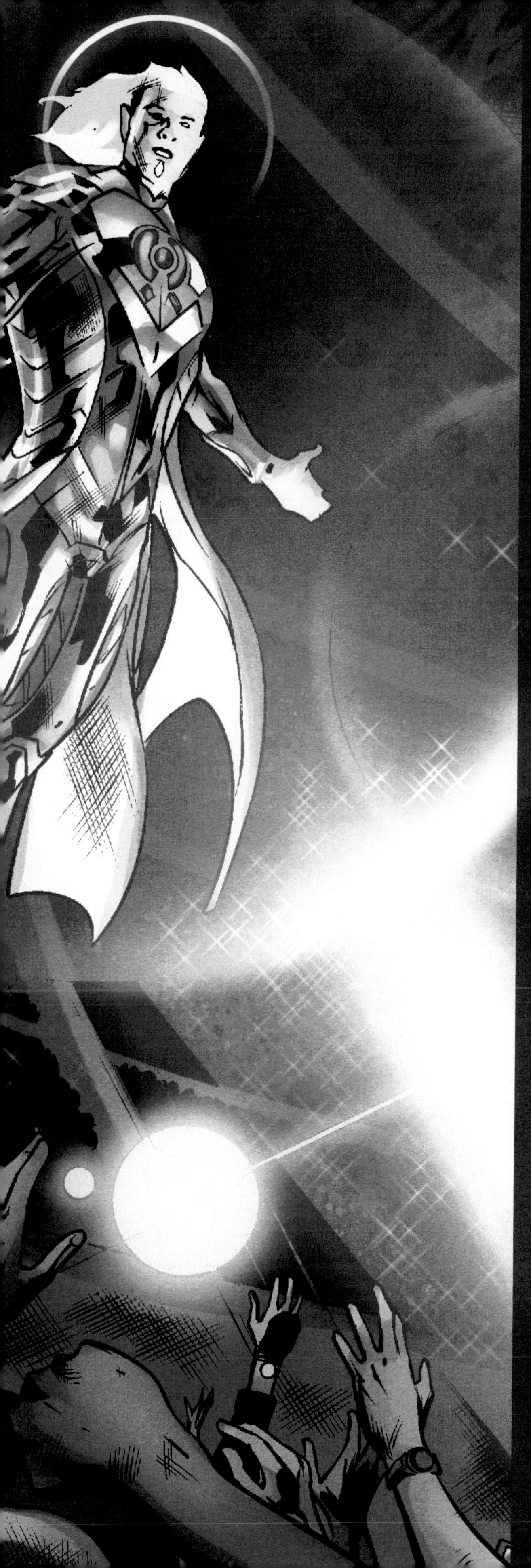

JUSTICE LEAGUE OF AMERICA

POWER AND GLORY

WRITTEN BY
BRYAN HITCH
TONY BEDARD

ART BY
BRYAN HITCH
DANIEL HENRIQUES
ANDREW CURRIE
WADE von GRAWBADGER
TOM DERENICK
SCOTT HANNA

COLOR BY
ALEX SINCLAIR
JEROMY COX
JEREMIAH SKIPPER

LETTERS BY
CHRIS ELIOPOULOS
CLAYTON COWLES

ORIGINAL SERIES & COLLECTION COVER ART
BRYAN HITCH & ALEX SINCLAIR

SUPERMAN CREATED BY
JERRY SIEGEL & JOE SHUSTER
BY SPECIAL ARRANGEMENT WITH THE JERRY SIEGEL FAMILY

BRIAN CUNNINGHAM Editor – Original Series
AMEDEO TURTURRO and DIEGO LOPEZ Assistant Editors – Original Series
JEB WOODARD Group Editor – Collected Editions
ERIKA ROTHBERG Editor – Collected Edition
STEVE COOK Design Director – Books
DAMIAN RYLAND Publication Design

BOB HARRAS Senior VP – Editor-in-Chief, DC Comics
PAT McCALLUM Executive Editor, DC Comics

DIANE NELSON President
DAN DiDIO Publisher
JIM LEE Publisher
GEOFF JOHNS President & Chief Creative Officer
AMIT DESAI Executive VP – Business & Marketing Strategy, Direct to Consumer & Global Franchise Management
SAM ADES Senior VP & General Manager, Digital Services
BOBBIE CHASE VP & Executive Editor, Young Reader & Talent Development
MARK CHIARELLO Senior VP – Art, Design & Collected Editions
JOHN CUNNINGHAM Senior VP – Sales & Trade Marketing
ANNE DePIES Senior VP – Business Strategy, Finance & Administration
DON FALLETTI VP – Manufacturing Operations
LAWRENCE GANEM VP – Editorial Administration & Talent Relations
ALISON GILL Senior VP – Manufacturing & Operations
HANK KANALZ Senior VP – Editorial Strategy & Administration
JAY KOGAN VP – Legal Affairs
JACK MAHAN VP – Business Affairs
NICK J. NAPOLITANO VP – Manufacturing Administration
EDDIE SCANNELL VP – Consumer Marketing
COURTNEY SIMMONS Senior VP – Publicity & Communications
JIM (SKI) SOKOLOWSKI VP – Comic Book Specialty Sales & Trade Marketing
NANCY SPEARS VP – Mass, Book, Digital Sales & Trade Marketing
MICHELE R. WELLS VP – Content Strategy

JUSTICE LEAGUE OF AMERICA: POWER AND GLORY

DC Comics, 2900 West Alameda Ave., Burbank, CA 91505
Printed by LSC Communications, Kendallville, IN, USA. 2/2/18. First Printing.
ISBN: 978-1-4012-7800-7

Library of Congress Cataloging-in-Publication Data is available.

PEFC Certified

Printed on paper from
sustainably managed
forests, controlled
sources

PEFC/29-31-337   www.pefc.org

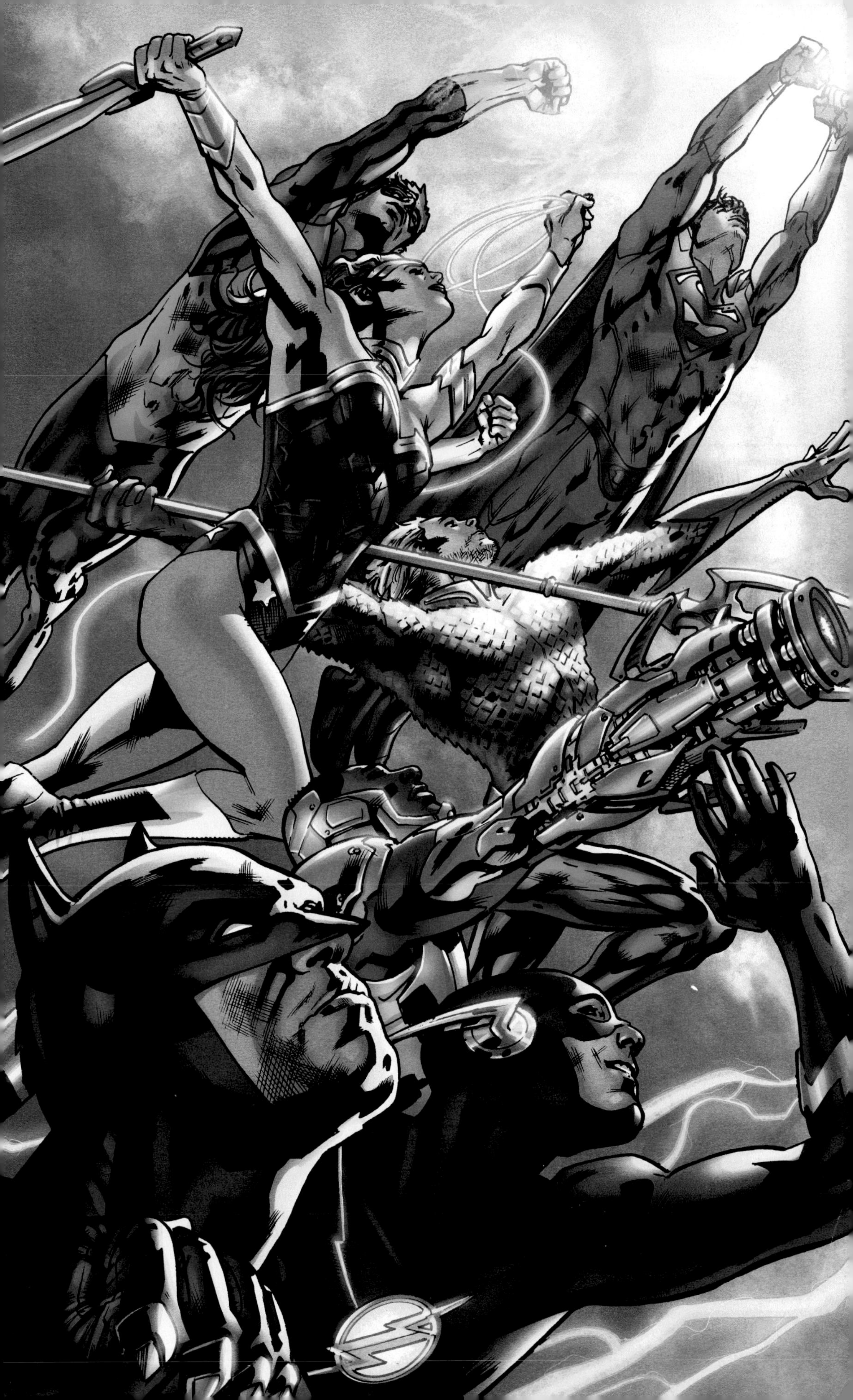

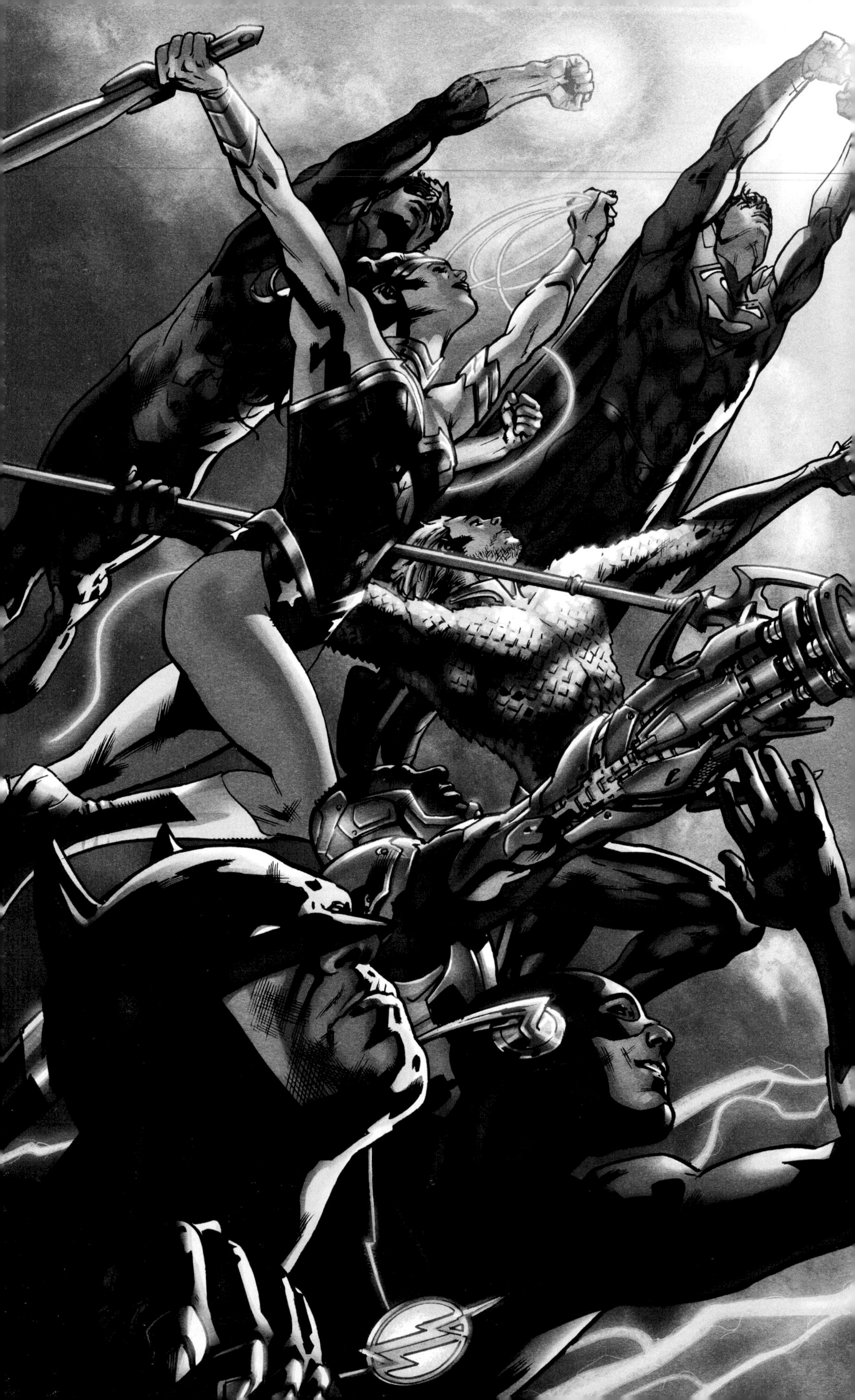

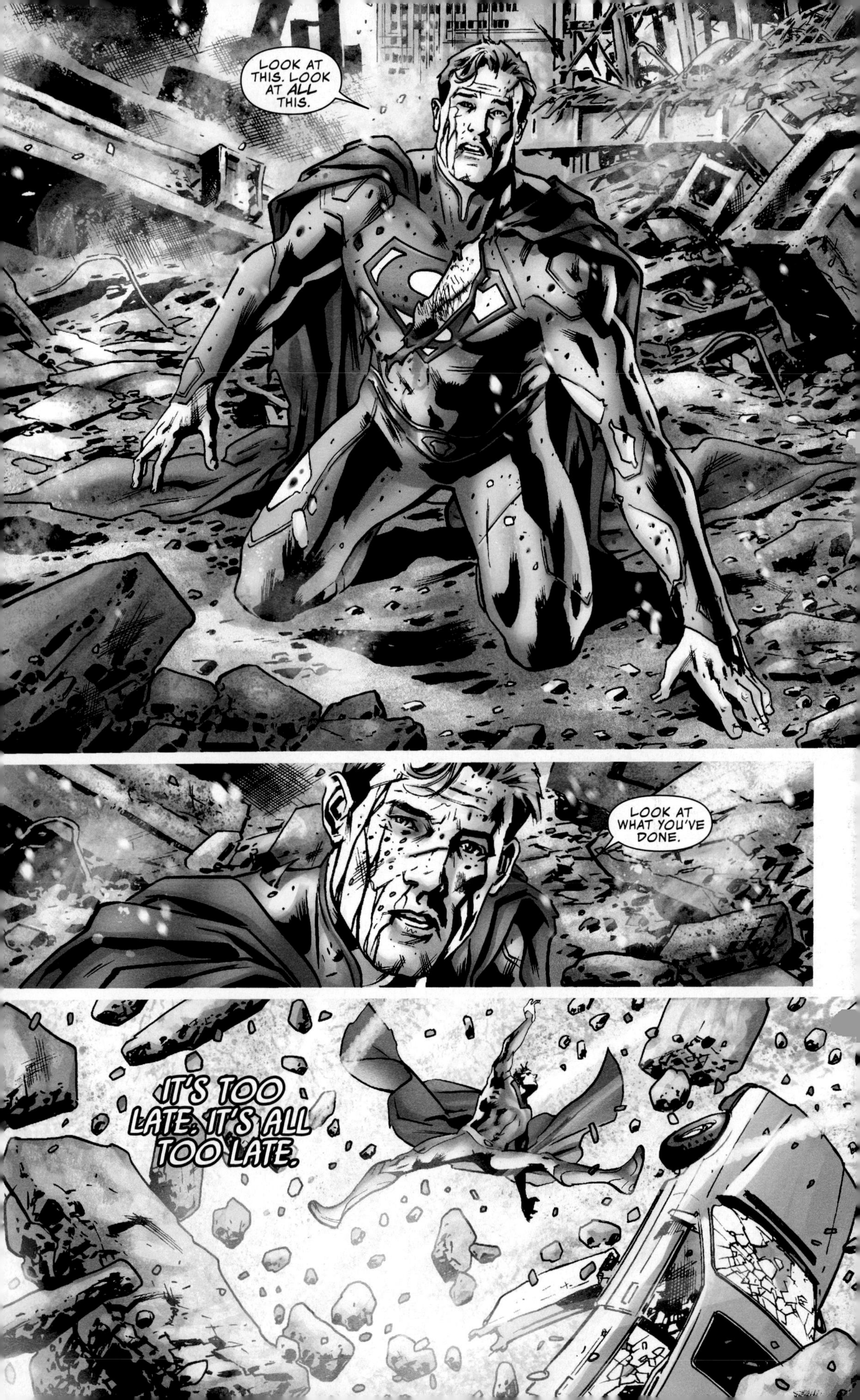
LOOK AT THIS. LOOK AT ALL THIS.
LOOK AT WHAT YOU'VE DONE.
IT'S TOO LATE. IT'S ALL TOO LATE.

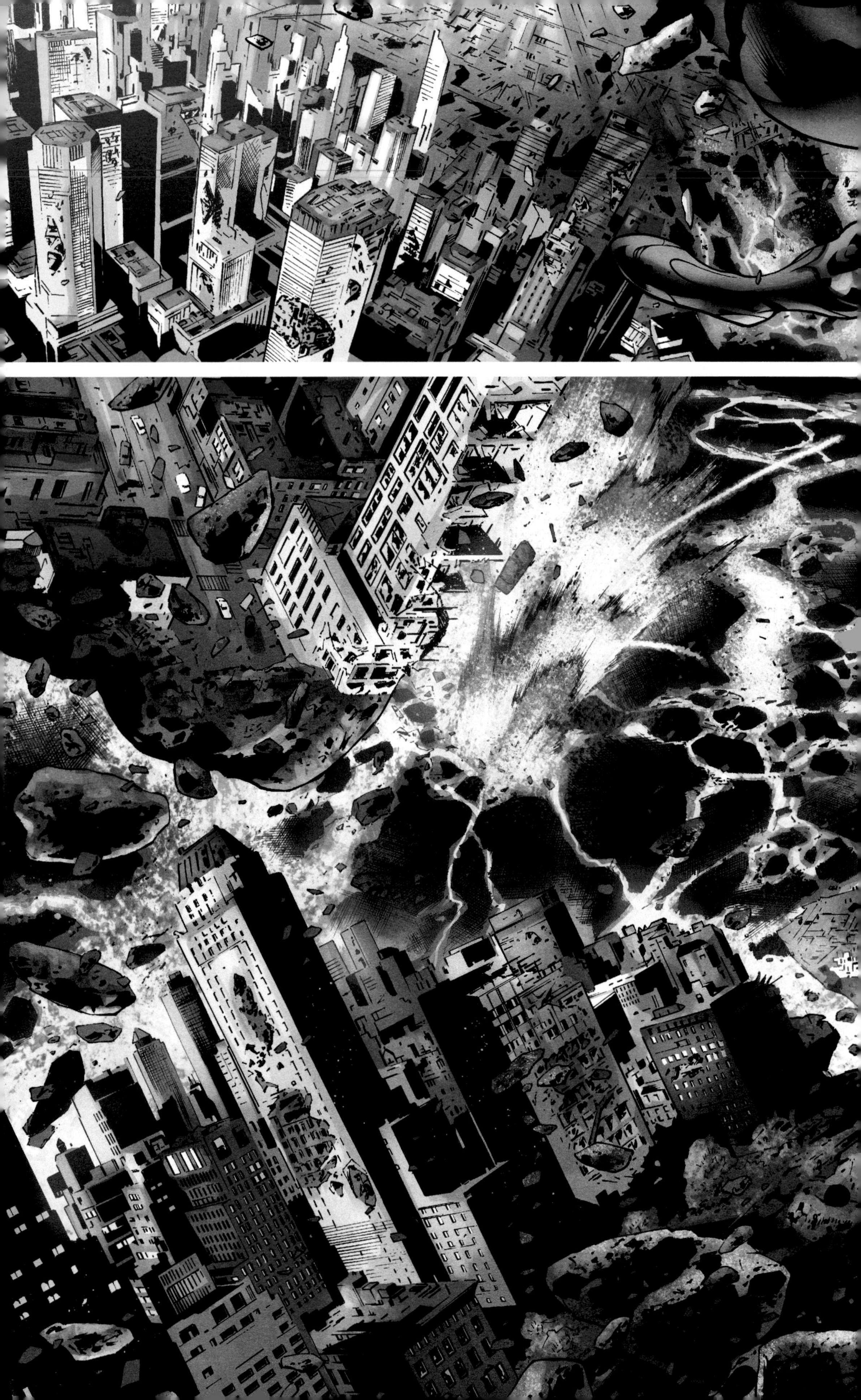

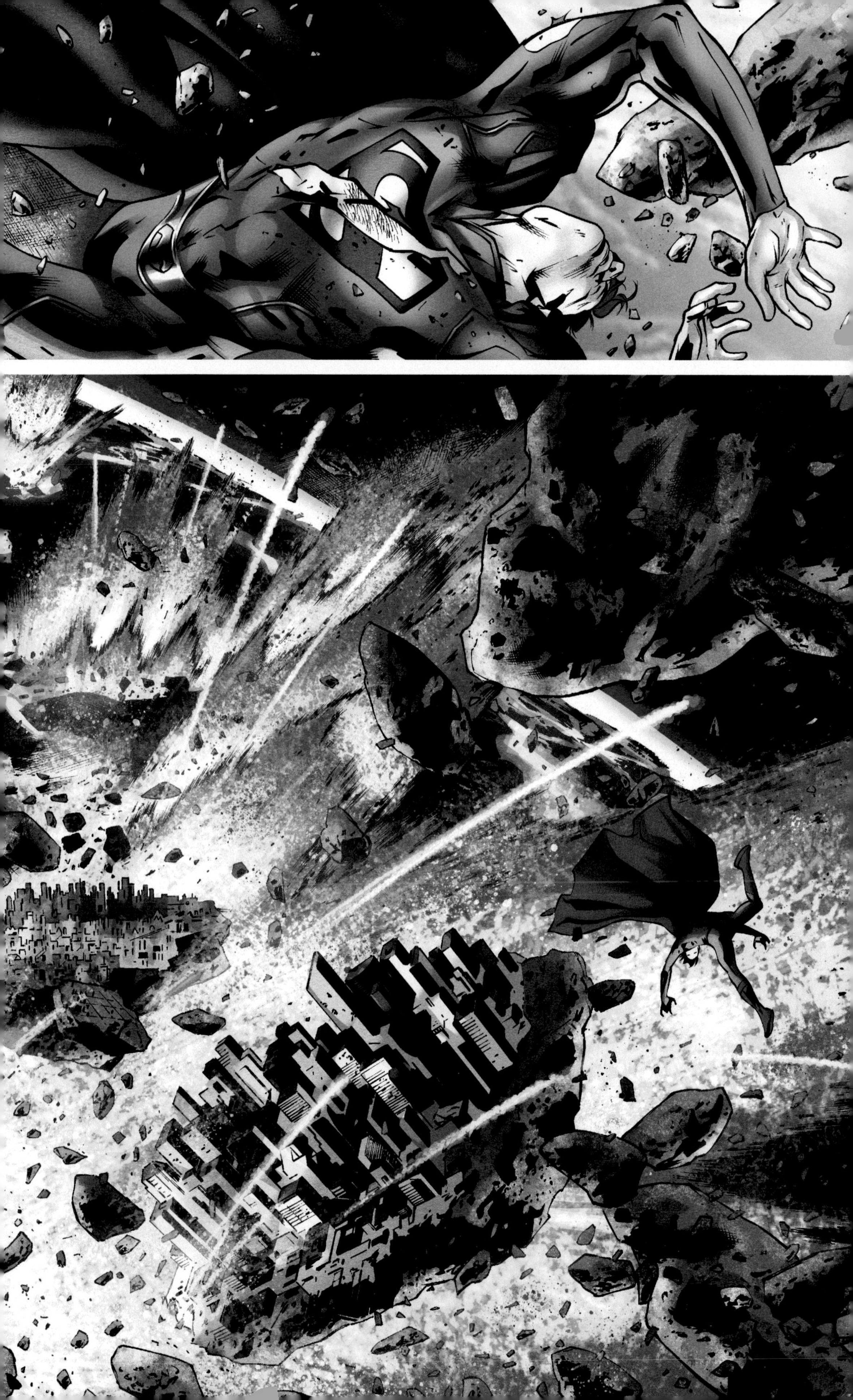

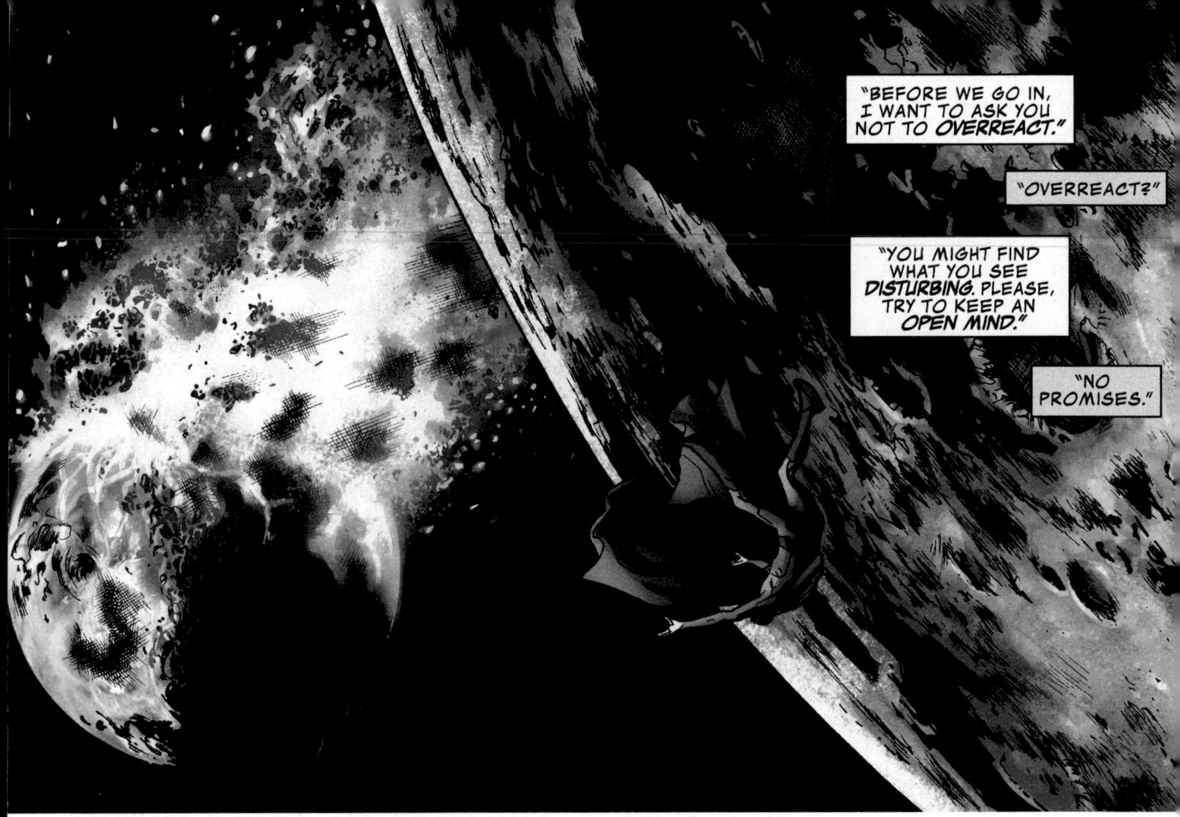
"BEFORE WE GO IN, I WANT TO ASK YOU NOT TO OVERREACT."
"OVERREACT?"
"YOU MIGHT FIND WHAT YOU SEE DISTURBING. PLEASE, TRY TO KEEP AN OPEN MIND."
"NO PROMISES."

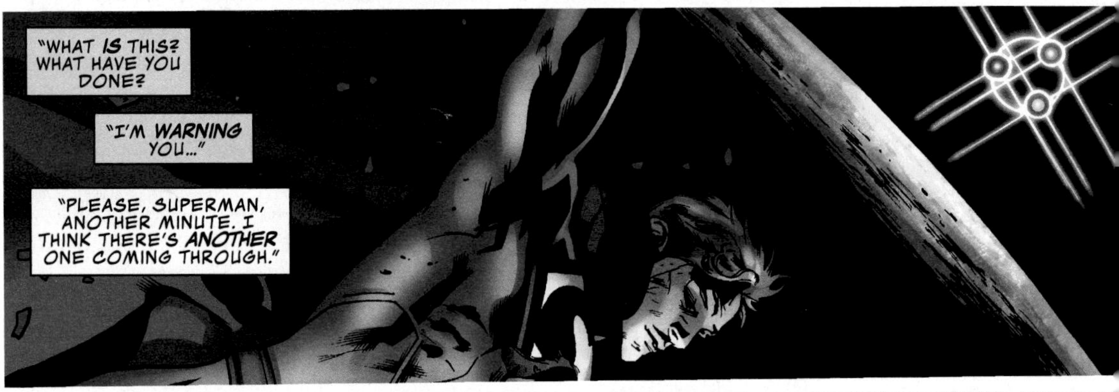
"WHAT IS THIS? WHAT HAVE YOU DONE?
"I'M WARNING YOU..."
"PLEASE, SUPERMAN, ANOTHER MINUTE. I THINK THERE'S ANOTHER ONE COMING THROUGH."

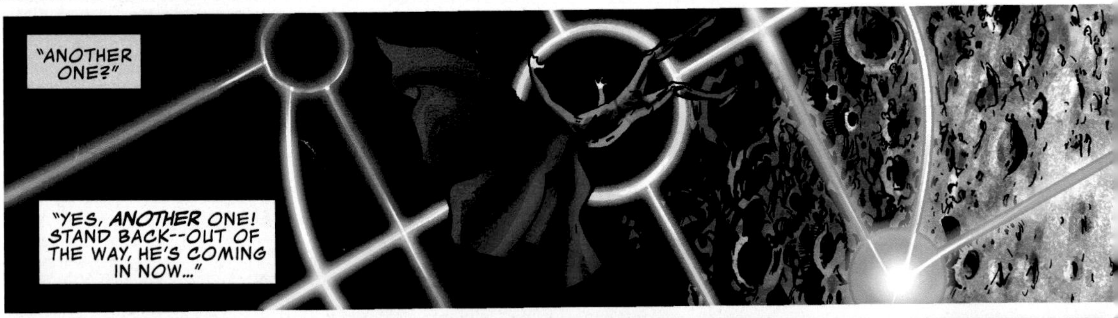
"ANOTHER ONE?"
"YES, ANOTHER ONE! STAND BACK--OUT OF THE WAY, HE'S COMING IN NOW..."

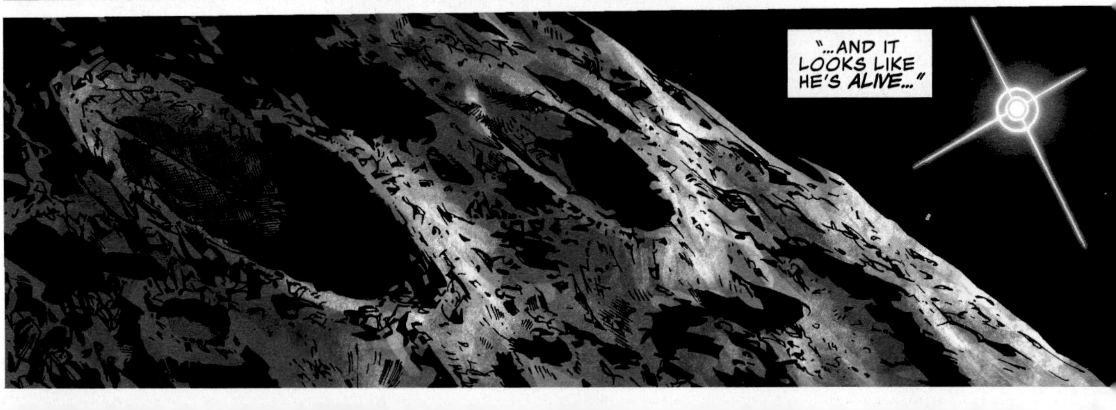
"...AND IT LOOKS LIKE HE'S ALIVE..."

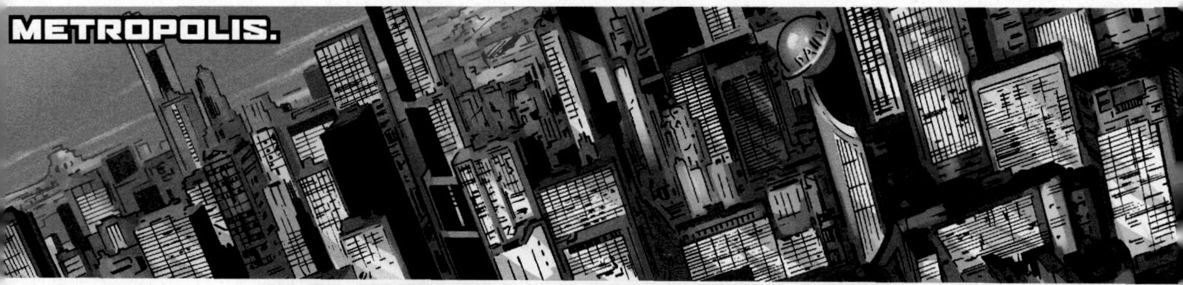
METROPOLIS.

DC COMICS PRESENTS
THE JUSTICE LEAGUE OF AMERICA

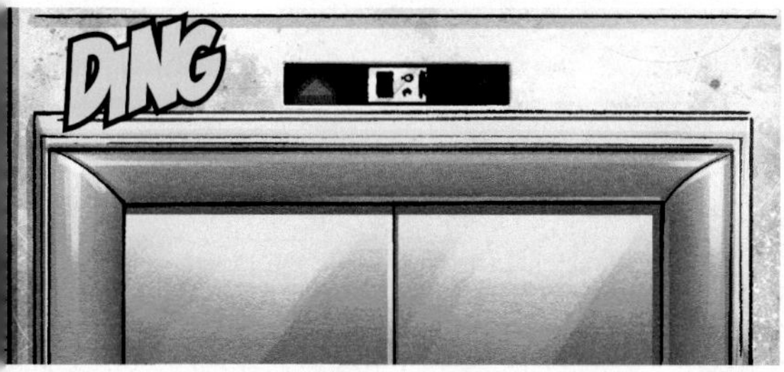
DING

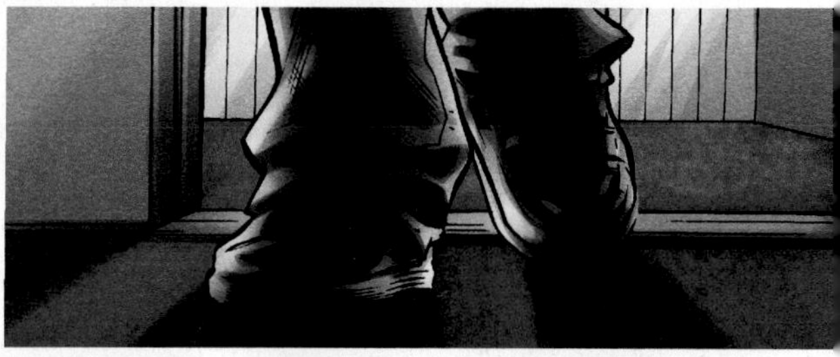

POWER AND GLORY
PART ONE
BY BRYAN HITCH

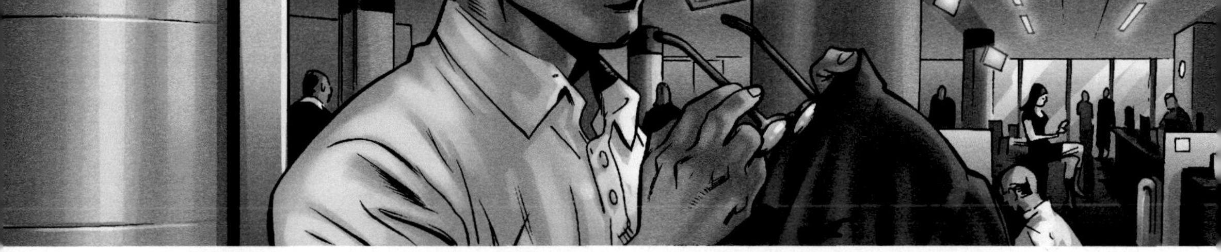

INKS BY **DANIEL HENRIQUES**
WITH **WADE VON GRAWBADGER** AND **ANDREW CURRIE**
COLORS BY **ALEX SINCLAIR** WITH **JEROMY COX**
LETTERS BY **CHRIS ELIOPOULOS**
ASSISTS BY **AMEDEO TURTURRO**
EDITS BY **BRIAN CUNNINGHAM**
COVER BY **BRYAN HITCH** AND **ALEX SINCLAIR**

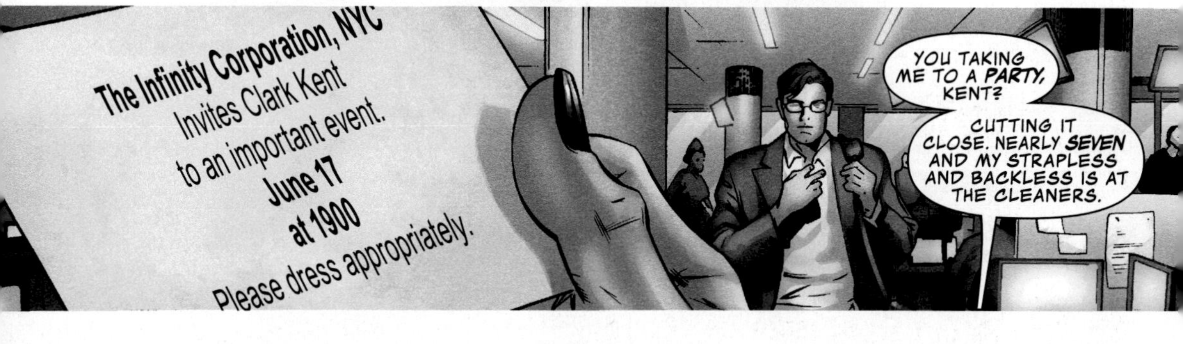
The Infinity Corporation, NYC
Invites Clark Kent
to an important event.
June 17
at 1900
Please dress appropriately.
YOU TAKING ME TO A PARTY, KENT?
CUTTING IT CLOSE. NEARLY SEVEN AND MY STRAPLESS AND BACKLESS IS AT THE CLEANERS.

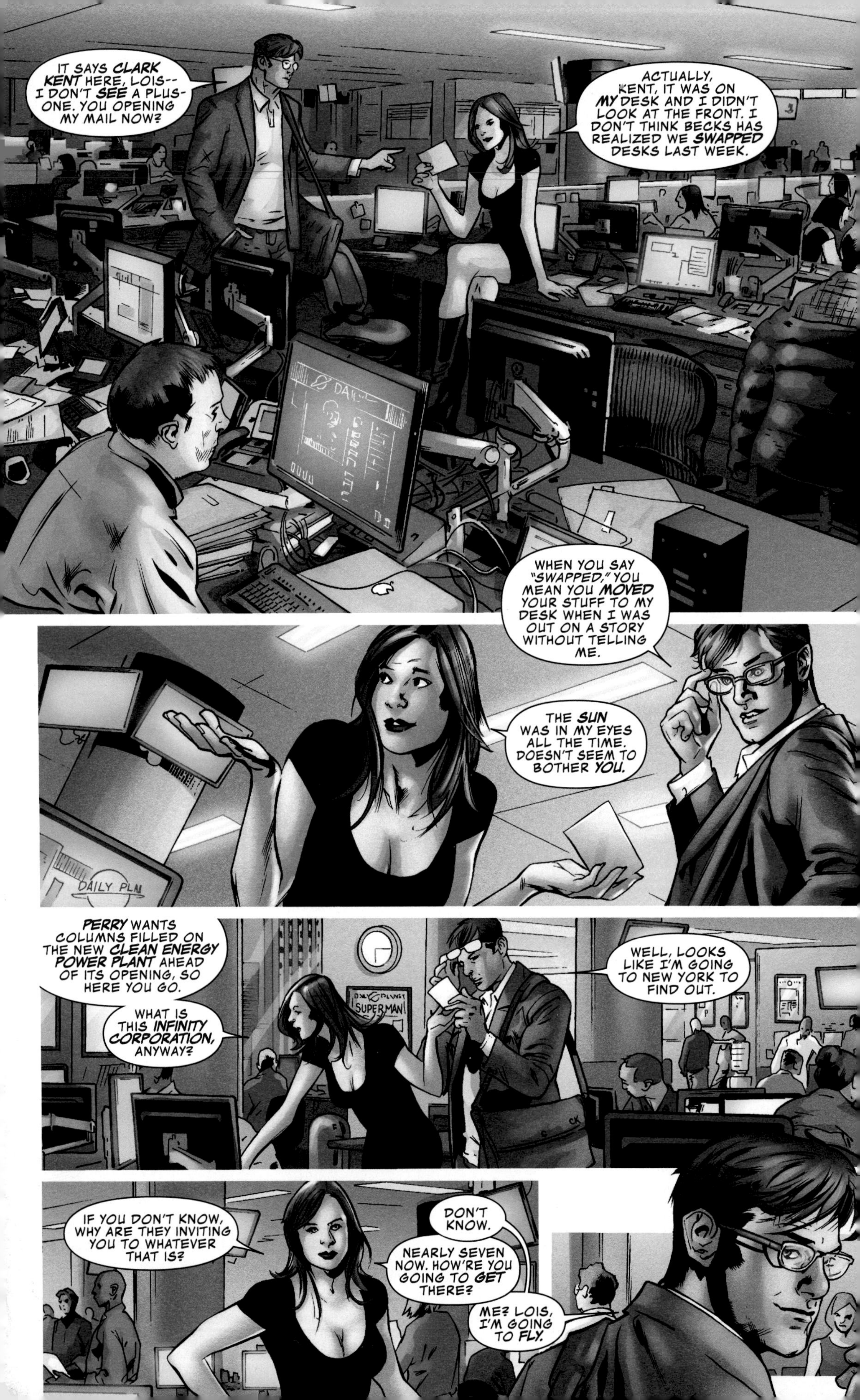
IT SAYS CLARK KENT HERE, LOIS-- I DON'T SEE A PLUS-ONE. YOU OPENING MY MAIL NOW?
ACTUALLY, KENT, IT WAS ON MY DESK AND I DIDN'T LOOK AT THE FRONT. I DON'T THINK BECKS HAS REALIZED WE SWAPPED DESKS LAST WEEK.
WHEN YOU SAY "SWAPPED," YOU MEAN YOU MOVED YOUR STUFF TO MY DESK WHEN I WAS OUT ON A STORY WITHOUT TELLING ME.
THE SUN WAS IN MY EYES ALL THE TIME. DOESN'T SEEM TO BOTHER YOU.
DAILY PLA
PERRY WANTS COLUMNS FILLED ON THE NEW CLEAN ENERGY POWER PLANT AHEAD OF ITS OPENING, SO HERE YOU GO.
WHAT IS THIS INFINITY CORPORATION, ANYWAY?
SUPERMAN!
WELL, LOOKS LIKE I'M GOING TO NEW YORK TO FIND OUT.
IF YOU DON'T KNOW, WHY ARE THEY INVITING YOU TO WHATEVER THAT IS?
DON'T KNOW.
NEARLY SEVEN NOW. HOW'RE YOU GOING TO GET THERE?
ME? LOIS, I'M GOING TO FLY.

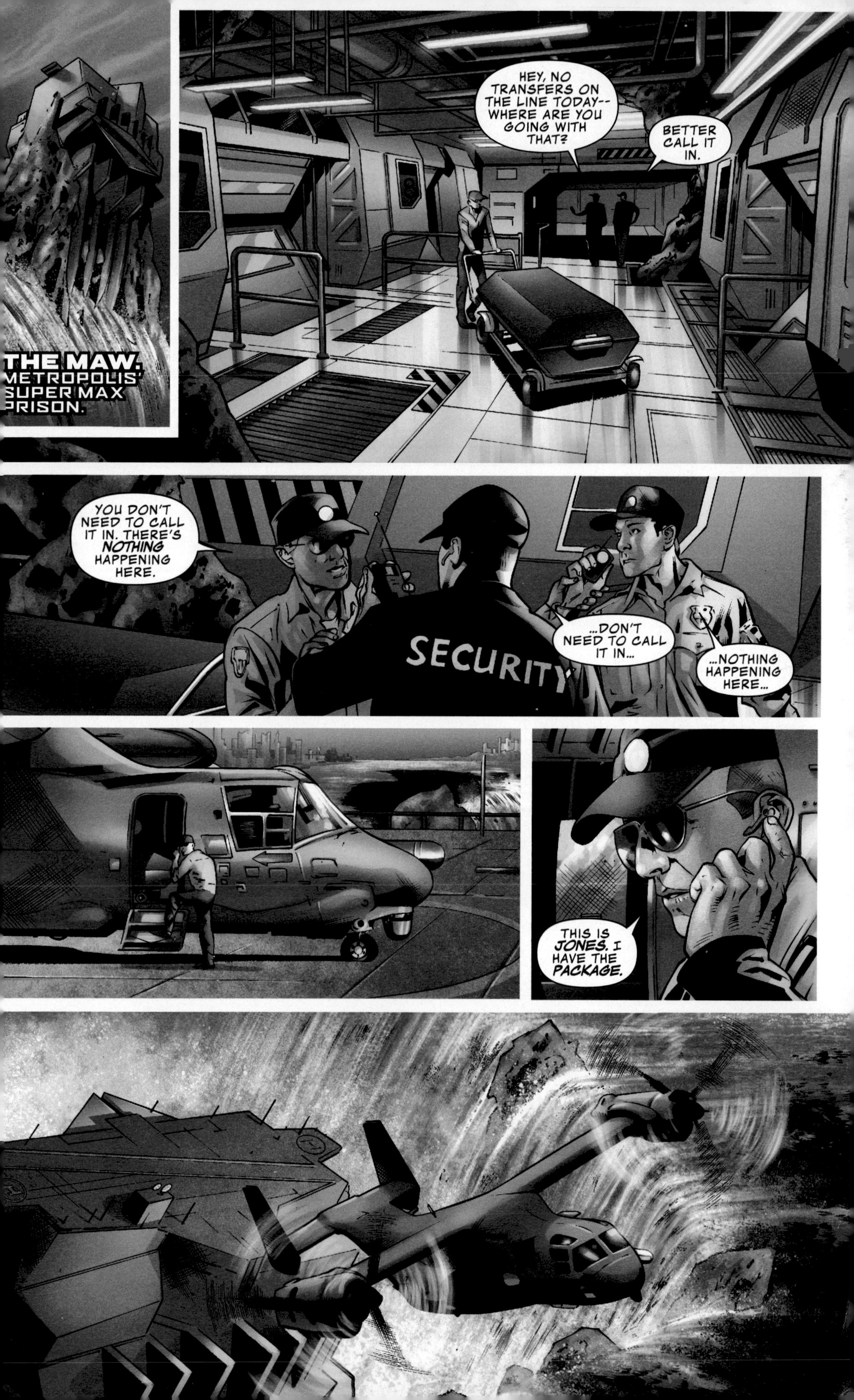
THE MAW. METROPOLIS' SUPER MAX PRISON.
HEY, NO TRANSFERS ON THE LINE TODAY-- WHERE ARE YOU GOING WITH THAT?
BETTER CALL IT IN.
YOU DON'T NEED TO CALL IT IN. THERE'S NOTHING HAPPENING HERE.
SECURITY
...DON'T NEED TO CALL IT IN...
...NOTHING HAPPENING HERE...
THIS IS JONES. I HAVE THE PACKAGE.

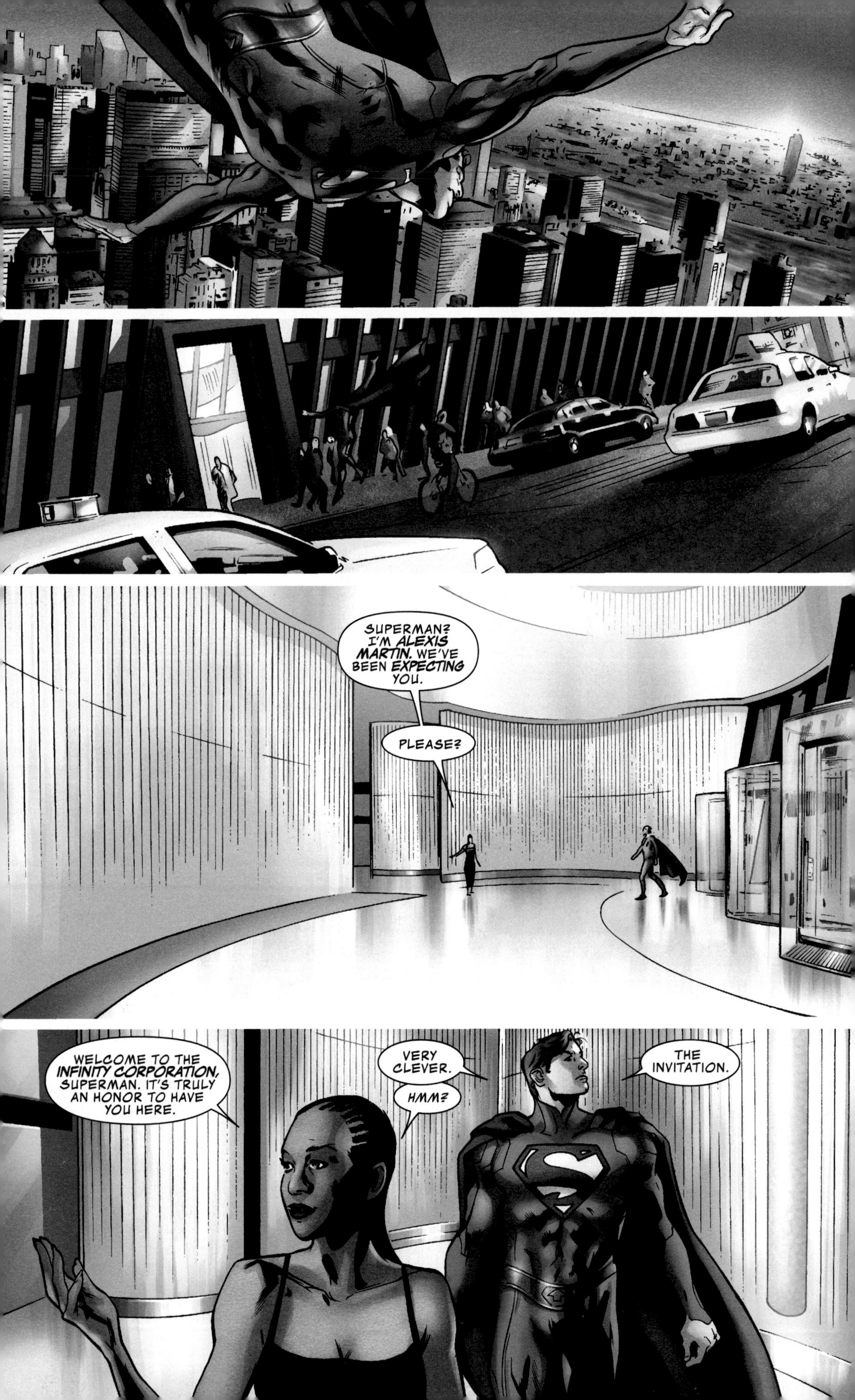
SUPERMAN? I'M ALEXIS MARTIN. WE'VE BEEN EXPECTING YOU.
PLEASE?
WELCOME TO THE INFINITY CORPORATION, SUPERMAN. IT'S TRULY AN HONOR TO HAVE YOU HERE.
VERY CLEVER.
HMM?
THE INVITATION.

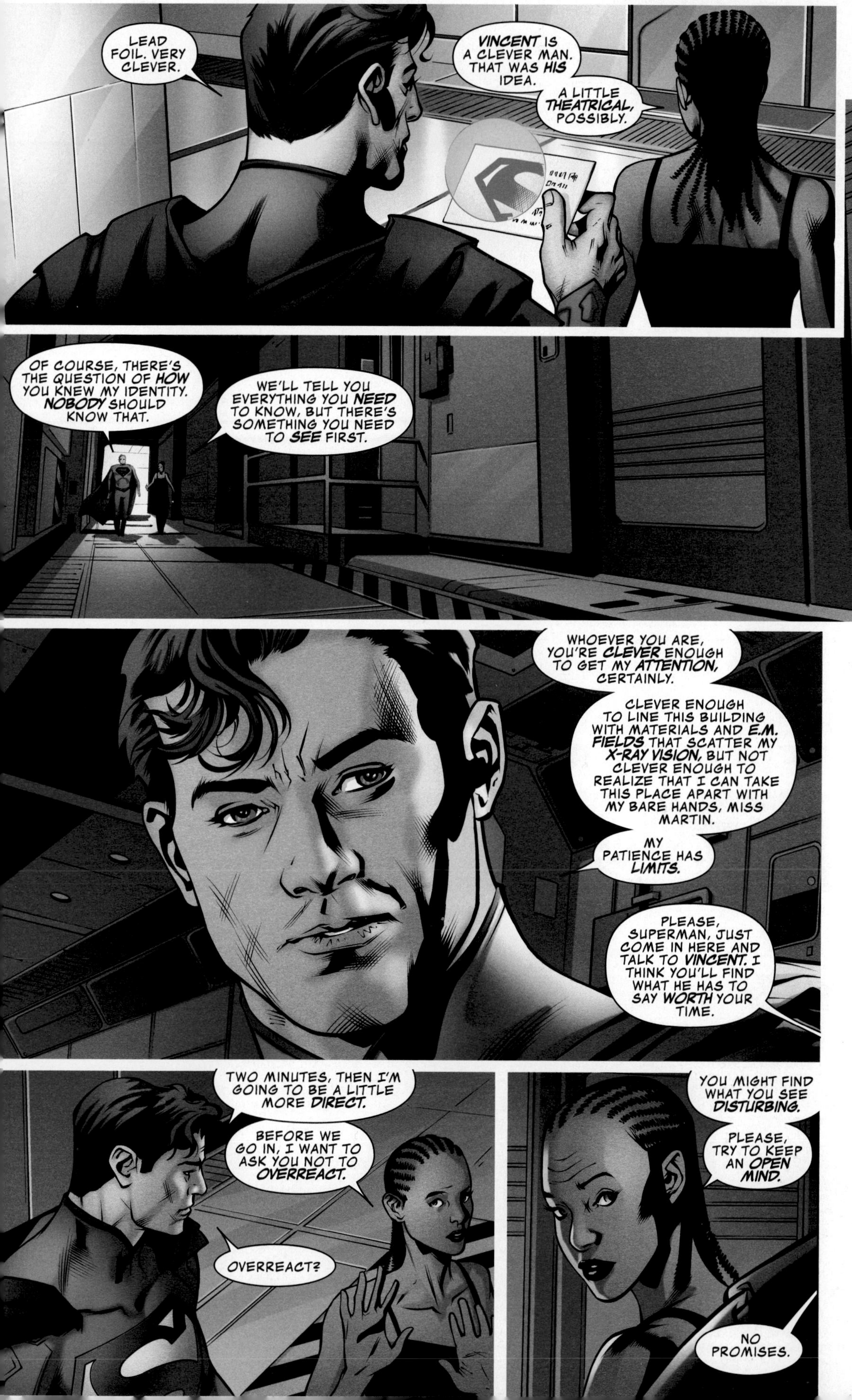
LEAD FOIL. VERY CLEVER.
VINCENT IS A CLEVER MAN. THAT WAS HIS IDEA.
A LITTLE THEATRICAL, POSSIBLY.
OF COURSE, THERE'S THE QUESTION OF HOW YOU KNEW MY IDENTITY. NOBODY SHOULD KNOW THAT.
WE'LL TELL YOU EVERYTHING YOU NEED TO KNOW, BUT THERE'S SOMETHING YOU NEED TO SEE FIRST.
WHOEVER YOU ARE, YOU'RE CLEVER ENOUGH TO GET MY ATTENTION, CERTAINLY.
CLEVER ENOUGH TO LINE THIS BUILDING WITH MATERIALS AND E.M. FIELDS THAT SCATTER MY X-RAY VISION, BUT NOT CLEVER ENOUGH TO REALIZE THAT I CAN TAKE THIS PLACE APART WITH MY BARE HANDS, MISS MARTIN.
MY PATIENCE HAS LIMITS.
PLEASE, SUPERMAN, JUST COME IN HERE AND TALK TO VINCENT. I THINK YOU'LL FIND WHAT HE HAS TO SAY WORTH YOUR TIME.
TWO MINUTES, THEN I'M GOING TO BE A LITTLE MORE DIRECT.
BEFORE WE GO IN, I WANT TO ASK YOU NOT TO OVERREACT.
OVERREACT?
YOU MIGHT FIND WHAT YOU SEE DISTURBING.
PLEASE, TRY TO KEEP AN OPEN MIND.
NO PROMISES.

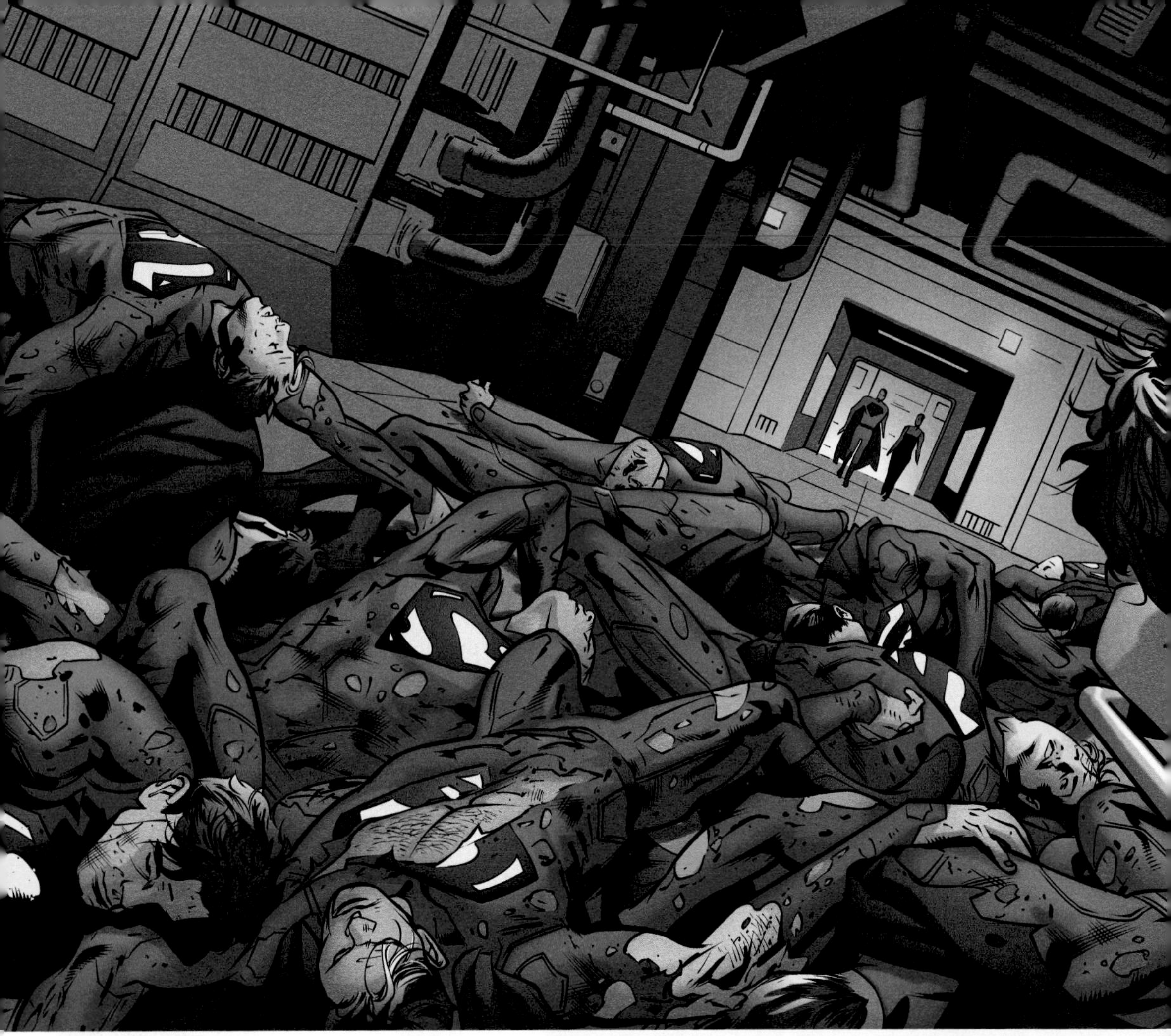

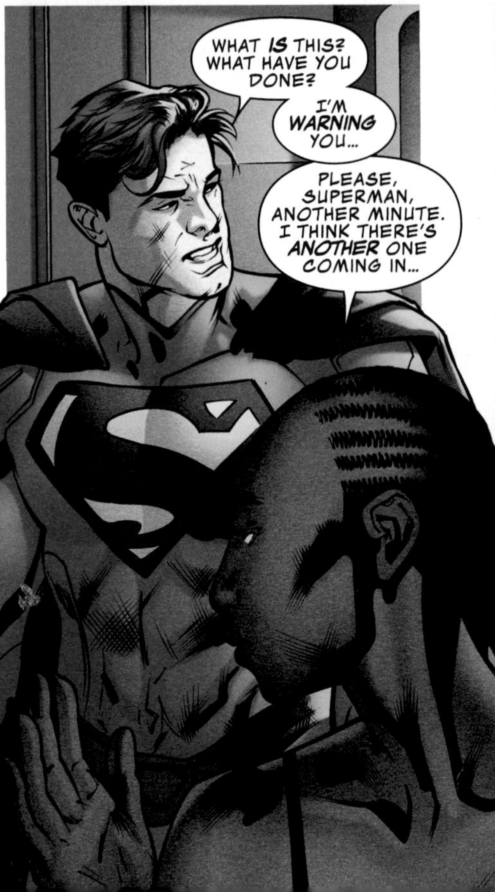
WHAT IS THIS? WHAT HAVE YOU DONE?
I'M WARNING YOU...
PLEASE, SUPERMAN, ANOTHER MINUTE. I THINK THERE'S ANOTHER ONE COMING IN...

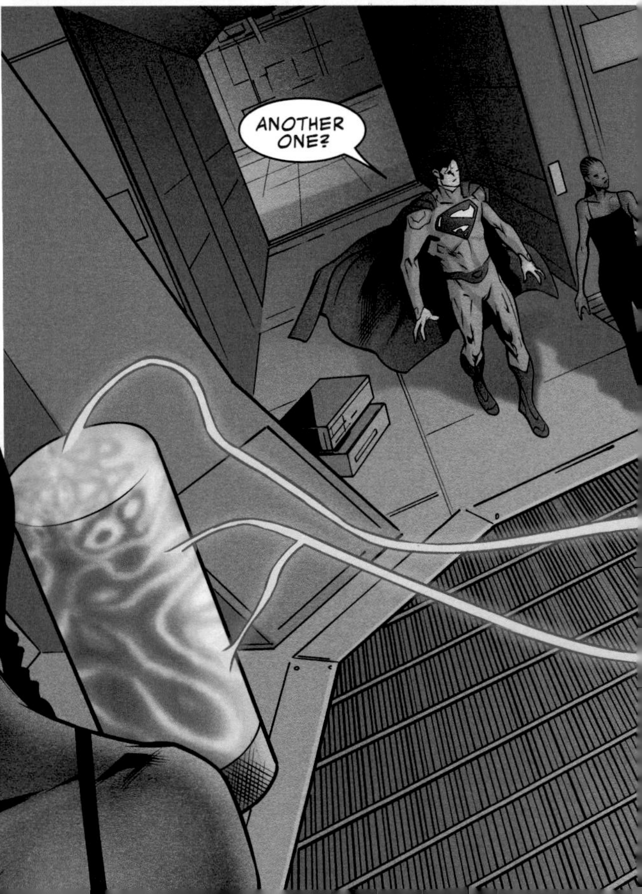
ANOTHER ONE?

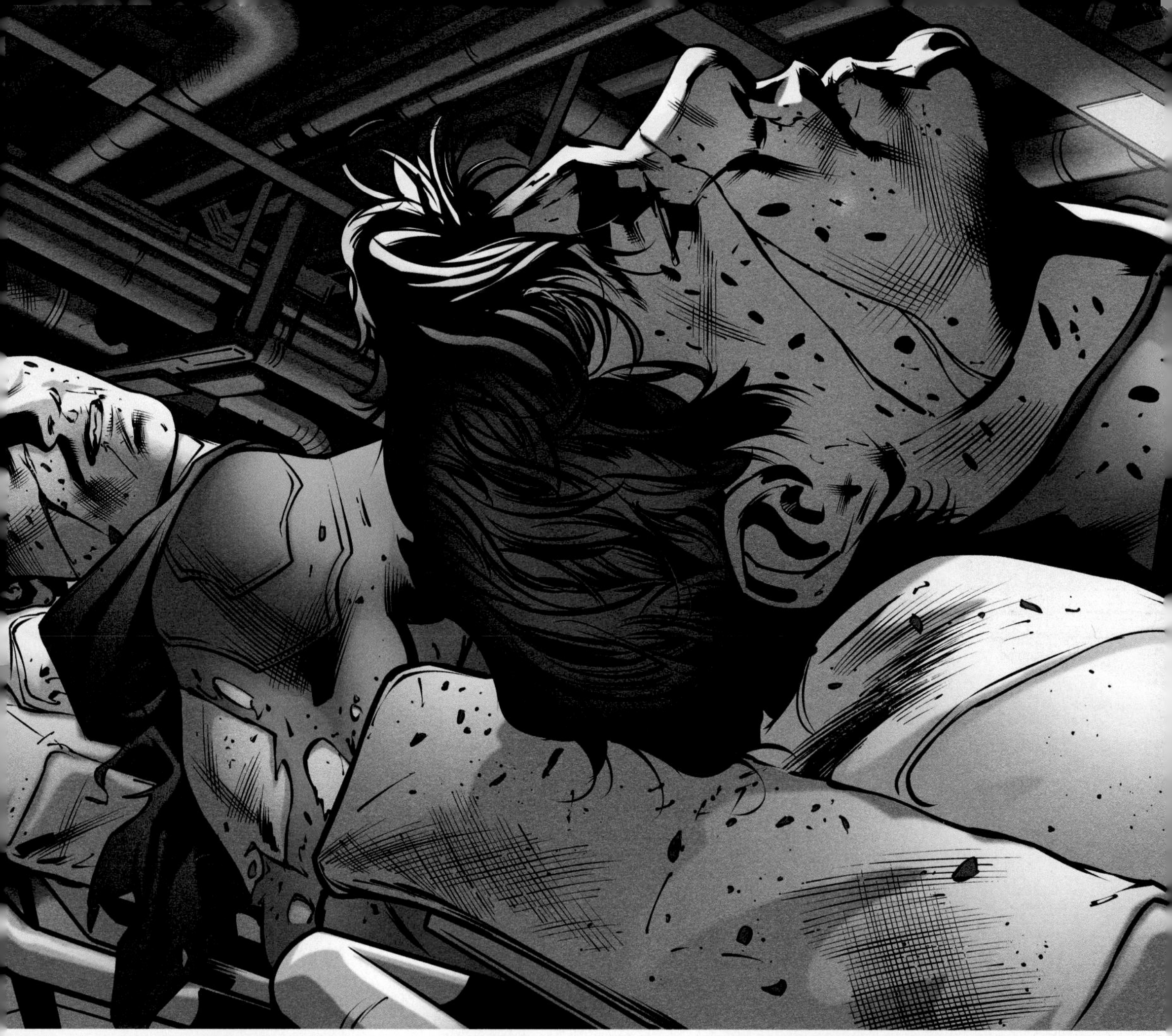

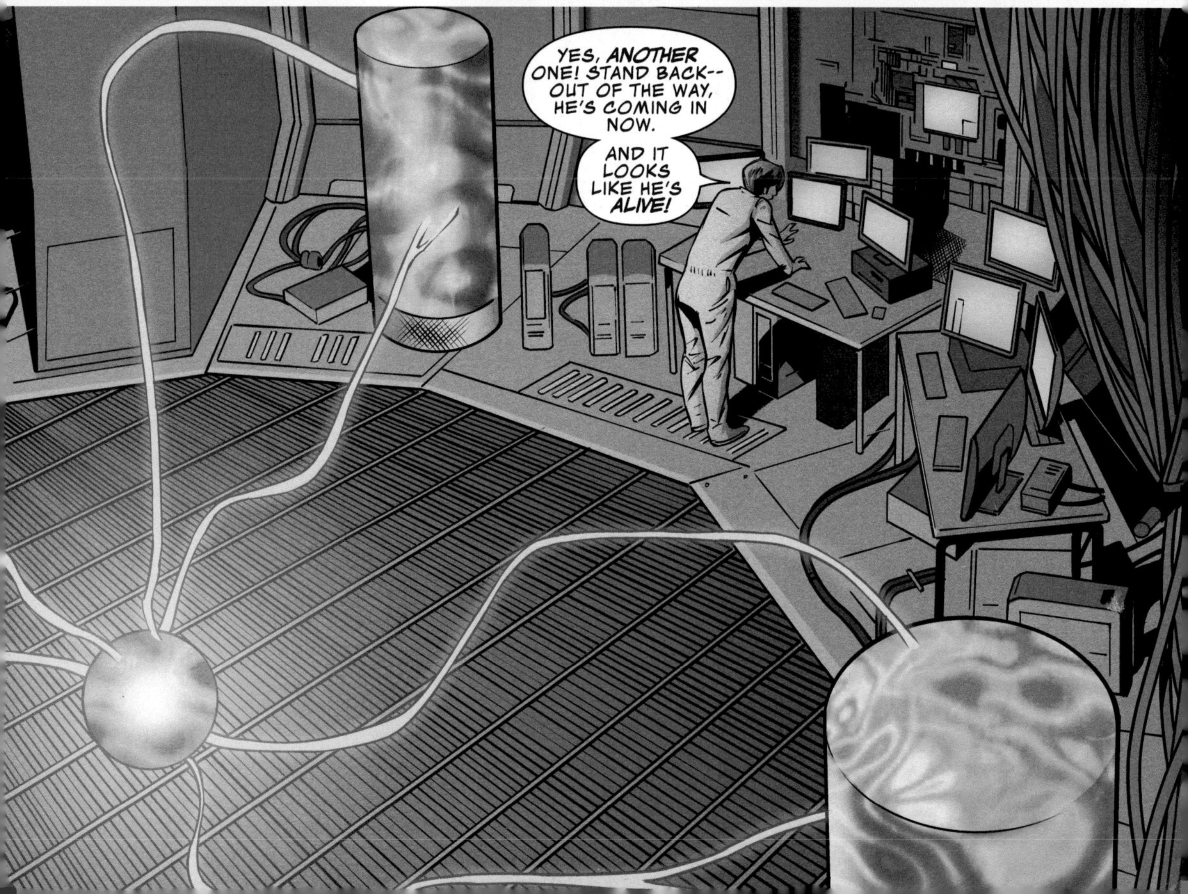
YES, ANOTHER ONE! STAND BACK--OUT OF THE WAY, HE'S COMING IN NOW.
AND IT LOOKS LIKE HE'S ALIVE!

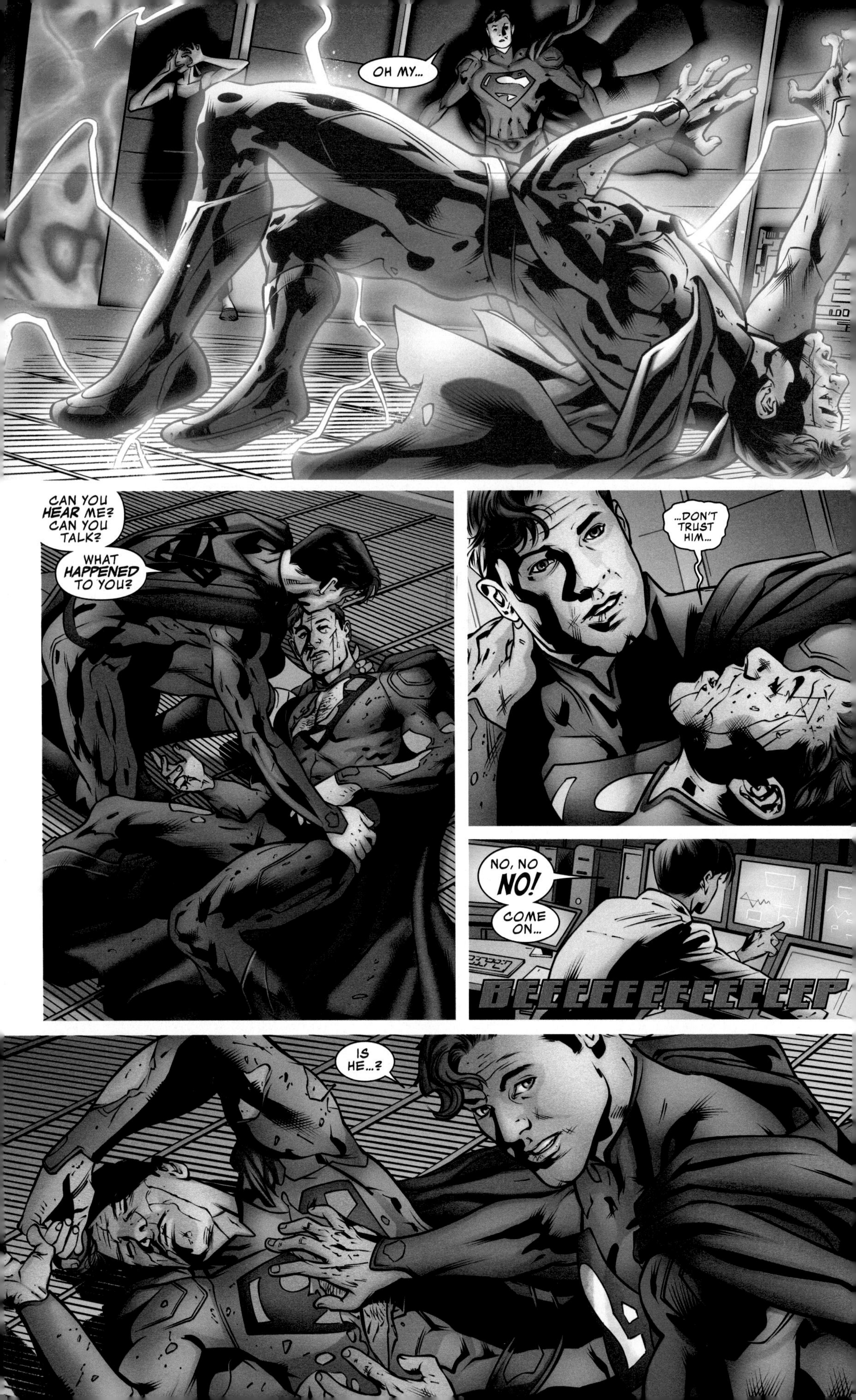
OH MY...
CAN YOU **HEAR** ME? CAN YOU TALK?
WHAT **HAPPENED** TO YOU?
...DON'T TRUST HIM...
NO, NO **NO!**
COME ON...
BEEEEEEEEEEEEEP
IS HE...?

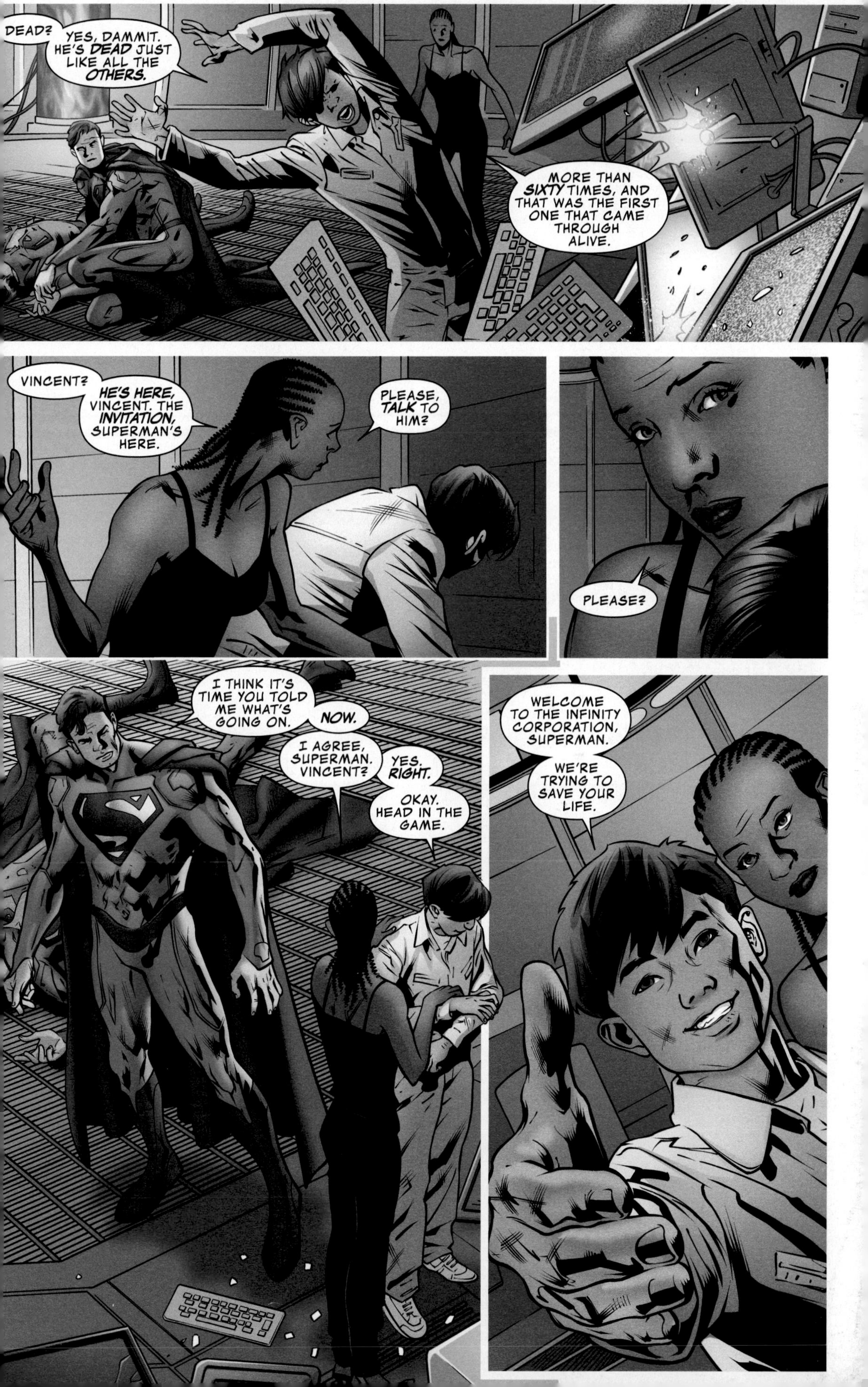
DEAD?
YES, DAMMIT. HE'S DEAD JUST LIKE ALL THE OTHERS.
MORE THAN SIXTY TIMES, AND THAT WAS THE FIRST ONE THAT CAME THROUGH ALIVE.
VINCENT?
HE'S HERE, VINCENT. THE INVITATION, SUPERMAN'S HERE.
PLEASE, TALK TO HIM?
PLEASE?
I THINK IT'S TIME YOU TOLD ME WHAT'S GOING ON.
NOW.
I AGREE, SUPERMAN. VINCENT?
YES. RIGHT.
OKAY. HEAD IN THE GAME.
WELCOME TO THE INFINITY CORPORATION, SUPERMAN.
WE'RE TRYING TO SAVE YOUR LIFE.

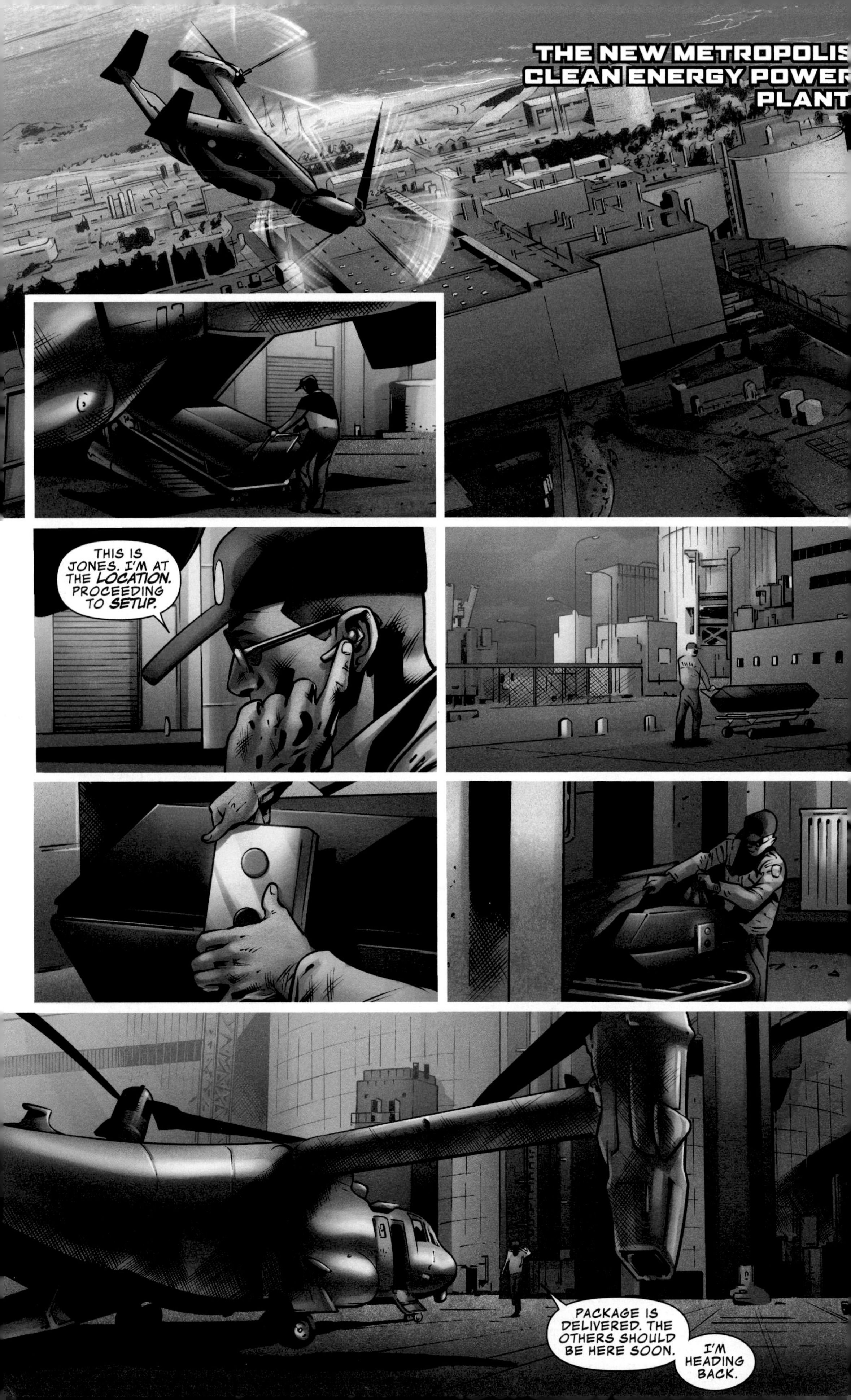
THE NEW METROPOLIS CLEAN ENERGY POWER PLANT
THIS IS JONES. I'M AT THE LOCATION. PROCEEDING TO SETUP.
PACKAGE IS DELIVERED. THE OTHERS SHOULD BE HERE SOON.
I'M HEADING BACK.

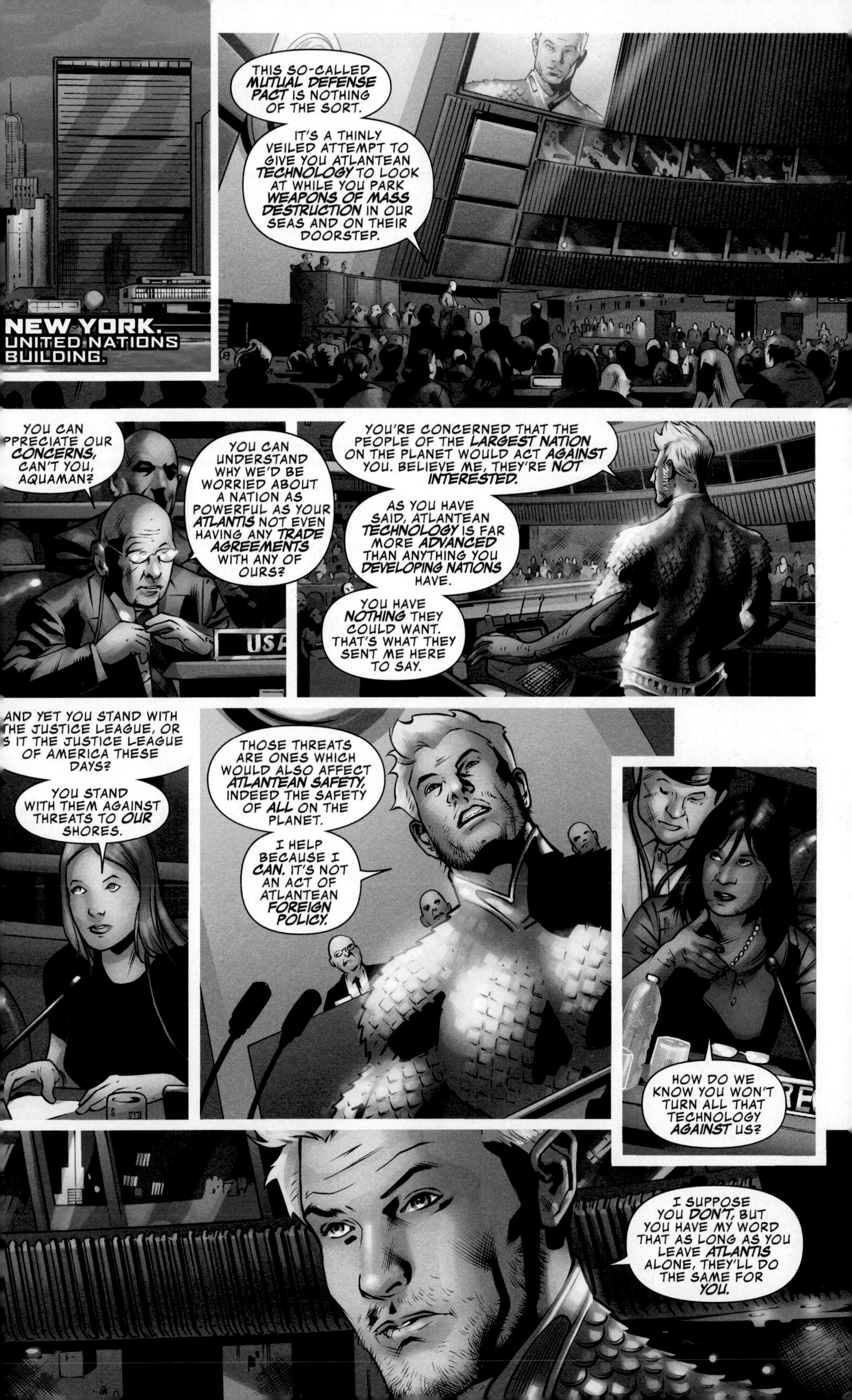
NEW YORK. UNITED NATIONS BUILDING.
THIS SO-CALLED MUTUAL DEFENSE PACT IS NOTHING OF THE SORT.
IT'S A THINLY VEILED ATTEMPT TO GIVE YOU ATLANTEAN TECHNOLOGY TO LOOK AT WHILE YOU PARK WEAPONS OF MASS DESTRUCTION IN OUR SEAS AND ON THEIR DOORSTEP.
YOU CAN APPRECIATE OUR CONCERNS, CAN'T YOU, AQUAMAN?
YOU CAN UNDERSTAND WHY WE'D BE WORRIED ABOUT A NATION AS POWERFUL AS YOUR ATLANTIS NOT EVEN HAVING ANY TRADE AGREEMENTS WITH ANY OF OURS?
USA
YOU'RE CONCERNED THAT THE PEOPLE OF THE LARGEST NATION ON THE PLANET WOULD ACT AGAINST YOU. BELIEVE ME, THEY'RE NOT INTERESTED.
AS YOU HAVE SAID, ATLANTEAN TECHNOLOGY IS FAR MORE ADVANCED THAN ANYTHING YOU DEVELOPING NATIONS HAVE.
YOU HAVE NOTHING THEY COULD WANT. THAT'S WHAT THEY SENT ME HERE TO SAY.
AND YET YOU STAND WITH THE JUSTICE LEAGUE, OR IS IT THE JUSTICE LEAGUE OF AMERICA THESE DAYS?
YOU STAND WITH THEM AGAINST THREATS TO OUR SHORES.
THOSE THREATS ARE ONES WHICH WOULD ALSO AFFECT ATLANTEAN SAFETY, INDEED THE SAFETY OF ALL ON THE PLANET.
I HELP BECAUSE I CAN. IT'S NOT AN ACT OF ATLANTEAN FOREIGN POLICY.
HOW DO WE KNOW YOU WON'T TURN ALL THAT TECHNOLOGY AGAINST US?
I SUPPOSE YOU DON'T, BUT YOU HAVE MY WORD THAT AS LONG AS YOU LEAVE ATLANTIS ALONE, THEY'LL DO THE SAME FOR YOU.

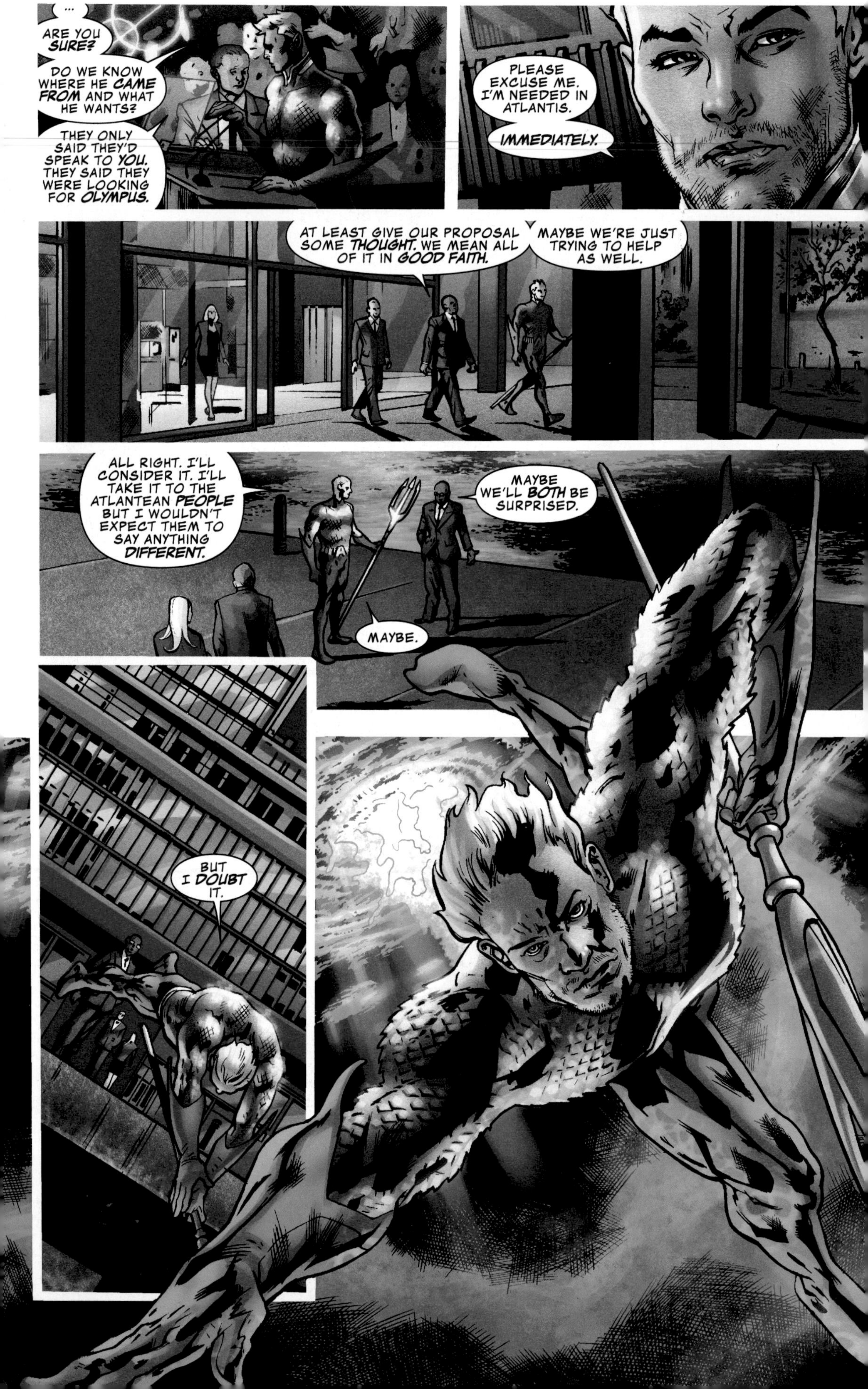
...
ARE YOU SURE?
DO WE KNOW WHERE HE CAME FROM AND WHAT HE WANTS?
THEY ONLY SAID THEY'D SPEAK TO YOU. THEY SAID THEY WERE LOOKING FOR OLYMPUS.
PLEASE EXCUSE ME. I'M NEEDED IN ATLANTIS.
IMMEDIATELY.
AT LEAST GIVE OUR PROPOSAL SOME THOUGHT. WE MEAN ALL OF IT IN GOOD FAITH.
MAYBE WE'RE JUST TRYING TO HELP AS WELL.
ALL RIGHT. I'LL CONSIDER IT. I'LL TAKE IT TO THE ATLANTEAN PEOPLE BUT I WOULDN'T EXPECT THEM TO SAY ANYTHING DIFFERENT.
MAYBE WE'LL BOTH BE SURPRISED.
MAYBE.
BUT I DOUBT IT.

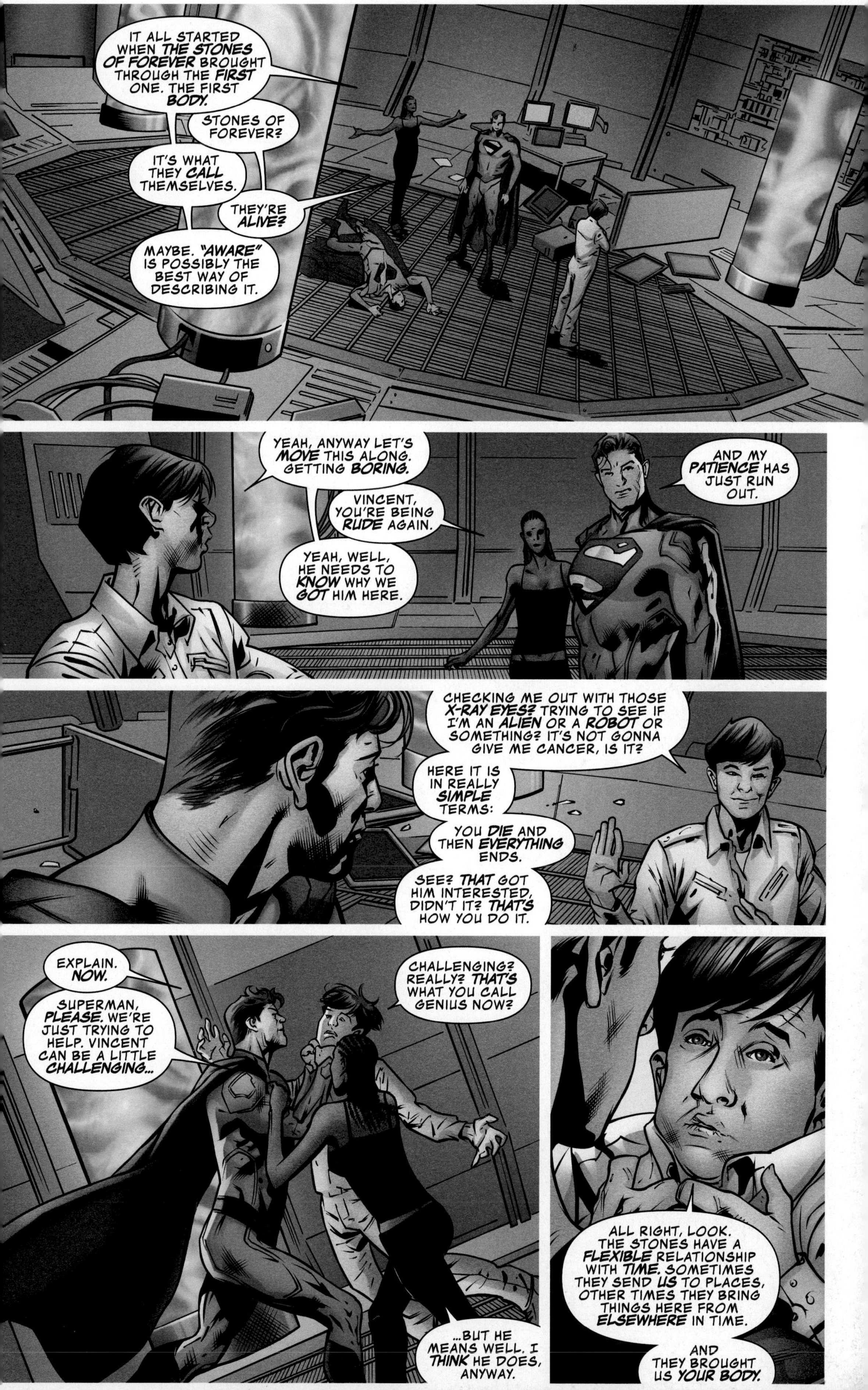
IT ALL STARTED WHEN THE STONES OF FOREVER BROUGHT THROUGH THE FIRST ONE. THE FIRST BODY.
STONES OF FOREVER?
IT'S WHAT THEY CALL THEMSELVES.
THEY'RE ALIVE?
MAYBE. "AWARE" IS POSSIBLY THE BEST WAY OF DESCRIBING IT.
YEAH, ANYWAY LET'S MOVE THIS ALONG. GETTING BORING.
VINCENT, YOU'RE BEING RUDE AGAIN.
YEAH, WELL, HE NEEDS TO KNOW WHY WE GOT HIM HERE.
AND MY PATIENCE HAS JUST RUN OUT.
CHECKING ME OUT WITH THOSE X-RAY EYES? TRYING TO SEE IF I'M AN ALIEN OR A ROBOT OR SOMETHING? IT'S NOT GONNA GIVE ME CANCER, IS IT?
HERE IT IS IN REALLY SIMPLE TERMS:
YOU DIE AND THEN EVERYTHING ENDS.
SEE? THAT GOT HIM INTERESTED, DIDN'T IT? THAT'S HOW YOU DO IT.
EXPLAIN. NOW.
SUPERMAN, PLEASE. WE'RE JUST TRYING TO HELP. VINCENT CAN BE A LITTLE CHALLENGING...
CHALLENGING? REALLY? THAT'S WHAT YOU CALL GENIUS NOW?
...BUT HE MEANS WELL. I THINK HE DOES, ANYWAY.
ALL RIGHT, LOOK. THE STONES HAVE A FLEXIBLE RELATIONSHIP WITH TIME. SOMETIMES THEY SEND US TO PLACES, OTHER TIMES THEY BRING THINGS HERE FROM ELSEWHERE IN TIME.
AND THEY BROUGHT US YOUR BODY.

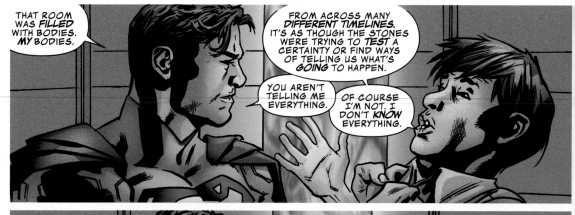

THAT ROOM WAS *FILLED* WITH BODIES. *MY* BODIES.

FROM ACROSS MANY *DIFFERENT TIMELINES.* IT'S AS THOUGH THE STONES WERE TRYING TO *TEST* A CERTAINTY OR FIND WAYS OF TELLING US WHAT'S *GOING* TO HAPPEN.

YOU AREN'T TELLING ME EVERYTHING.

OF COURSE I'M NOT. I DON'T *KNOW* EVERYTHING.

DO YOU KNOW *HOW* I DIE?

NO.

WHEN?

NO.

THEN YOU HAVE *NOTHING* TO TELL ME.

I'M TELLING YOU WHAT I'M *SURE* OF.

I CAN TELL YOU THAT THE *WHOLE FUTURE* IS GOING TO END. WHATEVER IS COMING IS GOING TO *CHANGE EVERYTHING.* THE FUTURE, THE PRESENT *AND* THE PAST.

IT'S *ALREADY* HAPPENING. WE ARE ALREADY *PART* OF IT. YOUR DEATH IS TIED UP IN THIS LIKE A *FIXED BEACON* IN TIME, ACROSS ALL TIME.

A *UNIVERSAL* EXTINCTION LEVEL EVENT AND THE SHOCKWAVE REACHES BACK TO THE *BEGINNING OF TIME.*

THOSE OTHER BODIES ARE JUST *RIPPLES,* SUPERMAN. WHATEVER IS GOING TO HAPPEN WILL HAPPEN *HERE.* THIS PLACE. *THIS* TIME. TO YOU, TO ALL OF US. *THAT'S* WHY WE INVITED YOU HERE, TO *TELL* YOU.

HOW CAN YOU *KNOW* THE FUTURE IS GONE?

I DON'T, BUT *THEY* DO.

THE STONES. *THEY* TOLD YOU?

WE HAVE A *SPECIAL* RELATIONSHIP.

I'M SURE YOU DO.

TIME IS *CONSTANTLY* IN FLUX, IT'S FAR MORE *FLUID* THAN YOU COULD IMAGINE.

IT'S NOT A *STREAM,* SUPERMAN, IT'S A ROILING *OCEAN* IN A CONSTANT *STORM.* THE PAST ISN'T FIXED AND THE FUTURE ISN'T WRITTEN. THE ONLY TIME THAT MATTERS, THE ONLY MOMENT THAT COUNTS, IS ALWAYS THE *NOW.*

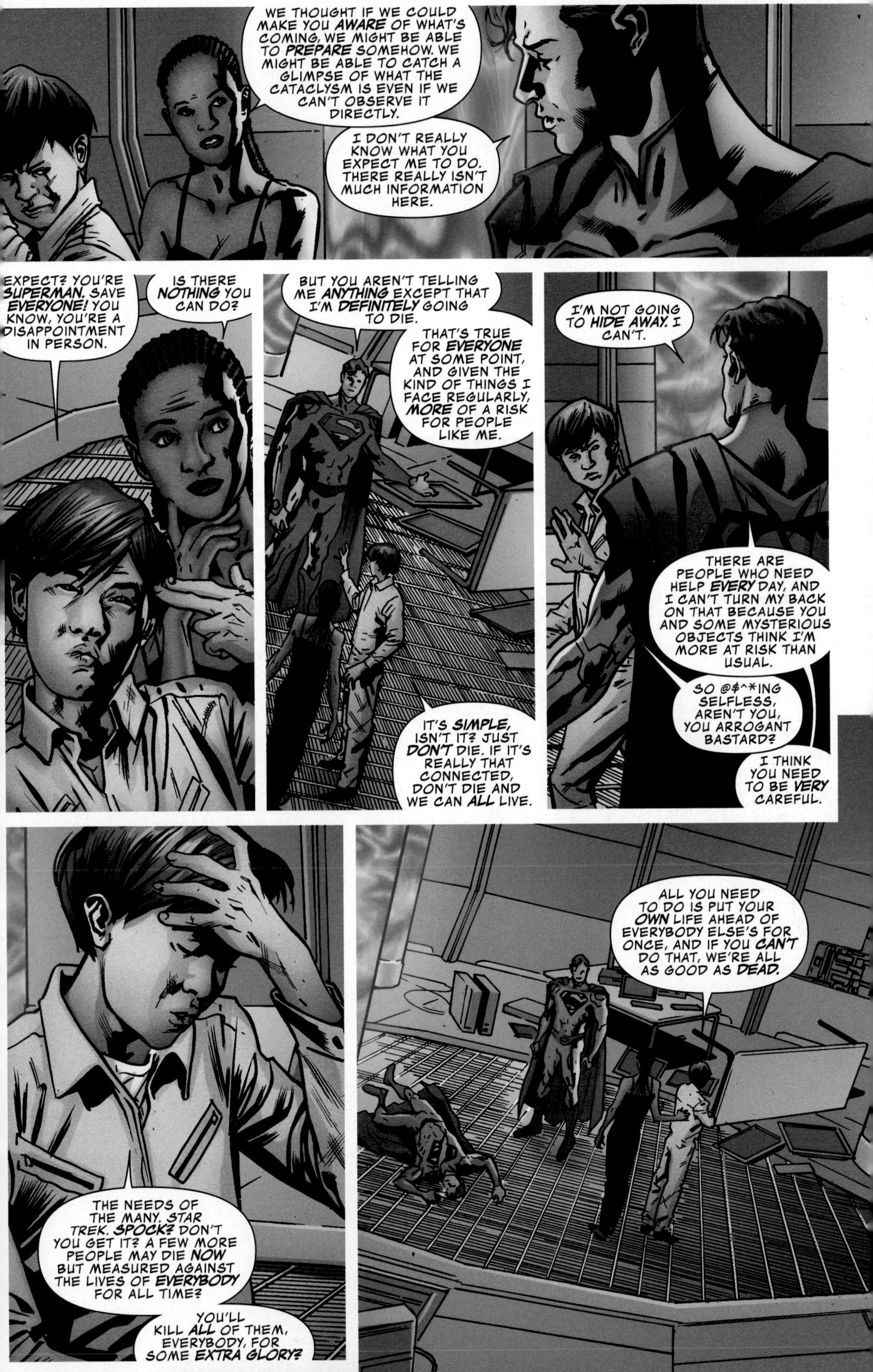

WE THOUGHT IF WE COULD MAKE YOU AWARE OF WHAT'S COMING, WE MIGHT BE ABLE TO PREPARE SOMEHOW. WE MIGHT BE ABLE TO CATCH A GLIMPSE OF WHAT THE CATACLYSM IS EVEN IF WE CAN'T OBSERVE IT DIRECTLY.
I DON'T REALLY KNOW WHAT YOU EXPECT ME TO DO. THERE REALLY ISN'T MUCH INFORMATION HERE.
EXPECT? YOU'RE SUPERMAN. SAVE EVERYONE! YOU KNOW, YOU'RE A DISAPPOINTMENT IN PERSON.
IS THERE NOTHING YOU CAN DO?
BUT YOU AREN'T TELLING ME ANYTHING EXCEPT THAT I'M DEFINITELY GOING TO DIE.
THAT'S TRUE FOR EVERYONE AT SOME POINT, AND GIVEN THE KIND OF THINGS I FACE REGULARLY, MORE OF A RISK FOR PEOPLE LIKE ME.
IT'S SIMPLE, ISN'T IT? JUST DON'T DIE. IF IT'S REALLY THAT CONNECTED, DON'T DIE AND WE CAN ALL LIVE.
I'M NOT GOING TO HIDE AWAY. I CAN'T.
THERE ARE PEOPLE WHO NEED HELP EVERY DAY, AND I CAN'T TURN MY BACK ON THAT BECAUSE YOU AND SOME MYSTERIOUS OBJECTS THINK I'M MORE AT RISK THAN USUAL.
SO @$^*ING SELFLESS, AREN'T YOU, YOU ARROGANT BASTARD?
I THINK YOU NEED TO BE VERY CAREFUL.
THE NEEDS OF THE MANY. STAR TREK. SPOCK? DON'T YOU GET IT? A FEW MORE PEOPLE MAY DIE NOW BUT MEASURED AGAINST THE LIVES OF EVERYBODY FOR ALL TIME?
YOU'LL KILL ALL OF THEM, EVERYBODY, FOR SOME EXTRA GLORY?
ALL YOU NEED TO DO IS PUT YOUR OWN LIFE AHEAD OF EVERYBODY ELSE'S FOR ONCE, AND IF YOU CAN'T DO THAT, WE'RE ALL AS GOOD AS DEAD.

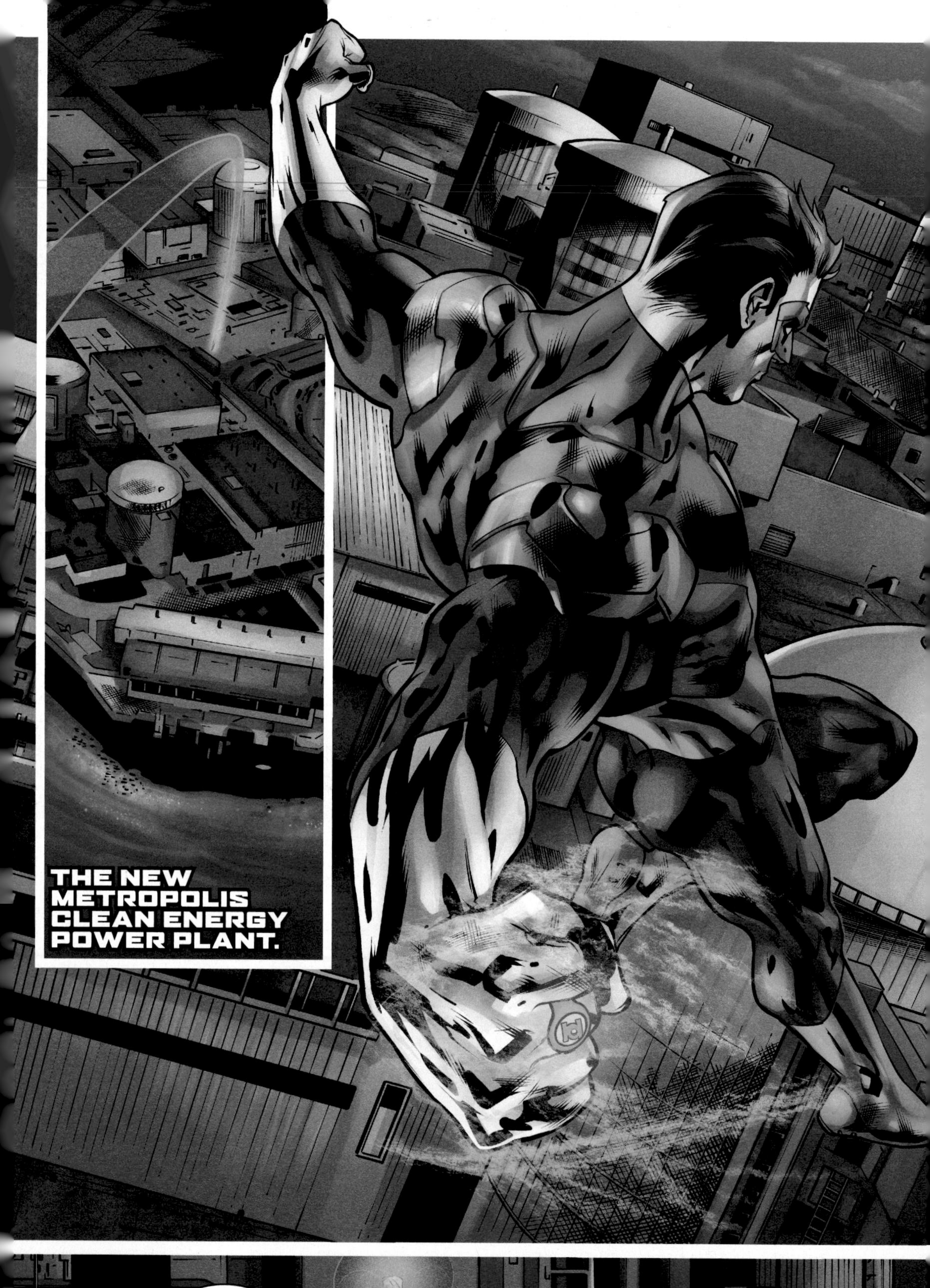
THE NEW METROPOLIS CLEAN ENERGY POWER PLANT.

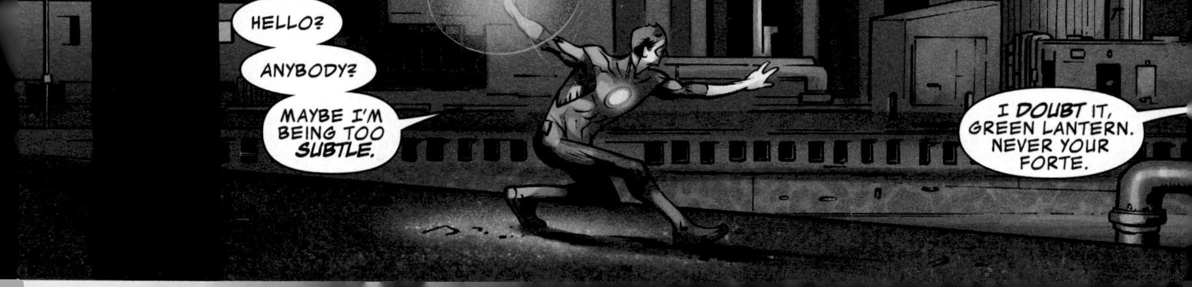
HELLO?
ANYBODY?
MAYBE I'M BEING TOO SUBTLE.
I DOUBT IT, GREEN LANTERN. NEVER YOUR FORTE.

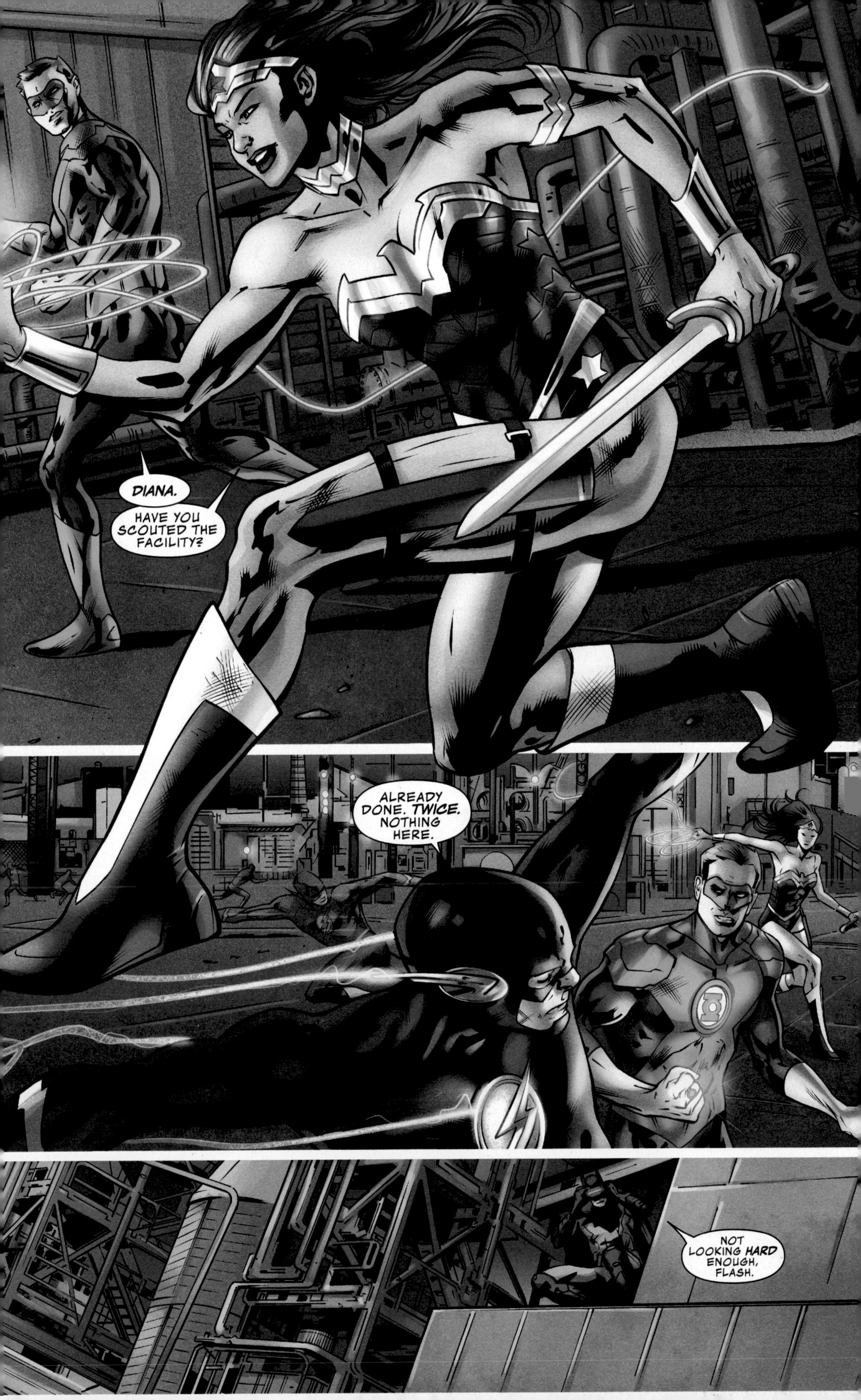
DIANA.
HAVE YOU SCOUTED THE FACILITY?
ALREADY DONE. TWICE. NOTHING HERE.
NOT LOOKING HARD ENOUGH, FLASH.

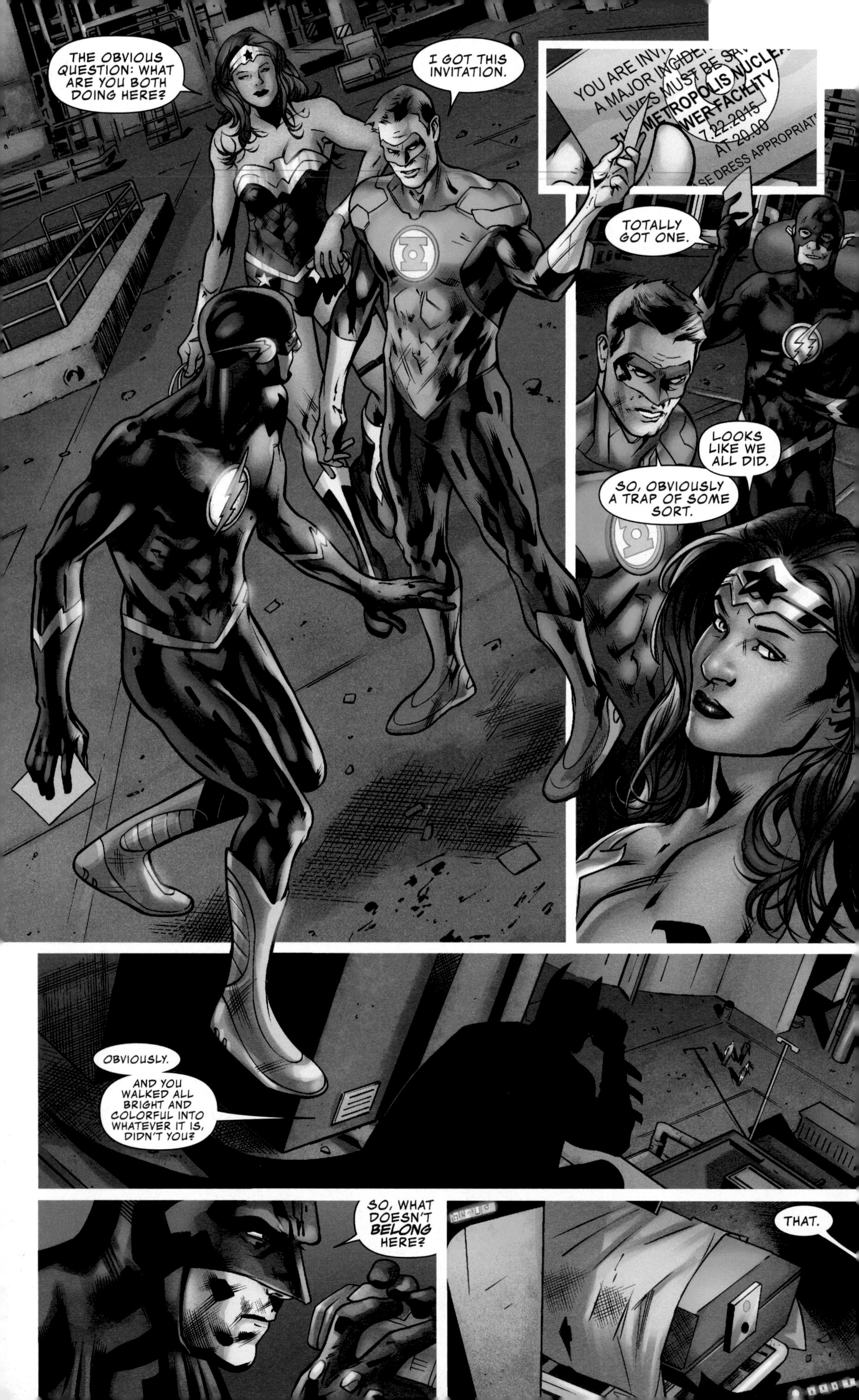
THE OBVIOUS QUESTION: WHAT ARE YOU BOTH DOING HERE?
I GOT THIS INVITATION.
YOU ARE INVITED... A MAJOR INCIDENT... LIVES MUST BE SA... METROPOLIS NUCLEAR POWER FACILITY 7.22.2015 AT 20.00 ...SE DRESS APPROPRIAT...
TOTALLY GOT ONE.
LOOKS LIKE WE ALL DID.
SO, OBVIOUSLY A TRAP OF SOME SORT.
OBVIOUSLY.
AND YOU WALKED ALL BRIGHT AND COLORFUL INTO WHATEVER IT IS, DIDN'T YOU?
SO, WHAT DOESN'T BELONG HERE?
THAT.

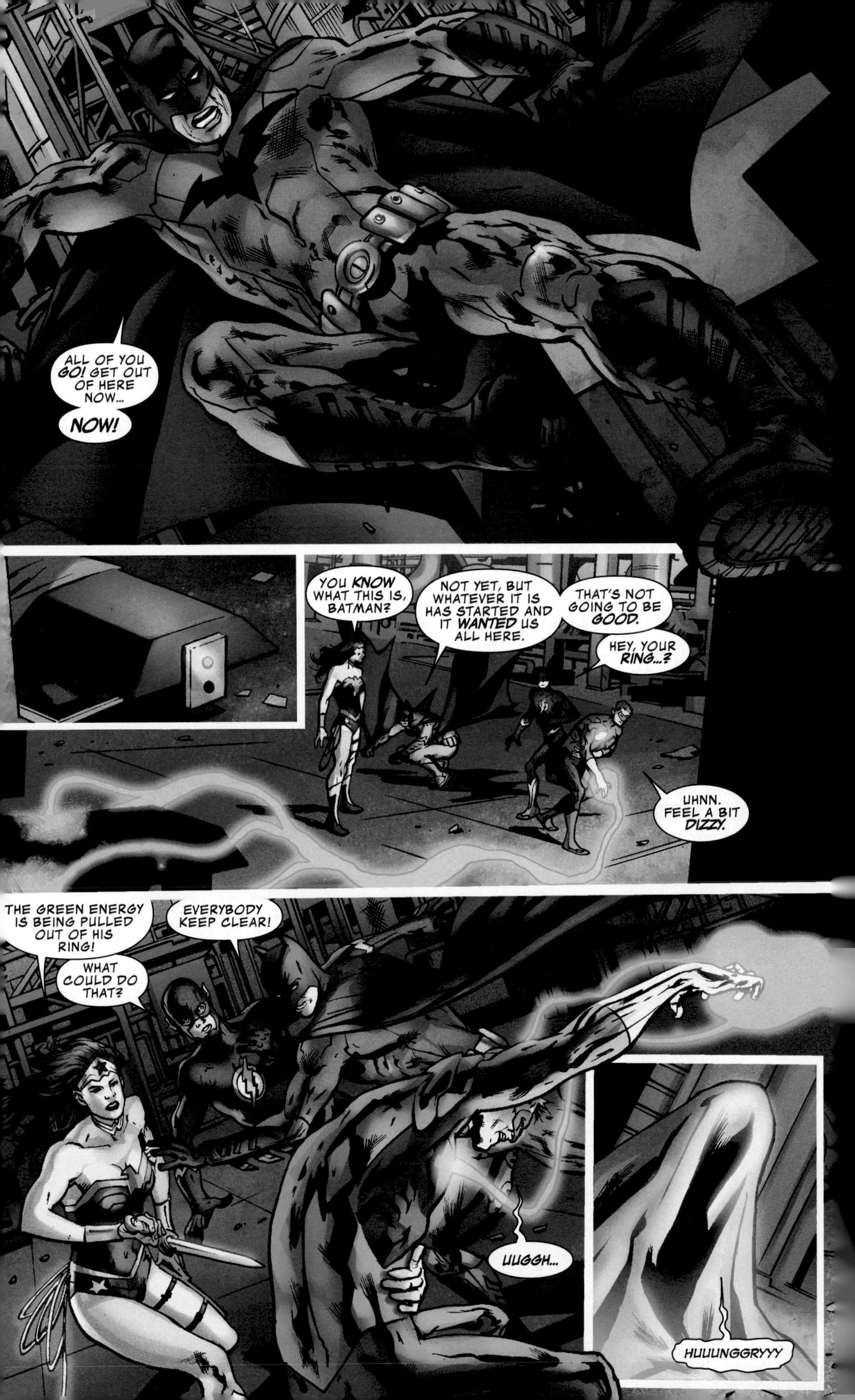
ALL OF YOU GO! GET OUT OF HERE NOW...
NOW!
YOU KNOW WHAT THIS IS, BATMAN?
NOT YET, BUT WHATEVER IT IS HAS STARTED AND IT WANTED US ALL HERE.
THAT'S NOT GOING TO BE GOOD.
HEY, YOUR RING...?
UHNN. FEEL A BIT DIZZY.
THE GREEN ENERGY IS BEING PULLED OUT OF HIS RING!
WHAT COULD DO THAT?
EVERYBODY KEEP CLEAR!
UUGGH...
HUUUNGGRYYY

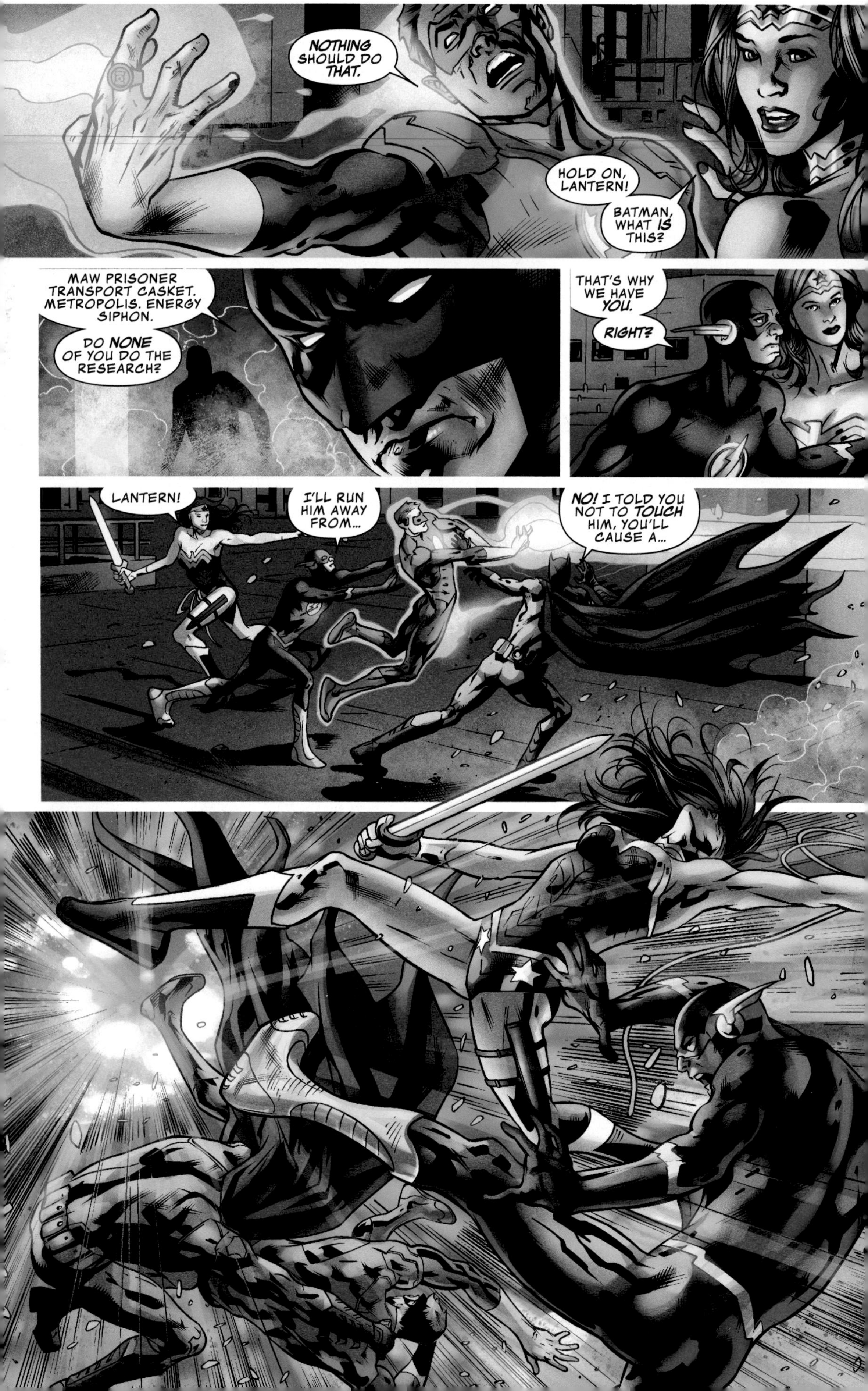
NOTHING SHOULD DO THAT.
HOLD ON, LANTERN!
BATMAN, WHAT IS THIS?
MAW PRISONER TRANSPORT CASKET. METROPOLIS. ENERGY SIPHON.
DO NONE OF YOU DO THE RESEARCH?
THAT'S WHY WE HAVE YOU.
RIGHT?
LANTERN!
I'LL RUN HIM AWAY FROM...
NO! I TOLD YOU NOT TO TOUCH HIM, YOU'LL CAUSE A...

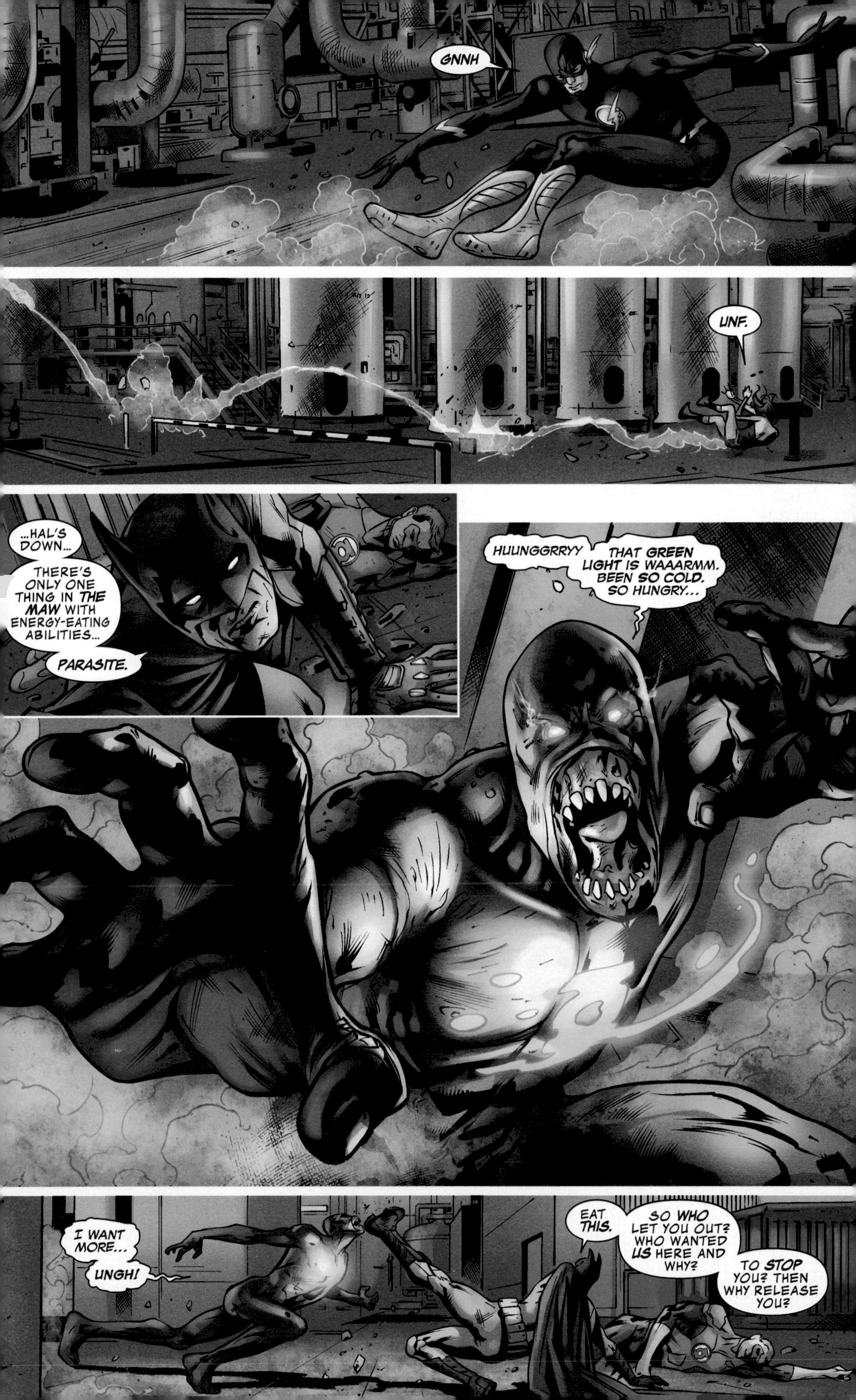
GNNH
UNF.
...HAL'S DOWN...
THERE'S ONLY ONE THING IN THE MAW WITH ENERGY-EATING ABILITIES...
PARASITE.
HUUNGGRRYY
THAT GREEN LIGHT IS WAAARMM. BEEN SO COLD. SO HUNGRY...
I WANT MORE...
UNGH!
EAT THIS.
SO WHO LET YOU OUT? WHO WANTED US HERE AND WHY?
TO STOP YOU? THEN WHY RELEASE YOU?

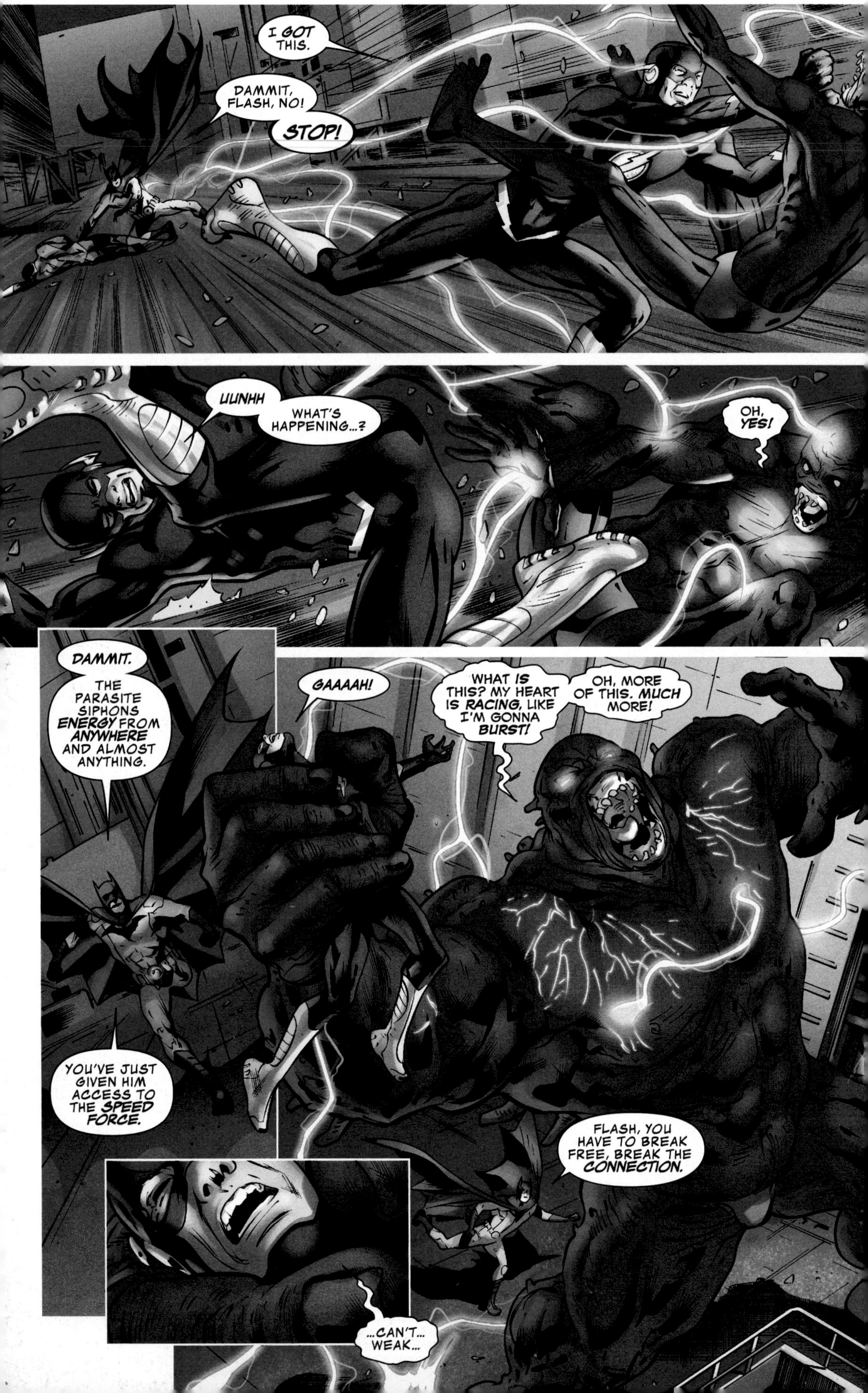
I GOT THIS.
DAMMIT, FLASH, NO!
STOP!
UUNHH
WHAT'S HAPPENING...?
OH, YES!
DAMMIT.
THE PARASITE SIPHONS ENERGY FROM ANYWHERE AND ALMOST ANYTHING.
GAAAAH!
WHAT IS THIS? MY HEART IS RACING, LIKE I'M GONNA BURST!
OH, MORE OF THIS. MUCH MORE!
YOU'VE JUST GIVEN HIM ACCESS TO THE SPEED FORCE.
FLASH, YOU HAVE TO BREAK FREE, BREAK THE CONNECTION.
...CAN'T... WEAK...

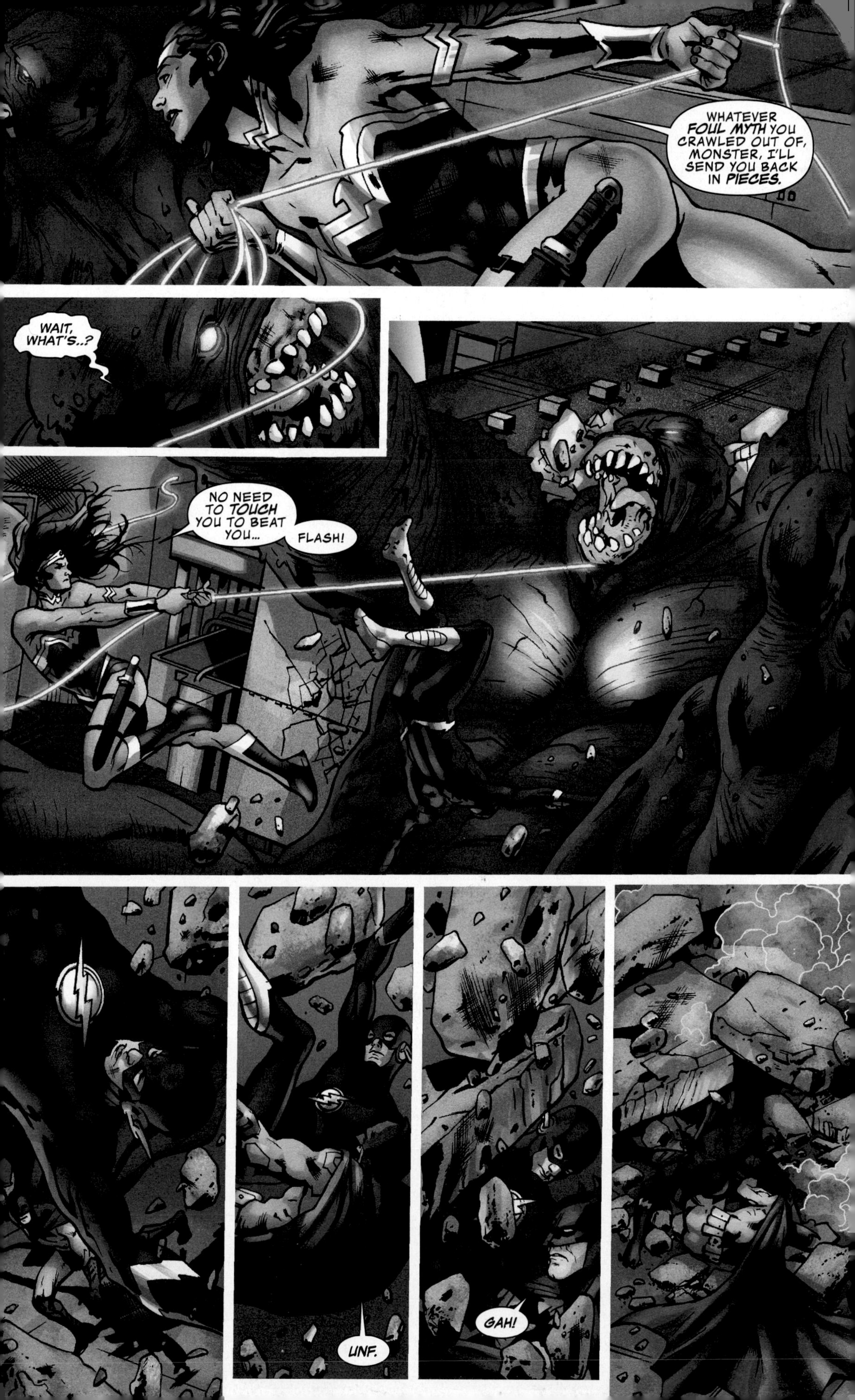
WHATEVER FOUL MYTH YOU CRAWLED OUT OF, MONSTER, I'LL SEND YOU BACK IN PIECES.
WAIT, WHAT'S..?
NO NEED TO TOUCH YOU TO BEAT YOU...
FLASH!
UNF.
GAH!

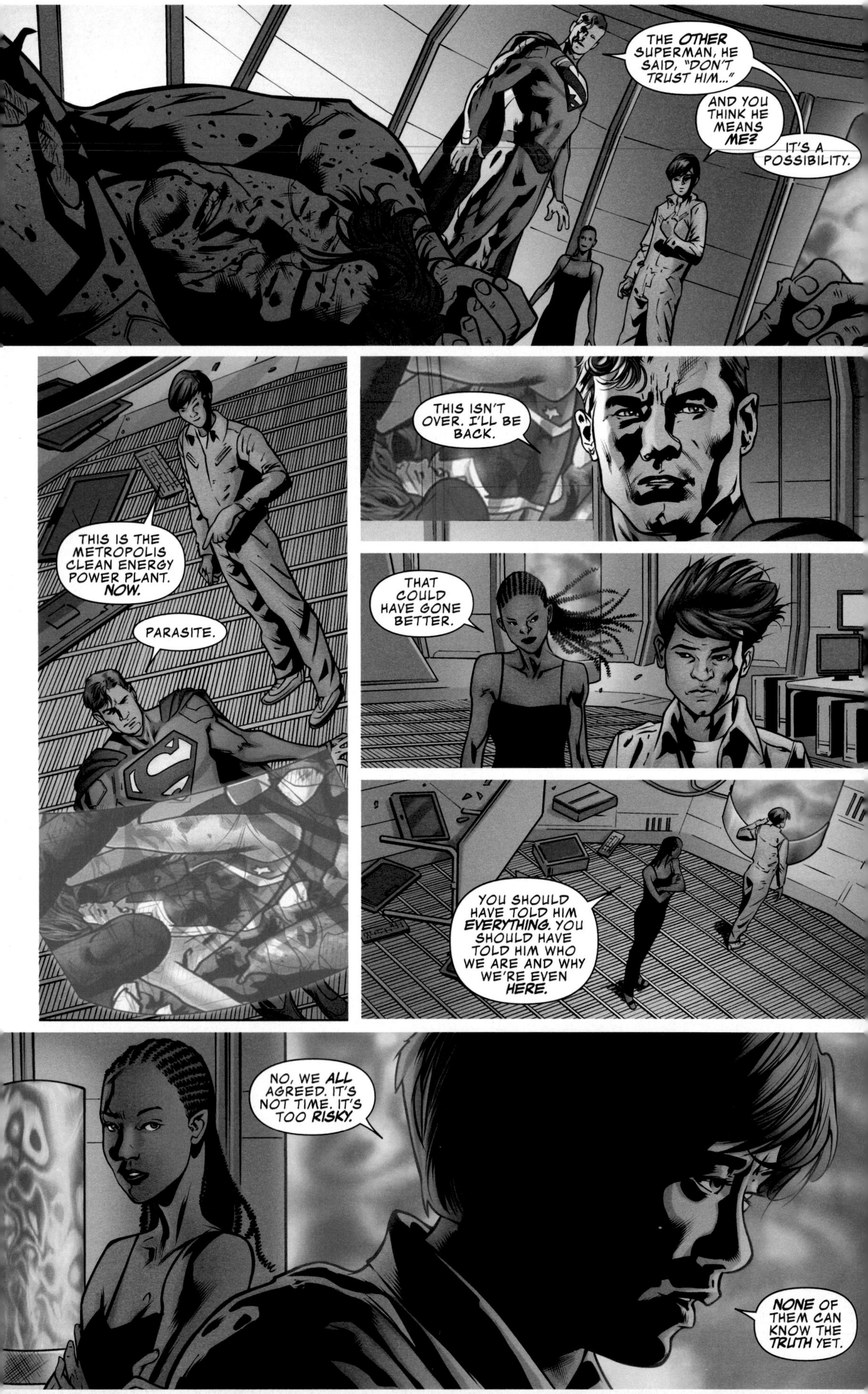
THE OTHER SUPERMAN, HE SAID, "DON'T TRUST HIM..."
AND YOU THINK HE MEANS ME?
IT'S A POSSIBILITY.
THIS IS THE METROPOLIS CLEAN ENERGY POWER PLANT. NOW.
PARASITE.
THIS ISN'T OVER. I'LL BE BACK.
THAT COULD HAVE GONE BETTER.
YOU SHOULD HAVE TOLD HIM EVERYTHING. YOU SHOULD HAVE TOLD HIM WHO WE ARE AND WHY WE'RE EVEN HERE.
NO, WE ALL AGREED. IT'S NOT TIME. IT'S TOO RISKY.
NONE OF THEM CAN KNOW THE TRUTH YET.

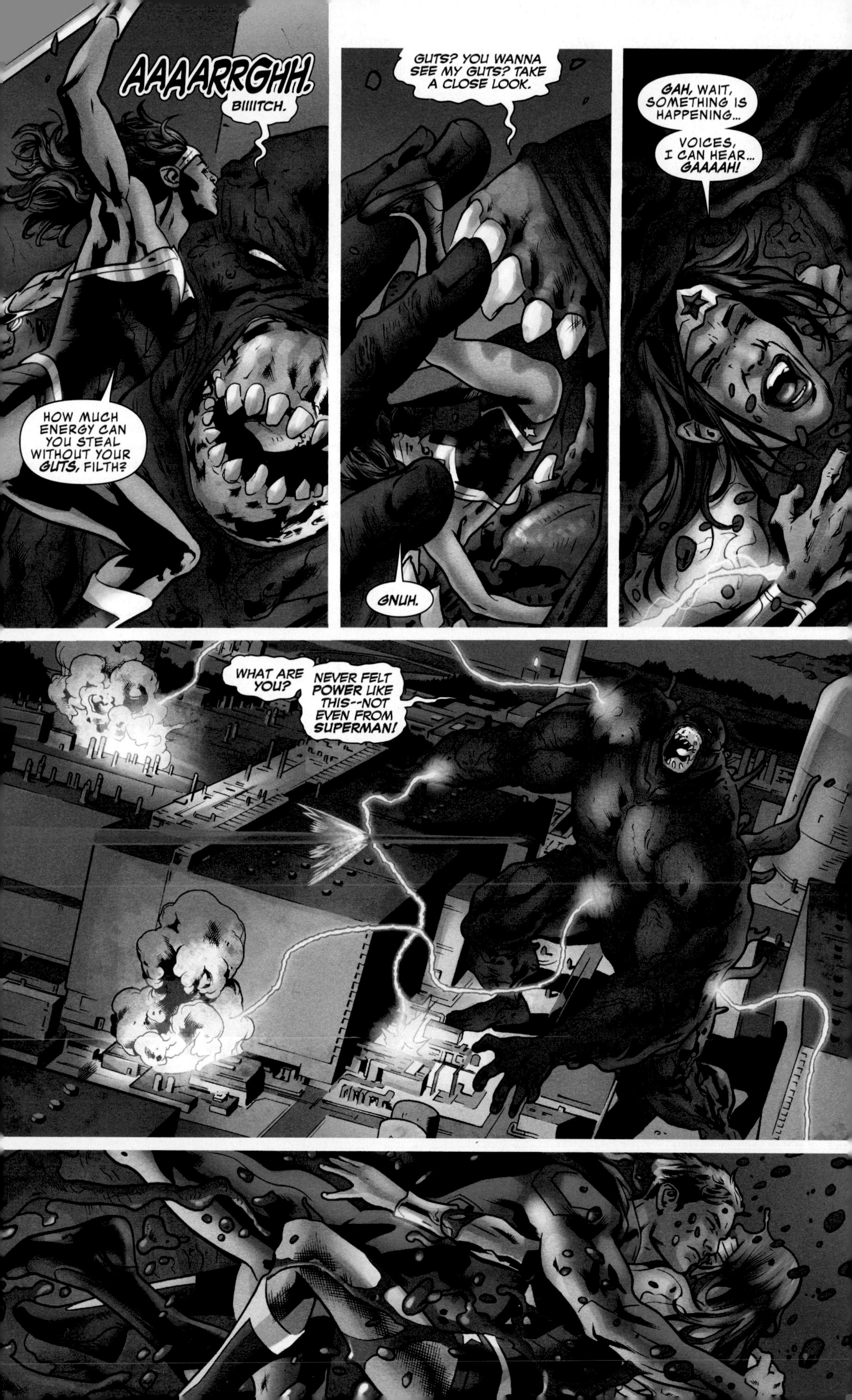
AAAARRGHH!
BIIIITCH.
HOW MUCH ENERGY CAN YOU STEAL WITHOUT YOUR GUTS, FILTH?
GUTS? YOU WANNA SEE MY GUTS? TAKE A CLOSE LOOK.
GNUH.
GAH, WAIT, SOMETHING IS HAPPENING...
VOICES, I CAN HEAR... GAAAAH!
WHAT ARE YOU?
NEVER FELT POWER LIKE THIS--NOT EVEN FROM SUPERMAN!

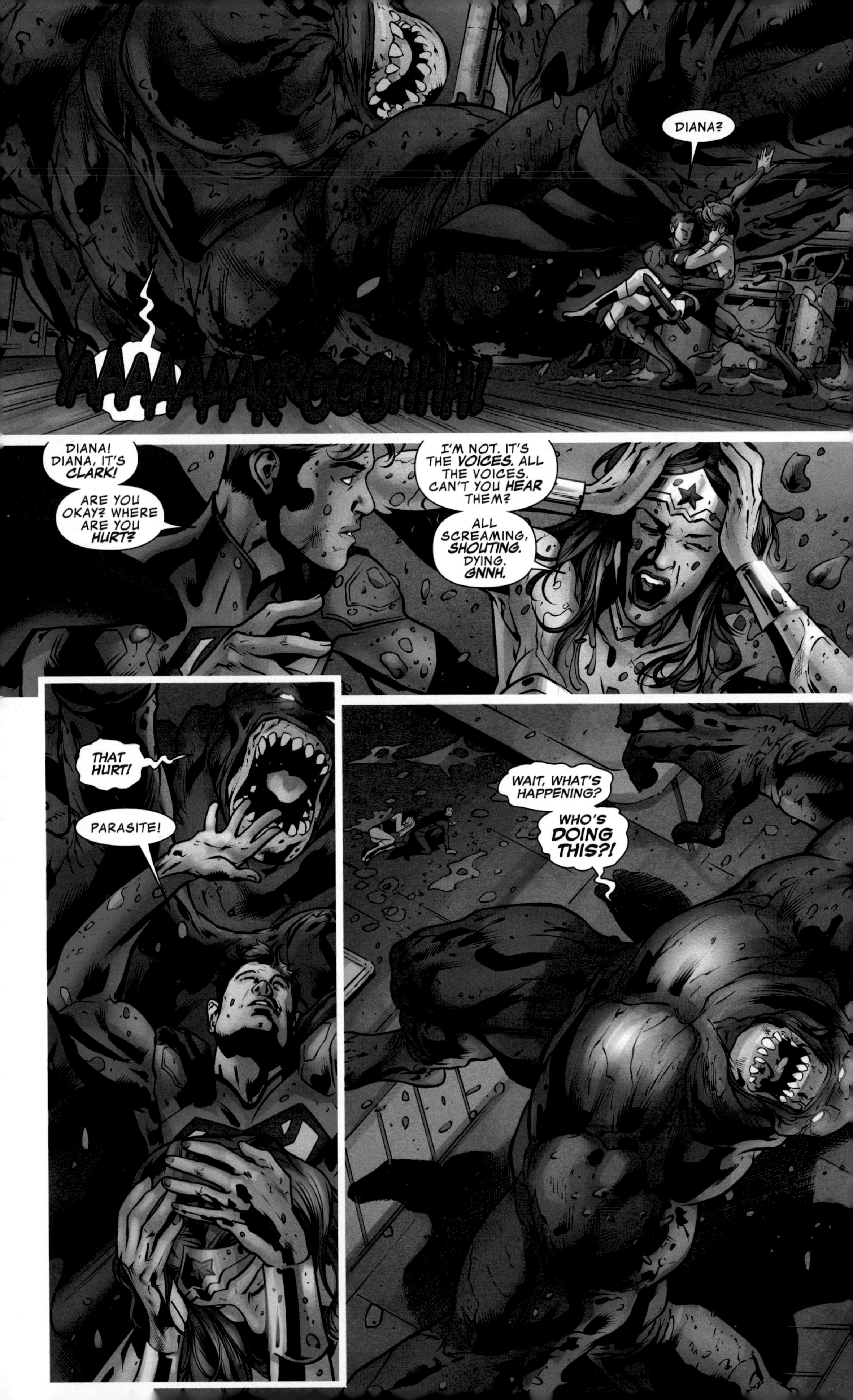

DIANA?
YAAAAAARRGGGHHH!
DIANA! DIANA, IT'S CLARK!
ARE YOU OKAY? WHERE ARE YOU HURT?
I'M NOT. IT'S THE VOICES. ALL THE VOICES. CAN'T YOU HEAR THEM?
ALL SCREAMING, SHOUTING. DYING. GNNH.
THAT HURT!
PARASITE!
WAIT, WHAT'S HAPPENING?
WHO'S DOING THIS?!

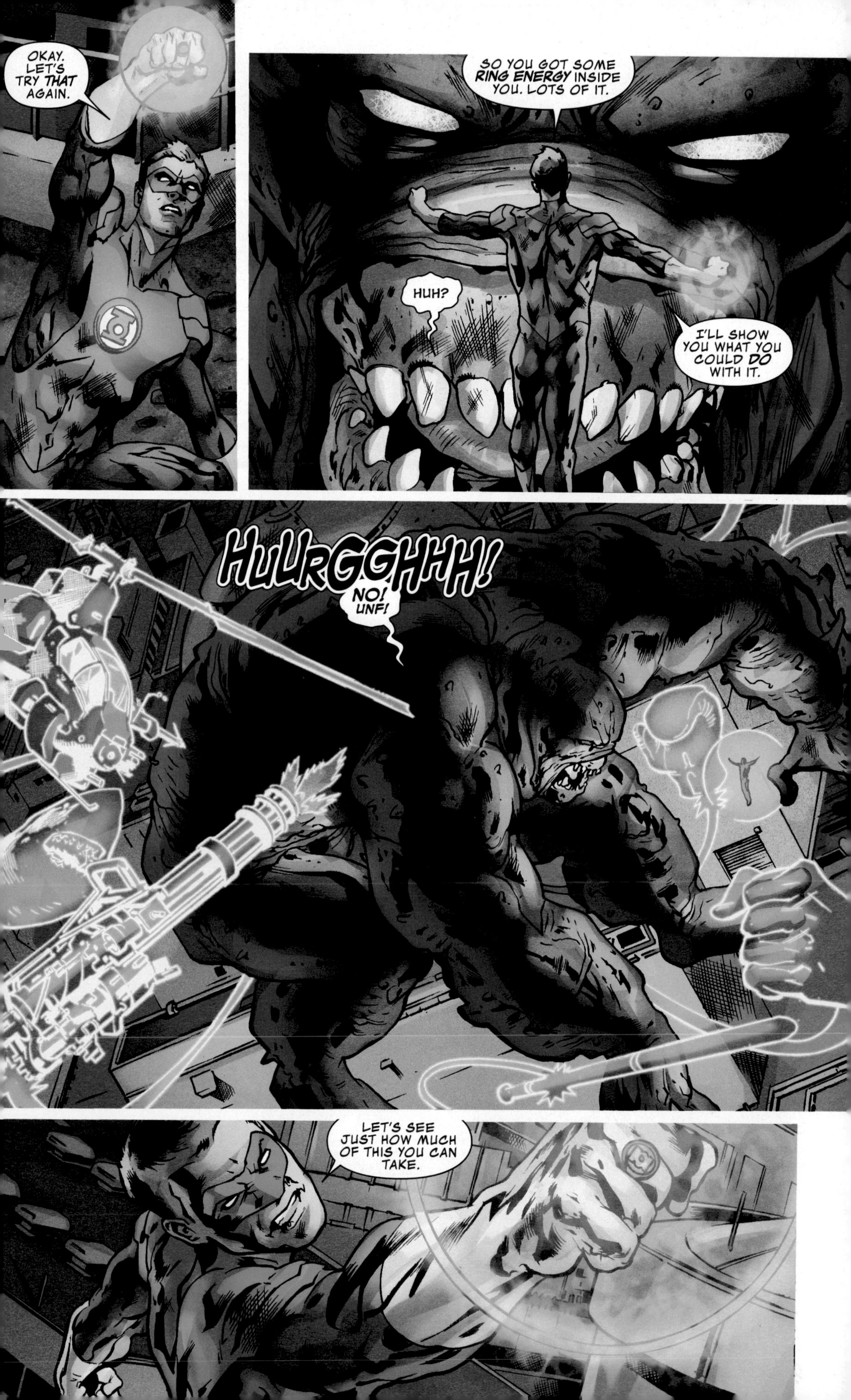

OKAY. LET'S TRY **THAT** AGAIN.
SO YOU GOT SOME **RING ENERGY** INSIDE YOU. LOTS OF IT.
HUH?
I'LL SHOW YOU WHAT YOU COULD **DO** WITH IT.
HULRGGHHH!
NO! UNF!
LET'S SEE JUST HOW MUCH OF THIS YOU CAN TAKE.

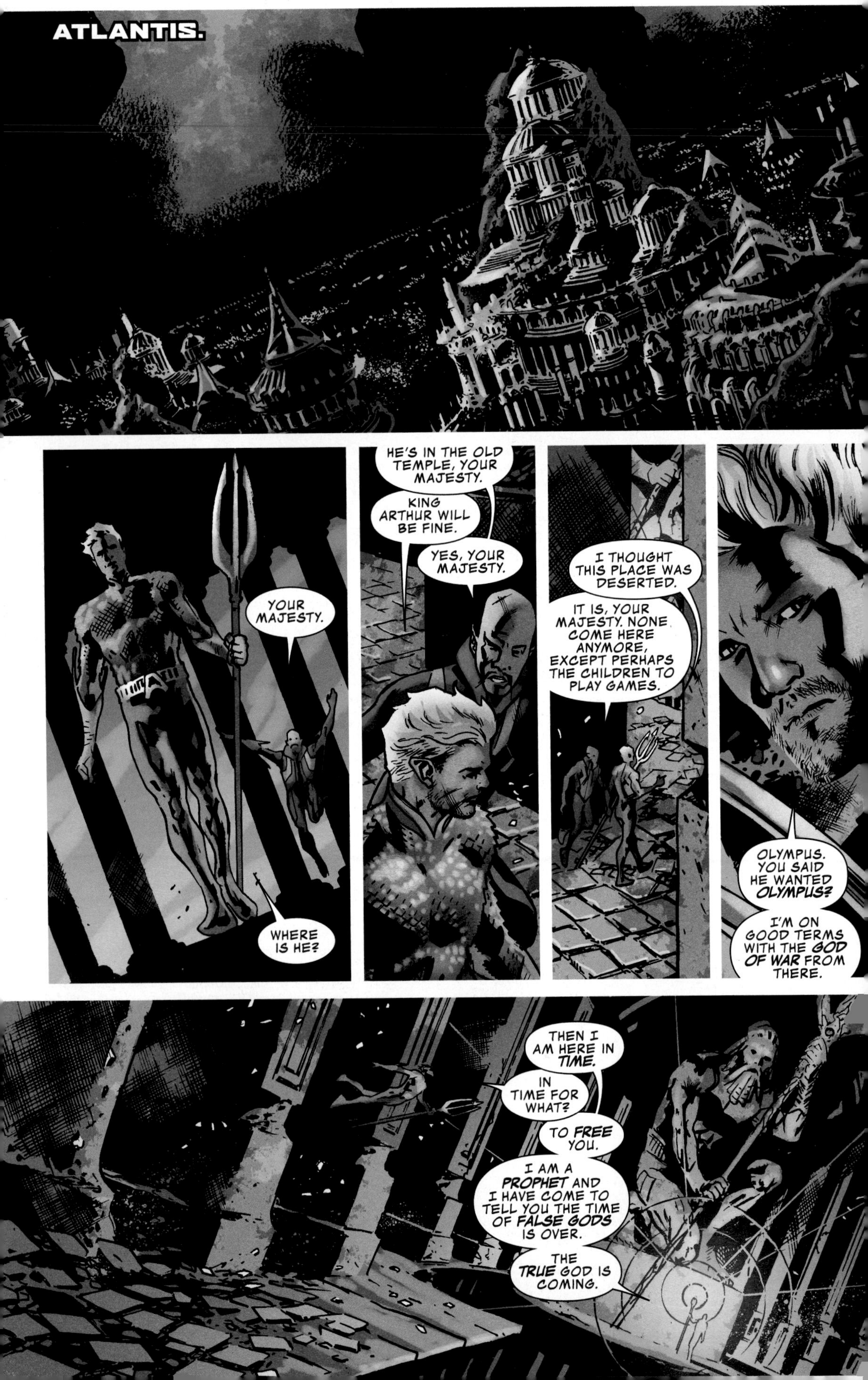
ATLANTIS.
YOUR MAJESTY.
WHERE IS HE?
HE'S IN THE OLD TEMPLE, YOUR MAJESTY.
KING ARTHUR WILL BE FINE.
YES, YOUR MAJESTY.
I THOUGHT THIS PLACE WAS DESERTED.
IT IS, YOUR MAJESTY. NONE COME HERE ANYMORE, EXCEPT PERHAPS THE CHILDREN TO PLAY GAMES.
OLYMPUS. YOU SAID HE WANTED OLYMPUS?
I'M ON GOOD TERMS WITH THE GOD OF WAR FROM THERE.
THEN I AM HERE IN TIME.
IN TIME FOR WHAT?
TO FREE YOU.
I AM A PROPHET AND I HAVE COME TO TELL YOU THE TIME OF FALSE GODS IS OVER.
THE TRUE GOD IS COMING.

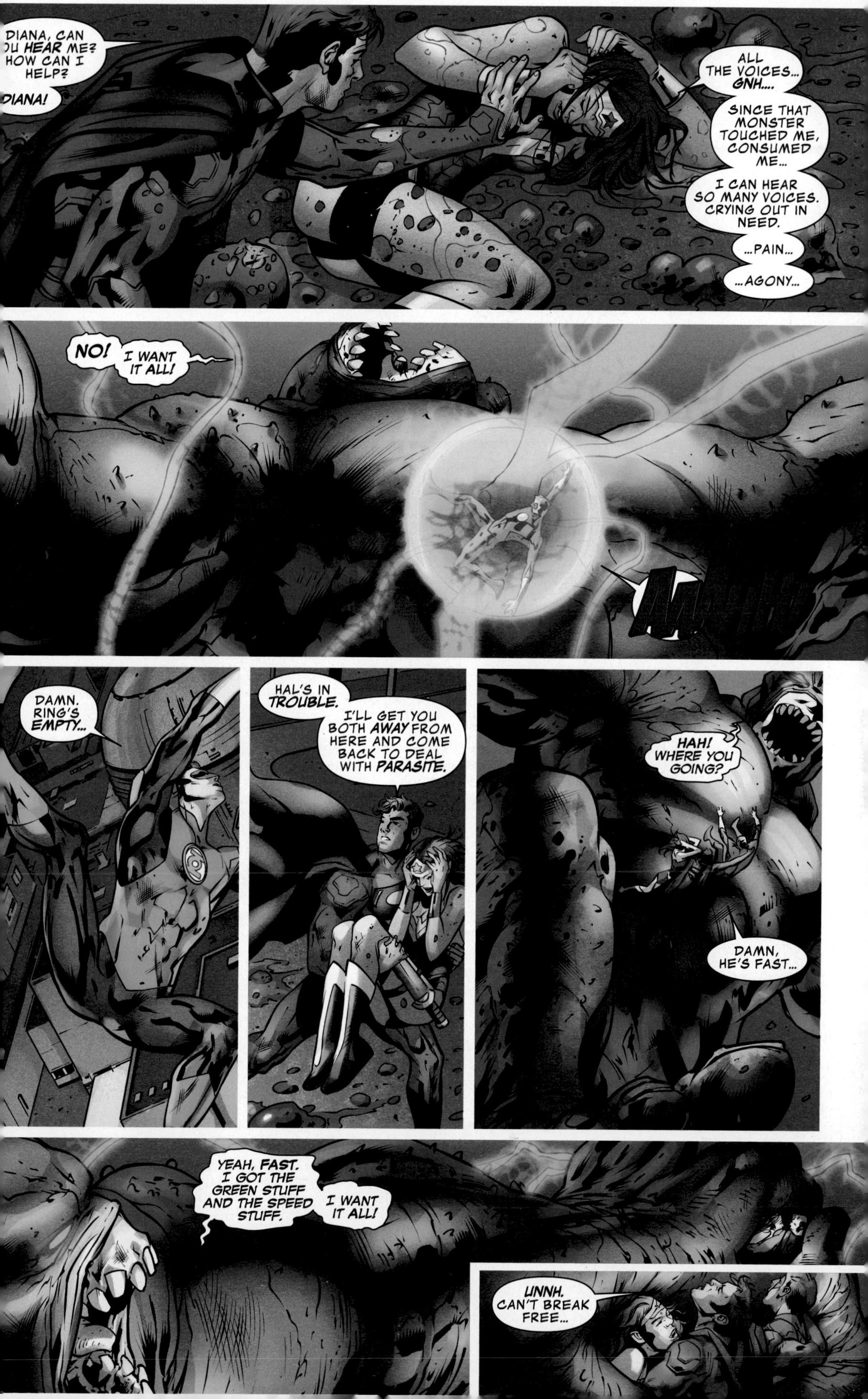
DIANA, CAN
U HEAR ME? HOW CAN I HELP?
DIANA!
ALL THE VOICES... GNH....
SINCE THAT MONSTER TOUCHED ME, CONSUMED ME...
I CAN HEAR SO MANY VOICES. CRYING OUT IN NEED.
...PAIN...
...AGONY...
NO!
I WANT IT ALL!
DAMN. RING'S EMPTY...
HAL'S IN TROUBLE.
I'LL GET YOU BOTH AWAY FROM HERE AND COME BACK TO DEAL WITH PARASITE.
HAH! WHERE YOU GOING?
DAMN, HE'S FAST...
YEAH, FAST. I GOT THE GREEN STUFF AND THE SPEED STUFF.
I WANT IT ALL!
UNNH. CAN'T BREAK FREE...

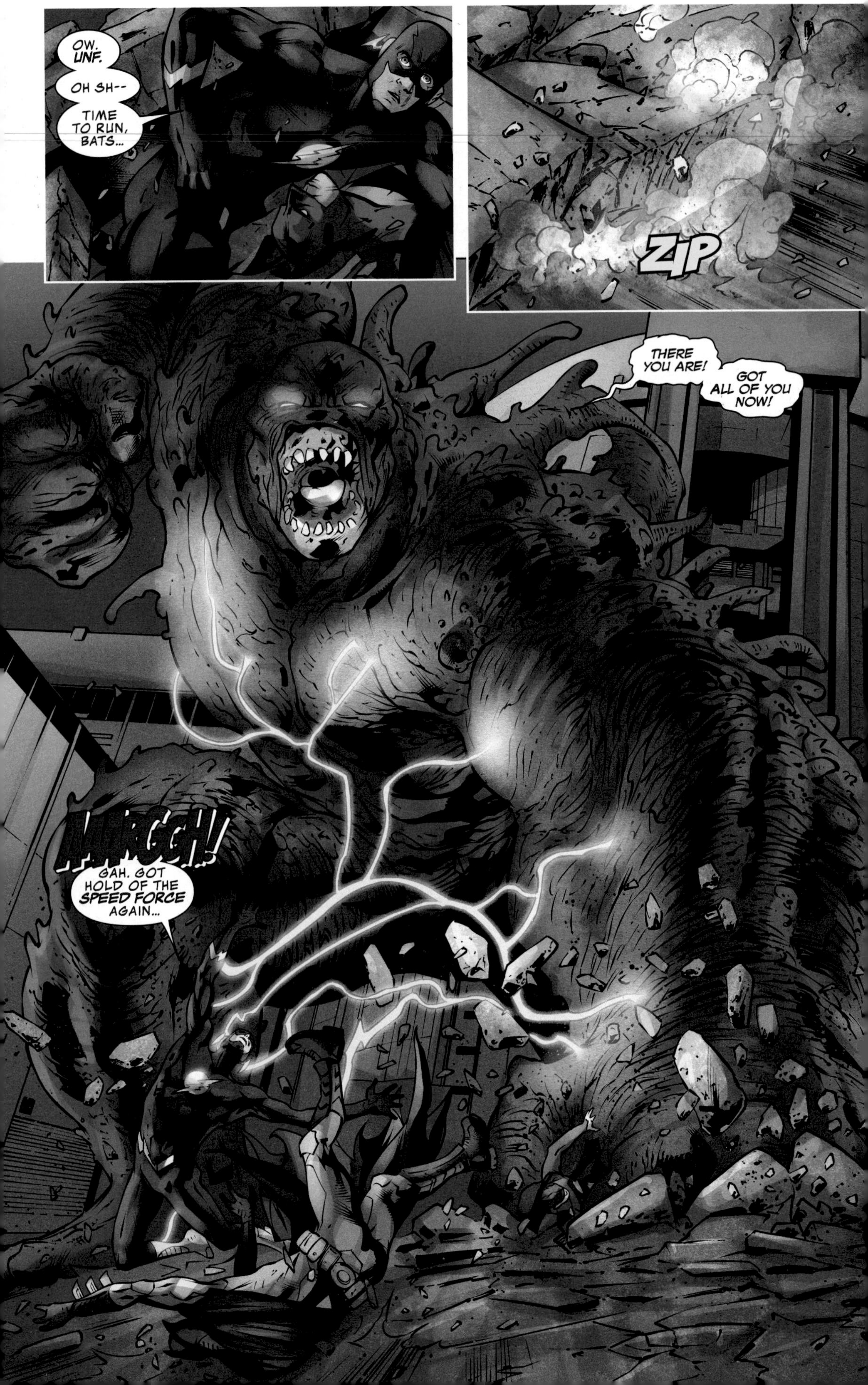
OW. UNF.
OH SH--
TIME TO RUN, BATS...
ZIP
THERE YOU ARE!
GOT ALL OF YOU NOW!
GAH. GOT HOLD OF THE SPEED FORCE AGAIN...

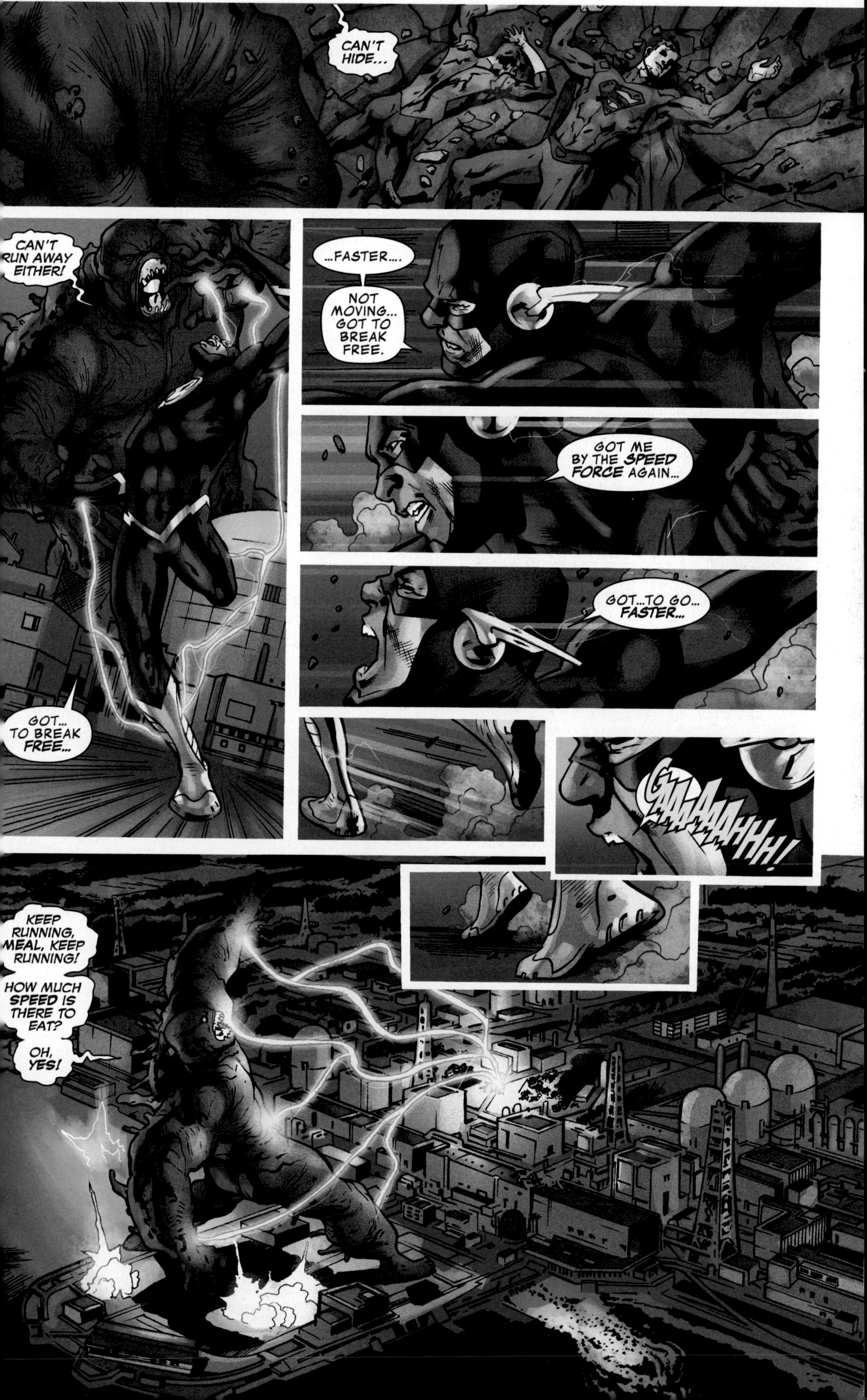
CAN'T HIDE...
CAN'T RUN AWAY EITHER!
...FASTER....
NOT MOVING... GOT TO BREAK FREE.
GOT ME BY THE SPEED FORCE AGAIN...
GOT...TO GO... FASTER...
GOT... TO BREAK FREE...
GAAAAAAHHH!
KEEP RUNNING, MEAL, KEEP RUNNING!
HOW MUCH SPEED IS THERE TO EAT?
OH, YES!

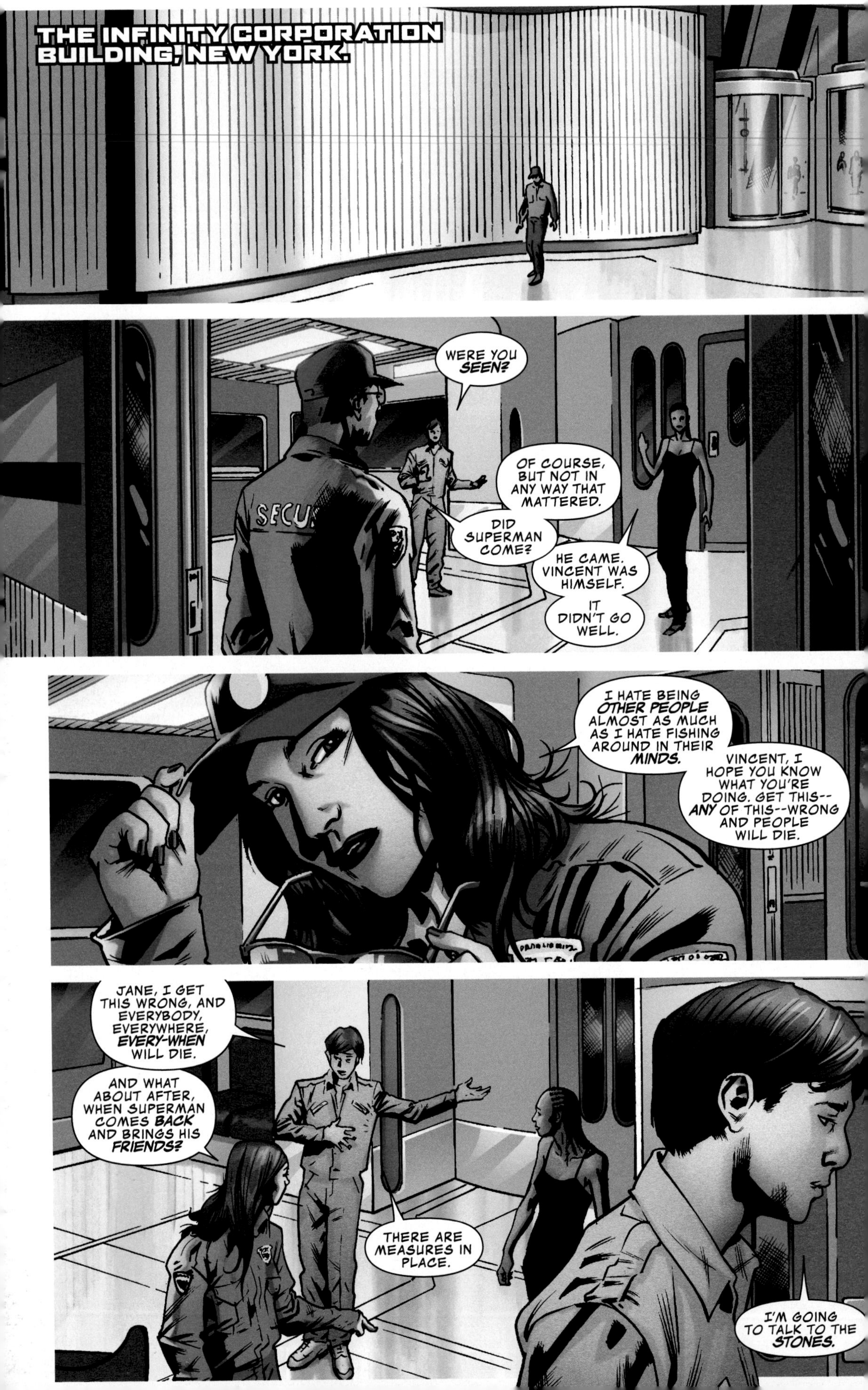
THE INFINITY CORPORATION BUILDING, NEW YORK.
WERE YOU SEEN?
OF COURSE, BUT NOT IN ANY WAY THAT MATTERED.
DID SUPERMAN COME?
HE CAME. VINCENT WAS HIMSELF.
IT DIDN'T GO WELL.
I HATE BEING OTHER PEOPLE ALMOST AS MUCH AS I HATE FISHING AROUND IN THEIR MINDS.
VINCENT, I HOPE YOU KNOW WHAT YOU'RE DOING. GET THIS--ANY OF THIS--WRONG AND PEOPLE WILL DIE.
JANE, I GET THIS WRONG, AND EVERYBODY, EVERYWHERE, EVERY-WHEN WILL DIE.
AND WHAT ABOUT AFTER, WHEN SUPERMAN COMES BACK AND BRINGS HIS FRIENDS?
THERE ARE MEASURES IN PLACE.
I'M GOING TO TALK TO THE STONES.

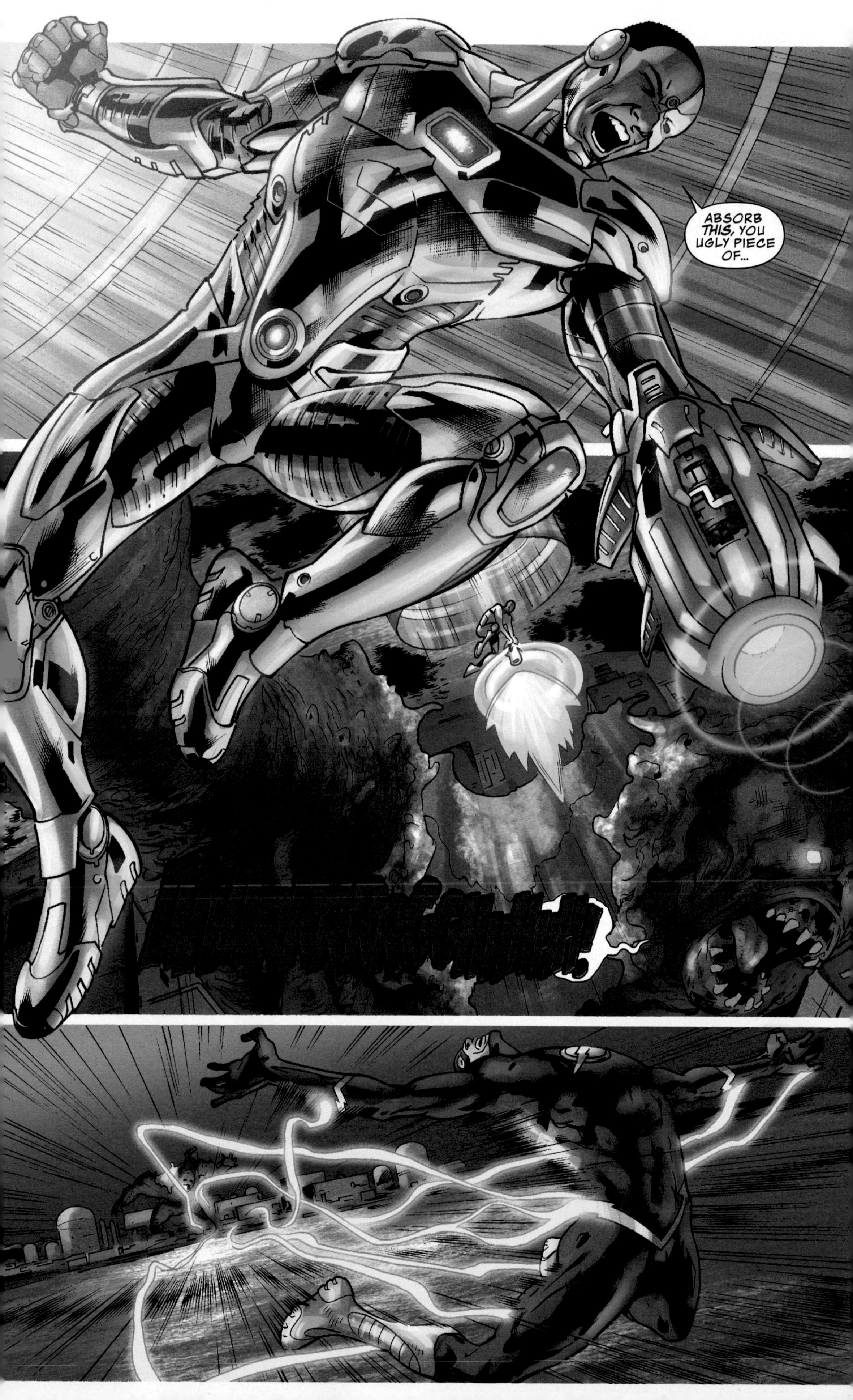
ABSORB THIS, YOU UGLY PIECE OF...

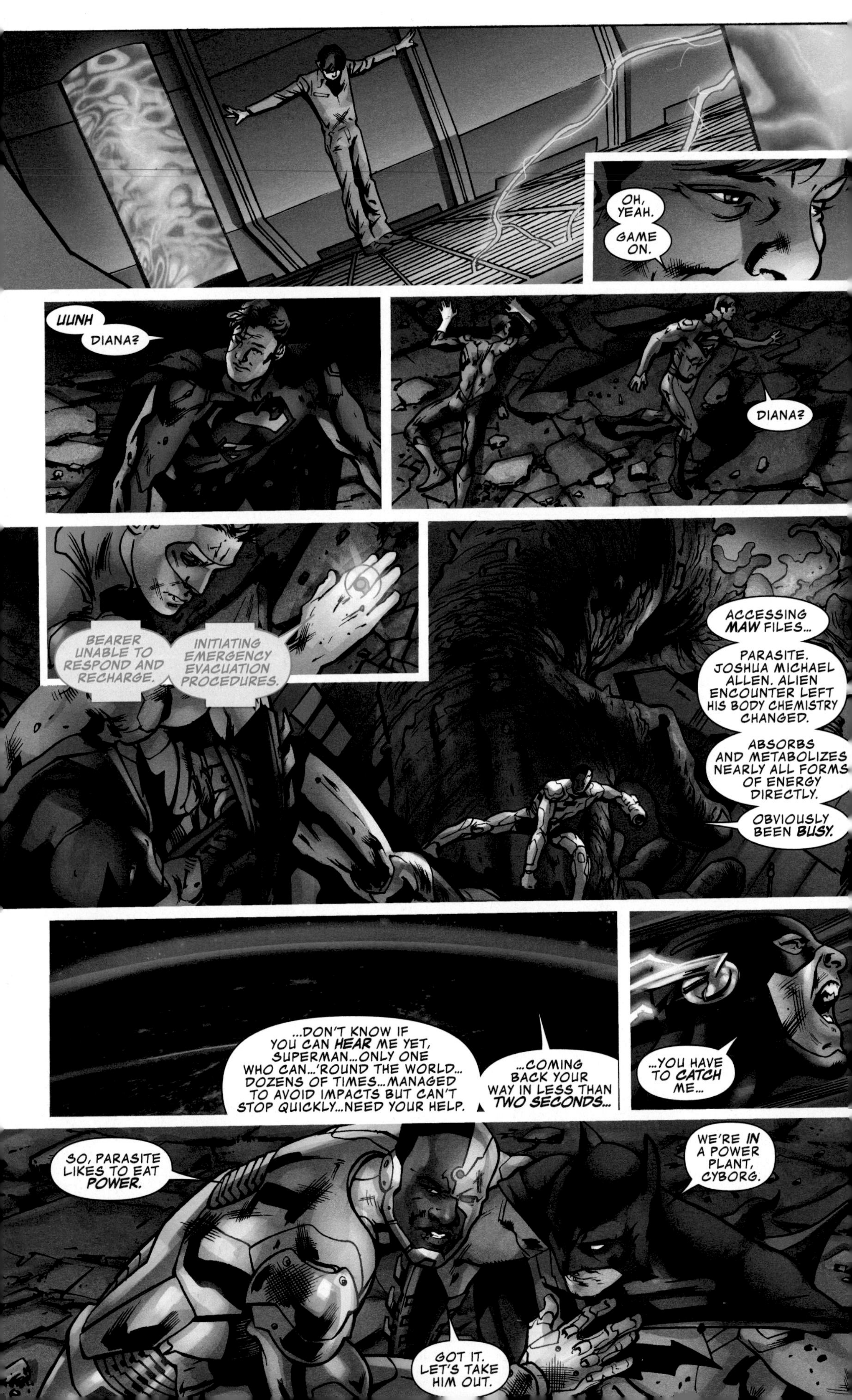
OH, YEAH.
GAME ON.
UUNH
DIANA?
DIANA?
BEARER UNABLE TO RESPOND AND RECHARGE.
INITIATING EMERGENCY EVACUATION PROCEDURES.
ACCESSING MAW FILES...
PARASITE. JOSHUA MICHAEL ALLEN. ALIEN ENCOUNTER LEFT HIS BODY CHEMISTRY CHANGED.
ABSORBS AND METABOLIZES NEARLY ALL FORMS OF ENERGY DIRECTLY.
OBVIOUSLY BEEN BUSY.
...DON'T KNOW IF YOU CAN HEAR ME YET, SUPERMAN...ONLY ONE WHO CAN...'ROUND THE WORLD... DOZENS OF TIMES...MANAGED TO AVOID IMPACTS BUT CAN'T STOP QUICKLY...NEED YOUR HELP.
...COMING BACK YOUR WAY IN LESS THAN TWO SECONDS...
...YOU HAVE TO CATCH ME...
SO, PARASITE LIKES TO EAT POWER.
WE'RE IN A POWER PLANT, CYBORG.
GOT IT. LET'S TAKE HIM OUT.

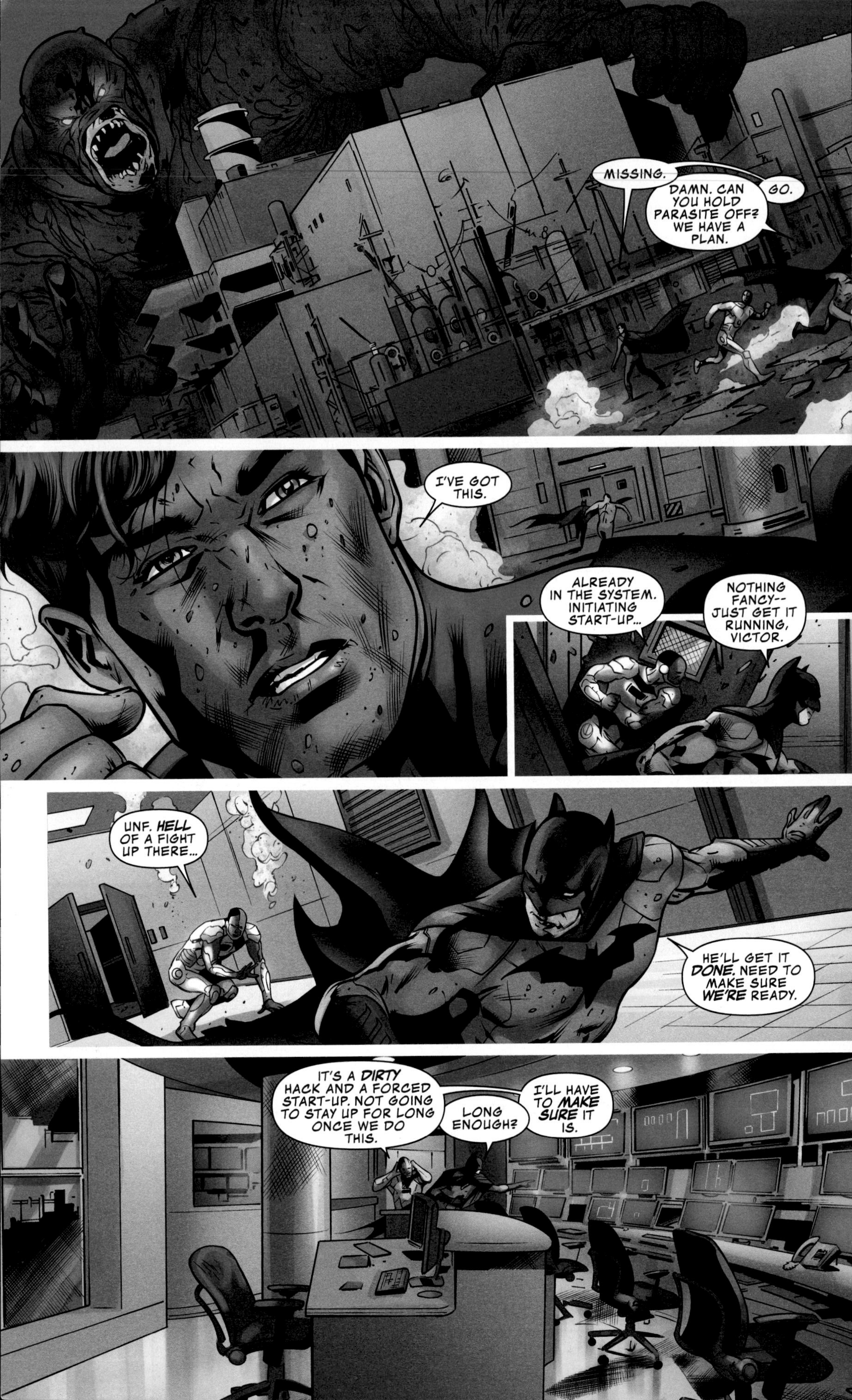
MISSING.
DAMN. CAN YOU HOLD PARASITE OFF? WE HAVE A PLAN.
GO.
I'VE GOT THIS.
ALREADY IN THE SYSTEM. INITIATING START-UP...
NOTHING FANCY-- JUST GET IT RUNNING, VICTOR.
UNF. HELL OF A FIGHT UP THERE...
HE'LL GET IT DONE. NEED TO MAKE SURE WE'RE READY.
IT'S A DIRTY HACK AND A FORCED START-UP. NOT GOING TO STAY UP FOR LONG ONCE WE DO THIS.
LONG ENOUGH?
I'LL HAVE TO MAKE SURE IT IS.

WHEN IT'S ALL RUNNING, YOU'LL NEED TO...

I KNOW WHAT TO DO.

OF COURSE YOU DO.

UFF.

SCHEMATICS I PULLED TELL ME THE CABLES I NEED ARE RIGHT...

...HERE. BATMAN, HOW WE DOING? THIS TRICK IS GOING TO FRY MY UPLINK SO YOU'LL HAVE TO KEEP SYSTEMS ONLINE THERE.

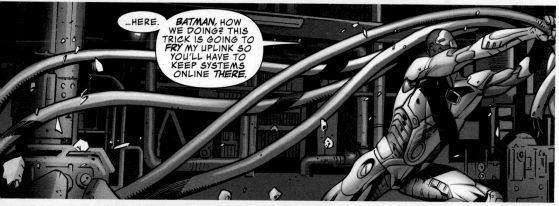

THE BOARD'S AS GREEN AS IT'S GOING TO GET.

SUPERMAN, BRING HIM IN.

...WAIT, I'M NOT READY...

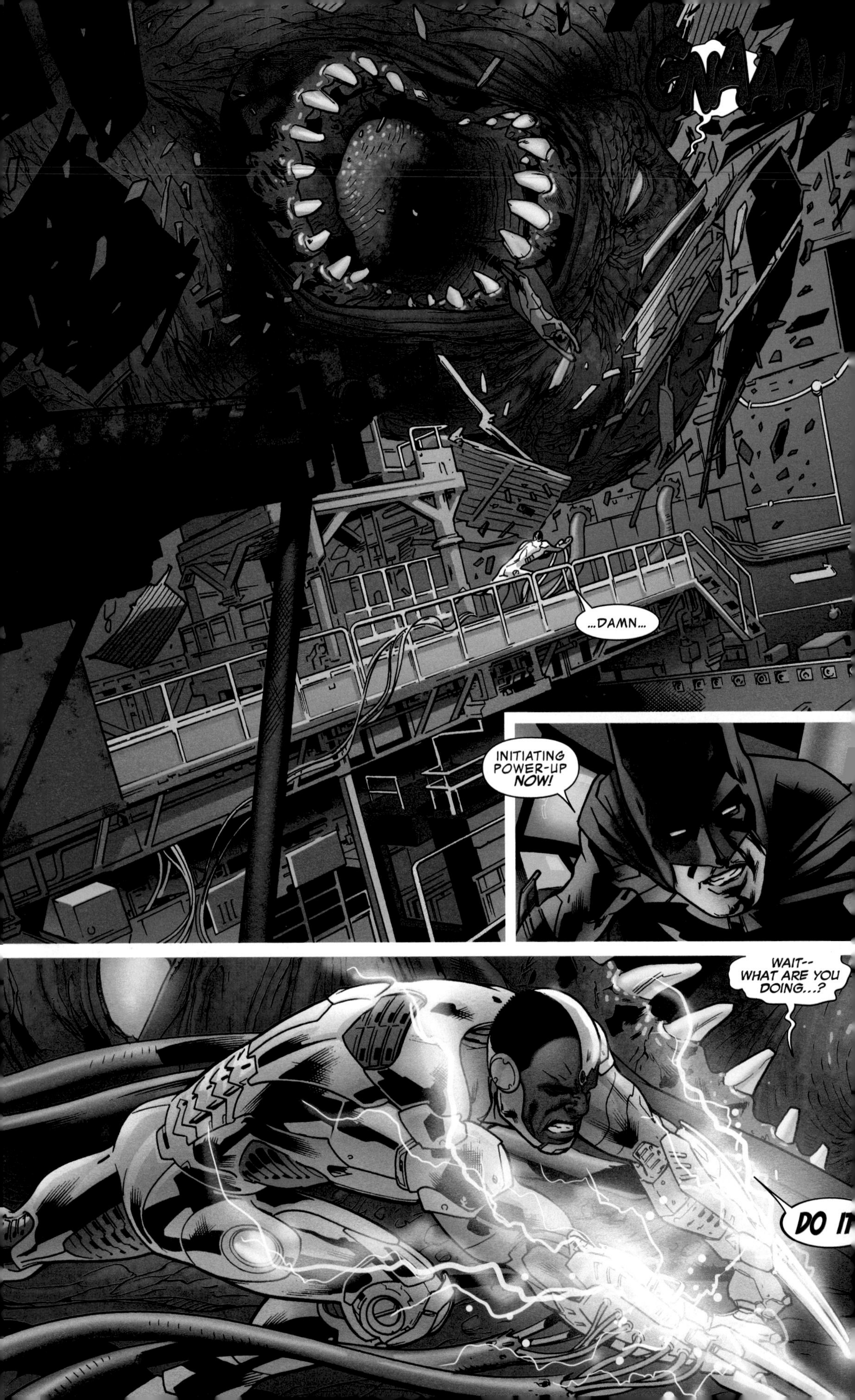
GNAAAH!
...DAMN...
INITIATING POWER-UP NOW!
WAIT-- WHAT ARE YOU DOING...?
DO IT

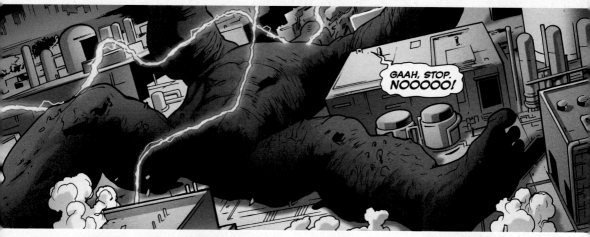

GAAH, STOP. NOOOOO!

SYSTEM'S BLOWING!

VICTOR, YOU'LL HAVE TO HOLD IT TOGETHER!

UNFF!

NOOO, PLEASE!

YOU'RE TAKING ALL THE POWER AWAY!

...AND DUMPING IT ALL INTO THE NATIONAL GRID...

GnAAAAAAHHHH!

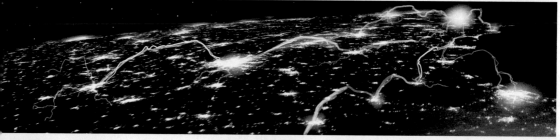

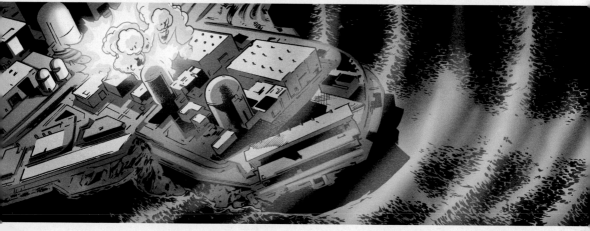

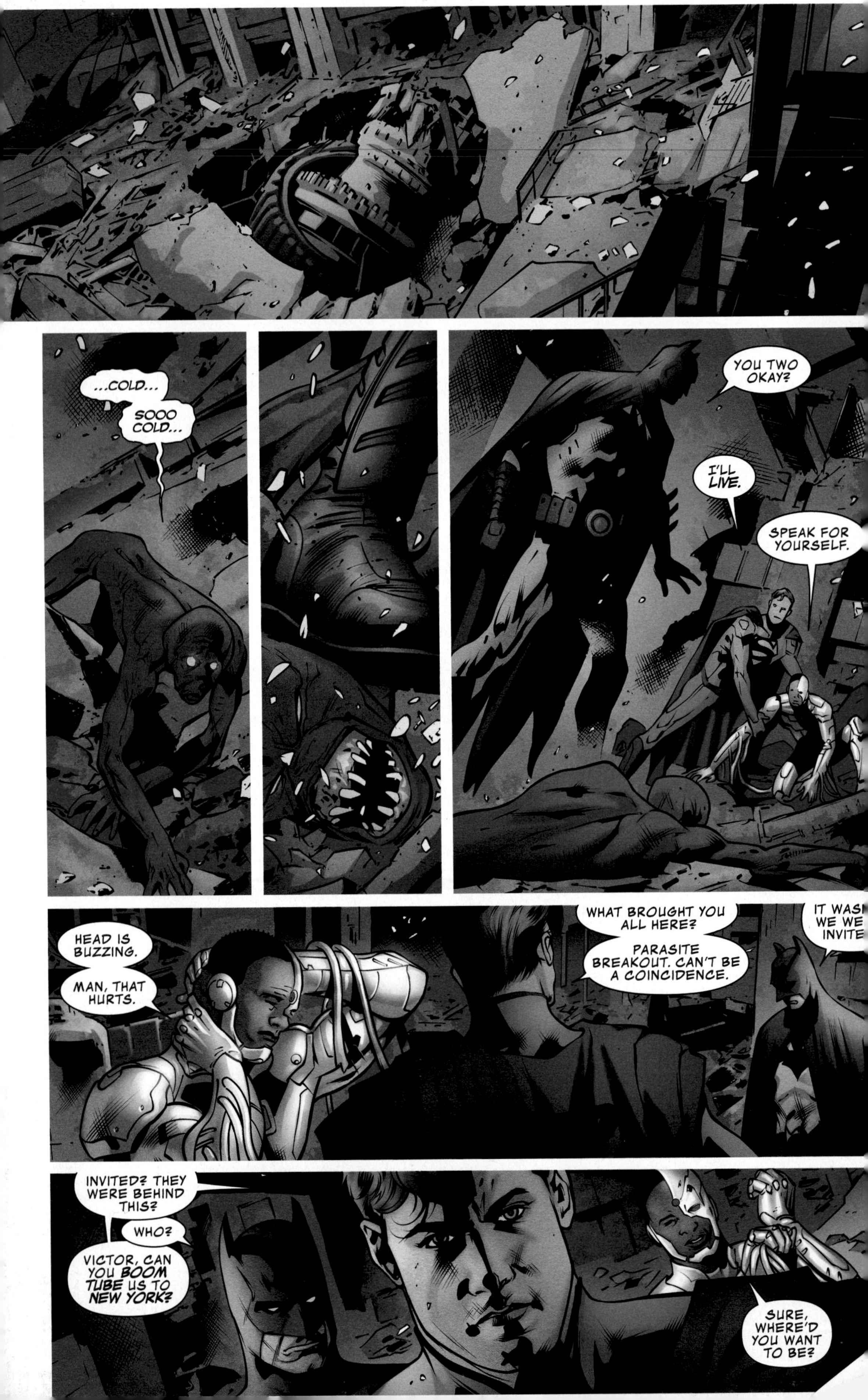
...COLD...
SOOO COLD...
YOU TWO OKAY?
I'LL *LIVE.*
SPEAK FOR YOURSELF.
HEAD IS BUZZING.
MAN, THAT HURTS.
WHAT BROUGHT YOU ALL HERE?
PARASITE BREAKOUT. CAN'T BE A COINCIDENCE.
INVITED? THEY WERE BEHIND THIS?
WHO?
VICTOR, CAN YOU *BOOM TUBE* US TO *NEW YORK?*
SURE, WHERE'D YOU WANT TO BE?

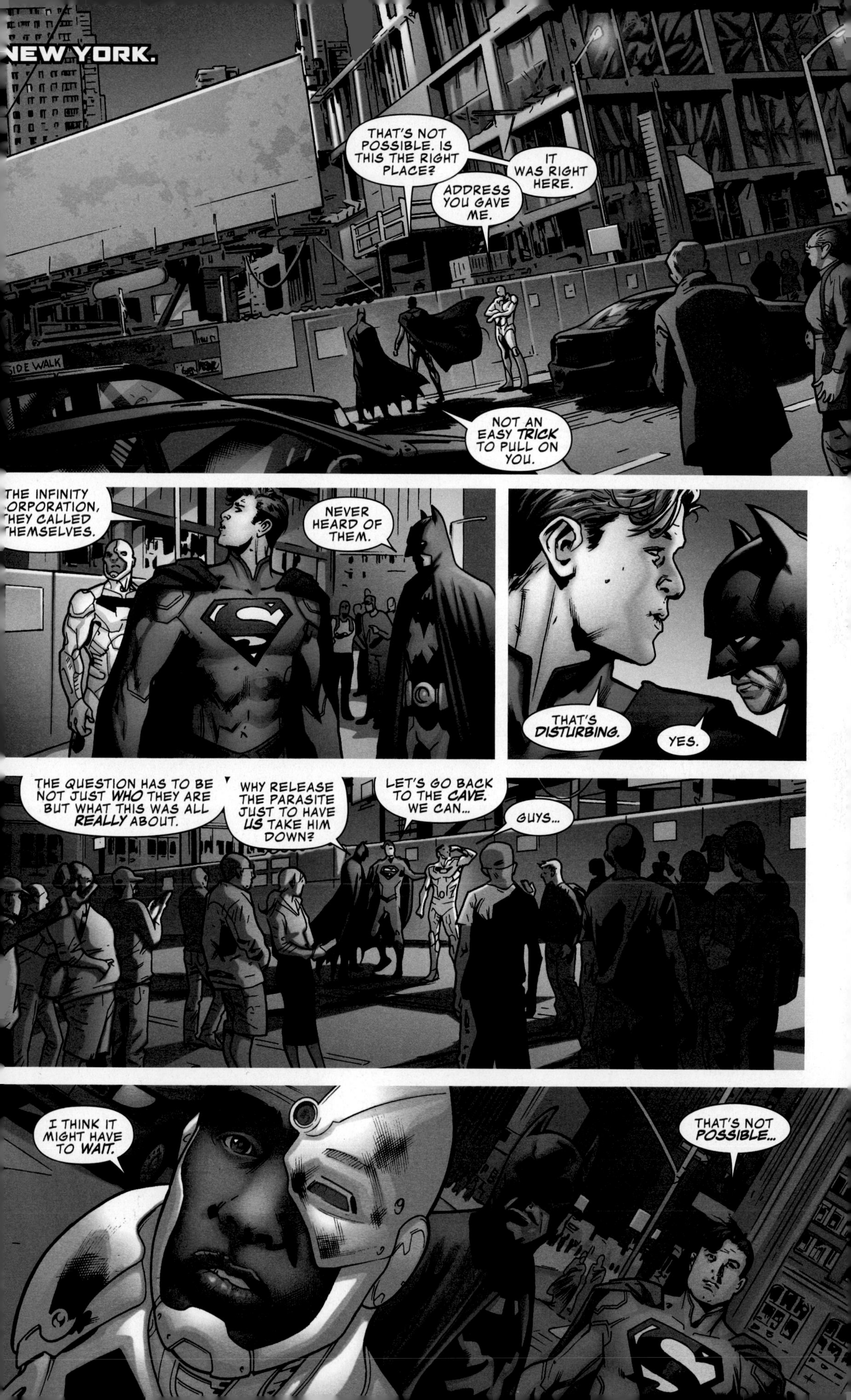
NEW YORK.
THAT'S NOT POSSIBLE. IS THIS THE RIGHT PLACE?
IT WAS RIGHT HERE.
ADDRESS YOU GAVE ME.
SIDE WALK
NOT AN EASY TRICK TO PULL ON YOU.
THE INFINITY CORPORATION, THEY CALLED THEMSELVES.
NEVER HEARD OF THEM.
THAT'S DISTURBING.
YES.
THE QUESTION HAS TO BE NOT JUST WHO THEY ARE BUT WHAT THIS WAS ALL REALLY ABOUT.
WHY RELEASE THE PARASITE JUST TO HAVE US TAKE HIM DOWN?
LET'S GO BACK TO THE CAVE. WE CAN...
GUYS...
I THINK IT MIGHT HAVE TO WAIT.
THAT'S NOT POSSIBLE...

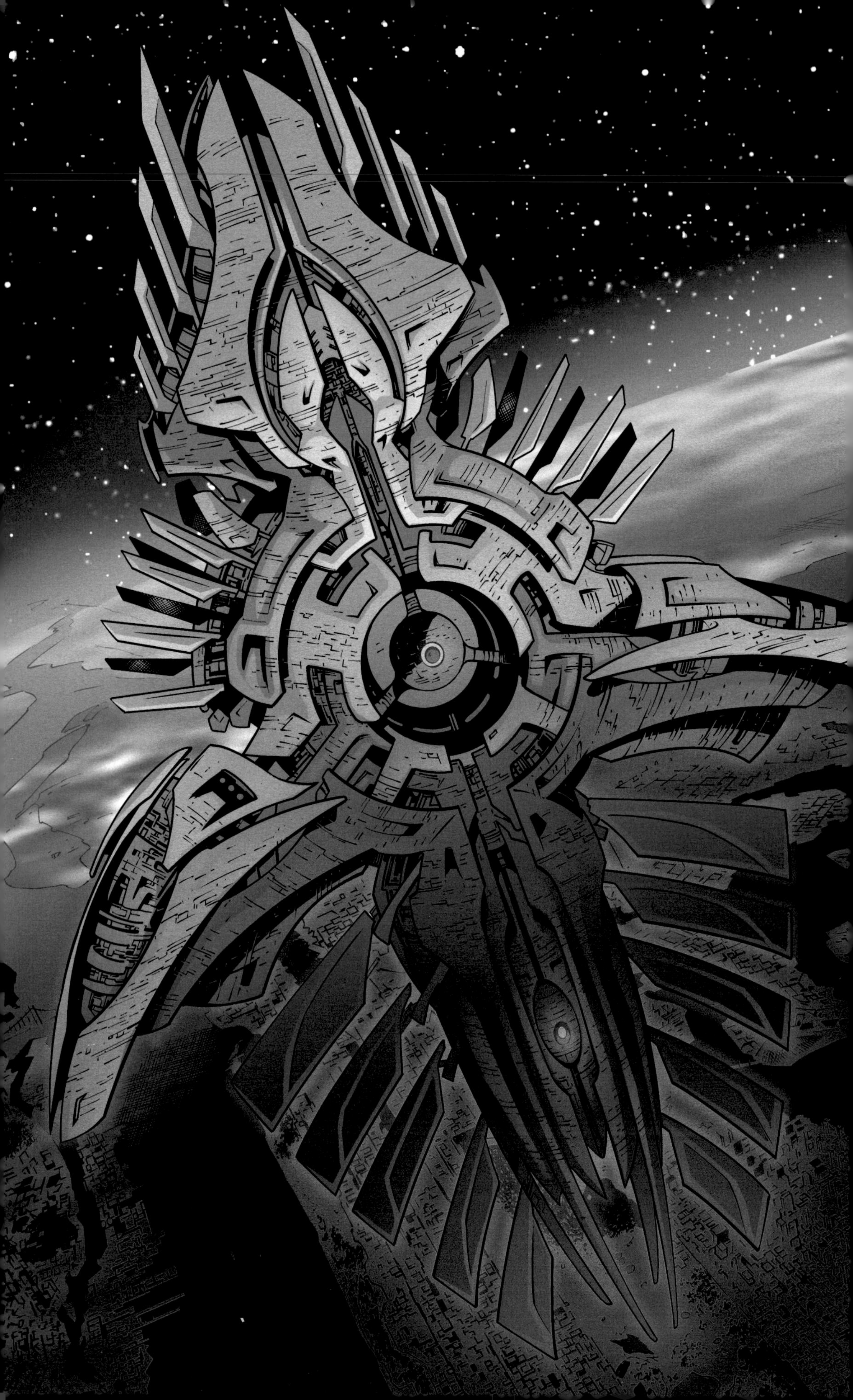

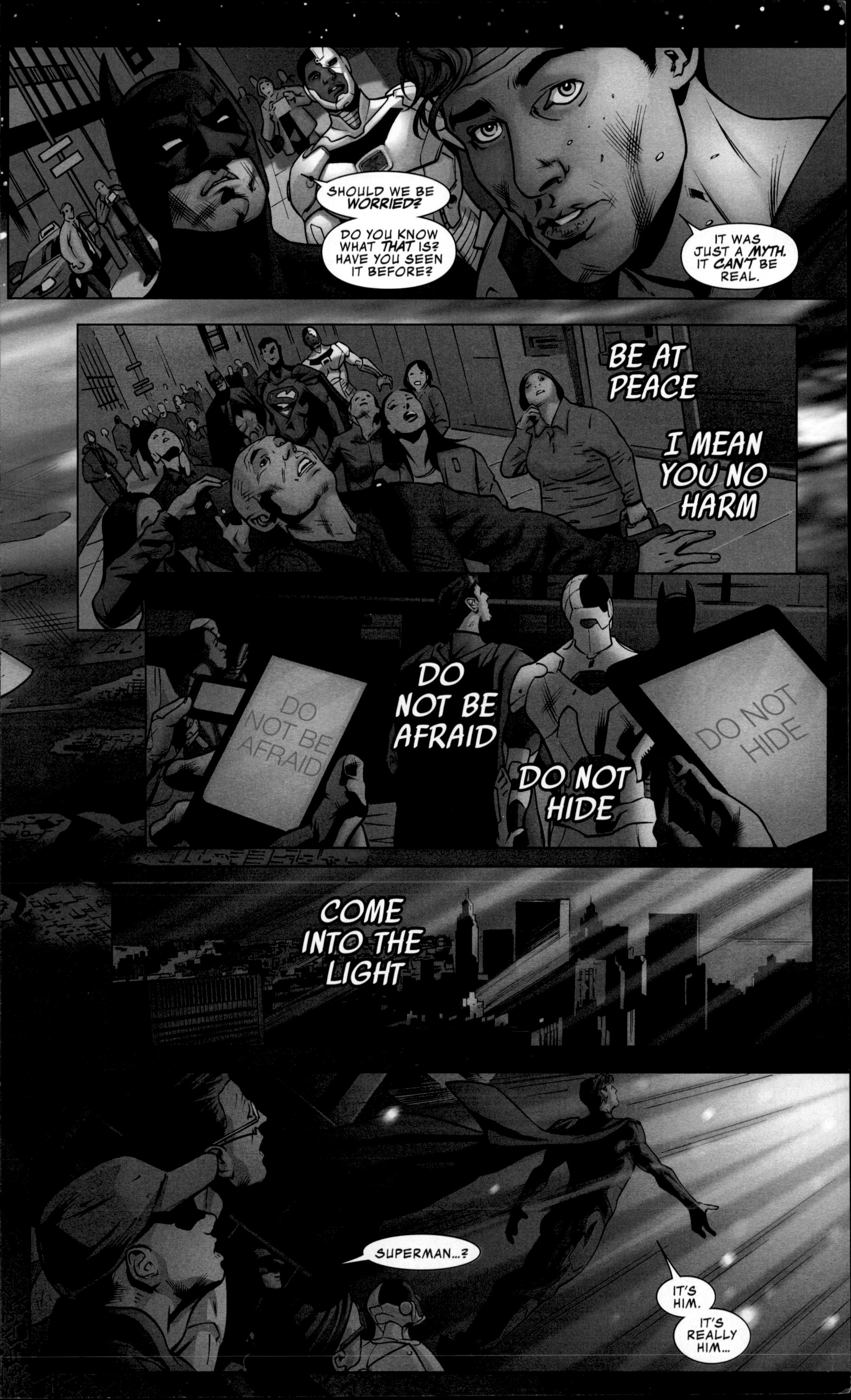
SHOULD WE BE WORRIED?
DO YOU KNOW WHAT THAT IS? HAVE YOU SEEN IT BEFORE?
IT WAS JUST A MYTH. IT CAN'T BE REAL.
BE AT PEACE
I MEAN YOU NO HARM
DO NOT BE AFRAID
DO NOT BE AFRAID
DO NOT HIDE
DO NOT HIDE
COME INTO THE LIGHT
SUPERMAN...?
IT'S HIM.
IT'S REALLY HIM...

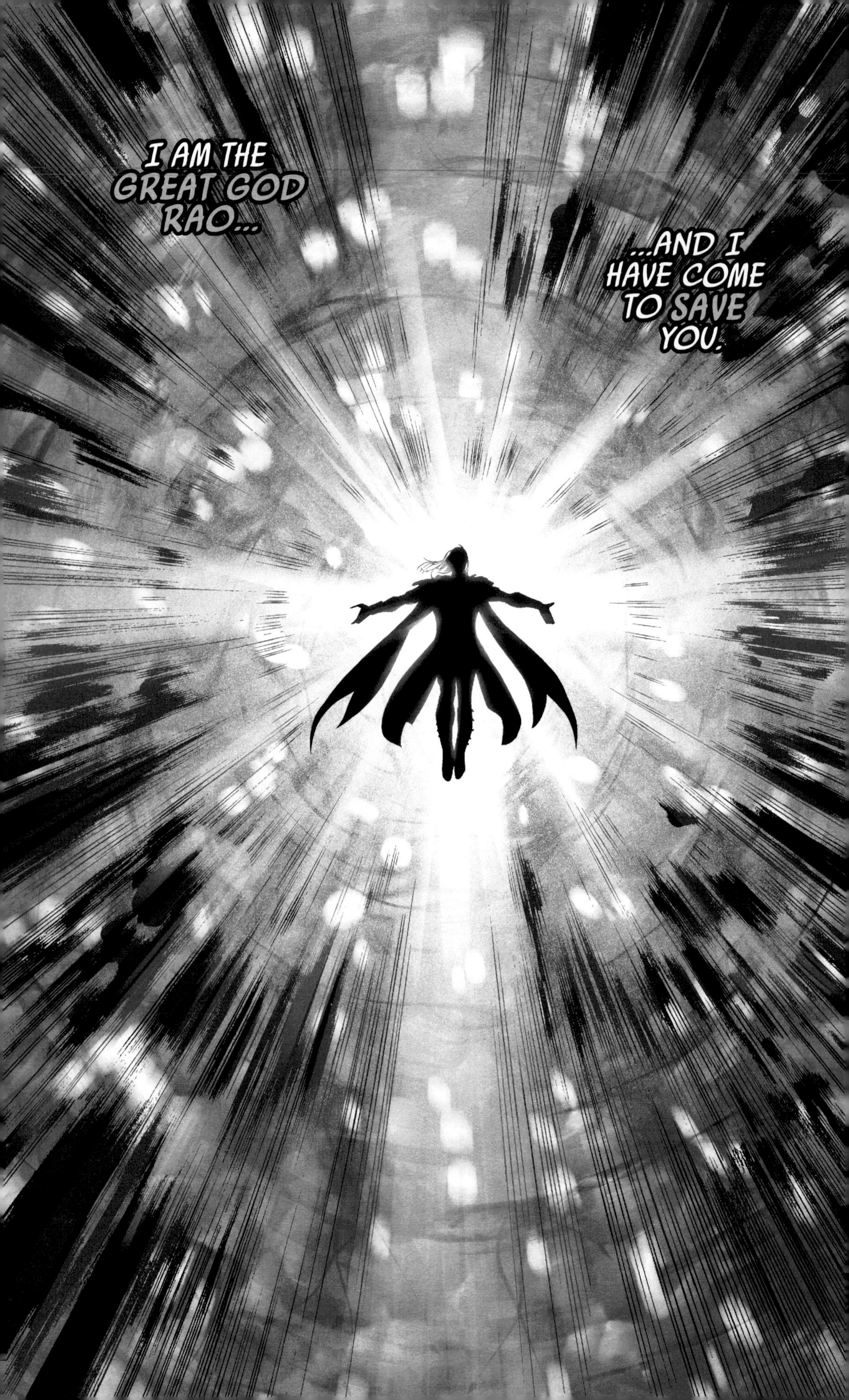
I AM THE GREAT GOD RAO...
...AND I HAVE COME TO SAVE YOU.

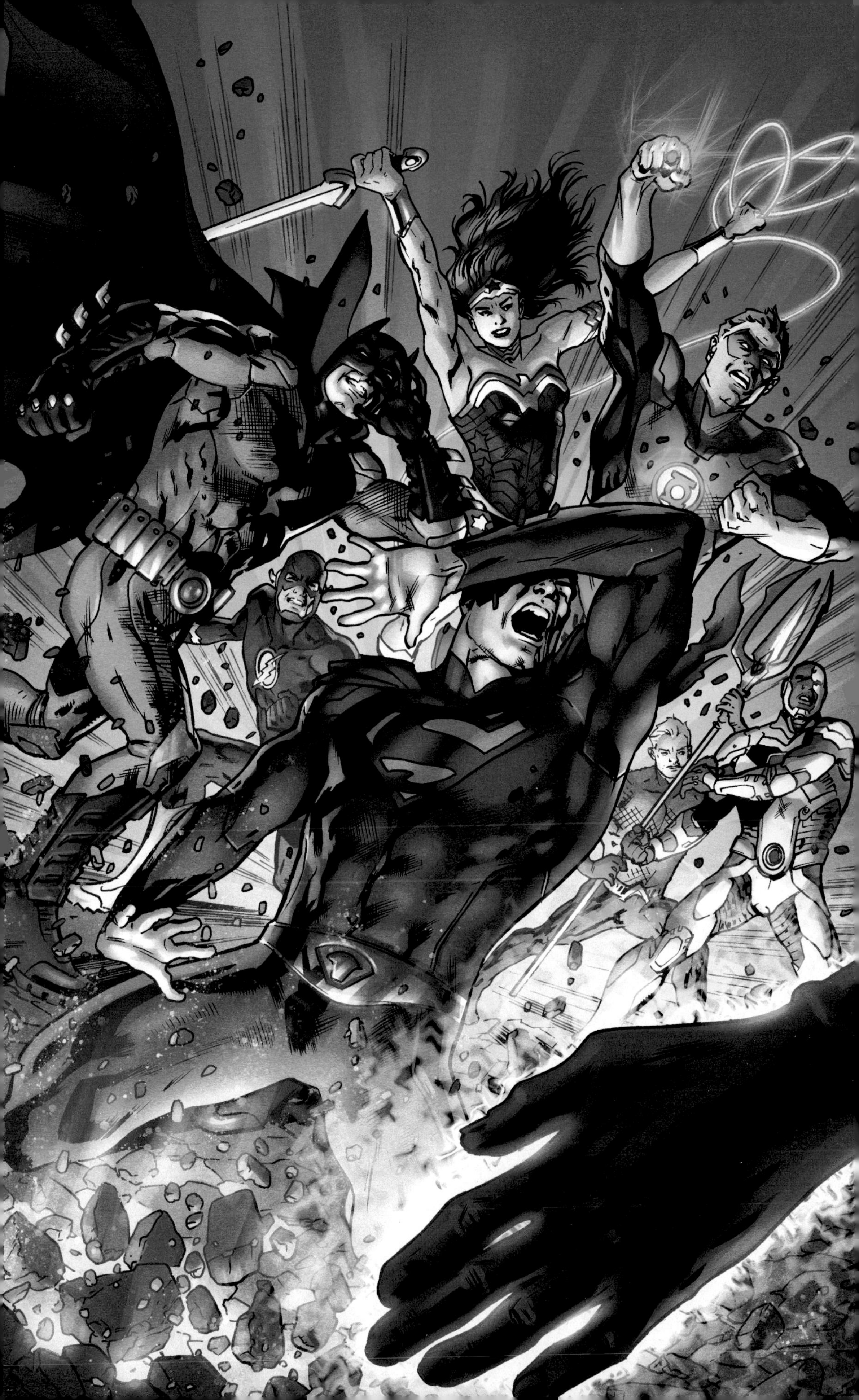

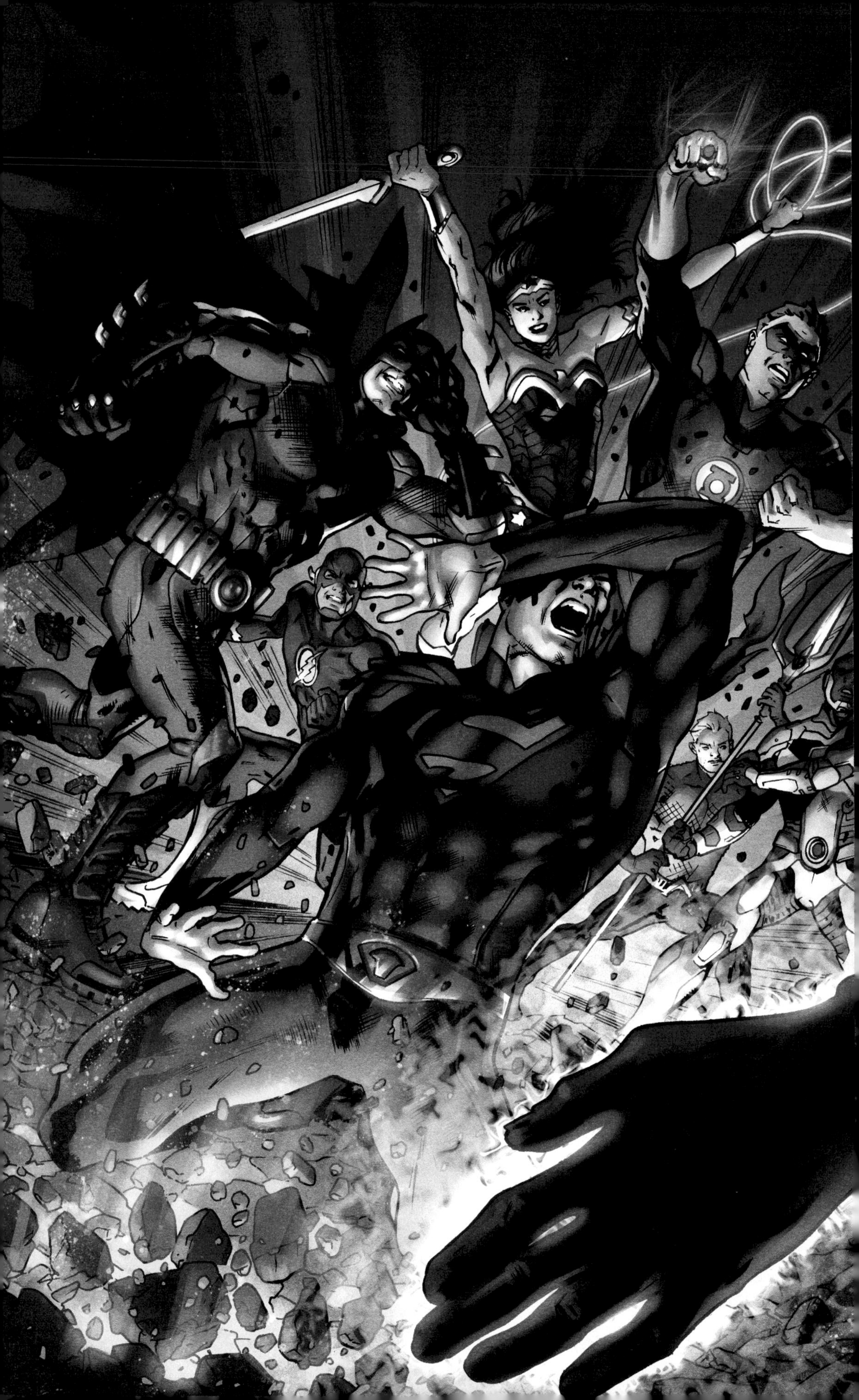

DC COMICS PRESENTS

THE JUSTICE LEAGUE OF AMERICA
POWER AND GLORY
PART TWO

BY BRYAN HITCH

INKS BY DANIEL HENRIQUES,
ANDREW CURRIE & BRYAN HITCH
COLORS BY ALEX SINCLAIR
LETTERS BY CHRIS ELIOPOULOS
ASSISTS BY AMEDEO TURTURRO
EDITS BY BRIAN CUNNINGHAM

COVER BY BRYAN HITCH AND ALEX SINCLAIR

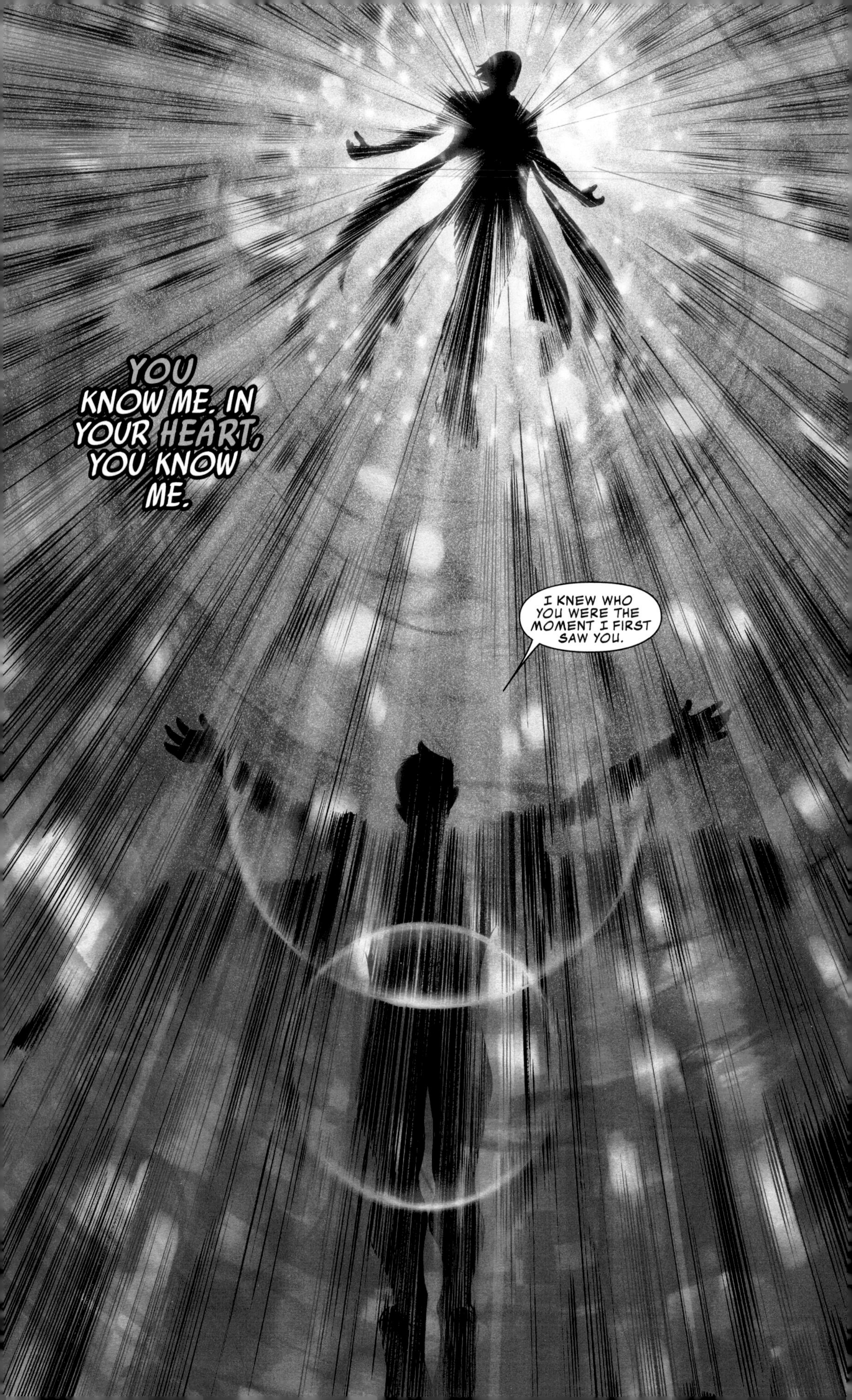
YOU KNOW ME. IN YOUR HEART, YOU KNOW ME.
I KNEW WHO YOU WERE THE MOMENT I FIRST SAW YOU.

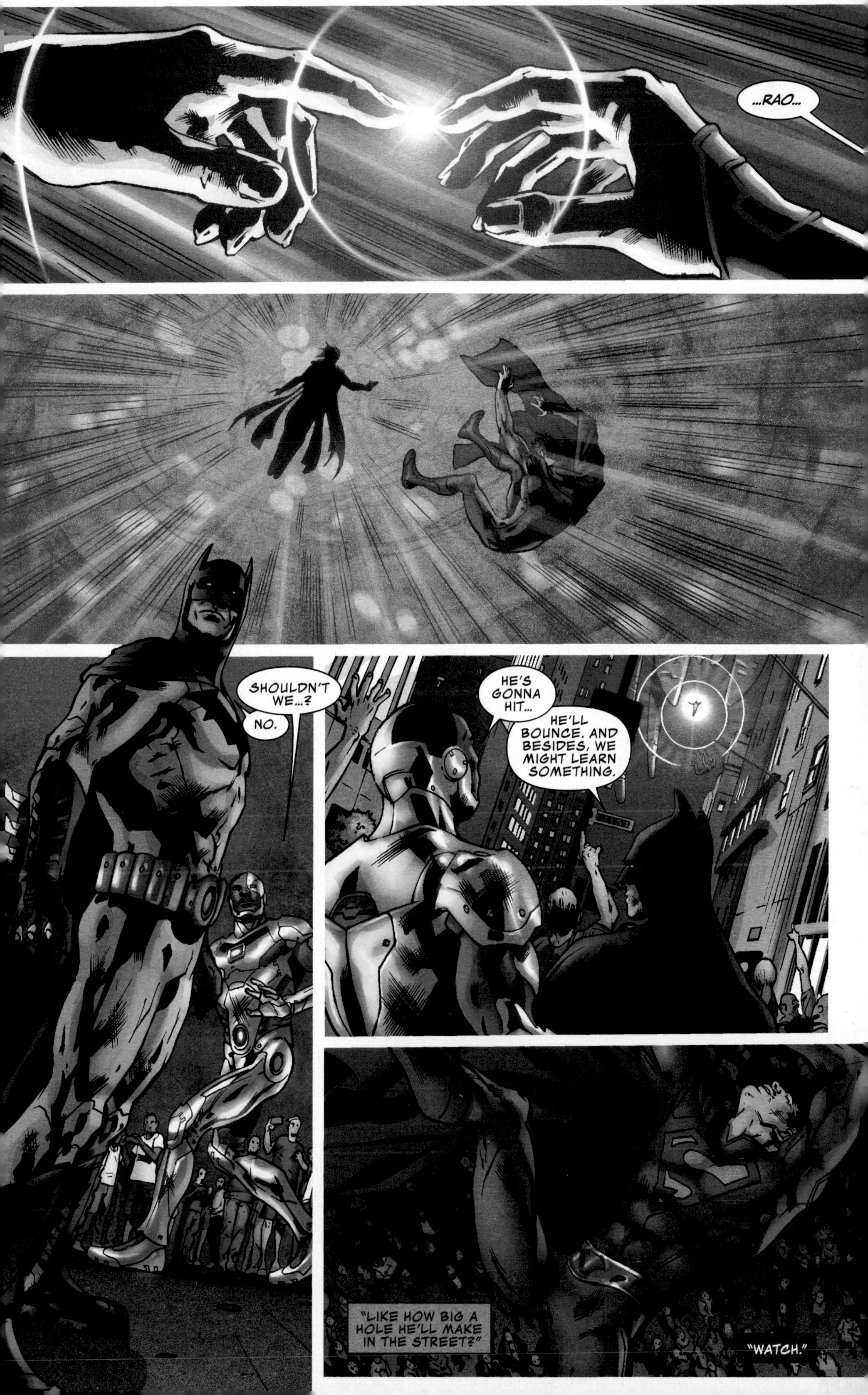
...RAO...
SHOULDN'T WE...?
NO.
HE'S GONNA HIT...
HE'LL BOUNCE. AND BESIDES, WE MIGHT LEARN SOMETHING.
"LIKE HOW BIG A HOLE HE'LL MAKE IN THE STREET?"
"WATCH."

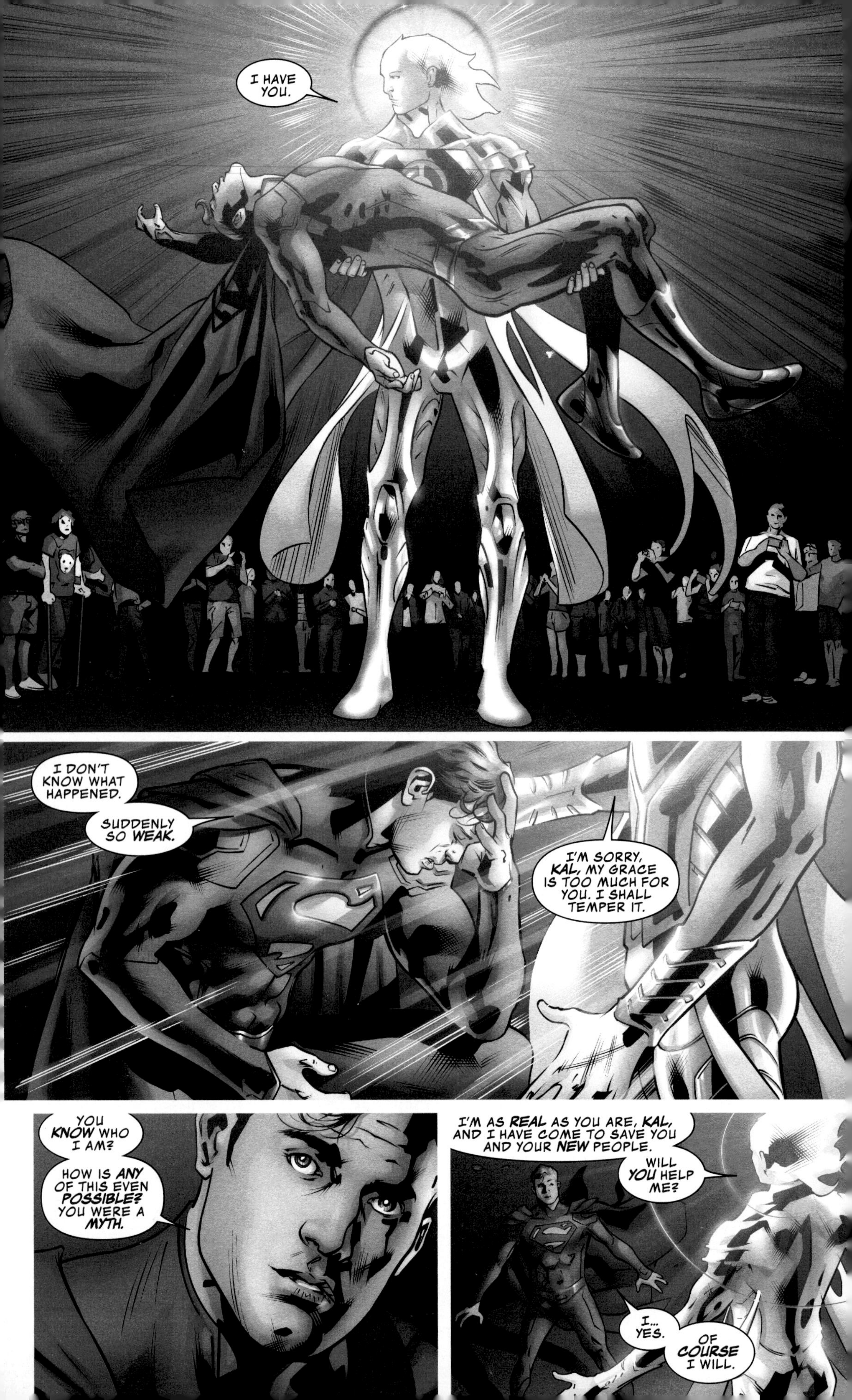

I HAVE YOU.
I DON'T KNOW WHAT HAPPENED.
SUDDENLY SO WEAK.
I'M SORRY, KAL, MY GRACE IS TOO MUCH FOR YOU. I SHALL TEMPER IT.
YOU KNOW WHO I AM?
HOW IS ANY OF THIS EVEN POSSIBLE? YOU WERE A MYTH.
I'M AS REAL AS YOU ARE, KAL, AND I HAVE COME TO SAVE YOU AND YOUR NEW PEOPLE.
WILL YOU HELP ME?
I... YES.
OF COURSE I WILL.

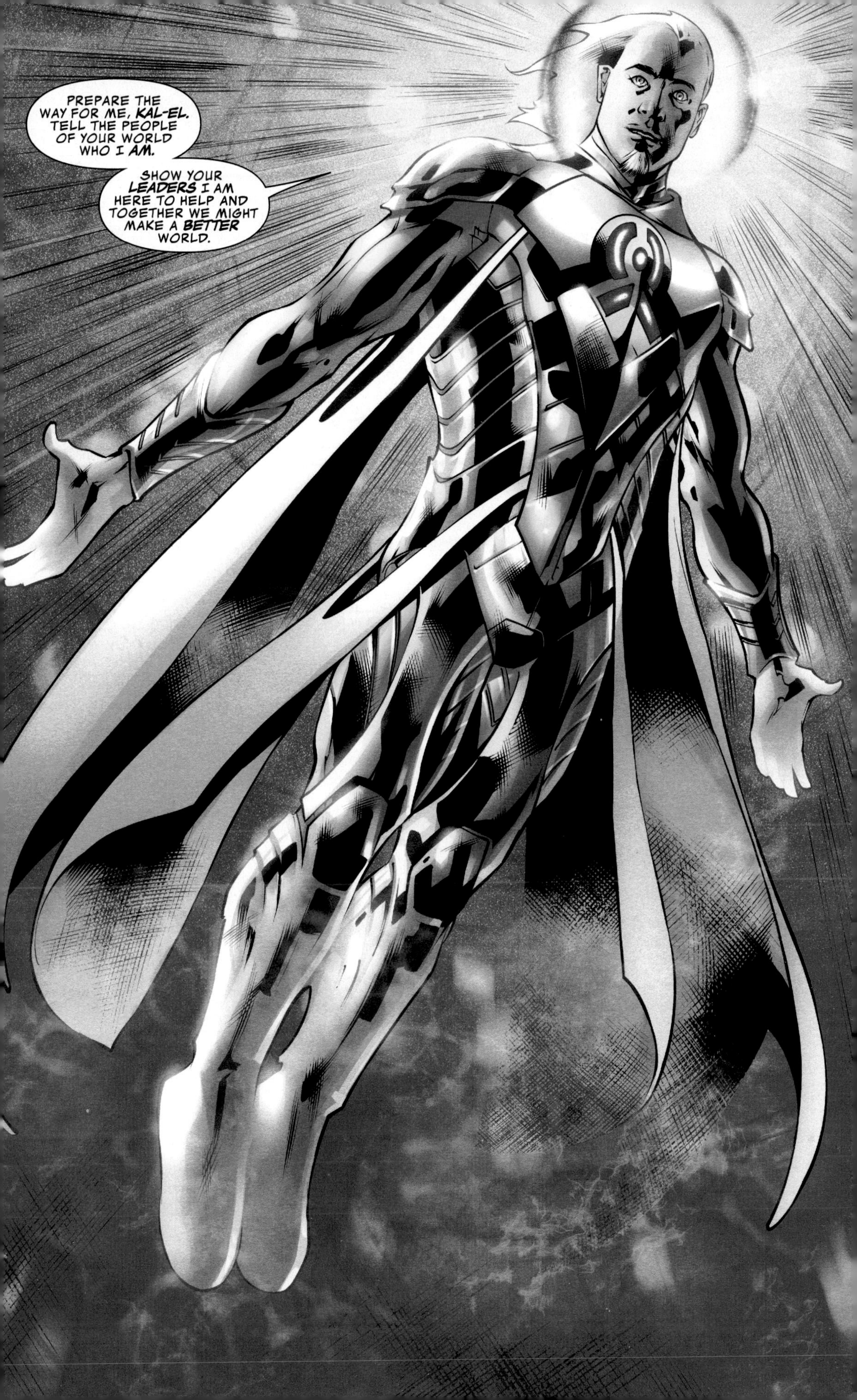
PREPARE THE WAY FOR ME, KAL-EL. TELL THE PEOPLE OF YOUR WORLD WHO I AM.
SHOW YOUR LEADERS I AM HERE TO HELP AND TOGETHER WE MIGHT MAKE A BETTER WORLD.

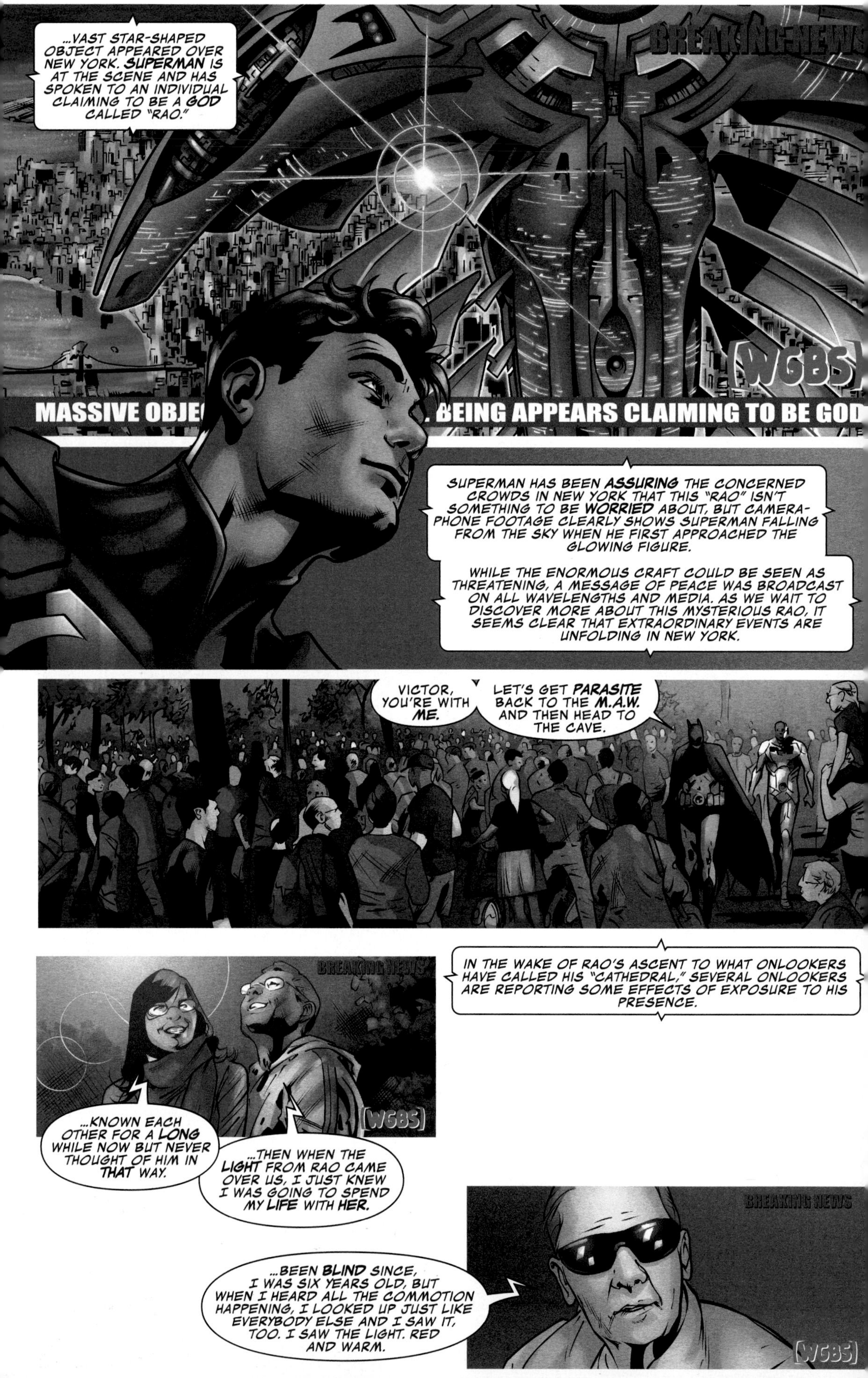

...VAST STAR-SHAPED OBJECT APPEARED OVER NEW YORK. SUPERMAN IS AT THE SCENE AND HAS SPOKEN TO AN INDIVIDUAL CLAIMING TO BE A GOD CALLED "RAO."
BREAKING NEWS
WGBS
MASSIVE OBJE
. BEING APPEARS CLAIMING TO BE GOD
SUPERMAN HAS BEEN ASSURING THE CONCERNED CROWDS IN NEW YORK THAT THIS "RAO" ISN'T SOMETHING TO BE WORRIED ABOUT, BUT CAMERA-PHONE FOOTAGE CLEARLY SHOWS SUPERMAN FALLING FROM THE SKY WHEN HE FIRST APPROACHED THE GLOWING FIGURE.
WHILE THE ENORMOUS CRAFT COULD BE SEEN AS THREATENING, A MESSAGE OF PEACE WAS BROADCAST ON ALL WAVELENGTHS AND MEDIA. AS WE WAIT TO DISCOVER MORE ABOUT THIS MYSTERIOUS RAO, IT SEEMS CLEAR THAT EXTRAORDINARY EVENTS ARE UNFOLDING IN NEW YORK.
VICTOR, YOU'RE WITH ME.
LET'S GET PARASITE BACK TO THE M.A.W. AND THEN HEAD TO THE CAVE.
BREAKING NEWS
IN THE WAKE OF RAO'S ASCENT TO WHAT ONLOOKERS HAVE CALLED HIS "CATHEDRAL," SEVERAL ONLOOKERS ARE REPORTING SOME EFFECTS OF EXPOSURE TO HIS PRESENCE.
WGBS
...KNOWN EACH OTHER FOR A LONG WHILE NOW BUT NEVER THOUGHT OF HIM IN THAT WAY.
...THEN WHEN THE LIGHT FROM RAO CAME OVER US, I JUST KNEW I WAS GOING TO SPEND MY LIFE WITH HER.
BREAKING NEWS
...BEEN BLIND SINCE, I WAS SIX YEARS OLD, BUT WHEN I HEARD ALL THE COMMOTION HAPPENING, I LOOKED UP JUST LIKE EVERYBODY ELSE AND I SAW IT, TOO. I SAW THE LIGHT. RED AND WARM.
WGBS

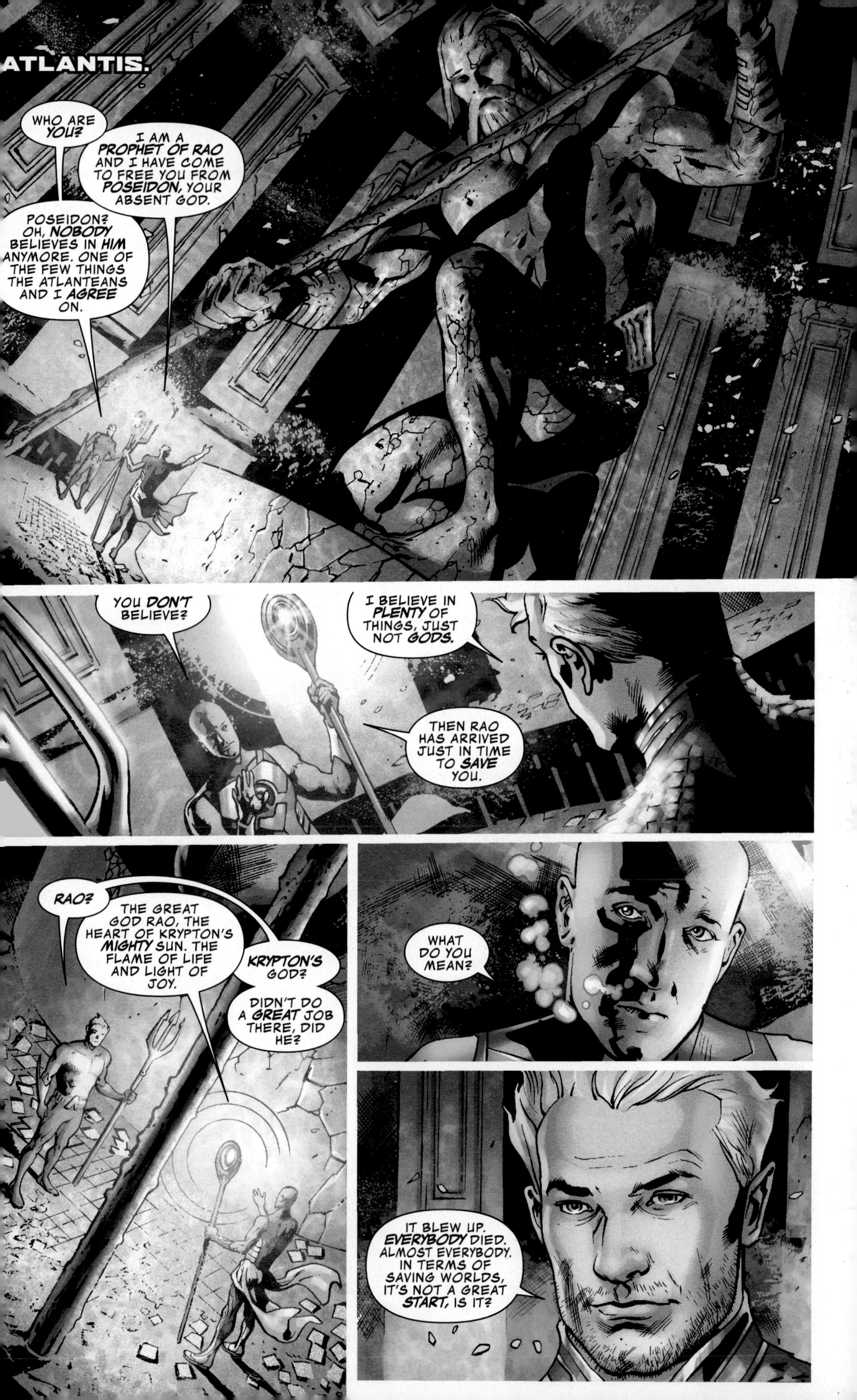
ATLANTIS.
WHO ARE YOU?
I AM A PROPHET OF RAO AND I HAVE COME TO FREE YOU FROM POSEIDON, YOUR ABSENT GOD.
POSEIDON? OH, NOBODY BELIEVES IN HIM ANYMORE. ONE OF THE FEW THINGS THE ATLANTEANS AND I AGREE ON.
YOU DON'T BELIEVE?
I BELIEVE IN PLENTY OF THINGS, JUST NOT GODS.
THEN RAO HAS ARRIVED JUST IN TIME TO SAVE YOU.
RAO?
THE GREAT GOD RAO, THE HEART OF KRYPTON'S MIGHTY SUN. THE FLAME OF LIFE AND LIGHT OF JOY.
KRYPTON'S GOD?
DIDN'T DO A GREAT JOB THERE, DID HE?
WHAT DO YOU MEAN?
IT BLEW UP. EVERYBODY DIED. ALMOST EVERYBODY. IN TERMS OF SAVING WORLDS, IT'S NOT A GREAT START, IS IT?

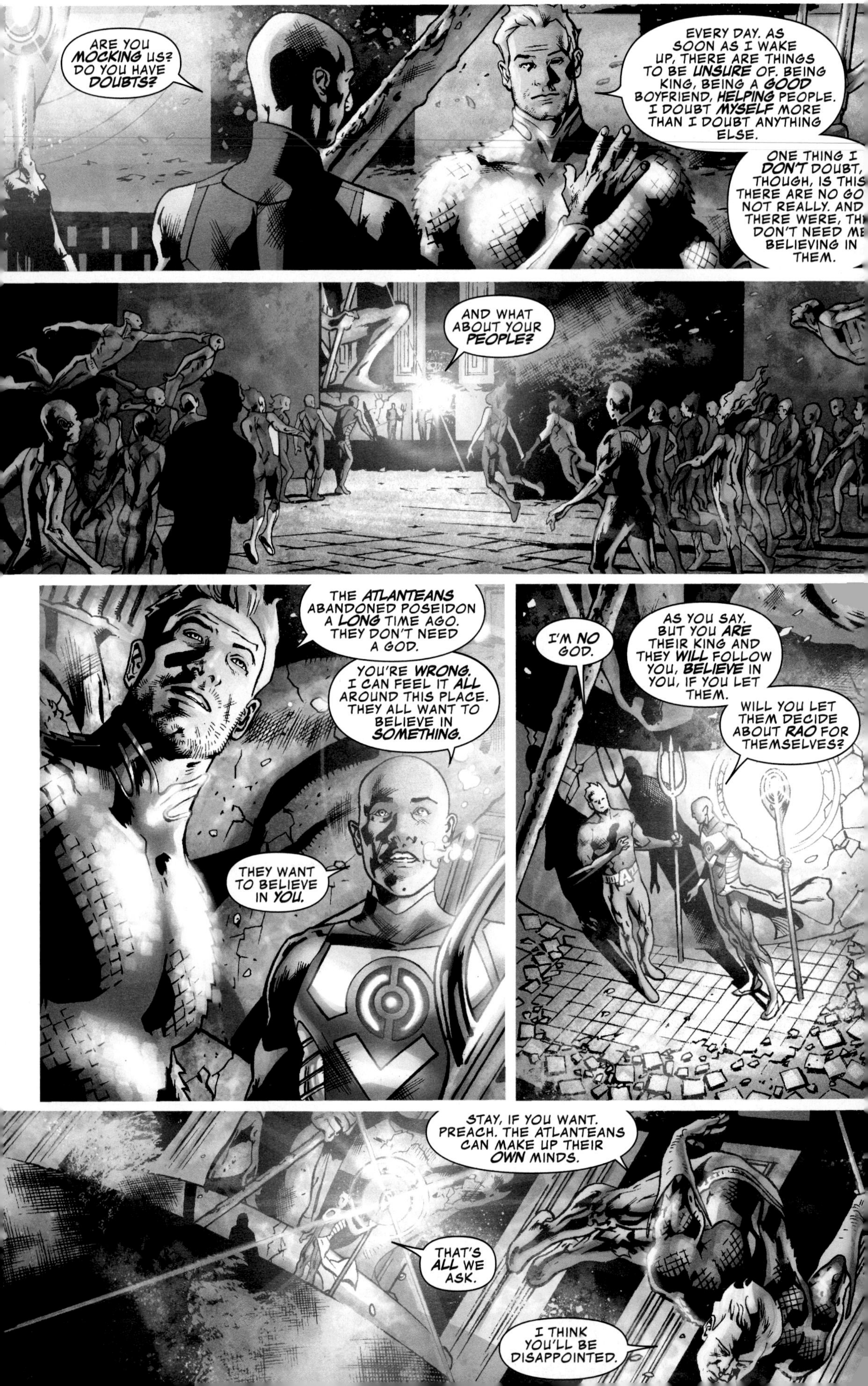
ARE YOU MOCKING US? DO YOU HAVE DOUBTS?
EVERY DAY. AS SOON AS I WAKE UP, THERE ARE THINGS TO BE UNSURE OF. BEING KING, BEING A GOOD BOYFRIEND, HELPING PEOPLE. I DOUBT MYSELF MORE THAN I DOUBT ANYTHING ELSE.
ONE THING I DON'T DOUBT, THOUGH, IS THIS THERE ARE NO GO NOT REALLY. AND THERE WERE, TH DON'T NEED ME BELIEVING IN THEM.
AND WHAT ABOUT YOUR PEOPLE?
THE ATLANTEANS ABANDONED POSEIDON A LONG TIME AGO. THEY DON'T NEED A GOD.
YOU'RE WRONG. I CAN FEEL IT ALL AROUND THIS PLACE. THEY ALL WANT TO BELIEVE IN SOMETHING.
THEY WANT TO BELIEVE IN YOU.
I'M NO GOD.
AS YOU SAY. BUT YOU ARE THEIR KING AND THEY WILL FOLLOW YOU, BELIEVE IN YOU, IF YOU LET THEM.
WILL YOU LET THEM DECIDE ABOUT RAO FOR THEMSELVES?
STAY, IF YOU WANT. PREACH. THE ATLANTEANS CAN MAKE UP THEIR OWN MINDS.
THAT'S ALL WE ASK.
I THINK YOU'LL BE DISAPPOINTED.

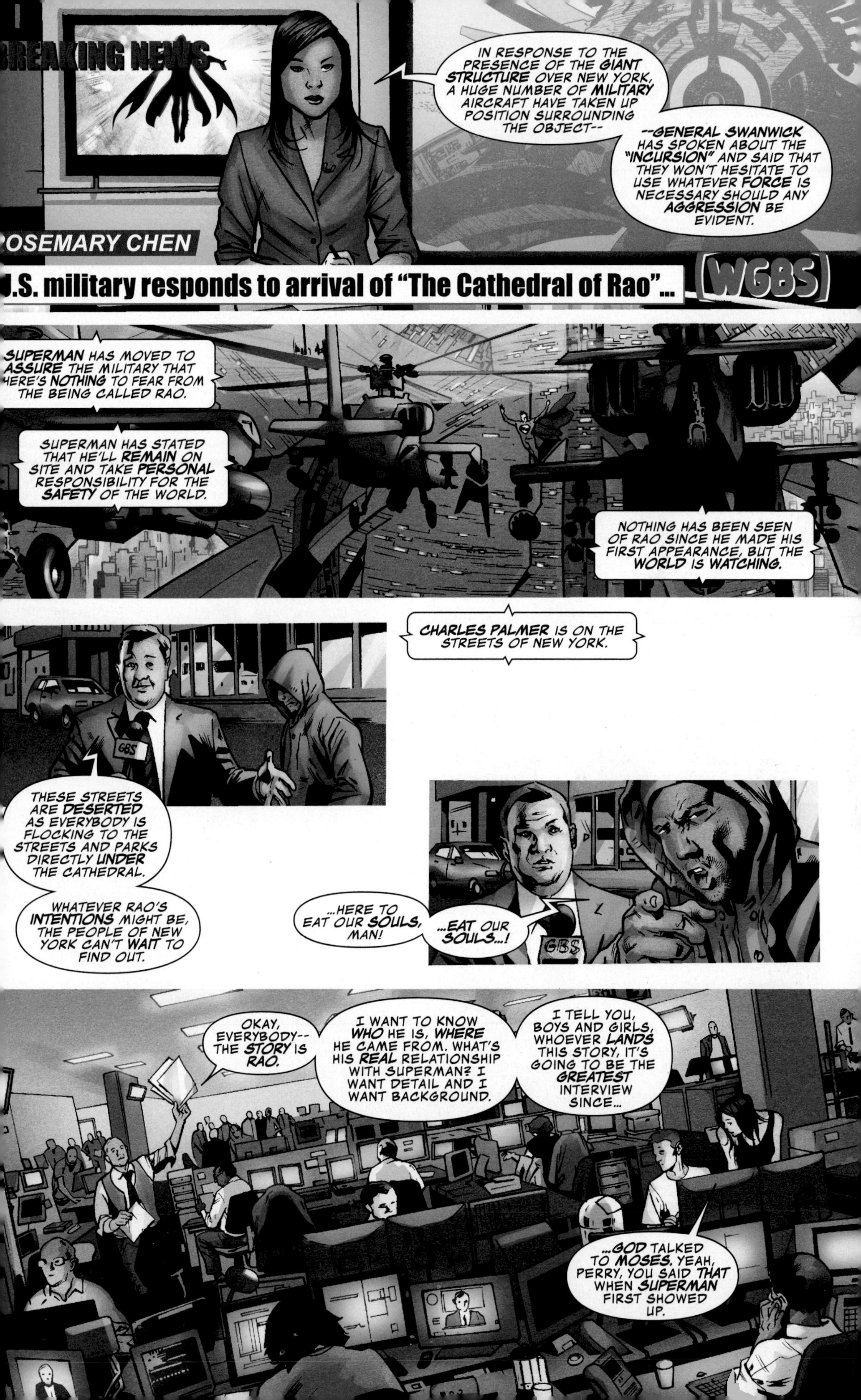
BREAKING NEWS
IN RESPONSE TO THE PRESENCE OF THE GIANT STRUCTURE OVER NEW YORK, A HUGE NUMBER OF MILITARY AIRCRAFT HAVE TAKEN UP POSITION SURROUNDING THE OBJECT--
--GENERAL SWANWICK HAS SPOKEN ABOUT THE "INCURSION" AND SAID THAT THEY WON'T HESITATE TO USE WHATEVER FORCE IS NECESSARY SHOULD ANY AGGRESSION BE EVIDENT.
OSEMARY CHEN
.S. military responds to arrival of "The Cathedral of Rao"...
WGBS
SUPERMAN HAS MOVED TO ASSURE THE MILITARY THAT HERE'S NOTHING TO FEAR FROM THE BEING CALLED RAO.
SUPERMAN HAS STATED THAT HE'LL REMAIN ON SITE AND TAKE PERSONAL RESPONSIBILITY FOR THE SAFETY OF THE WORLD.
NOTHING HAS BEEN SEEN OF RAO SINCE HE MADE HIS FIRST APPEARANCE, BUT THE WORLD IS WATCHING.
CHARLES PALMER IS ON THE STREETS OF NEW YORK.
GBS
THESE STREETS ARE DESERTED AS EVERYBODY IS FLOCKING TO THE STREETS AND PARKS DIRECTLY UNDER THE CATHEDRAL.
WHATEVER RAO'S INTENTIONS MIGHT BE, THE PEOPLE OF NEW YORK CAN'T WAIT TO FIND OUT.
...HERE TO EAT OUR SOULS, MAN!
...EAT OUR SOULS...!
GBS
OKAY, EVERYBODY-- THE STORY IS RAO.
I WANT TO KNOW WHO HE IS, WHERE HE CAME FROM. WHAT'S HIS REAL RELATIONSHIP WITH SUPERMAN? I WANT DETAIL AND I WANT BACKGROUND.
I TELL YOU, BOYS AND GIRLS, WHOEVER LANDS THIS STORY, IT'S GOING TO BE THE GREATEST INTERVIEW SINCE...
...GOD TALKED TO MOSES. YEAH, PERRY, YOU SAID THAT WHEN SUPERMAN FIRST SHOWED UP.

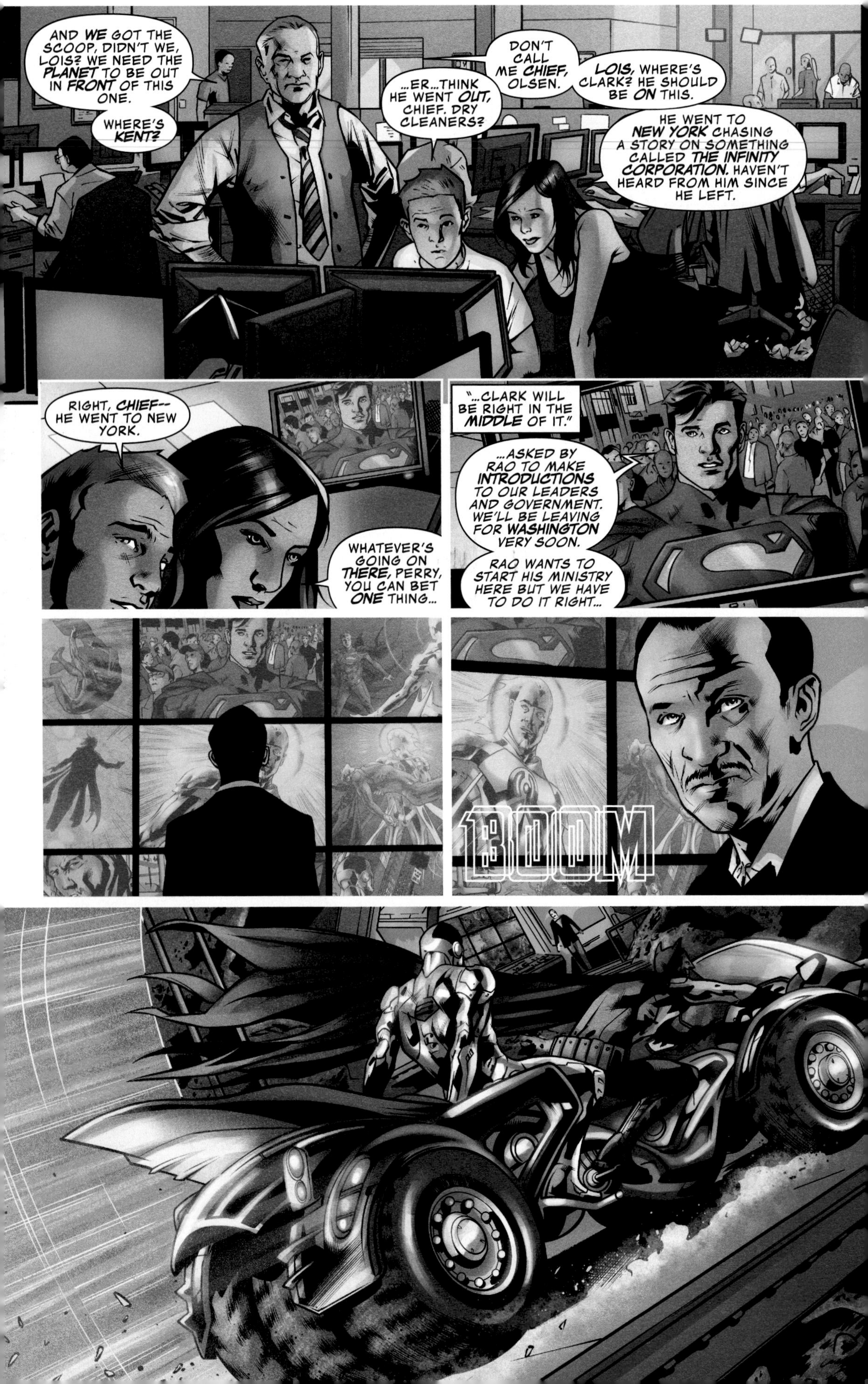
AND WE GOT THE SCOOP, DIDN'T WE, LOIS? WE NEED THE PLANET TO BE OUT IN FRONT OF THIS ONE.
WHERE'S KENT?
...ER...THINK HE WENT OUT, CHIEF. DRY CLEANERS?
DON'T CALL ME CHIEF, OLSEN.
LOIS, WHERE'S CLARK? HE SHOULD BE ON THIS.
HE WENT TO NEW YORK CHASING A STORY ON SOMETHING CALLED THE INFINITY CORPORATION. HAVEN'T HEARD FROM HIM SINCE HE LEFT.
RIGHT, CHIEF-- HE WENT TO NEW YORK.
WHATEVER'S GOING ON THERE, PERRY, YOU CAN BET ONE THING...
"...CLARK WILL BE RIGHT IN THE MIDDLE OF IT."
...ASKED BY RAO TO MAKE INTRODUCTIONS TO OUR LEADERS AND GOVERNMENT. WE'LL BE LEAVING FOR WASHINGTON VERY SOON.
RAO WANTS TO START HIS MINISTRY HERE BUT WE HAVE TO DO IT RIGHT...
BOOM

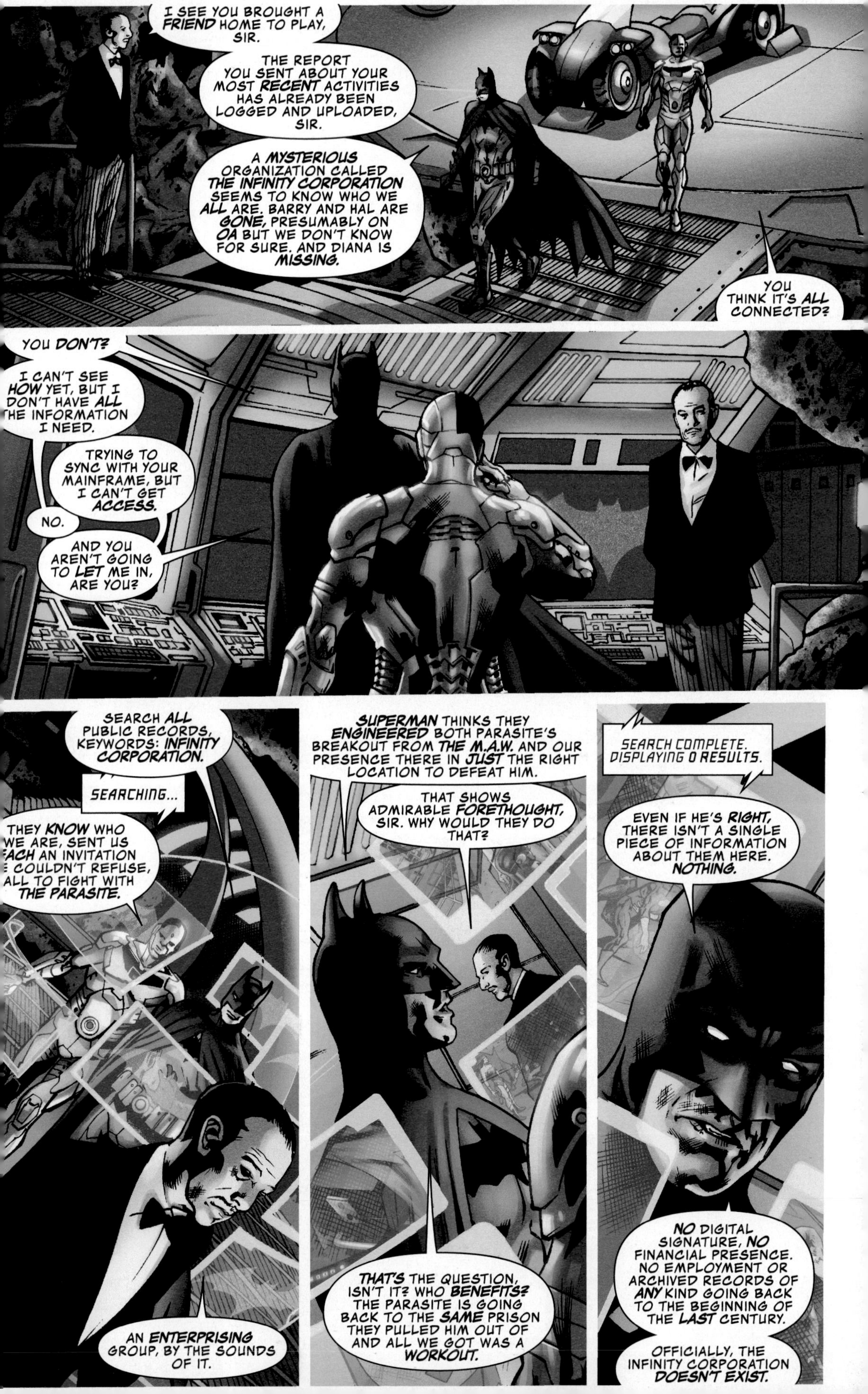
I SEE YOU BROUGHT A FRIEND HOME TO PLAY, SIR.
THE REPORT YOU SENT ABOUT YOUR MOST RECENT ACTIVITIES HAS ALREADY BEEN LOGGED AND UPLOADED, SIR.
A MYSTERIOUS ORGANIZATION CALLED THE INFINITY CORPORATION SEEMS TO KNOW WHO WE ALL ARE. BARRY AND HAL ARE GONE, PRESUMABLY ON OA BUT WE DON'T KNOW FOR SURE. AND DIANA IS MISSING.
YOU THINK IT'S ALL CONNECTED?
YOU DON'T?
I CAN'T SEE HOW YET, BUT I DON'T HAVE ALL THE INFORMATION I NEED.
TRYING TO SYNC WITH YOUR MAINFRAME, BUT I CAN'T GET ACCESS.
NO.
AND YOU AREN'T GOING TO LET ME IN, ARE YOU?
SEARCH ALL PUBLIC RECORDS, KEYWORDS: INFINITY CORPORATION.
SEARCHING...
THEY KNOW WHO WE ARE, SENT US EACH AN INVITATION WE COULDN'T REFUSE, ALL TO FIGHT WITH THE PARASITE.
AN ENTERPRISING GROUP, BY THE SOUNDS OF IT.
SUPERMAN THINKS THEY ENGINEERED BOTH PARASITE'S BREAKOUT FROM THE M.A.W. AND OUR PRESENCE THERE IN JUST THE RIGHT LOCATION TO DEFEAT HIM.
THAT SHOWS ADMIRABLE FORETHOUGHT, SIR. WHY WOULD THEY DO THAT?
THAT'S THE QUESTION, ISN'T IT? WHO BENEFITS? THE PARASITE IS GOING BACK TO THE SAME PRISON THEY PULLED HIM OUT OF AND ALL WE GOT WAS A WORKOUT.
SEARCH COMPLETE. DISPLAYING 0 RESULTS.
EVEN IF HE'S RIGHT, THERE ISN'T A SINGLE PIECE OF INFORMATION ABOUT THEM HERE. NOTHING.
NO DIGITAL SIGNATURE, NO FINANCIAL PRESENCE. NO EMPLOYMENT OR ARCHIVED RECORDS OF ANY KIND GOING BACK TO THE BEGINNING OF THE LAST CENTURY.
OFFICIALLY, THE INFINITY CORPORATION DOESN'T EXIST.

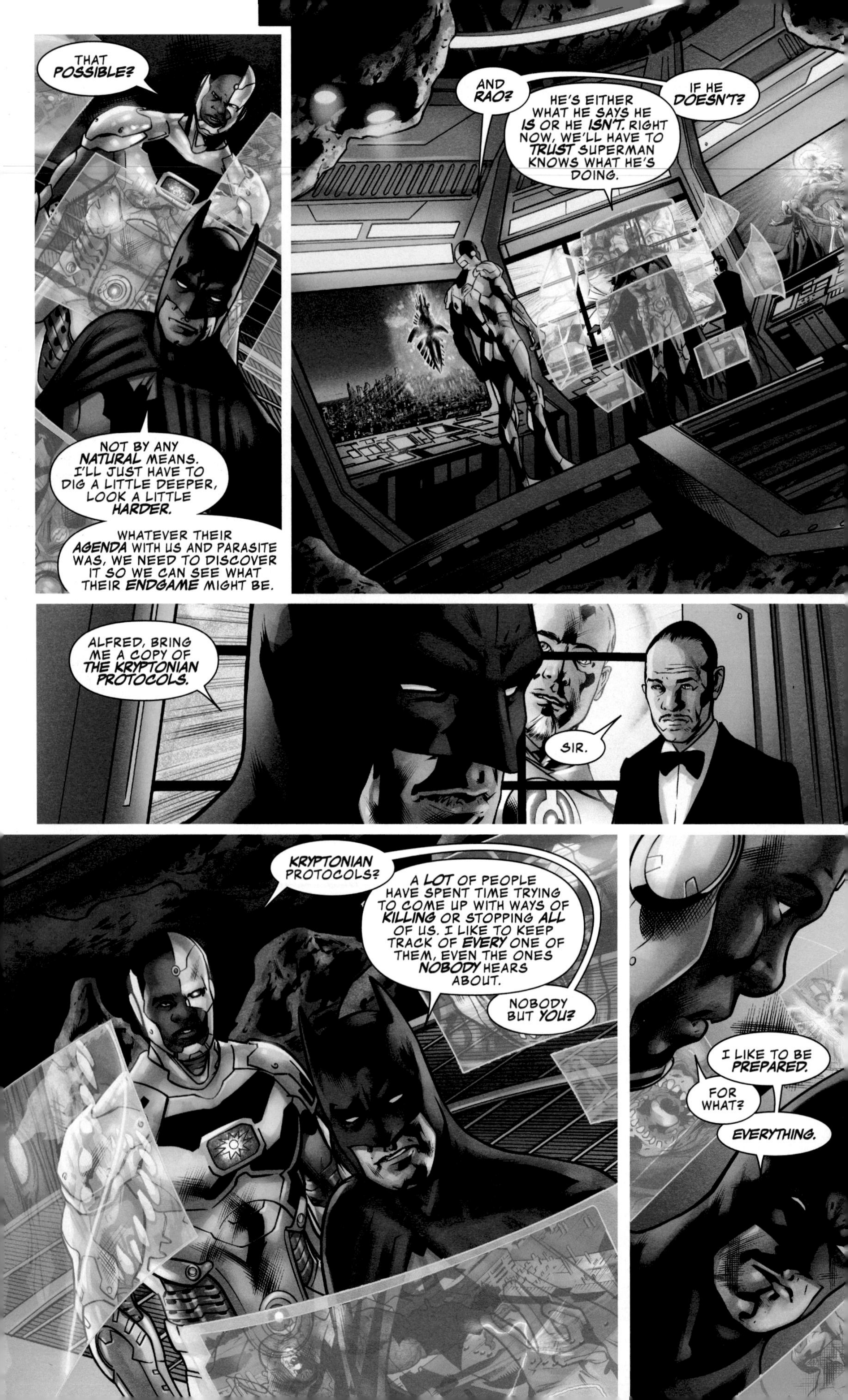
THAT POSSIBLE?
NOT BY ANY NATURAL MEANS. I'LL JUST HAVE TO DIG A LITTLE DEEPER, LOOK A LITTLE HARDER.
WHATEVER THEIR AGENDA WITH US AND PARASITE WAS, WE NEED TO DISCOVER IT SO WE CAN SEE WHAT THEIR ENDGAME MIGHT BE.
AND RAO?
HE'S EITHER WHAT HE SAYS HE IS OR HE ISN'T. RIGHT NOW, WE'LL HAVE TO TRUST SUPERMAN KNOWS WHAT HE'S DOING.
IF HE DOESN'T?
ALFRED, BRING ME A COPY OF THE KRYPTONIAN PROTOCOLS.
SIR.
KRYPTONIAN PROTOCOLS?
A LOT OF PEOPLE HAVE SPENT TIME TRYING TO COME UP WITH WAYS OF KILLING OR STOPPING ALL OF US. I LIKE TO KEEP TRACK OF EVERY ONE OF THEM, EVEN THE ONES NOBODY HEARS ABOUT.
NOBODY BUT YOU?
I LIKE TO BE PREPARED.
FOR WHAT?
EVERYTHING.

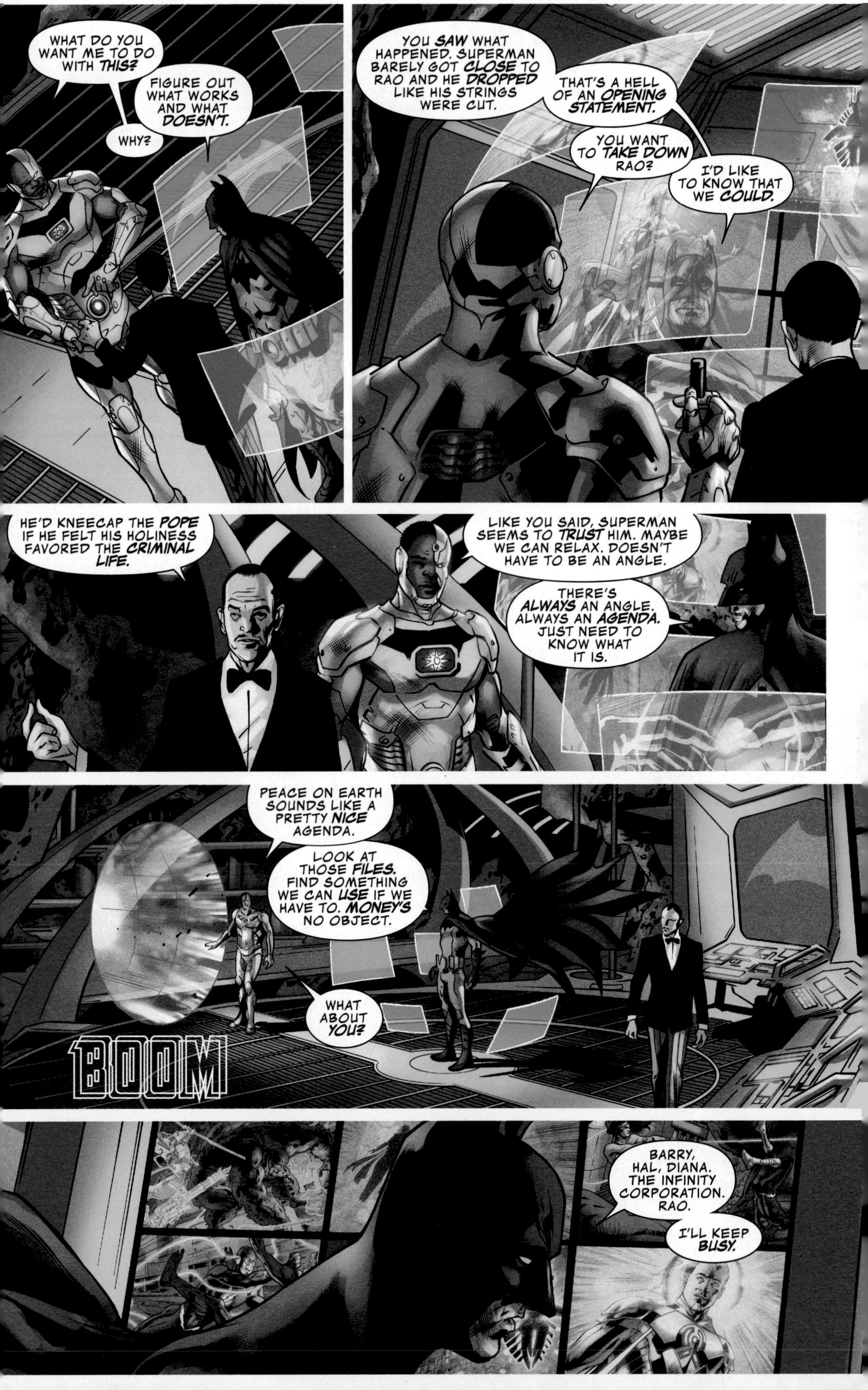
WHAT DO YOU WANT ME TO DO WITH THIS?
FIGURE OUT WHAT WORKS AND WHAT DOESN'T.
WHY?
YOU SAW WHAT HAPPENED. SUPERMAN BARELY GOT CLOSE TO RAO AND HE DROPPED LIKE HIS STRINGS WERE CUT.
THAT'S A HELL OF AN OPENING STATEMENT.
YOU WANT TO TAKE DOWN RAO?
I'D LIKE TO KNOW THAT WE COULD.
HE'D KNEECAP THE POPE IF HE FELT HIS HOLINESS FAVORED THE CRIMINAL LIFE.
LIKE YOU SAID, SUPERMAN SEEMS TO TRUST HIM. MAYBE WE CAN RELAX. DOESN'T HAVE TO BE AN ANGLE.
THERE'S ALWAYS AN ANGLE. ALWAYS AN AGENDA. JUST NEED TO KNOW WHAT IT IS.
PEACE ON EARTH SOUNDS LIKE A PRETTY NICE AGENDA.
LOOK AT THOSE FILES. FIND SOMETHING WE CAN USE IF WE HAVE TO. MONEY'S NO OBJECT.
WHAT ABOUT YOU?
BOOM
BARRY, HAL, DIANA. THE INFINITY CORPORATION. RAO.
I'LL KEEP BUSY.

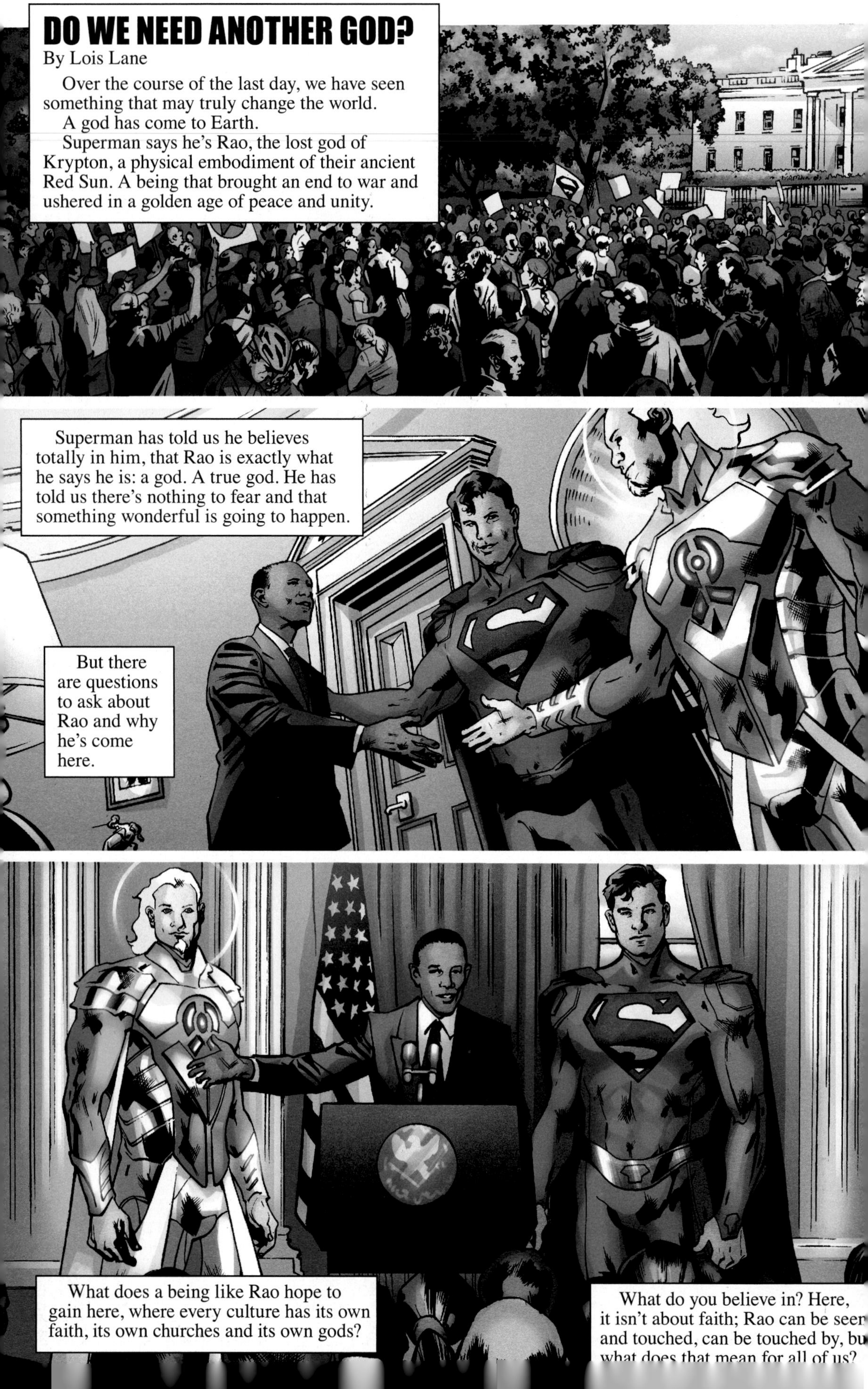
DO WE NEED ANOTHER GOD?
By Lois Lane
Over the course of the last day, we have seen something that may truly change the world.
A god has come to Earth.
Superman says he's Rao, the lost god of Krypton, a physical embodiment of their ancient Red Sun. A being that brought an end to war and ushered in a golden age of peace and unity.
Superman has told us he believes totally in him, that Rao is exactly what he says he is: a god. A true god. He has told us there's nothing to fear and that something wonderful is going to happen.
But there are questions to ask about Rao and why he's come here.
What does a being like Rao hope to gain here, where every culture has its own faith, its own churches and its own gods?
What do you believe in? Here, it isn't about faith; Rao can be seen and touched, can be touched by, but what does that mean for all of us?

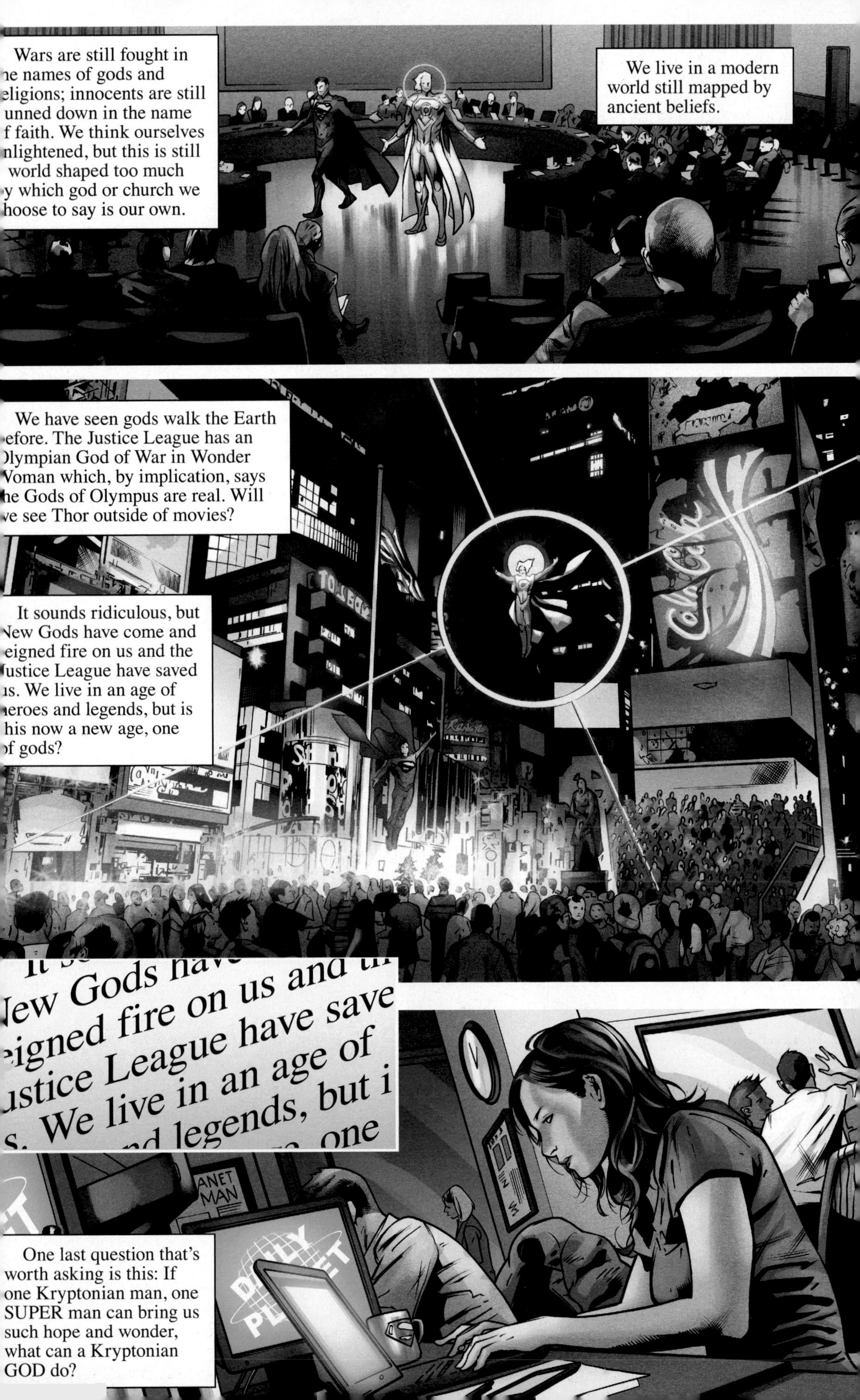
Wars are still fought in
ıe names of gods and
eligions; innocents are still
unned down in the name
f faith. We think ourselves
nlightened, but this is still
 world shaped too much
y which god or church we
hoose to say is our own.
We live in a modern
world still mapped by
ancient beliefs.
We have seen gods walk the Earth
efore. The Justice League has an
)lympian God of War in Wonder
Voman which, by implication, says
he Gods of Olympus are real. Will
ve see Thor outside of movies?
It sounds ridiculous, but
New Gods have come and
eigned fire on us and the
ustice League have saved
ıs. We live in an age of
ıeroes and legends, but is
his now a new age, one
of gods?
lew Gods hav
eigned fire on us and
ustice League have save
s. We live in an age of
nd legends, but i
one
ANET
MAN
DAILY
PLANET
One last question that's
worth asking is this: If
one Kryptonian man, one
SUPER man can bring us
such hope and wonder,
what can a Kryptonian
GOD do?

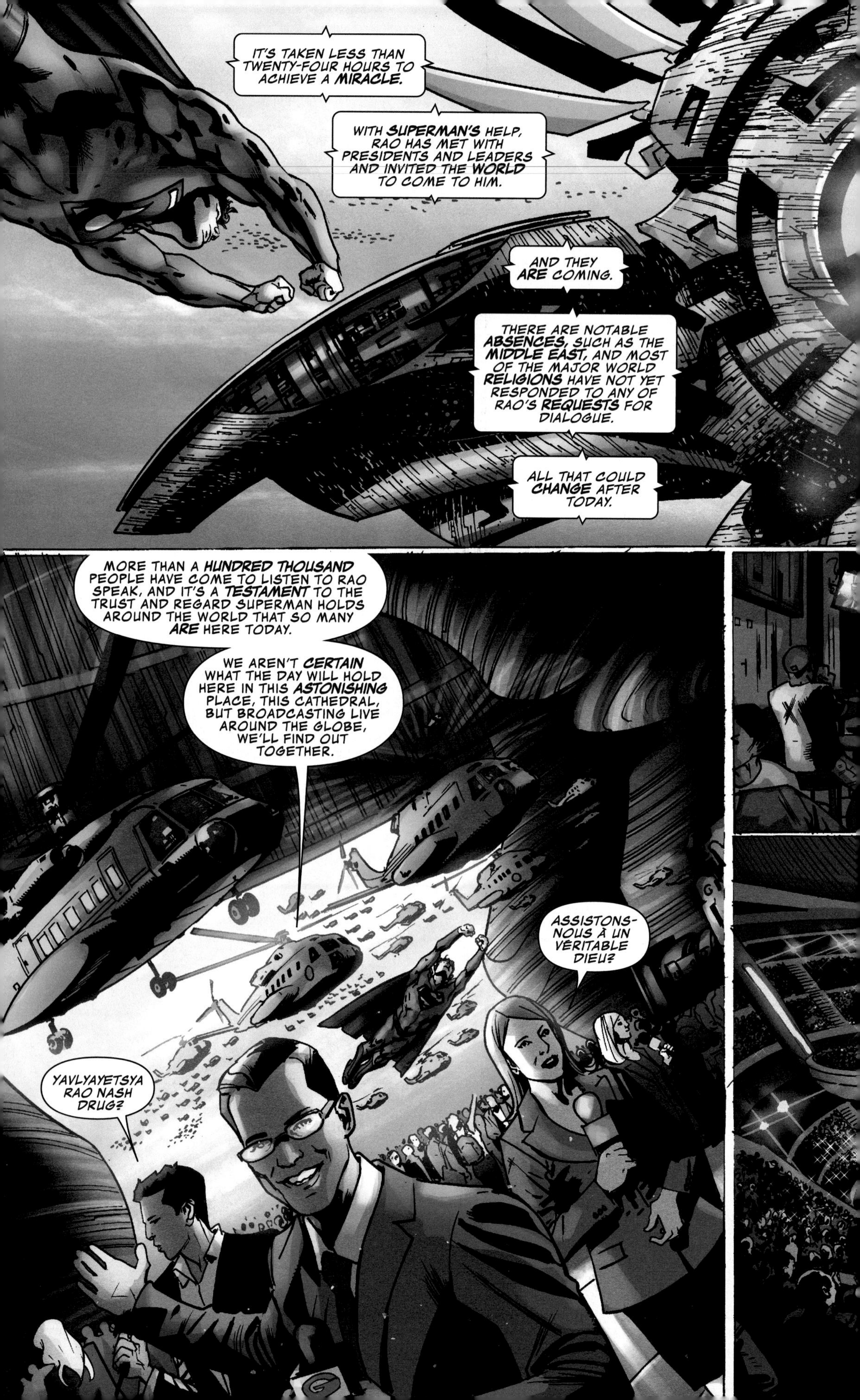
IT'S TAKEN LESS THAN TWENTY-FOUR HOURS TO ACHIEVE A MIRACLE.
WITH SUPERMAN'S HELP, RAO HAS MET WITH PRESIDENTS AND LEADERS AND INVITED THE WORLD TO COME TO HIM.
AND THEY ARE COMING.
THERE ARE NOTABLE ABSENCES, SUCH AS THE MIDDLE EAST, AND MOST OF THE MAJOR WORLD RELIGIONS HAVE NOT YET RESPONDED TO ANY OF RAO'S REQUESTS FOR DIALOGUE.
ALL THAT COULD CHANGE AFTER TODAY.
MORE THAN A HUNDRED THOUSAND PEOPLE HAVE COME TO LISTEN TO RAO SPEAK, AND IT'S A TESTAMENT TO THE TRUST AND REGARD SUPERMAN HOLDS AROUND THE WORLD THAT SO MANY ARE HERE TODAY.
WE AREN'T CERTAIN WHAT THE DAY WILL HOLD HERE IN THIS ASTONISHING PLACE, THIS CATHEDRAL, BUT BROADCASTING LIVE AROUND THE GLOBE, WE'LL FIND OUT TOGETHER.
ASSISTONS-NOUS À UN VÉRITABLE DIEU?
YAVLYAYETSYA RAO NASH DRUG?

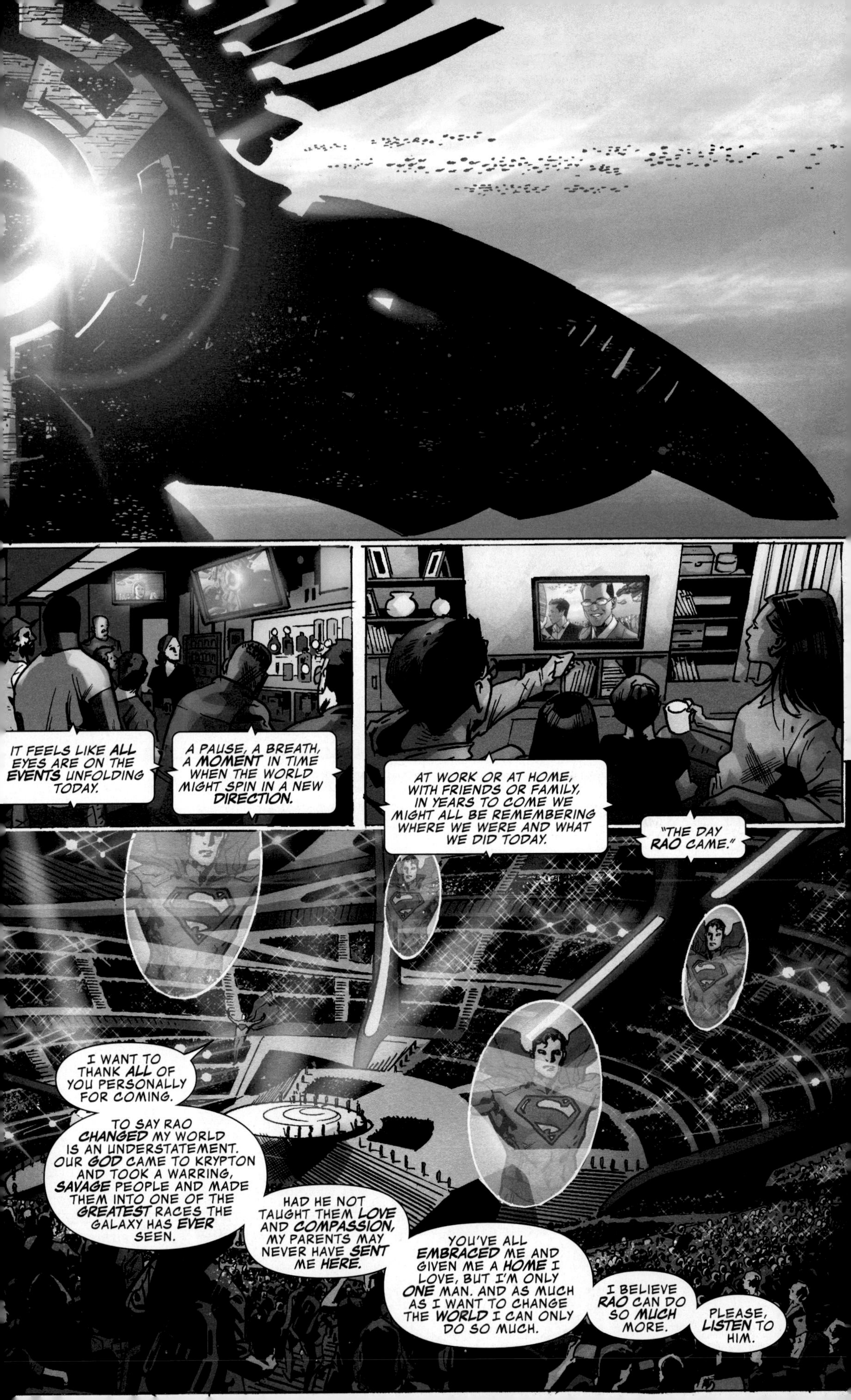
IT FEELS LIKE ALL EYES ARE ON THE EVENTS UNFOLDING TODAY.
A PAUSE, A BREATH, A MOMENT IN TIME WHEN THE WORLD MIGHT SPIN IN A NEW DIRECTION.
AT WORK OR AT HOME, WITH FRIENDS OR FAMILY, IN YEARS TO COME WE MIGHT ALL BE REMEMBERING WHERE WE WERE AND WHAT WE DID TODAY.
"THE DAY RAO CAME."
I WANT TO THANK ALL OF YOU PERSONALLY FOR COMING.
TO SAY RAO CHANGED MY WORLD IS AN UNDERSTATEMENT. OUR GOD CAME TO KRYPTON AND TOOK A WARRING, SAVAGE PEOPLE AND MADE THEM INTO ONE OF THE GREATEST RACES THE GALAXY HAS EVER SEEN.
HAD HE NOT TAUGHT THEM LOVE AND COMPASSION, MY PARENTS MAY NEVER HAVE SENT ME HERE.
YOU'VE ALL EMBRACED ME AND GIVEN ME A HOME I LOVE, BUT I'M ONLY ONE MAN. AND AS MUCH AS I WANT TO CHANGE THE WORLD I CAN ONLY DO SO MUCH.
I BELIEVE RAO CAN DO SO MUCH MORE.
PLEASE, LISTEN TO HIM.

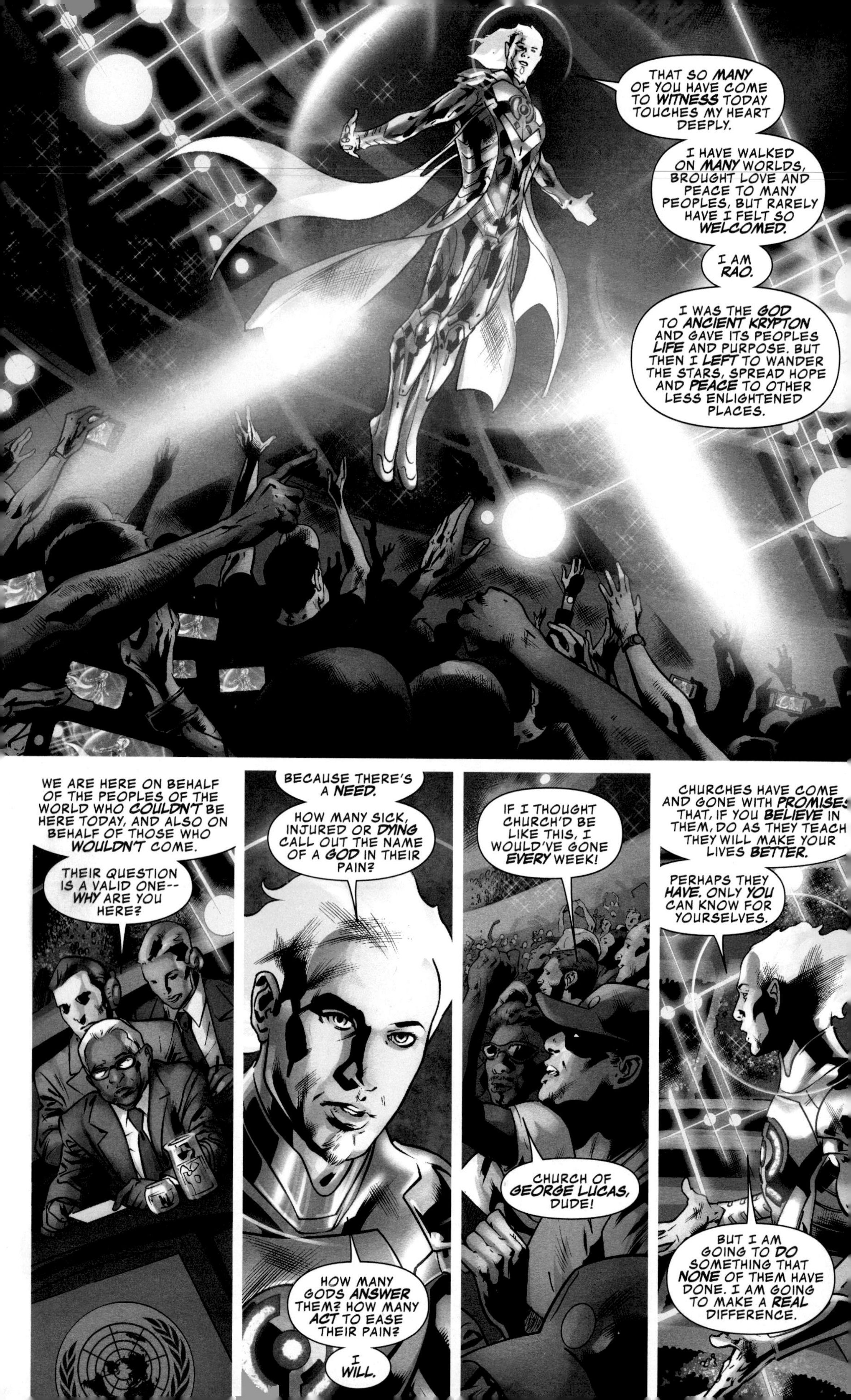
THAT SO MANY OF YOU HAVE COME TO WITNESS TODAY TOUCHES MY HEART DEEPLY.
I HAVE WALKED ON MANY WORLDS, BROUGHT LOVE AND PEACE TO MANY PEOPLES, BUT RARELY HAVE I FELT SO WELCOMED.
I AM RAO.
I WAS THE GOD TO ANCIENT KRYPTON AND GAVE ITS PEOPLES LIFE AND PURPOSE. BUT THEN I LEFT TO WANDER THE STARS, SPREAD HOPE AND PEACE TO OTHER LESS ENLIGHTENED PLACES.
WE ARE HERE ON BEHALF OF THE PEOPLES OF THE WORLD WHO COULDN'T BE HERE TODAY, AND ALSO ON BEHALF OF THOSE WHO WOULDN'T COME.
THEIR QUESTION IS A VALID ONE-- WHY ARE YOU HERE?
BECAUSE THERE'S A NEED.
HOW MANY SICK, INJURED OR DYING CALL OUT THE NAME OF A GOD IN THEIR PAIN?
HOW MANY GODS ANSWER THEM? HOW MANY ACT TO EASE THEIR PAIN?
I WILL.
IF I THOUGHT CHURCH'D BE LIKE THIS, I WOULD'VE GONE EVERY WEEK!
CHURCH OF GEORGE LUCAS, DUDE!
CHURCHES HAVE COME AND GONE WITH PROMISES THAT, IF YOU BELIEVE IN THEM, DO AS THEY TEACH THEY WILL MAKE YOUR LIVES BETTER.
PERHAPS THEY HAVE. ONLY YOU CAN KNOW FOR YOURSELVES.
BUT I AM GOING TO DO SOMETHING THAT NONE OF THEM HAVE DONE. I AM GOING TO MAKE A REAL DIFFERENCE.

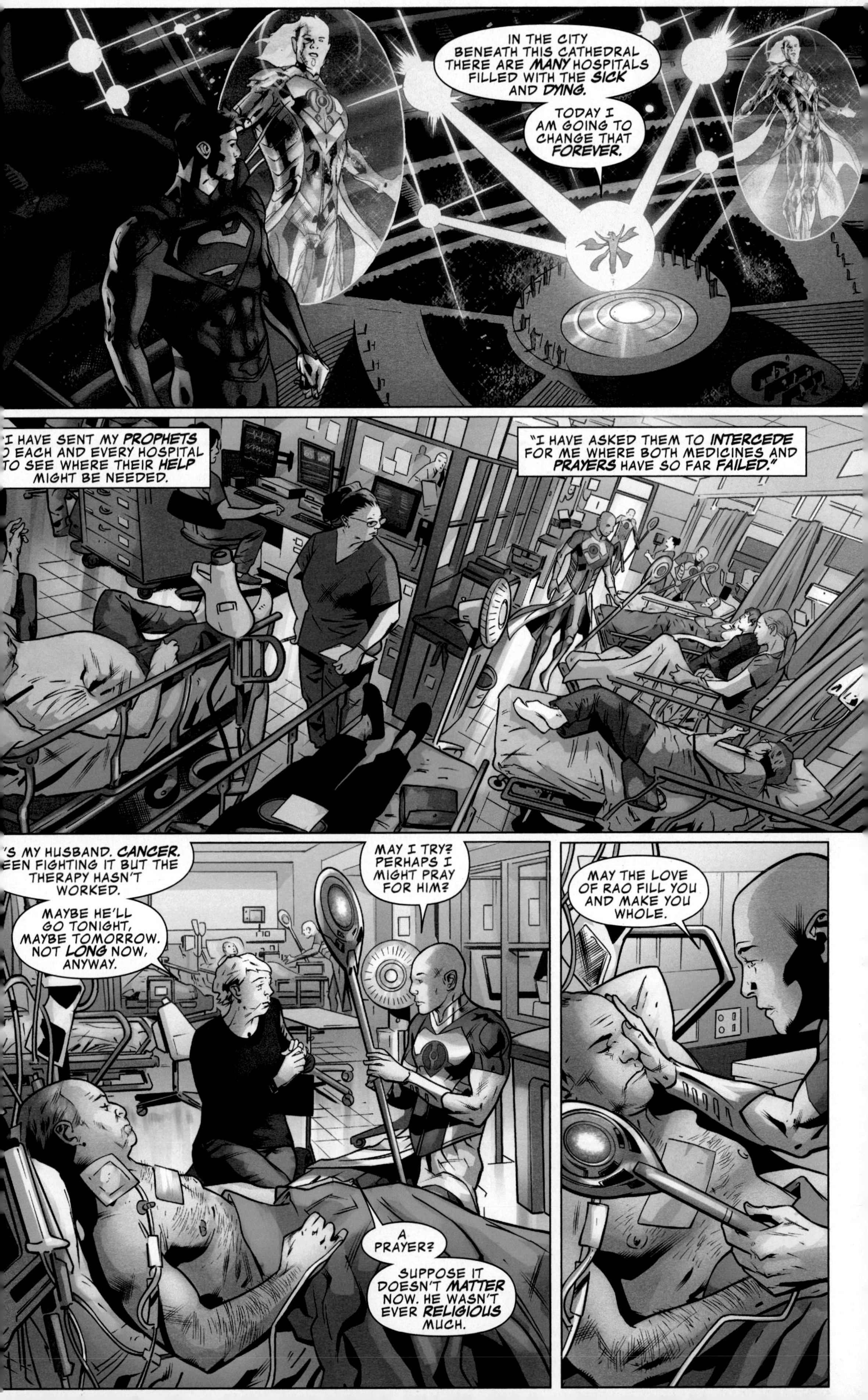
IN THE CITY BENEATH THIS CATHEDRAL THERE ARE MANY HOSPITALS FILLED WITH THE SICK AND DYING.
TODAY I AM GOING TO CHANGE THAT FOREVER.
"I HAVE SENT MY PROPHETS TO EACH AND EVERY HOSPITAL TO SEE WHERE THEIR HELP MIGHT BE NEEDED.
"I HAVE ASKED THEM TO INTERCEDE FOR ME WHERE BOTH MEDICINES AND PRAYERS HAVE SO FAR FAILED."
'S MY HUSBAND. CANCER. EEN FIGHTING IT BUT THE THERAPY HASN'T WORKED.
MAYBE HE'LL GO TONIGHT, MAYBE TOMORROW. NOT LONG NOW, ANYWAY.
MAY I TRY? PERHAPS I MIGHT PRAY FOR HIM?
A PRAYER?
SUPPOSE IT DOESN'T MATTER NOW. HE WASN'T EVER RELIGIOUS MUCH.
MAY THE LOVE OF RAO FILL YOU AND MAKE YOU WHOLE.

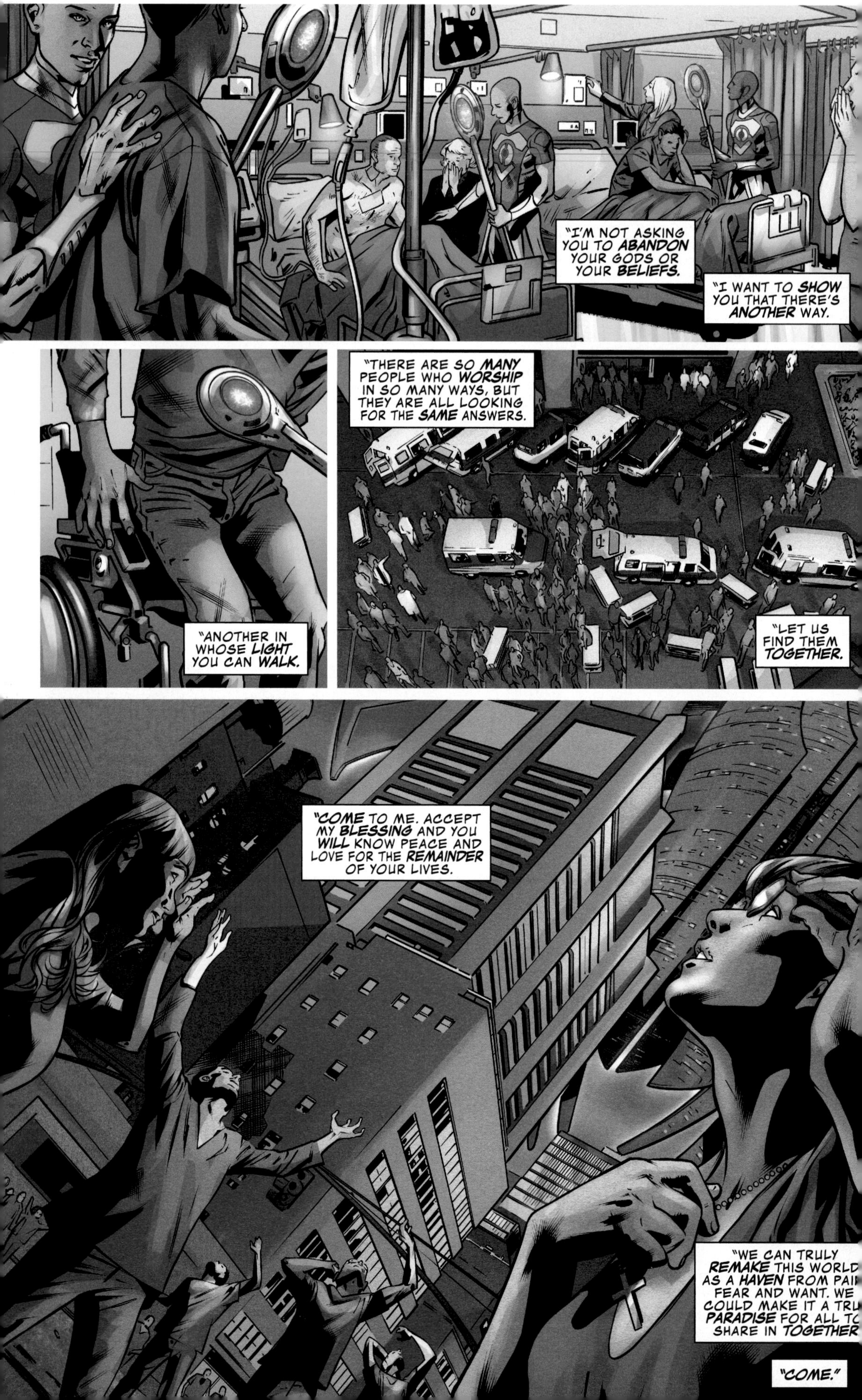
"I'M NOT ASKING YOU TO ABANDON YOUR GODS OR YOUR BELIEFS.
"I WANT TO SHOW YOU THAT THERE'S ANOTHER WAY.
"ANOTHER IN WHOSE LIGHT YOU CAN WALK.
"THERE ARE SO MANY PEOPLE WHO WORSHIP IN SO MANY WAYS, BUT THEY ARE ALL LOOKING FOR THE SAME ANSWERS.
"LET US FIND THEM TOGETHER.
"COME TO ME. ACCEPT MY BLESSING AND YOU WILL KNOW PEACE AND LOVE FOR THE REMAINDER OF YOUR LIVES.
"WE CAN TRULY REMAKE THIS WORLD AS A HAVEN FROM PAI FEAR AND WANT. WE COULD MAKE IT A TRU PARADISE FOR ALL TO SHARE IN TOGETHER
"COME."

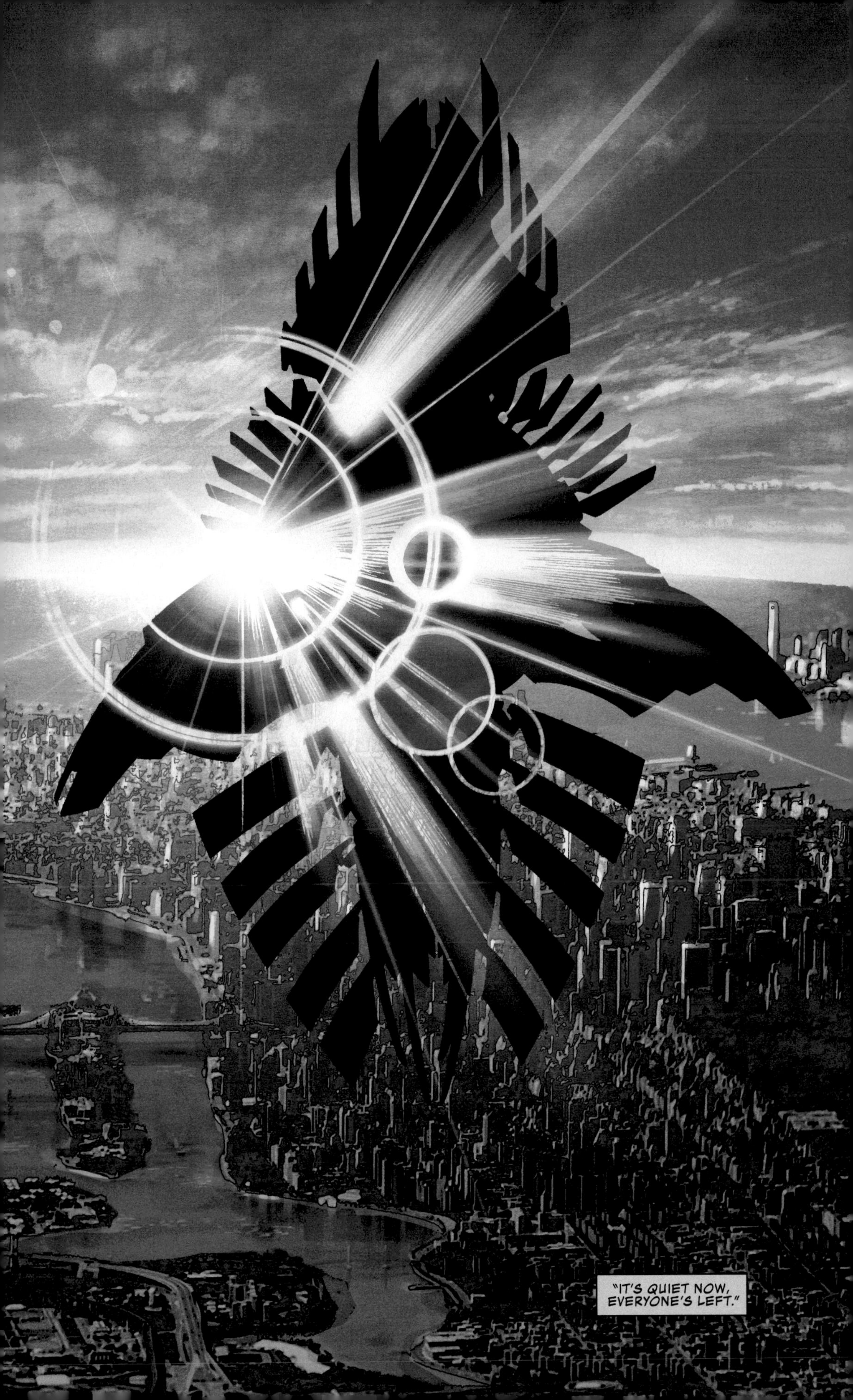
"IT'S QUIET NOW, EVERYONE'S LEFT."

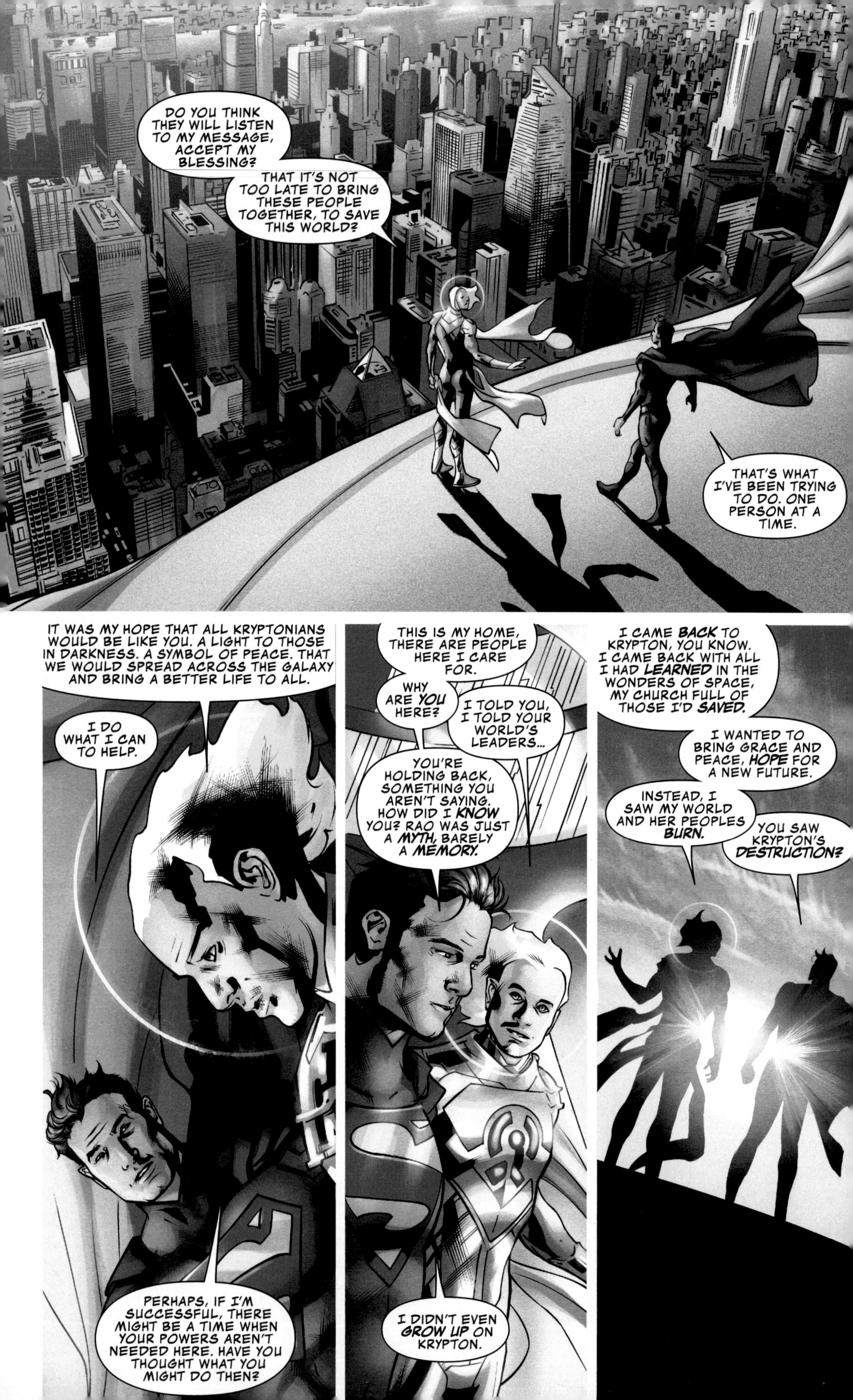
DO YOU THINK THEY WILL LISTEN TO MY MESSAGE, ACCEPT MY BLESSING?
THAT IT'S NOT TOO LATE TO BRING THESE PEOPLE TOGETHER, TO SAVE THIS WORLD?
THAT'S WHAT I'VE BEEN TRYING TO DO. ONE PERSON AT A TIME.
IT WAS MY HOPE THAT ALL KRYPTONIANS WOULD BE LIKE YOU. A LIGHT TO THOSE IN DARKNESS. A SYMBOL OF PEACE. THAT WE WOULD SPREAD ACROSS THE GALAXY AND BRING A BETTER LIFE TO ALL.
I DO WHAT I CAN TO HELP.
PERHAPS, IF I'M SUCCESSFUL, THERE MIGHT BE A TIME WHEN YOUR POWERS AREN'T NEEDED HERE. HAVE YOU THOUGHT WHAT YOU MIGHT DO THEN?
THIS IS MY HOME, THERE ARE PEOPLE HERE I CARE FOR.
WHY ARE YOU HERE?
I TOLD YOU, I TOLD YOUR WORLD'S LEADERS...
YOU'RE HOLDING BACK, SOMETHING YOU AREN'T SAYING. HOW DID I KNOW YOU? RAO WAS JUST A MYTH, BARELY A MEMORY.
I DIDN'T EVEN GROW UP ON KRYPTON.
I CAME BACK TO KRYPTON, YOU KNOW. I CAME BACK WITH ALL I HAD LEARNED IN THE WONDERS OF SPACE, MY CHURCH FULL OF THOSE I'D SAVED.
I WANTED TO BRING GRACE AND PEACE, HOPE FOR A NEW FUTURE.
INSTEAD, I SAW MY WORLD AND HER PEOPLES BURN.
YOU SAW KRYPTON'S DESTRUCTION?

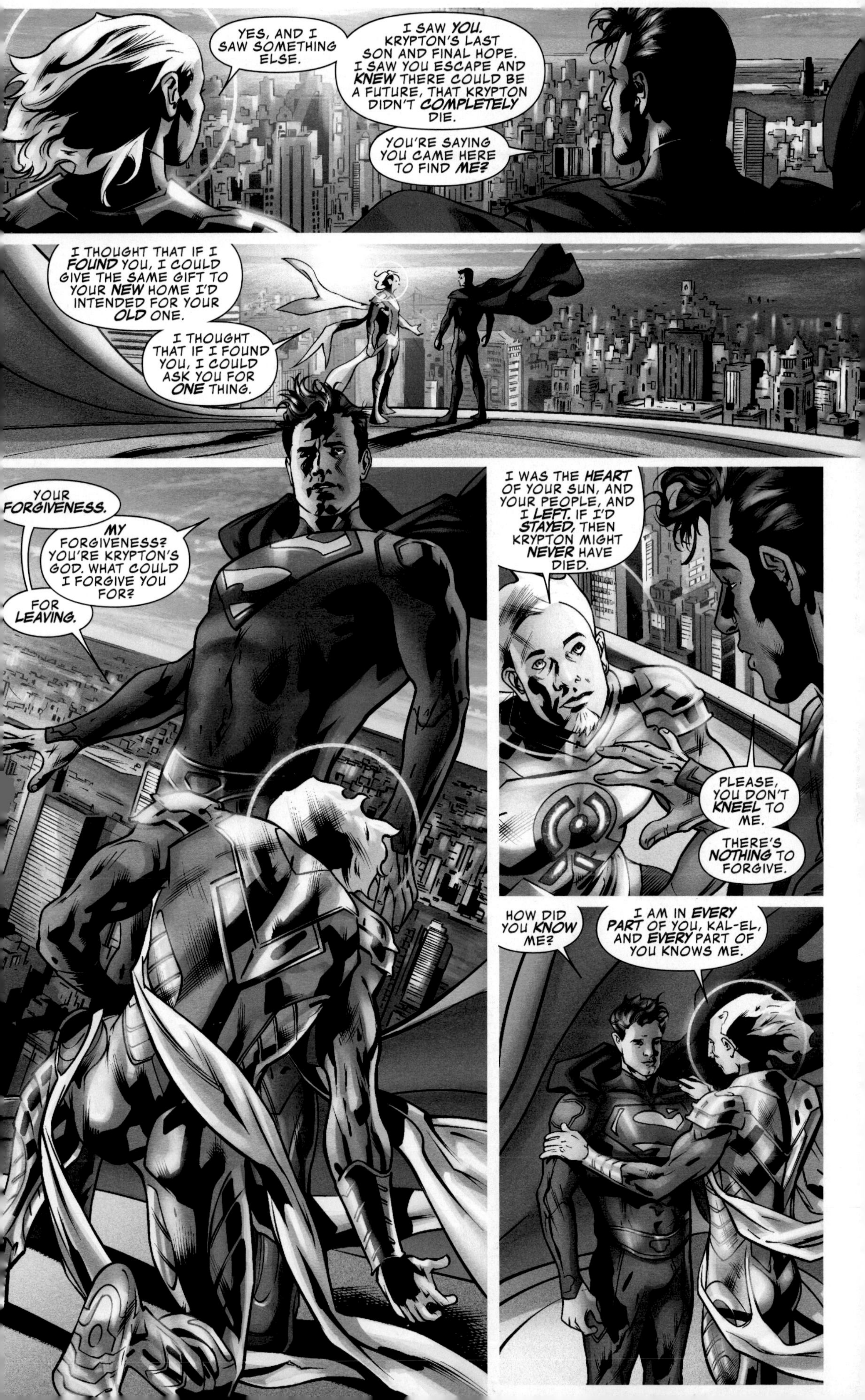
YES, AND I SAW SOMETHING ELSE.
I SAW YOU. KRYPTON'S LAST SON AND FINAL HOPE. I SAW YOU ESCAPE AND KNEW THERE COULD BE A FUTURE, THAT KRYPTON DIDN'T COMPLETELY DIE.
YOU'RE SAYING YOU CAME HERE TO FIND ME?
I THOUGHT THAT IF I FOUND YOU, I COULD GIVE THE SAME GIFT TO YOUR NEW HOME I'D INTENDED FOR YOUR OLD ONE.
I THOUGHT THAT IF I FOUND YOU, I COULD ASK YOU FOR ONE THING.
YOUR FORGIVENESS.
MY FORGIVENESS? YOU'RE KRYPTON'S GOD. WHAT COULD I FORGIVE YOU FOR?
FOR LEAVING.
I WAS THE HEART OF YOUR SUN, AND YOUR PEOPLE, AND I LEFT. IF I'D STAYED, THEN KRYPTON MIGHT NEVER HAVE DIED.
PLEASE, YOU DON'T KNEEL TO ME.
THERE'S NOTHING TO FORGIVE.
HOW DID YOU KNOW ME?
I AM IN EVERY PART OF YOU, KAL-EL, AND EVERY PART OF YOU KNOWS ME.

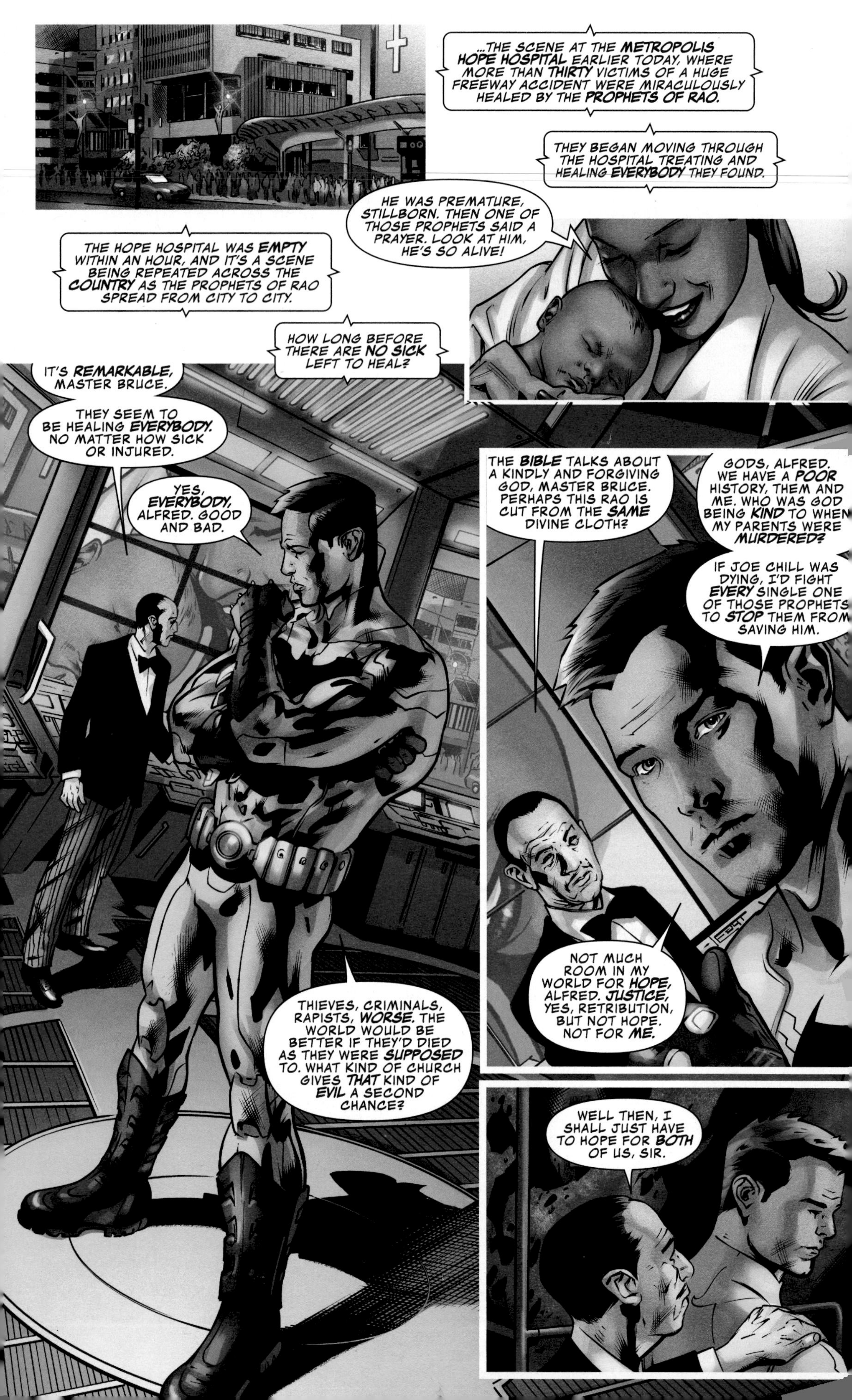
...THE SCENE AT THE METROPOLIS HOPE HOSPITAL EARLIER TODAY, WHERE MORE THAN THIRTY VICTIMS OF A HUGE FREEWAY ACCIDENT WERE MIRACULOUSLY HEALED BY THE PROPHETS OF RAO.
THEY BEGAN MOVING THROUGH THE HOSPITAL TREATING AND HEALING EVERYBODY THEY FOUND.
THE HOPE HOSPITAL WAS EMPTY WITHIN AN HOUR, AND IT'S A SCENE BEING REPEATED ACROSS THE COUNTRY AS THE PROPHETS OF RAO SPREAD FROM CITY TO CITY.
HE WAS PREMATURE, STILLBORN. THEN ONE OF THOSE PROPHETS SAID A PRAYER. LOOK AT HIM, HE'S SO ALIVE!
HOW LONG BEFORE THERE ARE NO SICK LEFT TO HEAL?
IT'S REMARKABLE, MASTER BRUCE.
THEY SEEM TO BE HEALING EVERYBODY. NO MATTER HOW SICK OR INJURED.
YES, EVERYBODY, ALFRED. GOOD AND BAD.
THIEVES, CRIMINALS, RAPISTS, WORSE. THE WORLD WOULD BE BETTER IF THEY'D DIED AS THEY WERE SUPPOSED TO. WHAT KIND OF CHURCH GIVES THAT KIND OF EVIL A SECOND CHANCE?
THE BIBLE TALKS ABOUT A KINDLY AND FORGIVING GOD, MASTER BRUCE. PERHAPS THIS RAO IS CUT FROM THE SAME DIVINE CLOTH?
GODS, ALFRED. WE HAVE A POOR HISTORY, THEM AND ME. WHO WAS GOD BEING KIND TO WHEN MY PARENTS WERE MURDERED?
IF JOE CHILL WAS DYING, I'D FIGHT EVERY SINGLE ONE OF THOSE PROPHETS TO STOP THEM FROM SAVING HIM.
NOT MUCH ROOM IN MY WORLD FOR HOPE, ALFRED. JUSTICE, YES, RETRIBUTION, BUT NOT HOPE. NOT FOR ME.
WELL THEN, I SHALL JUST HAVE TO HOPE FOR BOTH OF US, SIR.

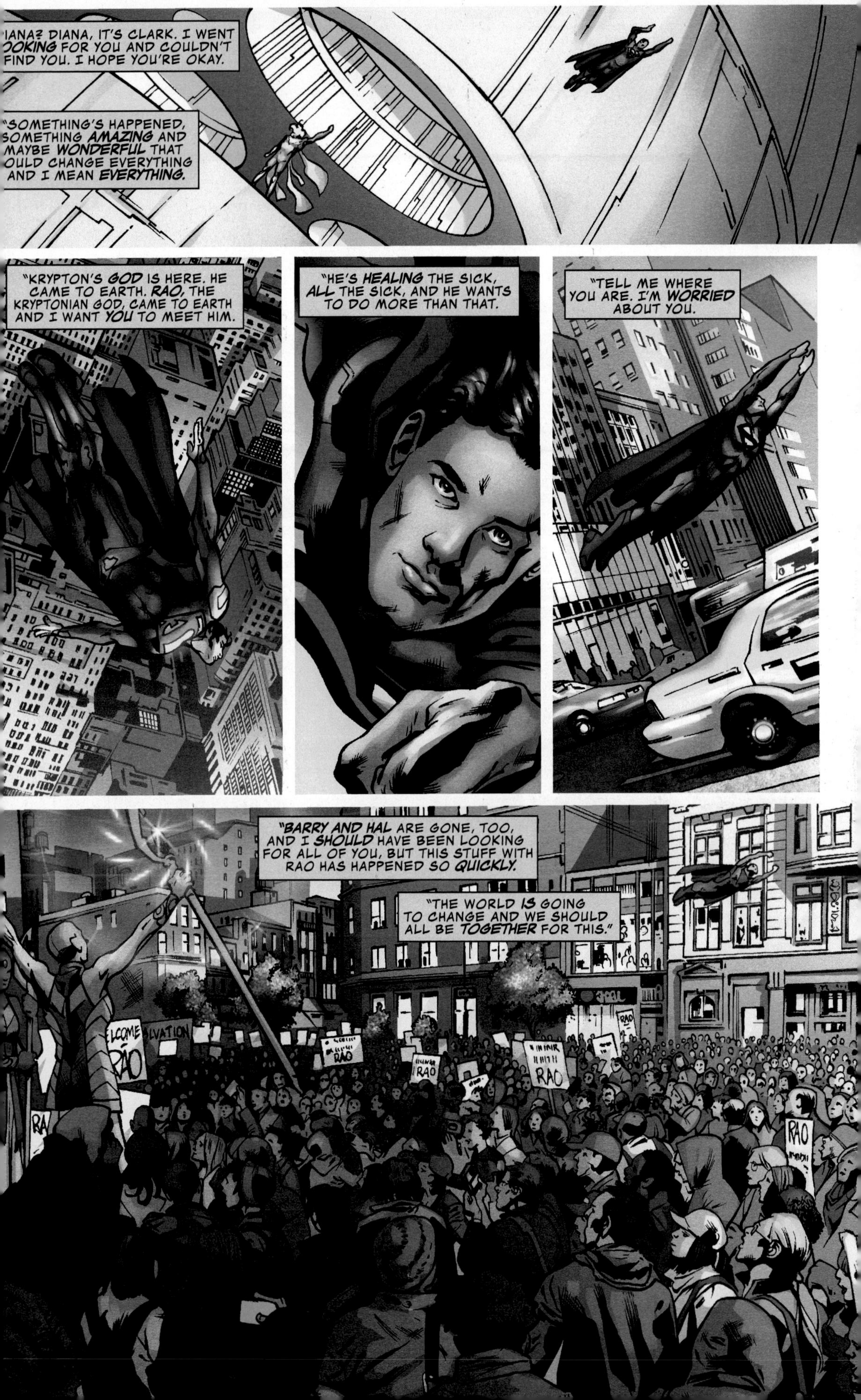
DIANA? DIANA, IT'S CLARK. I WENT LOOKING FOR YOU AND COULDN'T FIND YOU. I HOPE YOU'RE OKAY.
"SOMETHING'S HAPPENED, SOMETHING AMAZING AND MAYBE WONDERFUL THAT COULD CHANGE EVERYTHING AND I MEAN EVERYTHING.
"KRYPTON'S GOD IS HERE. HE CAME TO EARTH. RAO, THE KRYPTONIAN GOD, CAME TO EARTH AND I WANT YOU TO MEET HIM.
"HE'S HEALING THE SICK, ALL THE SICK, AND HE WANTS TO DO MORE THAN THAT.
"TELL ME WHERE YOU ARE. I'M WORRIED ABOUT YOU.
"BARRY AND HAL ARE GONE, TOO, AND I SHOULD HAVE BEEN LOOKING FOR ALL OF YOU, BUT THIS STUFF WITH RAO HAS HAPPENED SO QUICKLY.
"THE WORLD IS GOING TO CHANGE AND WE SHOULD ALL BE TOGETHER FOR THIS."
ELCOME RAO
LVATION
RAO
RAO
RAO
RAO
RAO

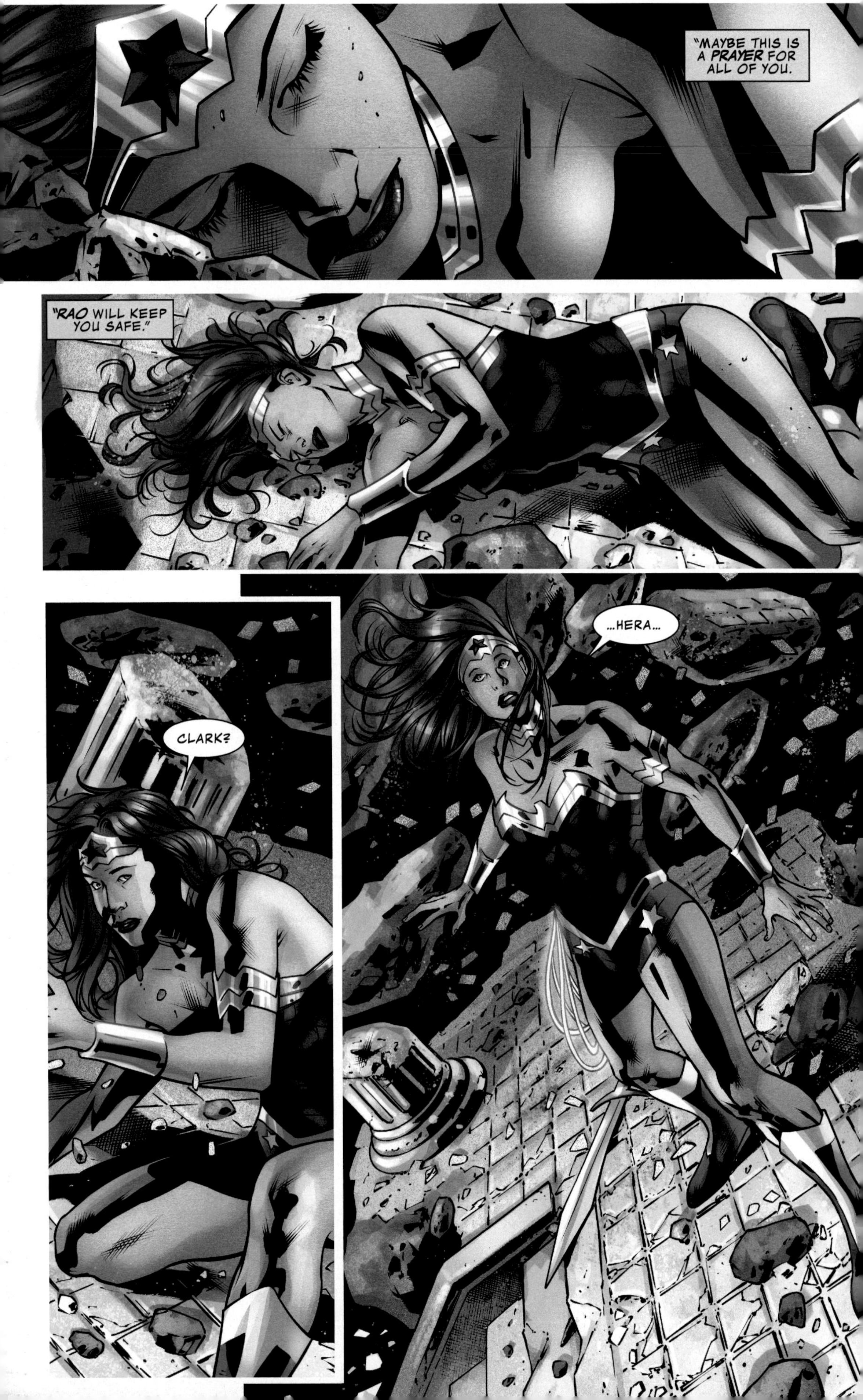
"MAYBE THIS IS A PRAYER FOR ALL OF YOU.
"RAO WILL KEEP YOU SAFE."
CLARK?
...HERA...

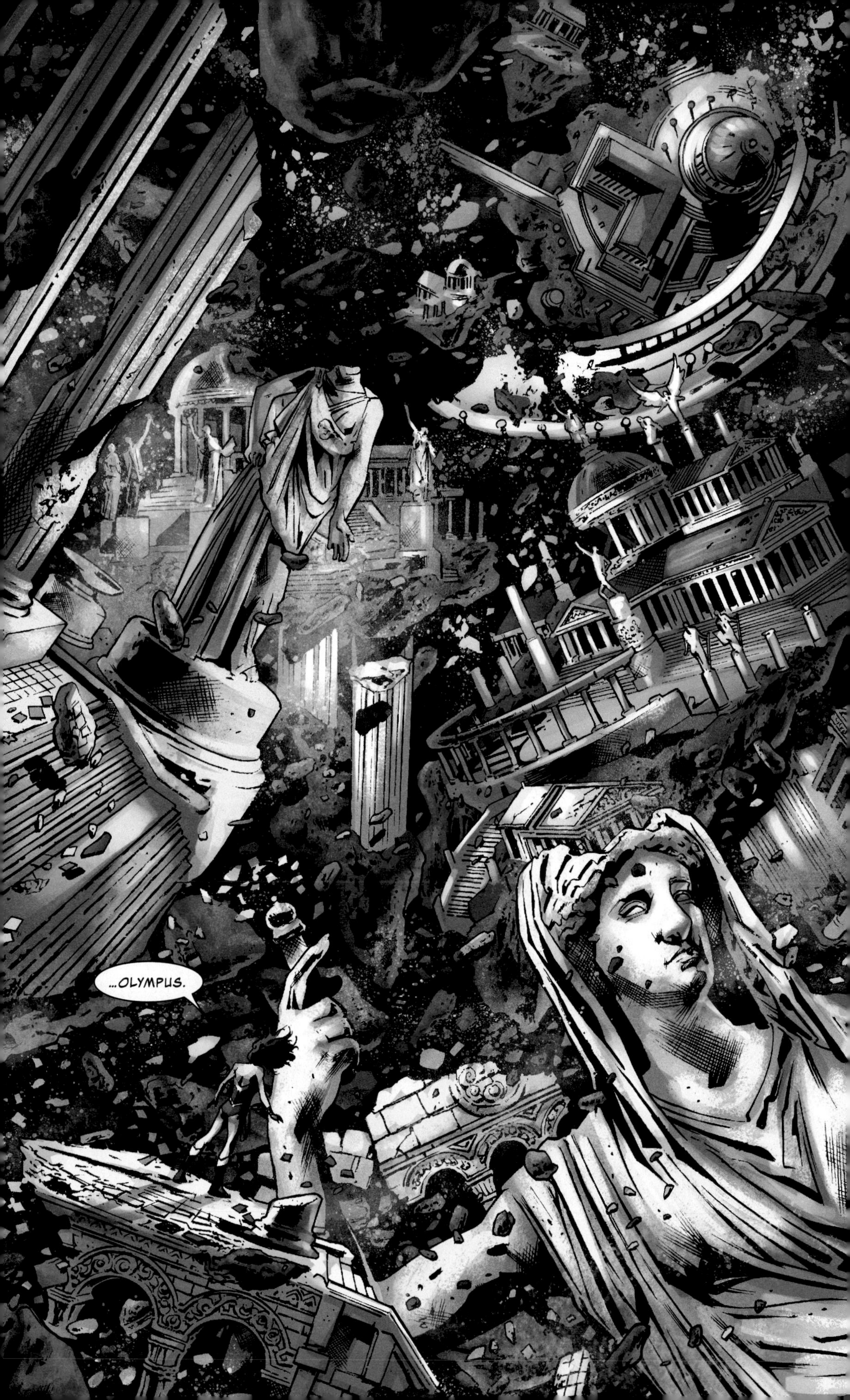
...OLYMPUS.

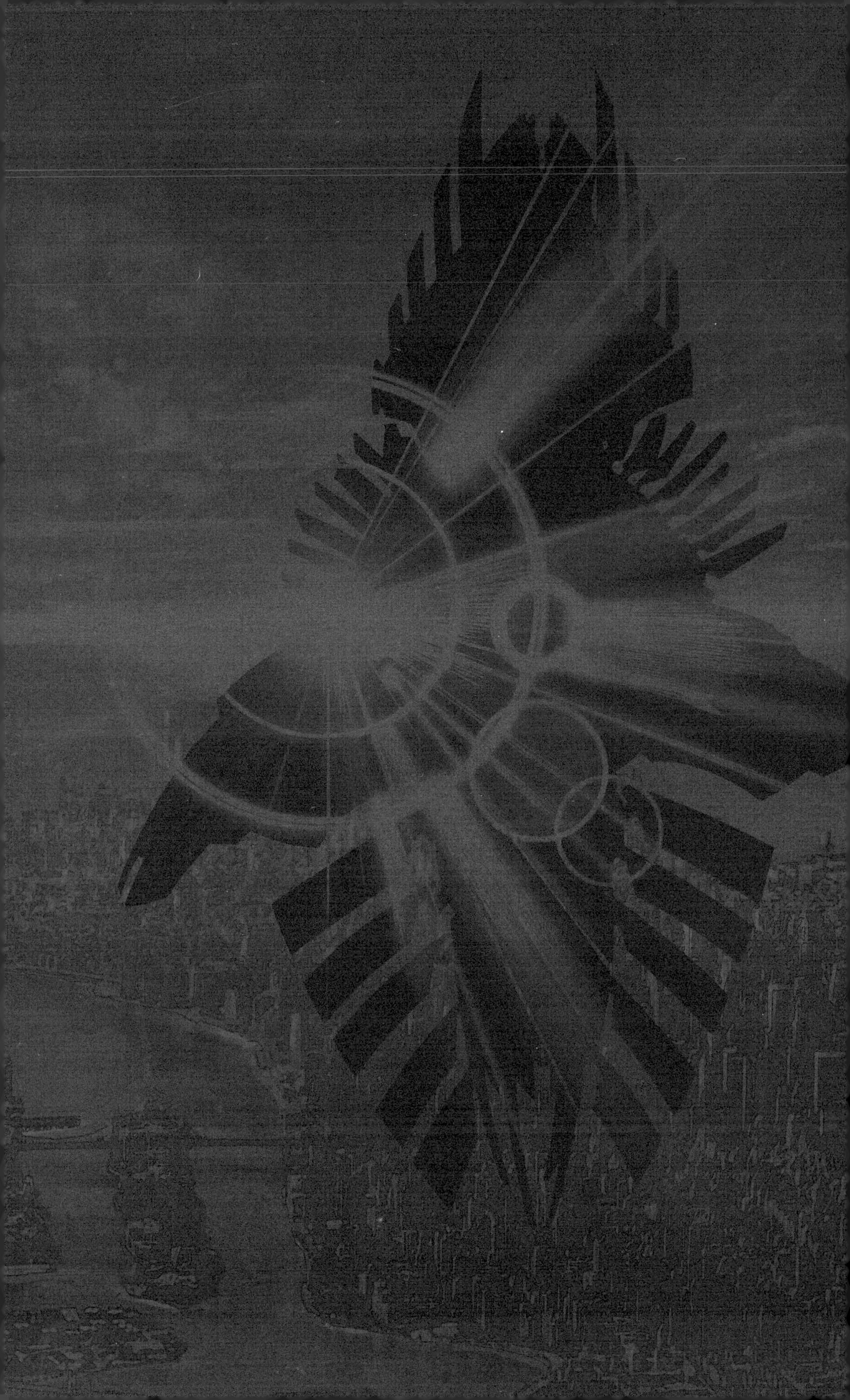

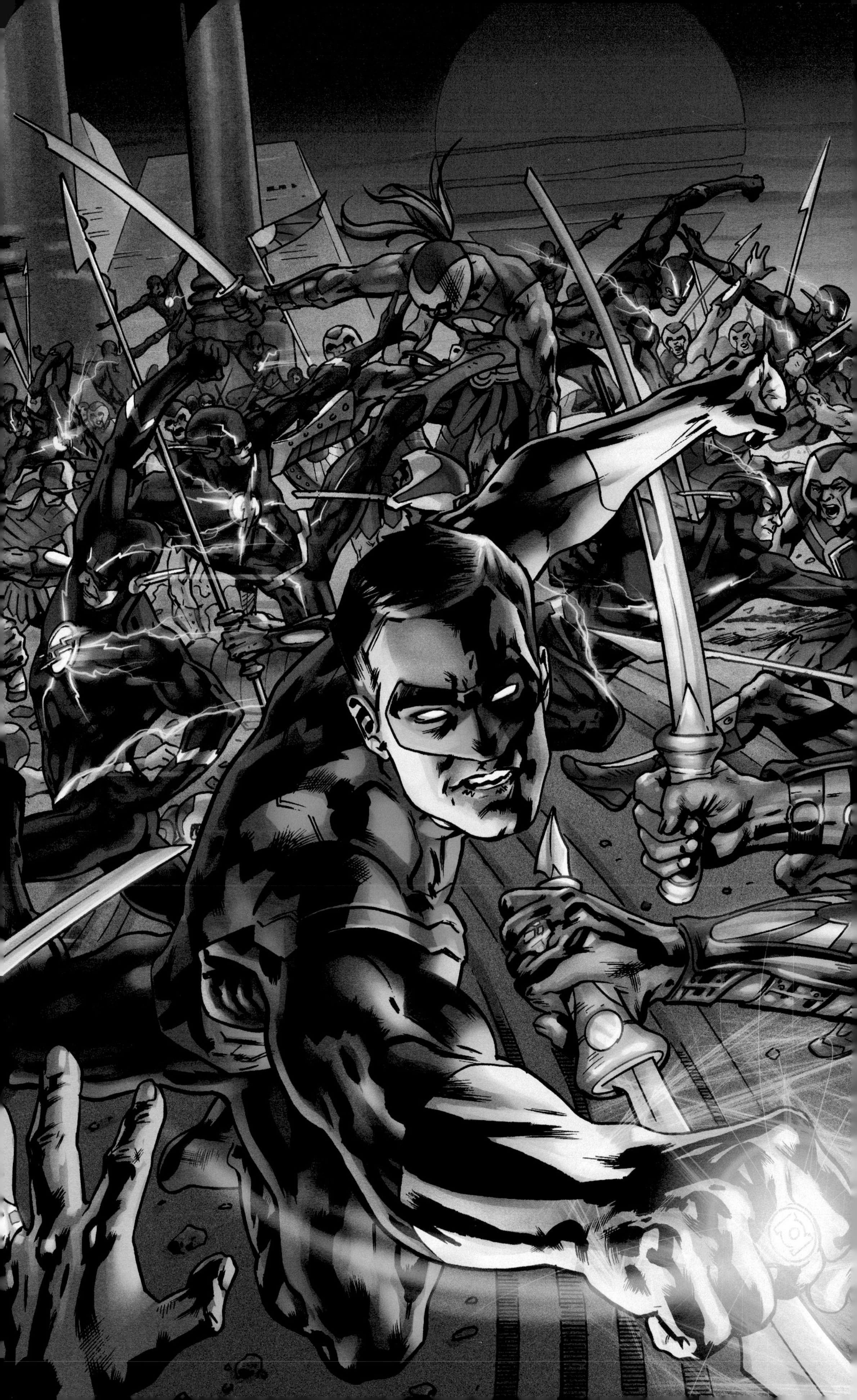

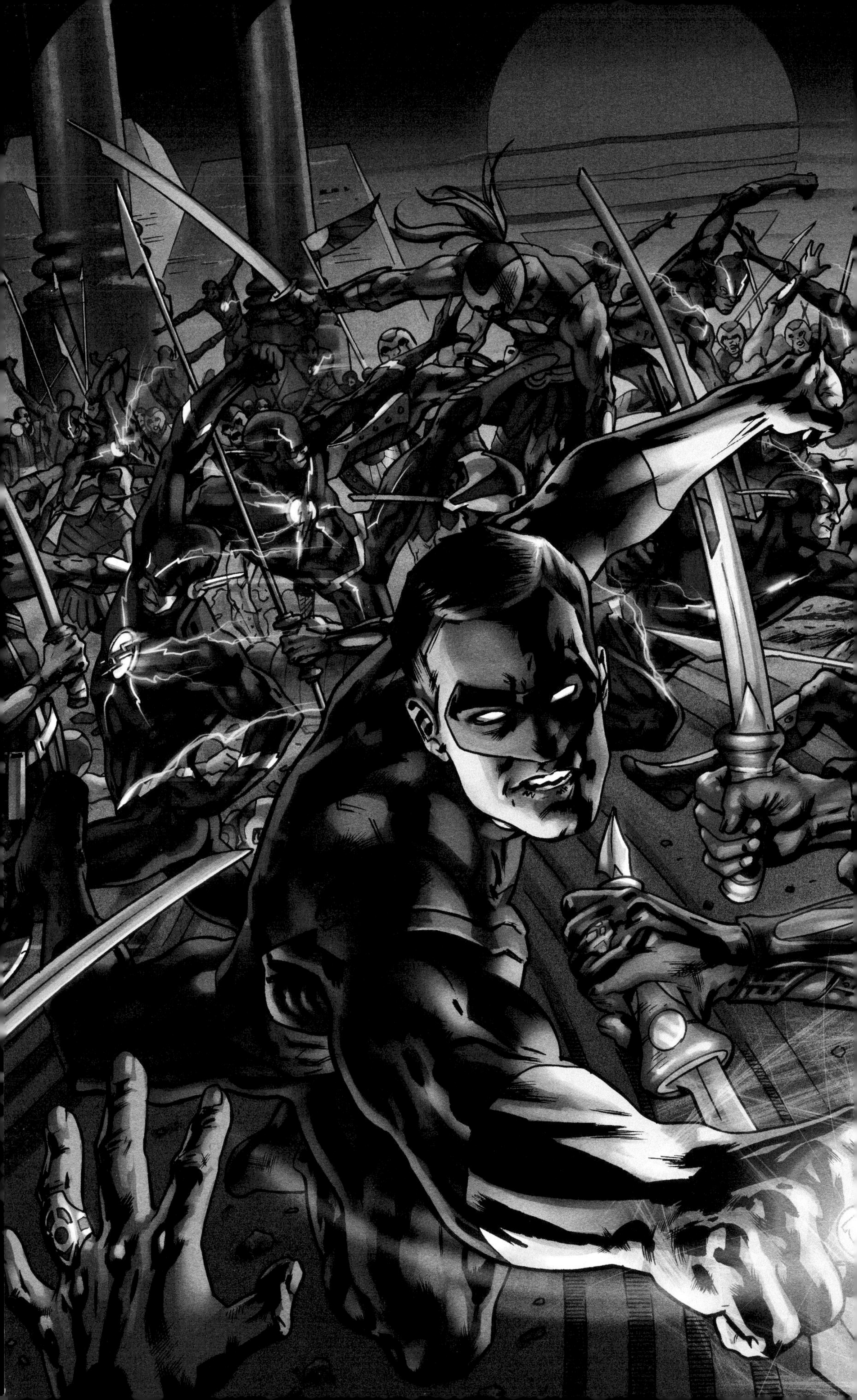

DC COMICS PRESENTS
THE JUSTICE LEAGUE OF AMERICA
POWER AND GLORY
PART THREE
BY BRYAN HITCH

INKS BY **DANIEL HENRIQUES**
COLORS BY **ALEX SINCLAIR**
LETTERS BY **CHRIS ELIOPOULOS**
ASSISTS BY **AMEDEO TURTURRO**
EDITS BY **BRIAN CUNNINGHAM**

COVER BY **BRYAN HITCH** AND **ALEX SINCLAIR**

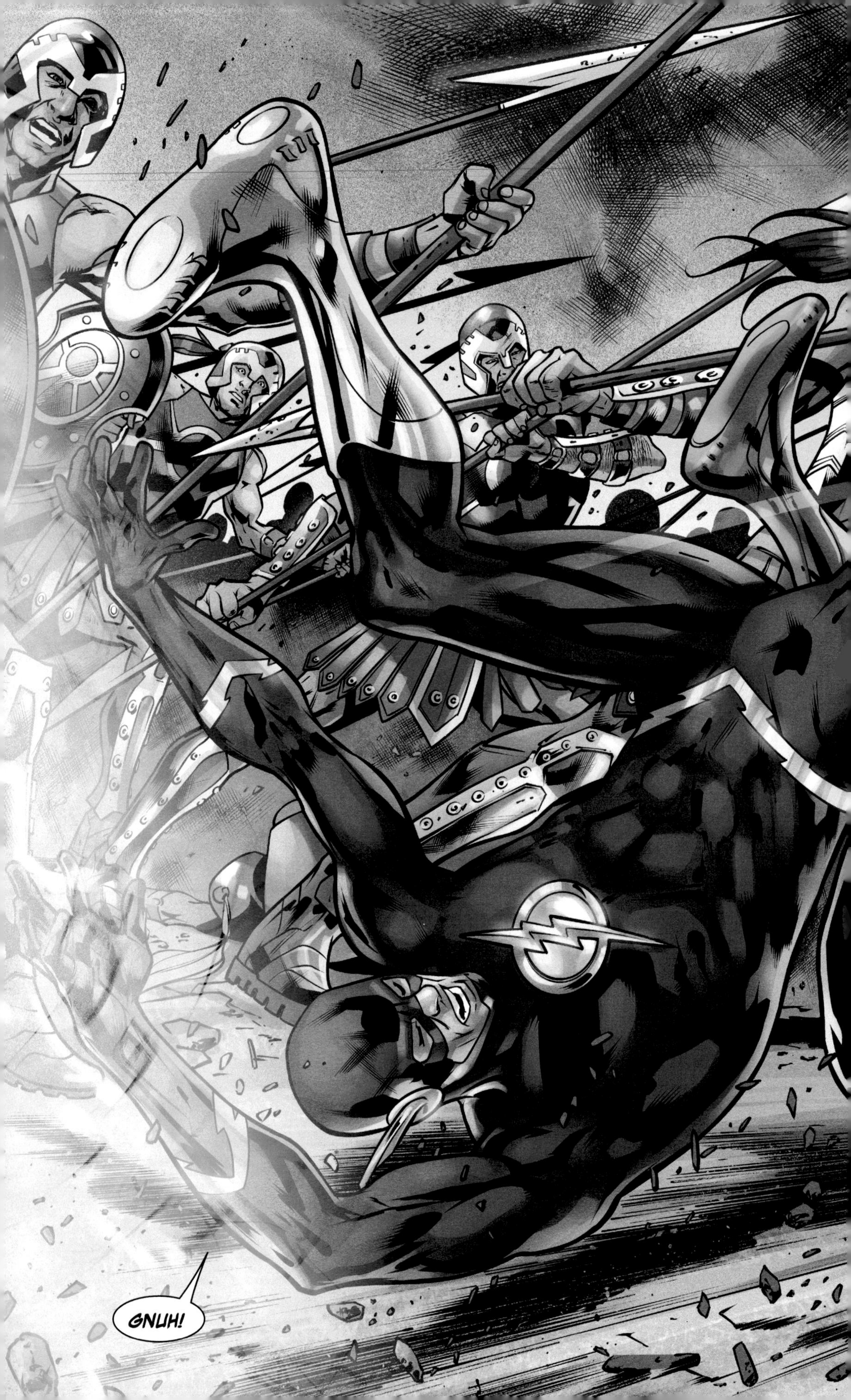
GNUH!

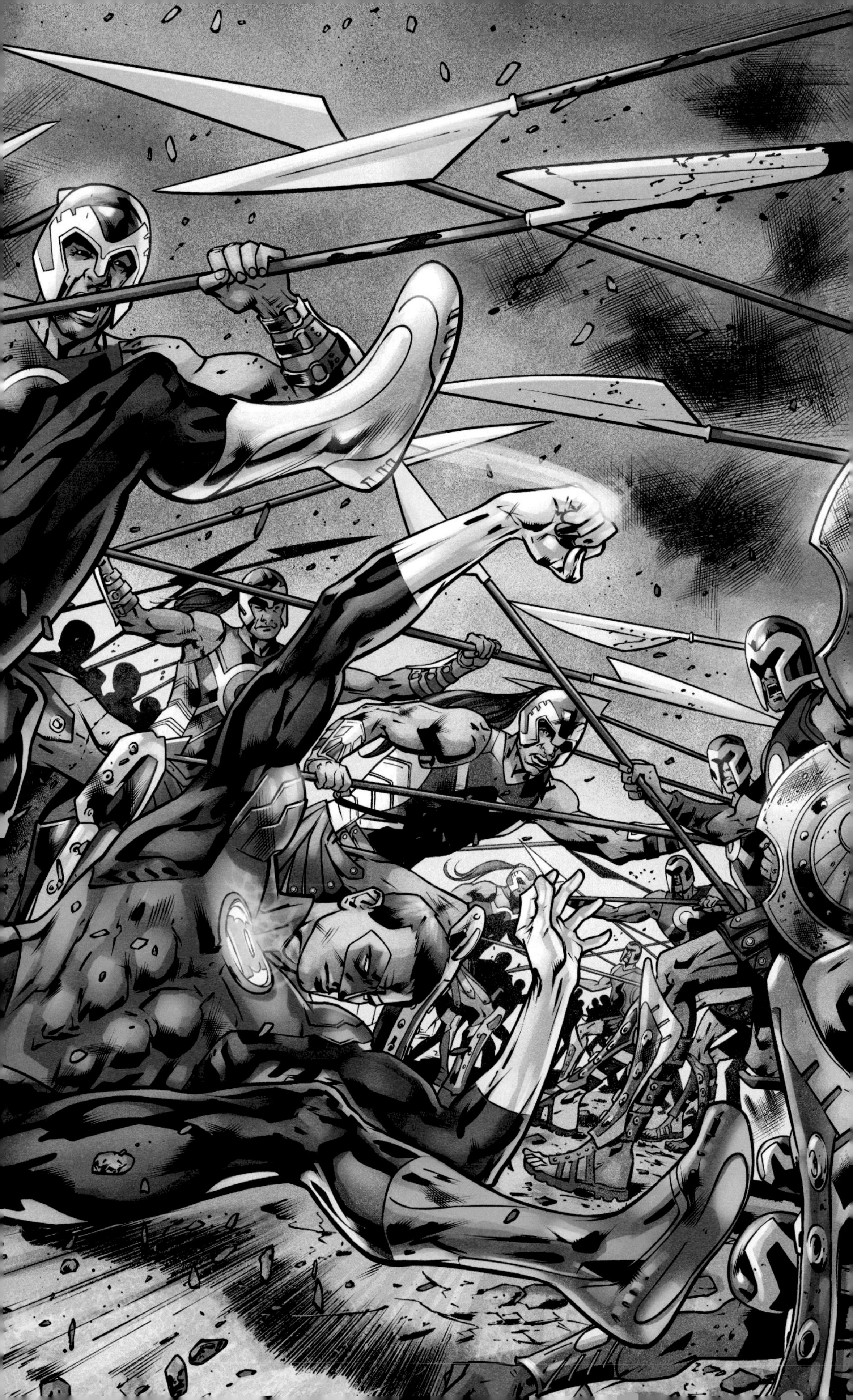

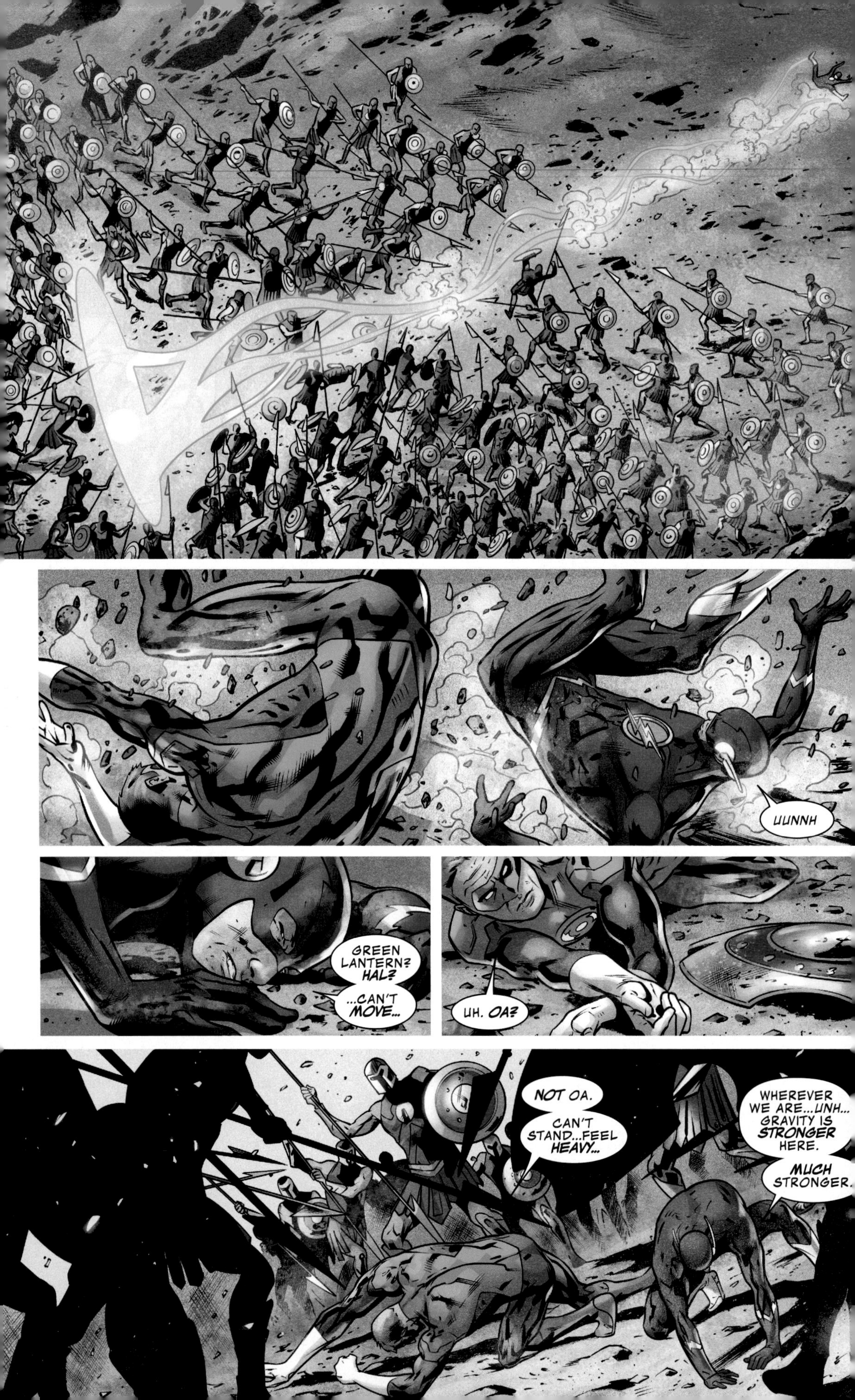
UUNNH
GREEN LANTERN? HAL?
...CAN'T MOVE...
UH. OA?
NOT OA.
CAN'T STAND...FEEL HEAVY...
WHEREVER WE ARE...UNH... GRAVITY IS STRONGER HERE.
MUCH STRONGER.

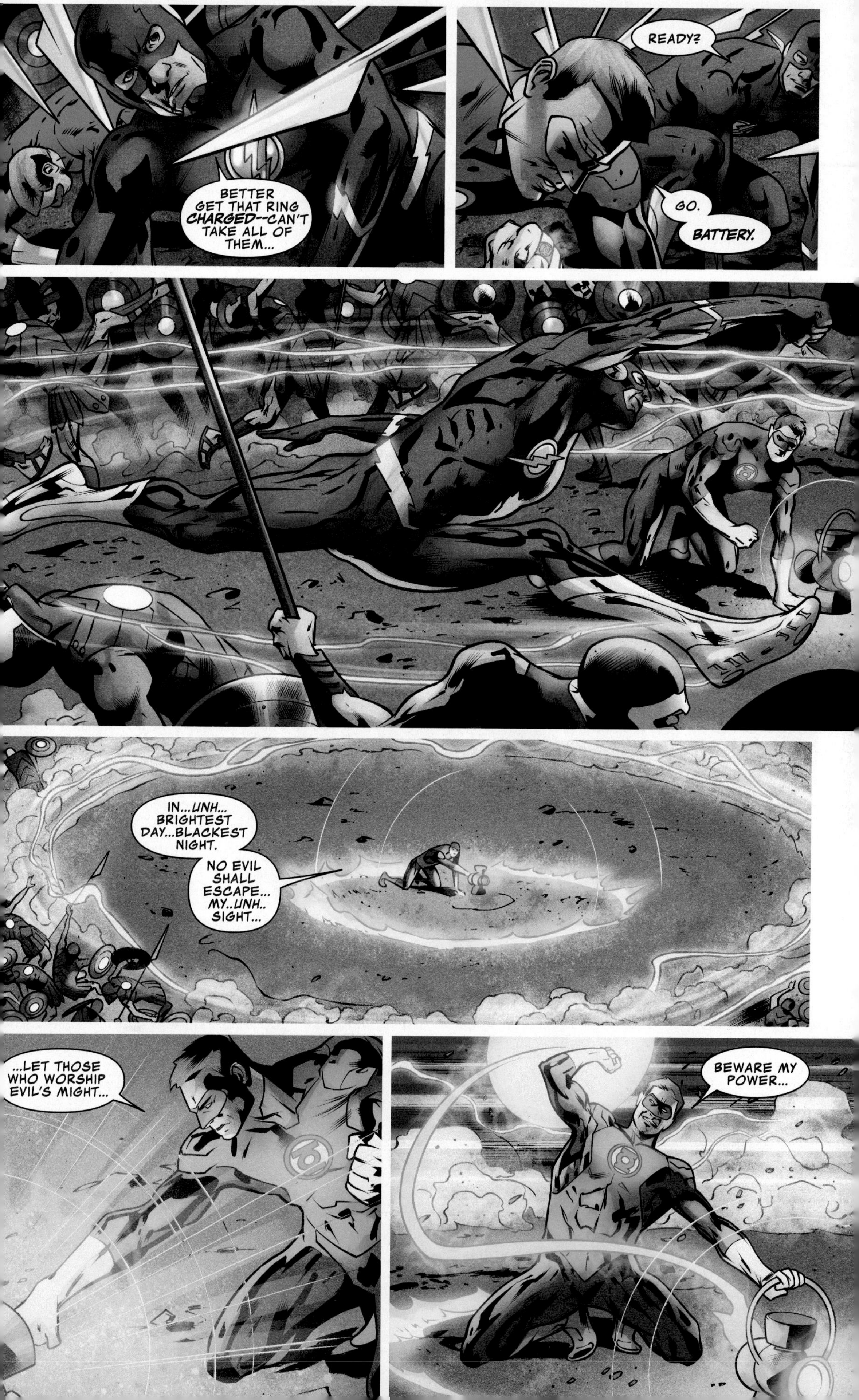
BETTER GET THAT RING CHARGED--CAN'T TAKE ALL OF THEM...
READY?
GO.
BATTERY.
IN...UNH... BRIGHTEST DAY...BLACKEST NIGHT.
NO EVIL SHALL ESCAPE... MY..UNH.. SIGHT...
...LET THOSE WHO WORSHIP EVIL'S MIGHT...
BEWARE MY POWER...

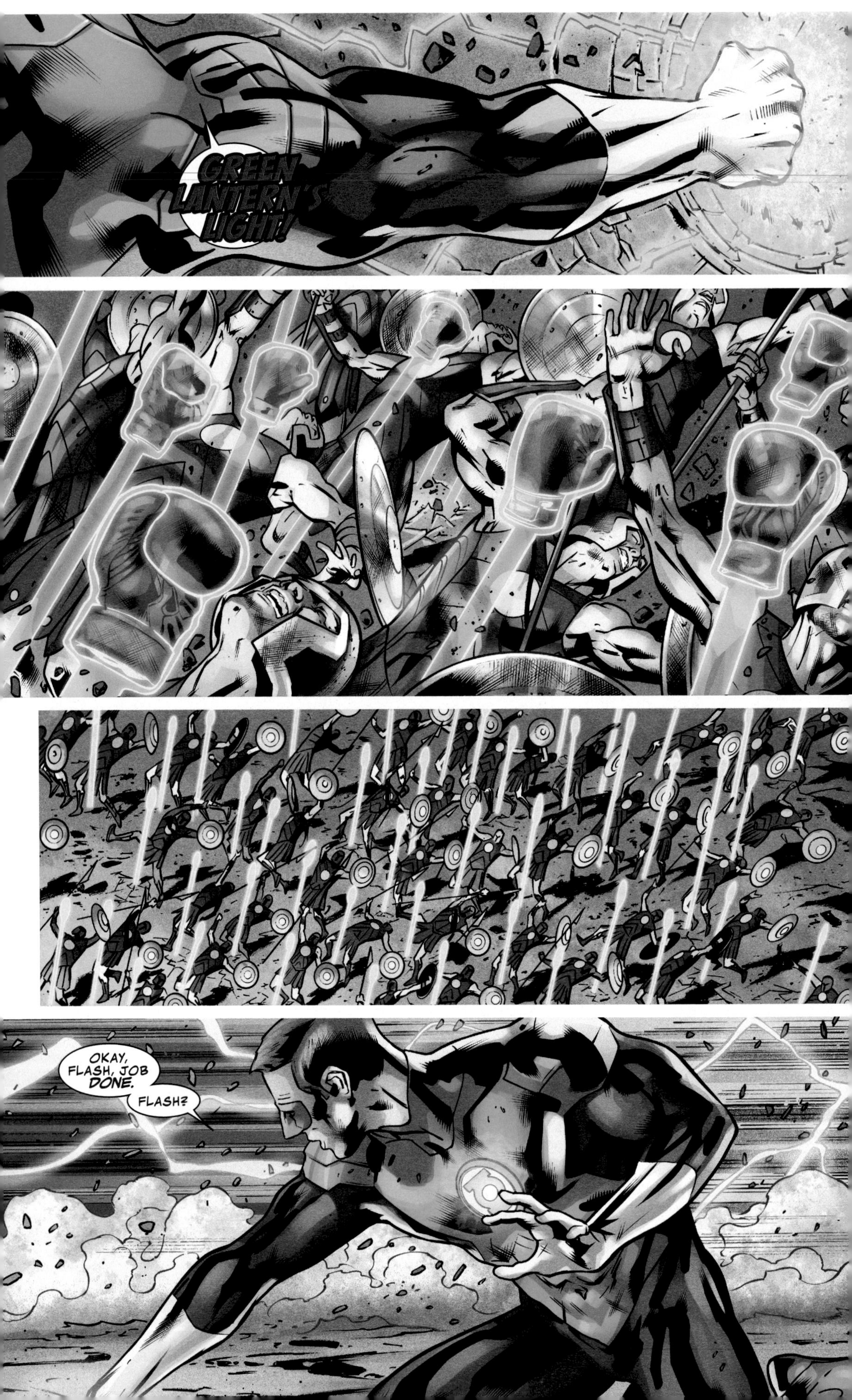
GREEN LANTERN'S LIGHT!
OKAY, FLASH, JOB DONE.
FLASH?

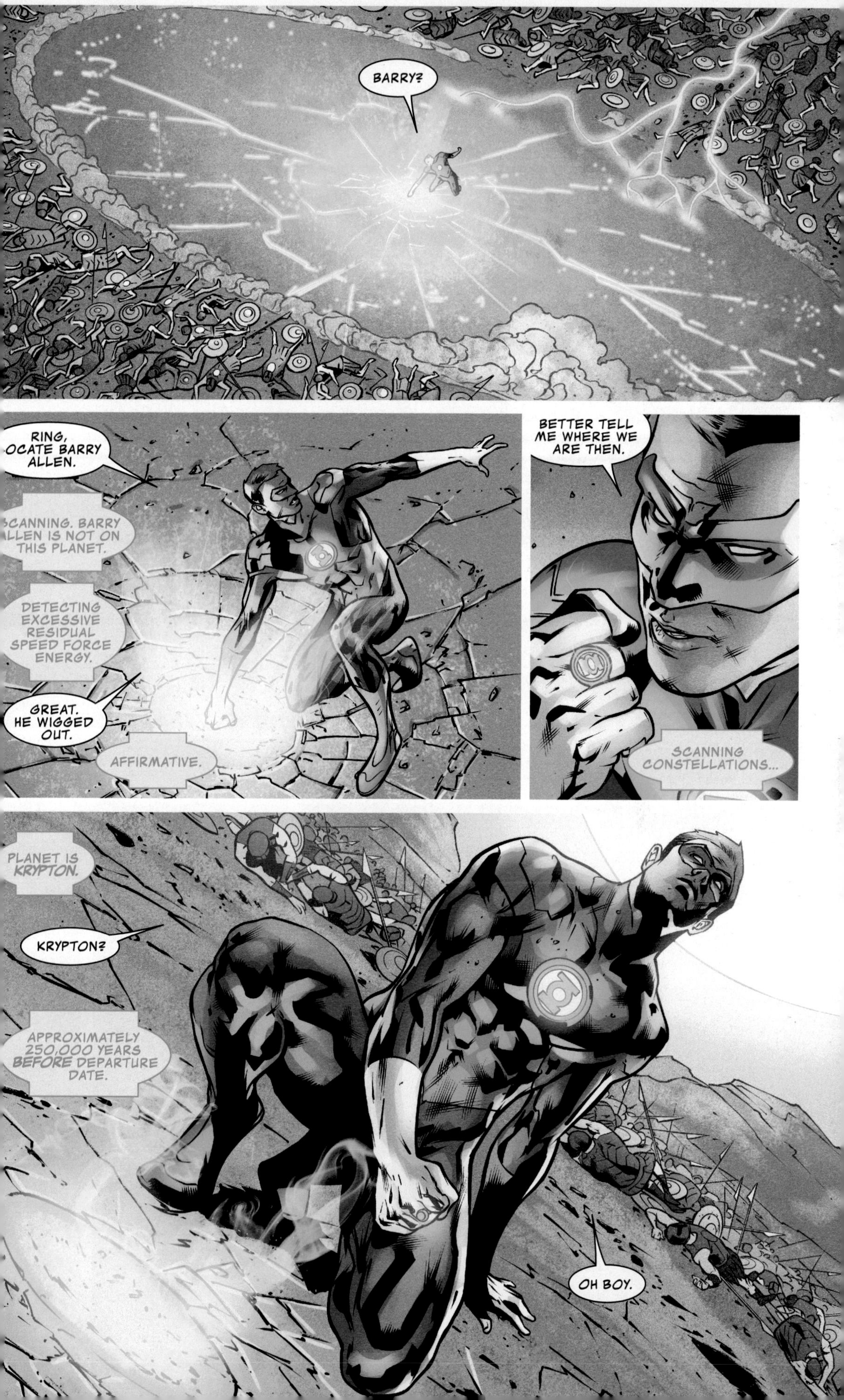
BARRY?
RING, OCATE BARRY ALLEN.
SCANNING. BARRY ALLEN IS NOT ON THIS PLANET.
DETECTING EXCESSIVE RESIDUAL SPEED FORCE ENERGY.
GREAT. HE WIGGED OUT.
AFFIRMATIVE.
BETTER TELL ME WHERE WE ARE THEN.
SCANNING CONSTELLATIONS...
PLANET IS *KRYPTON.*
KRYPTON?
APPROXIMATELY 250,000 YEARS *BEFORE* DEPARTURE DATE.
OH BOY.

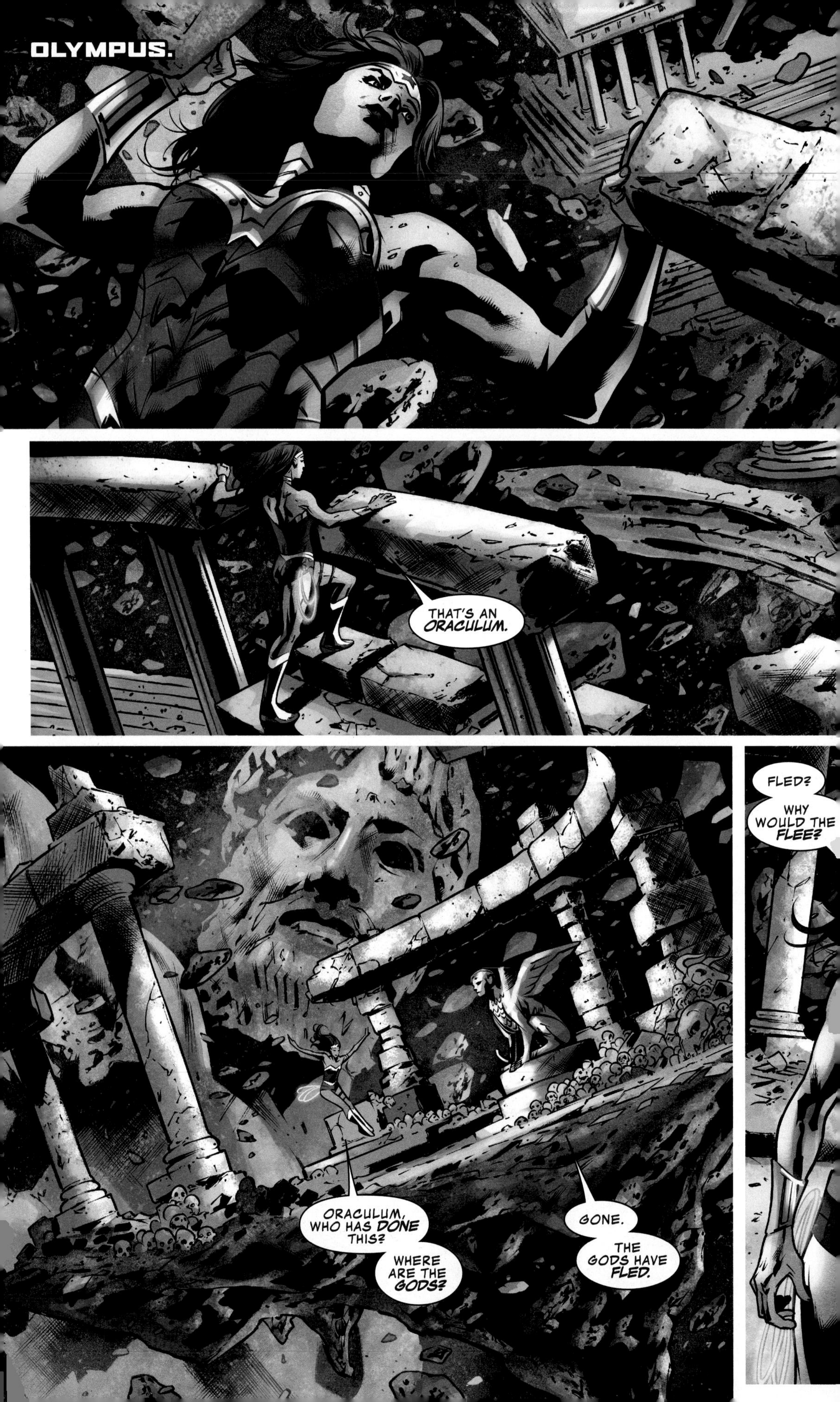
OLYMPUS.
THAT'S AN ORACULUM.
ORACULUM, WHO HAS DONE THIS?
WHERE ARE THE GODS?
GONE.
THE GODS HAVE FLED.
FLED?
WHY WOULD THE FLEE?

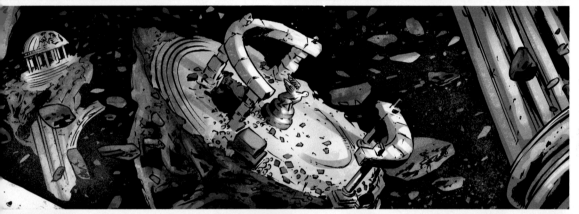

BECAUSE THEY **FEARED** WHAT WAS COMING.

AND WHAT **IS** COMING?

THE END OF **EVERYTHING.**

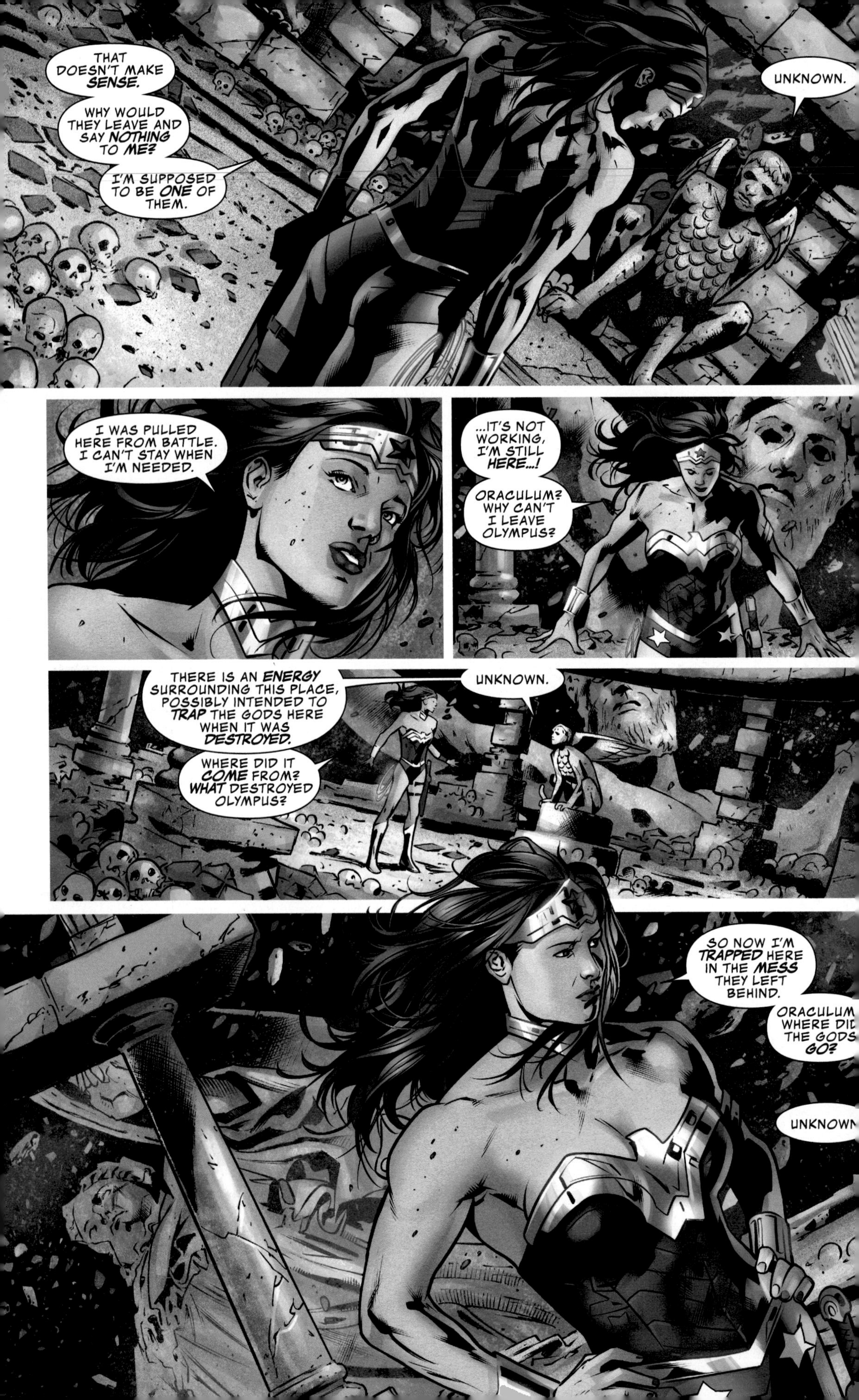
THAT DOESN'T MAKE SENSE.
WHY WOULD THEY LEAVE AND SAY NOTHING TO ME?
I'M SUPPOSED TO BE ONE OF THEM.
UNKNOWN.
I WAS PULLED HERE FROM BATTLE. I CAN'T STAY WHEN I'M NEEDED.
...IT'S NOT WORKING, I'M STILL HERE...!
ORACULUM? WHY CAN'T I LEAVE OLYMPUS?
THERE IS AN ENERGY SURROUNDING THIS PLACE, POSSIBLY INTENDED TO TRAP THE GODS HERE WHEN IT WAS DESTROYED.
UNKNOWN.
WHERE DID IT COME FROM? WHAT DESTROYED OLYMPUS?
SO NOW I'M TRAPPED HERE IN THE MESS THEY LEFT BEHIND.
ORACULUM WHERE DID THE GODS GO?
UNKNOWN

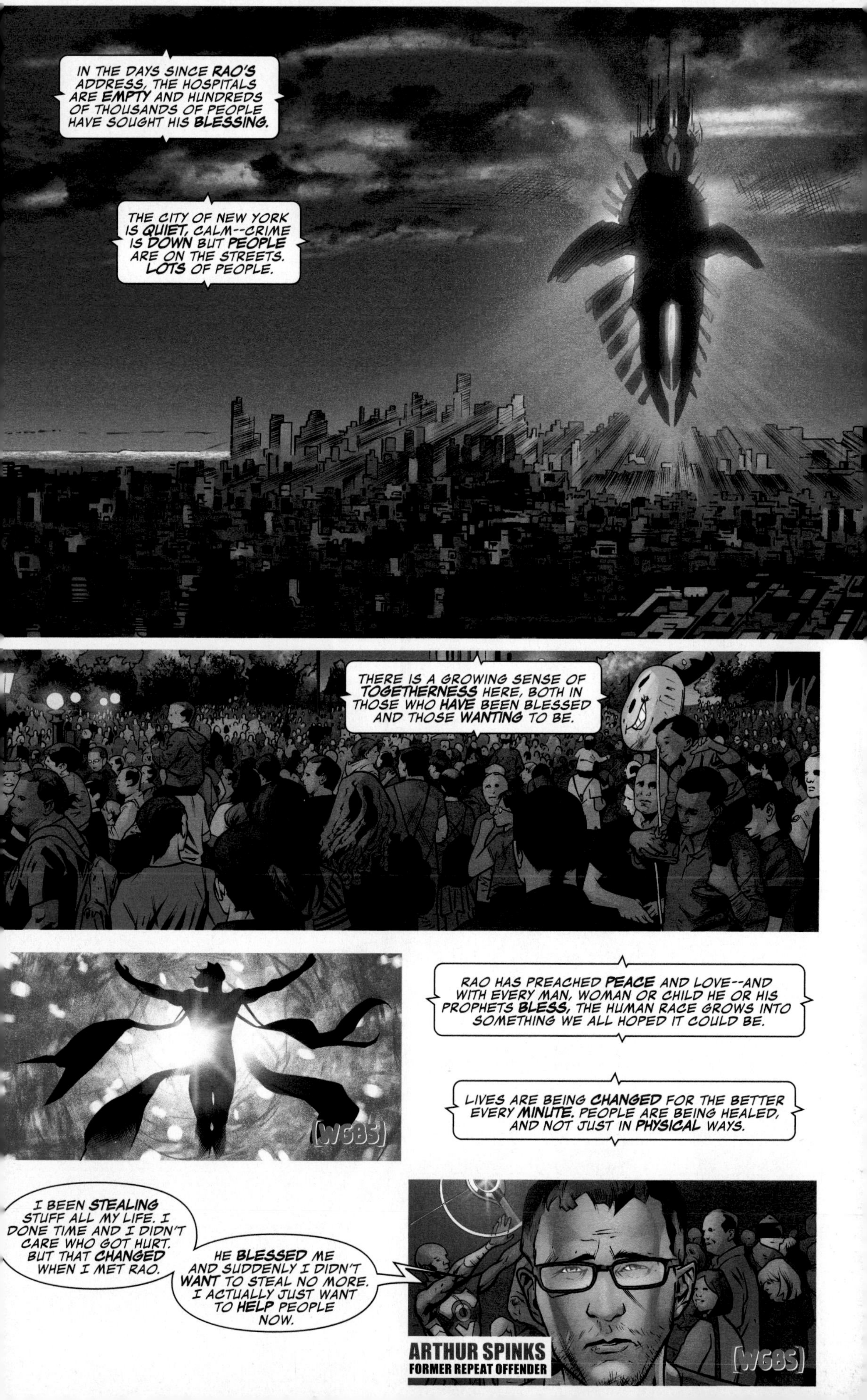
IN THE DAYS SINCE RAO'S ADDRESS, THE HOSPITALS ARE EMPTY AND HUNDREDS OF THOUSANDS OF PEOPLE HAVE SOUGHT HIS BLESSING.
THE CITY OF NEW YORK IS QUIET, CALM--CRIME IS DOWN BUT PEOPLE ARE ON THE STREETS. LOTS OF PEOPLE.
THERE IS A GROWING SENSE OF TOGETHERNESS HERE, BOTH IN THOSE WHO HAVE BEEN BLESSED AND THOSE WANTING TO BE.
[WGBS]
RAO HAS PREACHED PEACE AND LOVE--AND WITH EVERY MAN, WOMAN OR CHILD HE OR HIS PROPHETS BLESS, THE HUMAN RACE GROWS INTO SOMETHING WE ALL HOPED IT COULD BE.
LIVES ARE BEING CHANGED FOR THE BETTER EVERY MINUTE. PEOPLE ARE BEING HEALED, AND NOT JUST IN PHYSICAL WAYS.
I BEEN STEALING STUFF ALL MY LIFE. I DONE TIME AND I DIDN'T CARE WHO GOT HURT. BUT THAT CHANGED WHEN I MET RAO.
HE BLESSED ME AND SUDDENLY I DIDN'T WANT TO STEAL NO MORE. I ACTUALLY JUST WANT TO HELP PEOPLE NOW.
ARTHUR SPINKS
FORMER REPEAT OFFENDER
[WGBS]

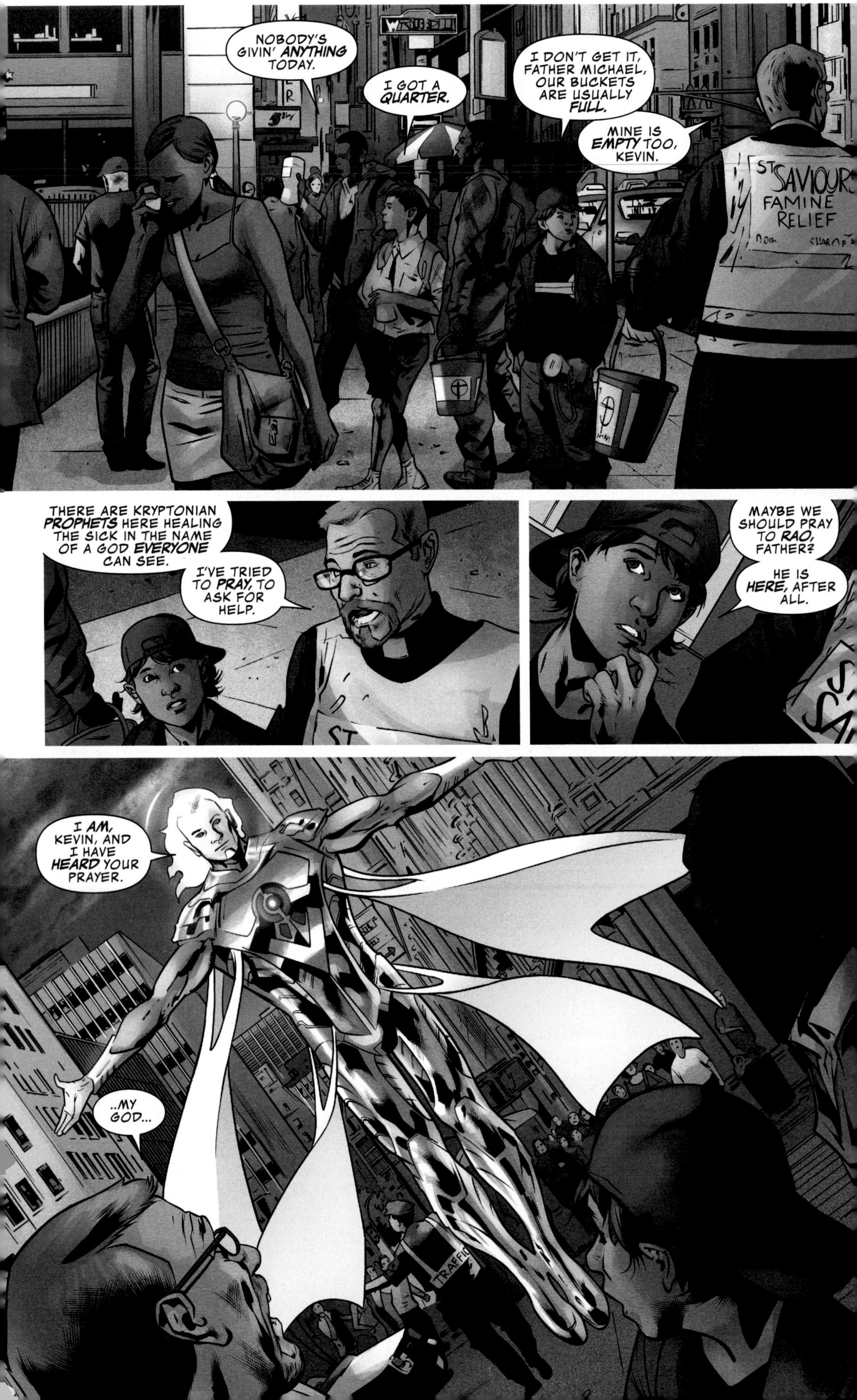
NOBODY'S GIVIN' ANYTHING TODAY.
I GOT A QUARTER.
I DON'T GET IT, FATHER MICHAEL, OUR BUCKETS ARE USUALLY FULL.
MINE IS EMPTY TOO, KEVIN.
ST SAVIOURS FAMINE RELIEF
THERE ARE KRYPTONIAN PROPHETS HERE HEALING THE SICK IN THE NAME OF A GOD EVERYONE CAN SEE.
I'VE TRIED TO PRAY, TO ASK FOR HELP.
MAYBE WE SHOULD PRAY TO RAO, FATHER?
HE IS HERE, AFTER ALL.
I AM, KEVIN, AND I HAVE HEARD YOUR PRAYER.
..MY GOD...
TRAFFIC

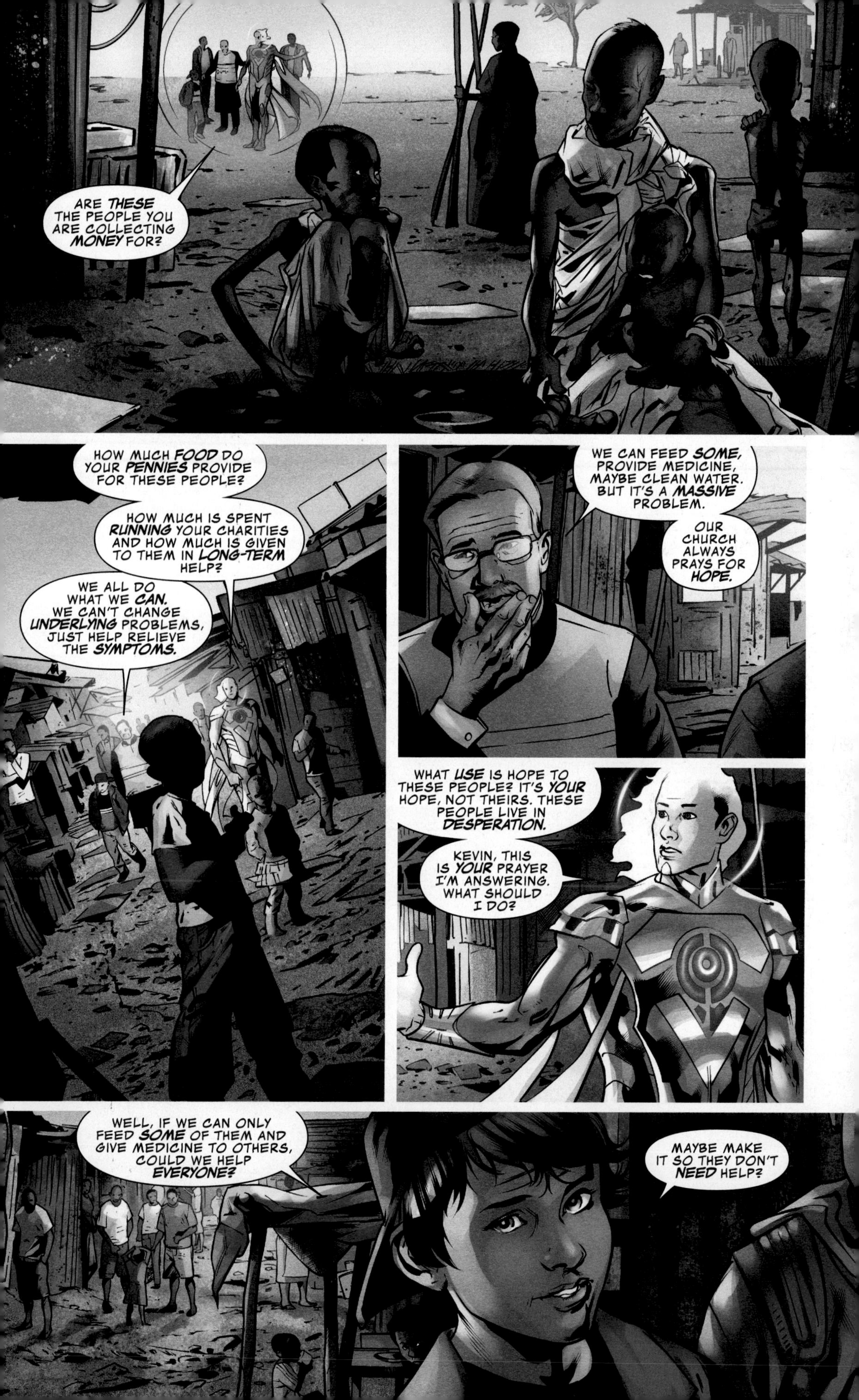
ARE THESE THE PEOPLE YOU ARE COLLECTING MONEY FOR?
HOW MUCH FOOD DO YOUR PENNIES PROVIDE FOR THESE PEOPLE?
HOW MUCH IS SPENT RUNNING YOUR CHARITIES AND HOW MUCH IS GIVEN TO THEM IN LONG-TERM HELP?
WE ALL DO WHAT WE CAN. WE CAN'T CHANGE UNDERLYING PROBLEMS, JUST HELP RELIEVE THE SYMPTOMS.
WE CAN FEED SOME, PROVIDE MEDICINE, MAYBE CLEAN WATER. BUT IT'S A MASSIVE PROBLEM.
OUR CHURCH ALWAYS PRAYS FOR HOPE.
WHAT USE IS HOPE TO THESE PEOPLE? IT'S YOUR HOPE, NOT THEIRS. THESE PEOPLE LIVE IN DESPERATION.
KEVIN, THIS IS YOUR PRAYER I'M ANSWERING. WHAT SHOULD I DO?
WELL, IF WE CAN ONLY FEED SOME OF THEM AND GIVE MEDICINE TO OTHERS, COULD WE HELP EVERYONE?
MAYBE MAKE IT SO THEY DON'T NEED HELP?

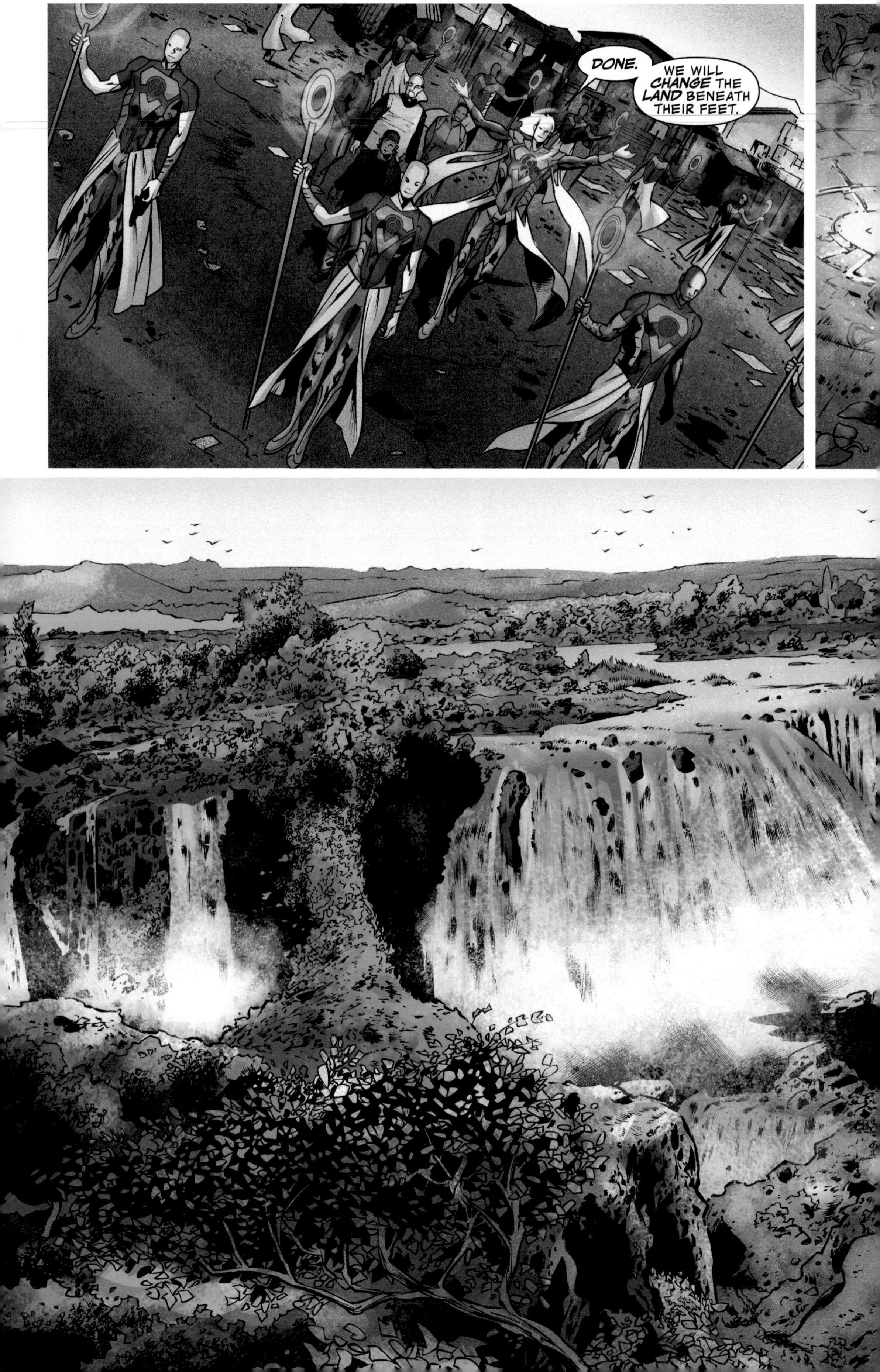
DONE.
WE WILL CHANGE THE LAND BENEATH THEIR FEET.

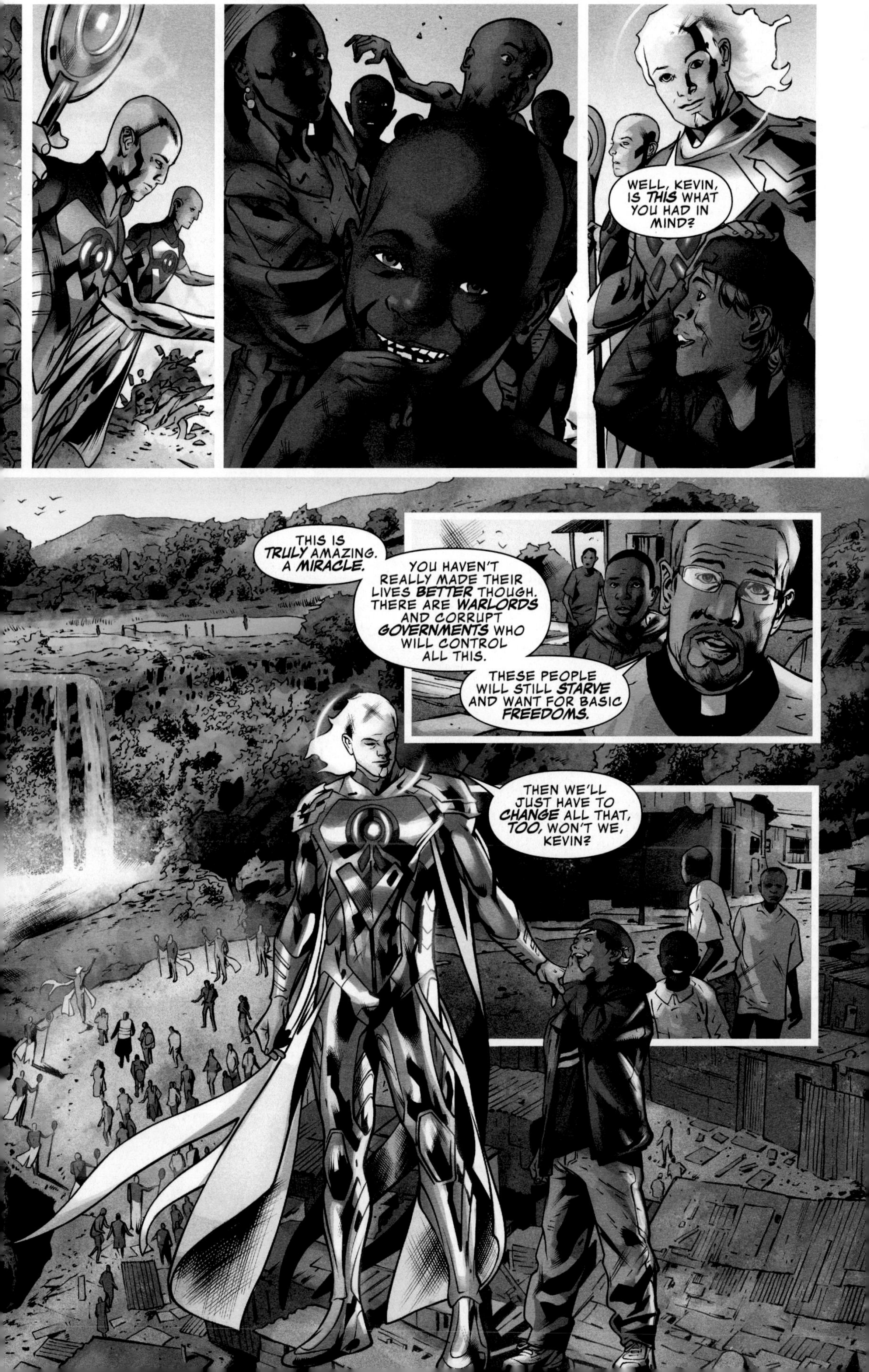
WELL, KEVIN, IS THIS WHAT YOU HAD IN MIND?
THIS IS TRULY AMAZING. A MIRACLE.
YOU HAVEN'T REALLY MADE THEIR LIVES BETTER THOUGH. THERE ARE WARLORDS AND CORRUPT GOVERNMENTS WHO WILL CONTROL ALL THIS.
THESE PEOPLE WILL STILL STARVE AND WANT FOR BASIC FREEDOMS.
THEN WE'LL JUST HAVE TO CHANGE ALL THAT, TOO, WON'T WE, KEVIN?

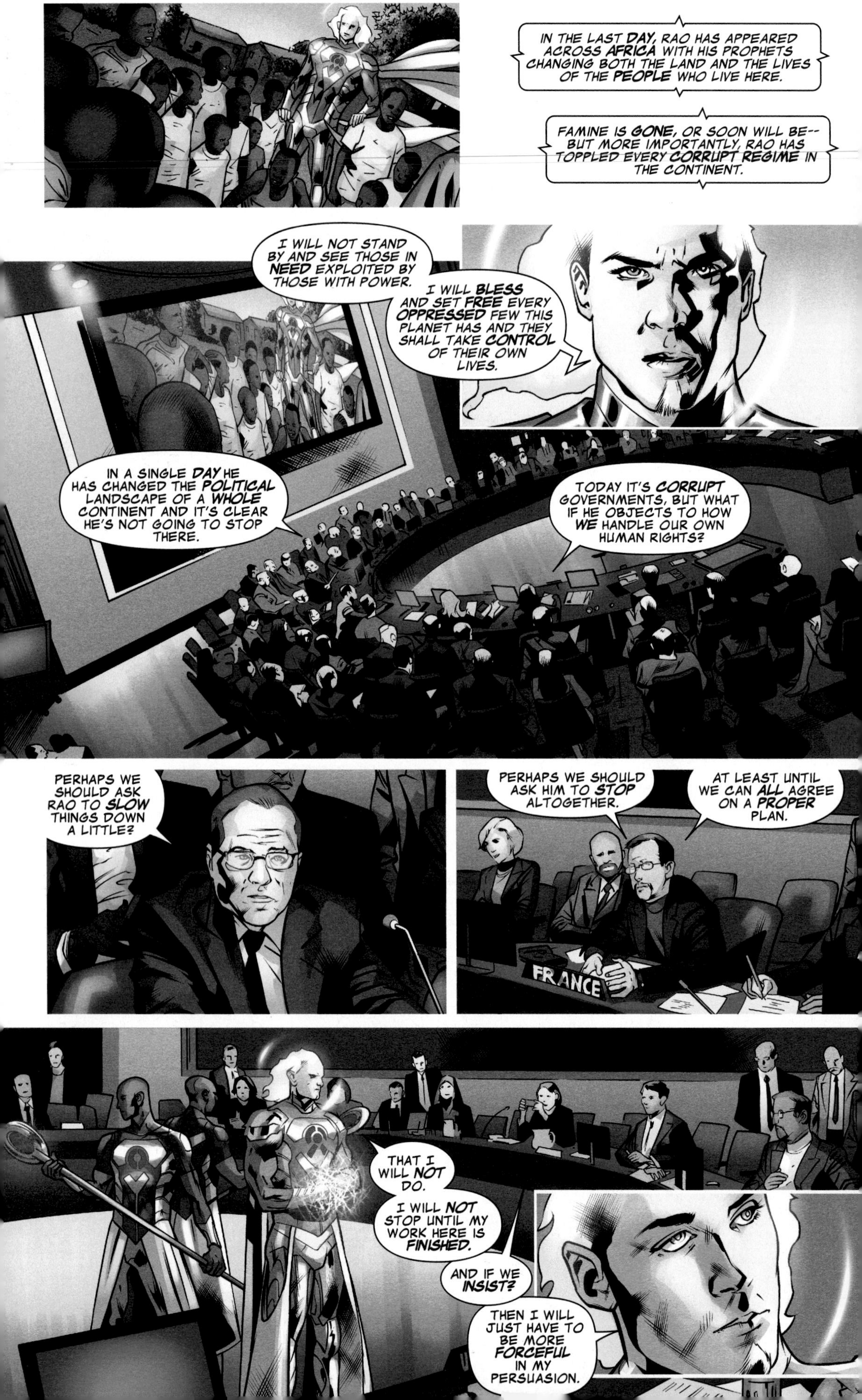
IN THE LAST DAY, RAO HAS APPEARED ACROSS AFRICA WITH HIS PROPHETS CHANGING BOTH THE LAND AND THE LIVES OF THE PEOPLE WHO LIVE HERE.
FAMINE IS GONE, OR SOON WILL BE-- BUT MORE IMPORTANTLY, RAO HAS TOPPLED EVERY CORRUPT REGIME IN THE CONTINENT.
I WILL NOT STAND BY AND SEE THOSE IN NEED EXPLOITED BY THOSE WITH POWER.
I WILL BLESS AND SET FREE EVERY OPPRESSED FEW THIS PLANET HAS AND THEY SHALL TAKE CONTROL OF THEIR OWN LIVES.
IN A SINGLE DAY HE HAS CHANGED THE POLITICAL LANDSCAPE OF A WHOLE CONTINENT AND IT'S CLEAR HE'S NOT GOING TO STOP THERE.
TODAY IT'S CORRUPT GOVERNMENTS, BUT WHAT IF HE OBJECTS TO HOW WE HANDLE OUR OWN HUMAN RIGHTS?
PERHAPS WE SHOULD ASK RAO TO SLOW THINGS DOWN A LITTLE?
PERHAPS WE SHOULD ASK HIM TO STOP ALTOGETHER.
AT LEAST UNTIL WE CAN ALL AGREE ON A PROPER PLAN.
FRANCE
THAT I WILL NOT DO.
I WILL NOT STOP UNTIL MY WORK HERE IS FINISHED.
AND IF WE INSIST?
THEN I WILL JUST HAVE TO BE MORE FORCEFUL IN MY PERSUASION.

YOU WANTED TO *SEE* ME?

I SUPPOSE I WANTED TO *ASK* YOU IF YOU WERE *SURE* ABOUT RAO BEFORE I TOOK MATTERS INTO MY *OWN* HANDS.

WHAT DOES *THAT* MEAN?

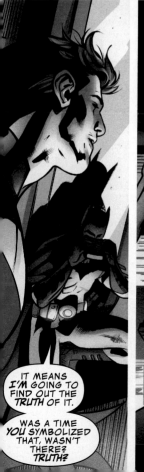

IT MEANS I'M GOING TO FIND OUT THE *TRUTH* OF IT.

WAS A TIME *YOU* SYMBOLIZED THAT, WASN'T THERE? *TRUTH*?

I STILL DO. *NOTHING* ABOUT RAO BEING HERE CHANGES THAT.

DOESN'T IT? YOU *GIFTED* HIM THE *WORLD* AS SOON AS HE APPEARED.

I DIDN'T *GIVE* HIM ANYTHING. THE WORLD *ACCEPTED* HIM.

BECAUSE YOU TOLD THEM TO.

YOU MADE YOUR SPEECHES, YOUR GRAND GESTURES. THE WORLD TRUSTED YOU AND YOU TURNED IT OVER TO RAO.

THE WORLD IS *BETTER* FOR RAO BEING HERE.

YES, *HEAL* THE SICK, *FEED* THE HUNGRY.

WHAT'S THE *COST*?

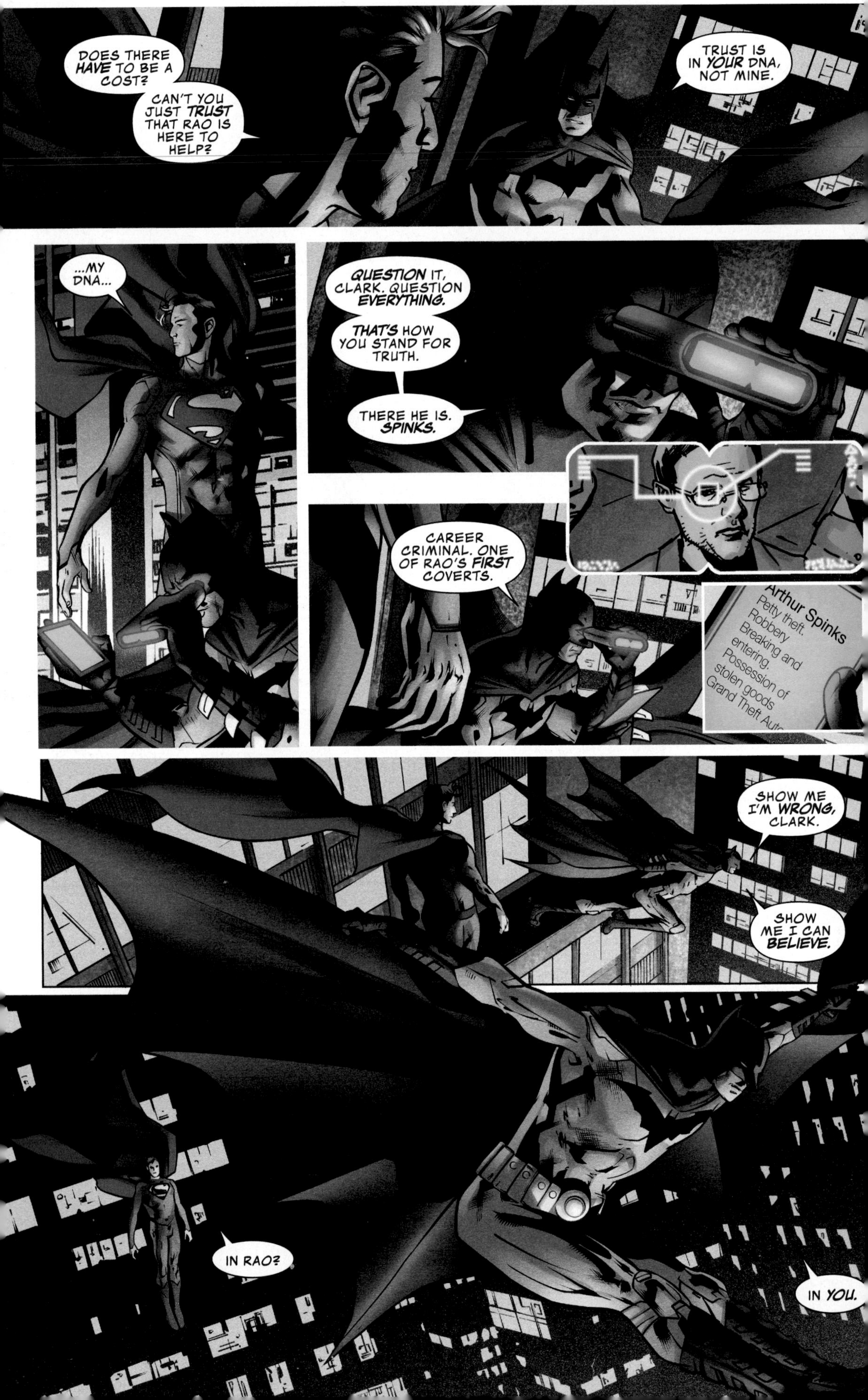
DOES THERE HAVE TO BE A COST?
CAN'T YOU JUST TRUST THAT RAO IS HERE TO HELP?
TRUST IS IN YOUR DNA, NOT MINE.
...MY DNA...
QUESTION IT, CLARK. QUESTION EVERYTHING.
THAT'S HOW YOU STAND FOR TRUTH.
THERE HE IS. SPINKS.
CAREER CRIMINAL. ONE OF RAO'S FIRST COVERTS.
Arthur Spinks
Petty theft.
Robbery
Breaking and entering.
Possession of stolen goods
SHOW ME I'M WRONG, CLARK.
SHOW ME I CAN BELIEVE.
IN RAO?
IN YOU.

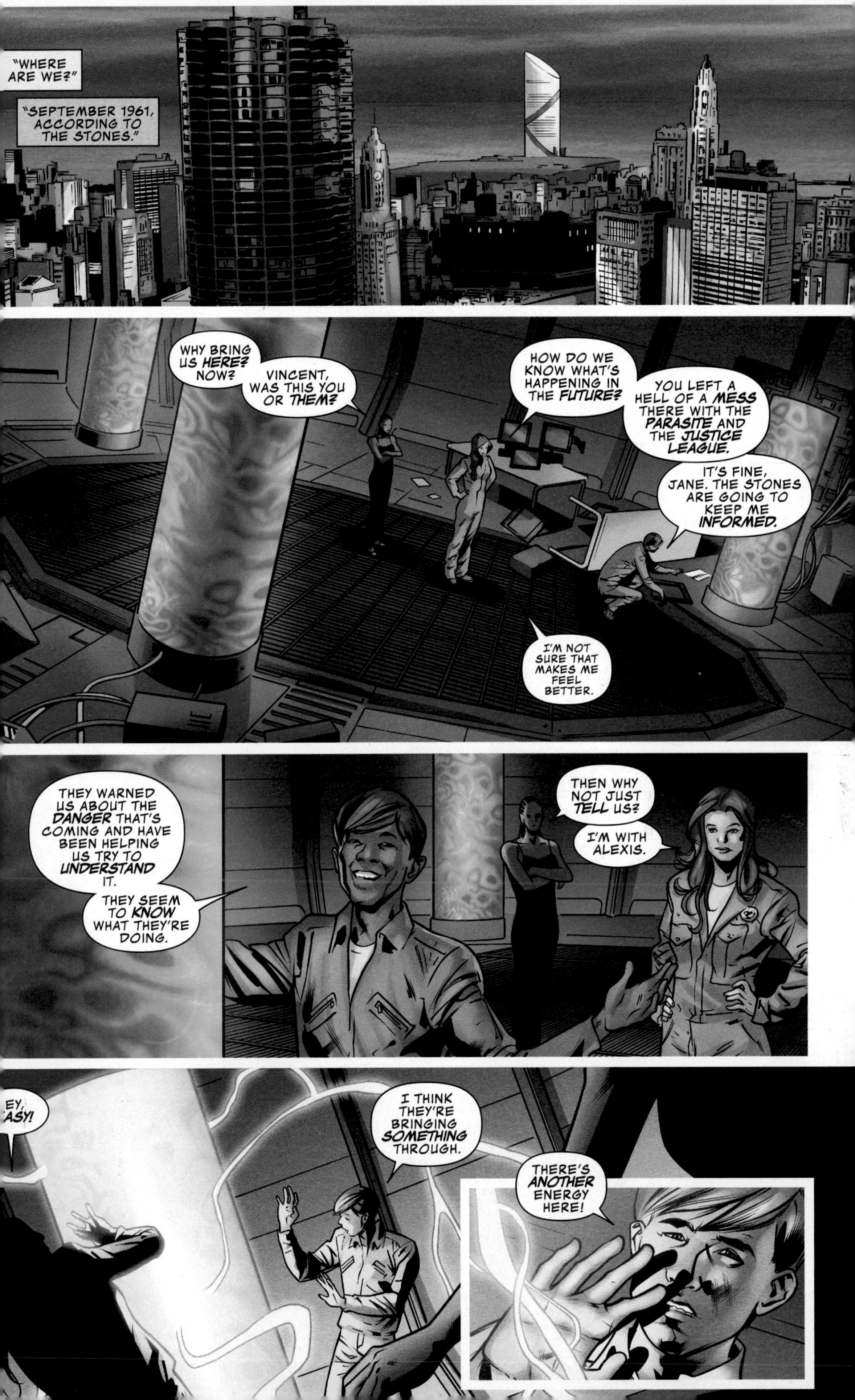
"WHERE ARE WE?"
"SEPTEMBER 1961, ACCORDING TO THE STONES."
WHY BRING US HERE? NOW?
VINCENT, WAS THIS YOU OR THEM?
HOW DO WE KNOW WHAT'S HAPPENING IN THE FUTURE?
YOU LEFT A HELL OF A MESS THERE WITH THE PARASITE AND THE JUSTICE LEAGUE.
IT'S FINE, JANE. THE STONES ARE GOING TO KEEP ME INFORMED.
I'M NOT SURE THAT MAKES ME FEEL BETTER.
THEY WARNED US ABOUT THE DANGER THAT'S COMING AND HAVE BEEN HELPING US TRY TO UNDERSTAND IT.
THEY SEEM TO KNOW WHAT THEY'RE DOING.
THEN WHY NOT JUST TELL US?
I'M WITH ALEXIS.
I THINK THEY'RE BRINGING SOMETHING THROUGH.
THERE'S ANOTHER ENERGY HERE!

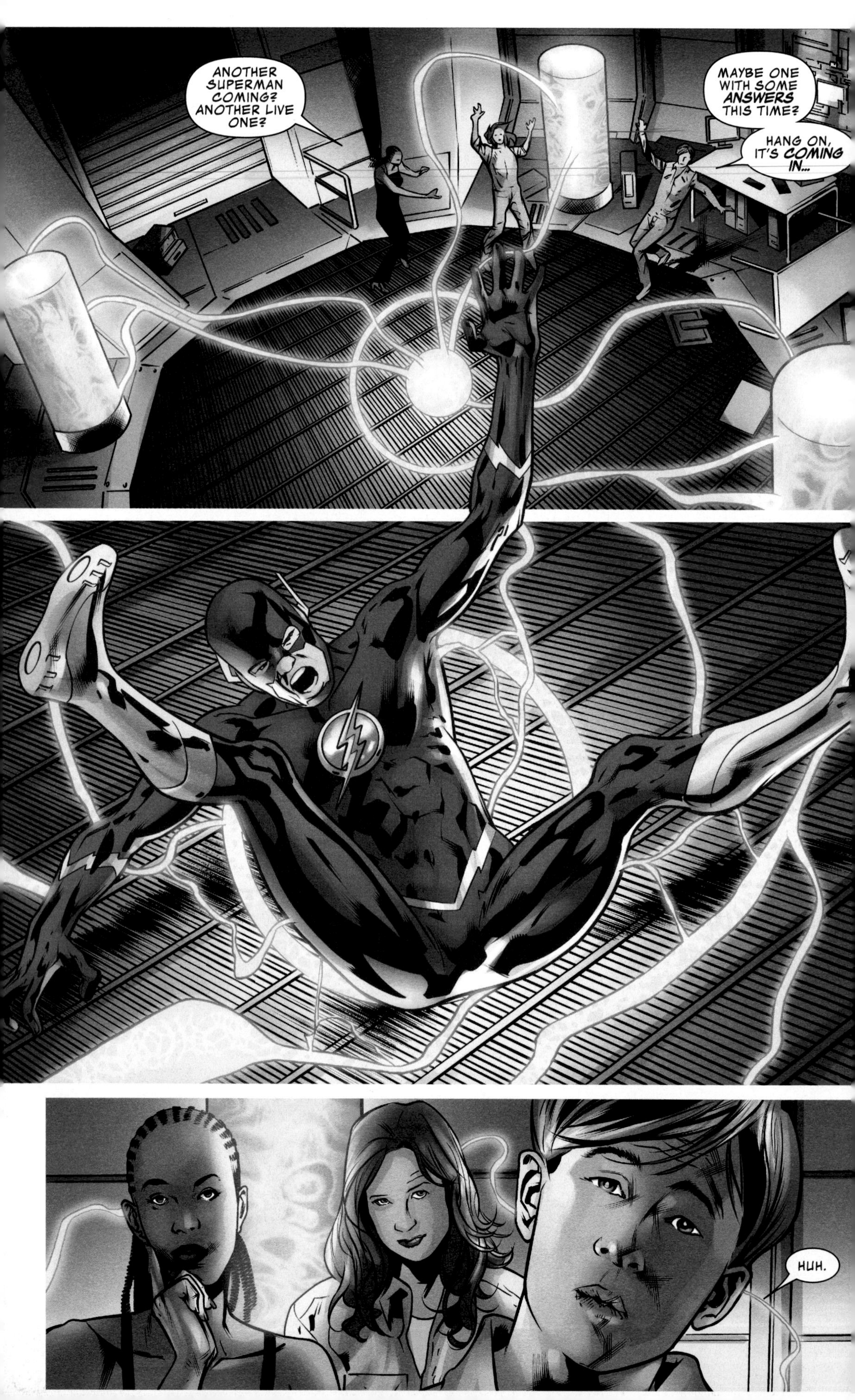
ANOTHER SUPERMAN COMING? ANOTHER LIVE ONE?
MAYBE ONE WITH SOME ANSWERS THIS TIME?
HANG ON, IT'S COMING IN...
HUH.

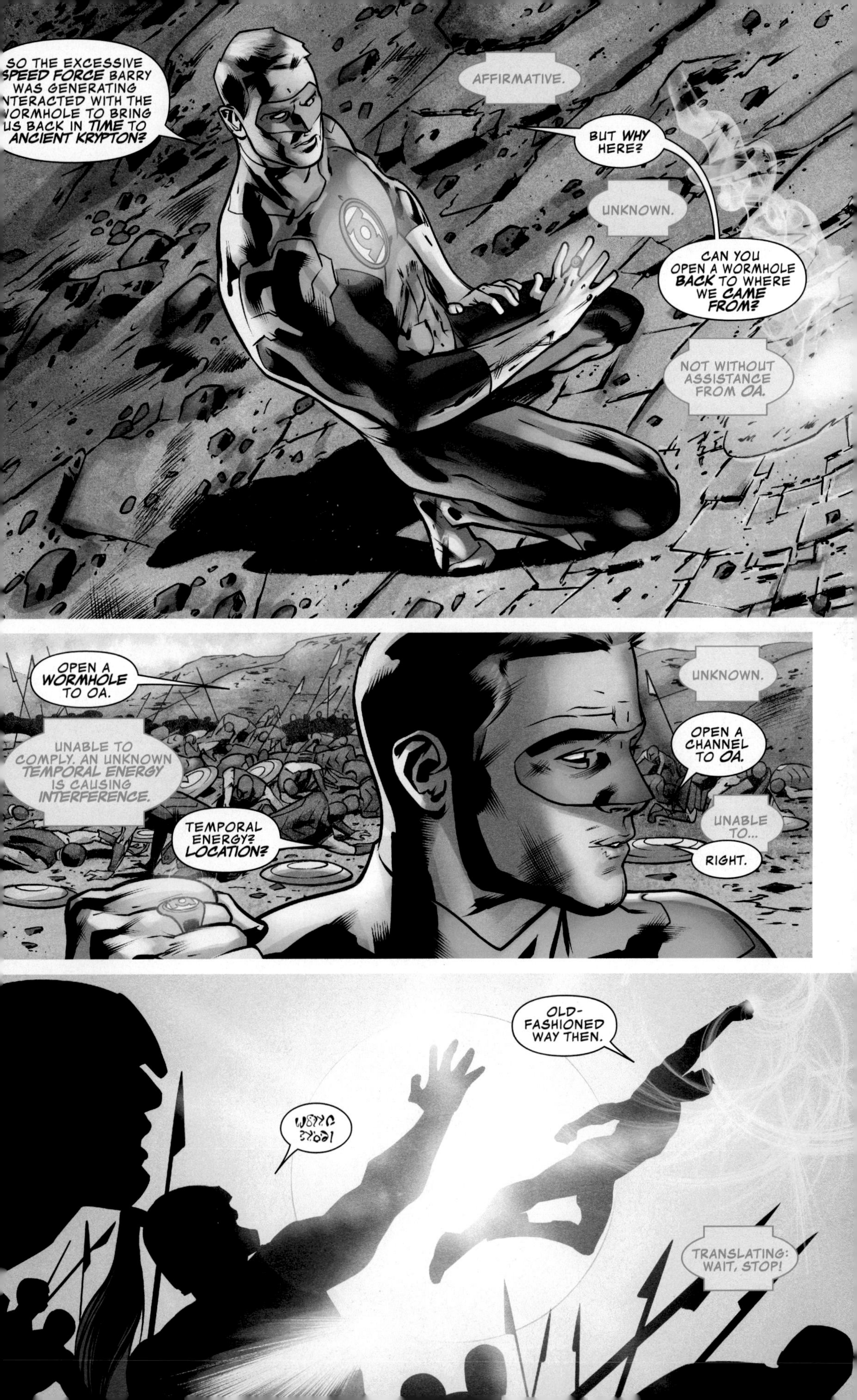
SO THE EXCESSIVE SPEED FORCE BARRY WAS GENERATING INTERACTED WITH THE WORMHOLE TO BRING US BACK IN TIME TO ANCIENT KRYPTON?
AFFIRMATIVE.
BUT WHY HERE?
UNKNOWN.
CAN YOU OPEN A WORMHOLE BACK TO WHERE WE CAME FROM?
NOT WITHOUT ASSISTANCE FROM OA.
OPEN A WORMHOLE TO OA.
UNABLE TO COMPLY. AN UNKNOWN TEMPORAL ENERGY IS CAUSING INTERFERENCE.
TEMPORAL ENERGY? LOCATION?
UNKNOWN.
OPEN A CHANNEL TO OA.
UNABLE TO...
RIGHT.
OLD-FASHIONED WAY THEN.
TRANSLATING: WAIT, STOP!

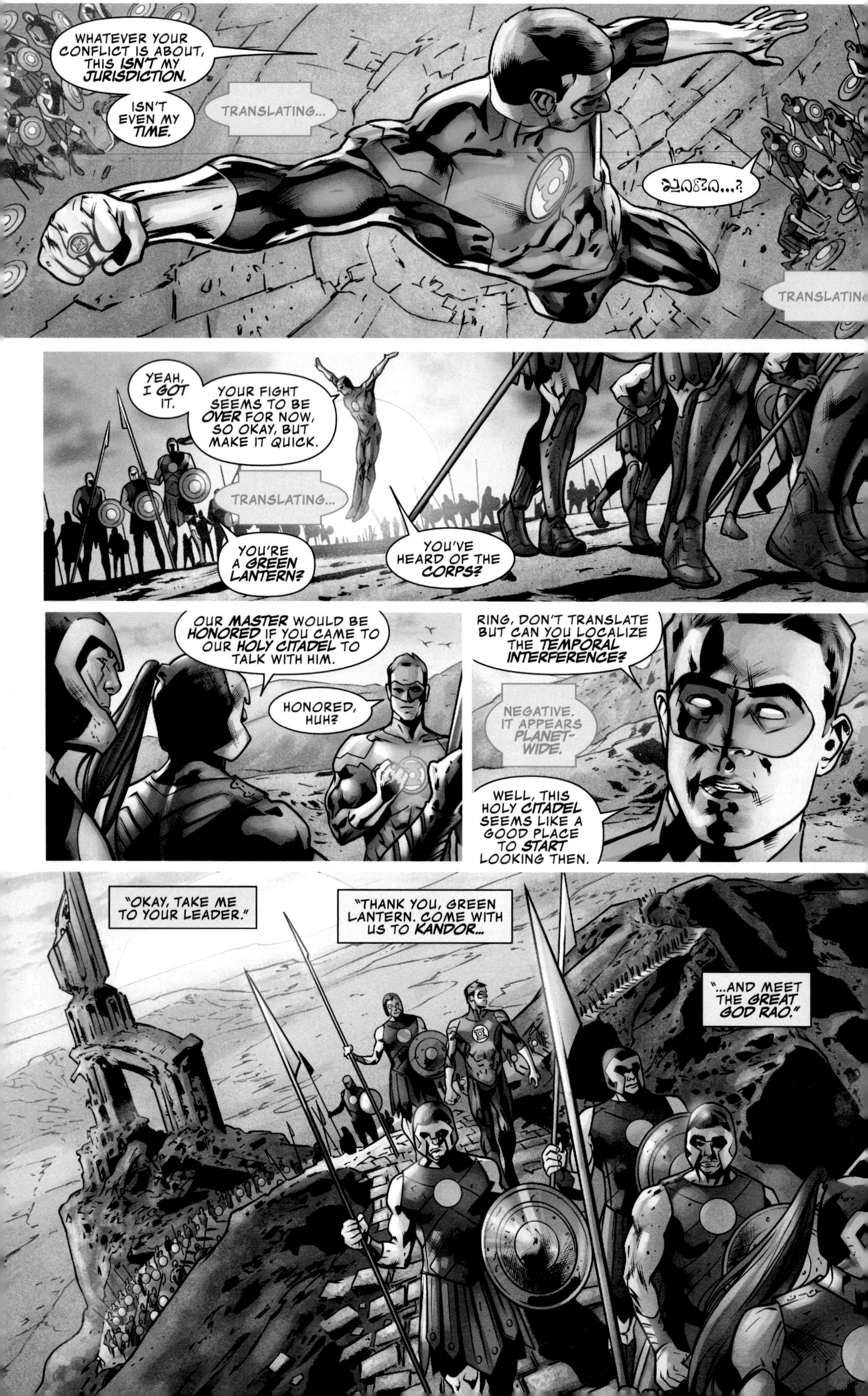
WHATEVER YOUR CONFLICT IS ABOUT, THIS ISN'T MY JURISDICTION.
ISN'T EVEN MY TIME.
TRANSLATING...
TRANSLATING
YEAH, I GOT IT.
YOUR FIGHT SEEMS TO BE OVER FOR NOW, SO OKAY, BUT MAKE IT QUICK.
TRANSLATING...
YOU'RE A GREEN LANTERN?
YOU'VE HEARD OF THE CORPS?
OUR MASTER WOULD BE HONORED IF YOU CAME TO OUR HOLY CITADEL TO TALK WITH HIM.
HONORED, HUH?
RING, DON'T TRANSLATE BUT CAN YOU LOCALIZE THE TEMPORAL INTERFERENCE?
NEGATIVE. IT APPEARS PLANET-WIDE.
WELL, THIS HOLY CITADEL SEEMS LIKE A GOOD PLACE TO START LOOKING THEN.
"OKAY, TAKE ME TO YOUR LEADER."
"THANK YOU, GREEN LANTERN. COME WITH US TO KANDOR...
"...AND MEET THE GREAT GOD RAO."

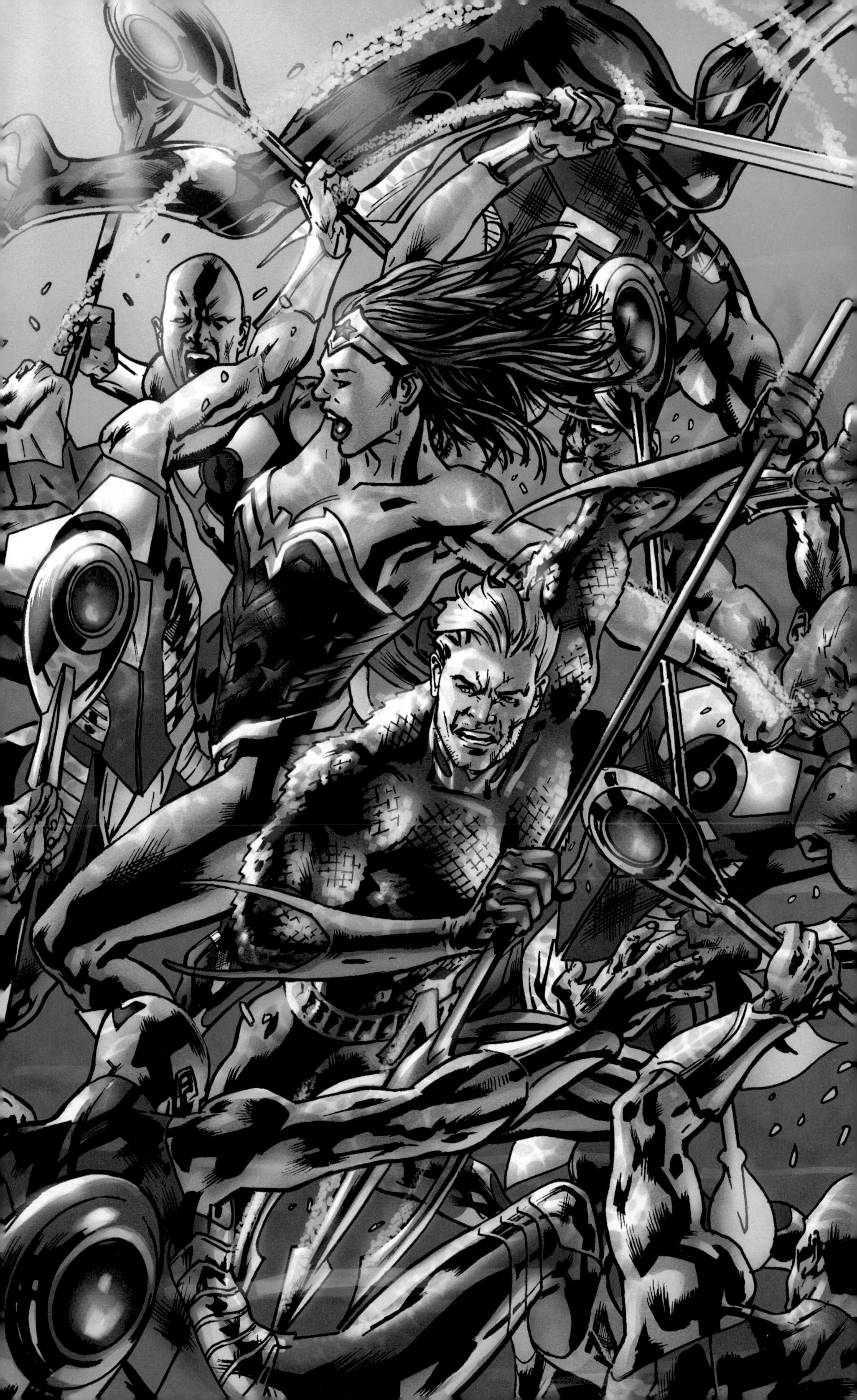

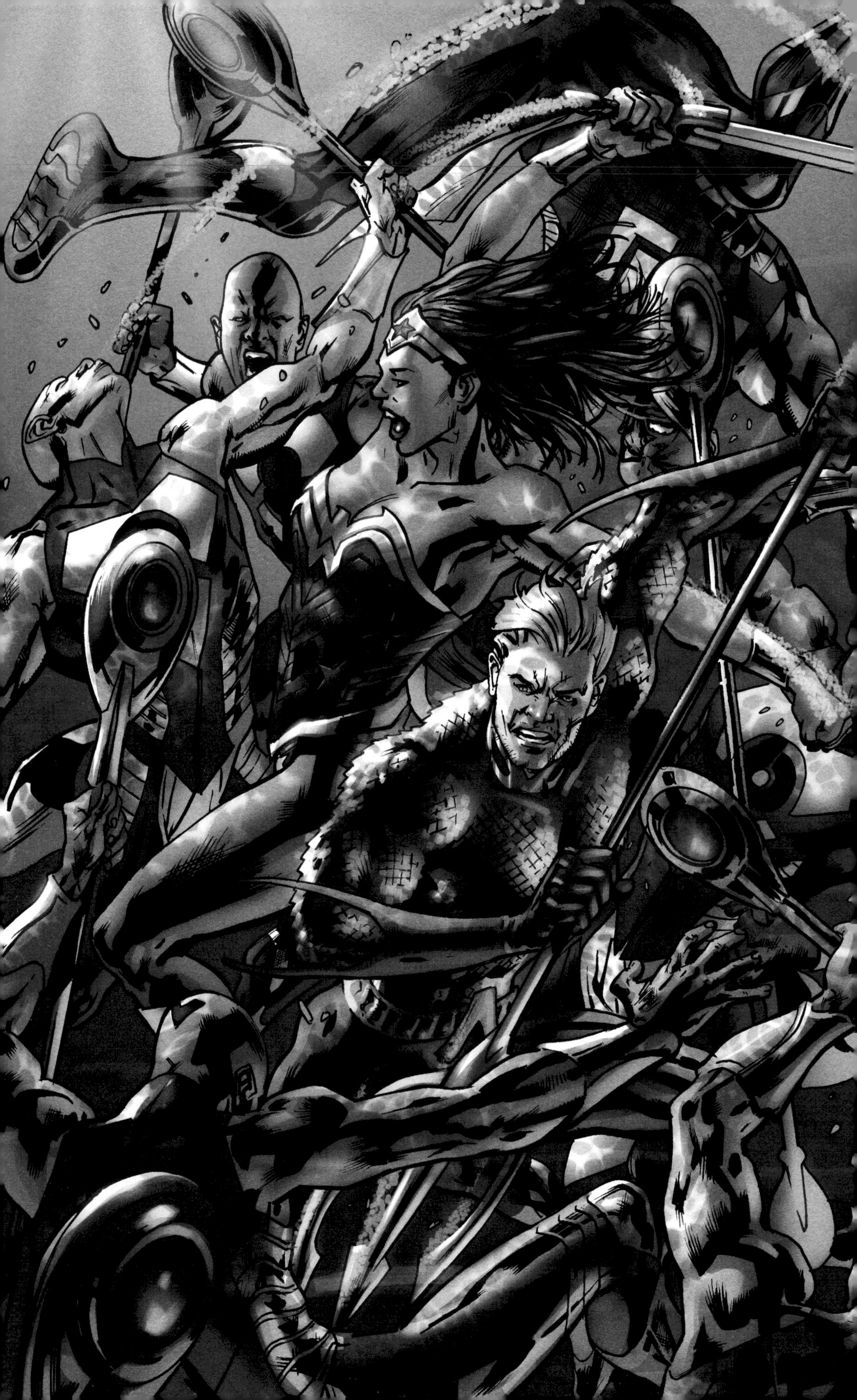

DC COMICS PRESENTS
THE JUSTICE LEAGUE OF AMERICA
POWER AND GLORY
PART FOUR
BY BRYAN HITCH

VICTOR, THIS IS *MY* BLOOD.

MY DNA.

INKS BY DANIEL HENRIQUES
COLORS BY ALEX SINCLAIR
LETTERS BY CHRIS ELIOPOULOS
ASSISTS BY AMEDEO TURTURRO
EDITS BY BRIAN CUNNINGHAM
COVER BY BRYAN HITCH AND ALEX SINCLAIR

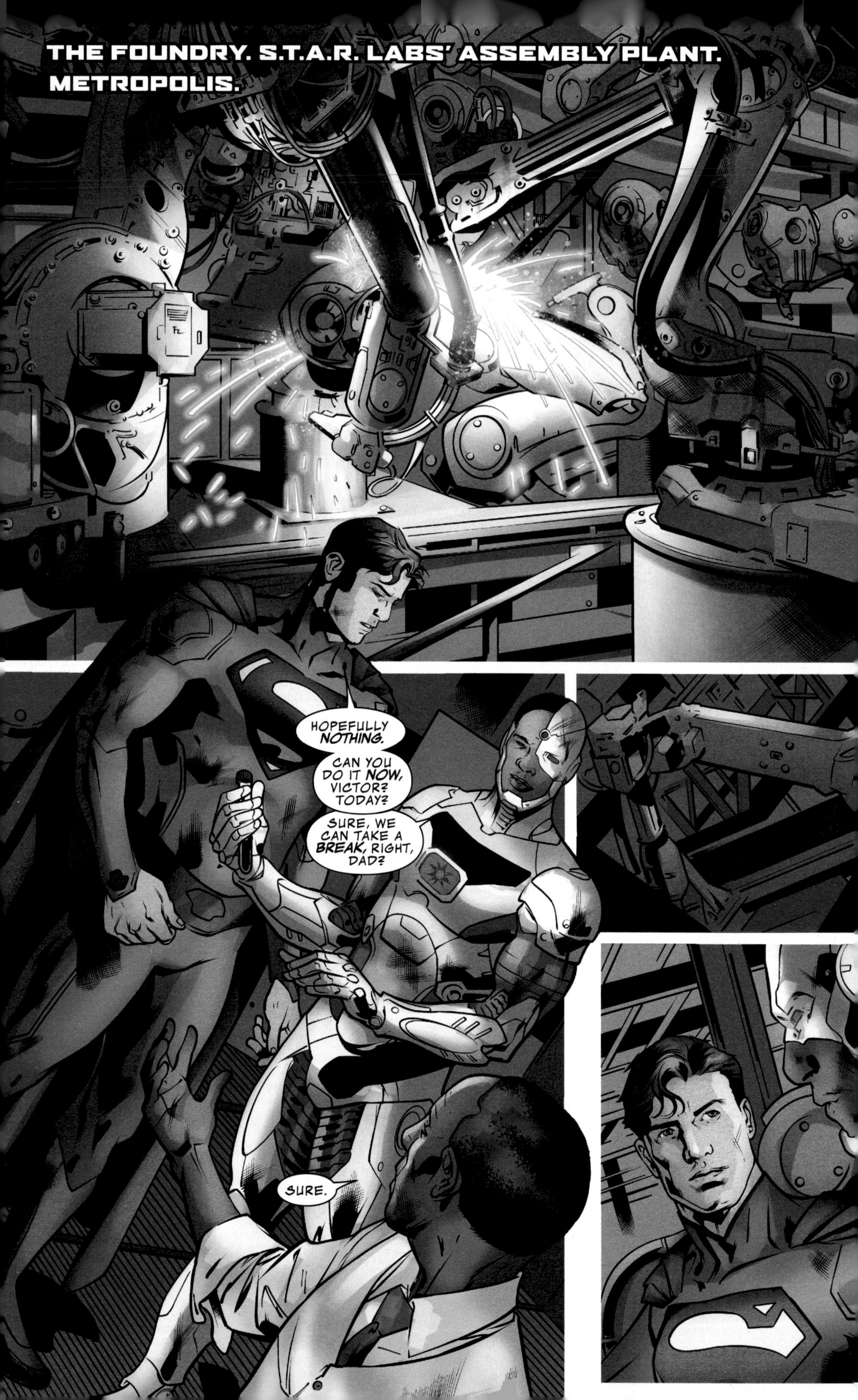
THE FOUNDRY. S.T.A.R. LABS' ASSEMBLY PLANT. METROPOLIS.
HOPEFULLY NOTHING.
CAN YOU DO IT NOW, VICTOR? TODAY?
SURE, WE CAN TAKE A BREAK, RIGHT, DAD?
SURE.

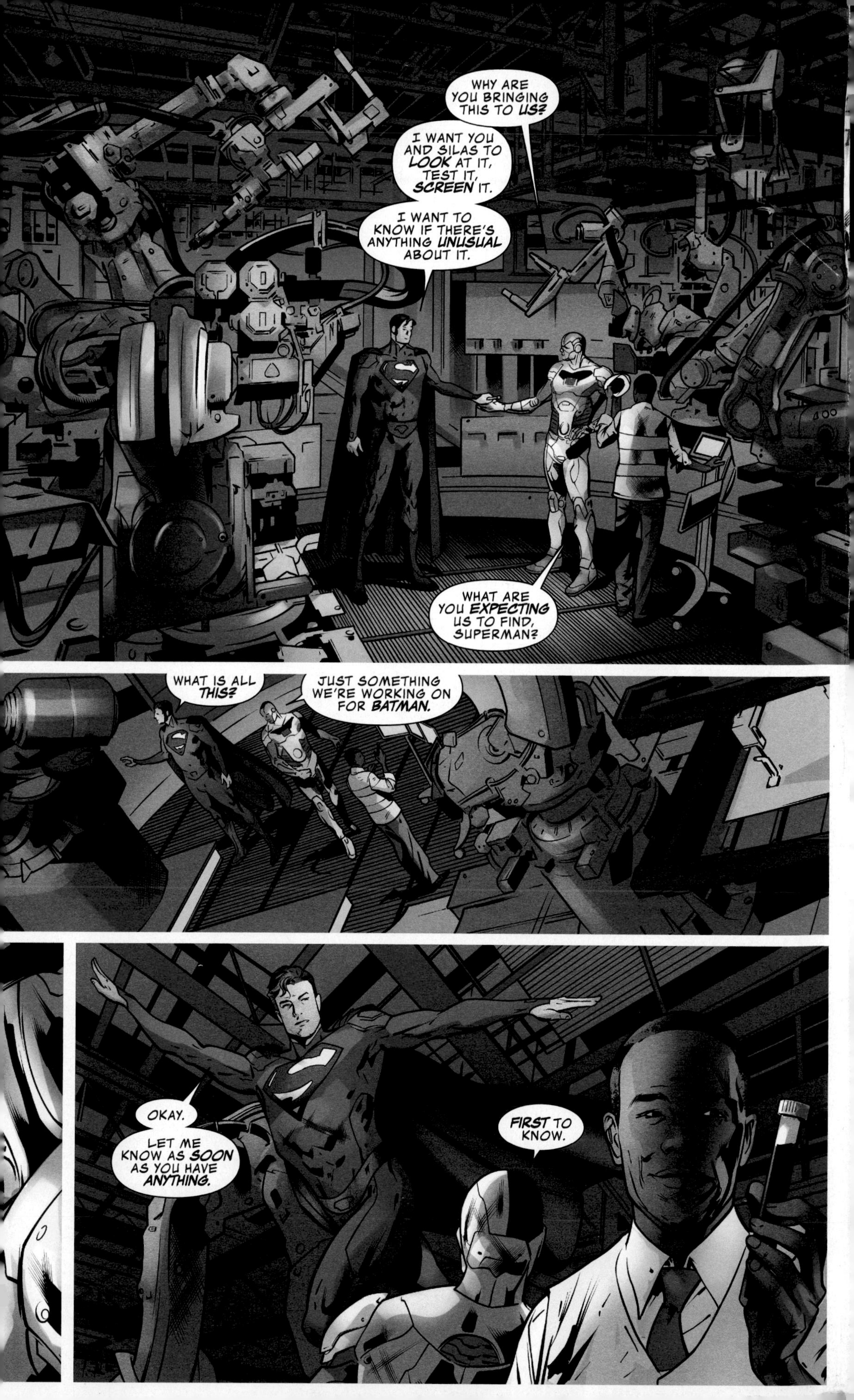
WHY ARE YOU BRINGING THIS TO US?
I WANT YOU AND SILAS TO LOOK AT IT, TEST IT, SCREEN IT.
I WANT TO KNOW IF THERE'S ANYTHING UNUSUAL ABOUT IT.
WHAT ARE YOU EXPECTING US TO FIND, SUPERMAN?
WHAT IS ALL THIS?
JUST SOMETHING WE'RE WORKING ON FOR BATMAN.
OKAY.
LET ME KNOW AS SOON AS YOU HAVE ANYTHING.
FIRST TO KNOW.

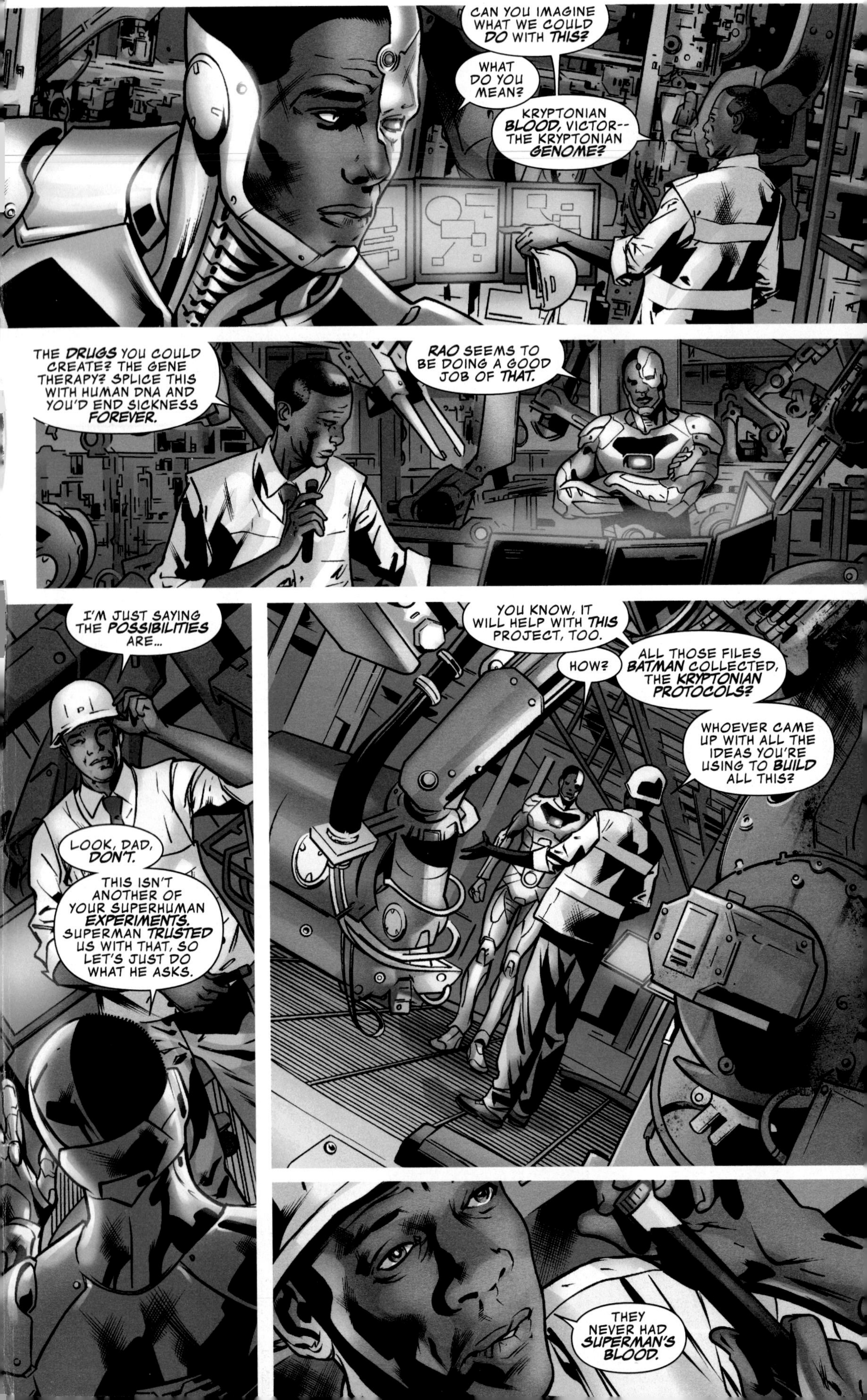
CAN YOU IMAGINE WHAT WE COULD DO WITH THIS?
WHAT DO YOU MEAN?
KRYPTONIAN BLOOD, VICTOR-- THE KRYPTONIAN GENOME?
THE DRUGS YOU COULD CREATE? THE GENE THERAPY? SPLICE THIS WITH HUMAN DNA AND YOU'D END SICKNESS FOREVER.
RAO SEEMS TO BE DOING A GOOD JOB OF THAT.
I'M JUST SAYING THE POSSIBILITIES ARE...
LOOK, DAD, DON'T.
THIS ISN'T ANOTHER OF YOUR SUPERHUMAN EXPERIMENTS. SUPERMAN TRUSTED US WITH THAT, SO LET'S JUST DO WHAT HE ASKS.
YOU KNOW, IT WILL HELP WITH THIS PROJECT, TOO.
HOW?
ALL THOSE FILES BATMAN COLLECTED, THE KRYPTONIAN PROTOCOLS?
WHOEVER CAME UP WITH ALL THE IDEAS YOU'RE USING TO BUILD ALL THIS?
THEY NEVER HAD SUPERMAN'S BLOOD.

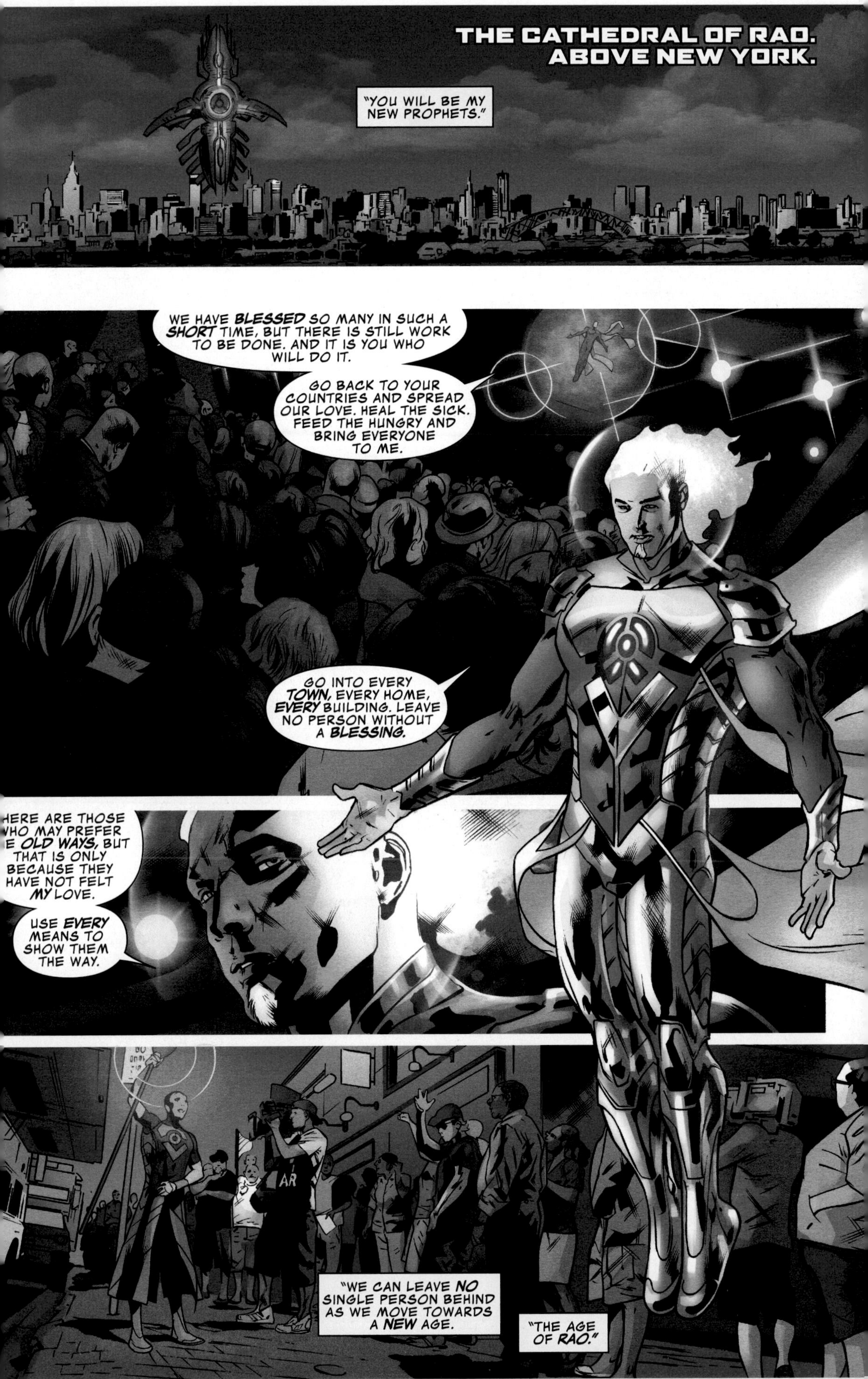
THE CATHEDRAL OF RAO. ABOVE NEW YORK.
"YOU WILL BE MY NEW PROPHETS."
WE HAVE BLESSED SO MANY IN SUCH A SHORT TIME, BUT THERE IS STILL WORK TO BE DONE. AND IT IS YOU WHO WILL DO IT.
GO BACK TO YOUR COUNTRIES AND SPREAD OUR LOVE. HEAL THE SICK. FEED THE HUNGRY AND BRING EVERYONE TO ME.
GO INTO EVERY TOWN, EVERY HOME, EVERY BUILDING. LEAVE NO PERSON WITHOUT A BLESSING.
HERE ARE THOSE WHO MAY PREFER E OLD WAYS, BUT THAT IS ONLY BECAUSE THEY HAVE NOT FELT MY LOVE.
USE EVERY MEANS TO SHOW THEM THE WAY.
"WE CAN LEAVE NO SINGLE PERSON BEHIND AS WE MOVE TOWARDS A NEW AGE.
"THE AGE OF RAO."

U.N. SECURITY COUNCIL.

THE UNITED NATIONS SECURITY COUNCIL TODAY INVITED ALL ITS MEMBER COUNTRIES TO OPEN THEIR BORDERS TO RAO AND HIS PROPHETS.

EVERY DAY *MILLIONS* OF PEOPLE ARE BEING BLESSED BY RAO.

ARE *YOU* AMONG THE BLESSED?

FEAR, HUNGER, POVERTY AND INEQUALITY SHOULD *NOT* BE AN INEVITABILITY.

IF WE ALL *EMBRACE* WHAT RAO HAS TO OFFER IT COULD BE THE *MOST ENLIGHTENED* TIME THE HUMAN RACE HAS EVER SEEN.

U.N. SECURITY COUNCIL.

GOTHAM GENERAL HOSPITAL.

...YES, SHOULD BE *DONE* IN ABOUT A HALF-HOUR. MEET YOU FOR DINNER?

YES, JUST GOT TO GET SOME RESULTS FROM THE *MRI.*

NO, VERY QUIET.

NOTHING HAPPENING HERE REALLY, JUST PAPERWORK.

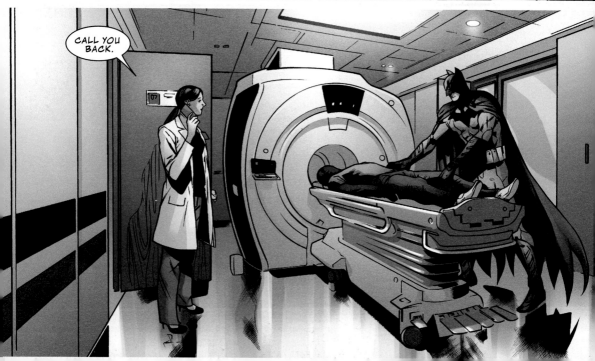

CALL YOU BACK.

WELL, OF COURSE THIS WEEK HAD TO GET STRANGER.

YOU TRYING TO MRI YOUR FRIEND TO SEE IF YOU HIT HIM TOO HARD?

TRYING TO FIND OUT WHAT SORT OF CRIME IS BEING COMMITTED.

AGAINST WHO?

THE WORLD.

YOU THINK YOU CAN FIND ALL THAT OUT WITH AN MRI SCAN ON THIS GUY? BEEN WATCHING TOO MUCH "HOUSE."

RAO. THE CONVERTED. I WANT TO KNOW WHAT HAPPENS WHEN HE BLESSES THEM.

THIS GUY SPINKS, LIFELONG PETTY CRIMINAL AND NOW CONVERT. I WANT TO SEE WHAT THEY DID TO HIM.

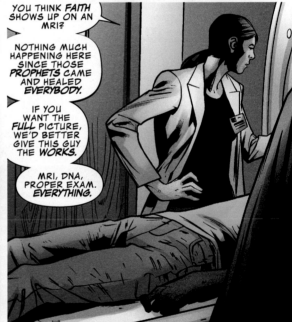

YOU THINK FAITH SHOWS UP ON AN MRI?

NOTHING MUCH HAPPENING HERE SINCE THOSE PROPHETS CAME AND HEALED EVERYBODY.

IF YOU WANT THE FULL PICTURE, WE'D BETTER GIVE THIS GUY THE WORKS.

MRI, DNA, PROPER EXAM. EVERYTHING.

MIGHT WANT TO STEP BACK. THIS MAGNET, METAL IN YOUR GEAR. COULD BE UNPLEASANT.

ALL YOURS.

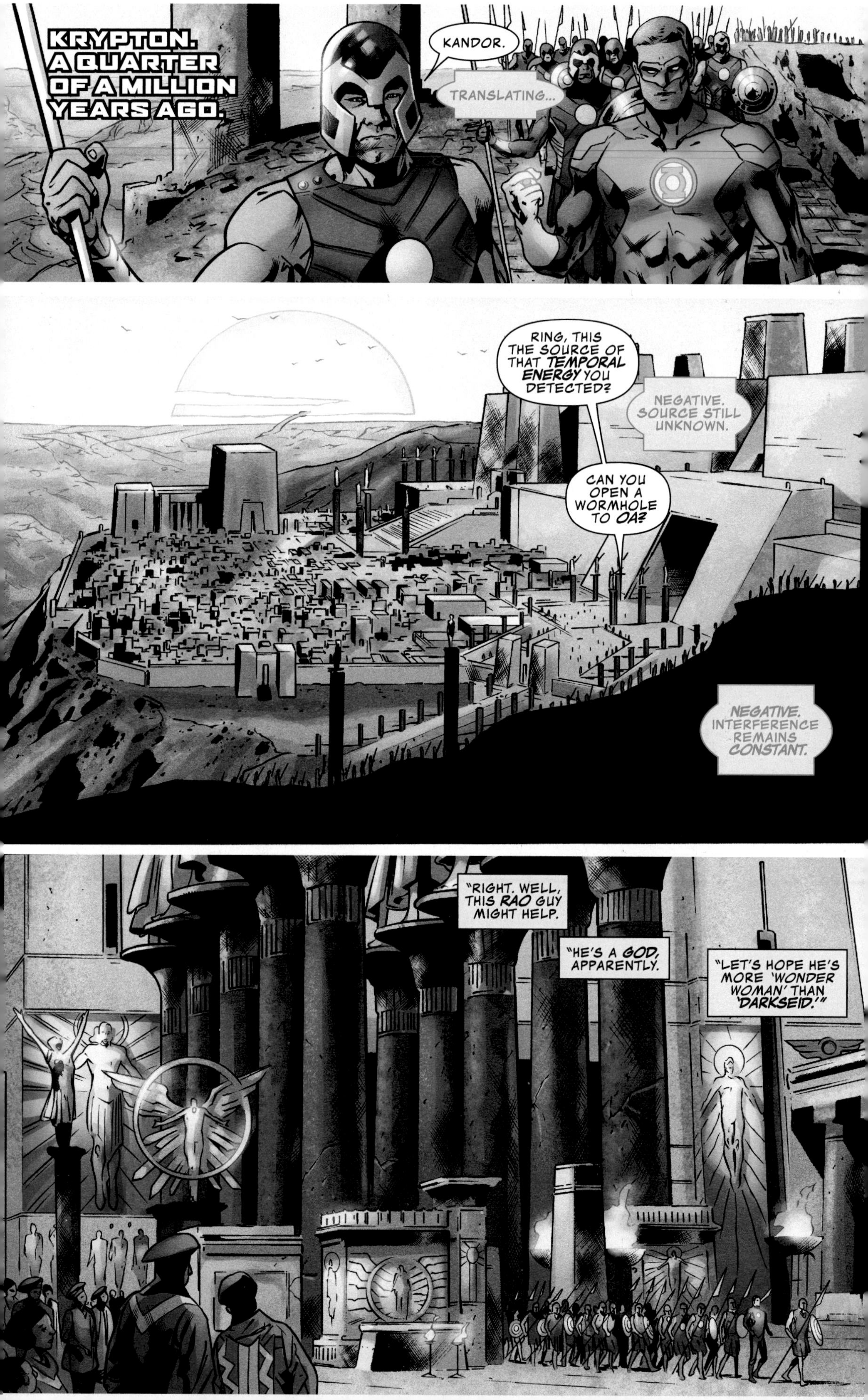
KRYPTON. A QUARTER OF A MILLION YEARS AGO.
KANDOR.
TRANSLATING...
RING, THIS THE SOURCE OF THAT TEMPORAL ENERGY YOU DETECTED?
NEGATIVE. SOURCE STILL UNKNOWN.
CAN YOU OPEN A WORMHOLE TO OA?
NEGATIVE. INTERFERENCE REMAINS CONSTANT.
"RIGHT. WELL, THIS RAO GUY MIGHT HELP.
"HE'S A GOD, APPARENTLY.
"LET'S HOPE HE'S MORE 'WONDER WOMAN' THAN 'DARKSEID.'"

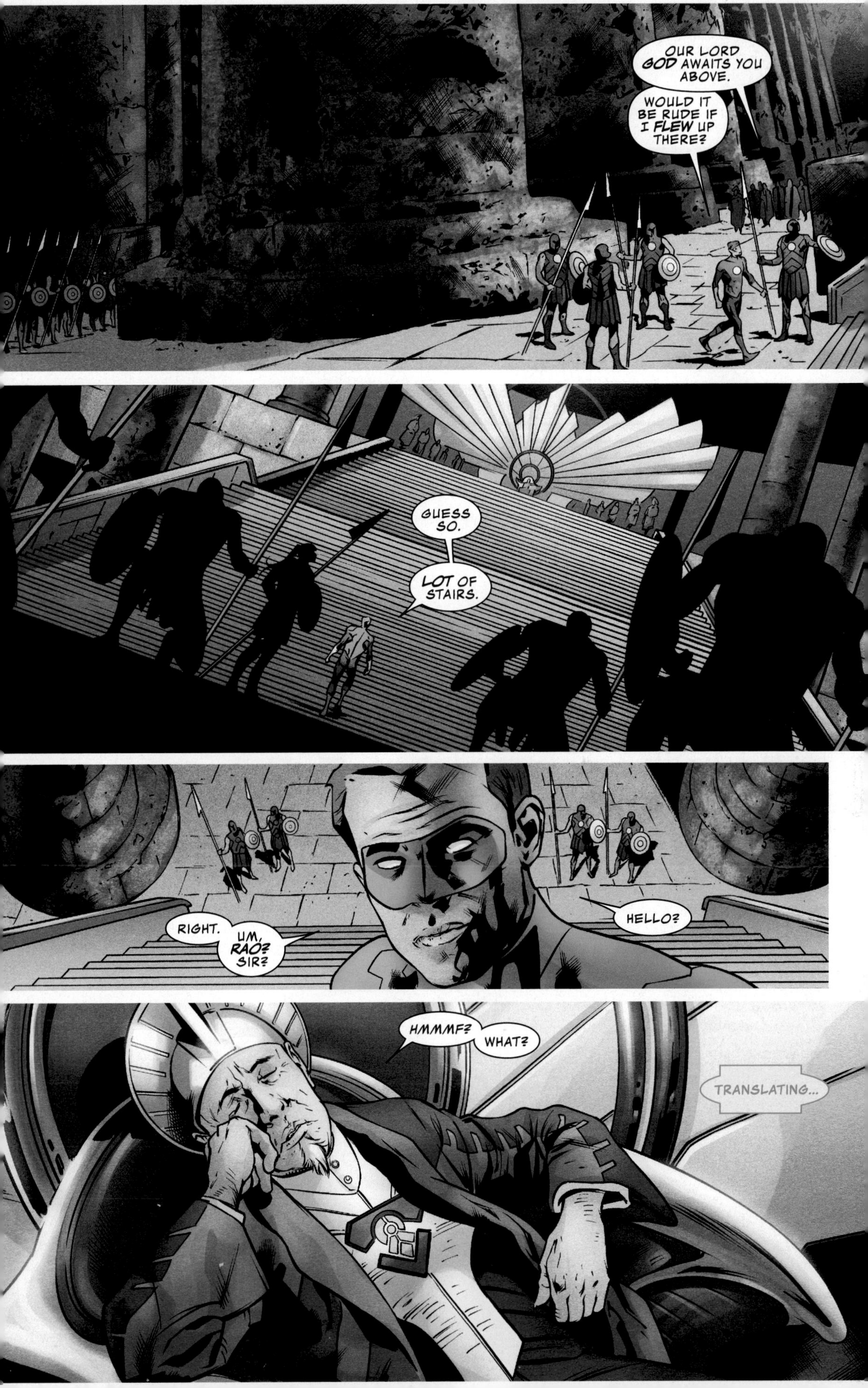
OUR LORD GOD AWAITS YOU ABOVE.
WOULD IT BE RUDE IF I FLEW UP THERE?
GUESS SO.
LOT OF STAIRS.
RIGHT.
UM, RAO? SIR?
HELLO?
HMMMF?
WHAT?
TRANSLATING...

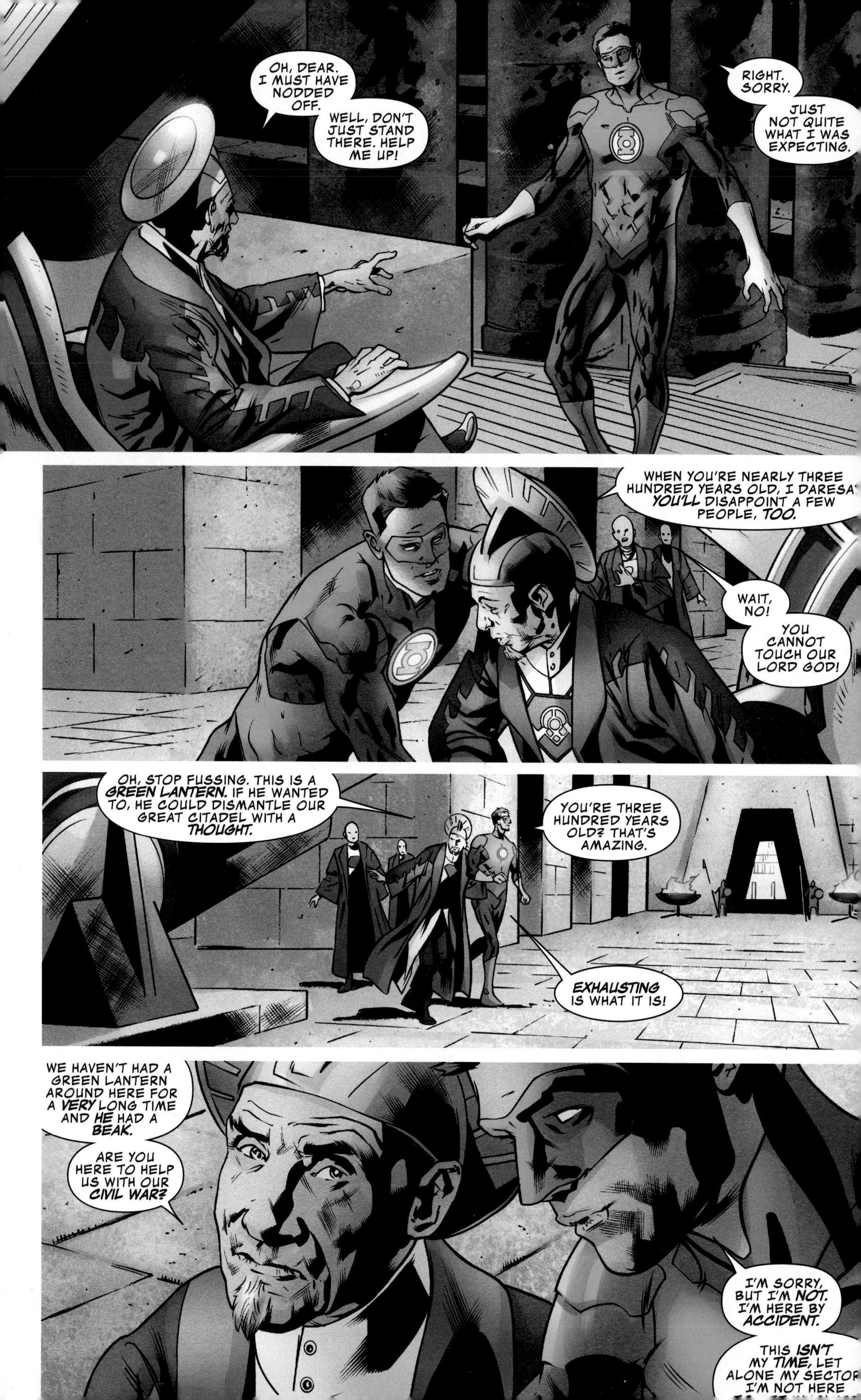
OH, DEAR. I MUST HAVE NODDED OFF.
WELL, DON'T JUST STAND THERE. HELP ME UP!
RIGHT. SORRY.
JUST NOT QUITE WHAT I WAS EXPECTING.
WHEN YOU'RE NEARLY THREE HUNDRED YEARS OLD, I DARESA YOU'LL DISAPPOINT A FEW PEOPLE, TOO.
WAIT, NO!
YOU CANNOT TOUCH OUR LORD GOD!
OH, STOP FUSSING. THIS IS A GREEN LANTERN. IF HE WANTED TO, HE COULD DISMANTLE OUR GREAT CITADEL WITH A THOUGHT.
YOU'RE THREE HUNDRED YEARS OLD? THAT'S AMAZING.
EXHAUSTING IS WHAT IT IS!
WE HAVEN'T HAD A GREEN LANTERN AROUND HERE FOR A VERY LONG TIME AND HE HAD A BEAK.
ARE YOU HERE TO HELP US WITH OUR CIVIL WAR?
I'M SORRY, BUT I'M NOT. I'M HERE BY ACCIDENT.
THIS ISN'T MY TIME, LET ALONE MY SECTOR I'M NOT HERE

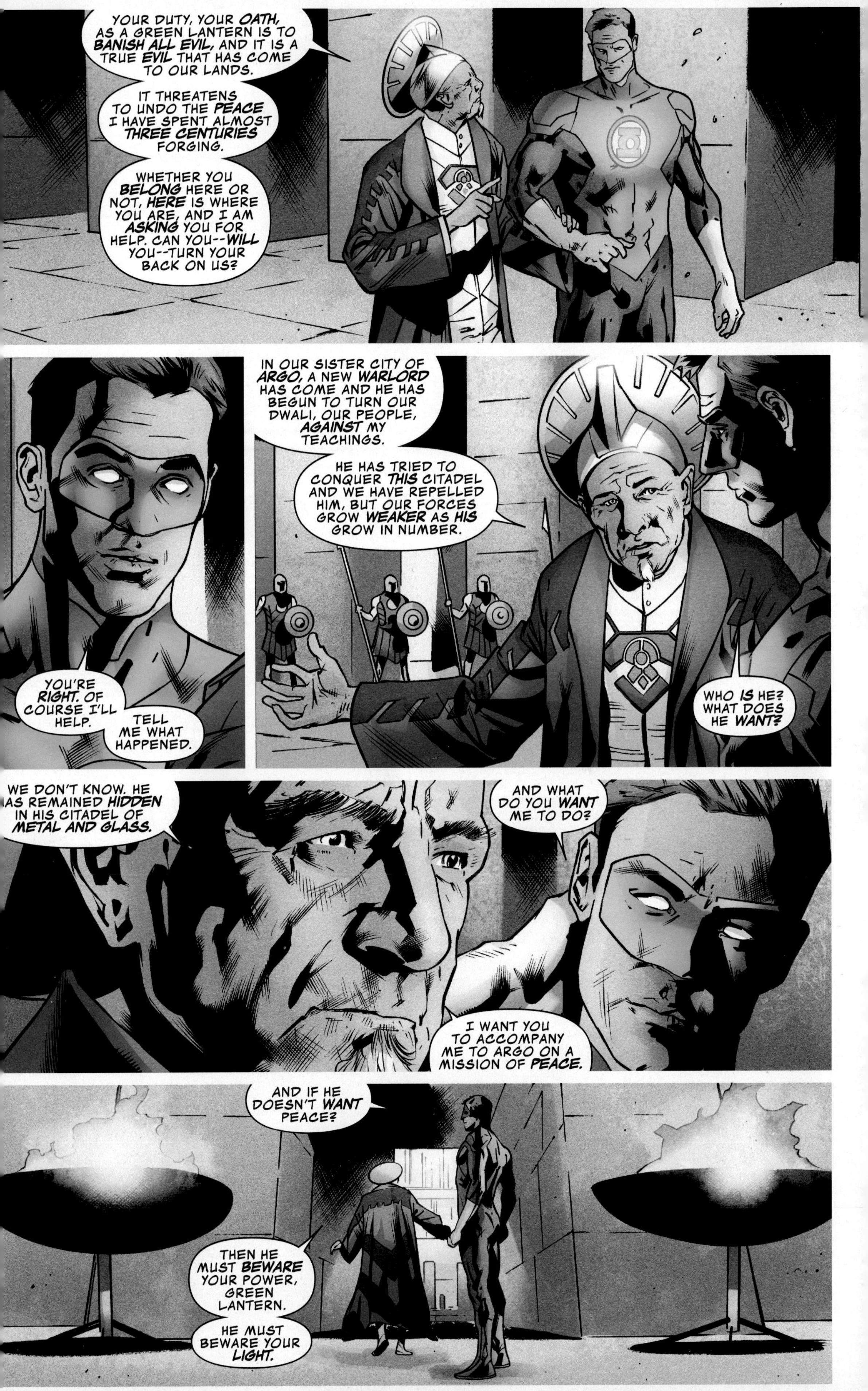
YOUR DUTY, YOUR OATH, AS A GREEN LANTERN IS TO BANISH ALL EVIL, AND IT IS A TRUE EVIL THAT HAS COME TO OUR LANDS.
IT THREATENS TO UNDO THE PEACE I HAVE SPENT ALMOST THREE CENTURIES FORGING.
WHETHER YOU BELONG HERE OR NOT, HERE IS WHERE YOU ARE, AND I AM ASKING YOU FOR HELP. CAN YOU--WILL YOU--TURN YOUR BACK ON US?
YOU'RE RIGHT. OF COURSE I'LL HELP.
TELL ME WHAT HAPPENED.
IN OUR SISTER CITY OF ARGO, A NEW WARLORD HAS COME AND HE HAS BEGUN TO TURN OUR DWALI, OUR PEOPLE, AGAINST MY TEACHINGS.
HE HAS TRIED TO CONQUER THIS CITADEL AND WE HAVE REPELLED HIM, BUT OUR FORCES GROW WEAKER AS HIS GROW IN NUMBER.
WHO IS HE? WHAT DOES HE WANT?
WE DON'T KNOW. HE AS REMAINED HIDDEN IN HIS CITADEL OF METAL AND GLASS.
AND WHAT DO YOU WANT ME TO DO?
I WANT YOU TO ACCOMPANY ME TO ARGO ON A MISSION OF PEACE.
AND IF HE DOESN'T WANT PEACE?
THEN HE MUST BEWARE YOUR POWER, GREEN LANTERN.
HE MUST BEWARE YOUR LIGHT.

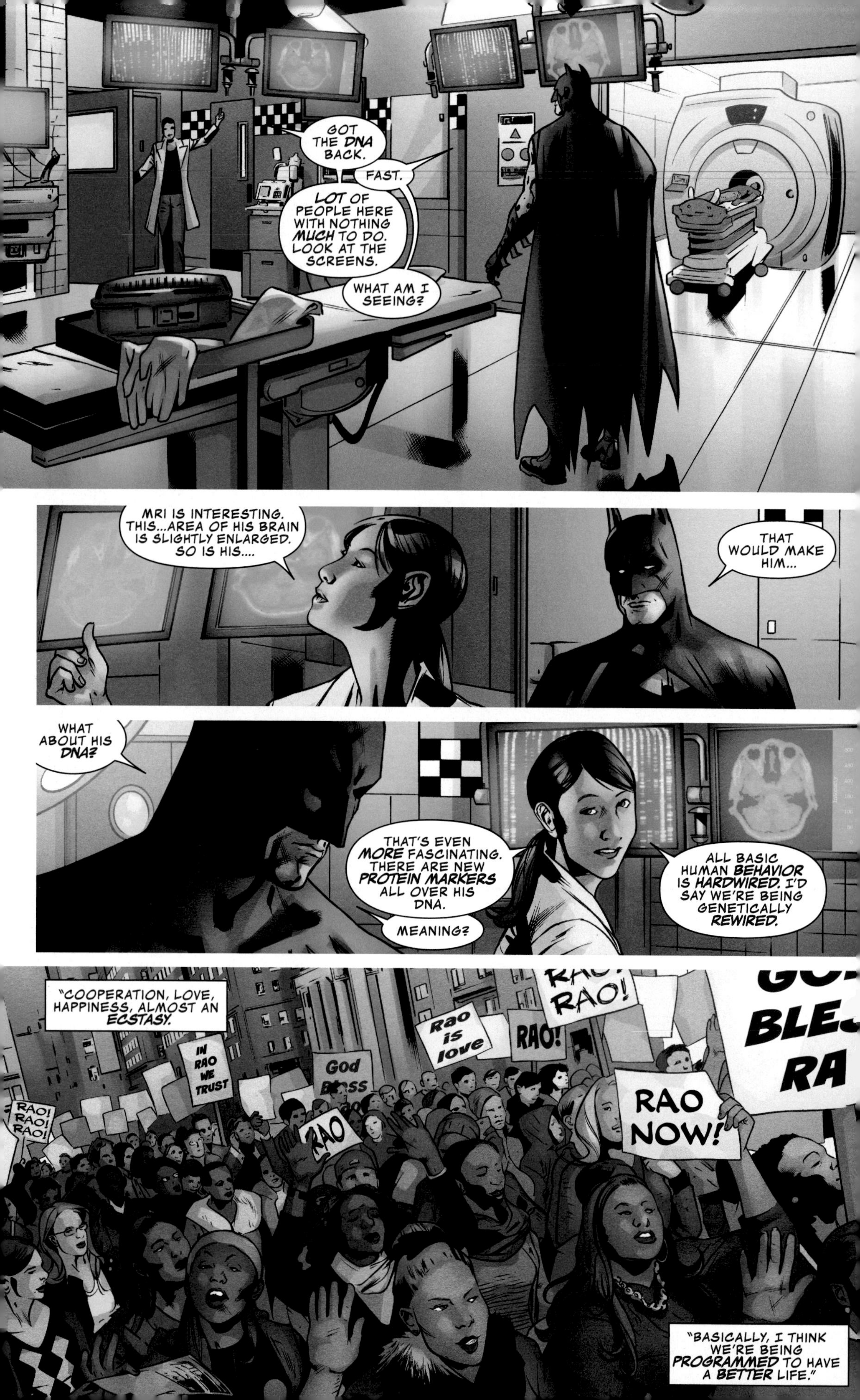
GOT THE DNA BACK.
FAST.
LOT OF PEOPLE HERE WITH NOTHING MUCH TO DO. LOOK AT THE SCREENS.
WHAT AM I SEEING?
MRI IS INTERESTING. THIS...AREA OF HIS BRAIN IS SLIGHTLY ENLARGED. SO IS HIS....
THAT WOULD MAKE HIM...
WHAT ABOUT HIS DNA?
THAT'S EVEN MORE FASCINATING. THERE ARE NEW PROTEIN MARKERS ALL OVER HIS DNA.
MEANING?
ALL BASIC HUMAN BEHAVIOR IS HARDWIRED. I'D SAY WE'RE BEING GENETICALLY REWIRED.
"COOPERATION, LOVE, HAPPINESS, ALMOST AN ECSTASY.
RAO!
Rao is love
RAO!
IN RAO WE TRUST
RAO! RAO! RAO!
RAO
RAO NOW!
"BASICALLY, I THINK WE'RE BEING PROGRAMMED TO HAVE A BETTER LIFE."

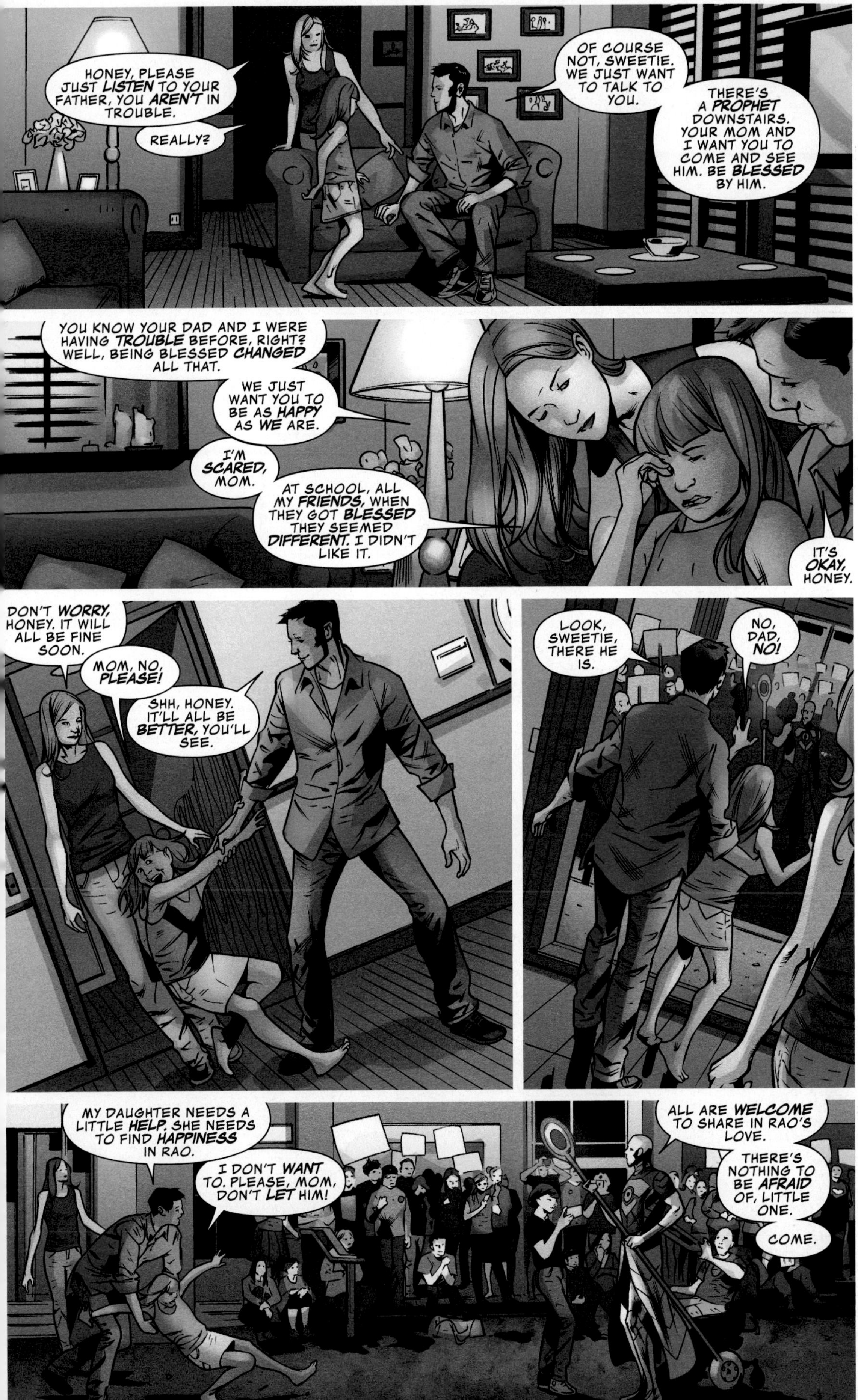
HONEY, PLEASE JUST LISTEN TO YOUR FATHER, YOU AREN'T IN TROUBLE.
REALLY?
OF COURSE NOT, SWEETIE. WE JUST WANT TO TALK TO YOU.
THERE'S A PROPHET DOWNSTAIRS. YOUR MOM AND I WANT YOU TO COME AND SEE HIM. BE BLESSED BY HIM.
YOU KNOW YOUR DAD AND I WERE HAVING TROUBLE BEFORE, RIGHT? WELL, BEING BLESSED CHANGED ALL THAT.
WE JUST WANT YOU TO BE AS HAPPY AS WE ARE.
I'M SCARED, MOM.
AT SCHOOL, ALL MY FRIENDS, WHEN THEY GOT BLESSED THEY SEEMED DIFFERENT. I DIDN'T LIKE IT.
IT'S OKAY, HONEY.
DON'T WORRY, HONEY. IT WILL ALL BE FINE SOON.
MOM, NO, PLEASE!
SHH, HONEY. IT'LL ALL BE BETTER, YOU'LL SEE.
LOOK, SWEETIE, THERE HE IS.
NO, DAD, NO!
MY DAUGHTER NEEDS A LITTLE HELP. SHE NEEDS TO FIND HAPPINESS IN RAO.
I DON'T WANT TO. PLEASE, MOM, DON'T LET HIM!
ALL ARE WELCOME TO SHARE IN RAO'S LOVE.
THERE'S NOTHING TO BE AFRAID OF, LITTLE ONE.
COME.

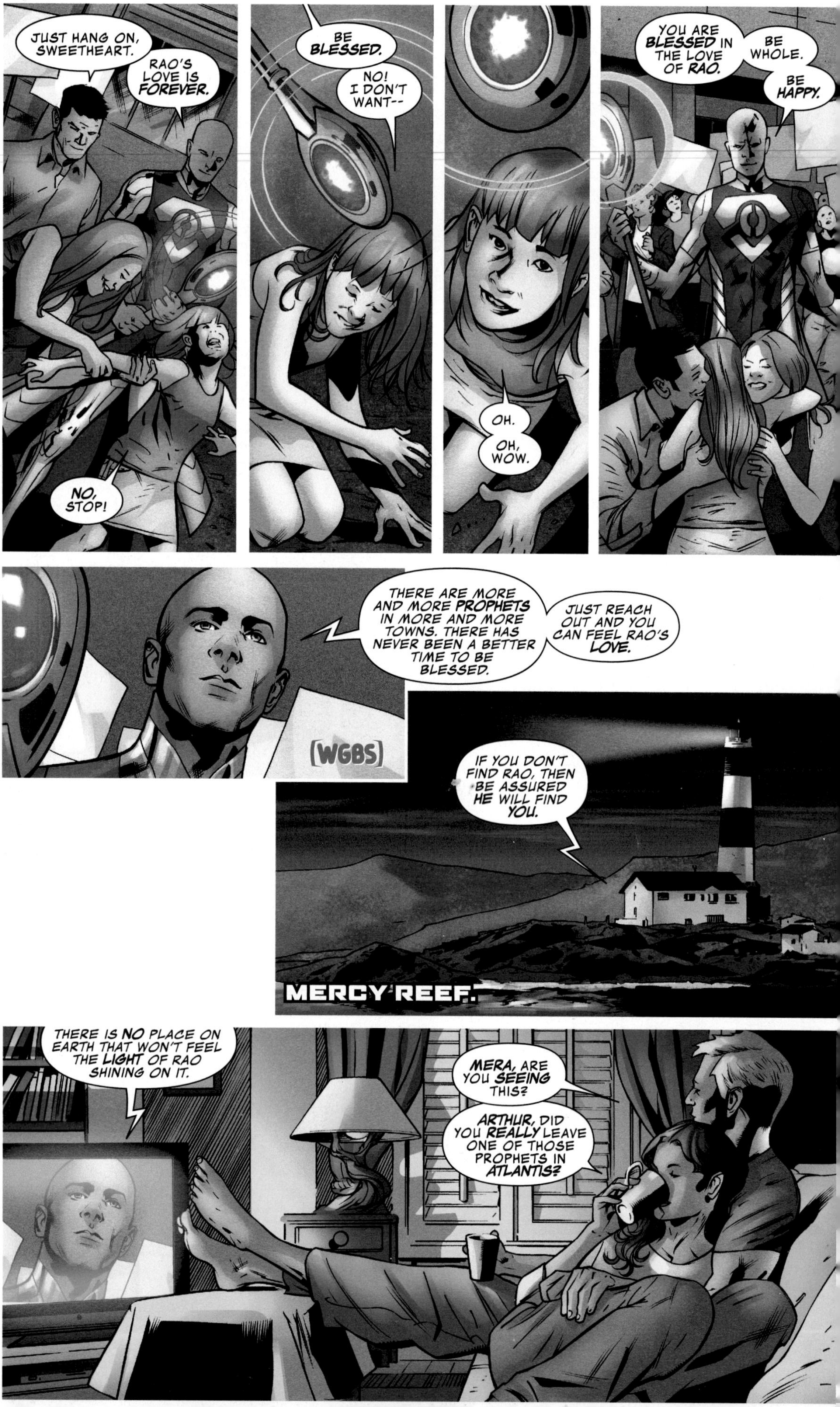
JUST HANG ON, SWEETHEART.
RAO'S LOVE IS FOREVER.
NO, STOP!
BE BLESSED.
NO! I DON'T WANT--
OH.
OH, WOW.
YOU ARE BLESSED IN THE LOVE OF RAO.
BE WHOLE.
BE HAPPY.
THERE ARE MORE AND MORE PROPHETS IN MORE AND MORE TOWNS. THERE HAS NEVER BEEN A BETTER TIME TO BE BLESSED.
JUST REACH OUT AND YOU CAN FEEL RAO'S LOVE.
[WGBS]
IF YOU DON'T FIND RAO, THEN BE ASSURED HE WILL FIND YOU.
MERCY REEF.
THERE IS NO PLACE ON EARTH THAT WON'T FEEL THE LIGHT OF RAO SHINING ON IT.
MERA, ARE YOU SEEING THIS?
ARTHUR, DID YOU REALLY LEAVE ONE OF THOSE PROPHETS IN ATLANTIS?

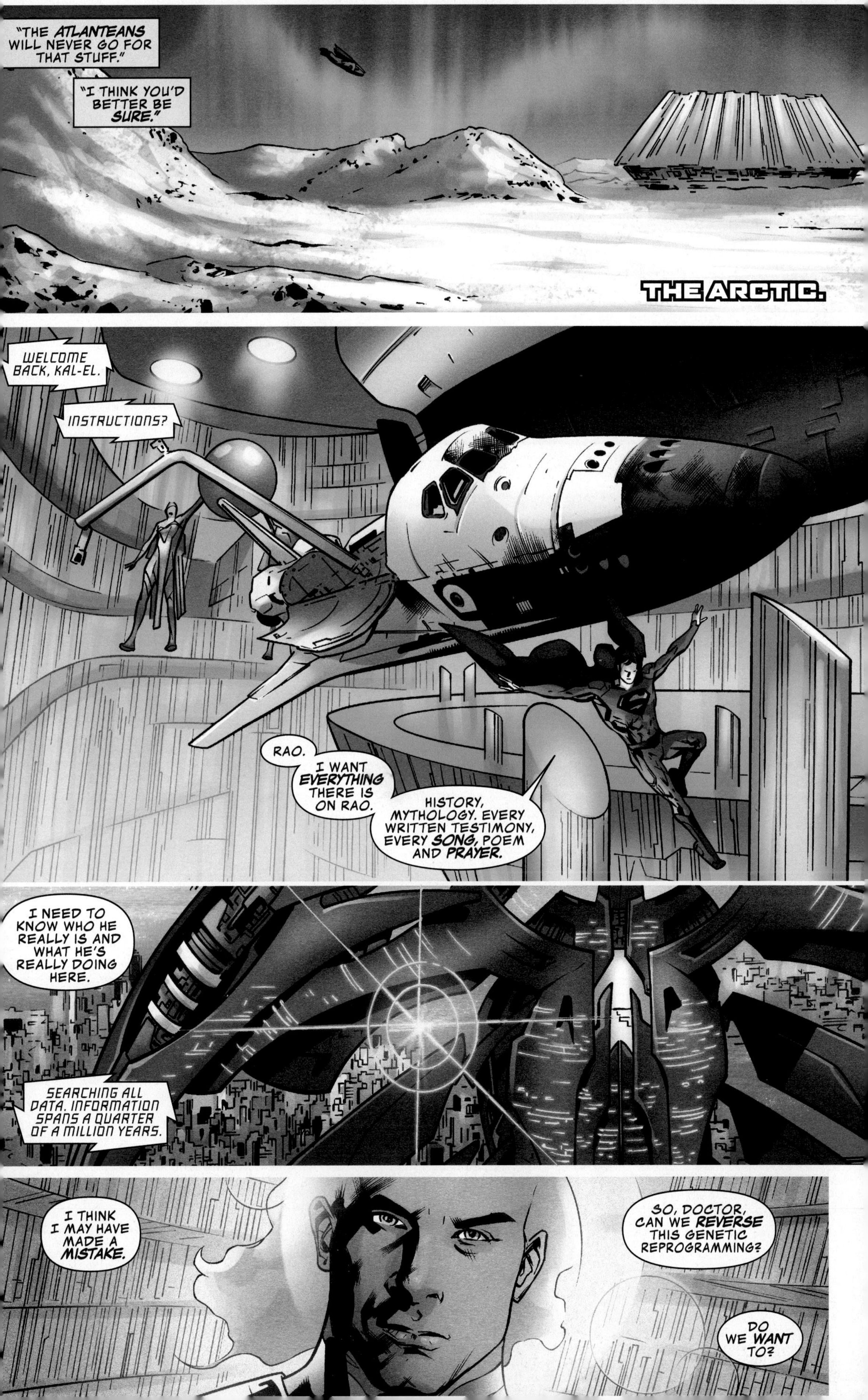
"THE ATLANTEANS WILL NEVER GO FOR THAT STUFF."
"I THINK YOU'D BETTER BE SURE."
THE ARCTIC.
WELCOME BACK, KAL-EL.
INSTRUCTIONS?
RAO.
I WANT EVERYTHING THERE IS ON RAO.
HISTORY, MYTHOLOGY. EVERY WRITTEN TESTIMONY, EVERY SONG, POEM AND PRAYER.
I NEED TO KNOW WHO HE REALLY IS AND WHAT HE'S REALLY DOING HERE.
SEARCHING ALL DATA. INFORMATION SPANS A QUARTER OF A MILLION YEARS.
I THINK I MAY HAVE MADE A MISTAKE.
SO, DOCTOR, CAN WE REVERSE THIS GENETIC REPROGRAMMING?
DO WE WANT TO?

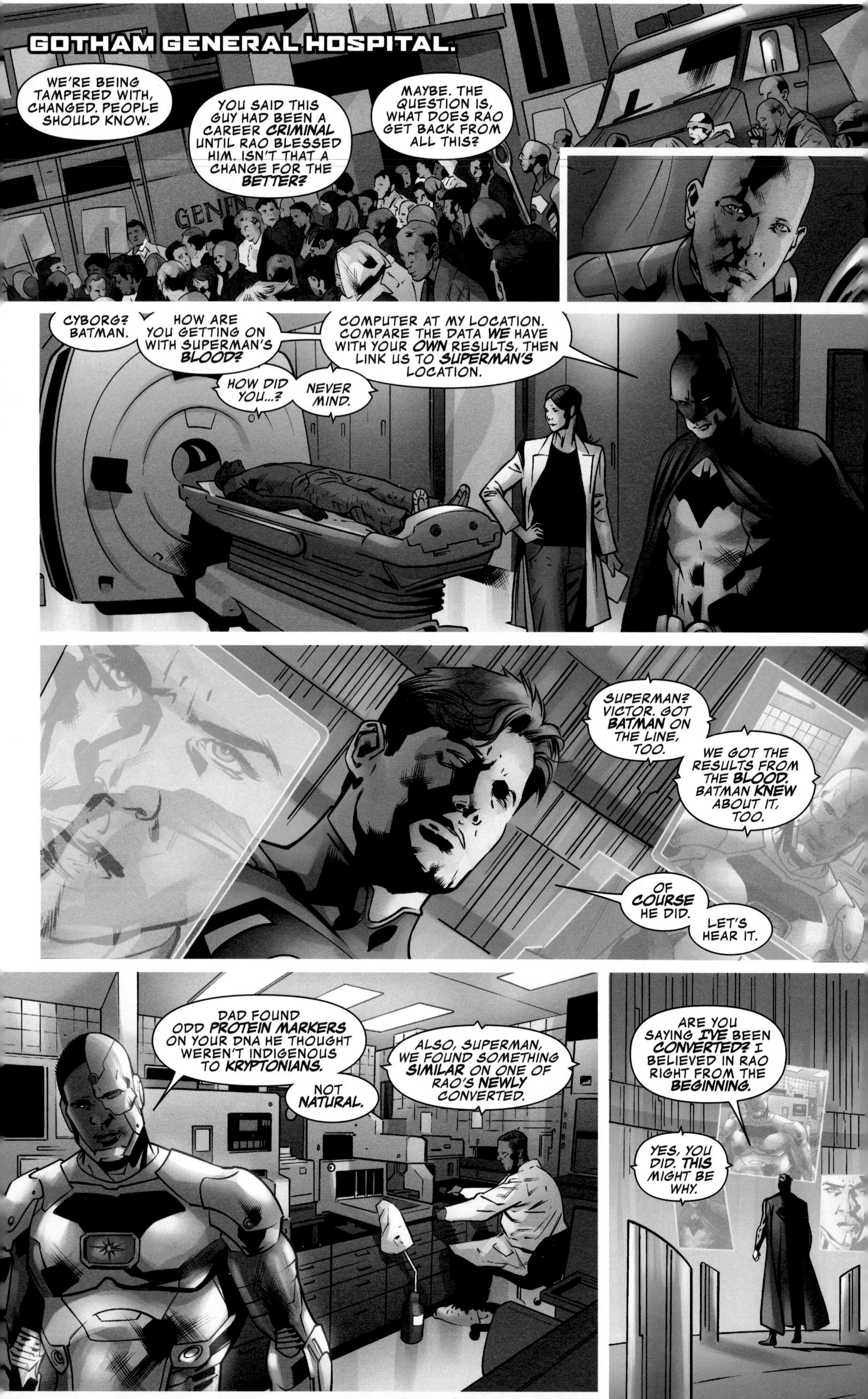
GOTHAM GENERAL HOSPITAL.
WE'RE BEING TAMPERED WITH, CHANGED. PEOPLE SHOULD KNOW.
YOU SAID THIS GUY HAD BEEN A CAREER CRIMINAL UNTIL RAO BLESSED HIM. ISN'T THAT A CHANGE FOR THE BETTER?
MAYBE. THE QUESTION IS, WHAT DOES RAO GET BACK FROM ALL THIS?
CYBORG? BATMAN.
HOW ARE YOU GETTING ON WITH SUPERMAN'S BLOOD?
COMPUTER AT MY LOCATION. COMPARE THE DATA WE HAVE WITH YOUR OWN RESULTS, THEN LINK US TO SUPERMAN'S LOCATION.
HOW DID YOU...?
NEVER MIND.
SUPERMAN? VICTOR. GOT BATMAN ON THE LINE, TOO.
WE GOT THE RESULTS FROM THE BLOOD. BATMAN KNEW ABOUT IT, TOO.
OF COURSE HE DID.
LET'S HEAR IT.
DAD FOUND ODD PROTEIN MARKERS ON YOUR DNA HE THOUGHT WEREN'T INDIGENOUS TO KRYPTONIANS.
NOT NATURAL.
ALSO, SUPERMAN, WE FOUND SOMETHING SIMILAR ON ONE OF RAO'S NEWLY CONVERTED.
ARE YOU SAYING I'VE BEEN CONVERTED? I BELIEVED IN RAO RIGHT FROM THE BEGINNING.
YES, YOU DID. THIS MIGHT BE WHY.

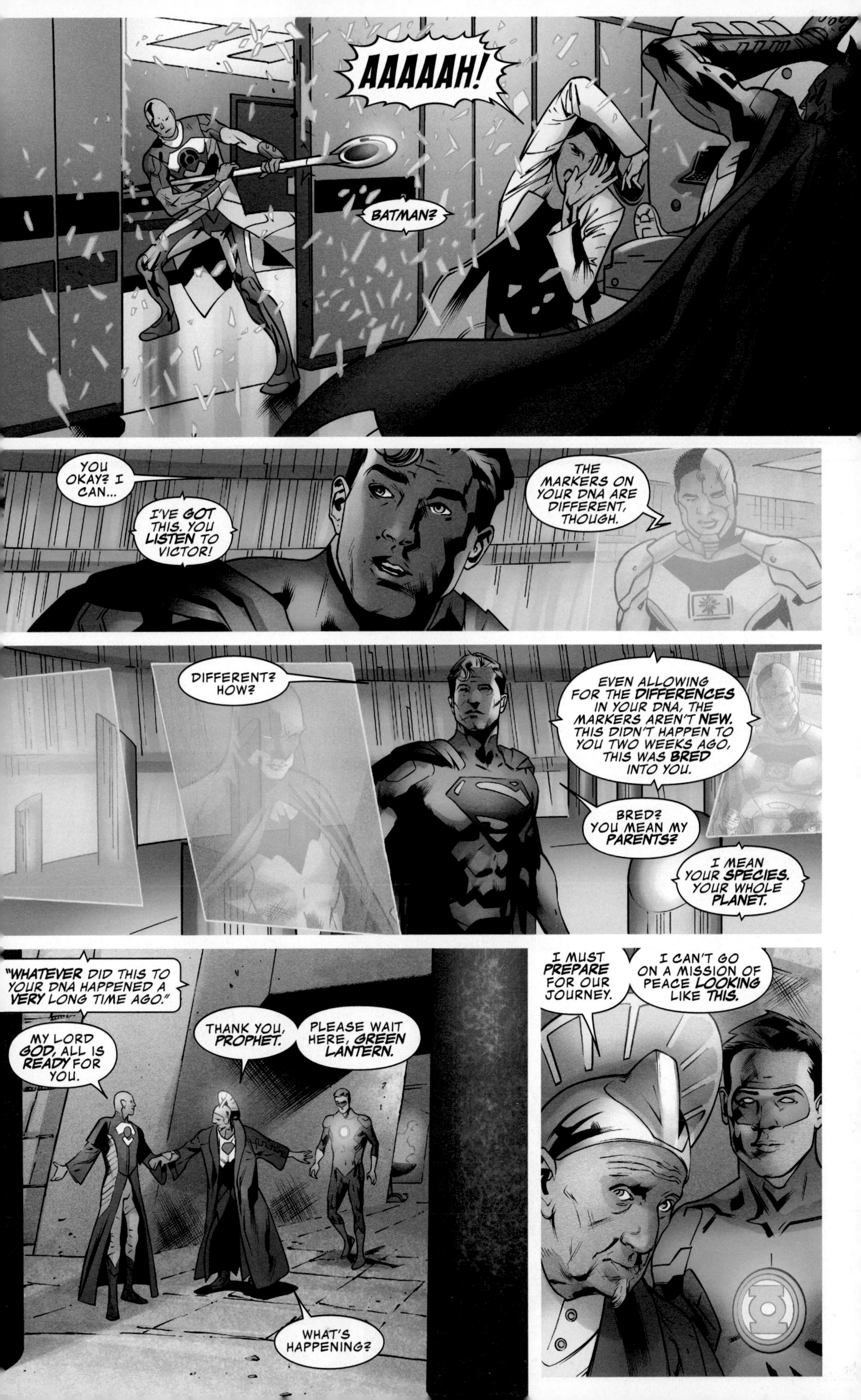
AAAAAH!
BATMAN?
YOU OKAY? I CAN...
I'VE **GOT** THIS. YOU **LISTEN** TO VICTOR!
THE MARKERS ON YOUR DNA ARE DIFFERENT, THOUGH.
DIFFERENT? HOW?
EVEN ALLOWING FOR THE **DIFFERENCES** IN YOUR DNA, THE MARKERS AREN'T **NEW.** THIS DIDN'T HAPPEN TO YOU TWO WEEKS AGO, THIS WAS **BRED** INTO YOU.
BRED? YOU MEAN MY **PARENTS?**
I MEAN YOUR **SPECIES.** YOUR WHOLE **PLANET.**
"**WHATEVER** DID THIS TO YOUR DNA HAPPENED A **VERY** LONG TIME AGO."
MY LORD **GOD,** ALL IS **READY** FOR YOU.
THANK YOU, **PROPHET.**
PLEASE WAIT HERE, **GREEN LANTERN.**
WHAT'S HAPPENING?
I MUST **PREPARE** FOR OUR JOURNEY.
I CAN'T GO ON A MISSION OF PEACE **LOOKING** LIKE **THIS.**

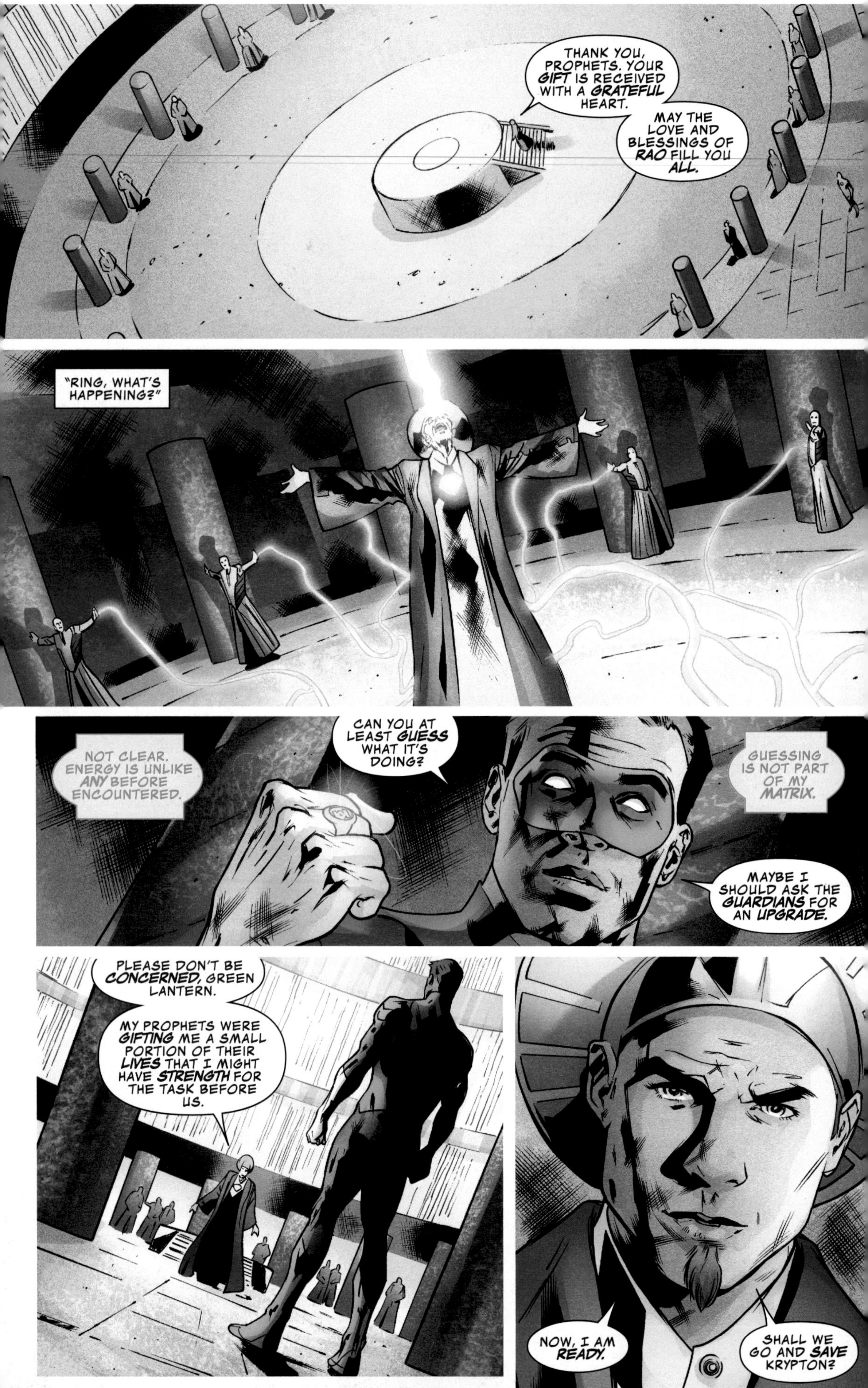
THANK YOU, PROPHETS. YOUR GIFT IS RECEIVED WITH A GRATEFUL HEART.
MAY THE LOVE AND BLESSINGS OF RAO FILL YOU ALL.
"RING, WHAT'S HAPPENING?"
NOT CLEAR. ENERGY IS UNLIKE ANY BEFORE ENCOUNTERED.
CAN YOU AT LEAST GUESS WHAT IT'S DOING?
GUESSING IS NOT PART OF MY MATRIX.
MAYBE I SHOULD ASK THE GUARDIANS FOR AN UPGRADE.
PLEASE DON'T BE CONCERNED, GREEN LANTERN.
MY PROPHETS WERE GIFTING ME A SMALL PORTION OF THEIR LIVES THAT I MIGHT HAVE STRENGTH FOR THE TASK BEFORE US.
NOW, I AM READY.
SHALL WE GO AND SAVE KRYPTON?

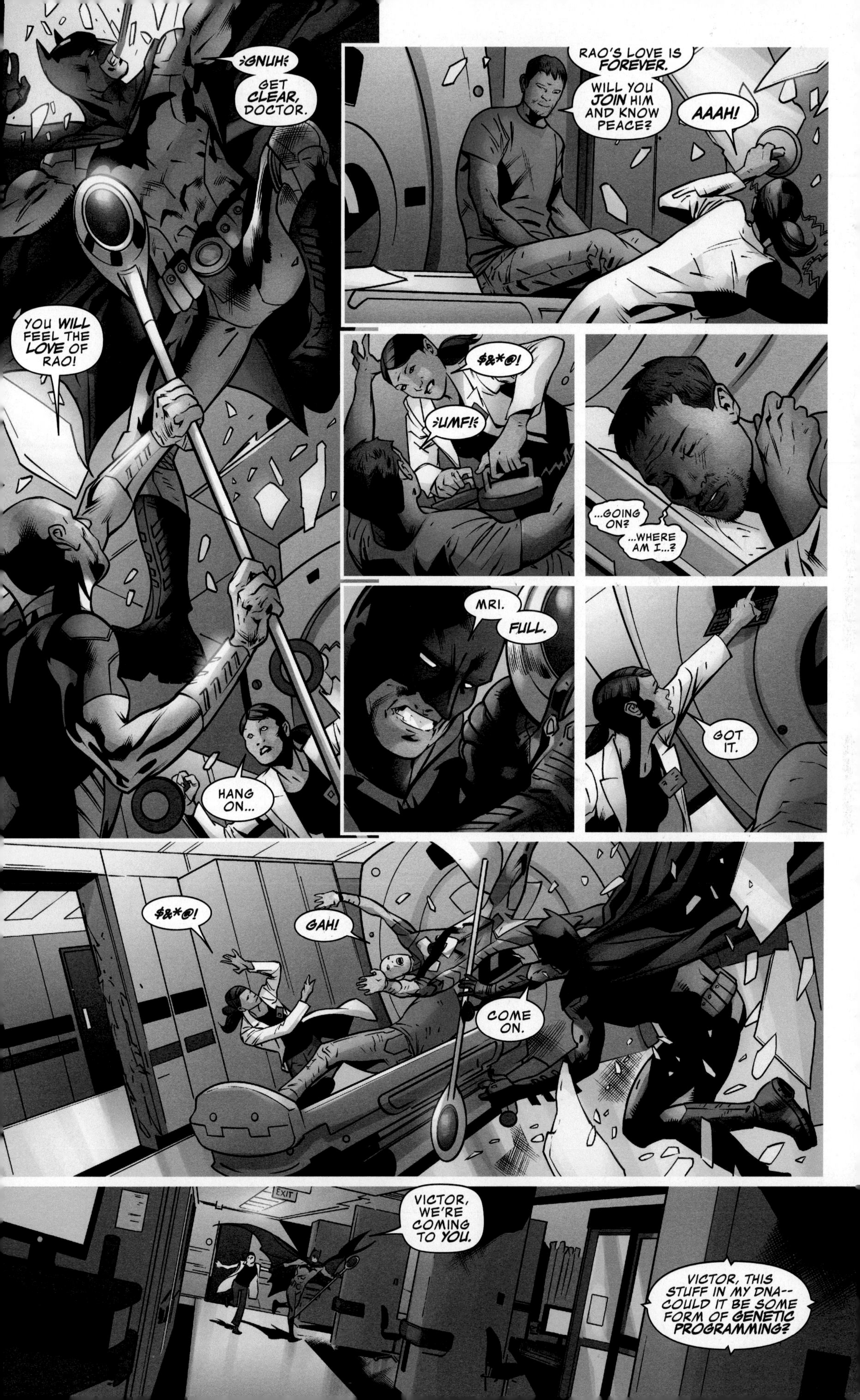

:GNUH:
GET CLEAR, DOCTOR.
YOU WILL FEEL THE LOVE OF RAO!
HANG ON...
RAO'S LOVE IS FOREVER.
WILL YOU JOIN HIM AND KNOW PEACE?
AAAH!
$&*@!
:UMF!:
...GOING ON?
...WHERE AM I...?
MRI.
FULL.
GOT IT.
$&*@!
GAH!
COME ON.
EXIT
VICTOR, WE'RE COMING TO YOU.
VICTOR, THIS STUFF IN MY DNA--COULD IT BE SOME FORM OF GENETIC PROGRAMMING?

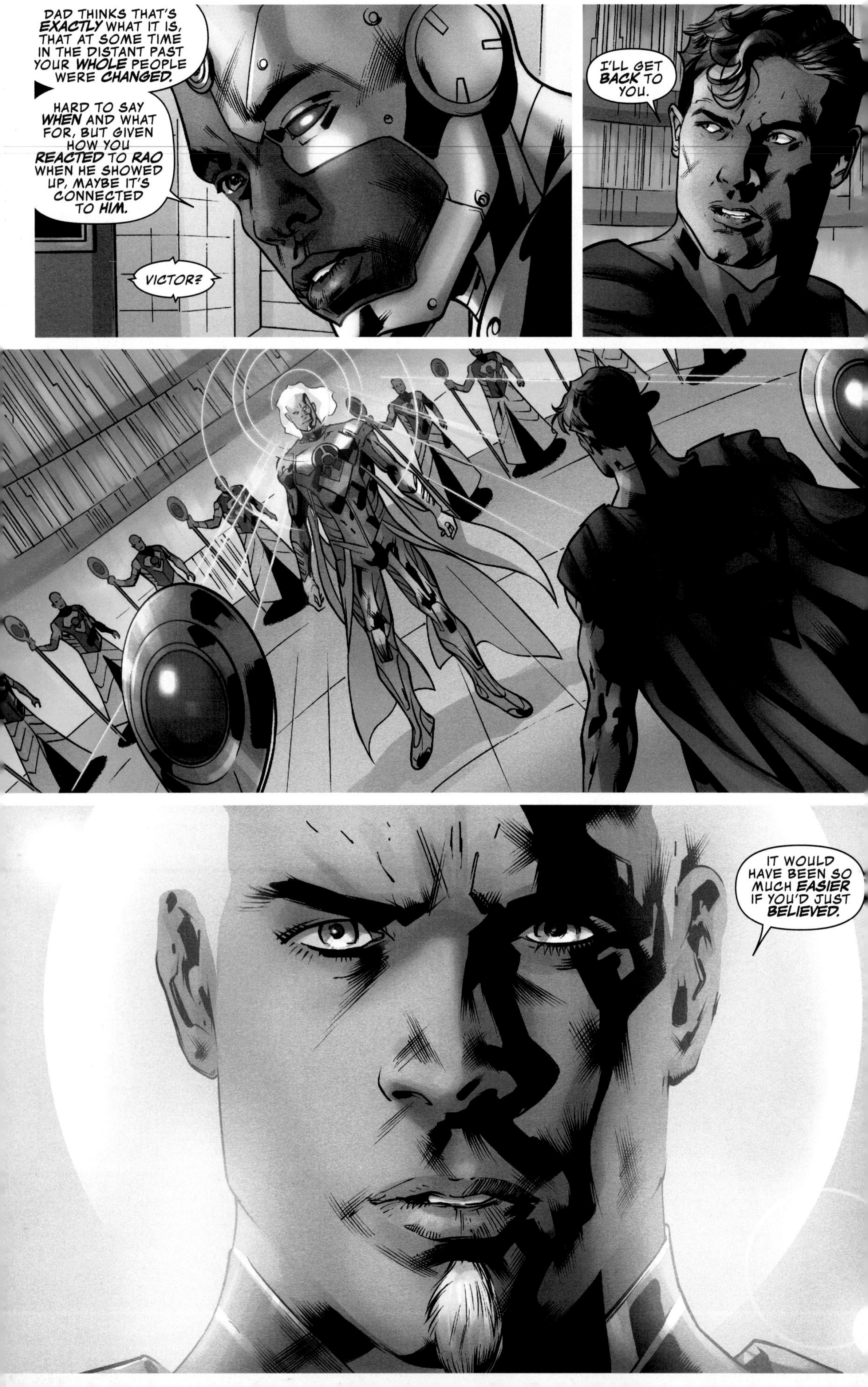
DAD THINKS THAT'S EXACTLY WHAT IT IS, THAT AT SOME TIME IN THE DISTANT PAST YOUR WHOLE PEOPLE WERE CHANGED.
HARD TO SAY WHEN AND WHAT FOR, BUT GIVEN HOW YOU REACTED TO RAO WHEN HE SHOWED UP, MAYBE IT'S CONNECTED TO HIM.
VICTOR?
I'LL GET BACK TO YOU.
IT WOULD HAVE BEEN SO MUCH EASIER IF YOU'D JUST BELIEVED.

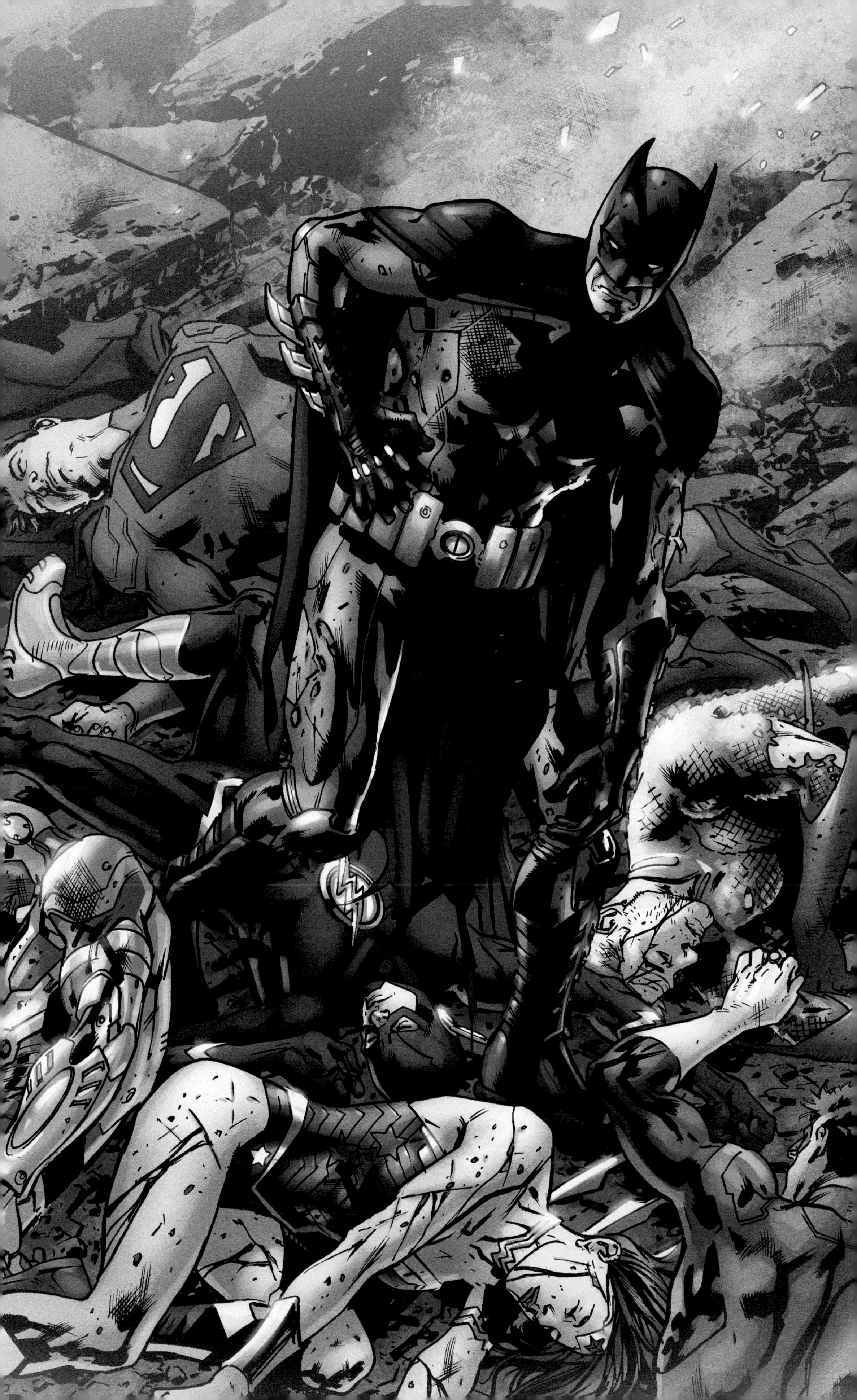

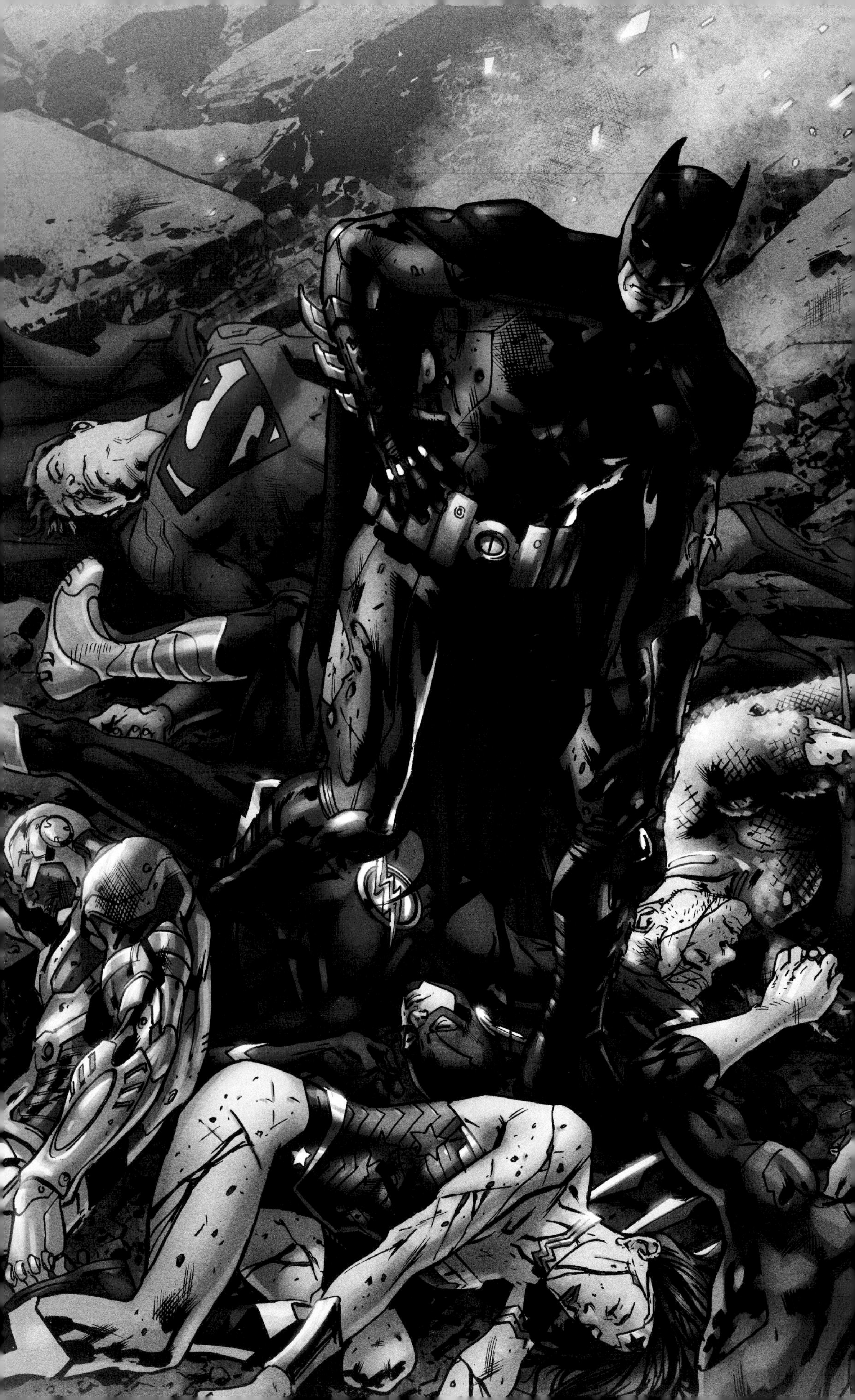

DC COMICS PRESENTS

THE JUSTICE LEAGUE OF AMERICA

POWER AND GLORY

PART FIVE

BY BRYAN HITCH

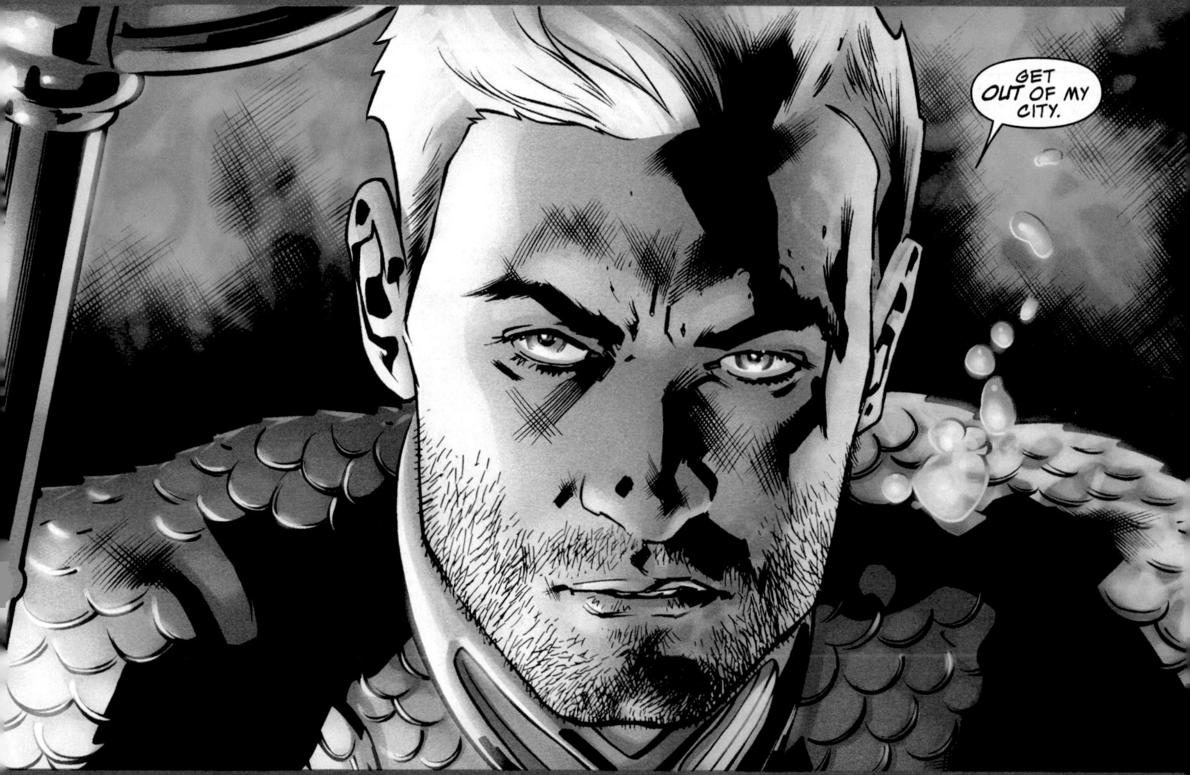
GET OUT OF MY CITY.

INKS BY DANIEL HENRIQUES, ANDREW CURRIE & BRYAN HITCH
COLORS BY ALEX SINCLAIR
LETTERS BY CHRIS ELIOPOULOS
ASSISTS BY AMEDEO TURTURRO
EDITS BY BRIAN CUNNINGHAM
COVER BY BRYAN HITCH AND ALEX SINCLAIR

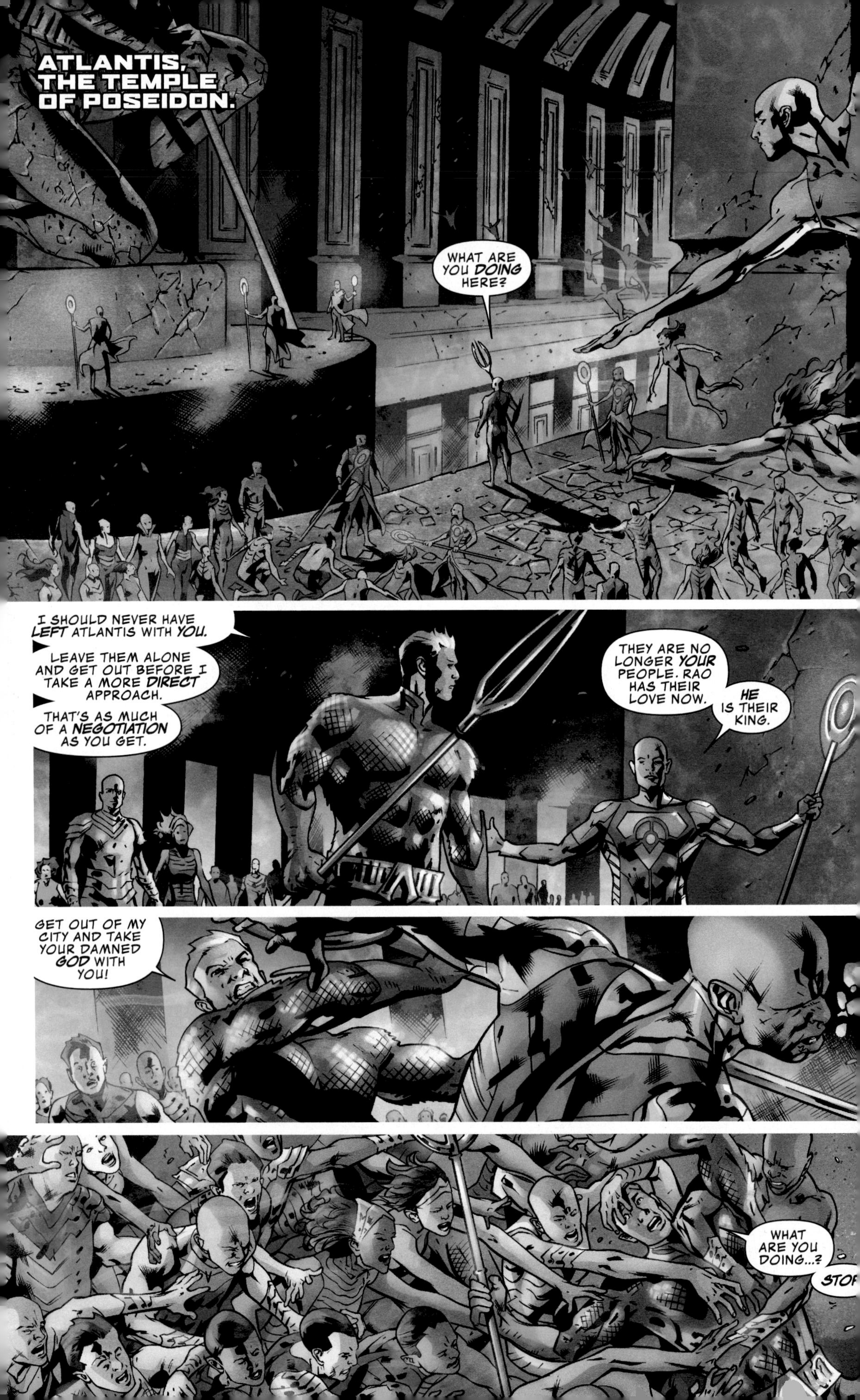
ATLANTIS, THE TEMPLE OF POSEIDON.
WHAT ARE YOU DOING HERE?
I SHOULD NEVER HAVE LEFT ATLANTIS WITH YOU.
LEAVE THEM ALONE AND GET OUT BEFORE I TAKE A MORE DIRECT APPROACH.
THAT'S AS MUCH OF A NEGOTIATION AS YOU GET.
THEY ARE NO LONGER YOUR PEOPLE. RAO HAS THEIR LOVE NOW.
HE IS THEIR KING.
GET OUT OF MY CITY AND TAKE YOUR DAMNED GOD WITH YOU!
WHAT ARE YOU DOING...?
STOP

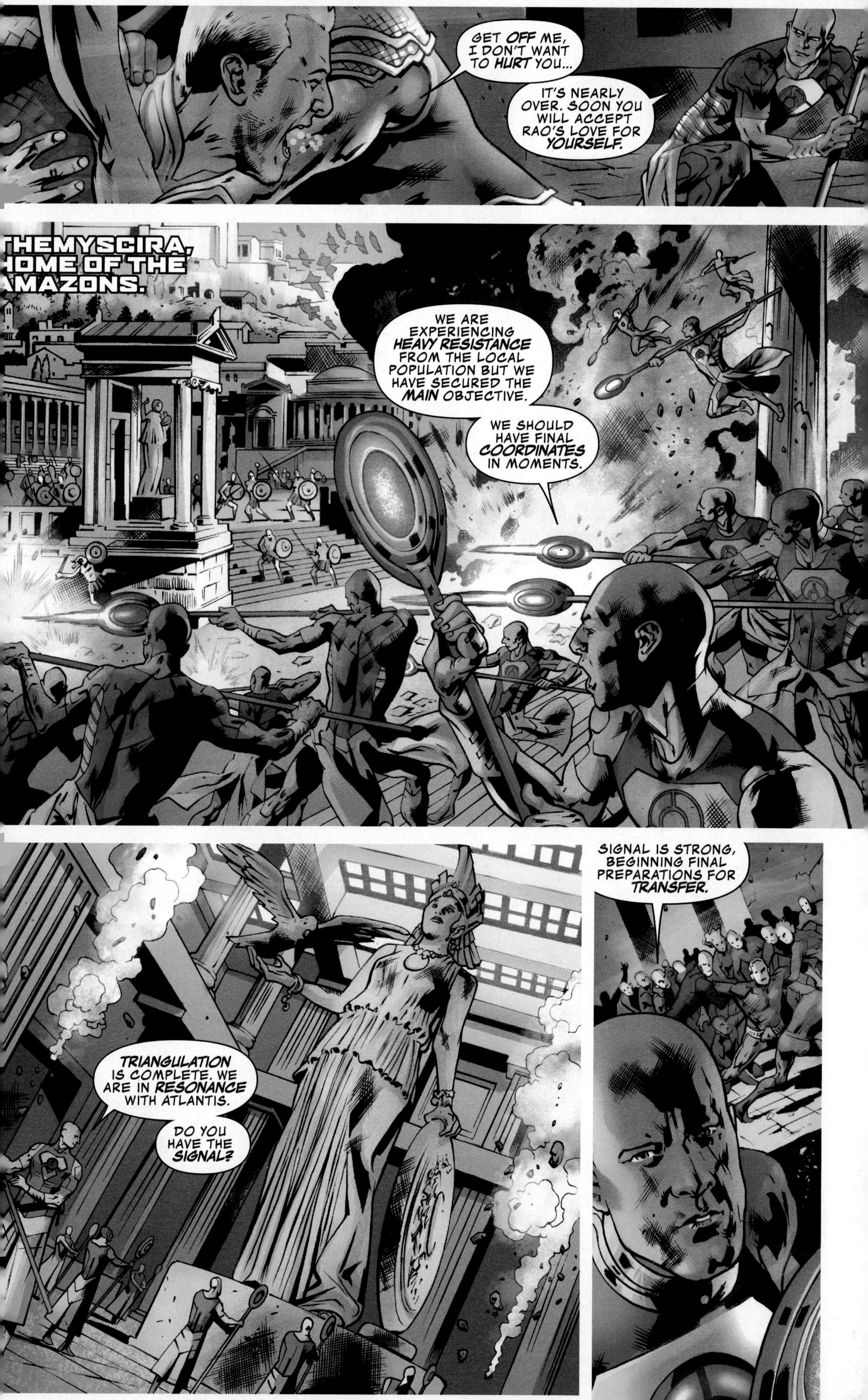

GET OFF ME, I DON'T WANT TO HURT YOU...
IT'S NEARLY OVER. SOON YOU WILL ACCEPT RAO'S LOVE FOR YOURSELF.
THEMYSCIRA, HOME OF THE AMAZONS.
WE ARE EXPERIENCING HEAVY RESISTANCE FROM THE LOCAL POPULATION BUT WE HAVE SECURED THE MAIN OBJECTIVE.
WE SHOULD HAVE FINAL COORDINATES IN MOMENTS.
TRIANGULATION IS COMPLETE. WE ARE IN RESONANCE WITH ATLANTIS.
DO YOU HAVE THE SIGNAL?
SIGNAL IS STRONG, BEGINNING FINAL PREPARATIONS FOR TRANSFER.

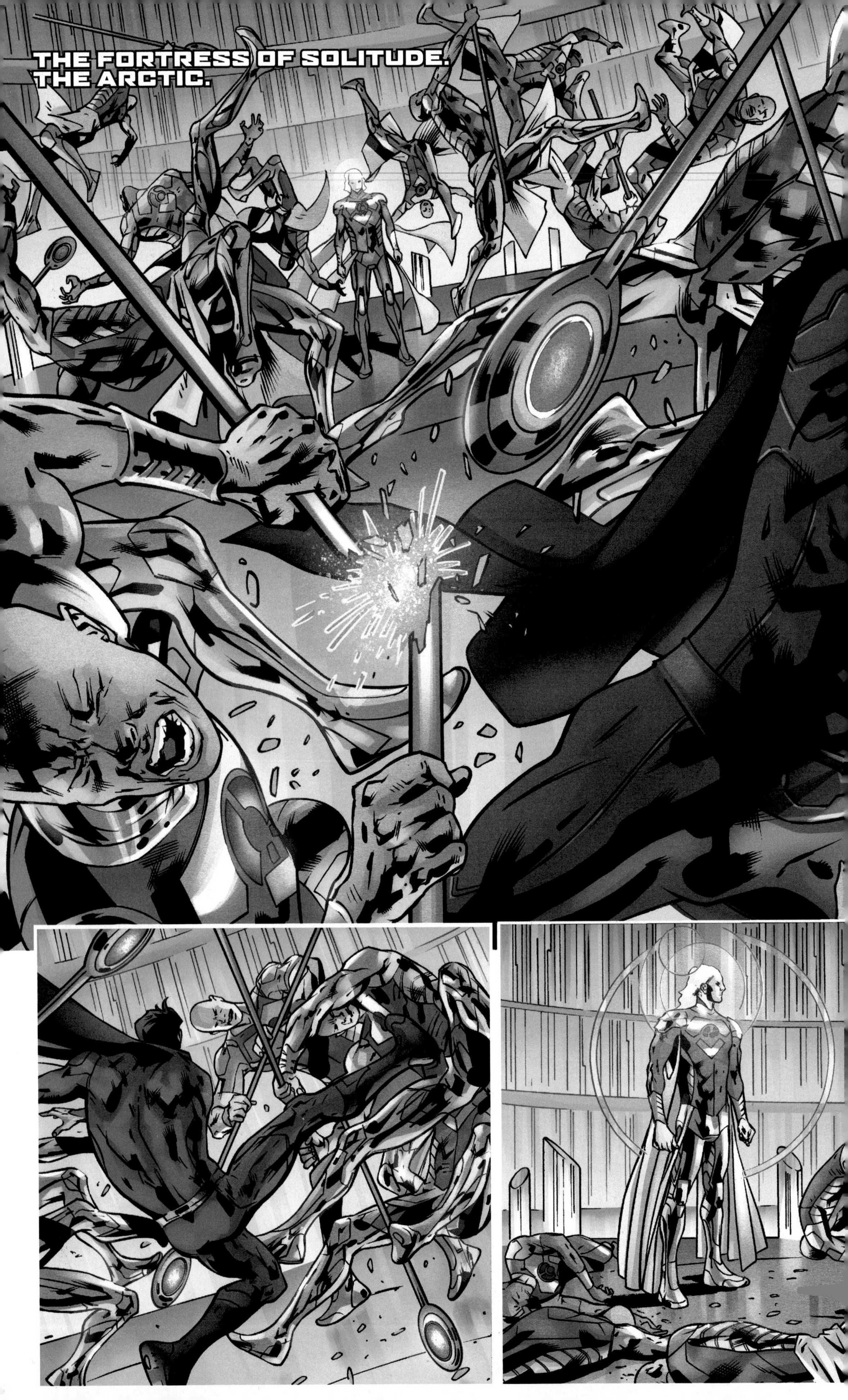
THE FORTRESS OF SOLITUDE. THE ARCTIC.

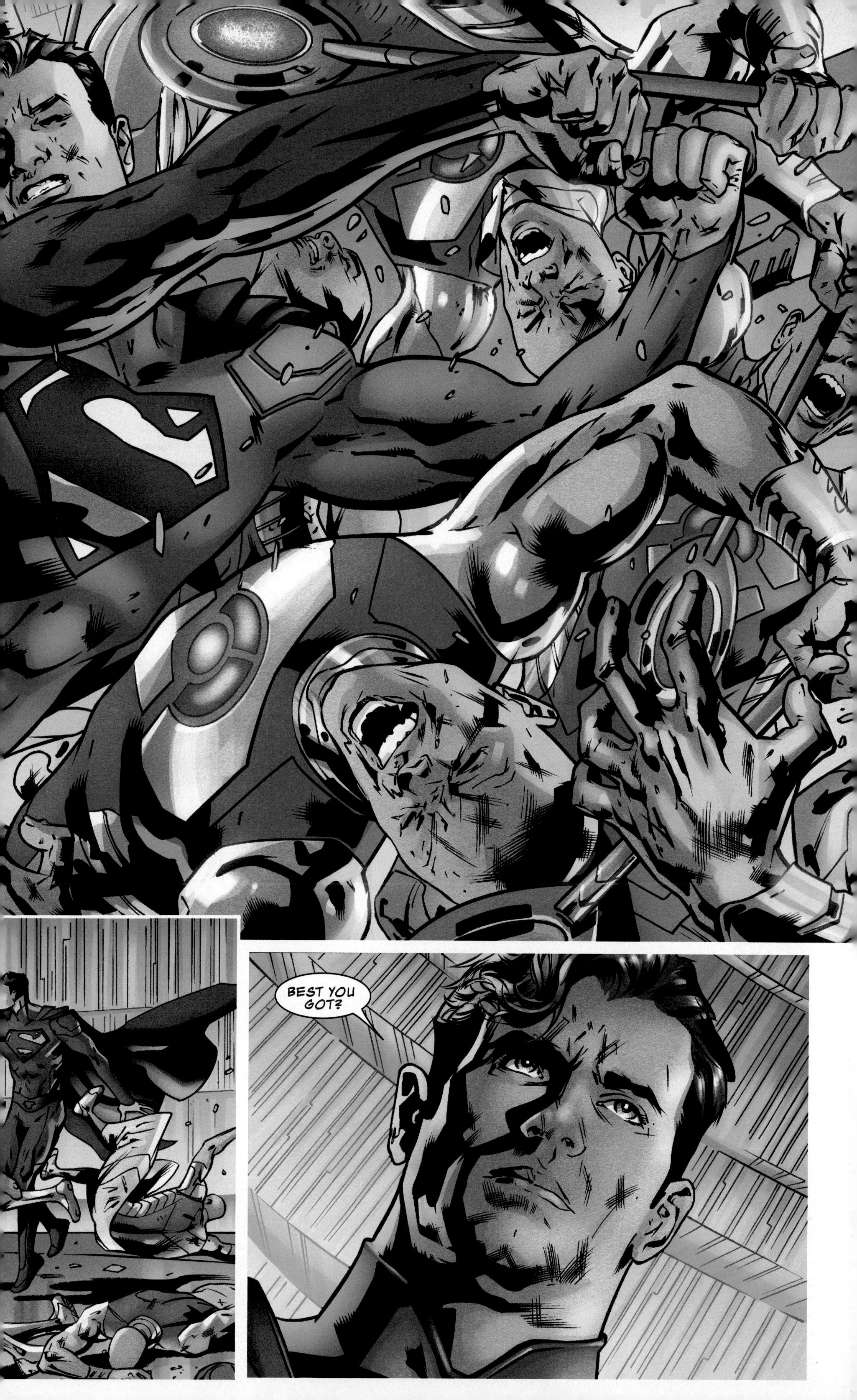
BEST YOU GOT?

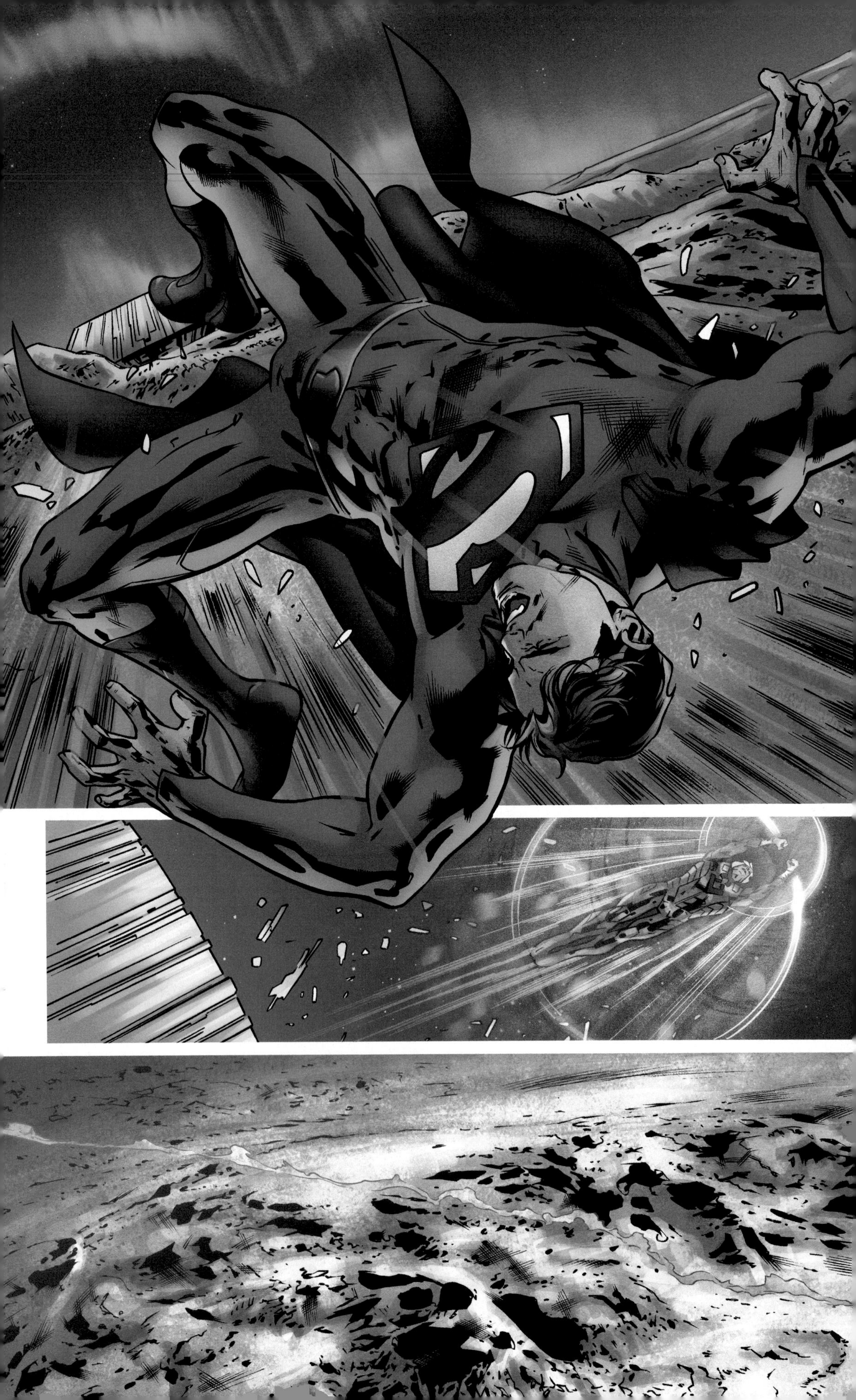

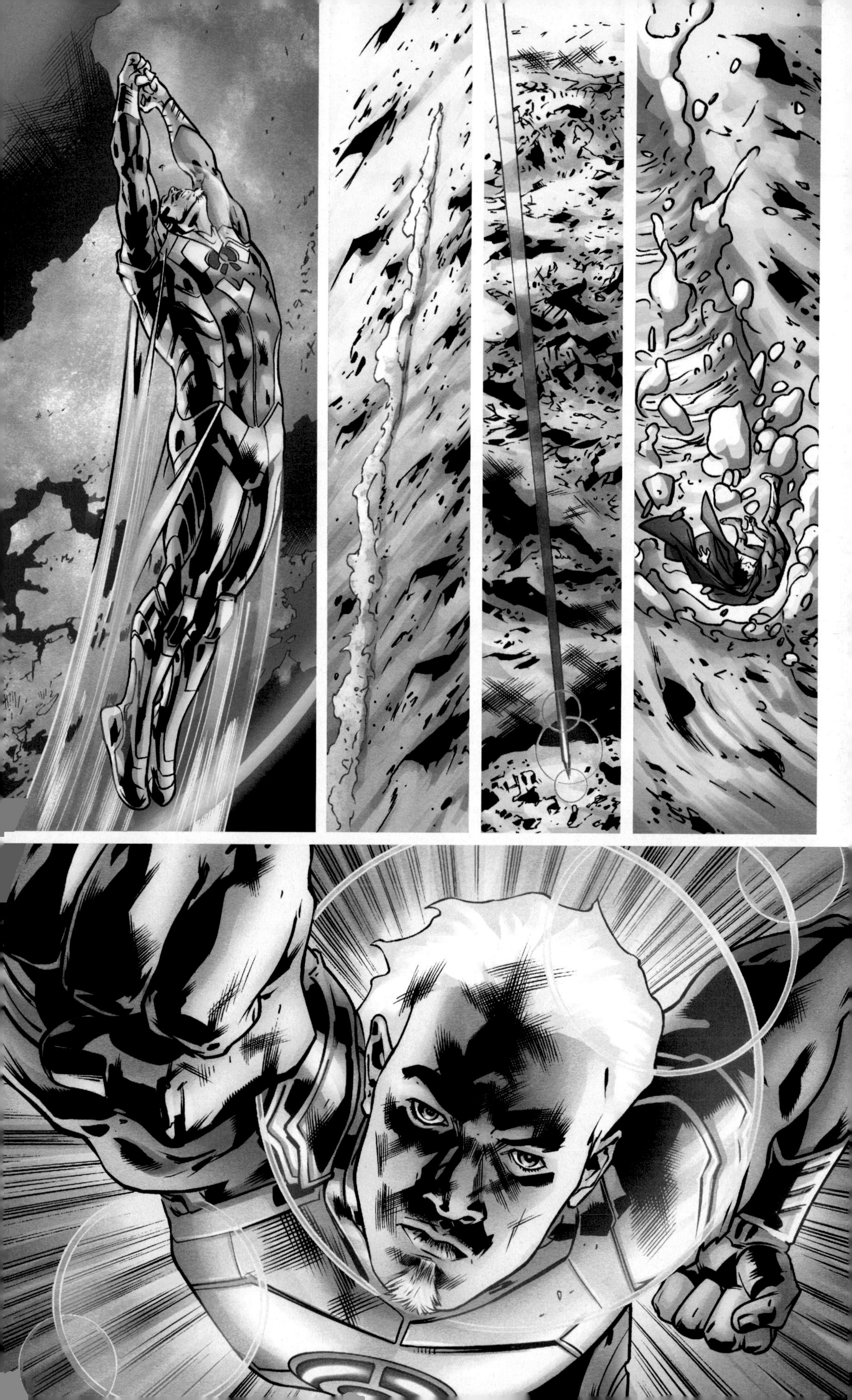

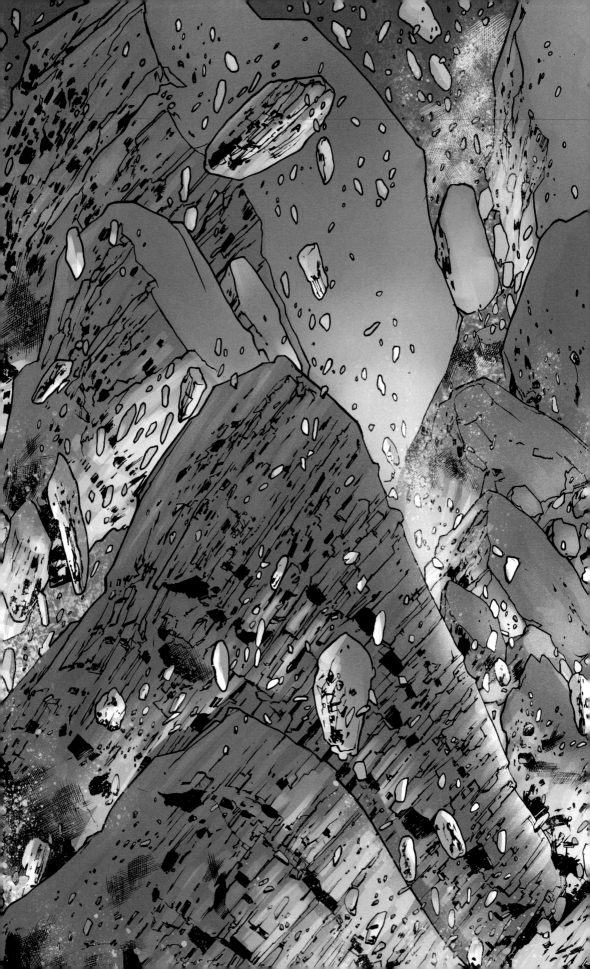

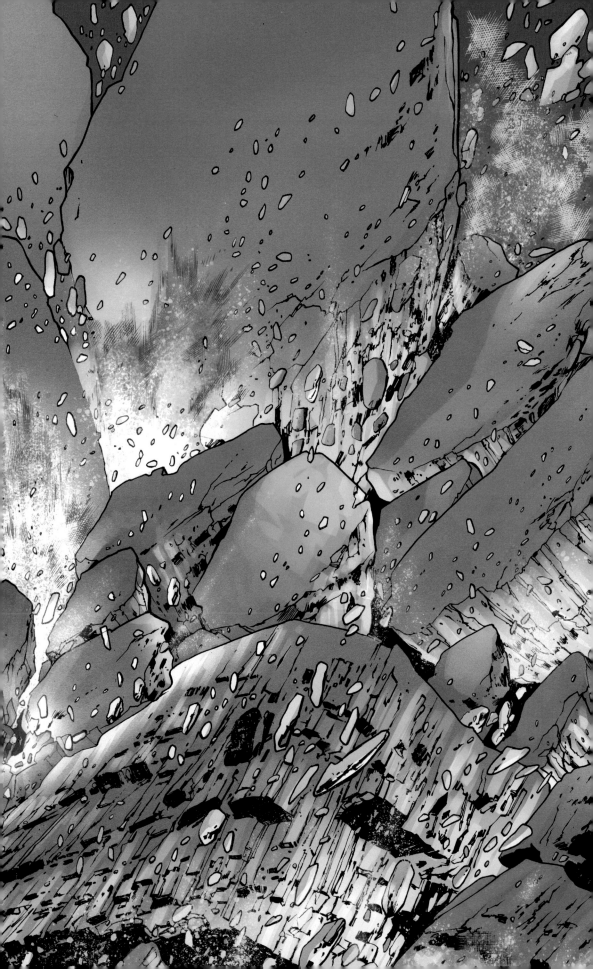

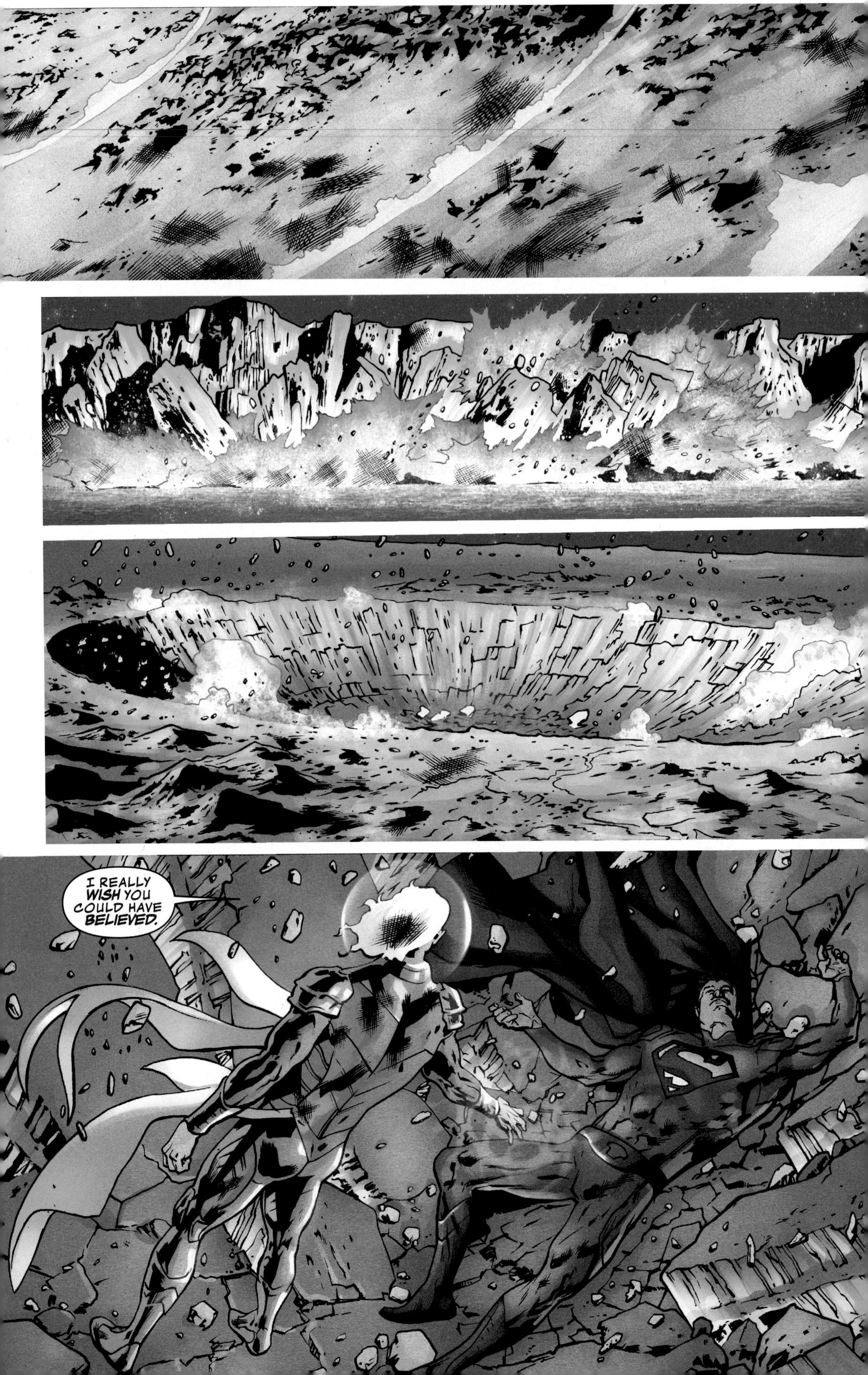
I REALLY WISH YOU COULD HAVE BELIEVED.

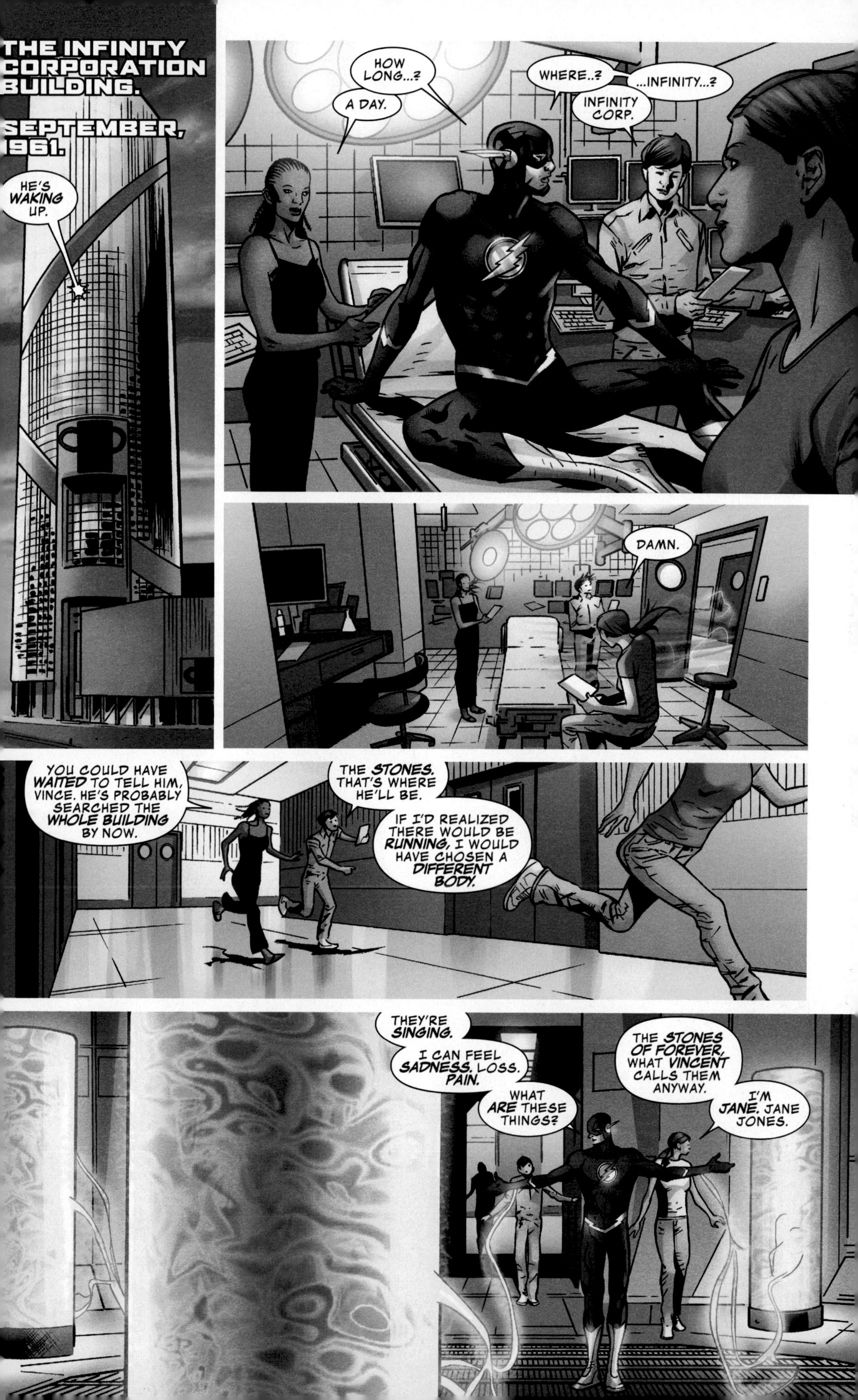
THE INFINITY CORPORATION BUILDING.
SEPTEMBER, 1961.
HE'S WAKING UP.
HOW LONG...?
A DAY.
WHERE..?
...INFINITY...?
INFINITY CORP.
DAMN.
YOU COULD HAVE WAITED TO TELL HIM, VINCE. HE'S PROBABLY SEARCHED THE WHOLE BUILDING BY NOW.
THE STONES. THAT'S WHERE HE'LL BE.
IF I'D REALIZED THERE WOULD BE RUNNING, I WOULD HAVE CHOSEN A DIFFERENT BODY.
THEY'RE SINGING.
I CAN FEEL SADNESS. LOSS. PAIN.
WHAT ARE THESE THINGS?
THE STONES OF FOREVER, WHAT VINCENT CALLS THEM ANYWAY.
I'M JANE. JANE JONES.

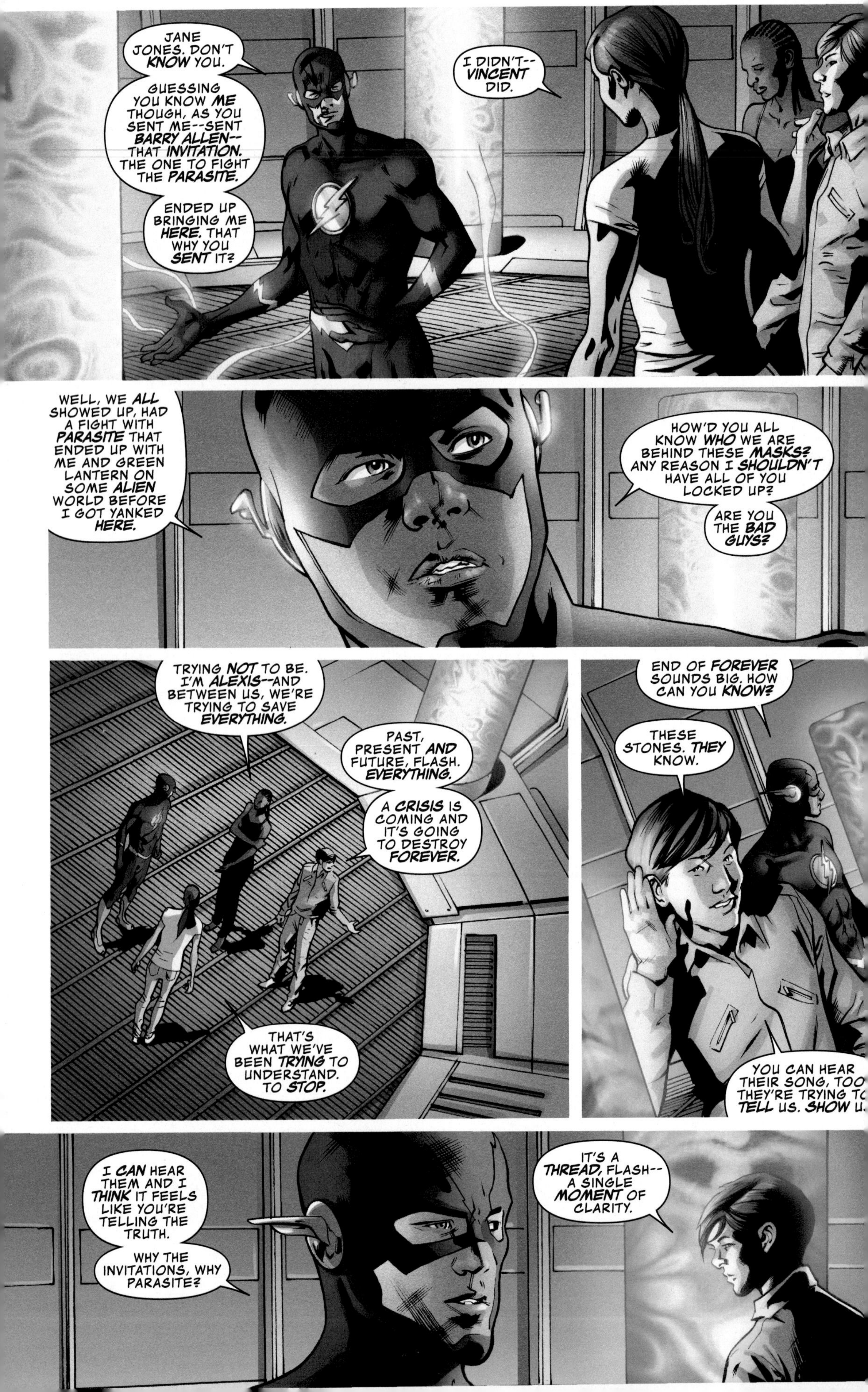
JANE JONES. DON'T KNOW YOU.
GUESSING YOU KNOW ME THOUGH, AS YOU SENT ME--SENT BARRY ALLEN--THAT INVITATION. THE ONE TO FIGHT THE PARASITE.
ENDED UP BRINGING ME HERE. THAT WHY YOU SENT IT?
I DIDN'T--VINCENT DID.
WELL, WE ALL SHOWED UP, HAD A FIGHT WITH PARASITE THAT ENDED UP WITH ME AND GREEN LANTERN ON SOME ALIEN WORLD BEFORE I GOT YANKED HERE.
HOW'D YOU ALL KNOW WHO WE ARE BEHIND THESE MASKS? ANY REASON I SHOULDN'T HAVE ALL OF YOU LOCKED UP?
ARE YOU THE BAD GUYS?
TRYING NOT TO BE. I'M ALEXIS--AND BETWEEN US, WE'RE TRYING TO SAVE EVERYTHING.
PAST, PRESENT AND FUTURE, FLASH. EVERYTHING.
A CRISIS IS COMING AND IT'S GOING TO DESTROY FOREVER.
THAT'S WHAT WE'VE BEEN TRYING TO UNDERSTAND. TO STOP.
END OF FOREVER SOUNDS BIG. HOW CAN YOU KNOW?
THESE STONES. THEY KNOW.
YOU CAN HEAR THEIR SONG, TOO THEY'RE TRYING TO TELL US. SHOW U
I CAN HEAR THEM AND I THINK IT FEELS LIKE YOU'RE TELLING THE TRUTH.
WHY THE INVITATIONS, WHY PARASITE?
IT'S A THREAD, FLASH--A SINGLE MOMENT OF CLARITY.

WE DON'T HAVE A FULL PICTURE. JUST THE CERTAINTY THAT THE END IS COMING.

IT'S LIKE TRYING TO SEE THE WHOLE TAPESTRY BY LOOKING AT A FEW RANDOM THREADS.

THE PARASITE, THE JUSTICE LEAGUE, SUPERMAN'S DEATH--ALL SEEMED TO BE CLEAR THREADS.

WAIT, SUPERMAN'S DEATH?

WE'VE ALREADY SPOKEN TO HIM ABOUT IT.

WE THOUGHT THAT IF WE PUT THOSE THREADS TOGETHER UNDER SOME CONTROLLED CIRCUMSTANCES, NOBODY WOULD BE HARMED AND WE MIGHT LEARN SOMETHING.

MIGHT GET JUST A GLIMPSE OF THE BIGGER PICTURE.

WELL, IT'S A THREAD THAT LED ME HERE AND LEFT LANTERN SOMEWHERE ELSE.

DO WE THINK THAT'S A COINCIDENCE?

ACTUALLY, DON'T ANSWER THAT.

I LOOKED OUTSIDE. LOOKS LIKE CHICAGO BUT NOT NOW. NOT MY NOW, ANYWAY.

1961.

THE STONES CAN DO THINGS WITH TIME.

RIGHT.

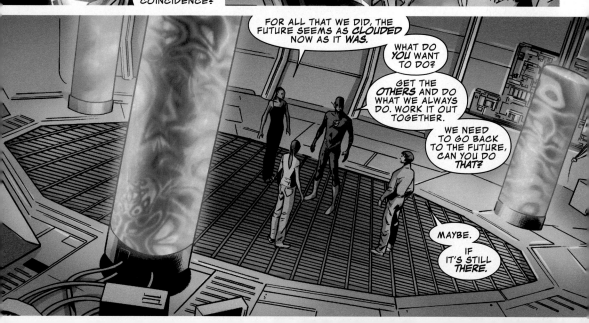

FOR ALL THAT WE DID, THE FUTURE SEEMS AS CLOUDED NOW AS IT WAS.

WHAT DO YOU WANT TO DO?

GET THE OTHERS AND DO WHAT WE ALWAYS DO. WORK IT OUT TOGETHER.

WE NEED TO GO BACK TO THE FUTURE, CAN YOU DO THAT?

MAYBE.

IF IT'S STILL THERE.

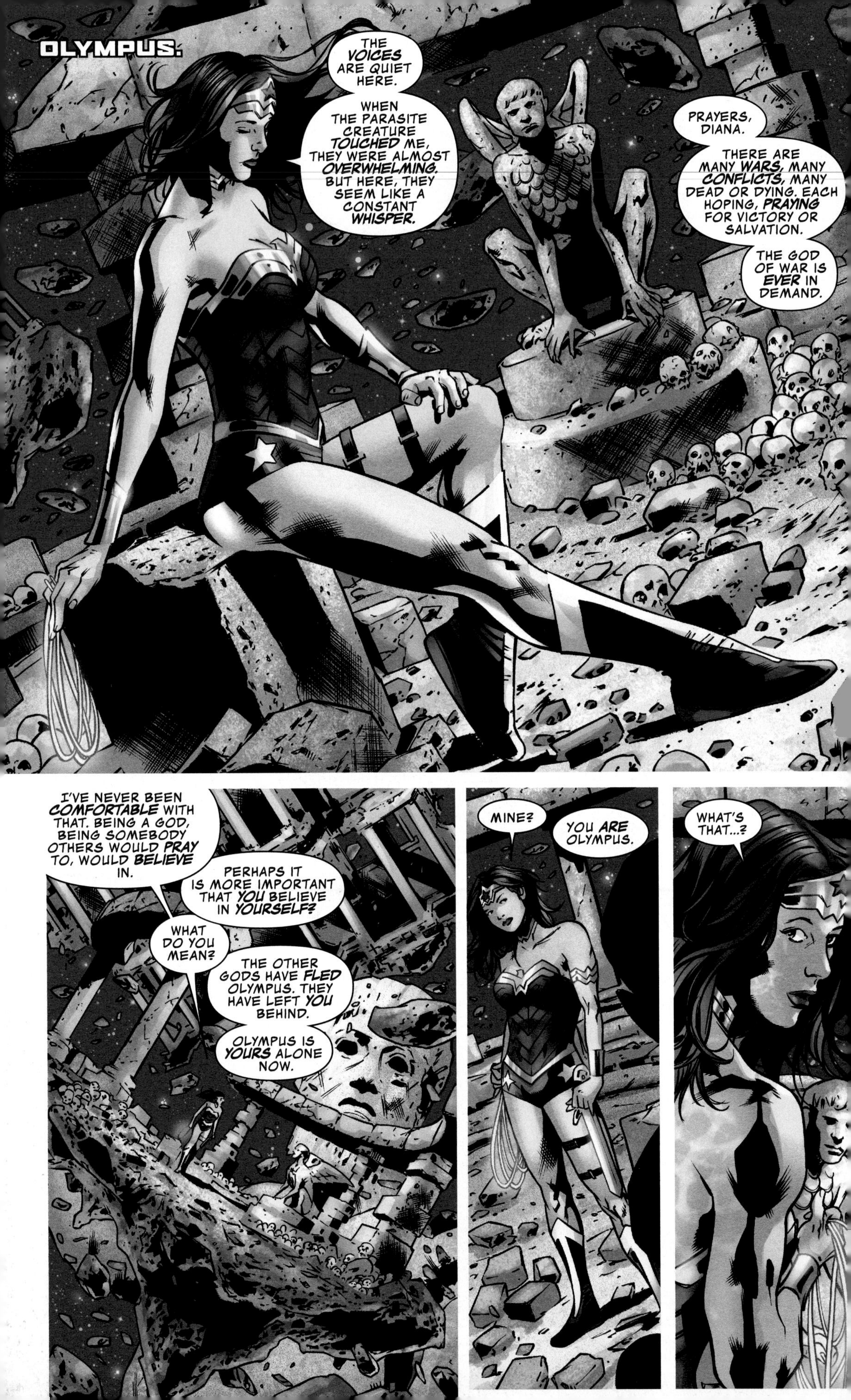
OLYMPUS.
THE VOICES ARE QUIET HERE.
WHEN THE PARASITE CREATURE TOUCHED ME, THEY WERE ALMOST OVERWHELMING. BUT HERE, THEY SEEM LIKE A CONSTANT WHISPER.
PRAYERS, DIANA.
THERE ARE MANY WARS, MANY CONFLICTS, MANY DEAD OR DYING. EACH HOPING, PRAYING FOR VICTORY OR SALVATION.
THE GOD OF WAR IS EVER IN DEMAND.
I'VE NEVER BEEN COMFORTABLE WITH THAT. BEING A GOD, BEING SOMEBODY OTHERS WOULD PRAY TO, WOULD BELIEVE IN.
PERHAPS IT IS MORE IMPORTANT THAT YOU BELIEVE IN YOURSELF?
WHAT DO YOU MEAN?
THE OTHER GODS HAVE FLED OLYMPUS. THEY HAVE LEFT YOU BEHIND.
OLYMPUS IS YOURS ALONE NOW.
MINE?
YOU ARE OLYMPUS.
WHAT'S THAT...?

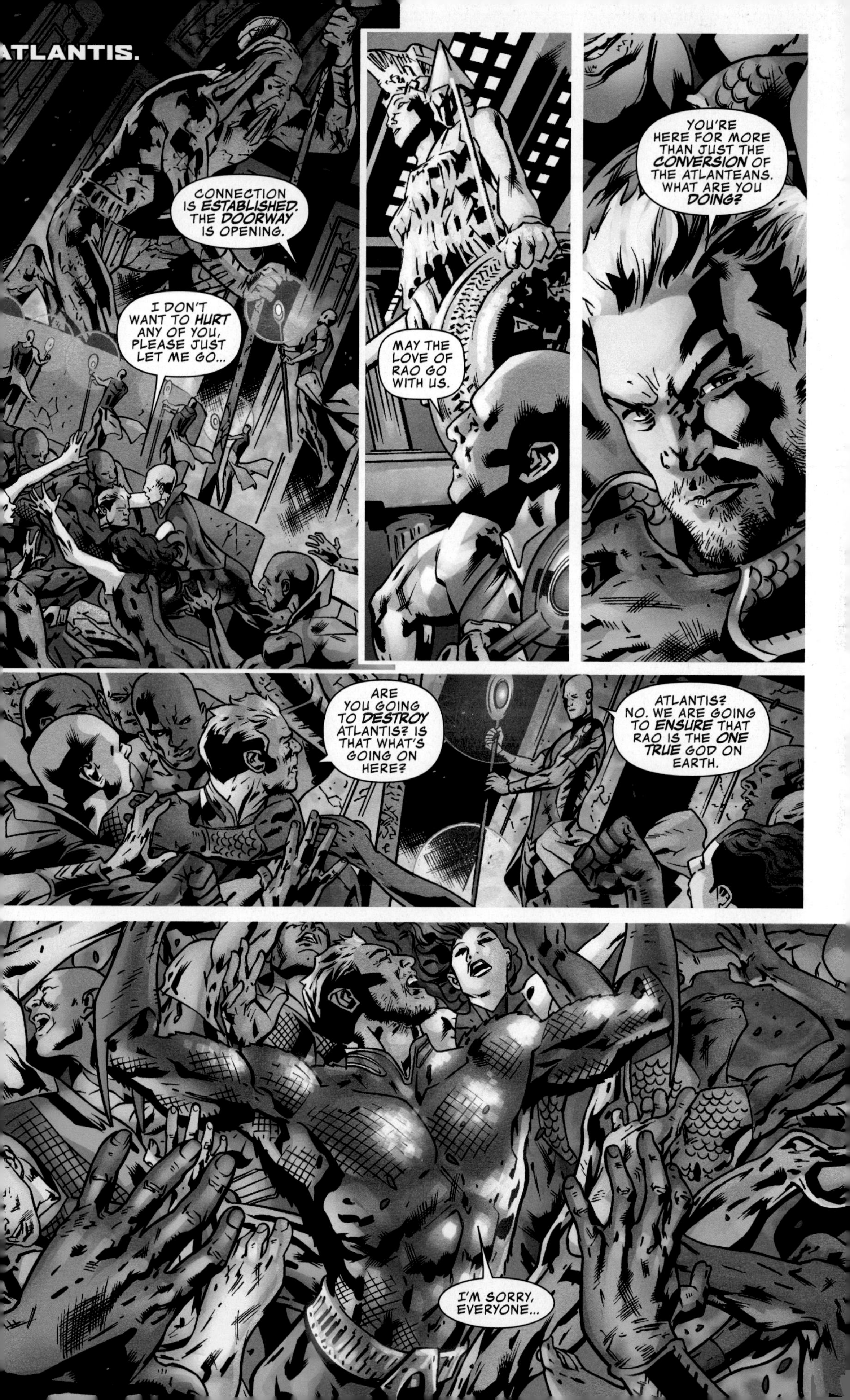
ATLANTIS.
CONNECTION IS ESTABLISHED. THE DOORWAY IS OPENING.
I DON'T WANT TO HURT ANY OF YOU, PLEASE JUST LET ME GO...
MAY THE LOVE OF RAO GO WITH US.
YOU'RE HERE FOR MORE THAN JUST THE CONVERSION OF THE ATLANTEANS. WHAT ARE YOU DOING?
ARE YOU GOING TO DESTROY ATLANTIS? IS THAT WHAT'S GOING ON HERE?
ATLANTIS? NO. WE ARE GOING TO ENSURE THAT RAO IS THE ONE TRUE GOD ON EARTH.
I'M SORRY, EVERYONE...

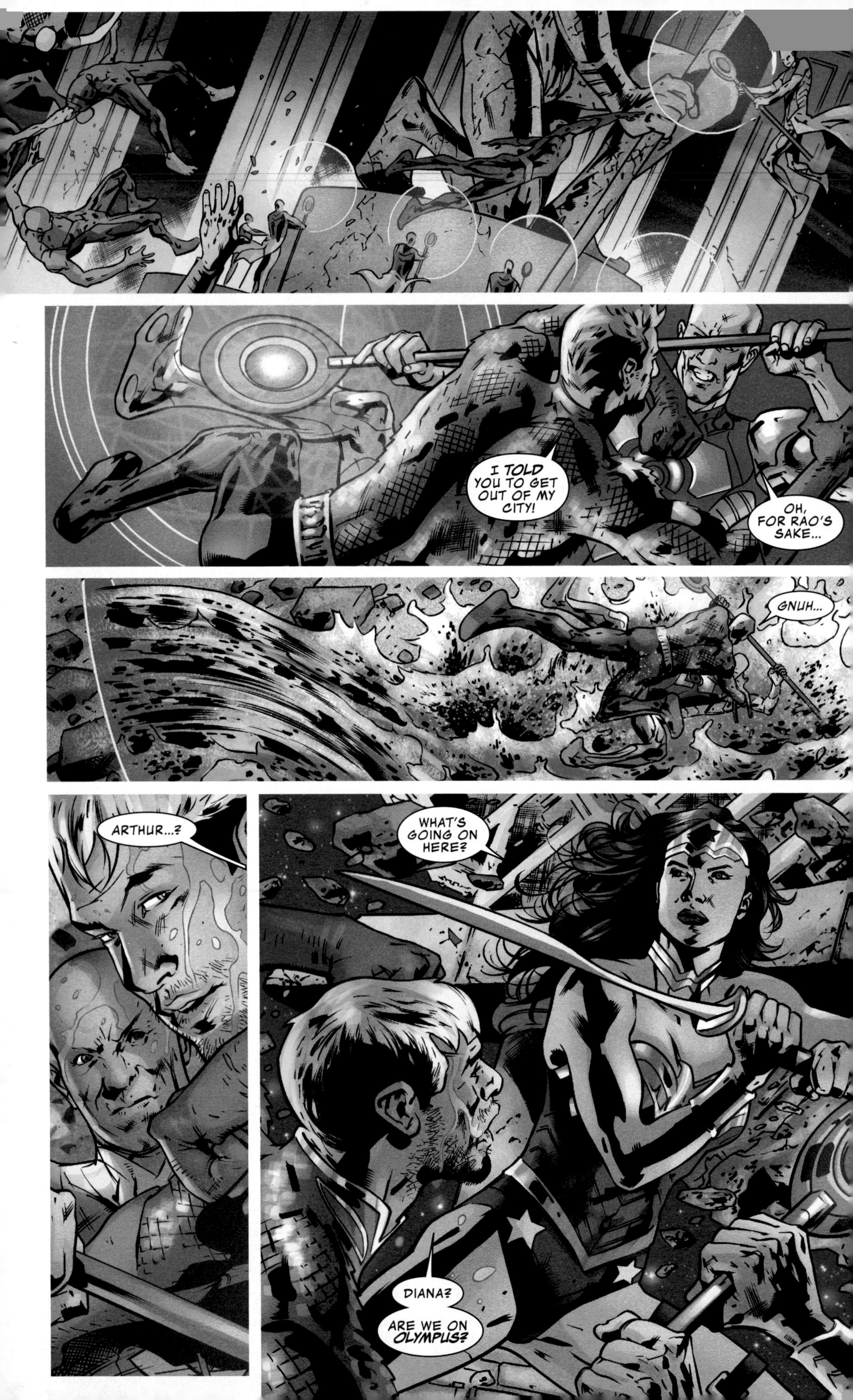
I TOLD YOU TO GET OUT OF MY CITY!
OH, FOR RAO'S SAKE...
GNUH...
ARTHUR...?
WHAT'S GOING ON HERE?
DIANA?
ARE WE ON OLYMPUS?

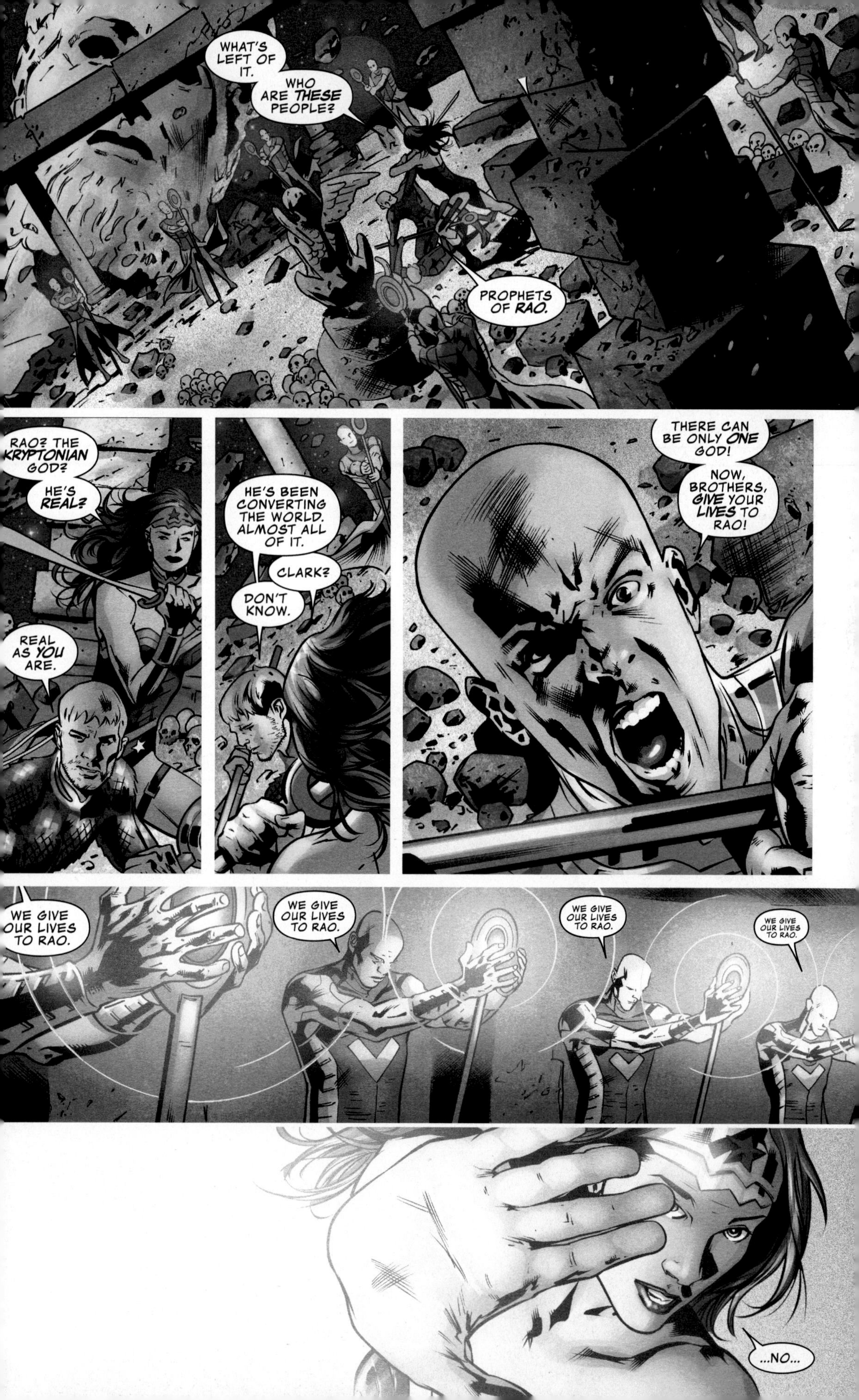
WHAT'S LEFT OF IT.
WHO ARE THESE PEOPLE?
PROPHETS OF RAO.
RAO? THE KRYPTONIAN GOD?
HE'S REAL?
REAL AS YOU ARE.
HE'S BEEN CONVERTING THE WORLD. ALMOST ALL OF IT.
CLARK?
DON'T KNOW.
THERE CAN BE ONLY ONE GOD!
NOW, BROTHERS, GIVE YOUR LIVES TO RAO!
WE GIVE OUR LIVES TO RAO.
WE GIVE OUR LIVES TO RAO.
WE GIVE OUR LIVES TO RAO.
WE GIVE OUR LIVES TO RAO.
...NO...

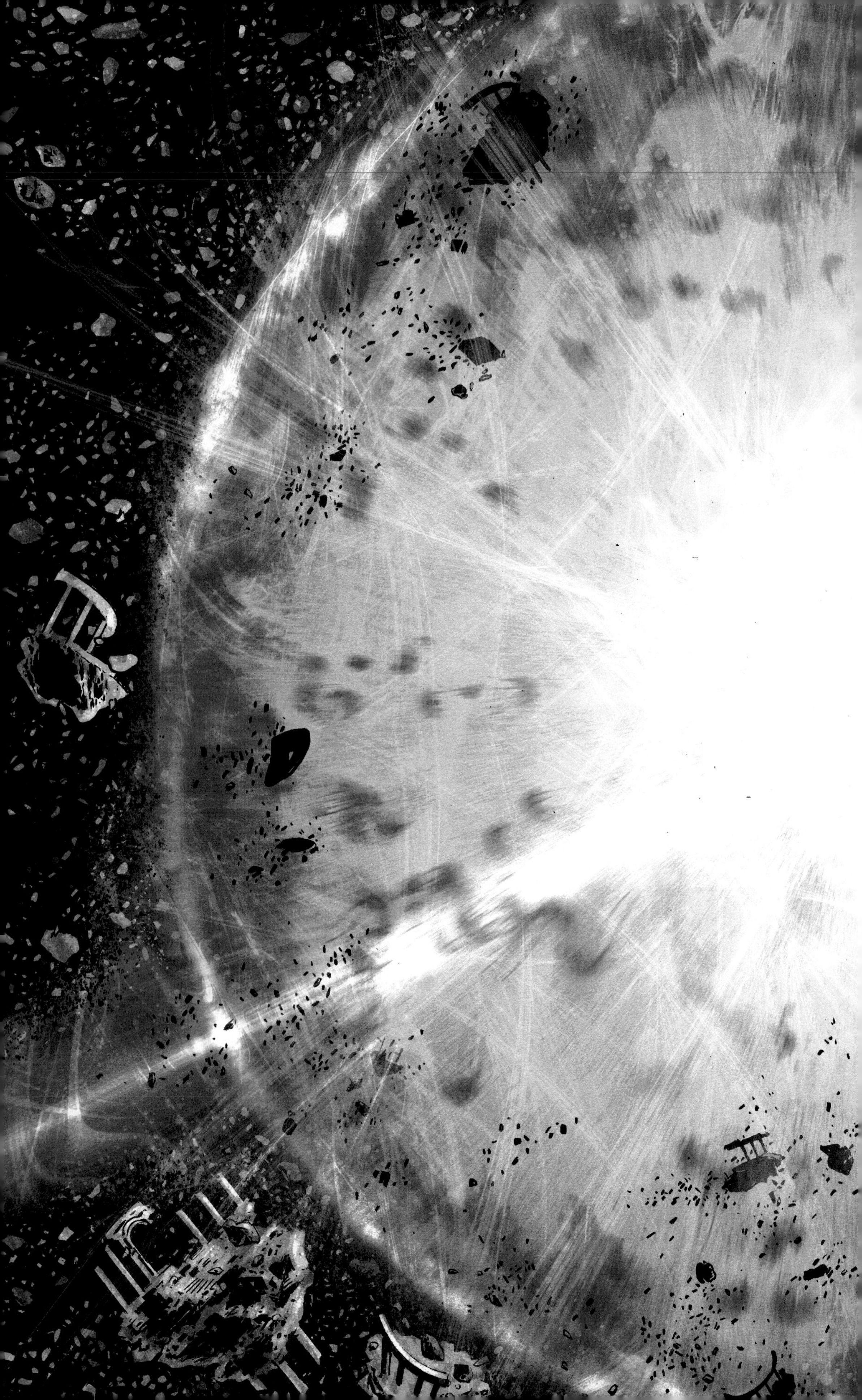

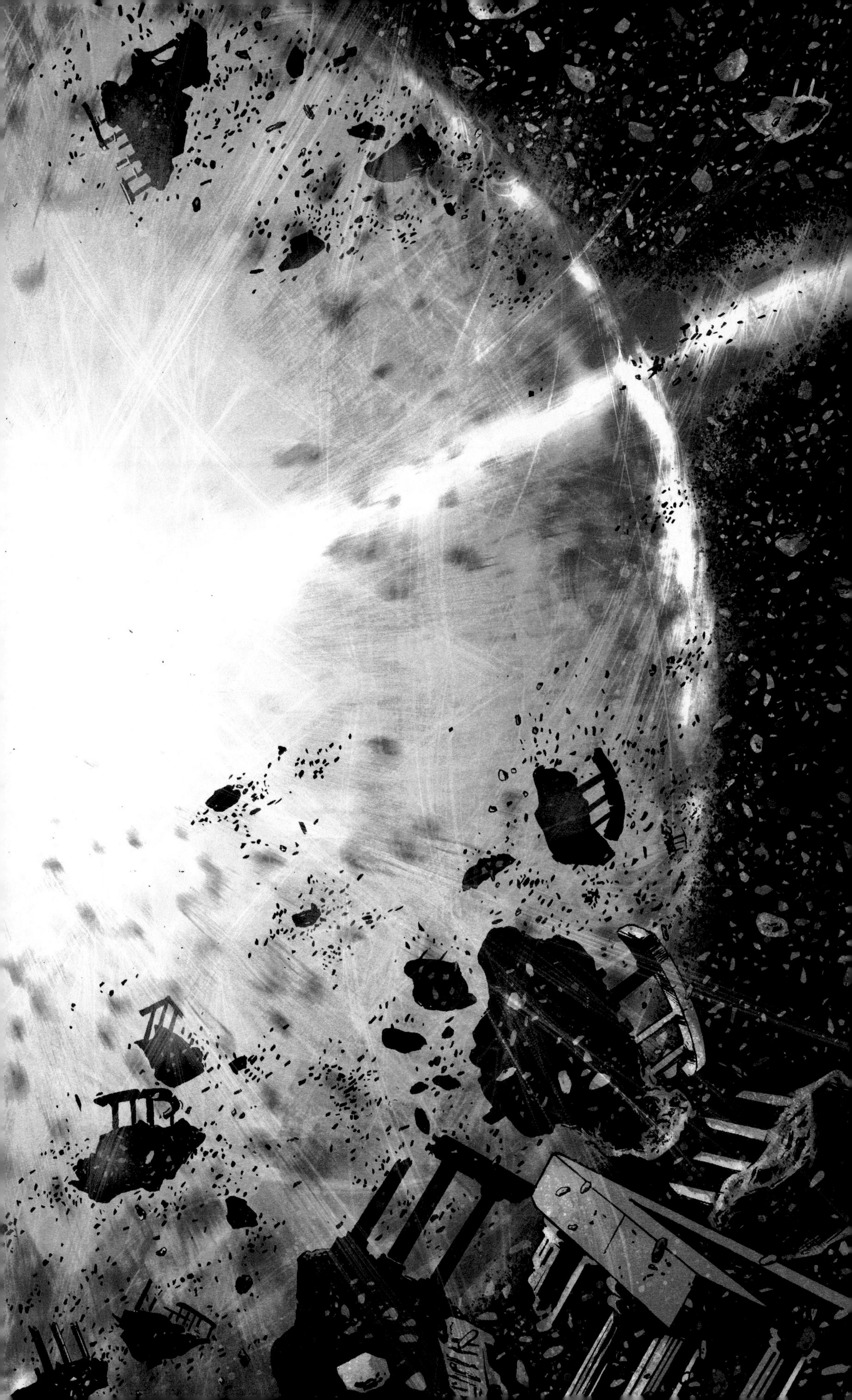

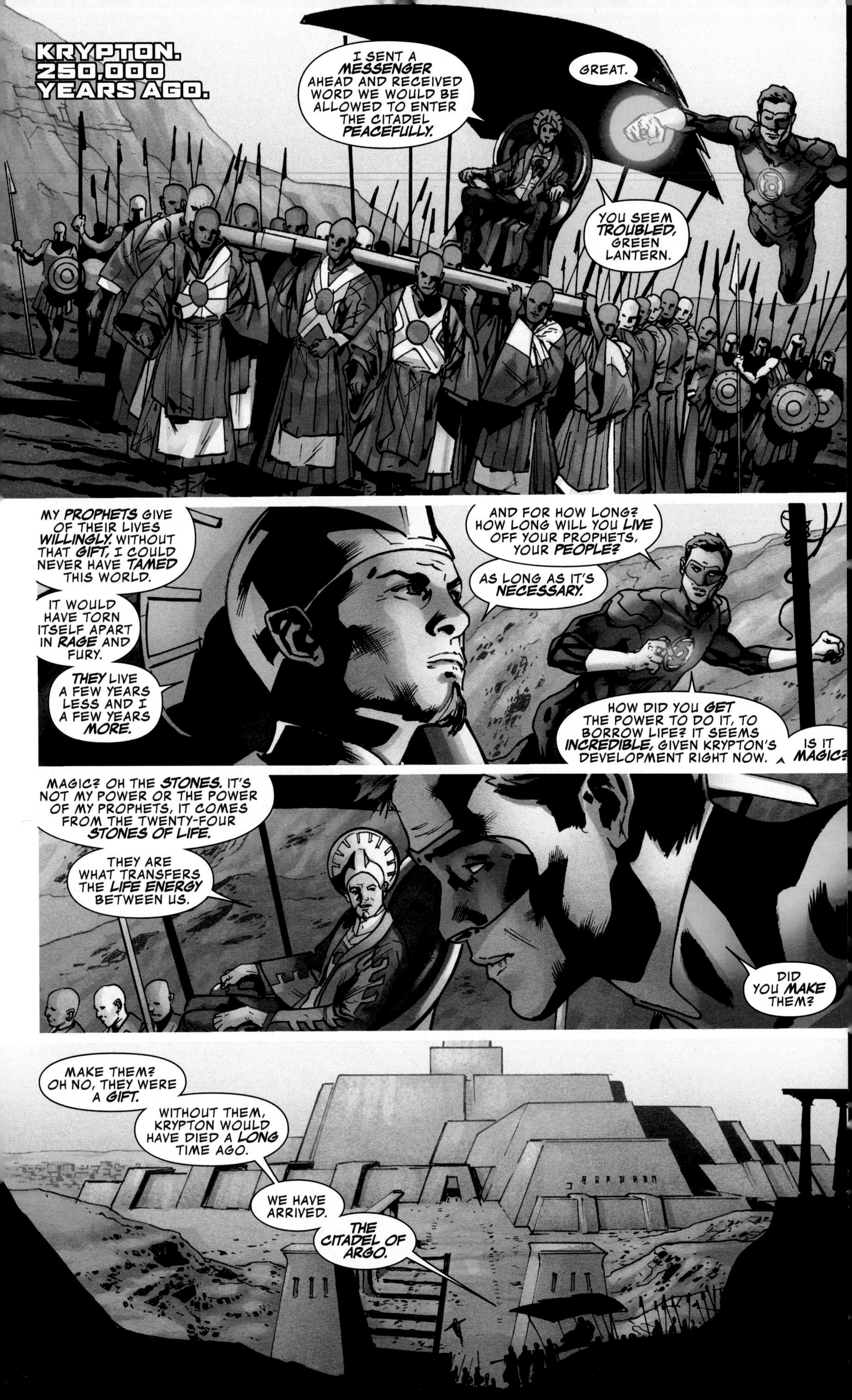

KRYPTON. 250,000 YEARS AGO.
I SENT A MESSENGER AHEAD AND RECEIVED WORD WE WOULD BE ALLOWED TO ENTER THE CITADEL PEACEFULLY.
GREAT.
YOU SEEM TROUBLED, GREEN LANTERN.
MY PROPHETS GIVE OF THEIR LIVES WILLINGLY. WITHOUT THAT GIFT, I COULD NEVER HAVE TAMED THIS WORLD.
IT WOULD HAVE TORN ITSELF APART IN RAGE AND FURY.
THEY LIVE A FEW YEARS LESS AND I A FEW YEARS MORE.
AND FOR HOW LONG? HOW LONG WILL YOU LIVE OFF YOUR PROPHETS, YOUR PEOPLE?
AS LONG AS IT'S NECESSARY.
HOW DID YOU GET THE POWER TO DO IT, TO BORROW LIFE? IT SEEMS INCREDIBLE, GIVEN KRYPTON'S DEVELOPMENT RIGHT NOW.
IS IT MAGIC?
MAGIC? OH THE STONES. IT'S NOT MY POWER OR THE POWER OF MY PROPHETS, IT COMES FROM THE TWENTY-FOUR STONES OF LIFE.
THEY ARE WHAT TRANSFERS THE LIFE ENERGY BETWEEN US.
DID YOU MAKE THEM?
MAKE THEM? OH NO, THEY WERE A GIFT.
WITHOUT THEM, KRYPTON WOULD HAVE DIED A LONG TIME AGO.
WE HAVE ARRIVED.
THE CITADEL OF ARGO.

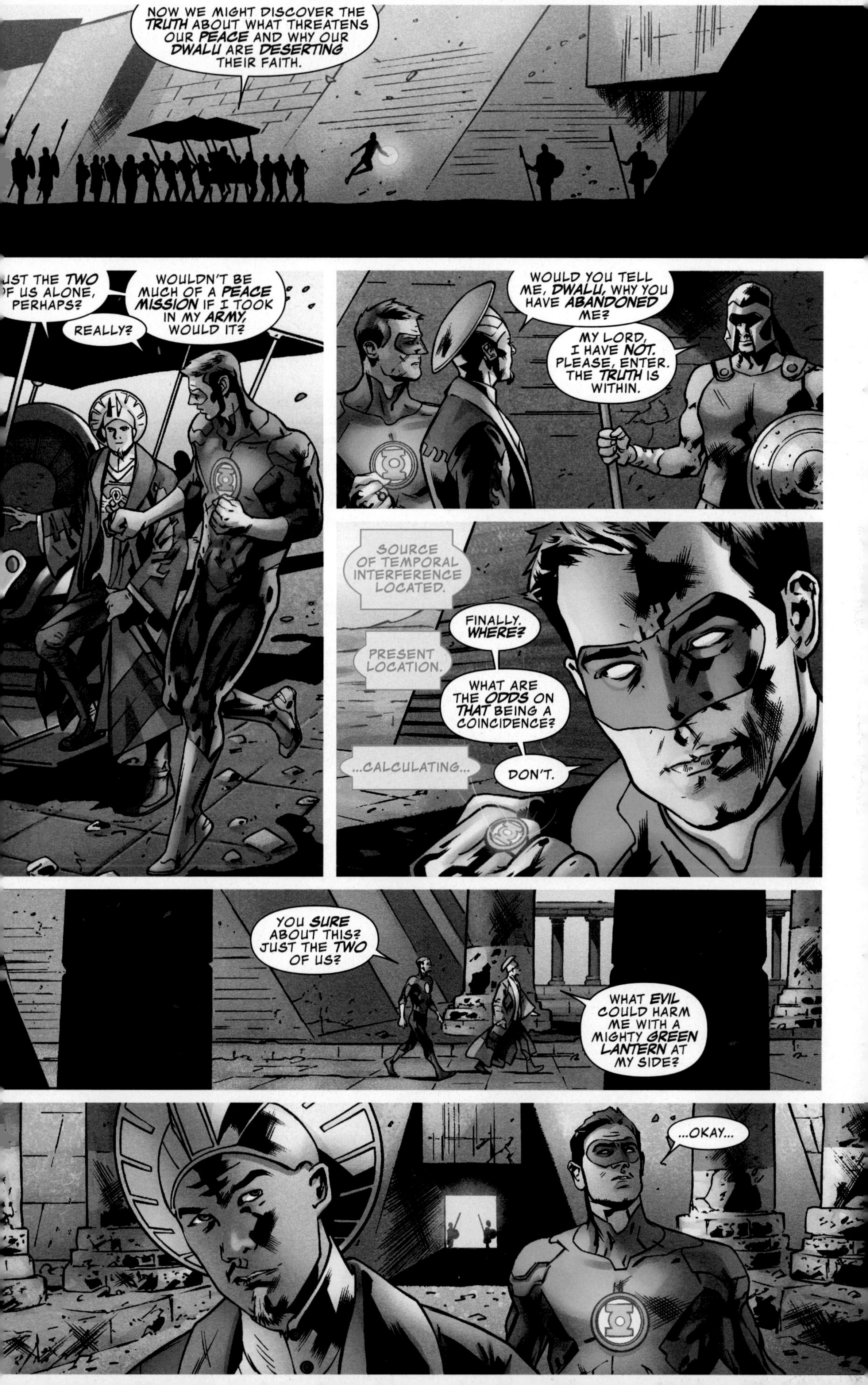
NOW WE MIGHT DISCOVER THE TRUTH ABOUT WHAT THREATENS OUR PEACE AND WHY OUR DWALU ARE DESERTING THEIR FAITH.
UST THE TWO F US ALONE, PERHAPS?
REALLY?
WOULDN'T BE MUCH OF A PEACE MISSION IF I TOOK IN MY ARMY, WOULD IT?
WOULD YOU TELL ME, DWALU, WHY YOU HAVE ABANDONED ME?
MY LORD, I HAVE NOT. PLEASE, ENTER. THE TRUTH IS WITHIN.
SOURCE OF TEMPORAL INTERFERENCE LOCATED.
FINALLY. WHERE?
PRESENT LOCATION.
WHAT ARE THE ODDS ON THAT BEING A COINCIDENCE?
...CALCULATING...
DON'T.
YOU SURE ABOUT THIS? JUST THE TWO OF US?
WHAT EVIL COULD HARM ME WITH A MIGHTY GREEN LANTERN AT MY SIDE?
...OKAY...

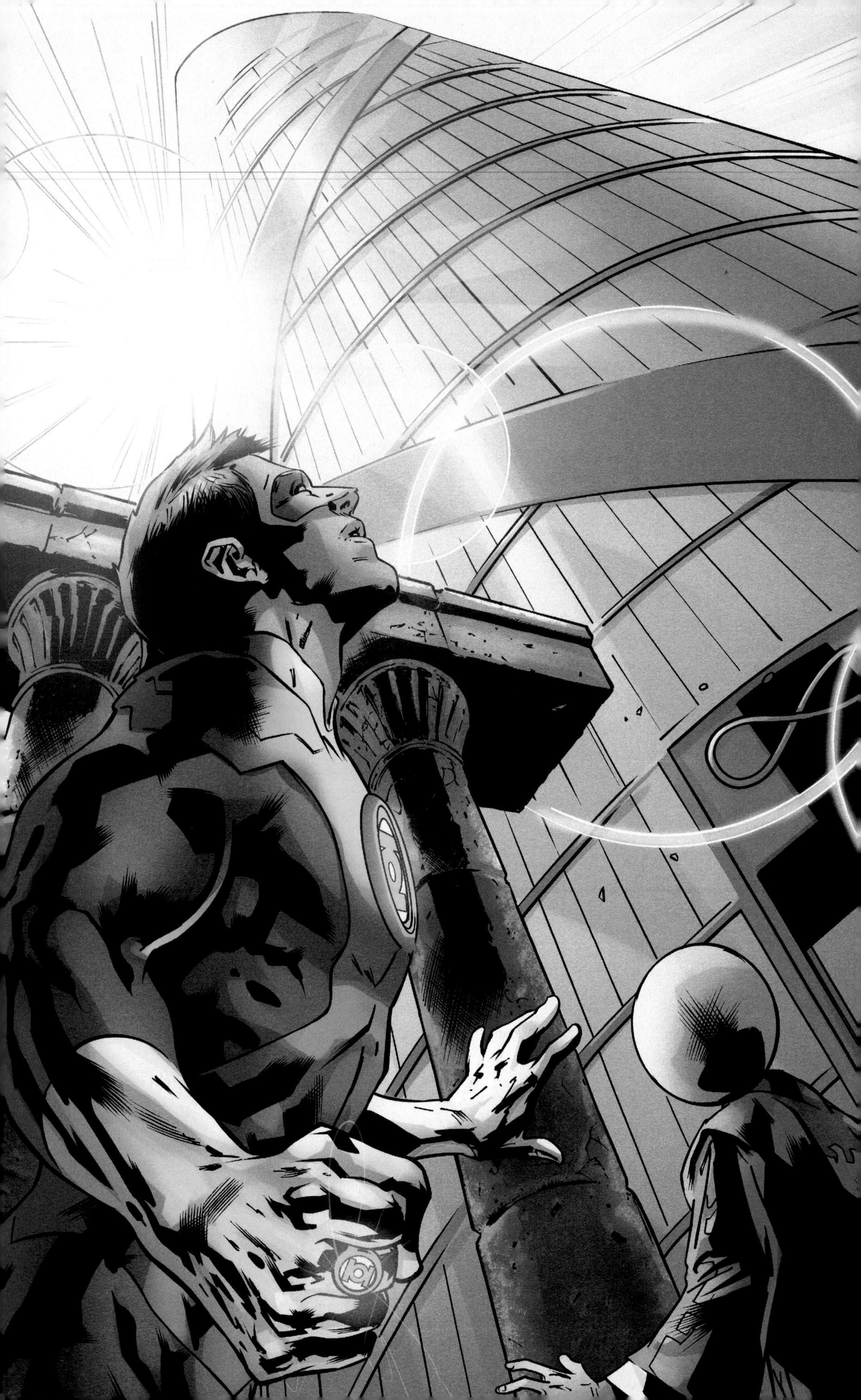

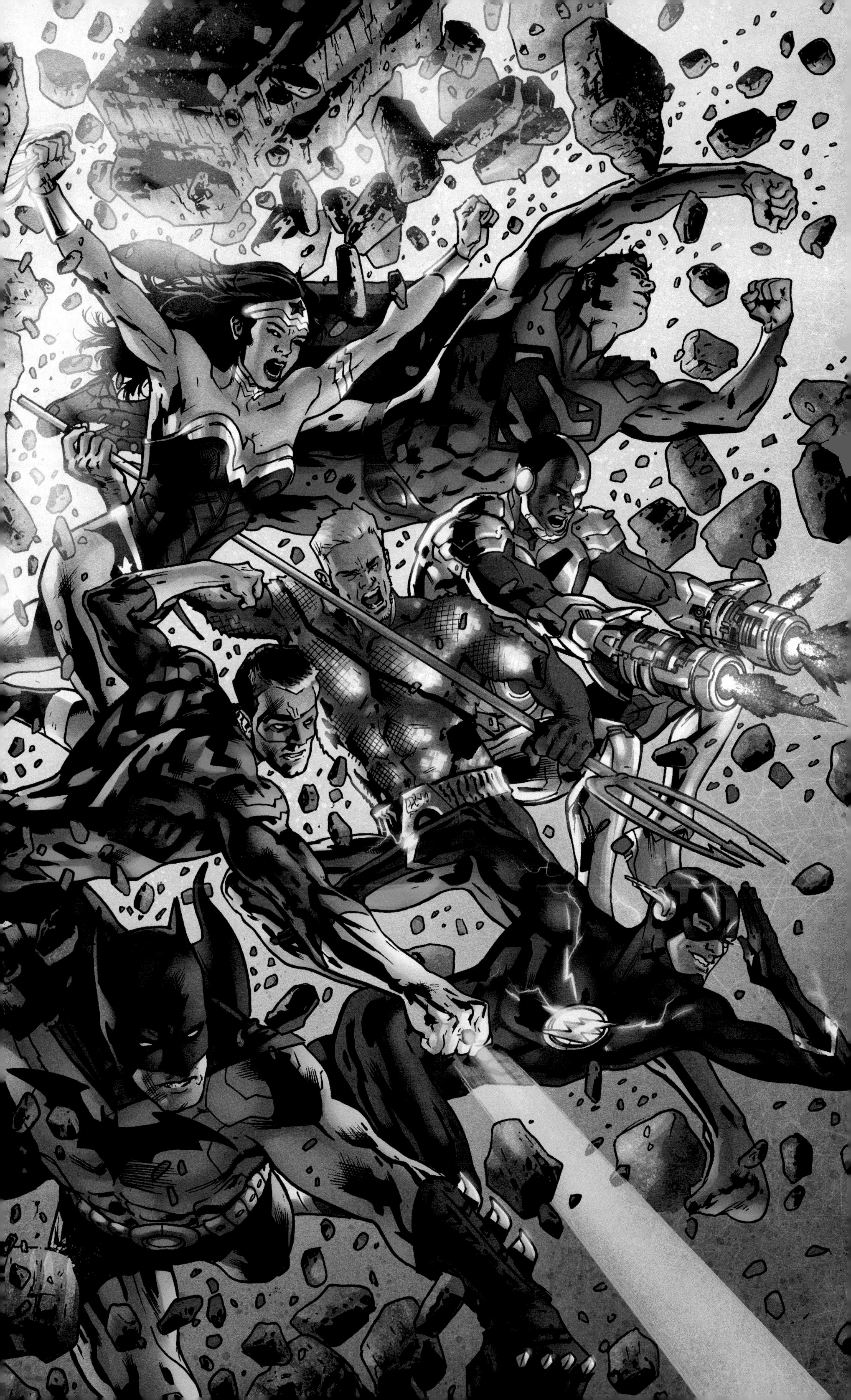

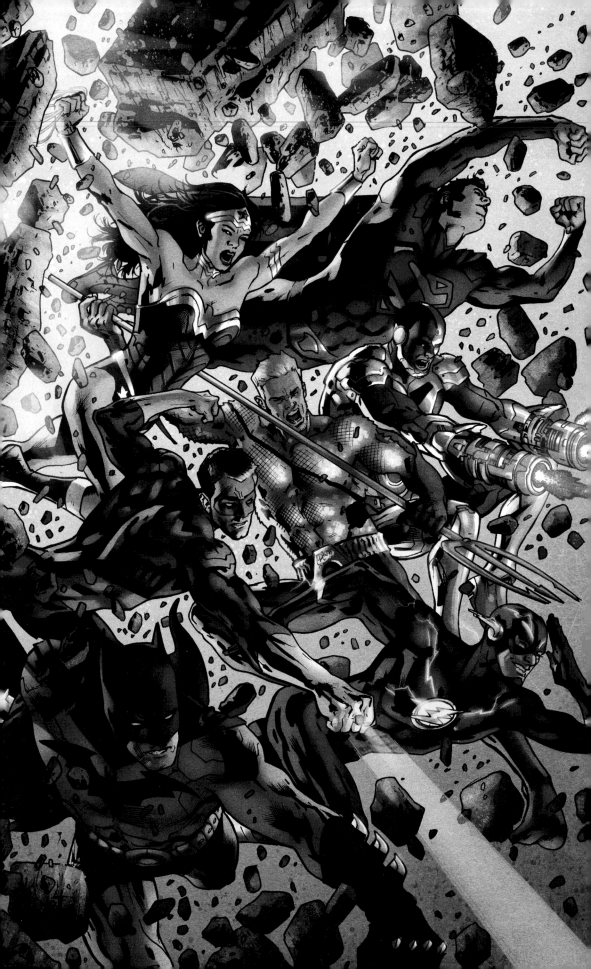

DC COMICS PRESENTS

THE JUSTICE LEAGUE OF AMERICA

POWER AND GLORY

PART SIX

BY BRYAN HITCH

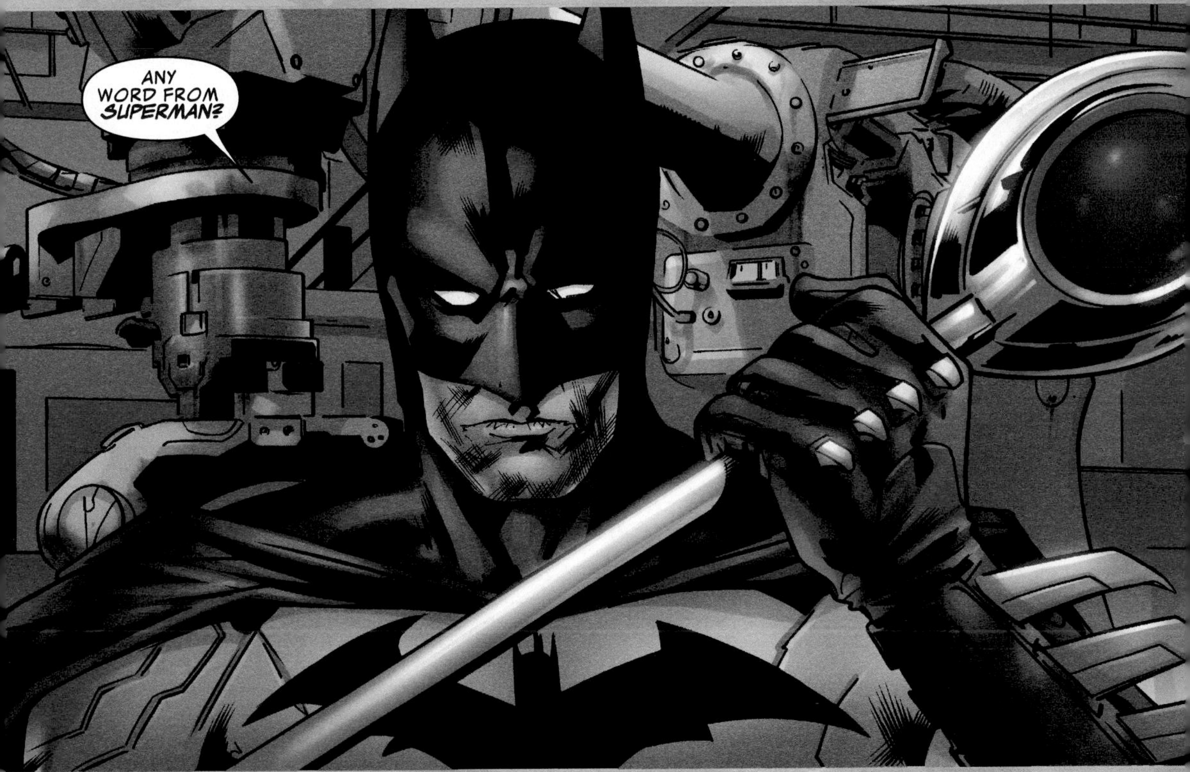
ANY WORD FROM SUPERMAN?

INKS BY DANIEL HENRIQUES,
WITH ANDREW CURRIE
COLORS BY ALEX SINCLAIR
LETTERS BY CHRIS ELIOPOULOS
ASSISTS BY AMEDEO TURTURRO
EDITS BY BRIAN CUNNINGHAM
COVER BY BRYAN HITCH AND ALEX SINCLAIR

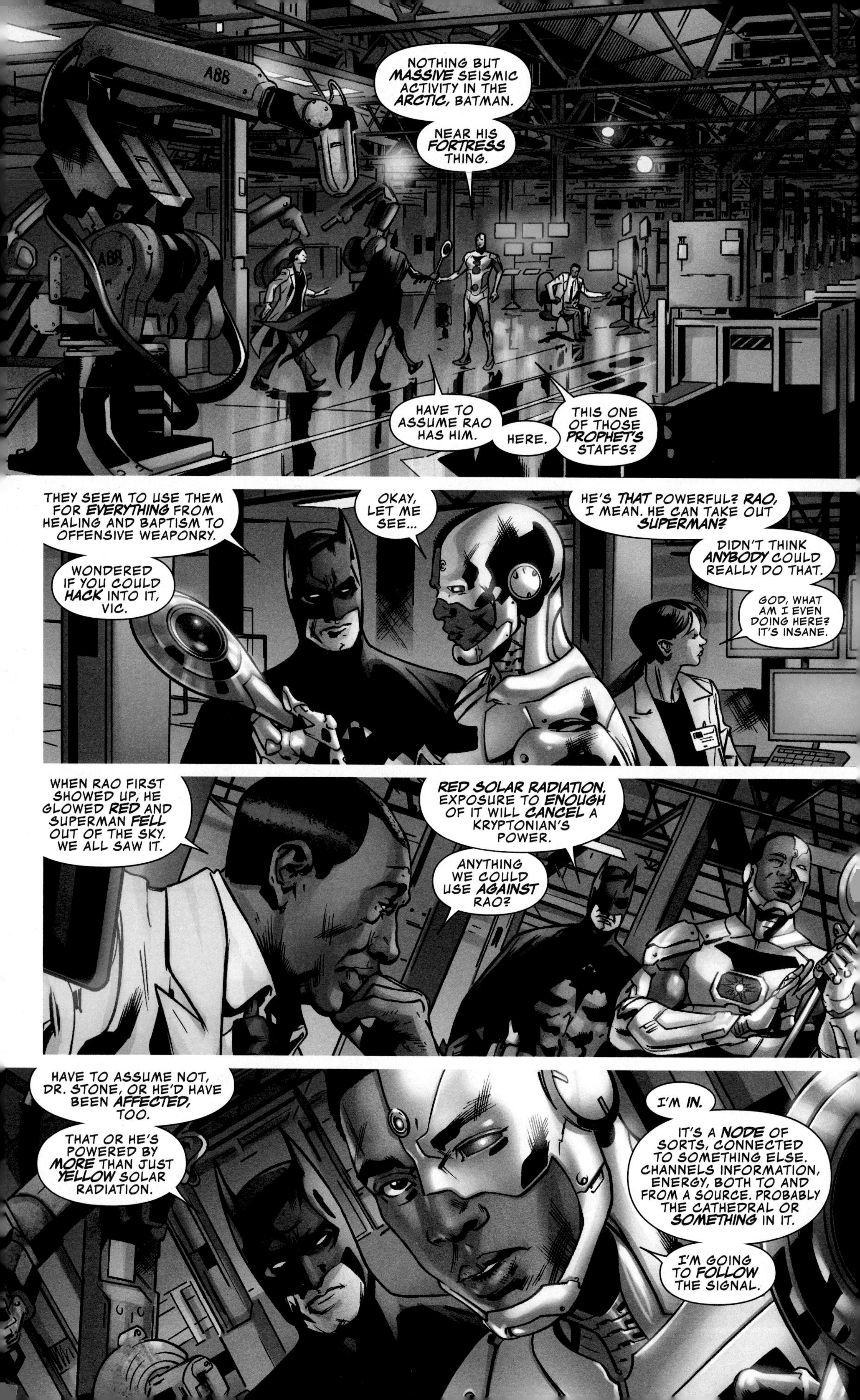
NOTHING BUT MASSIVE SEISMIC ACTIVITY IN THE ARCTIC, BATMAN.
NEAR HIS FORTRESS THING.
HAVE TO ASSUME RAO HAS HIM.
HERE.
THIS ONE OF THOSE PROPHET'S STAFFS?
THEY SEEM TO USE THEM FOR EVERYTHING FROM HEALING AND BAPTISM TO OFFENSIVE WEAPONRY.
WONDERED IF YOU COULD HACK INTO IT, VIC.
OKAY, LET ME SEE...
HE'S THAT POWERFUL? RAO, I MEAN. HE CAN TAKE OUT SUPERMAN?
DIDN'T THINK ANYBODY COULD REALLY DO THAT.
GOD, WHAT AM I EVEN DOING HERE? IT'S INSANE.
WHEN RAO FIRST SHOWED UP, HE GLOWED RED AND SUPERMAN FELL OUT OF THE SKY. WE ALL SAW IT.
RED SOLAR RADIATION. EXPOSURE TO ENOUGH OF IT WILL CANCEL A KRYPTONIAN'S POWER.
ANYTHING WE COULD USE AGAINST RAO?
HAVE TO ASSUME NOT, DR. STONE, OR HE'D HAVE BEEN AFFECTED, TOO.
THAT OR HE'S POWERED BY MORE THAN JUST YELLOW SOLAR RADIATION.
I'M IN.
IT'S A NODE OF SORTS, CONNECTED TO SOMETHING ELSE. CHANNELS INFORMATION, ENERGY, BOTH TO AND FROM A SOURCE. PROBABLY THE CATHEDRAL OR SOMETHING IN IT.
I'M GOING TO FOLLOW THE SIGNAL.

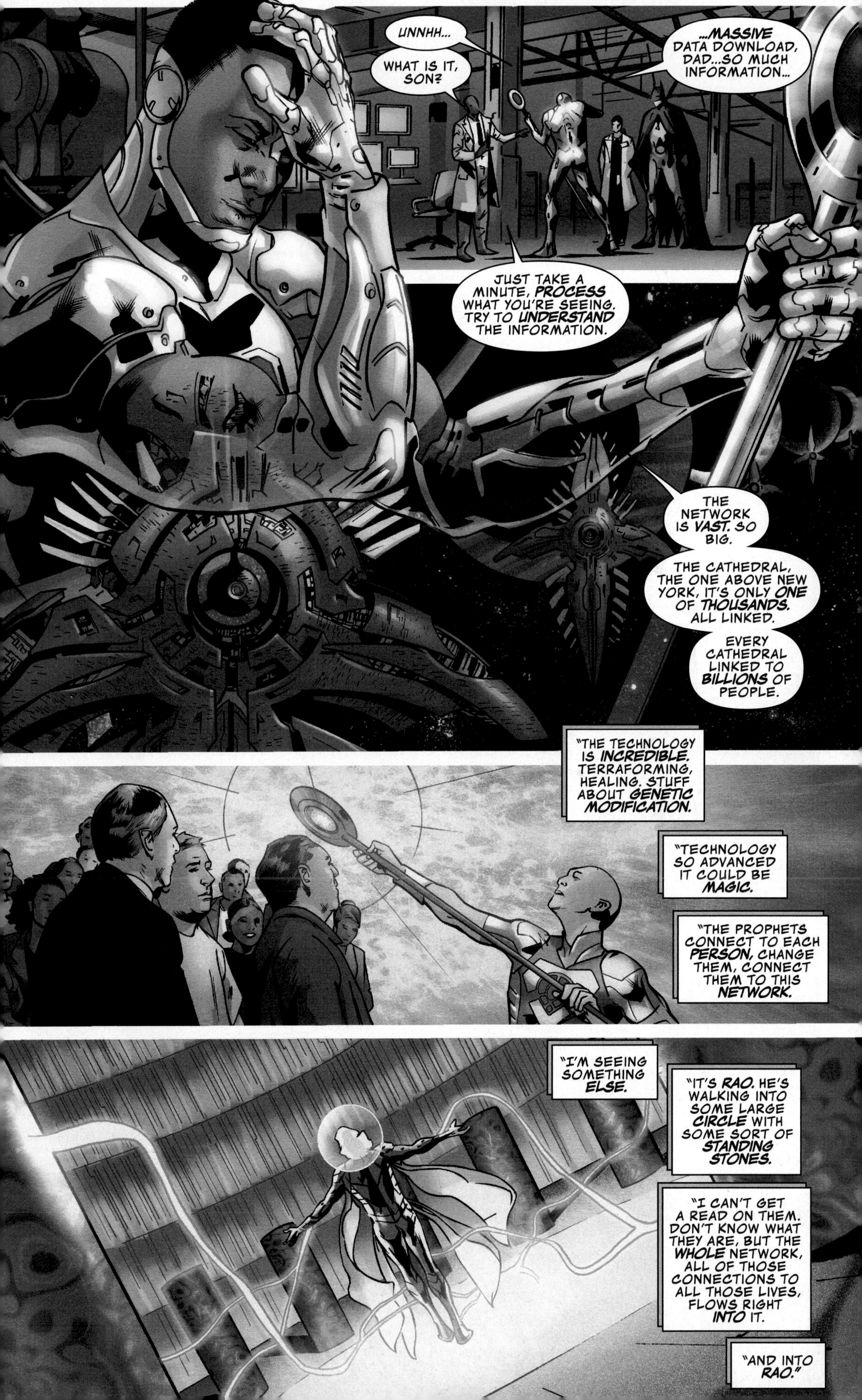
UNNHH...
WHAT IS IT, SON?
...MASSIVE DATA DOWNLOAD, DAD...SO MUCH INFORMATION...
JUST TAKE A MINUTE, PROCESS WHAT YOU'RE SEEING. TRY TO UNDERSTAND THE INFORMATION.
THE NETWORK IS VAST. SO BIG.
THE CATHEDRAL, THE ONE ABOVE NEW YORK, IT'S ONLY ONE OF THOUSANDS. ALL LINKED.
EVERY CATHEDRAL LINKED TO BILLIONS OF PEOPLE.
"THE TECHNOLOGY IS INCREDIBLE. TERRAFORMING, HEALING. STUFF ABOUT GENETIC MODIFICATION.
"TECHNOLOGY SO ADVANCED IT COULD BE MAGIC.
"THE PROPHETS CONNECT TO EACH PERSON, CHANGE THEM, CONNECT THEM TO THIS NETWORK.
"I'M SEEING SOMETHING ELSE.
"IT'S RAO. HE'S WALKING INTO SOME LARGE CIRCLE WITH SOME SORT OF STANDING STONES.
"I CAN'T GET A READ ON THEM. DON'T KNOW WHAT THEY ARE, BUT THE WHOLE NETWORK, ALL OF THOSE CONNECTIONS TO ALL THOSE LIVES, FLOWS RIGHT INTO IT.
"AND INTO RAO."

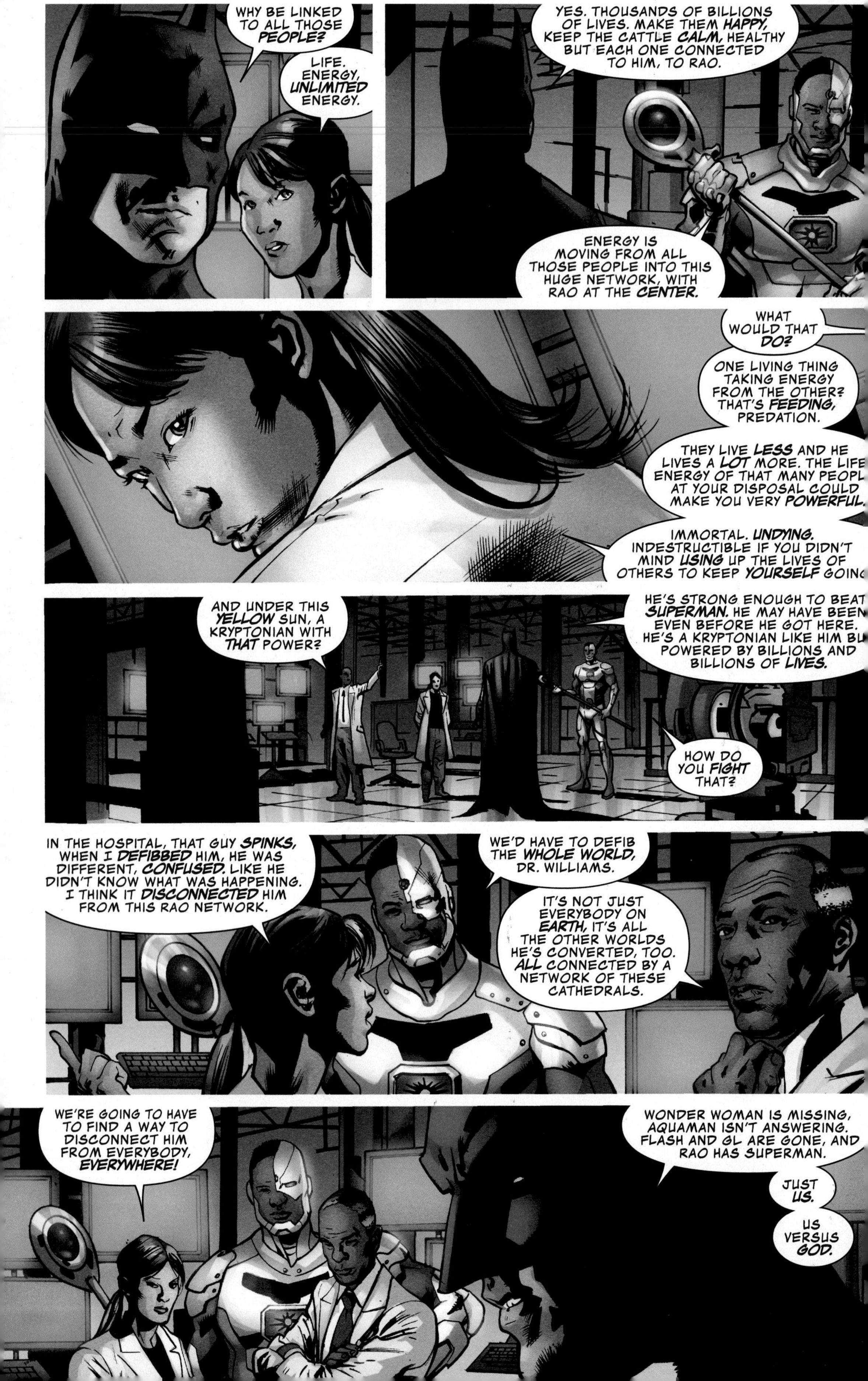
WHY BE LINKED TO ALL THOSE PEOPLE?
LIFE. ENERGY, UNLIMITED ENERGY.
YES. THOUSANDS OF BILLIONS OF LIVES. MAKE THEM HAPPY, KEEP THE CATTLE CALM, HEALTHY BUT EACH ONE CONNECTED TO HIM, TO RAO.
ENERGY IS MOVING FROM ALL THOSE PEOPLE INTO THIS HUGE NETWORK, WITH RAO AT THE CENTER.
WHAT WOULD THAT DO?
ONE LIVING THING TAKING ENERGY FROM THE OTHER? THAT'S FEEDING, PREDATION.
THEY LIVE LESS AND HE LIVES A LOT MORE. THE LIFE ENERGY OF THAT MANY PEOPL AT YOUR DISPOSAL COULD MAKE YOU VERY POWERFUL.
IMMORTAL. UNDYING. INDESTRUCTIBLE IF YOU DIDN'T MIND USING UP THE LIVES OF OTHERS TO KEEP YOURSELF GOIN
AND UNDER THIS YELLOW SUN, A KRYPTONIAN WITH THAT POWER?
HE'S STRONG ENOUGH TO BEAT SUPERMAN. HE MAY HAVE BEEN EVEN BEFORE HE GOT HERE. HE'S A KRYPTONIAN LIKE HIM BU POWERED BY BILLIONS AND BILLIONS OF LIVES.
HOW DO YOU FIGHT THAT?
IN THE HOSPITAL, THAT GUY SPINKS, WHEN I DEFIBBED HIM, HE WAS DIFFERENT, CONFUSED. LIKE HE DIDN'T KNOW WHAT WAS HAPPENING. I THINK IT DISCONNECTED HIM FROM THIS RAO NETWORK.
WE'D HAVE TO DEFIB THE WHOLE WORLD, DR. WILLIAMS.
IT'S NOT JUST EVERYBODY ON EARTH, IT'S ALL THE OTHER WORLDS HE'S CONVERTED, TOO. ALL CONNECTED BY A NETWORK OF THESE CATHEDRALS.
WE'RE GOING TO HAVE TO FIND A WAY TO DISCONNECT HIM FROM EVERYBODY, EVERYWHERE!
WONDER WOMAN IS MISSING, AQUAMAN ISN'T ANSWERING. FLASH AND GL ARE GONE, AND RAO HAS SUPERMAN.
JUST US.
US VERSUS GOD.

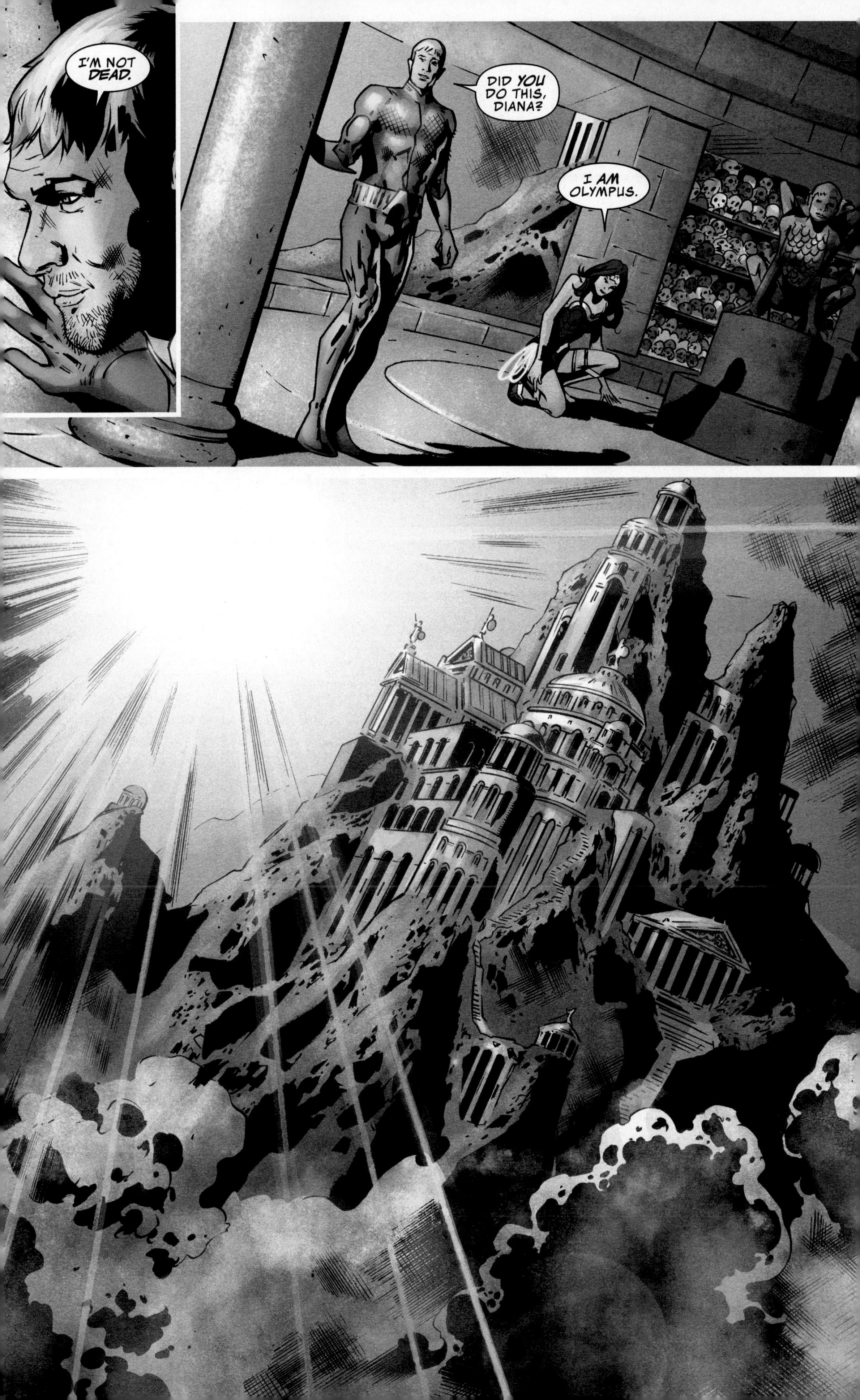
I'M NOT DEAD.
DID YOU DO THIS, DIANA?
I AM OLYMPUS.

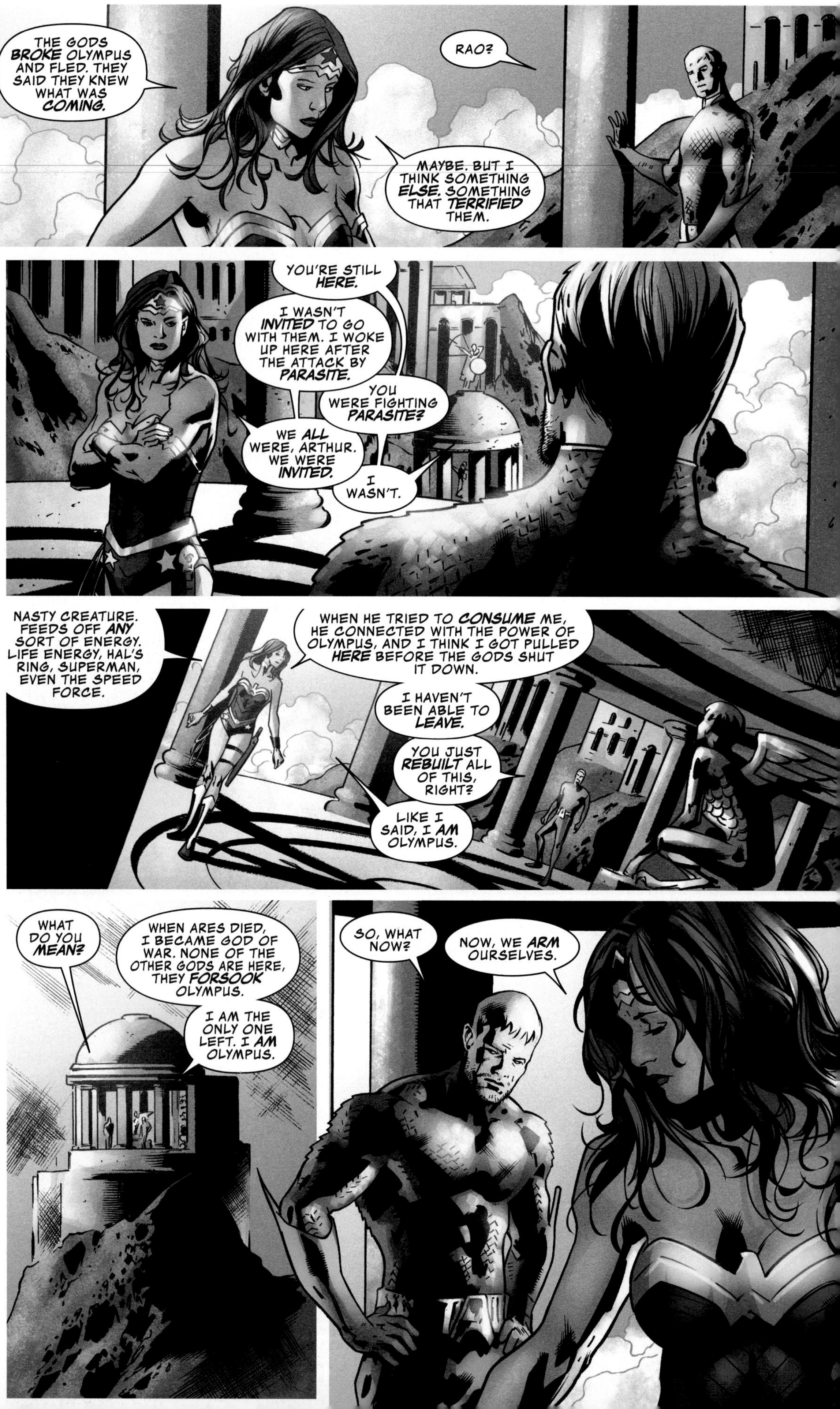

THE GODS BROKE OLYMPUS AND FLED. THEY SAID THEY KNEW WHAT WAS COMING.
RAO?
MAYBE. BUT I THINK SOMETHING ELSE. SOMETHING THAT TERRIFIED THEM.
YOU'RE STILL HERE.
I WASN'T INVITED TO GO WITH THEM. I WOKE UP HERE AFTER THE ATTACK BY PARASITE.
YOU WERE FIGHTING PARASITE?
WE ALL WERE, ARTHUR. WE WERE INVITED.
I WASN'T.
NASTY CREATURE. FEEDS OFF ANY SORT OF ENERGY. LIFE ENERGY, HAL'S RING, SUPERMAN, EVEN THE SPEED FORCE.
WHEN HE TRIED TO CONSUME ME, HE CONNECTED WITH THE POWER OF OLYMPUS, AND I THINK I GOT PULLED HERE BEFORE THE GODS SHUT IT DOWN.
I HAVEN'T BEEN ABLE TO LEAVE.
YOU JUST REBUILT ALL OF THIS, RIGHT?
LIKE I SAID, I AM OLYMPUS.
WHAT DO YOU MEAN?
WHEN ARES DIED, I BECAME GOD OF WAR. NONE OF THE OTHER GODS ARE HERE, THEY FORSOOK OLYMPUS.
I AM THE ONLY ONE LEFT. I AM OLYMPUS.
SO, WHAT NOW?
NOW, WE ARM OURSELVES.

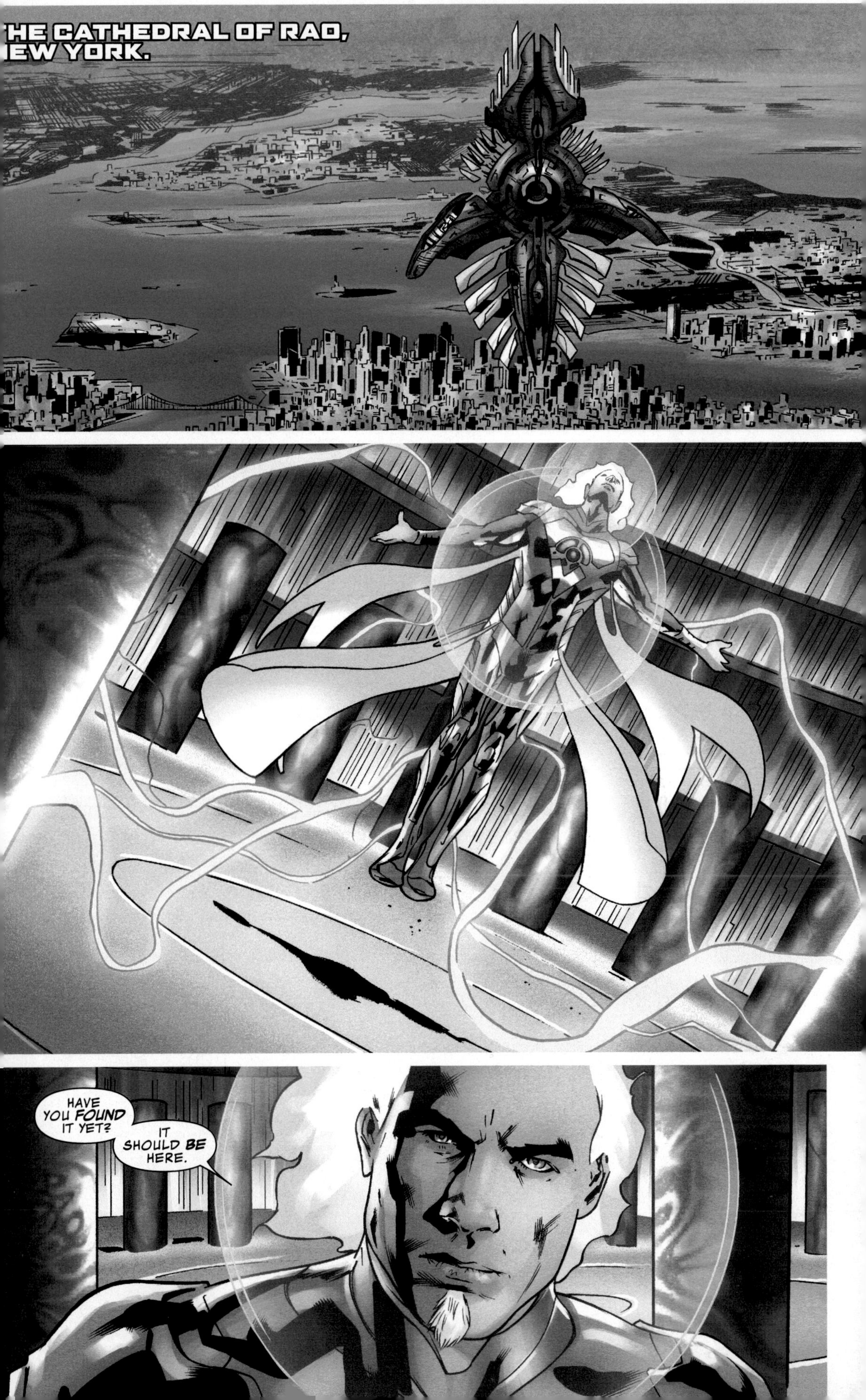
HE CATHEDRAL OF RAO,
EW YORK.
HAVE YOU FOUND IT YET?
IT SHOULD BE HERE.

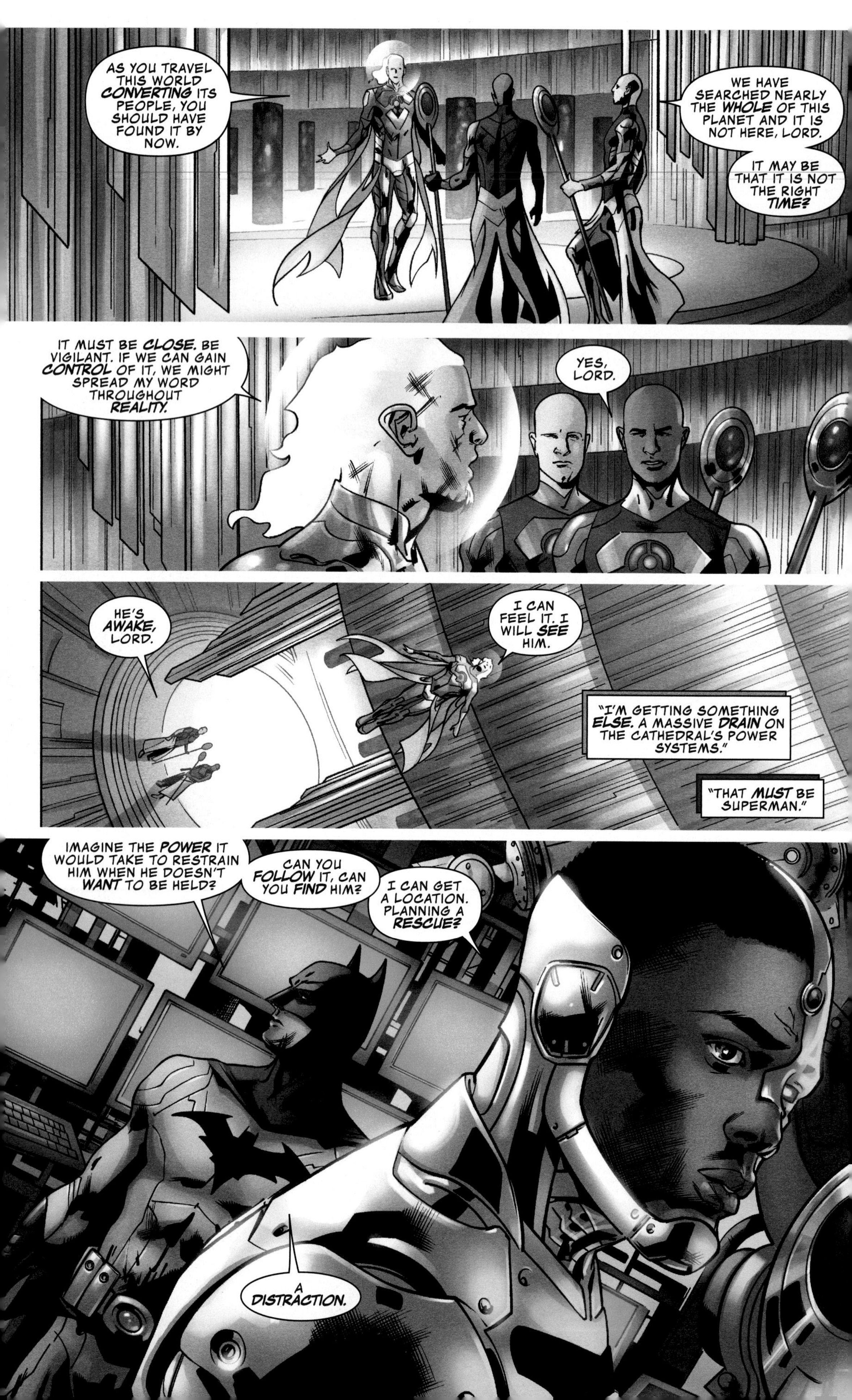
AS YOU TRAVEL THIS WORLD CONVERTING ITS PEOPLE, YOU SHOULD HAVE FOUND IT BY NOW.
WE HAVE SEARCHED NEARLY THE WHOLE OF THIS PLANET AND IT IS NOT HERE, LORD.
IT MAY BE THAT IT IS NOT THE RIGHT TIME?
IT MUST BE CLOSE. BE VIGILANT. IF WE CAN GAIN CONTROL OF IT, WE MIGHT SPREAD MY WORD THROUGHOUT REALITY.
YES, LORD.
HE'S AWAKE, LORD.
I CAN FEEL IT. I WILL SEE HIM.
"I'M GETTING SOMETHING ELSE. A MASSIVE DRAIN ON THE CATHEDRAL'S POWER SYSTEMS."
"THAT MUST BE SUPERMAN."
IMAGINE THE POWER IT WOULD TAKE TO RESTRAIN HIM WHEN HE DOESN'T WANT TO BE HELD?
CAN YOU FOLLOW IT, CAN YOU FIND HIM?
I CAN GET A LOCATION. PLANNING A RESCUE?
A DISTRACTION.

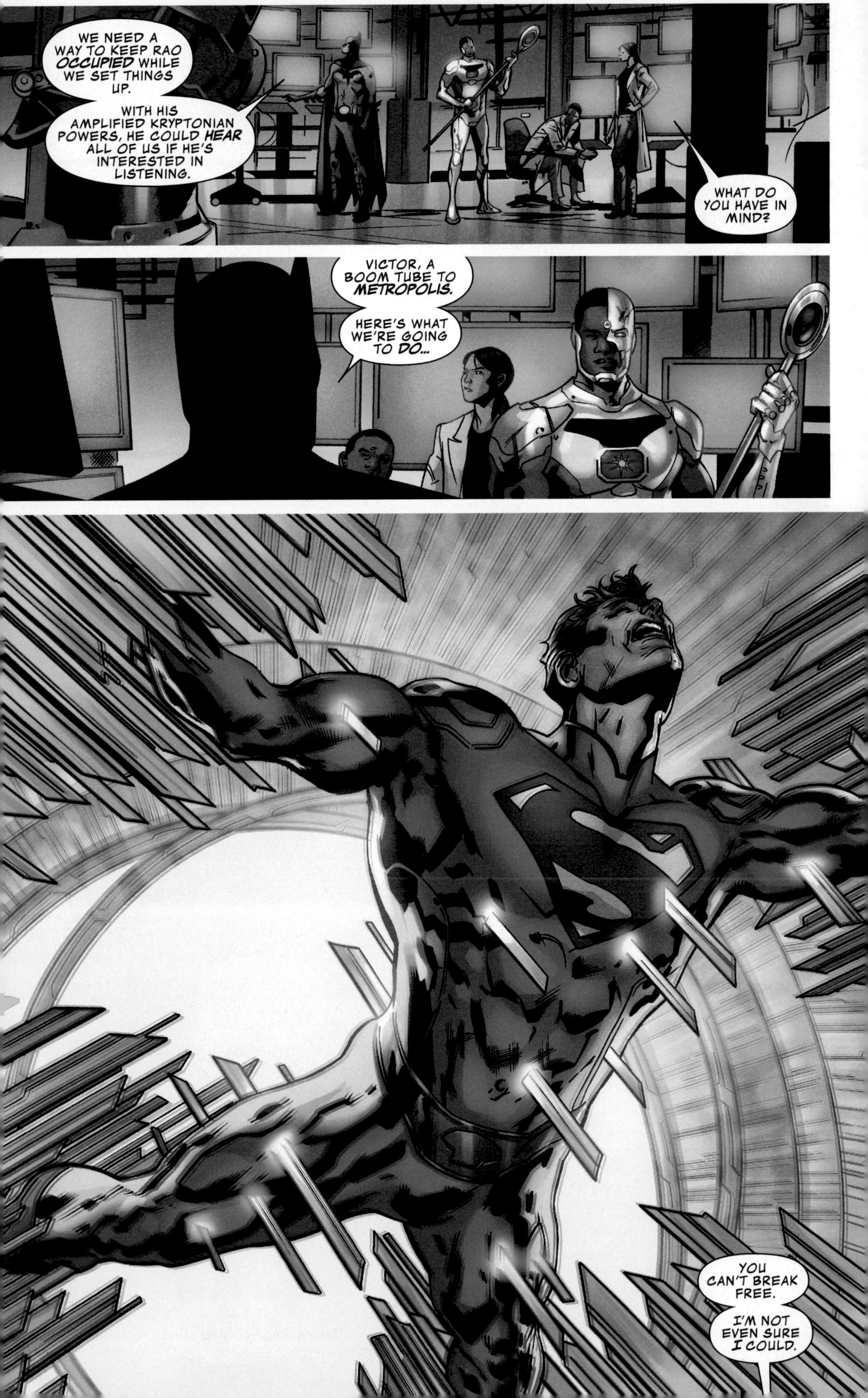
WE NEED A WAY TO KEEP RAO OCCUPIED WHILE WE SET THINGS UP.
WITH HIS AMPLIFIED KRYPTONIAN POWERS, HE COULD HEAR ALL OF US IF HE'S INTERESTED IN LISTENING.
WHAT DO YOU HAVE IN MIND?
VICTOR, A BOOM TUBE TO METROPOLIS.
HERE'S WHAT WE'RE GOING TO DO...
YOU CAN'T BREAK FREE.
I'M NOT EVEN SURE I COULD.

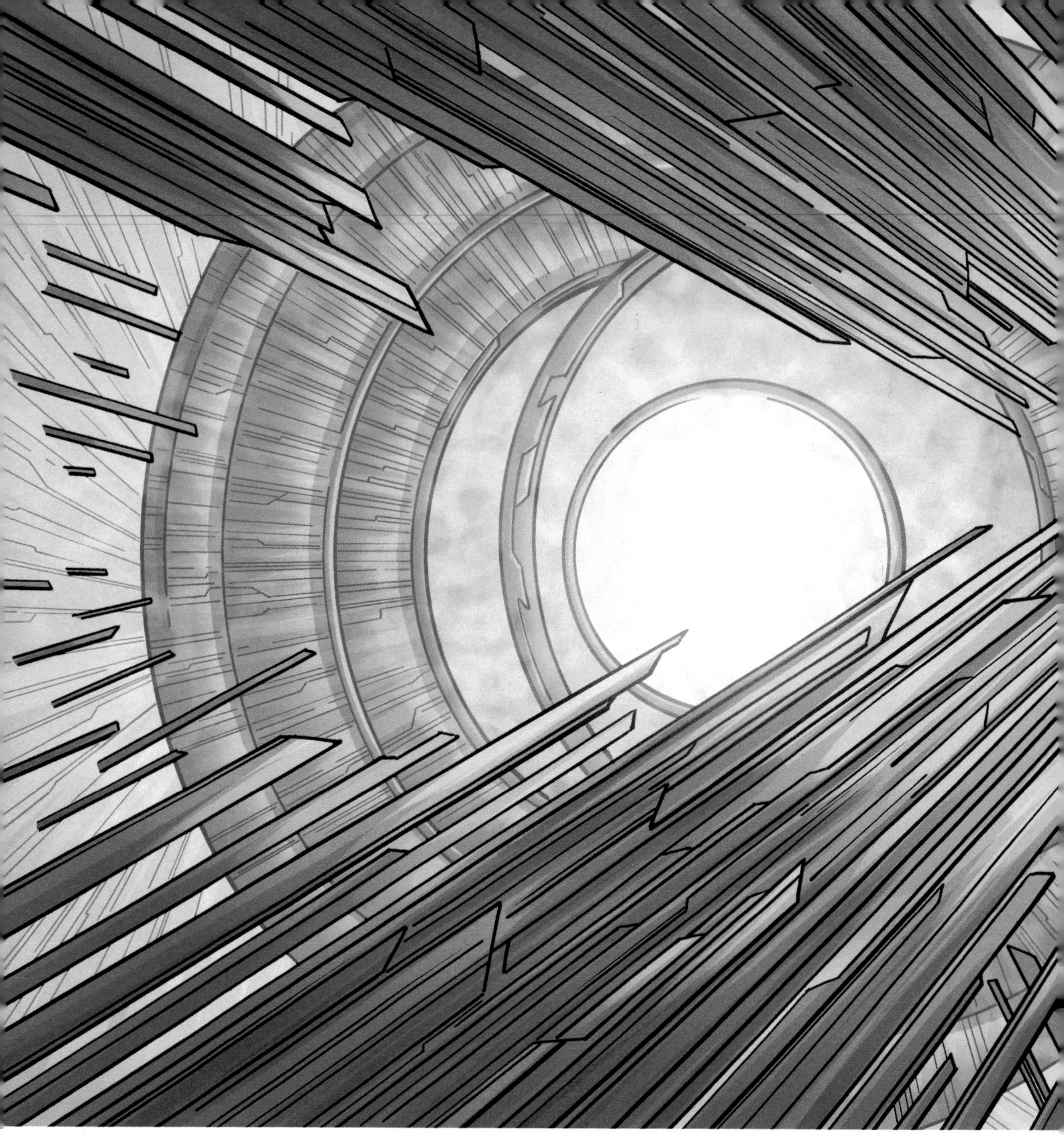

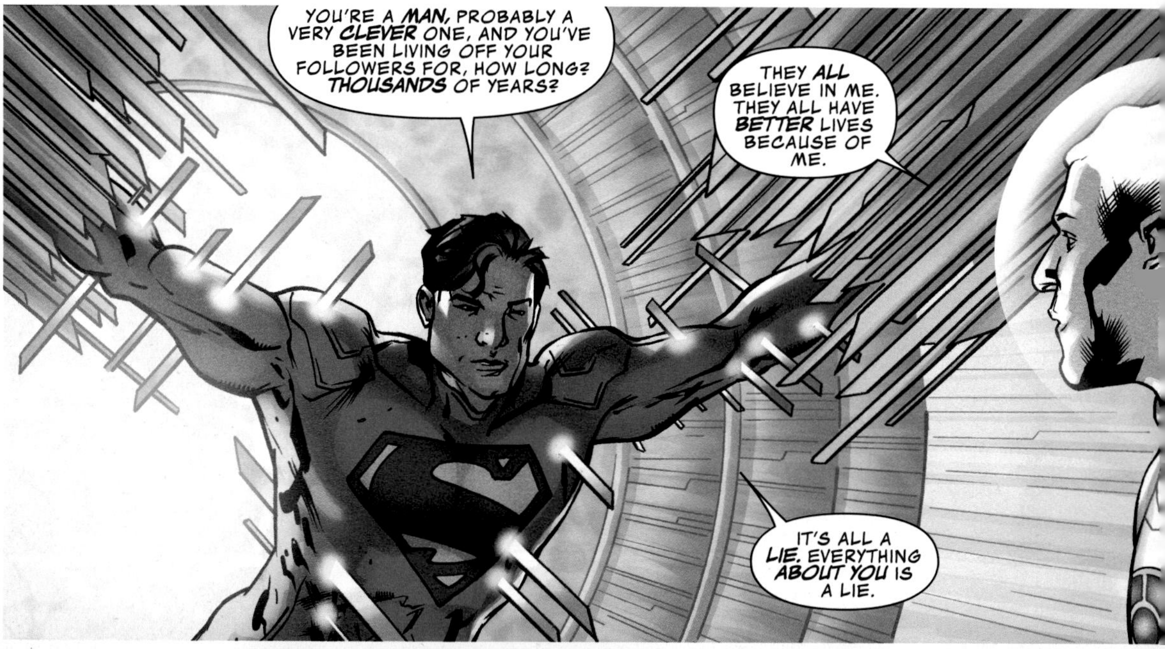

YOU'RE A MAN, PROBABLY A VERY CLEVER ONE, AND YOU'VE BEEN LIVING OFF YOUR FOLLOWERS FOR, HOW LONG? THOUSANDS OF YEARS?
THEY ALL BELIEVE IN ME. THEY ALL HAVE BETTER LIVES BECAUSE OF ME.
IT'S ALL A LIE. EVERYTHING ABOUT YOU IS A LIE.

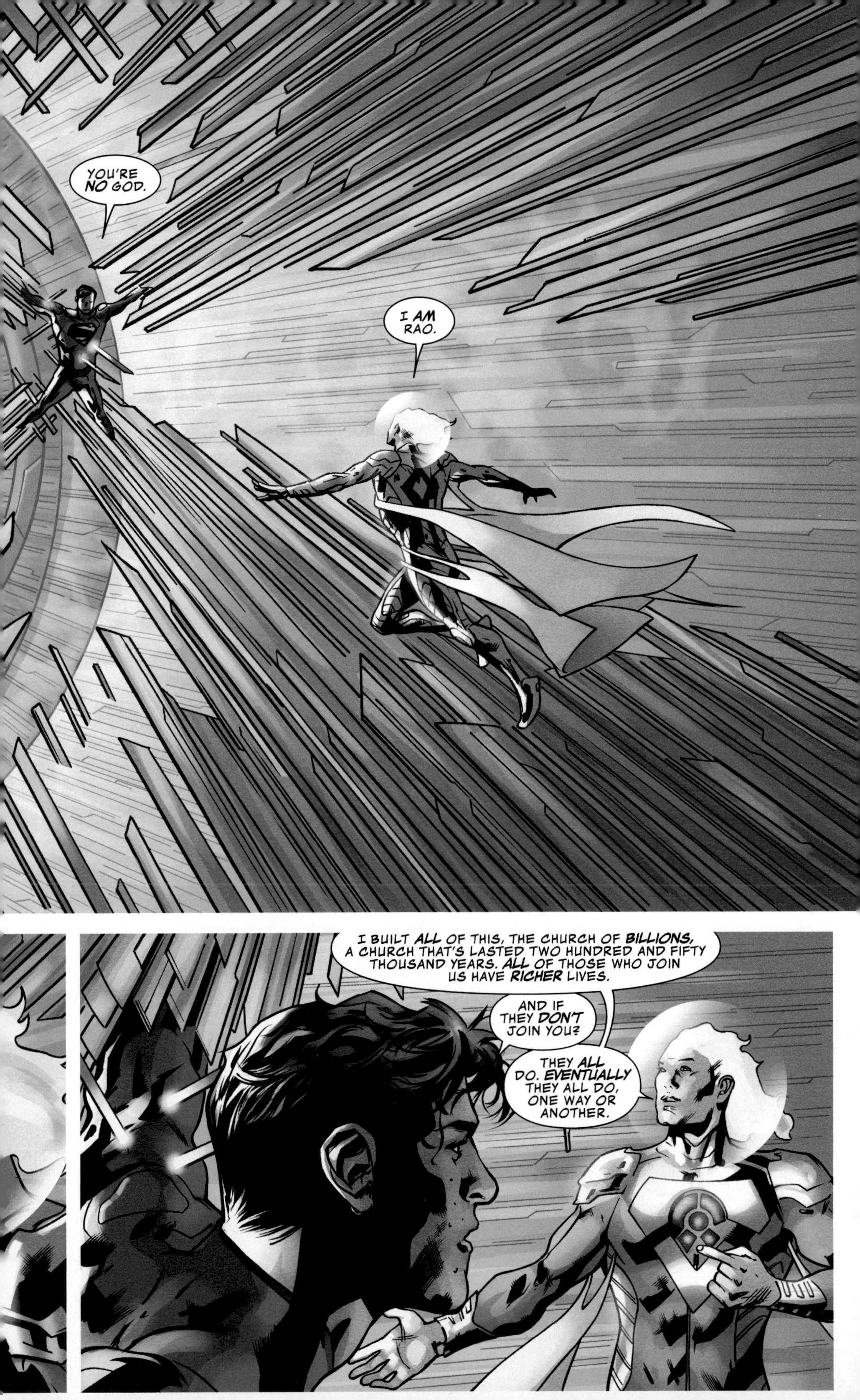
YOU'RE NO GOD.
I AM RAO.
I BUILT ALL OF THIS, THE CHURCH OF BILLIONS, A CHURCH THAT'S LASTED TWO HUNDRED AND FIFTY THOUSAND YEARS. ALL OF THOSE WHO JOIN US HAVE RICHER LIVES.
AND IF THEY DON'T JOIN YOU?
THEY ALL DO. EVENTUALLY THEY ALL DO, ONE WAY OR ANOTHER.

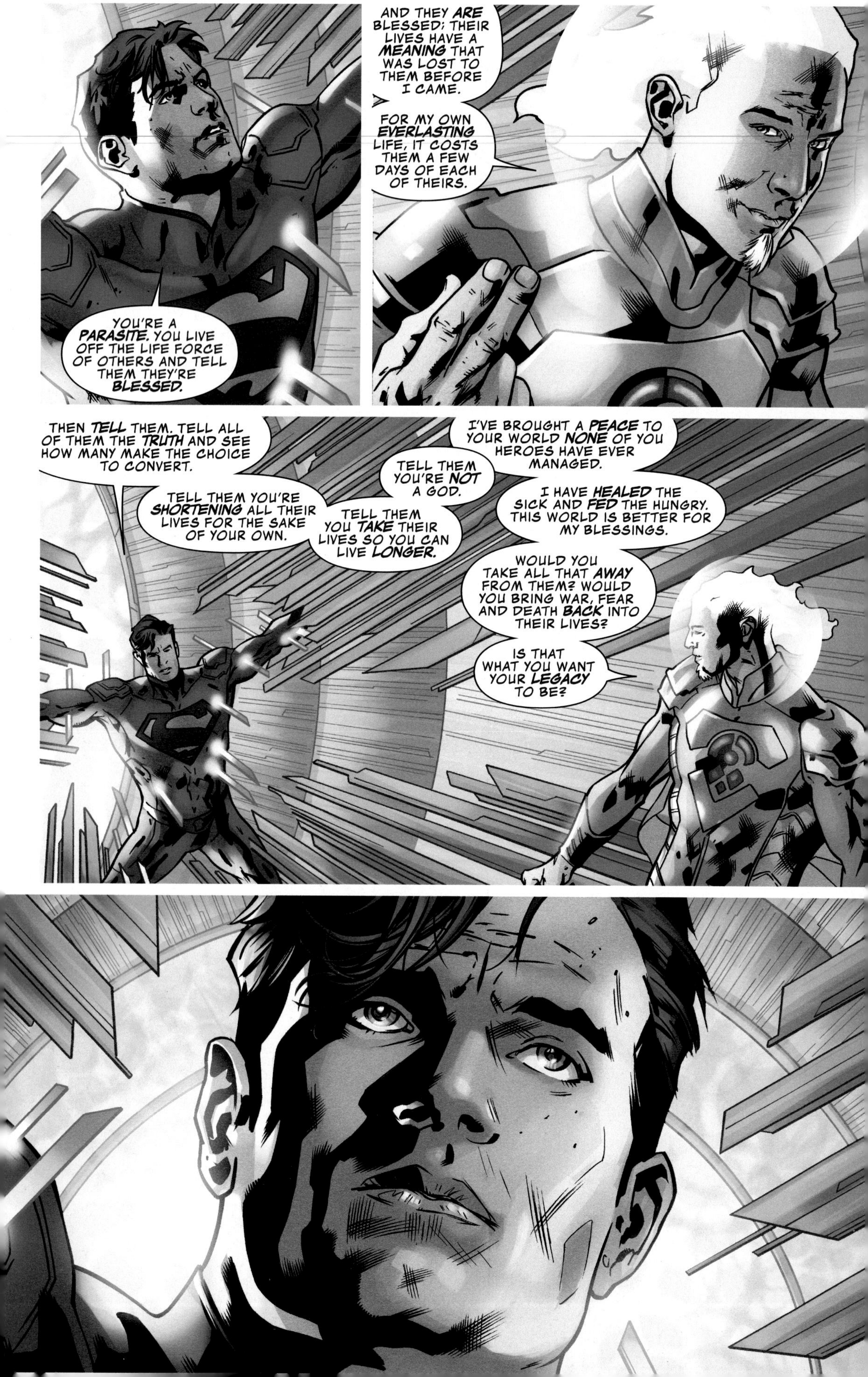

YOU'RE A PARASITE. YOU LIVE OFF THE LIFE FORCE OF OTHERS AND TELL THEM THEY'RE BLESSED.
AND THEY ARE BLESSED; THEIR LIVES HAVE A MEANING THAT WAS LOST TO THEM BEFORE I CAME.
FOR MY OWN EVERLASTING LIFE, IT COSTS THEM A FEW DAYS OF EACH OF THEIRS.
THEN TELL THEM. TELL ALL OF THEM THE TRUTH AND SEE HOW MANY MAKE THE CHOICE TO CONVERT.
TELL THEM YOU'RE SHORTENING ALL THEIR LIVES FOR THE SAKE OF YOUR OWN.
TELL THEM YOU TAKE THEIR LIVES SO YOU CAN LIVE LONGER.
TELL THEM YOU'RE NOT A GOD.
I'VE BROUGHT A PEACE TO YOUR WORLD NONE OF YOU HEROES HAVE EVER MANAGED.
I HAVE HEALED THE SICK AND FED THE HUNGRY. THIS WORLD IS BETTER FOR MY BLESSINGS.
WOULD YOU TAKE ALL THAT AWAY FROM THEM? WOULD YOU BRING WAR, FEAR AND DEATH BACK INTO THEIR LIVES?
IS THAT WHAT YOU WANT YOUR LEGACY TO BE?

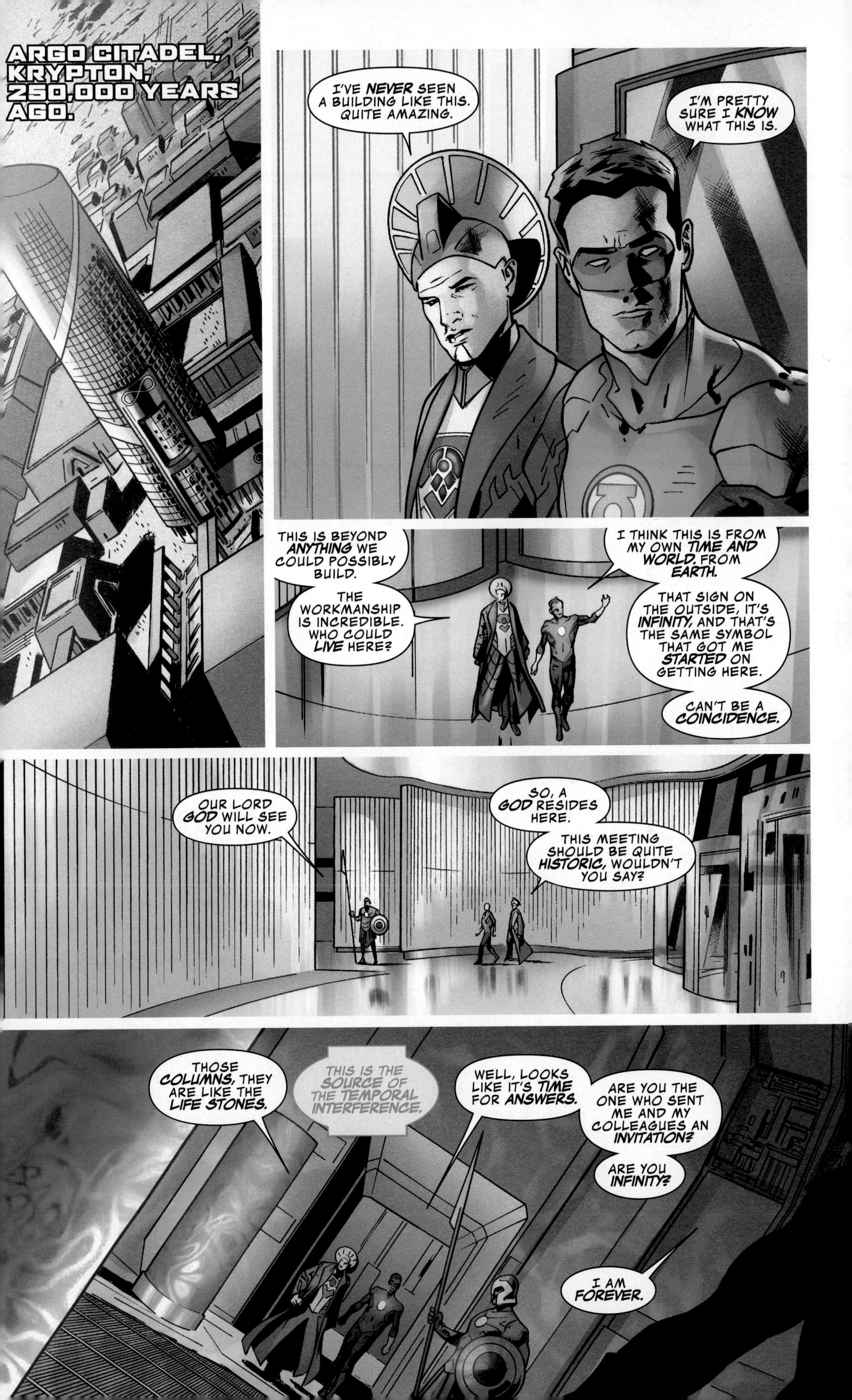
ARGO CITADEL, KRYPTON, 250,000 YEARS AGO.
I'VE NEVER SEEN A BUILDING LIKE THIS. QUITE AMAZING.
I'M PRETTY SURE I KNOW WHAT THIS IS.
THIS IS BEYOND ANYTHING WE COULD POSSIBLY BUILD.
THE WORKMANSHIP IS INCREDIBLE. WHO COULD LIVE HERE?
I THINK THIS IS FROM MY OWN TIME AND WORLD. FROM EARTH.
THAT SIGN ON THE OUTSIDE, IT'S INFINITY, AND THAT'S THE SAME SYMBOL THAT GOT ME STARTED ON GETTING HERE.
CAN'T BE A COINCIDENCE.
OUR LORD GOD WILL SEE YOU NOW.
SO, A GOD RESIDES HERE.
THIS MEETING SHOULD BE QUITE HISTORIC, WOULDN'T YOU SAY?
THOSE COLUMNS, THEY ARE LIKE THE LIFE STONES.
THIS IS THE SOURCE OF THE TEMPORAL INTERFERENCE.
WELL, LOOKS LIKE IT'S TIME FOR ANSWERS.
ARE YOU THE ONE WHO SENT ME AND MY COLLEAGUES AN INVITATION?
ARE YOU INFINITY?
I AM FOREVER.

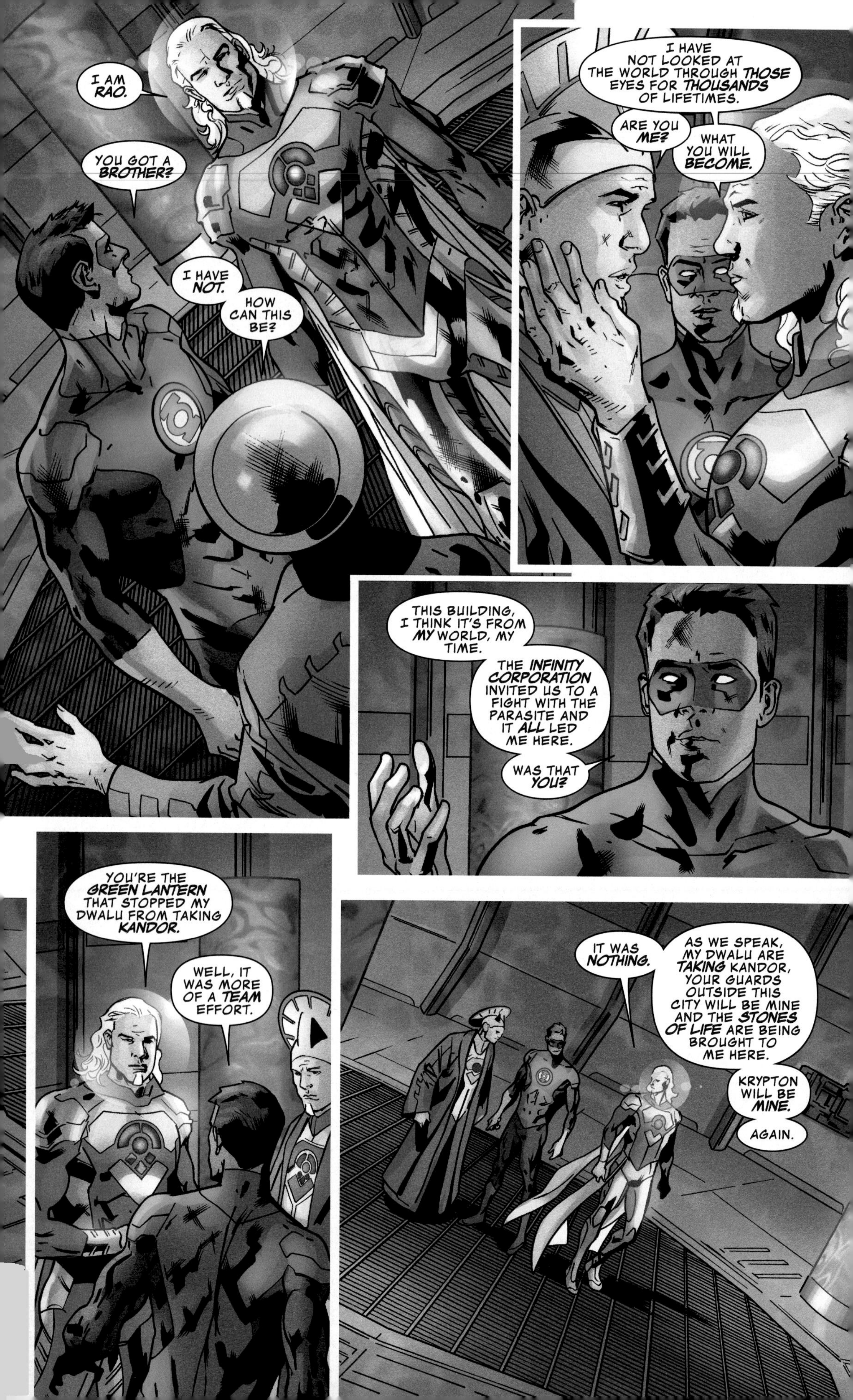
I AM RAO.
YOU GOT A BROTHER?
I HAVE NOT.
HOW CAN THIS BE?
I HAVE NOT LOOKED AT THE WORLD THROUGH THOSE EYES FOR THOUSANDS OF LIFETIMES.
ARE YOU ME?
WHAT YOU WILL BECOME.
THIS BUILDING, I THINK IT'S FROM MY WORLD, MY TIME.
THE INFINITY CORPORATION INVITED US TO A FIGHT WITH THE PARASITE AND IT ALL LED ME HERE.
WAS THAT YOU?
YOU'RE THE GREEN LANTERN THAT STOPPED MY DWALU FROM TAKING KANDOR.
WELL, IT WAS MORE OF A TEAM EFFORT.
IT WAS NOTHING.
AS WE SPEAK, MY DWALU ARE TAKING KANDOR, YOUR GUARDS OUTSIDE THIS CITY WILL BE MINE AND THE STONES OF LIFE ARE BEING BROUGHT TO ME HERE.
KRYPTON WILL BE MINE.
AGAIN.

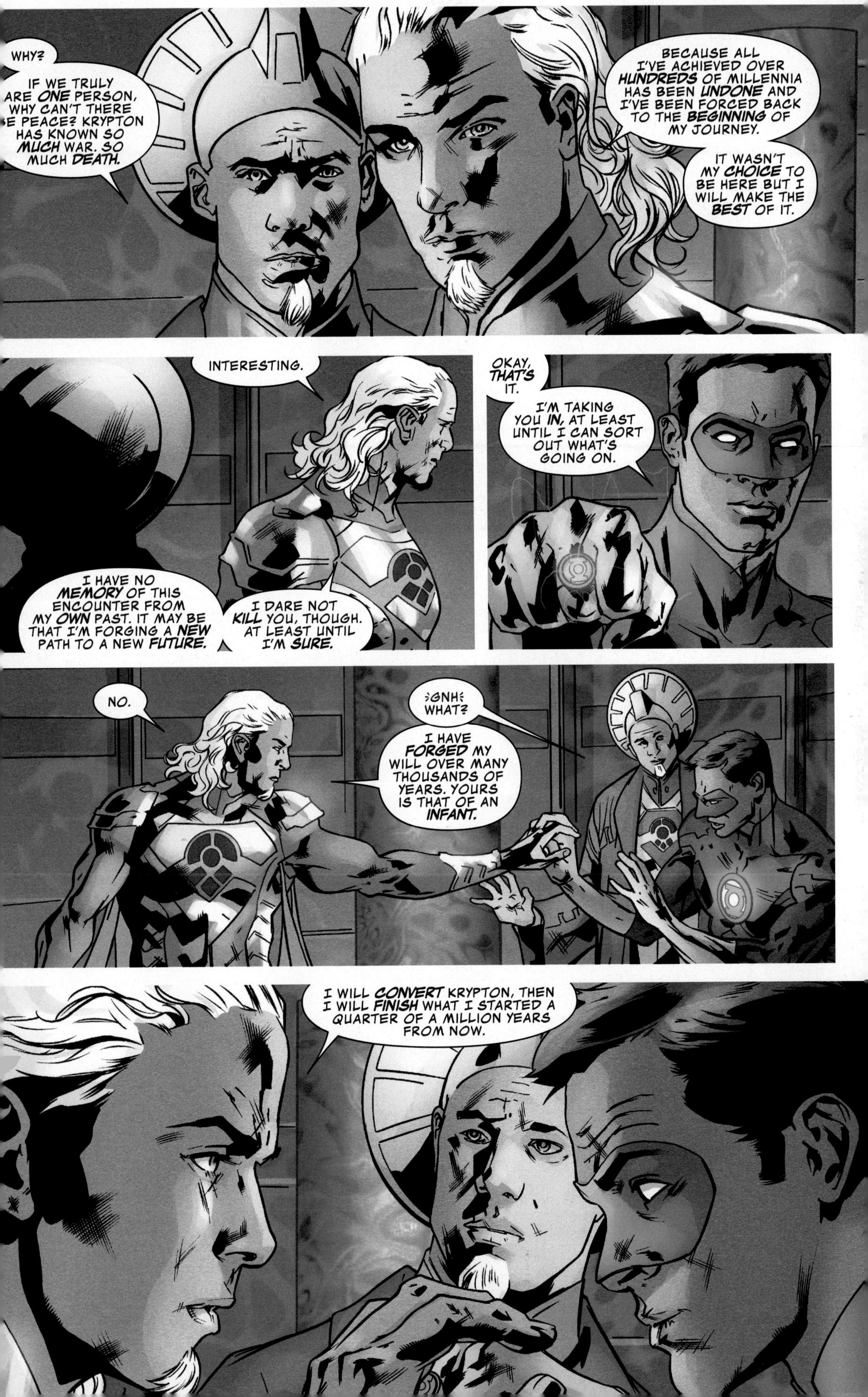
WHY?
IF WE TRULY ARE ONE PERSON, WHY CAN'T THERE E PEACE? KRYPTON HAS KNOWN SO MUCH WAR. SO MUCH DEATH.
BECAUSE ALL I'VE ACHIEVED OVER HUNDREDS OF MILLENNIA HAS BEEN UNDONE AND I'VE BEEN FORCED BACK TO THE BEGINNING OF MY JOURNEY.
IT WASN'T MY CHOICE TO BE HERE BUT I WILL MAKE THE BEST OF IT.
INTERESTING.
I HAVE NO MEMORY OF THIS ENCOUNTER FROM MY OWN PAST. IT MAY BE THAT I'M FORGING A NEW PATH TO A NEW FUTURE.
I DARE NOT KILL YOU, THOUGH. AT LEAST UNTIL I'M SURE.
OKAY, THAT'S IT.
I'M TAKING YOU IN, AT LEAST UNTIL I CAN SORT OUT WHAT'S GOING ON.
NO.
GNH WHAT?
I HAVE FORGED MY WILL OVER MANY THOUSANDS OF YEARS. YOURS IS THAT OF AN INFANT.
I WILL CONVERT KRYPTON, THEN I WILL FINISH WHAT I STARTED A QUARTER OF A MILLION YEARS FROM NOW.

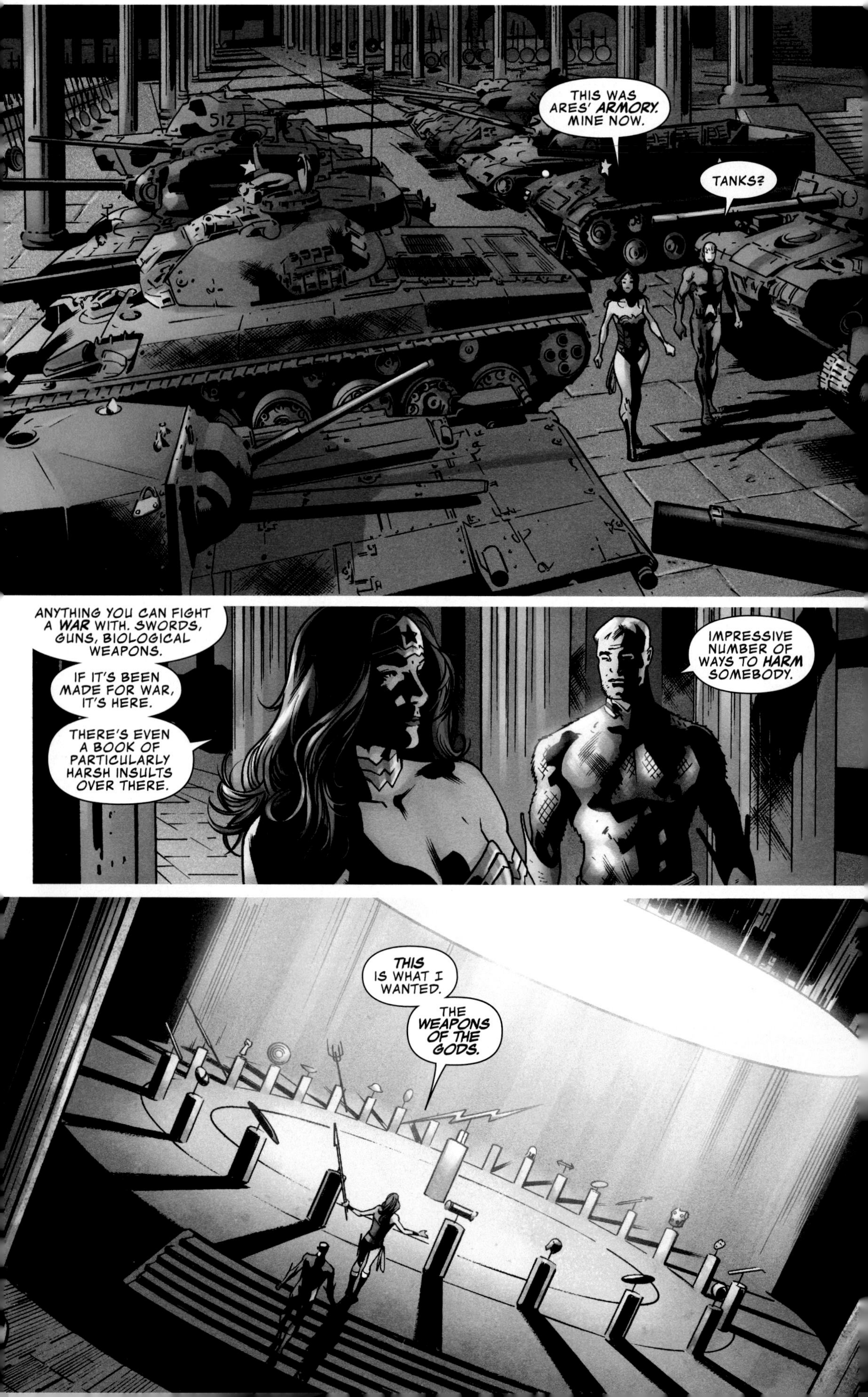
THIS WAS ARES' ARMORY. MINE NOW.
TANKS?
ANYTHING YOU CAN FIGHT A WAR WITH. SWORDS, GUNS, BIOLOGICAL WEAPONS.
IF IT'S BEEN MADE FOR WAR, IT'S HERE.
THERE'S EVEN A BOOK OF PARTICULARLY HARSH INSULTS OVER THERE.
IMPRESSIVE NUMBER OF WAYS TO HARM SOMEBODY.
THIS IS WHAT I WANTED.
THE WEAPONS OF THE GODS.

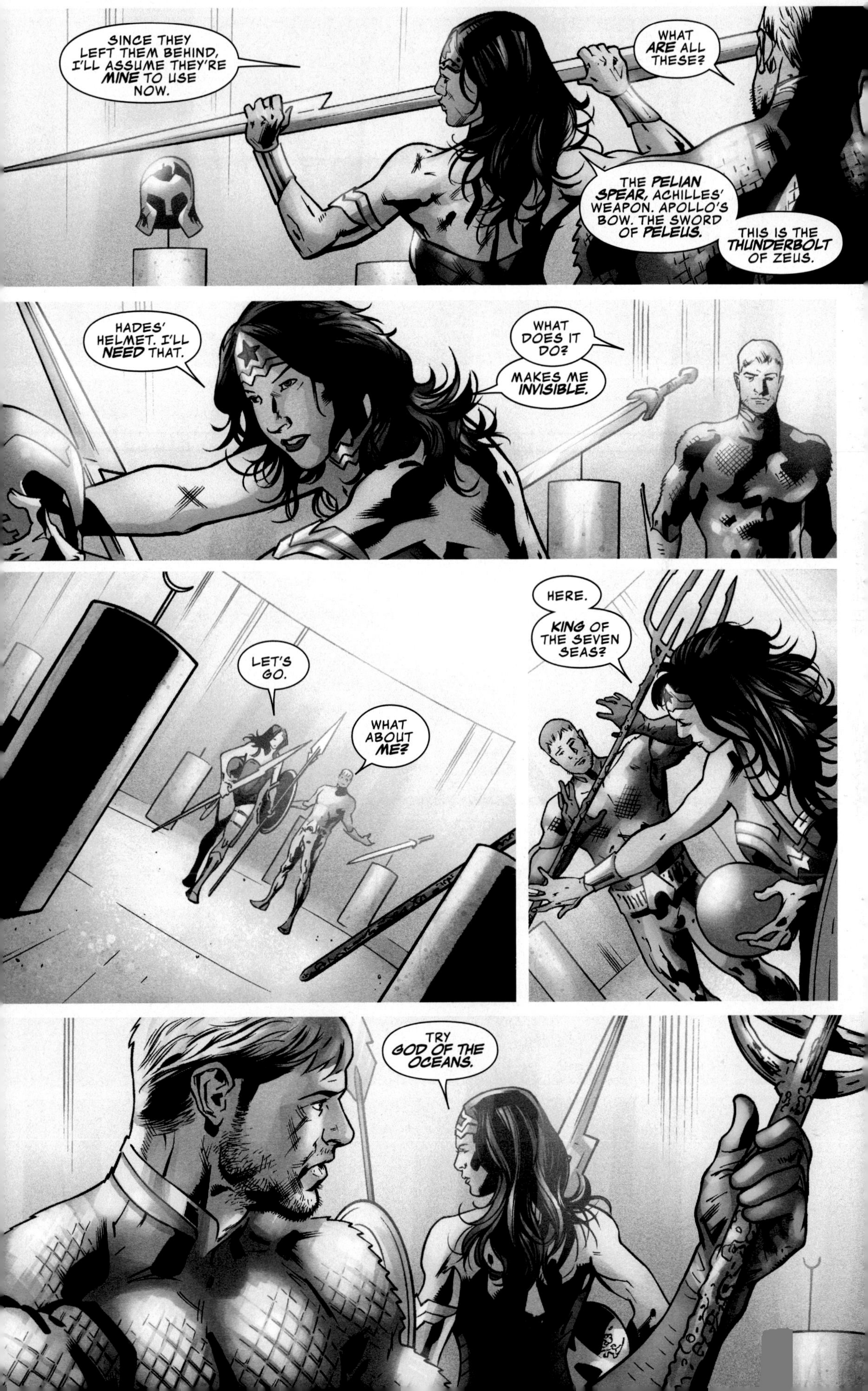
SINCE THEY LEFT THEM BEHIND, I'LL ASSUME THEY'RE MINE TO USE NOW.
WHAT ARE ALL THESE?
THE PELIAN SPEAR, ACHILLES' WEAPON. APOLLO'S BOW. THE SWORD OF PELEUS.
THIS IS THE THUNDERBOLT OF ZEUS.
HADES' HELMET. I'LL NEED THAT.
WHAT DOES IT DO?
MAKES ME INVISIBLE.
LET'S GO.
WHAT ABOUT ME?
HERE.
KING OF THE SEVEN SEAS?
TRY GOD OF THE OCEANS.

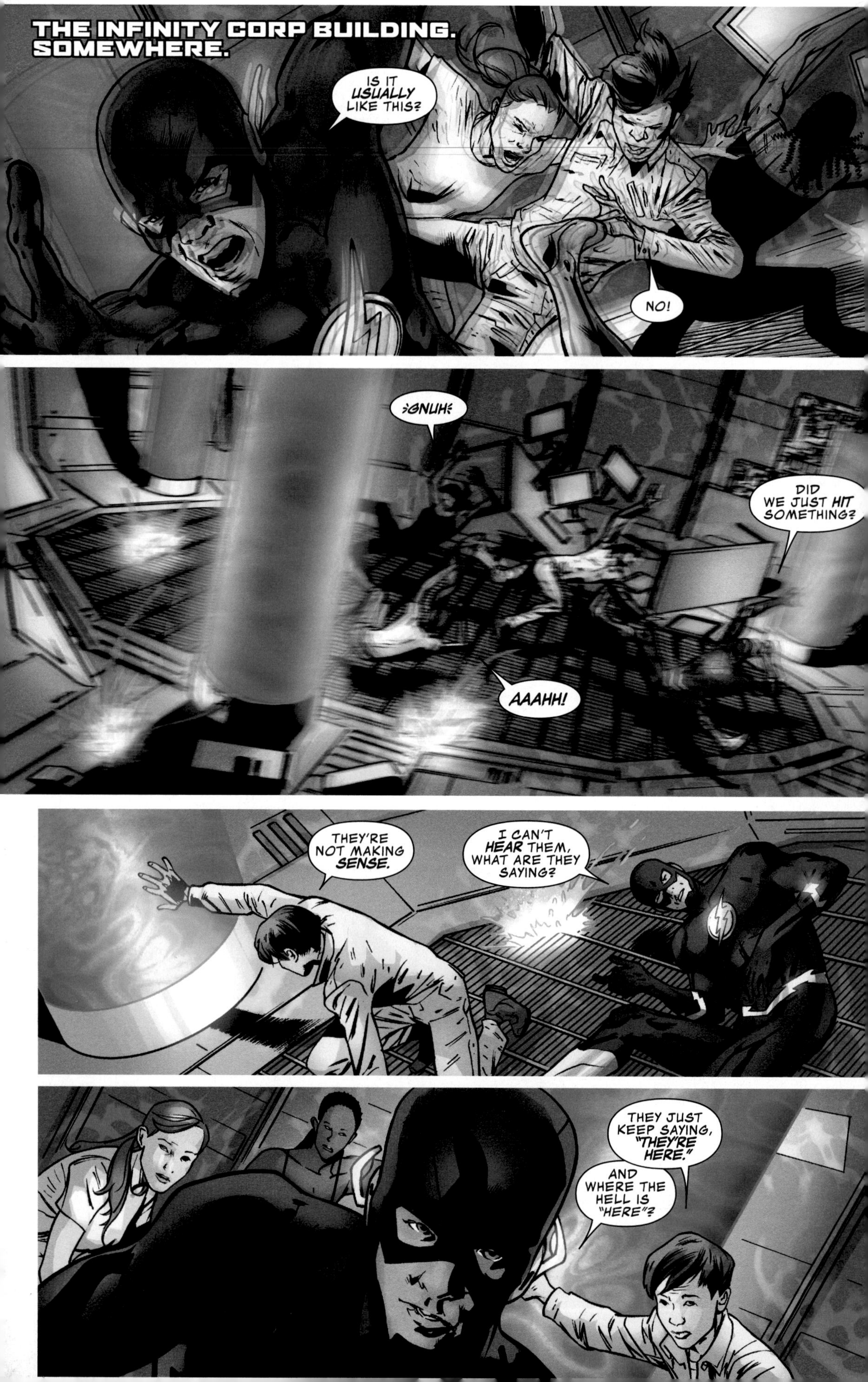
THE INFINITY CORP BUILDING. SOMEWHERE.
IS IT USUALLY LIKE THIS?
NO!
GNUH
DID WE JUST HIT SOMETHING?
AAAHH!
THEY'RE NOT MAKING SENSE.
I CAN'T HEAR THEM, WHAT ARE THEY SAYING?
THEY JUST KEEP SAYING, "THEY'RE HERE."
AND WHERE THE HELL IS "HERE"?

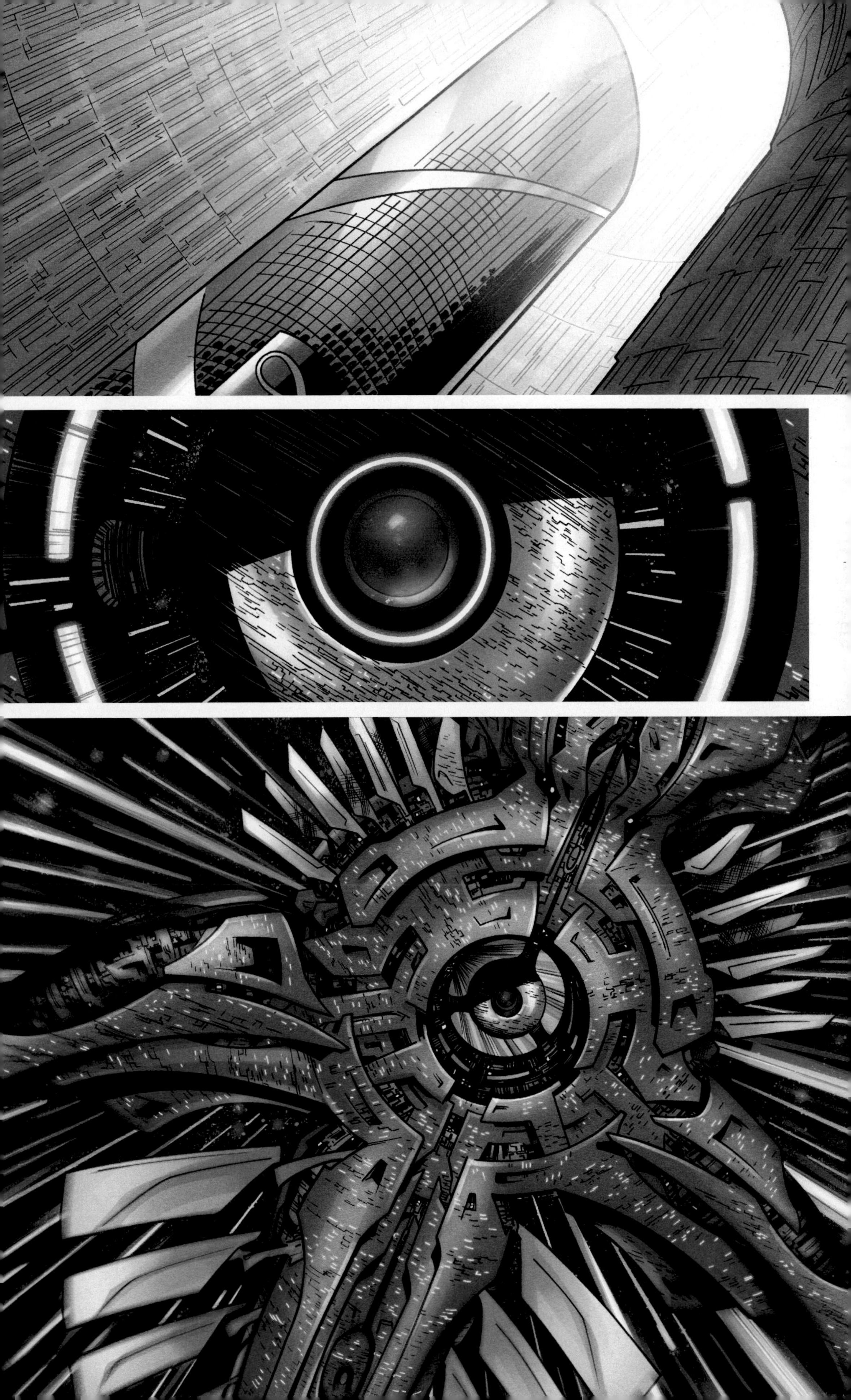

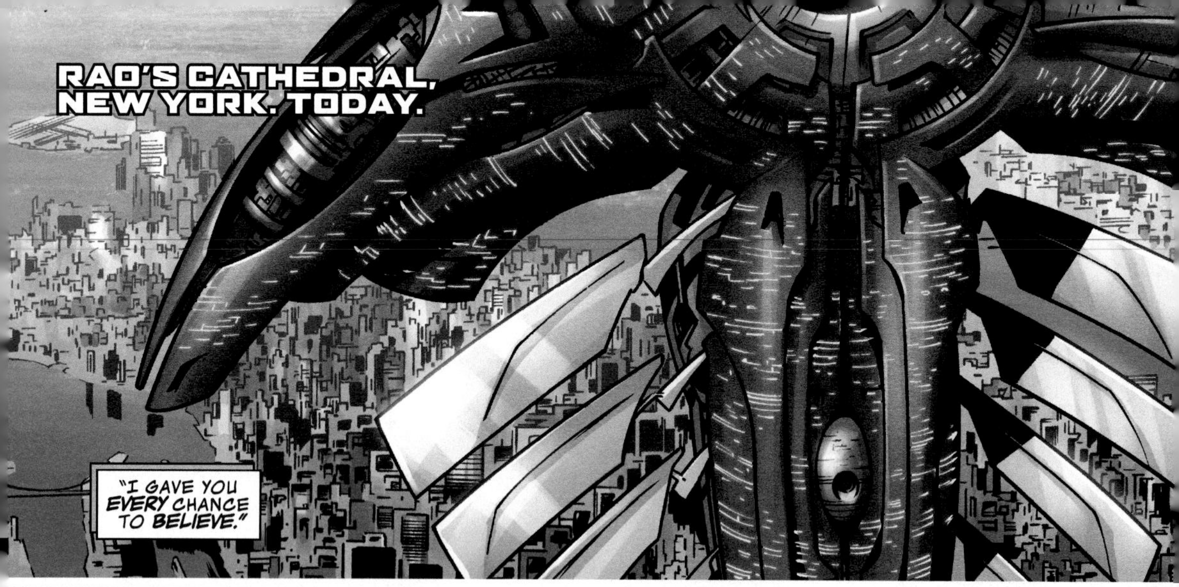
RAO'S CATHEDRAL, NEW YORK. TODAY.
"I GAVE YOU EVERY CHANCE TO BELIEVE."

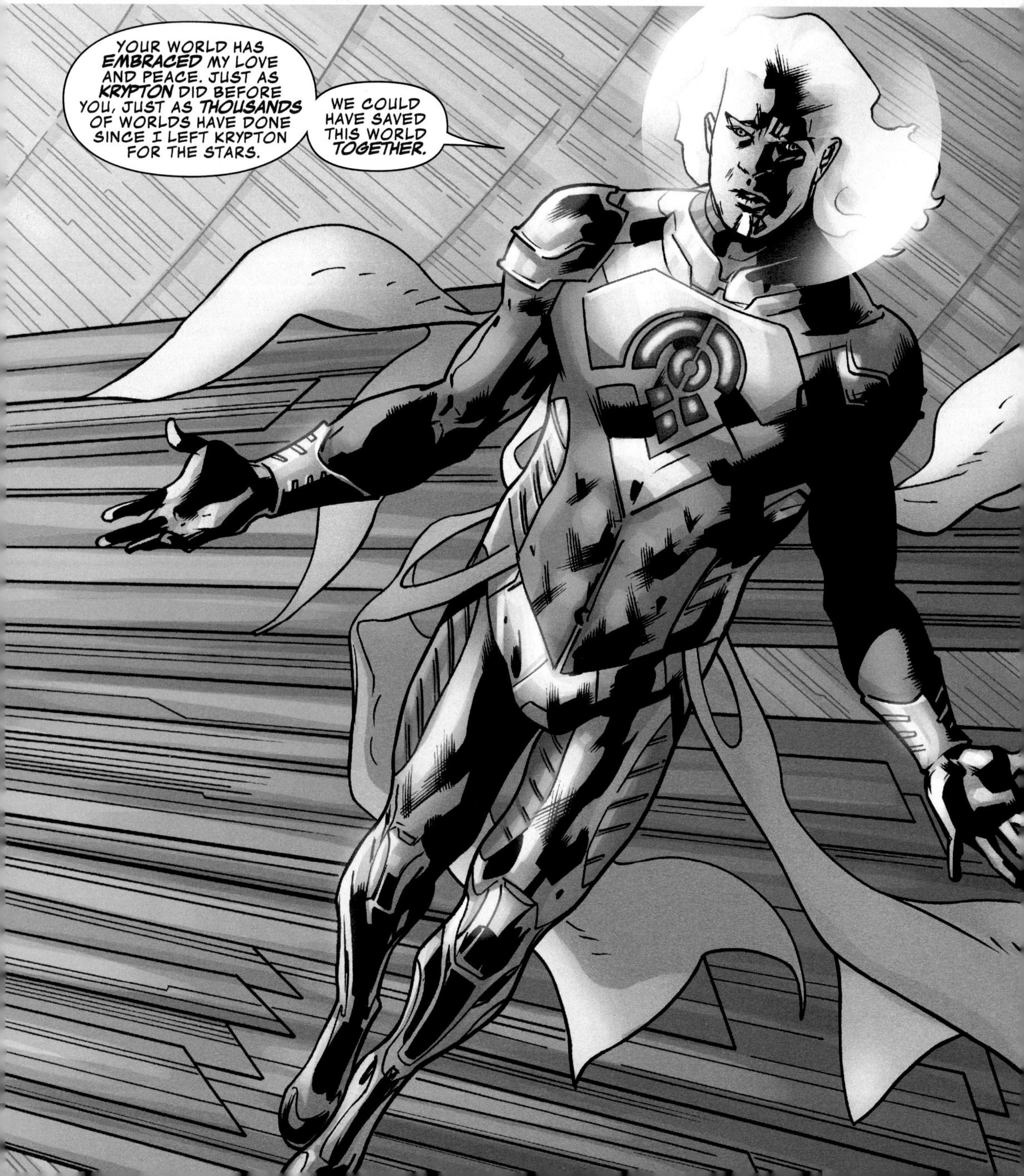
YOUR WORLD HAS EMBRACED MY LOVE AND PEACE. JUST AS KRYPTON DID BEFORE YOU, JUST AS THOUSANDS OF WORLDS HAVE DONE SINCE I LEFT KRYPTON FOR THE STARS.
WE COULD HAVE SAVED THIS WORLD TOGETHER.

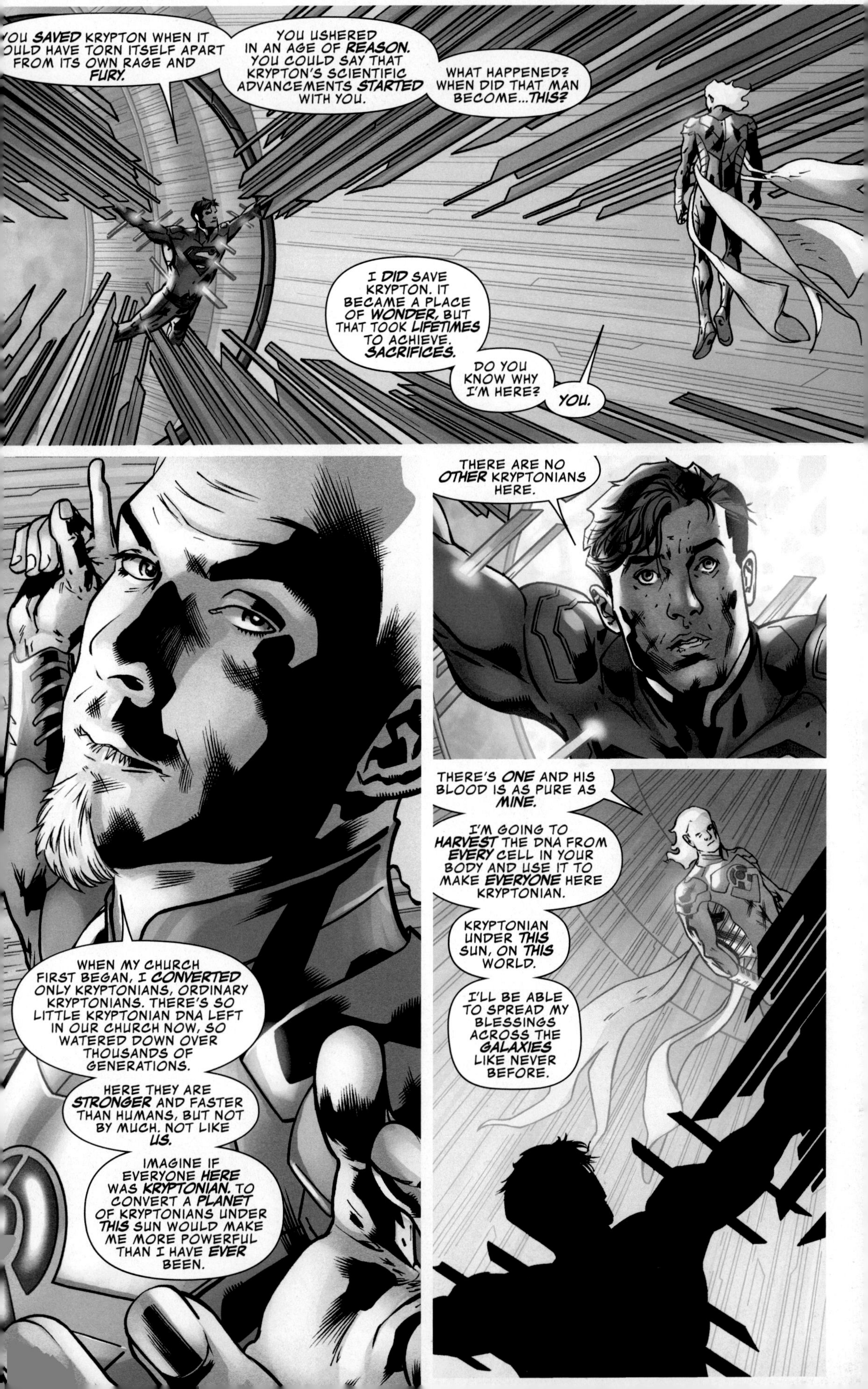
YOU SAVED KRYPTON WHEN IT COULD HAVE TORN ITSELF APART FROM ITS OWN RAGE AND FURY.
YOU USHERED IN AN AGE OF REASON. YOU COULD SAY THAT KRYPTON'S SCIENTIFIC ADVANCEMENTS STARTED WITH YOU.
WHAT HAPPENED? WHEN DID THAT MAN BECOME...THIS?
I DID SAVE KRYPTON. IT BECAME A PLACE OF WONDER, BUT THAT TOOK LIFETIMES TO ACHIEVE. SACRIFICES.
DO YOU KNOW WHY I'M HERE?
YOU.
WHEN MY CHURCH FIRST BEGAN, I CONVERTED ONLY KRYPTONIANS, ORDINARY KRYPTONIANS. THERE'S SO LITTLE KRYPTONIAN DNA LEFT IN OUR CHURCH NOW, SO WATERED DOWN OVER THOUSANDS OF GENERATIONS.
HERE THEY ARE STRONGER AND FASTER THAN HUMANS, BUT NOT BY MUCH. NOT LIKE US.
IMAGINE IF EVERYONE HERE WAS KRYPTONIAN. TO CONVERT A PLANET OF KRYPTONIANS UNDER THIS SUN WOULD MAKE ME MORE POWERFUL THAN I HAVE EVER BEEN.
THERE ARE NO OTHER KRYPTONIANS HERE.
THERE'S ONE AND HIS BLOOD IS AS PURE AS MINE.
I'M GOING TO HARVEST THE DNA FROM EVERY CELL IN YOUR BODY AND USE IT TO MAKE EVERYONE HERE KRYPTONIAN.
KRYPTONIAN UNDER THIS SUN, ON THIS WORLD.
I'LL BE ABLE TO SPREAD MY BLESSINGS ACROSS THE GALAXIES LIKE NEVER BEFORE.

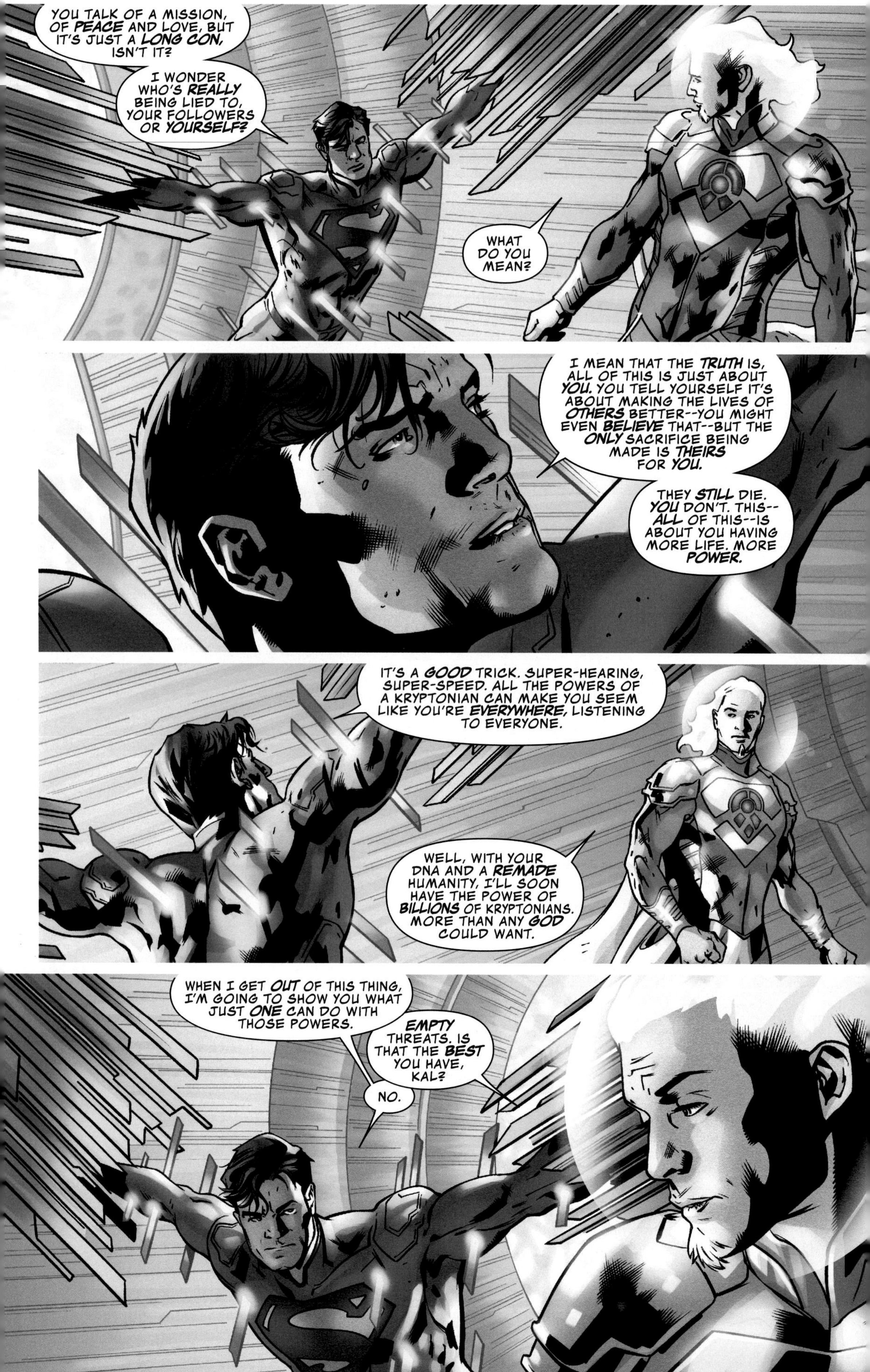
YOU TALK OF A MISSION, OF PEACE AND LOVE, BUT IT'S JUST A LONG CON, ISN'T IT?
I WONDER WHO'S REALLY BEING LIED TO, YOUR FOLLOWERS OR YOURSELF?
WHAT DO YOU MEAN?
I MEAN THAT THE TRUTH IS, ALL OF THIS IS JUST ABOUT YOU. YOU TELL YOURSELF IT'S ABOUT MAKING THE LIVES OF OTHERS BETTER--YOU MIGHT EVEN BELIEVE THAT--BUT THE ONLY SACRIFICE BEING MADE IS THEIRS FOR YOU.
THEY STILL DIE. YOU DON'T. THIS--ALL OF THIS--IS ABOUT YOU HAVING MORE LIFE. MORE POWER.
IT'S A GOOD TRICK. SUPER-HEARING, SUPER-SPEED. ALL THE POWERS OF A KRYPTONIAN CAN MAKE YOU SEEM LIKE YOU'RE EVERYWHERE, LISTENING TO EVERYONE.
WELL, WITH YOUR DNA AND A REMADE HUMANITY, I'LL SOON HAVE THE POWER OF BILLIONS OF KRYPTONIANS. MORE THAN ANY GOD COULD WANT.
WHEN I GET OUT OF THIS THING, I'M GOING TO SHOW YOU WHAT JUST ONE CAN DO WITH THOSE POWERS.
EMPTY THREATS. IS THAT THE BEST YOU HAVE, KAL?
NO.

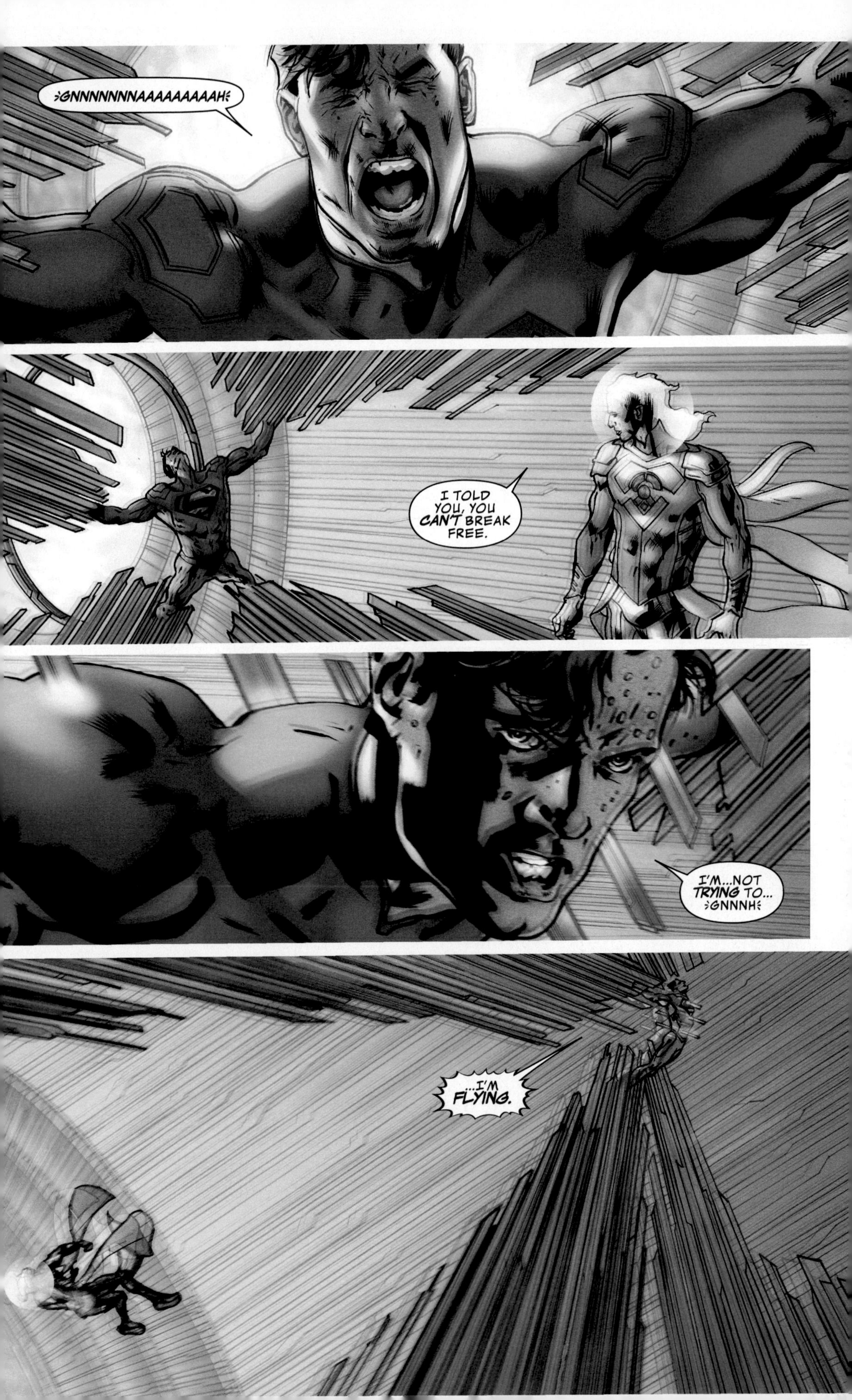
GNNNNNNNAAAAAAAAAAH
I TOLD YOU, YOU CAN'T BREAK FREE.
I'M...NOT TRYING TO... GNNNH
...I'M FLYING.

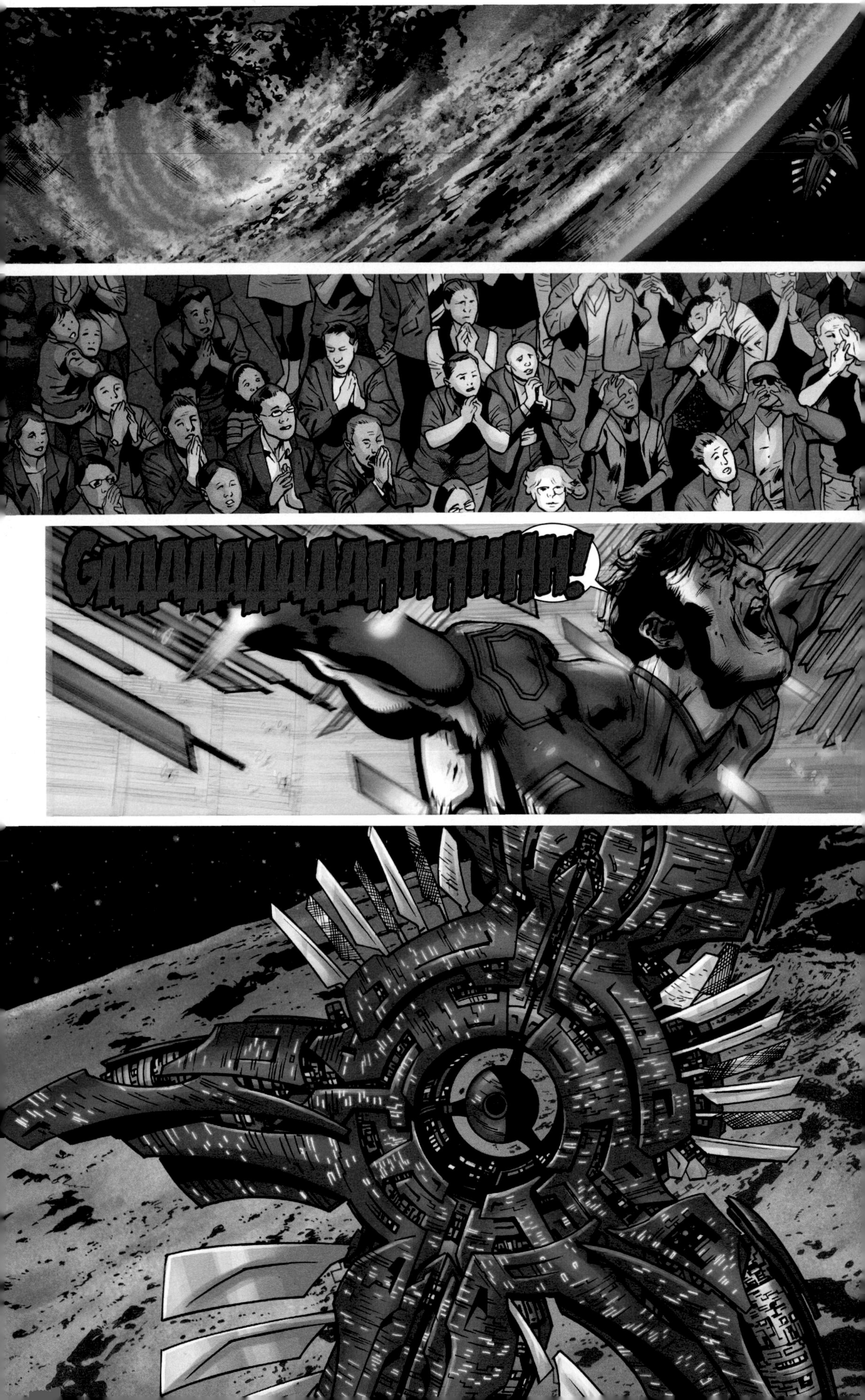
GAAAAAAAAHHHHHHHH!

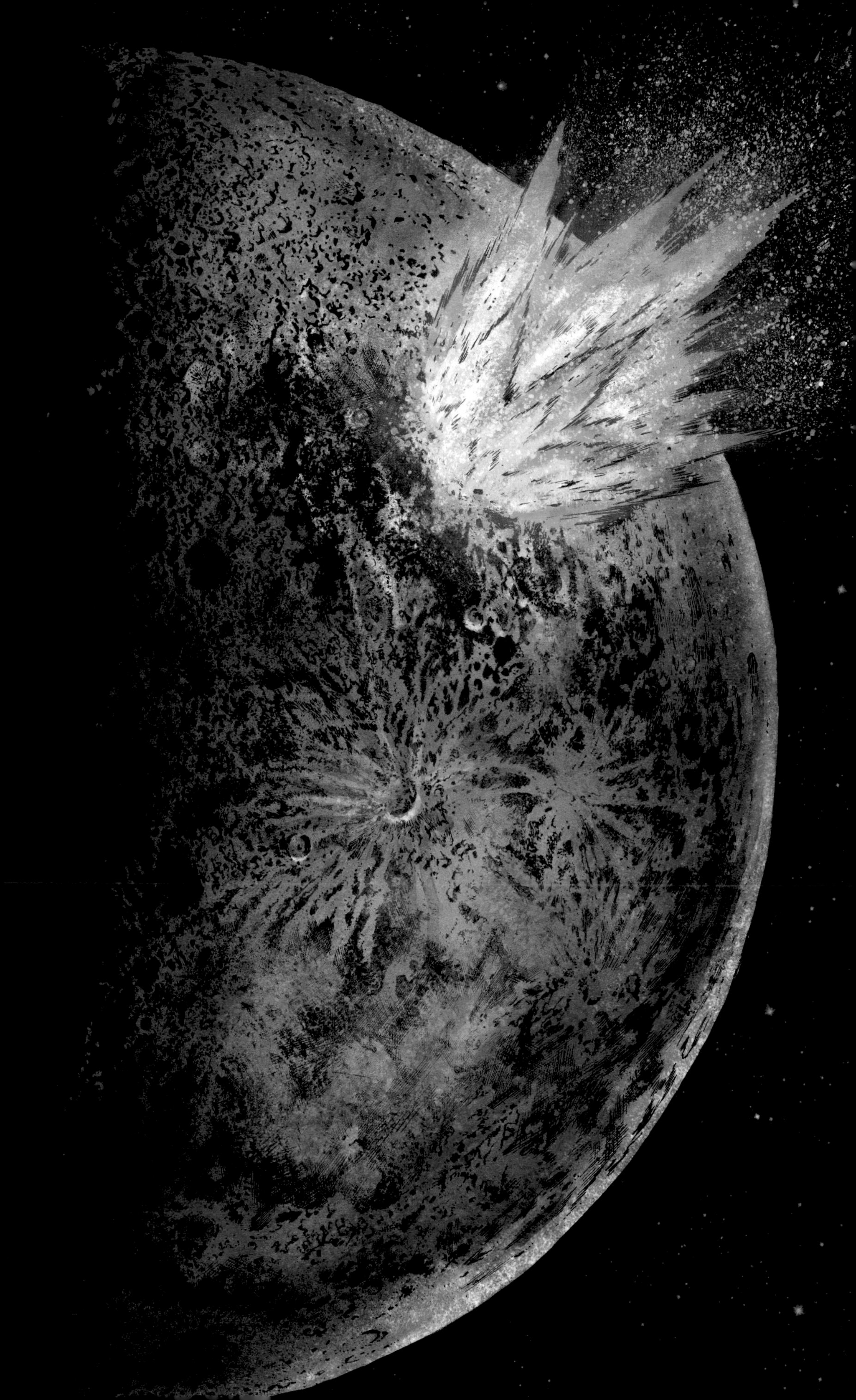

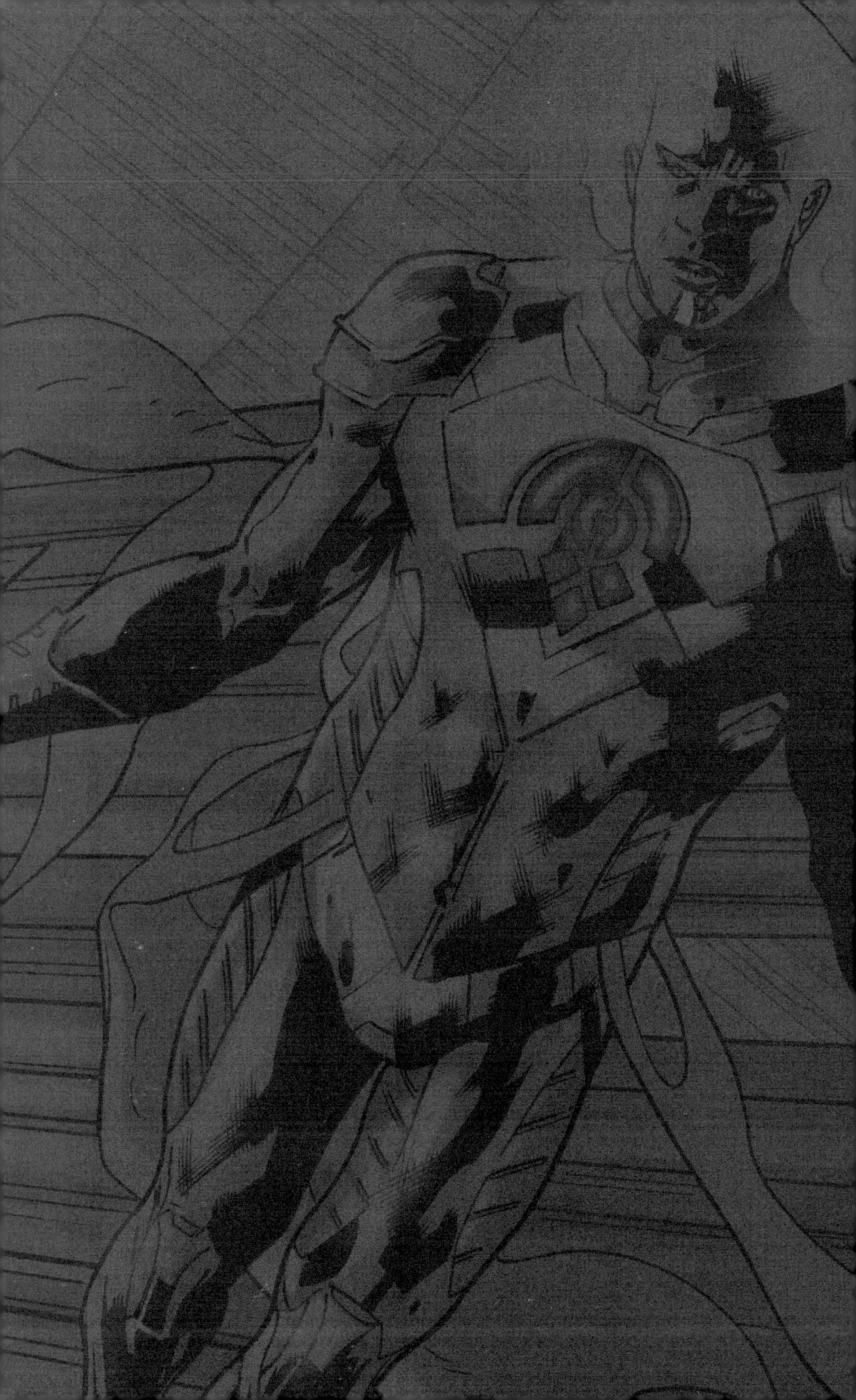

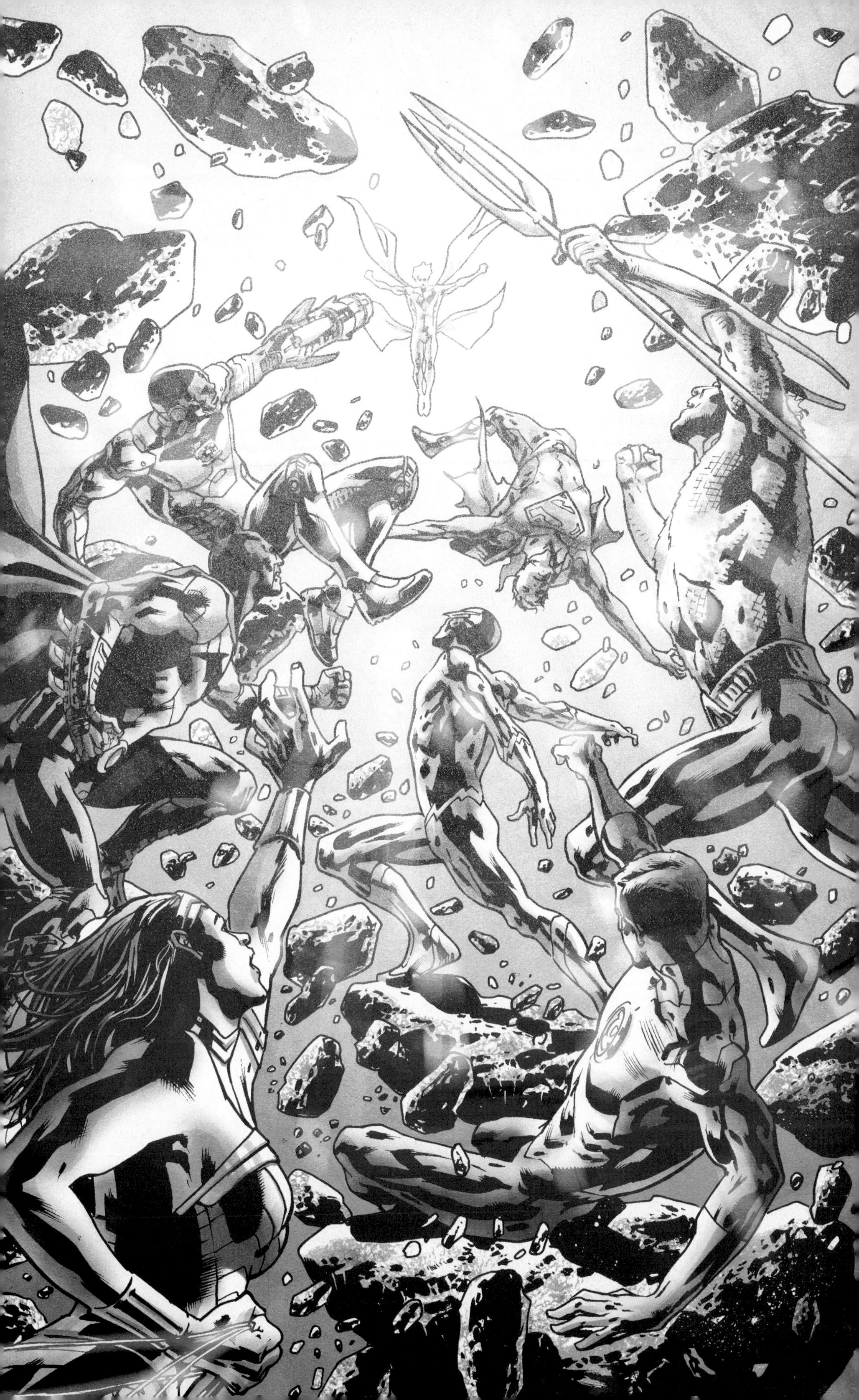

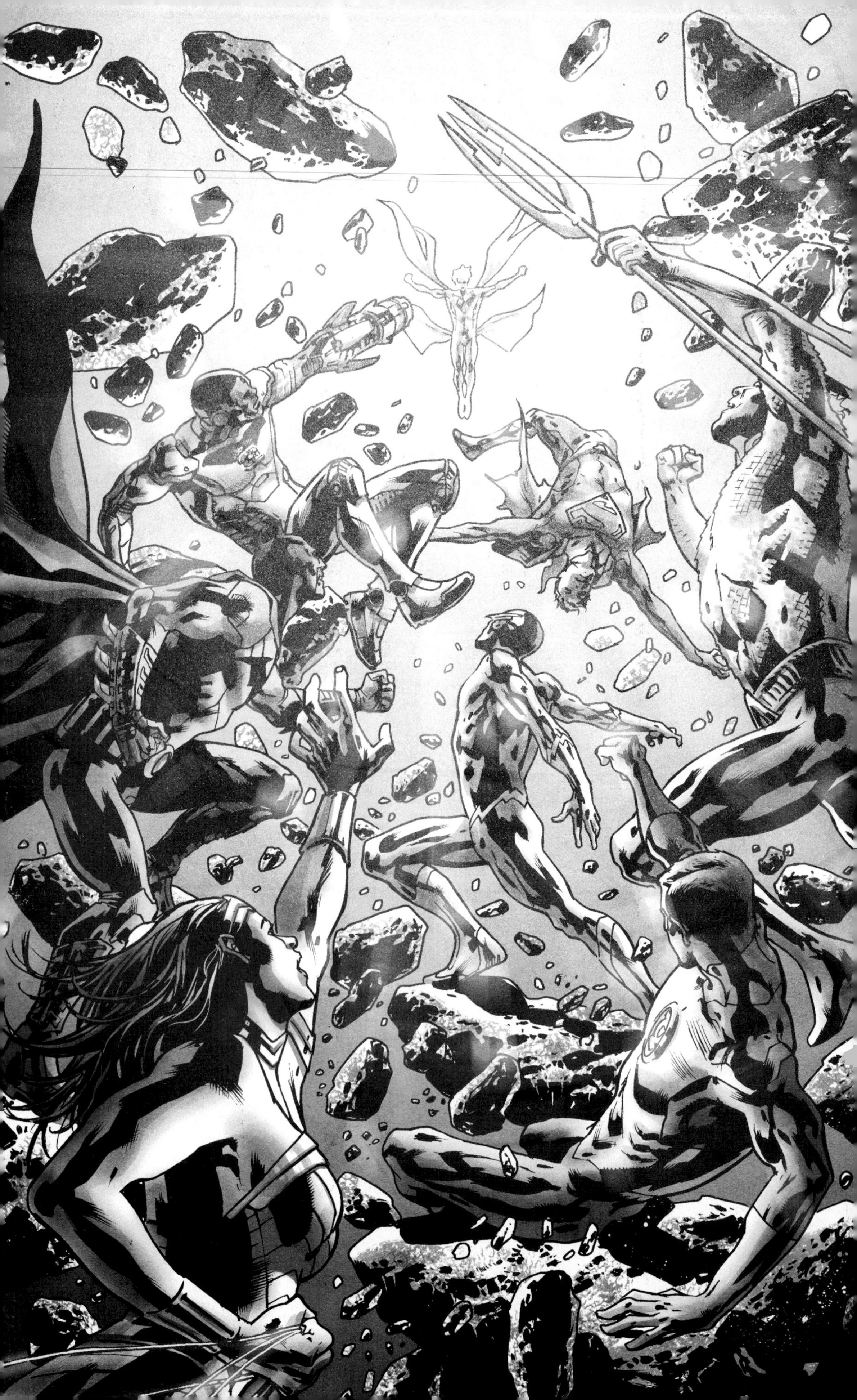

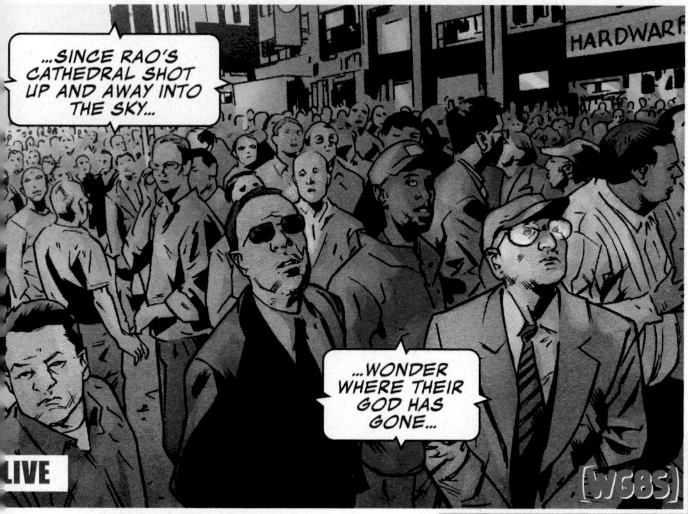
...SINCE RAO'S CATHEDRAL SHOT UP AND AWAY INTO THE SKY...
HARDWARE
...WONDER WHERE THEIR GOD HAS GONE...
LIVE
[WGBS]

DC COMICS PRESENTS

THE JUSTICE LEAGUE OF AMERICA

POWER AND GLORY PART SEVEN

BY **BRYAN HITCH**

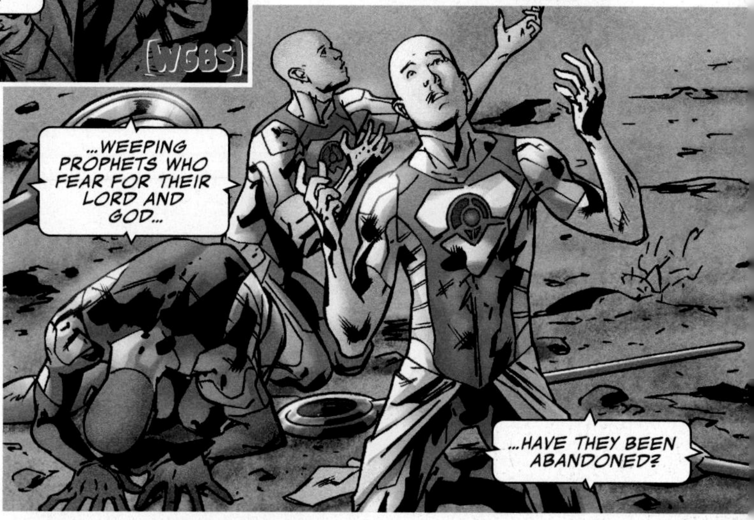
...WEEPING PROPHETS WHO FEAR FOR THEIR LORD AND GOD...
...HAVE THEY BEEN ABANDONED?

INKS BY **DANIEL HENRIQUES**
COLORS BY **ALEX SINCLAIR**
LETTERS BY **CHRIS ELIOPOULOS**
ASSISTS BY **AMEDEO TURTURRO**
EDITS BY **BRIAN CUNNINGHAM**

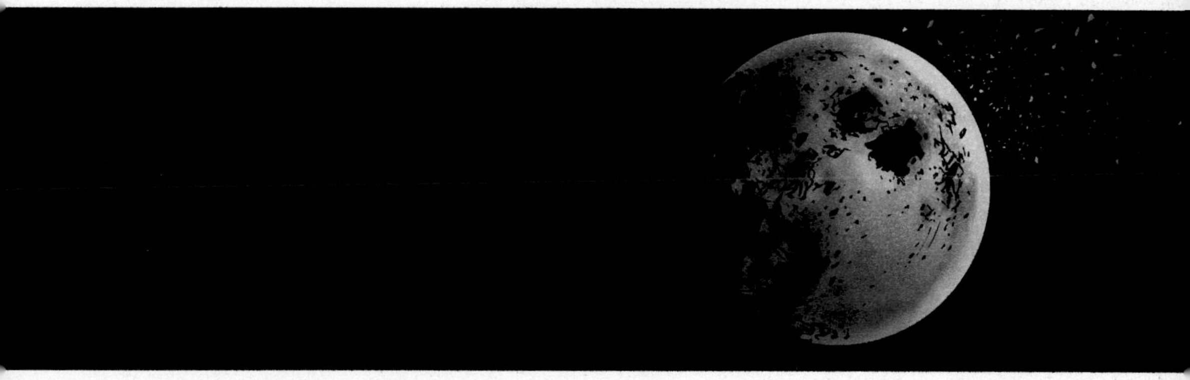

COVER BY **BRYAN HITCH & ALEX SINCLAIR**

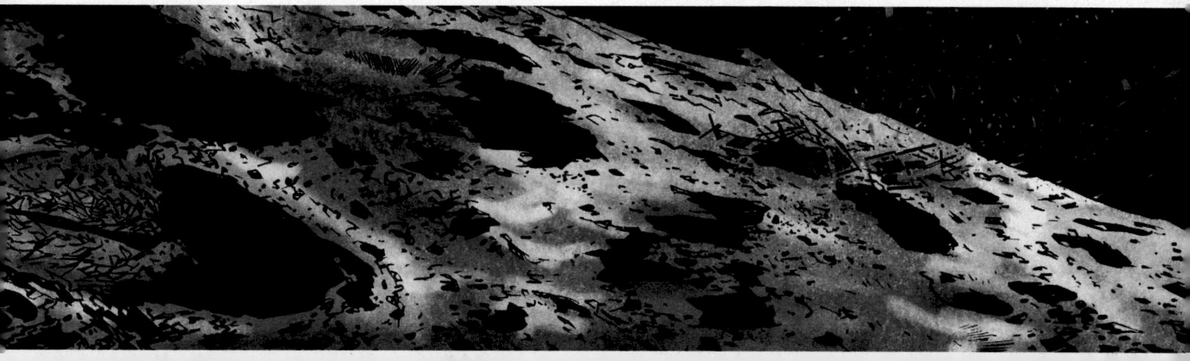

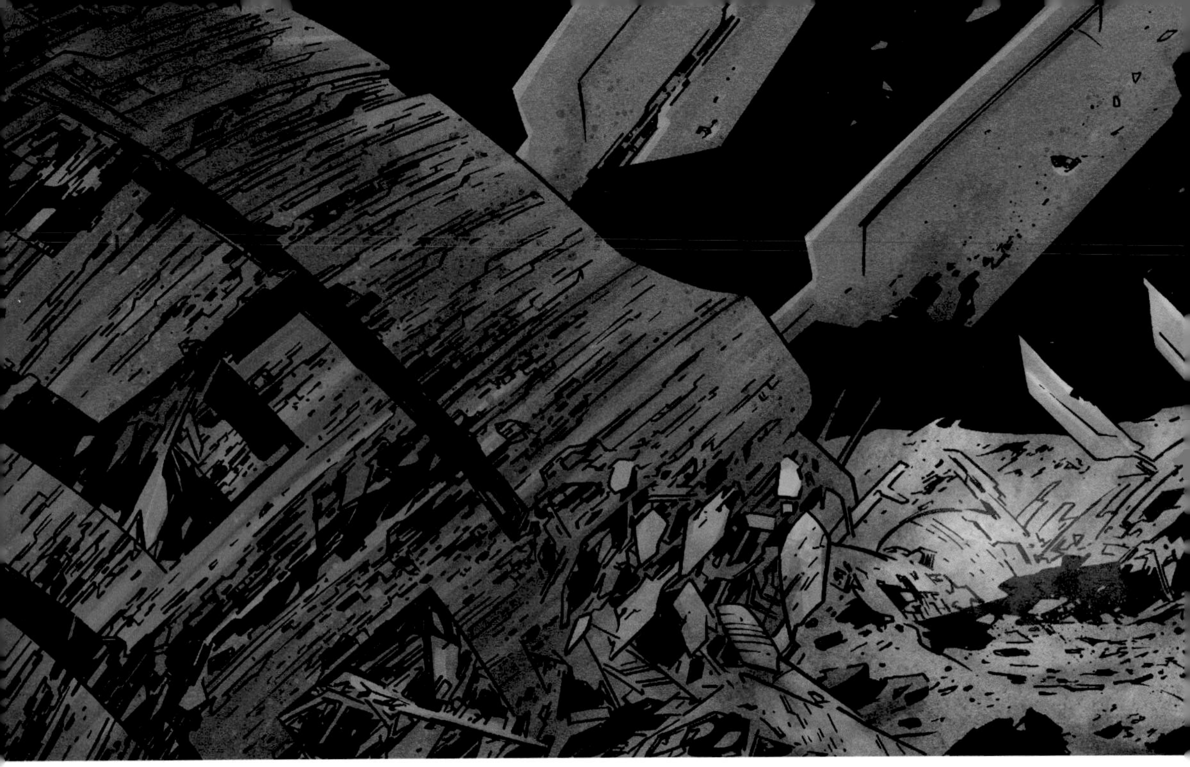

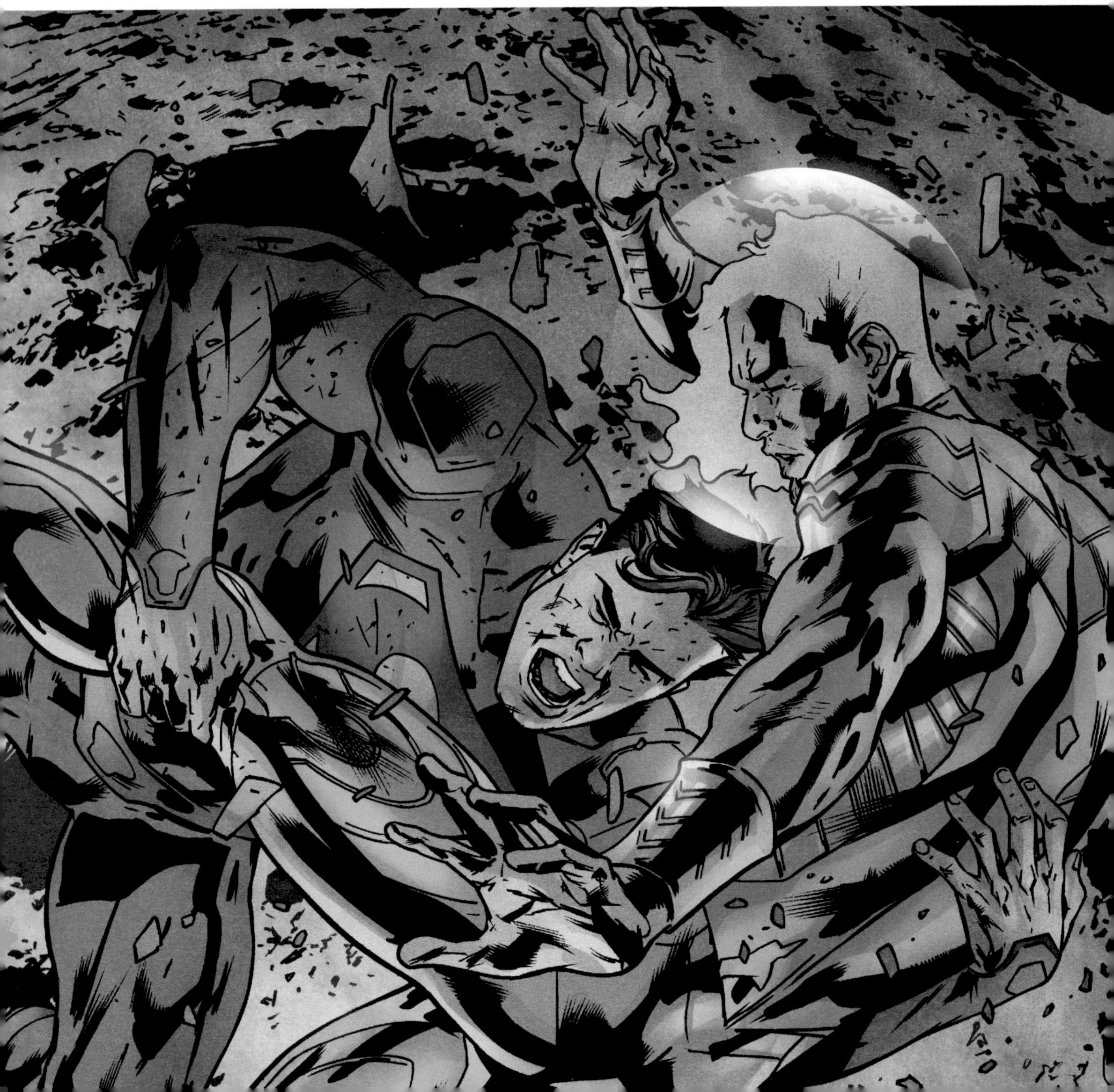

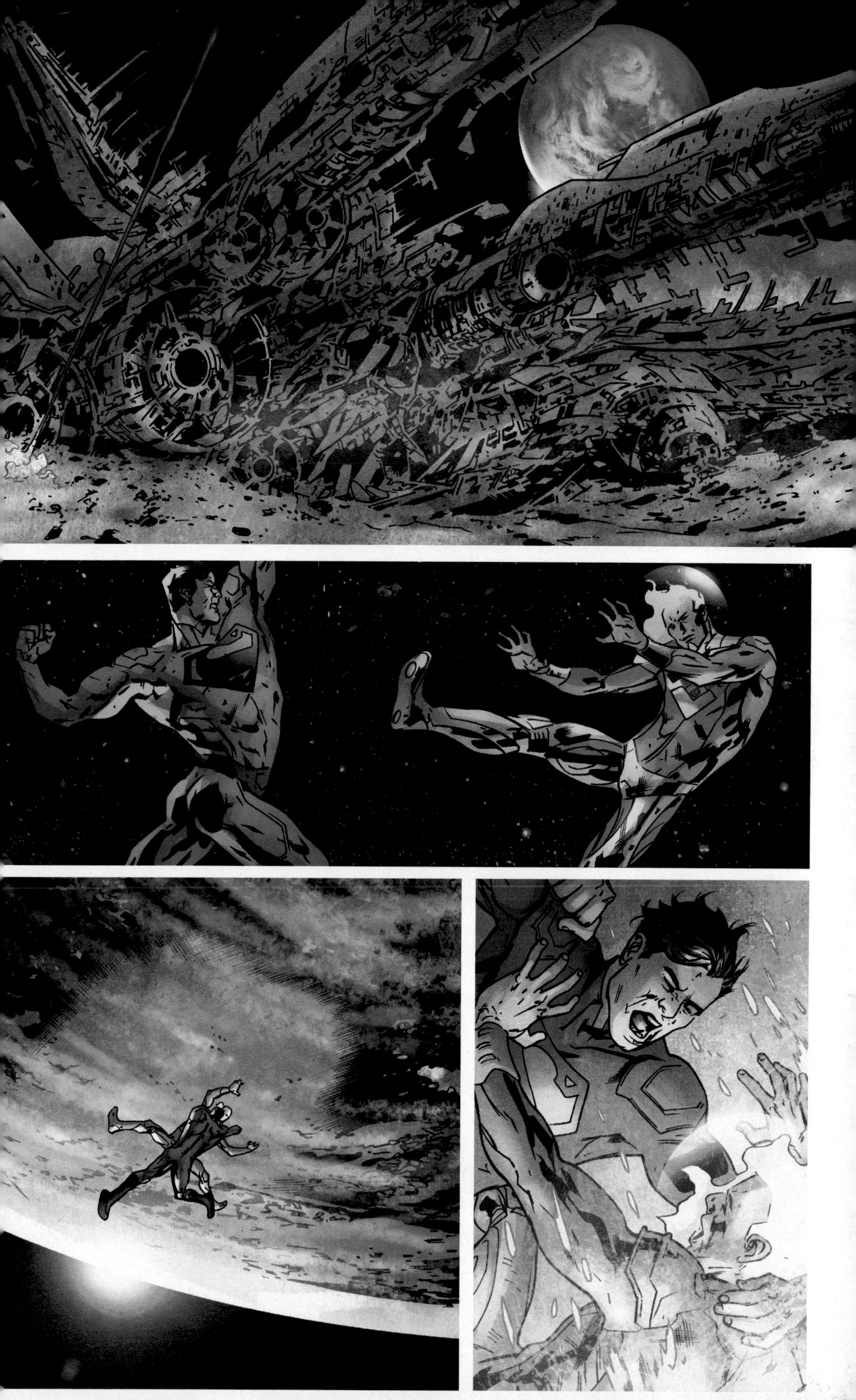

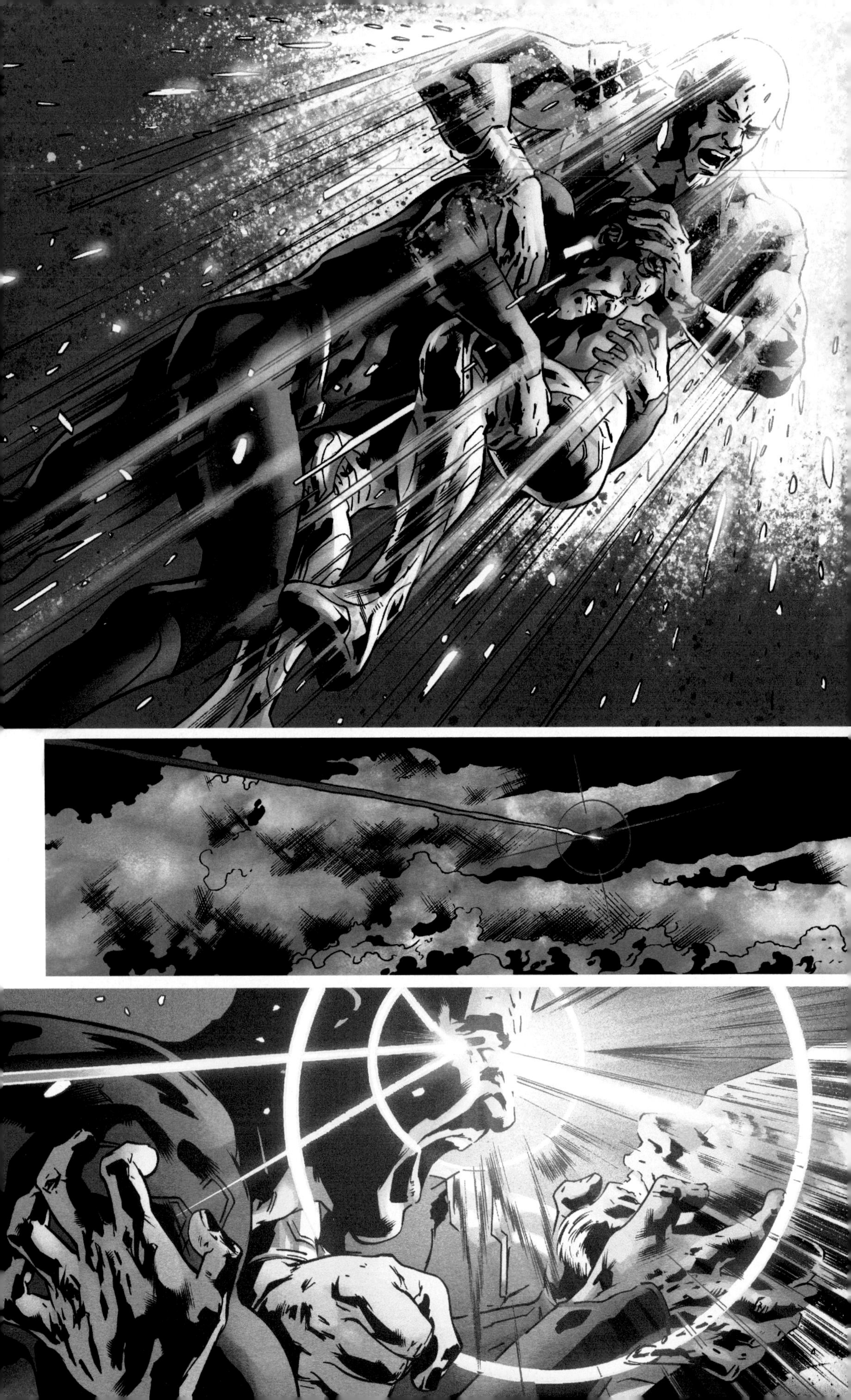

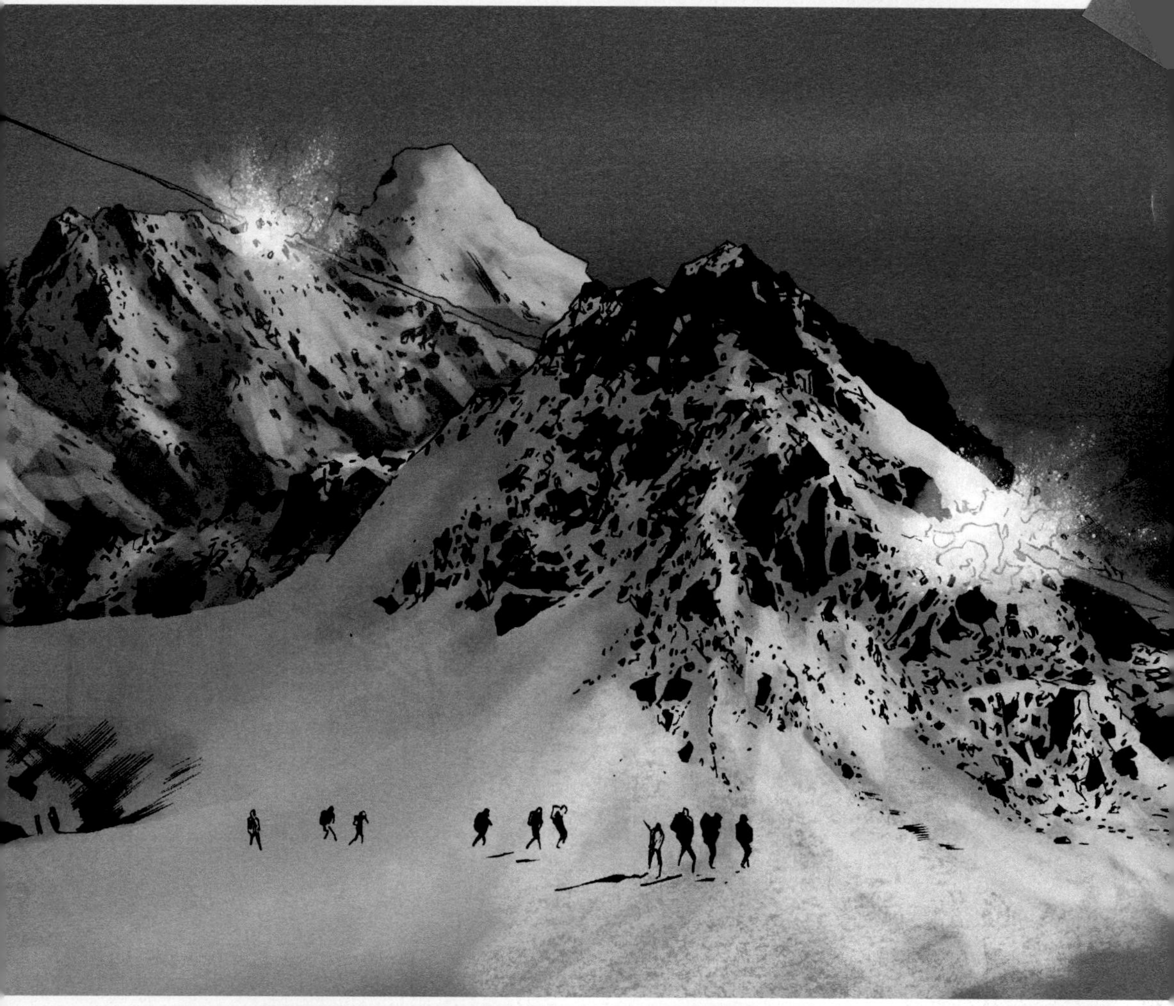

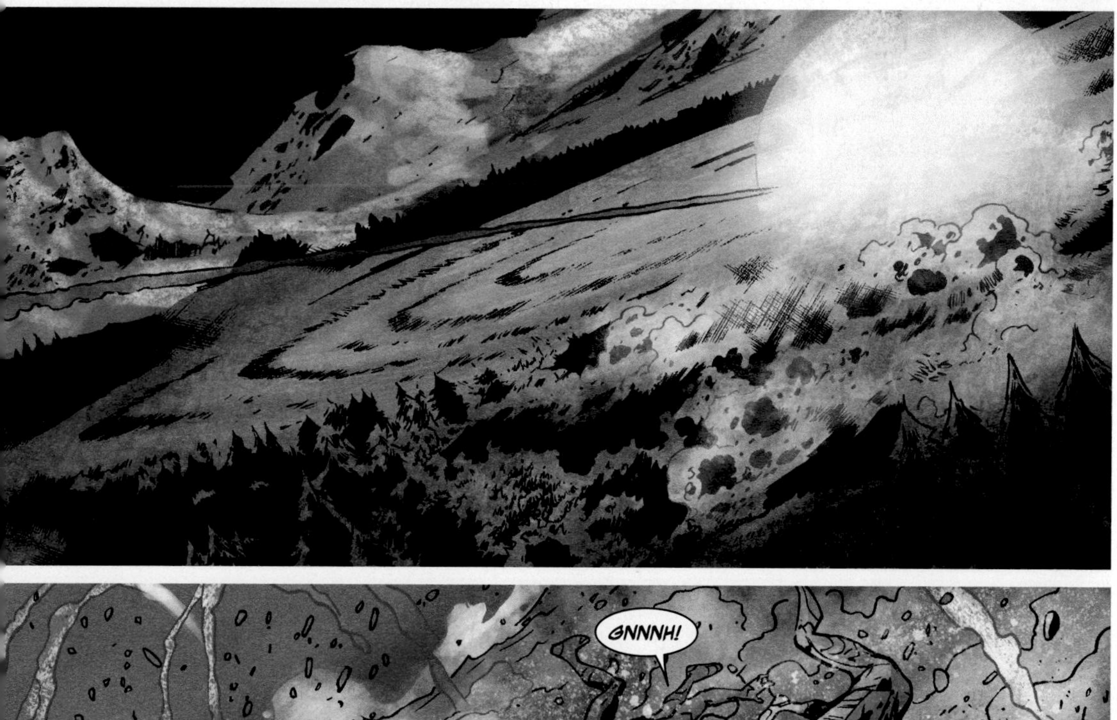

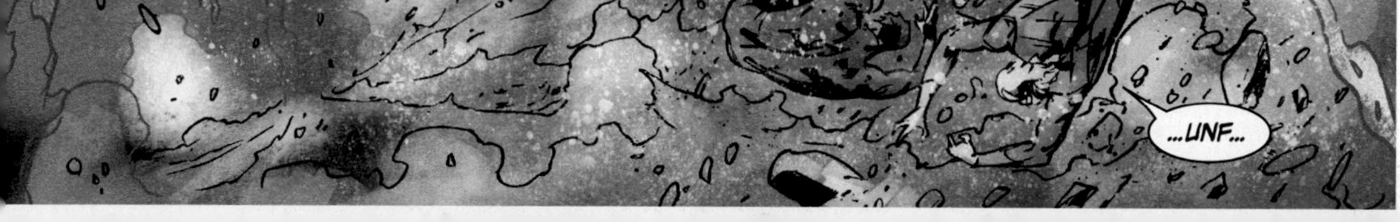
GNNNH!
...UNF...

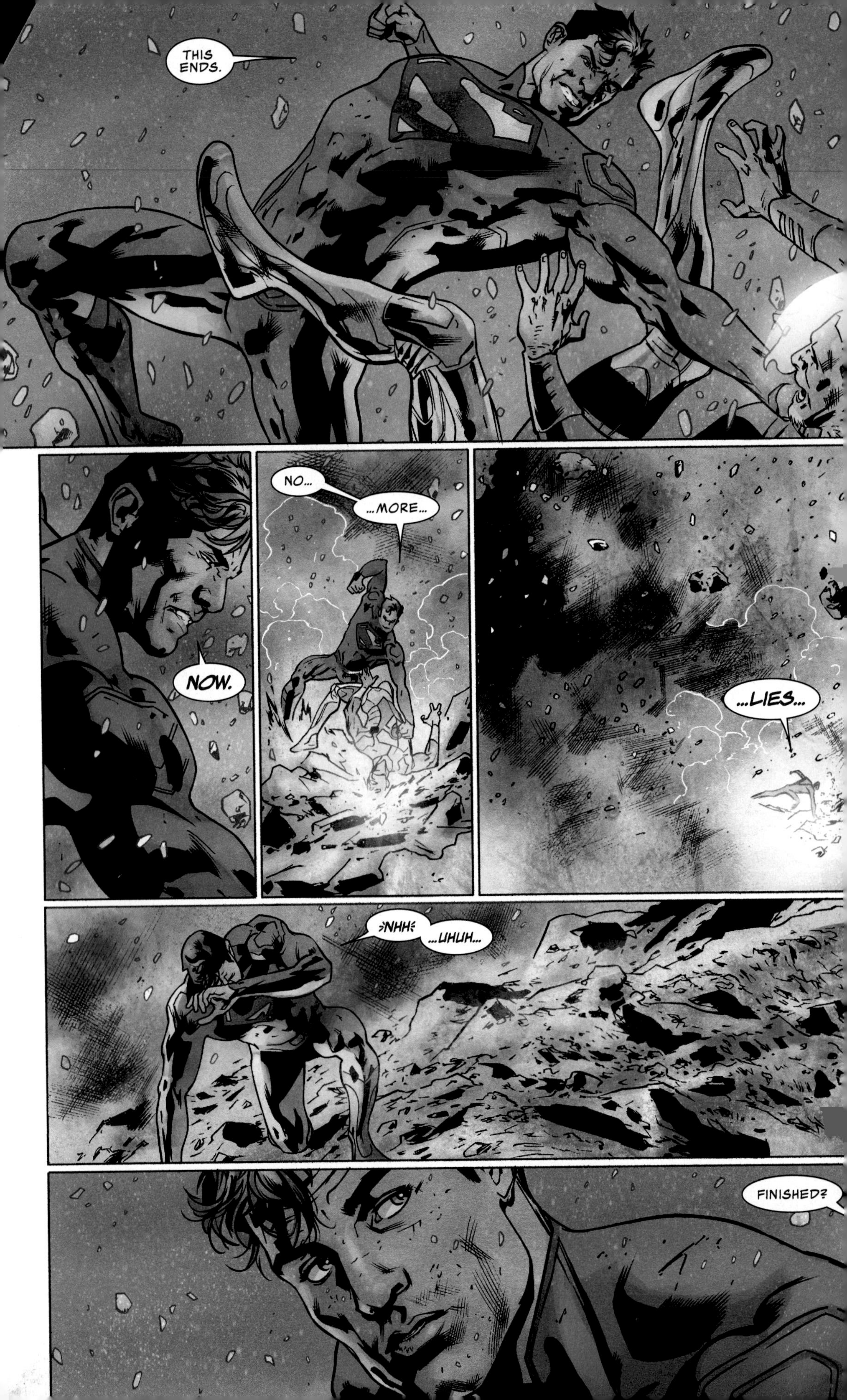
THIS ENDS.
NOW.
NO...
...MORE...
...LIES...
NHH ...UHUH...
FINISHED?

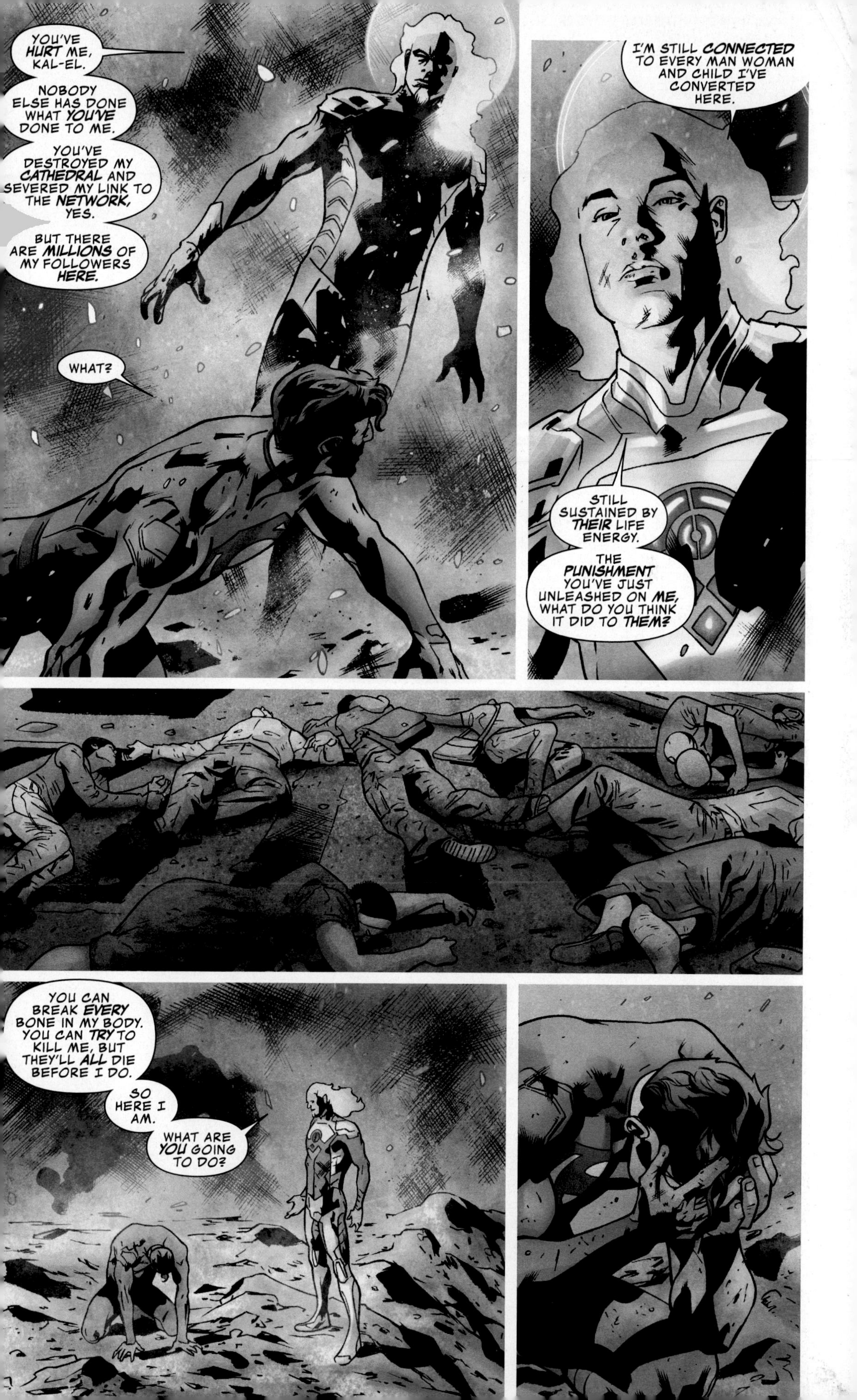
YOU'VE HURT ME, KAL-EL.
NOBODY ELSE HAS DONE WHAT YOU'VE DONE TO ME.
YOU'VE DESTROYED MY CATHEDRAL AND SEVERED MY LINK TO THE NETWORK, YES.
BUT THERE ARE MILLIONS OF MY FOLLOWERS HERE.
WHAT?
I'M STILL CONNECTED TO EVERY MAN WOMAN AND CHILD I'VE CONVERTED HERE.
STILL SUSTAINED BY THEIR LIFE ENERGY.
THE PUNISHMENT YOU'VE JUST UNLEASHED ON ME, WHAT DO YOU THINK IT DID TO THEM?
YOU CAN BREAK EVERY BONE IN MY BODY. YOU CAN TRY TO KILL ME, BUT THEY'LL ALL DIE BEFORE I DO.
SO HERE I AM.
WHAT ARE YOU GOING TO DO?

HNNF...

FIGHT BACK. I DARE YOU.

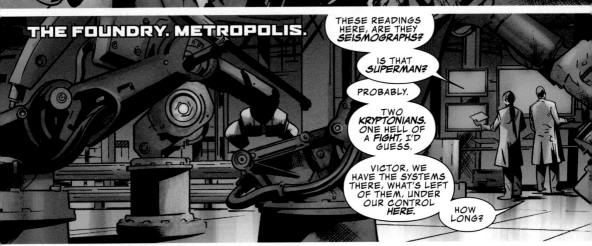

THE FOUNDRY. METROPOLIS.

THESE READINGS HERE, ARE THEY SEISMOGRAPHS?

IS THAT SUPERMAN?

PROBABLY.

TWO KRYPTONIANS. ONE HELL OF A FIGHT, I'D GUESS.

VICTOR, WE HAVE THE SYSTEMS THERE, WHAT'S LEFT OF THEM, UNDER OUR CONTROL HERE.

HOW LONG?

GONNA BE A WHILE YET. PLACE IS TRASHED.

BATMAN IS INBOUND WITH THE PACKAGE.

OKAY. BETTER BE QUICK.

SO, BATMAN NEVER TOLD US YOUR NAME.

HE NEVER ASKED.

THEN I SHALL. I'M SILAS STONE. VICTOR'S FATHER.

ANISA WILLIAMS.

BATMAN SAVED MY LIFE ONCE. THOUGH, I'M SURE HE DOESN'T REMEMBER.

REALLY?

GANG OF THUGS WITH IDEAS ABOUT HOW THEY LIKE TO ENTERTAIN THEMSELVES.

THEY ENDED UP IN MY E.R.

THESE SEISMOGRAPH READINGS ARE OFF THE SCALE.

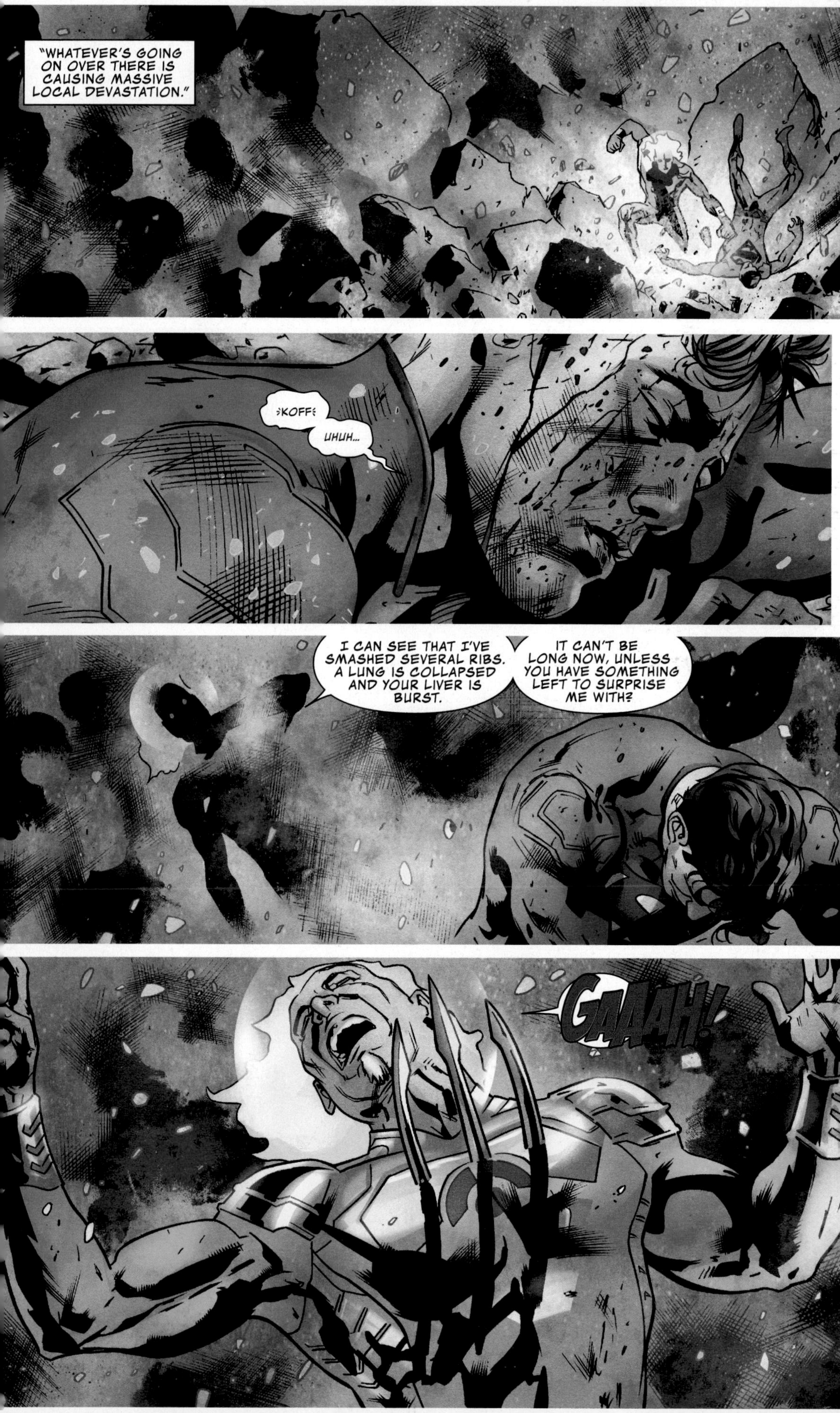
"WHATEVER'S GOING ON OVER THERE IS CAUSING MASSIVE LOCAL DEVASTATION."
KOFF
UHUH...
I CAN SEE THAT I'VE SMASHED SEVERAL RIBS. A LUNG IS COLLAPSED AND YOUR LIVER IS BURST.
IT CAN'T BE LONG NOW, UNLESS YOU HAVE SOMETHING LEFT TO SURPRISE ME WITH?
GAAAH!

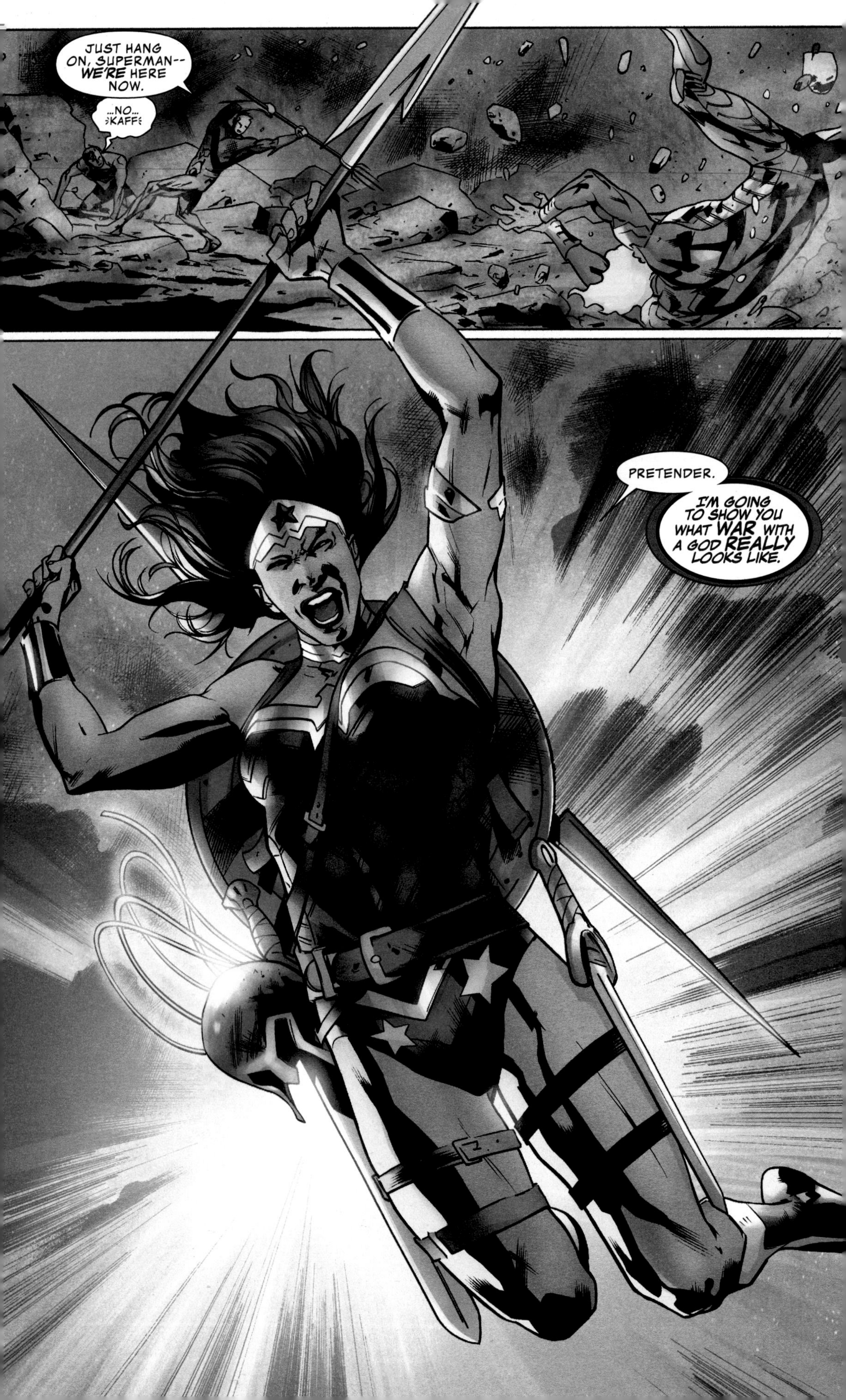
JUST HANG ON, SUPERMAN-- WE'RE HERE NOW.
...NO... KAFF
PRETENDER.
I'M GOING TO SHOW YOU WHAT WAR WITH A GOD REALLY LOOKS LIKE.

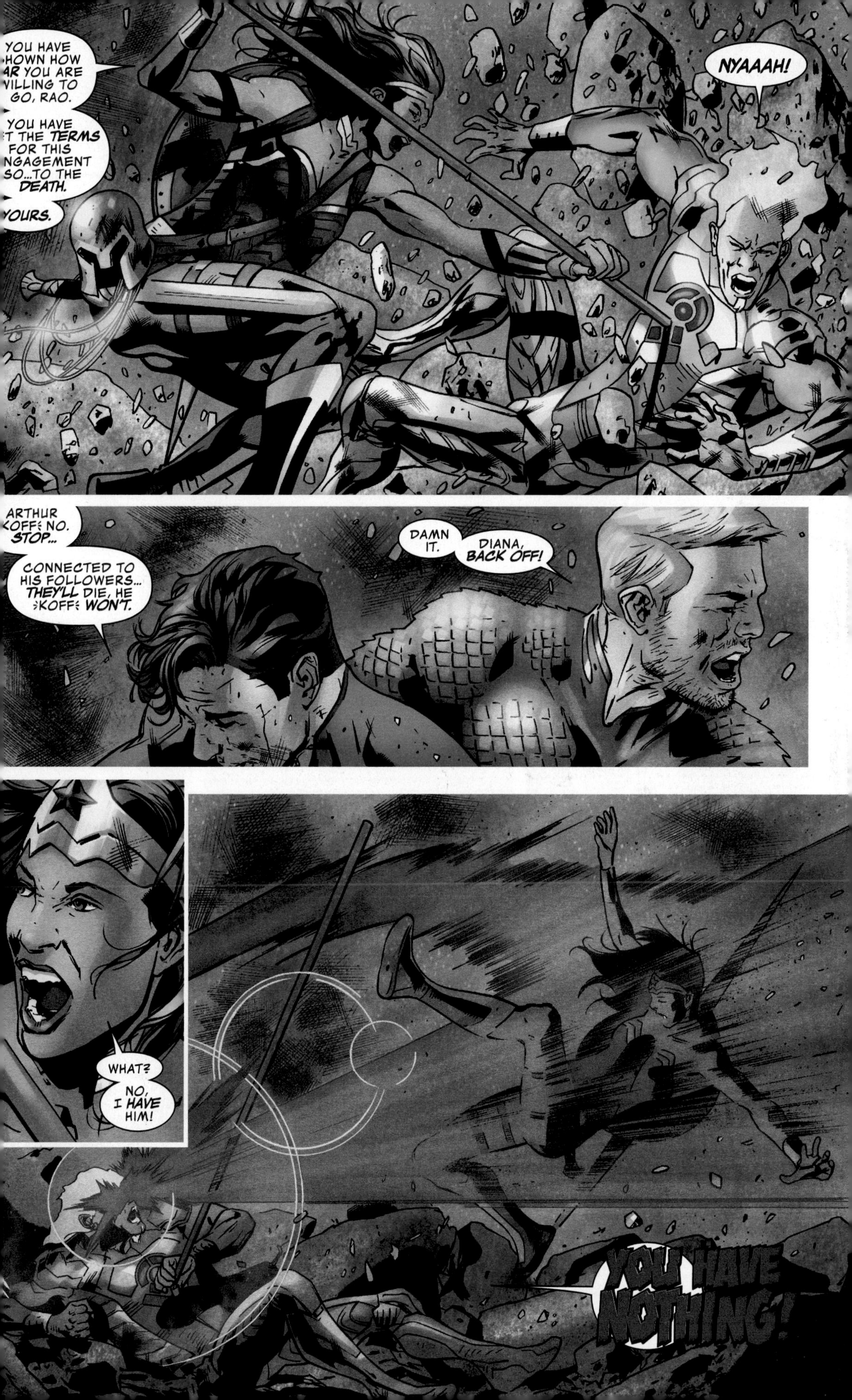
YOU HAVE SHOWN HOW FAR YOU ARE WILLING TO GO, RAO.
YOU HAVE SET THE TERMS FOR THIS ENGAGEMENT SO...TO THE DEATH.
YOURS.
NYAAAH!
ARTHUR KOFF NO. STOP...
CONNECTED TO HIS FOLLOWERS... THEY'LL DIE, HE KOFF WON'T.
DAMN IT.
DIANA, BACK OFF!
WHAT?
NO, I HAVE HIM!
YOU HAVE NOTHING!

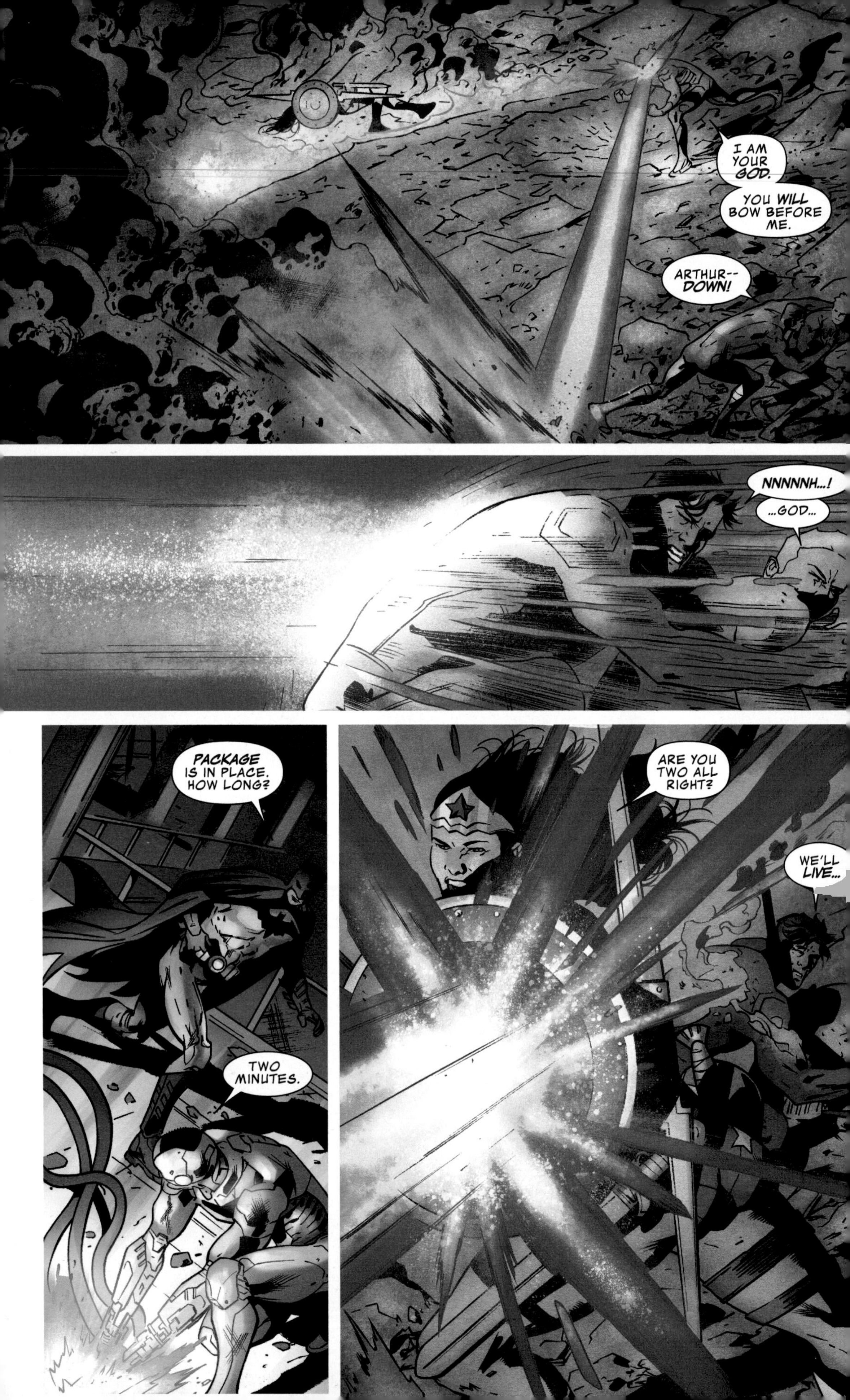
I AM YOUR GOD.
YOU WILL BOW BEFORE ME.
ARTHUR-- DOWN!
NNNNNH...!
...GOD...
PACKAGE IS IN PLACE. HOW LONG?
TWO MINUTES.
ARE YOU TWO ALL RIGHT?
WE'LL LIVE...

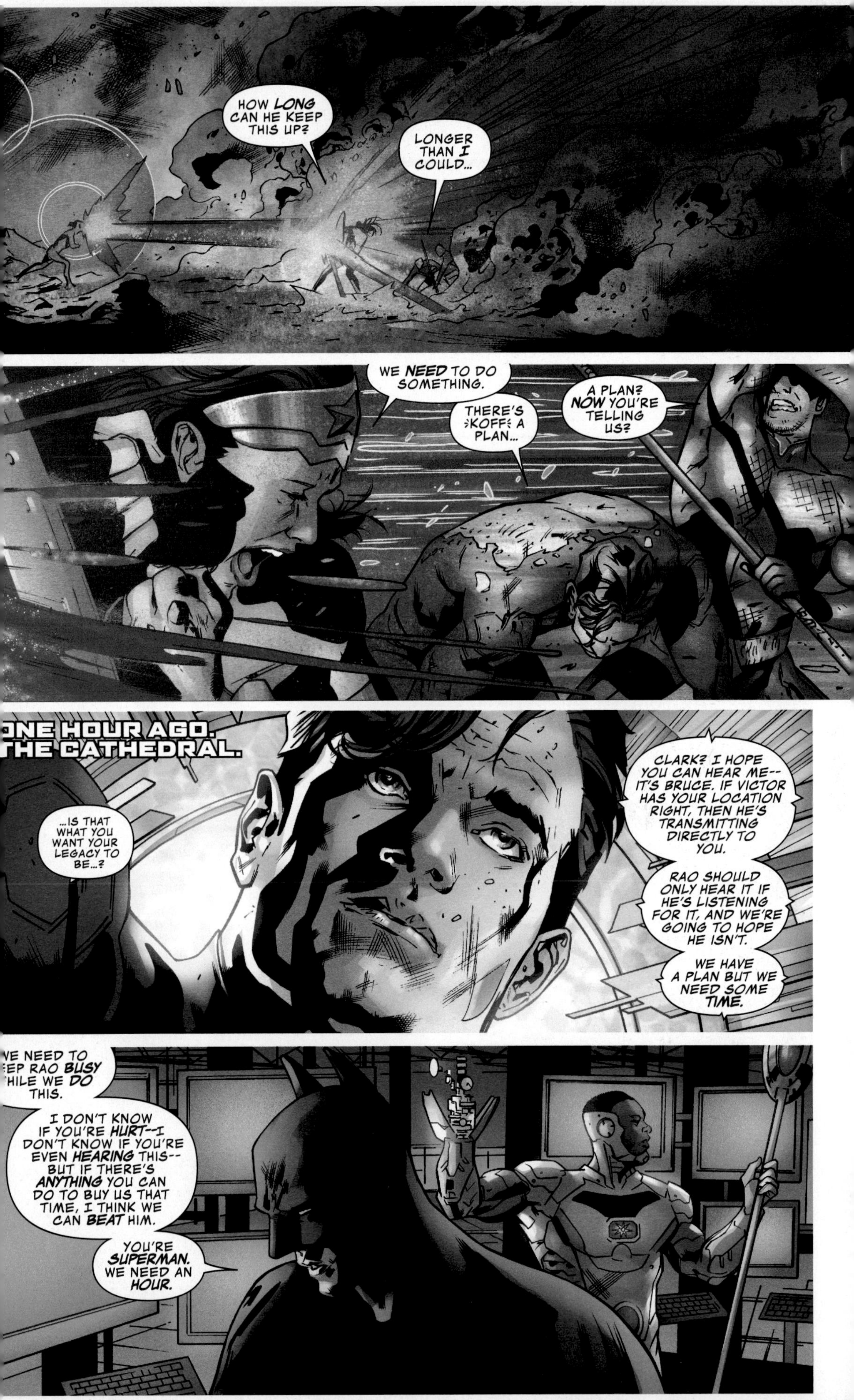
HOW LONG CAN HE KEEP THIS UP?
LONGER THAN I COULD...
WE NEED TO DO SOMETHING.
THERE'S *KOFF* A PLAN...
A PLAN? NOW YOU'RE TELLING US?
ONE HOUR AGO. THE CATHEDRAL.
...IS THAT WHAT YOU WANT YOUR LEGACY TO BE...?
CLARK? I HOPE YOU CAN HEAR ME-- IT'S BRUCE. IF VICTOR HAS YOUR LOCATION RIGHT, THEN HE'S TRANSMITTING DIRECTLY TO YOU.
RAO SHOULD ONLY HEAR IT IF HE'S LISTENING FOR IT, AND WE'RE GOING TO HOPE HE ISN'T.
WE HAVE A PLAN BUT WE NEED SOME TIME.
WE NEED TO KEEP RAO BUSY WHILE WE DO THIS.
I DON'T KNOW IF YOU'RE HURT--I DON'T KNOW IF YOU'RE EVEN HEARING THIS-- BUT IF THERE'S ANYTHING YOU CAN DO TO BUY US THAT TIME, I THINK WE CAN BEAT HIM.
YOU'RE SUPERMAN. WE NEED AN HOUR.

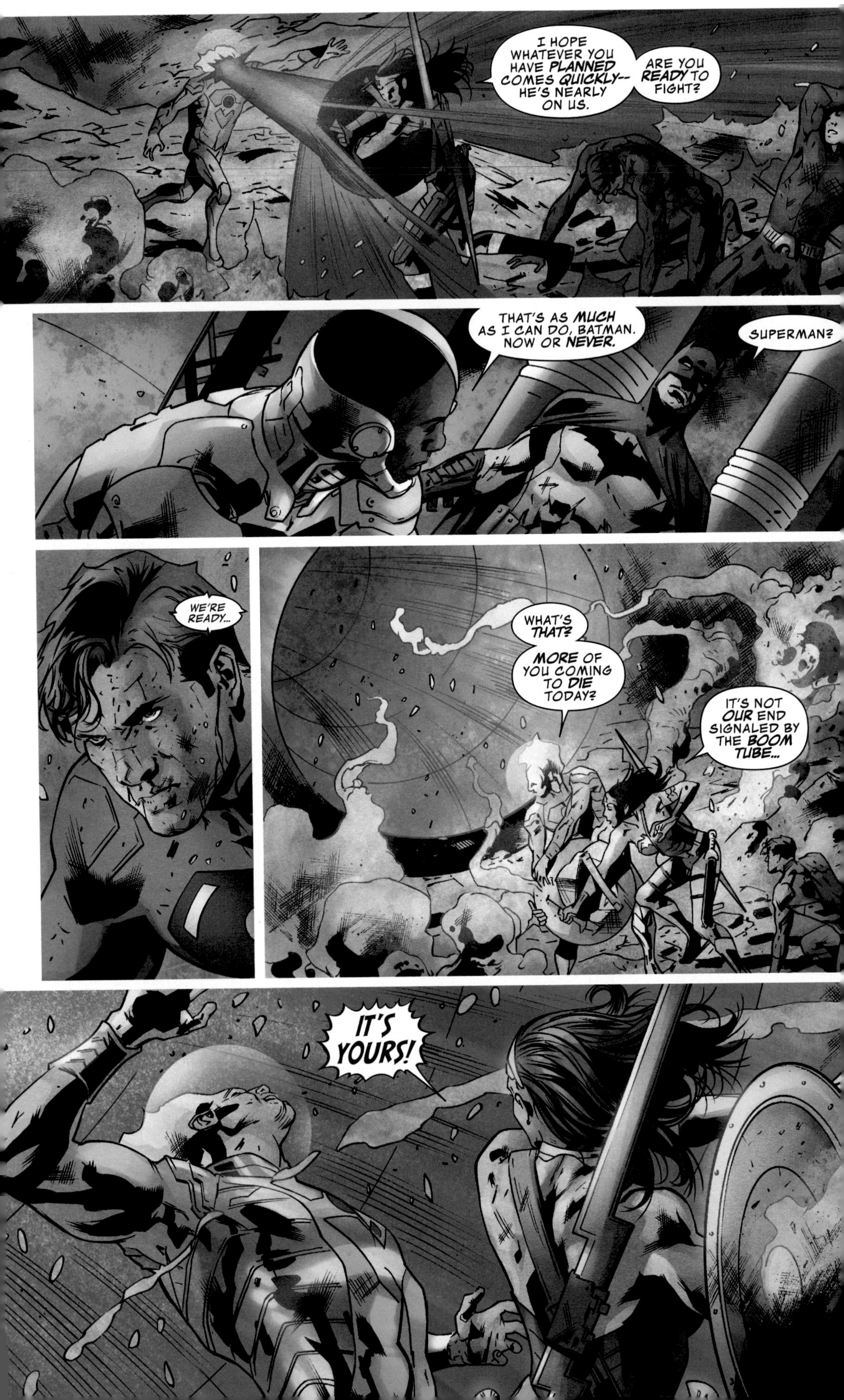
I HOPE WHATEVER YOU HAVE PLANNED COMES QUICKLY-- HE'S NEARLY ON US.
ARE YOU READY TO FIGHT?
THAT'S AS MUCH AS I CAN DO, BATMAN. NOW OR NEVER.
SUPERMAN?
WE'RE READY...
WHAT'S THAT?
MORE OF YOU COMING TO DIE TODAY?
IT'S NOT OUR END SIGNALED BY THE BOOM TUBE...
IT'S YOURS!

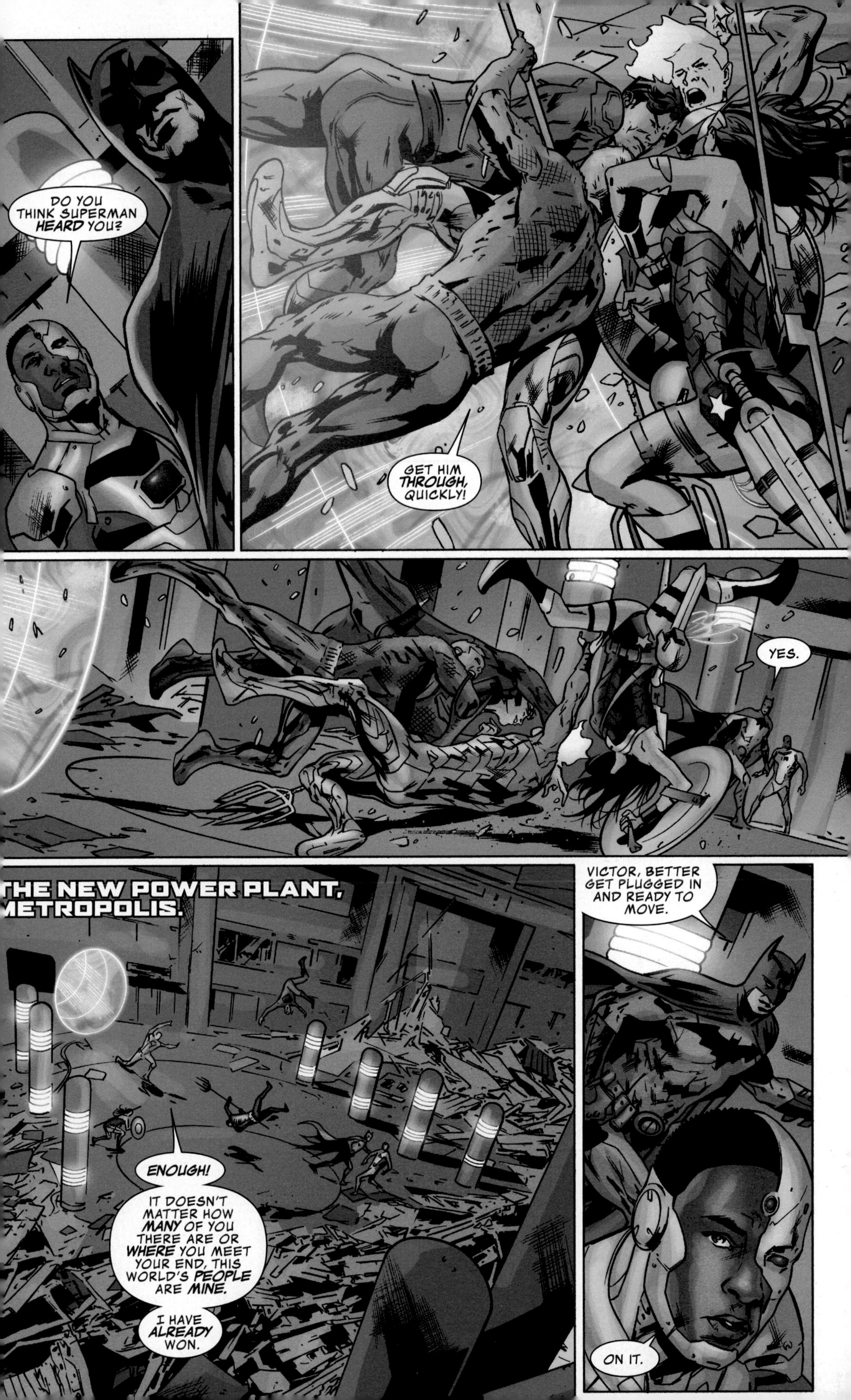
DO YOU THINK SUPERMAN HEARD YOU?
GET HIM THROUGH, QUICKLY!
YES.
THE NEW POWER PLANT, METROPOLIS.
ENOUGH!
IT DOESN'T MATTER HOW MANY OF YOU THERE ARE OR WHERE YOU MEET YOUR END, THIS WORLD'S PEOPLE ARE MINE.
I HAVE ALREADY WON.
VICTOR, BETTER GET PLUGGED IN AND READY TO MOVE.
ON IT.

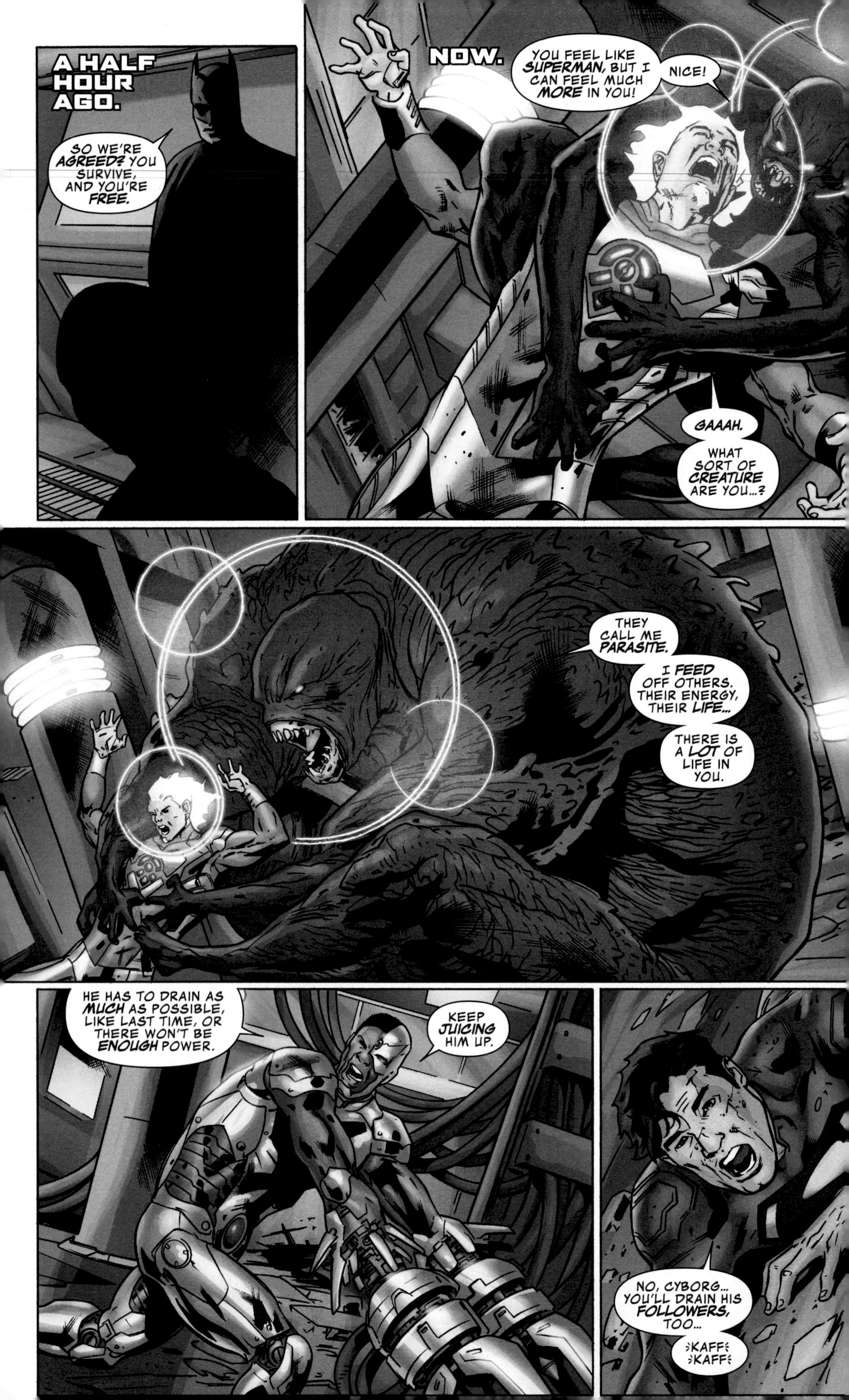

A HALF HOUR AGO.
SO WE'RE AGREED? YOU SURVIVE, AND YOU'RE FREE.
NOW.
YOU FEEL LIKE SUPERMAN, BUT I CAN FEEL MUCH MORE IN YOU!
NICE!
GAAAH.
WHAT SORT OF CREATURE ARE YOU...?
THEY CALL ME PARASITE.
I FEED OFF OTHERS. THEIR ENERGY, THEIR LIFE...
THERE IS A LOT OF LIFE IN YOU.
HE HAS TO DRAIN AS MUCH AS POSSIBLE, LIKE LAST TIME, OR THERE WON'T BE ENOUGH POWER.
KEEP JUICING HIM UP.
NO, CYBORG... YOU'LL DRAIN HIS FOLLOWERS, TOO...
KAFF KAFF

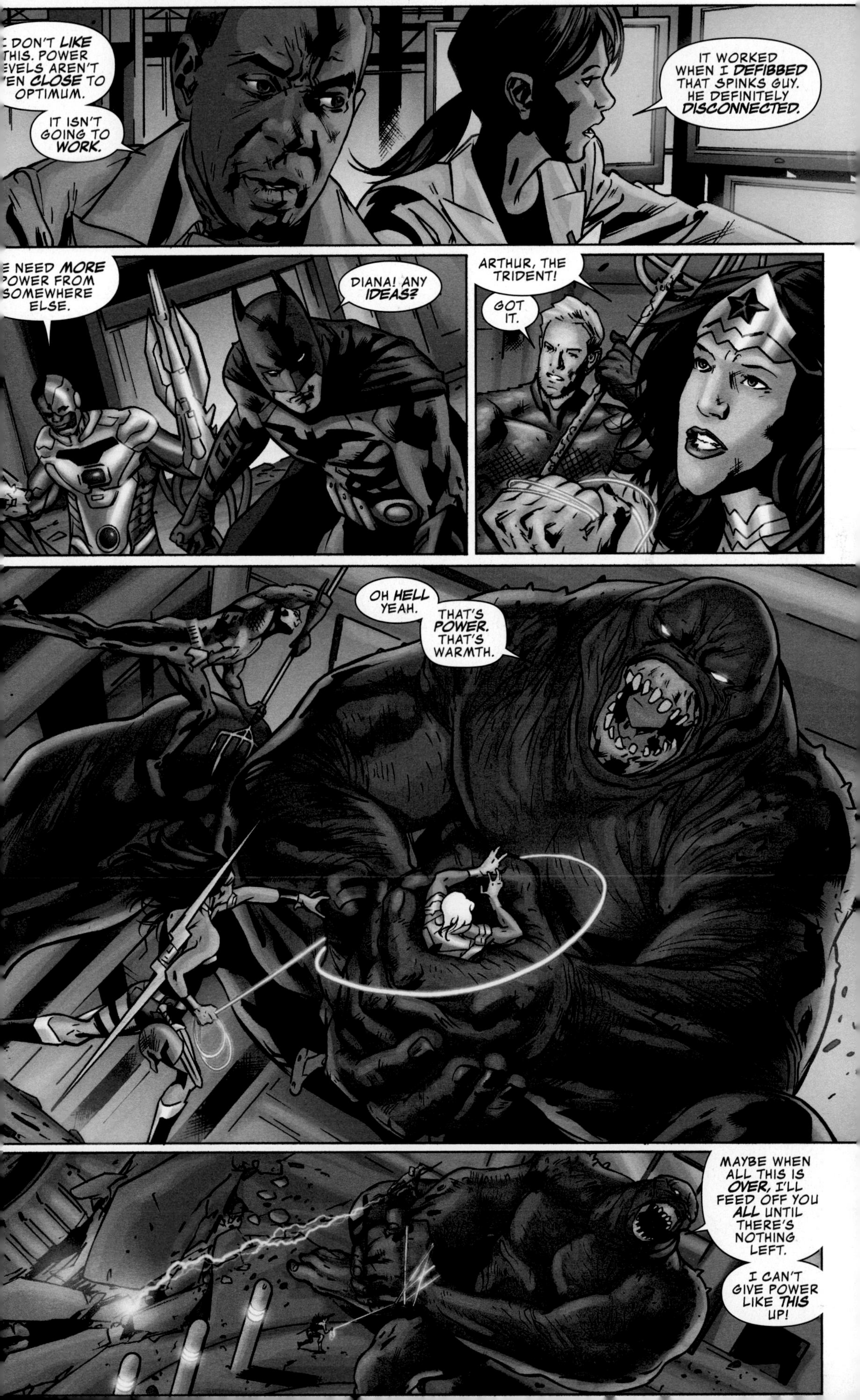

I DON'T LIKE THIS. POWER LEVELS AREN'T EVEN CLOSE TO OPTIMUM.
IT ISN'T GOING TO WORK.
IT WORKED WHEN I DEFIBBED THAT SPINKS GUY. HE DEFINITELY DISCONNECTED.
WE NEED MORE POWER FROM SOMEWHERE ELSE.
DIANA! ANY IDEAS?
ARTHUR, THE TRIDENT!
GOT IT.
OH HELL YEAH.
THAT'S POWER. THAT'S WARMTH.
MAYBE WHEN ALL THIS IS OVER, I'LL FEED OFF YOU ALL UNTIL THERE'S NOTHING LEFT.
I CAN'T GIVE POWER LIKE THIS UP!

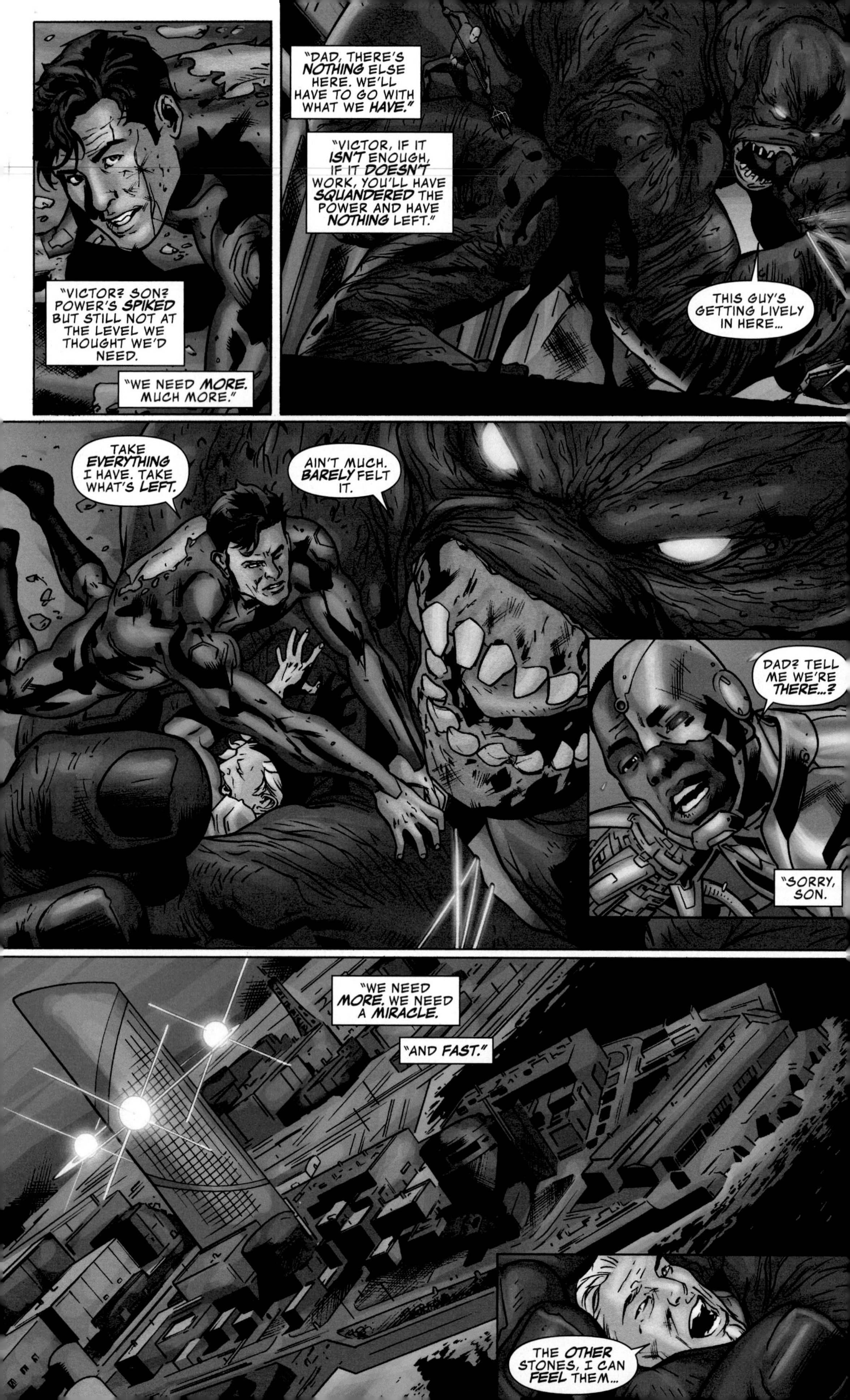
"VICTOR? SON? POWER'S SPIKED BUT STILL NOT AT THE LEVEL WE THOUGHT WE'D NEED.
"WE NEED MORE. MUCH MORE."
"DAD, THERE'S NOTHING ELSE HERE. WE'LL HAVE TO GO WITH WHAT WE HAVE."
"VICTOR, IF IT ISN'T ENOUGH, IF IT DOESN'T WORK, YOU'LL HAVE SQUANDERED THE POWER AND HAVE NOTHING LEFT."
THIS GUY'S GETTING LIVELY IN HERE...
TAKE EVERYTHING I HAVE. TAKE WHAT'S LEFT.
AIN'T MUCH. BARELY FELT IT.
DAD? TELL ME WE'RE THERE...?
"SORRY, SON.
"WE NEED MORE. WE NEED A MIRACLE.
"AND FAST."
THE OTHER STONES, I CAN FEEL THEM...

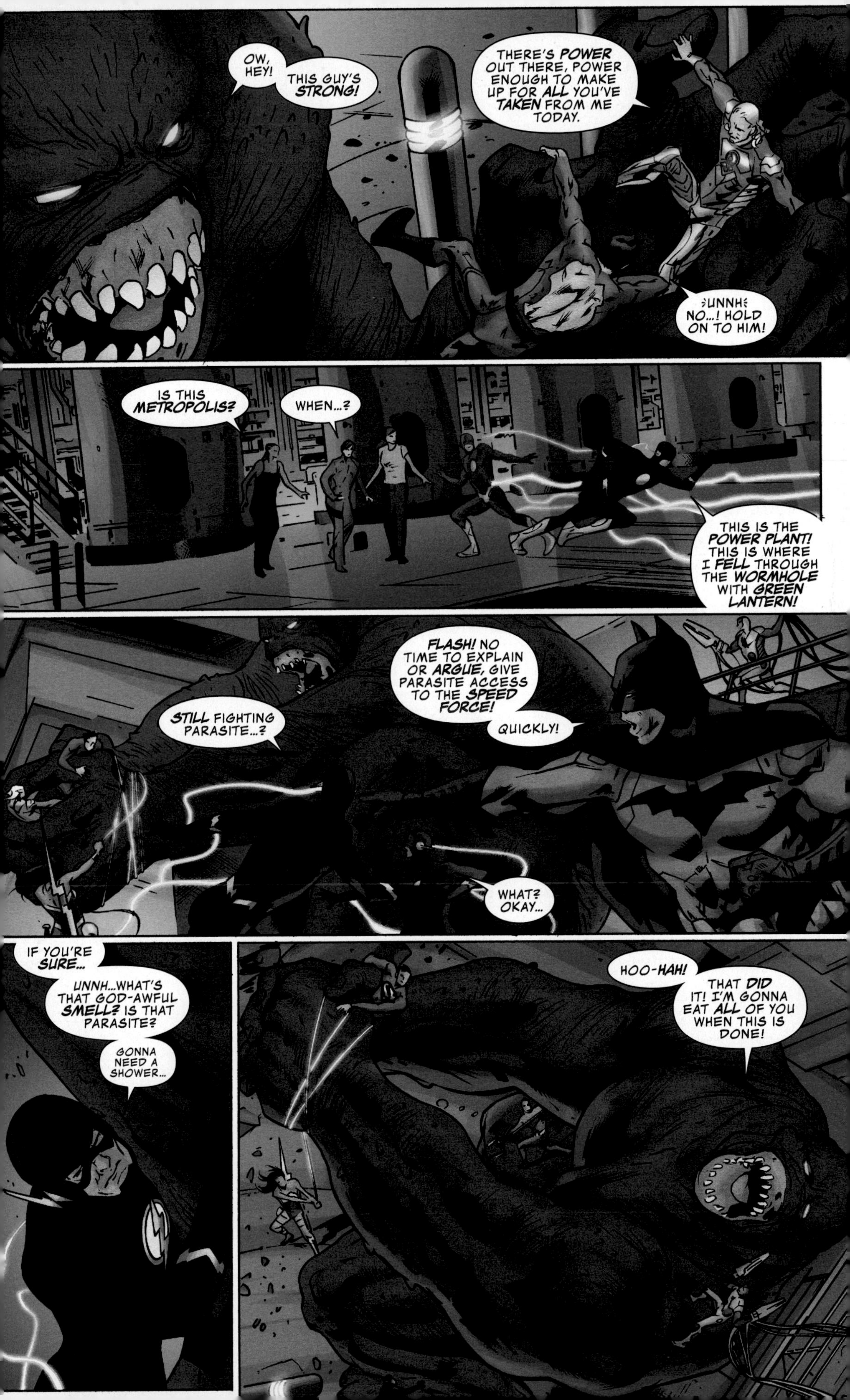
OW, HEY!
THIS GUY'S STRONG!
THERE'S POWER OUT THERE, POWER ENOUGH TO MAKE UP FOR ALL YOU'VE TAKEN FROM ME TODAY.
UNNH NO...! HOLD ON TO HIM!
IS THIS METROPOLIS?
WHEN...?
THIS IS THE POWER PLANT! THIS IS WHERE I FELL THROUGH THE WORMHOLE WITH GREEN LANTERN!
STILL FIGHTING PARASITE...?
FLASH! NO TIME TO EXPLAIN OR ARGUE, GIVE PARASITE ACCESS TO THE SPEED FORCE!
QUICKLY!
WHAT? OKAY...
IF YOU'RE SURE...
UNNH...WHAT'S THAT GOD-AWFUL SMELL? IS THAT PARASITE?
GONNA NEED A SHOWER...
HOO-HAH!
THAT DID IT! I'M GONNA EAT ALL OF YOU WHEN THIS IS DONE!

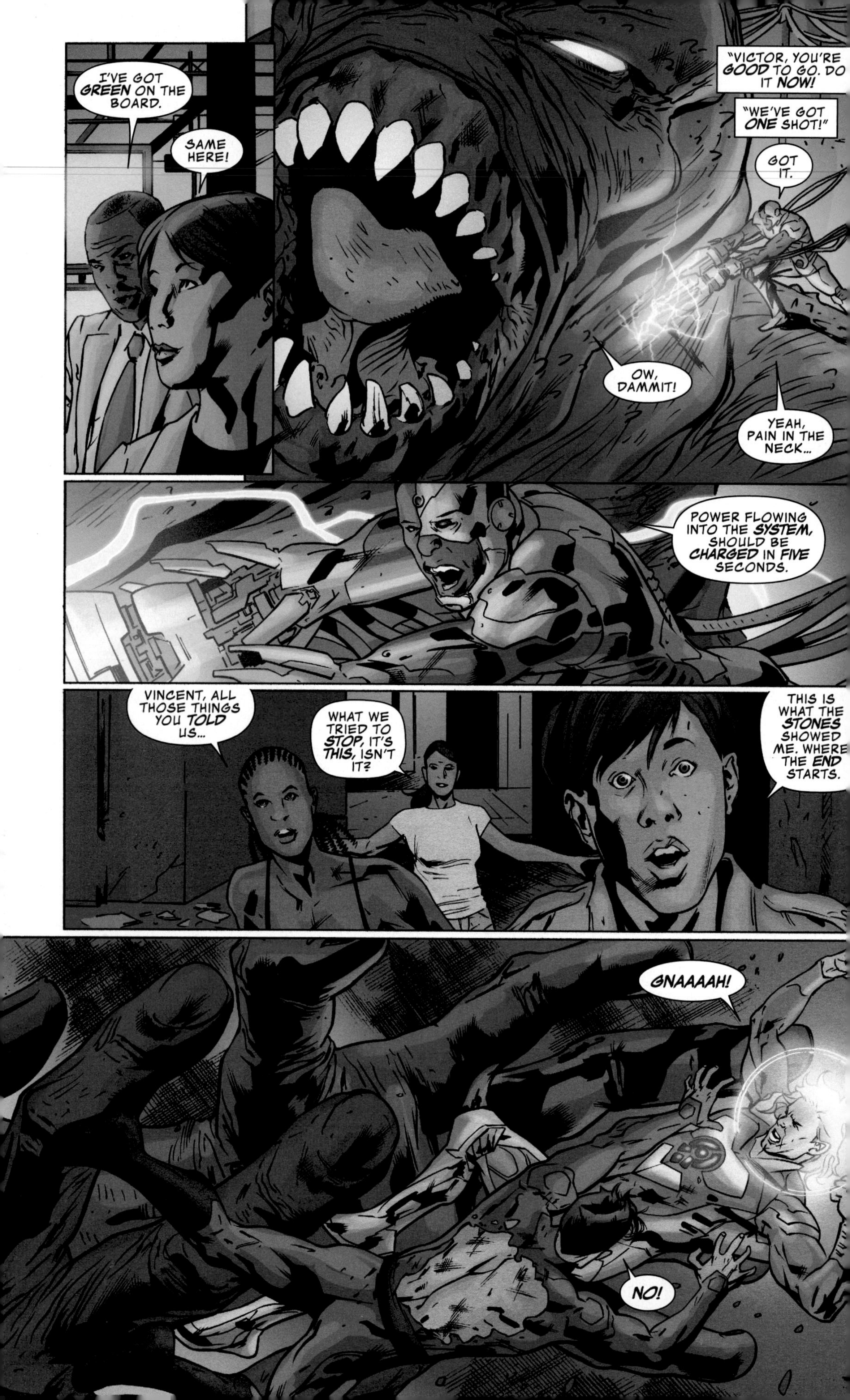
I'VE GOT GREEN ON THE BOARD.
SAME HERE!
"VICTOR, YOU'RE GOOD TO GO. DO IT NOW!
"WE'VE GOT ONE SHOT!"
GOT IT.
OW, DAMMIT!
YEAH, PAIN IN THE NECK...
POWER FLOWING INTO THE SYSTEM, SHOULD BE CHARGED IN FIVE SECONDS.
VINCENT, ALL THOSE THINGS YOU TOLD US...
WHAT WE TRIED TO STOP, IT'S THIS, ISN'T IT?
THIS IS WHAT THE STONES SHOWED ME. WHERE THE END STARTS.
GNAAAAH!
NO!

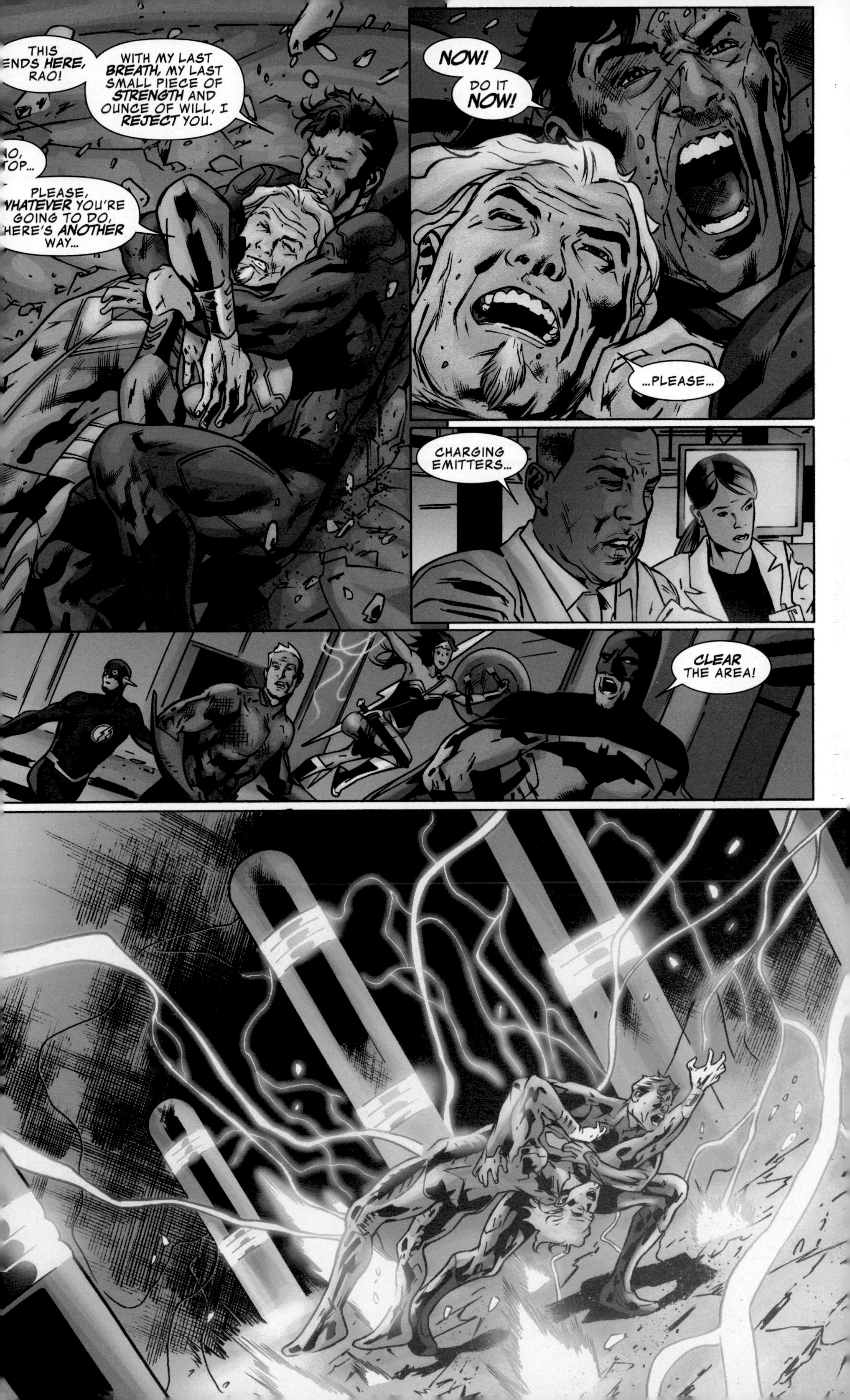
THIS
ENDS HERE,
RAO!
WITH MY LAST BREATH, MY LAST SMALL PIECE OF STRENGTH AND OUNCE OF WILL, I REJECT YOU.
NO,
STOP...
PLEASE, WHATEVER YOU'RE GOING TO DO, THERE'S ANOTHER WAY...
NOW!
DO IT NOW!
...PLEASE...
CHARGING EMITTERS...
CLEAR THE AREA!

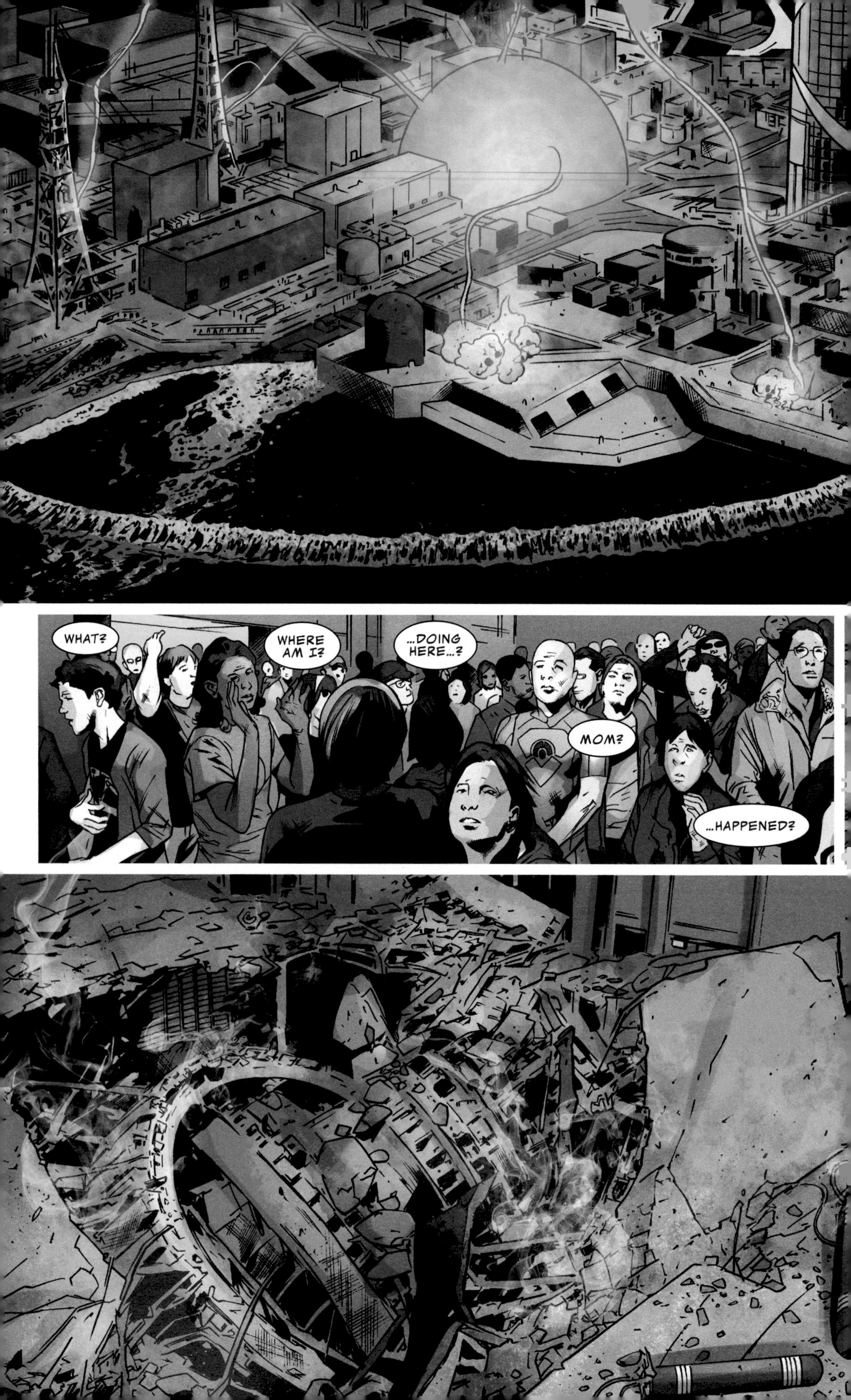
WHAT?
WHERE AM I?
...DOING HERE...?
MOM?
...HAPPENED?

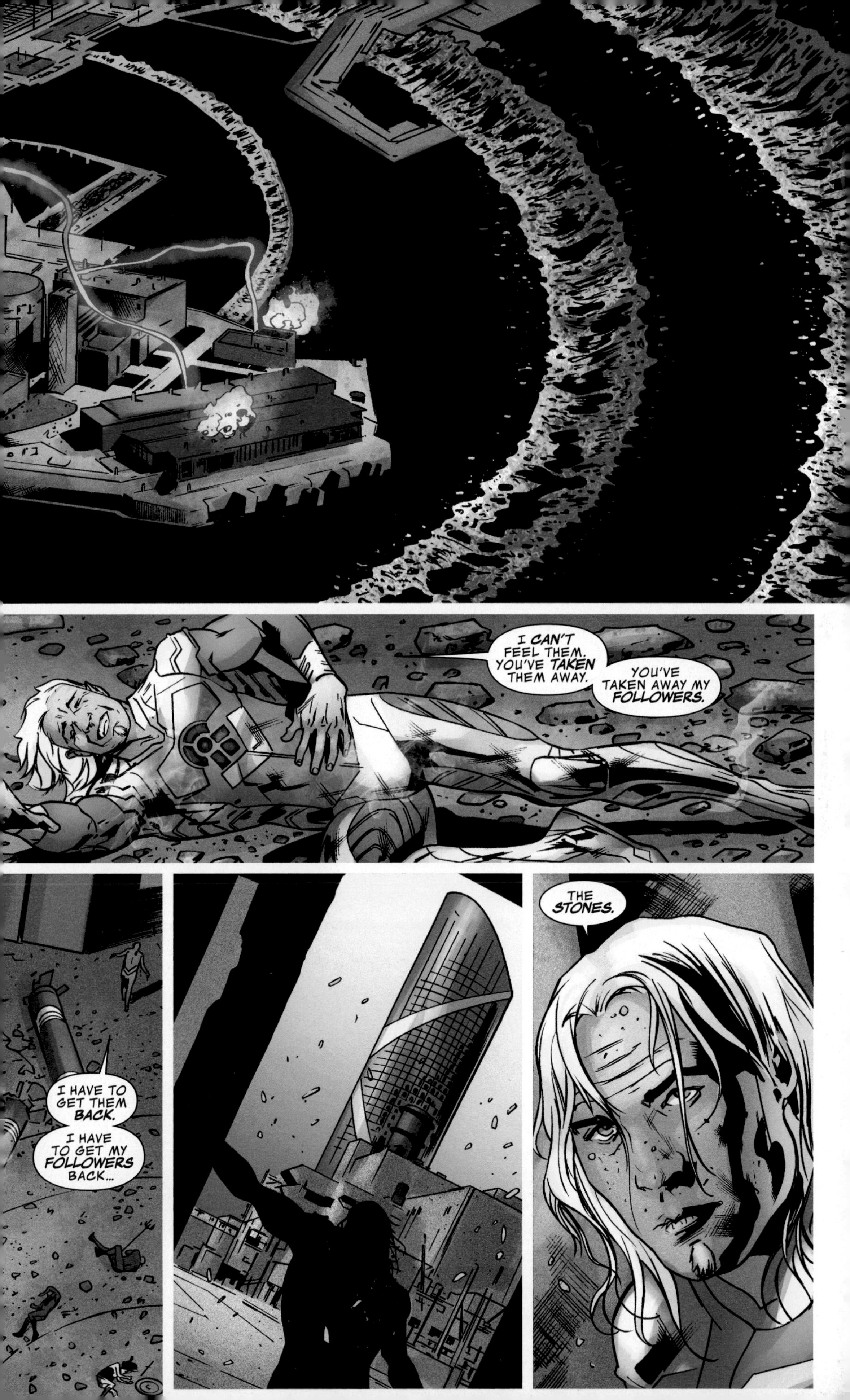
I CAN'T FEEL THEM. YOU'VE TAKEN THEM AWAY.
YOU'VE TAKEN AWAY MY FOLLOWERS.
I HAVE TO GET THEM BACK.
I HAVE TO GET MY FOLLOWERS BACK...
THE STONES.

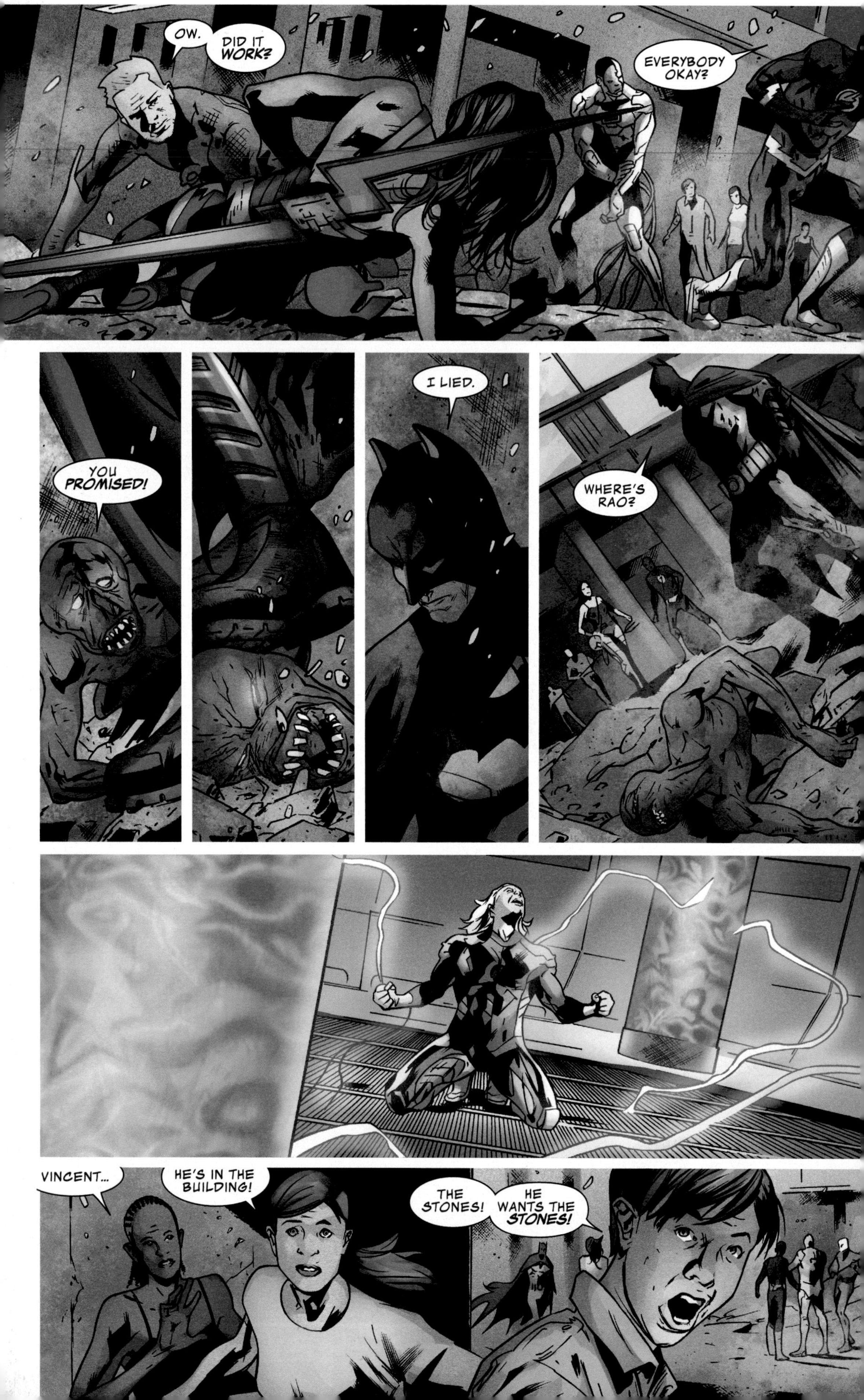
OW.
DID IT WORK?
EVERYBODY OKAY?
YOU PROMISED!
I LIED.
WHERE'S RAO?
VINCENT...
HE'S IN THE BUILDING!
THE STONES!
HE WANTS THE STONES!

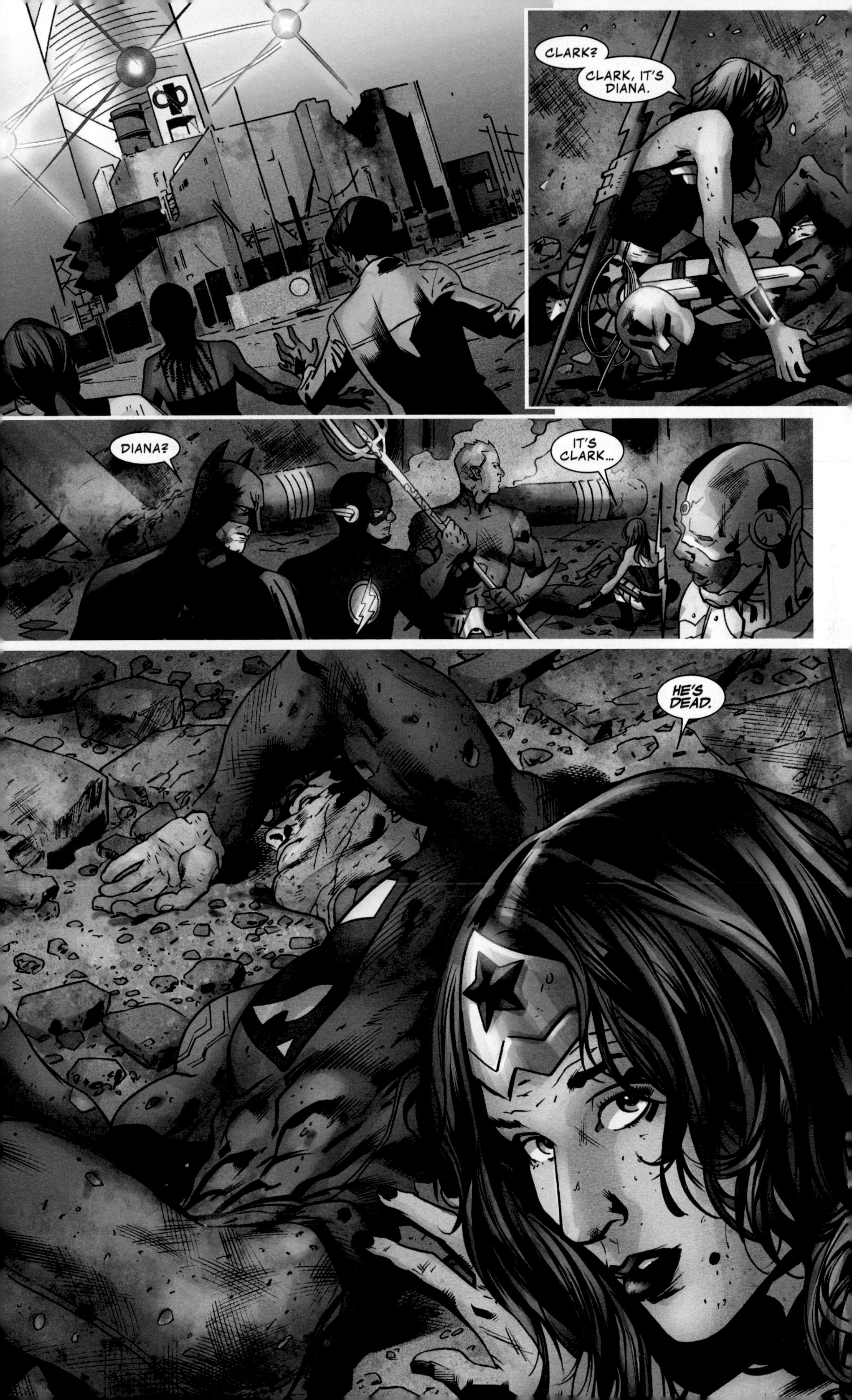
CLARK?
CLARK, IT'S DIANA.
DIANA?
IT'S CLARK...
HE'S DEAD.

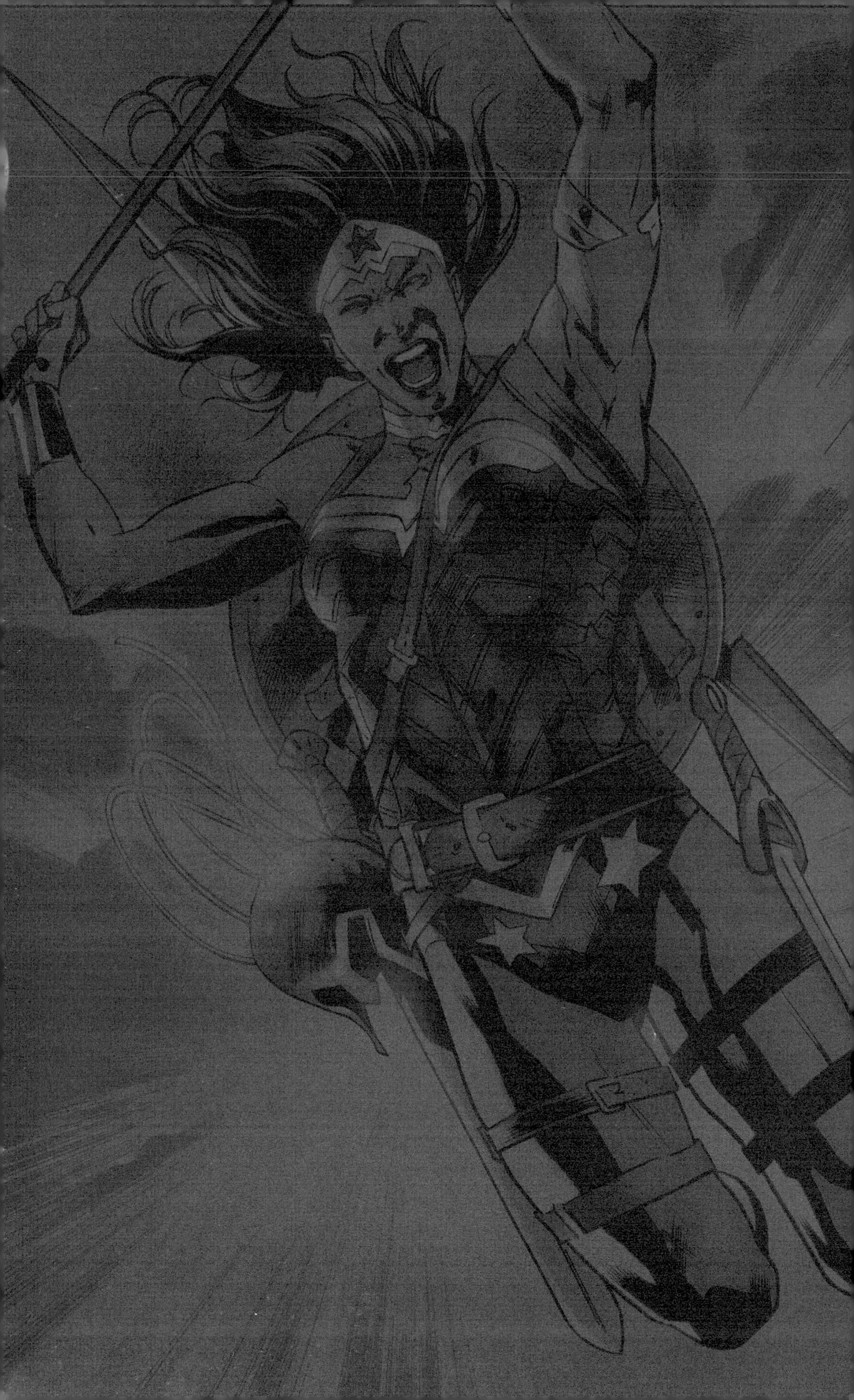

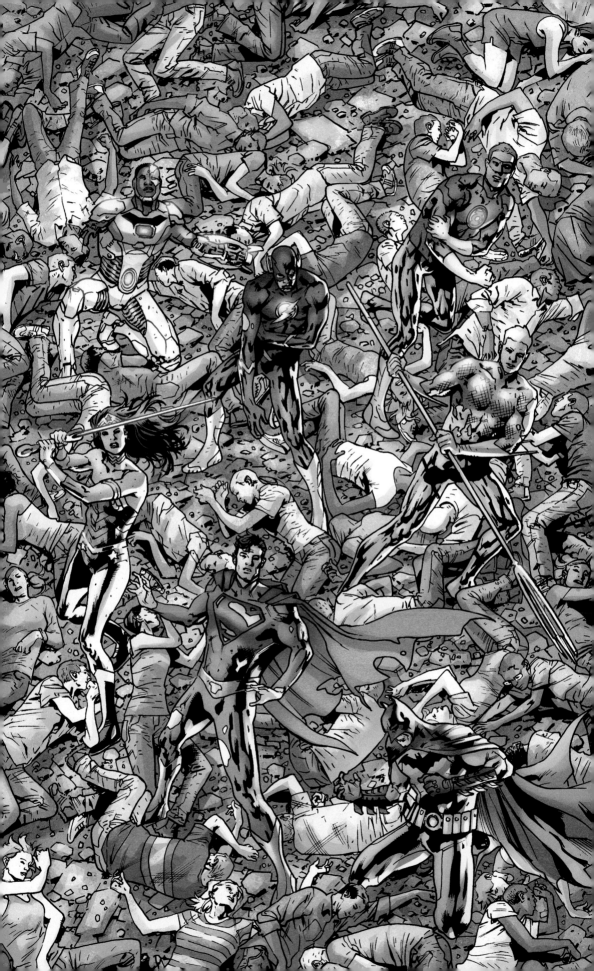

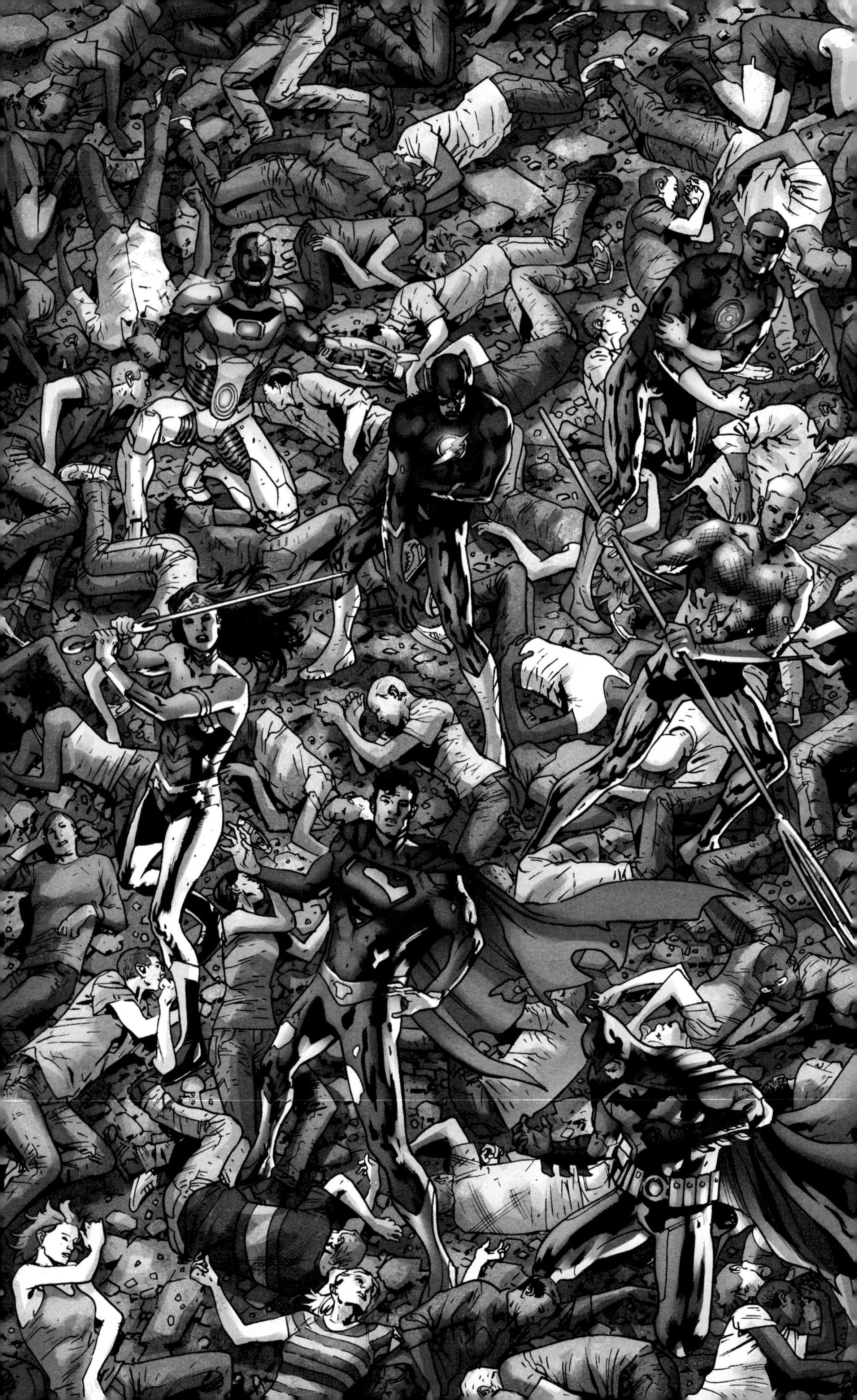

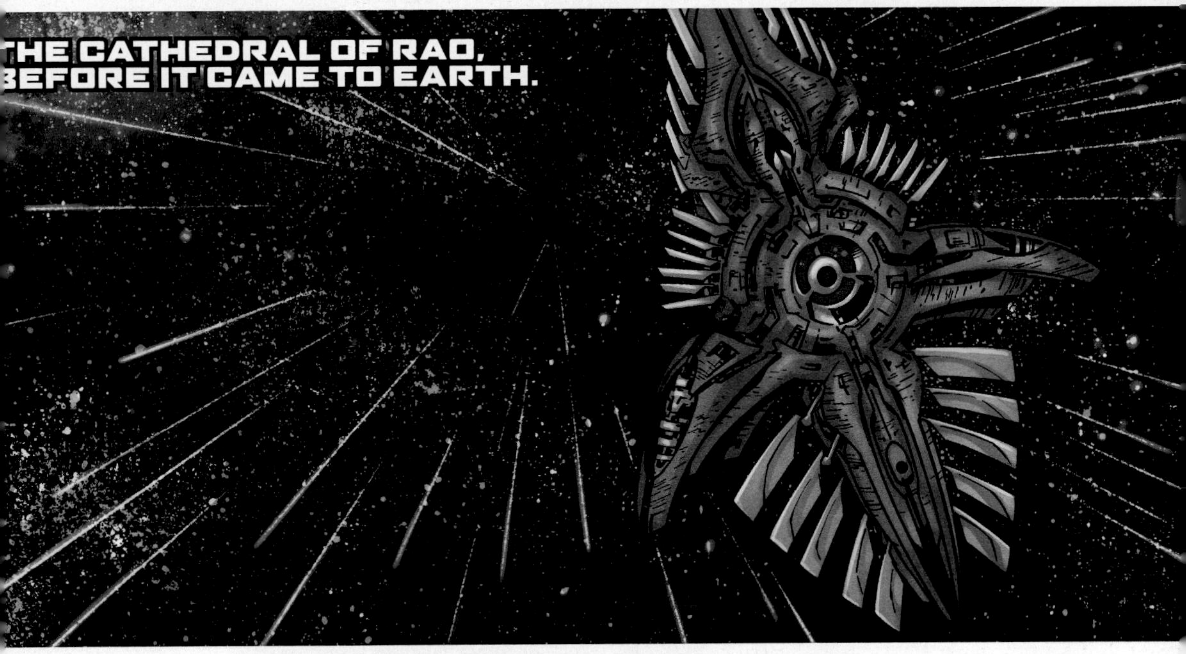
THE CATHEDRAL OF RAO,
BEFORE IT CAME TO EARTH.

DC COMICS PRESENTS

THE JUSTICE LEAGUE OF AMERICA
POWER AND GLORY

PART EIGHT

BY BRYAN HITCH

DANIEL HENRIQUES INKER
ALEX SINCLAIR COLORIST
CHRIS ELIOPOULOS LETTERER
AMEDEO TURTURRO ASSISTANT EDITOR
BRIAN CUNNINGHAM EDITOR

COVER BY **BRYAN HITCH** AND **ALEX SINCLAIR**

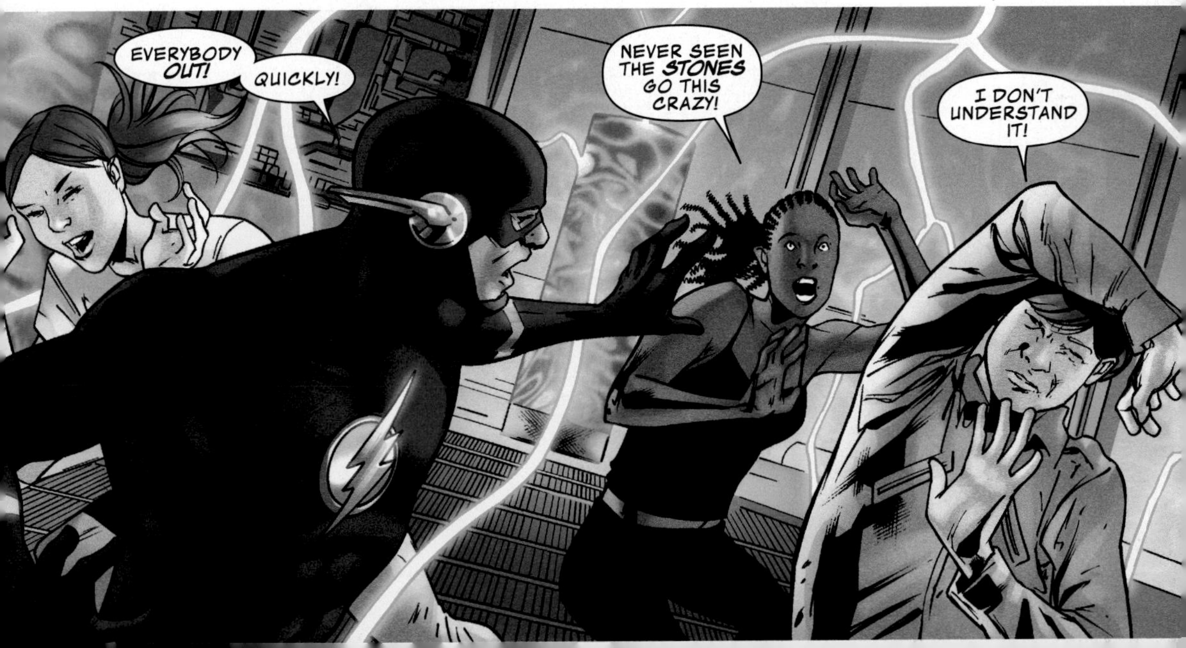
EVERYBODY OUT!
QUICKLY!
NEVER SEEN THE STONES GO THIS CRAZY!
I DON'T UNDERSTAND IT!

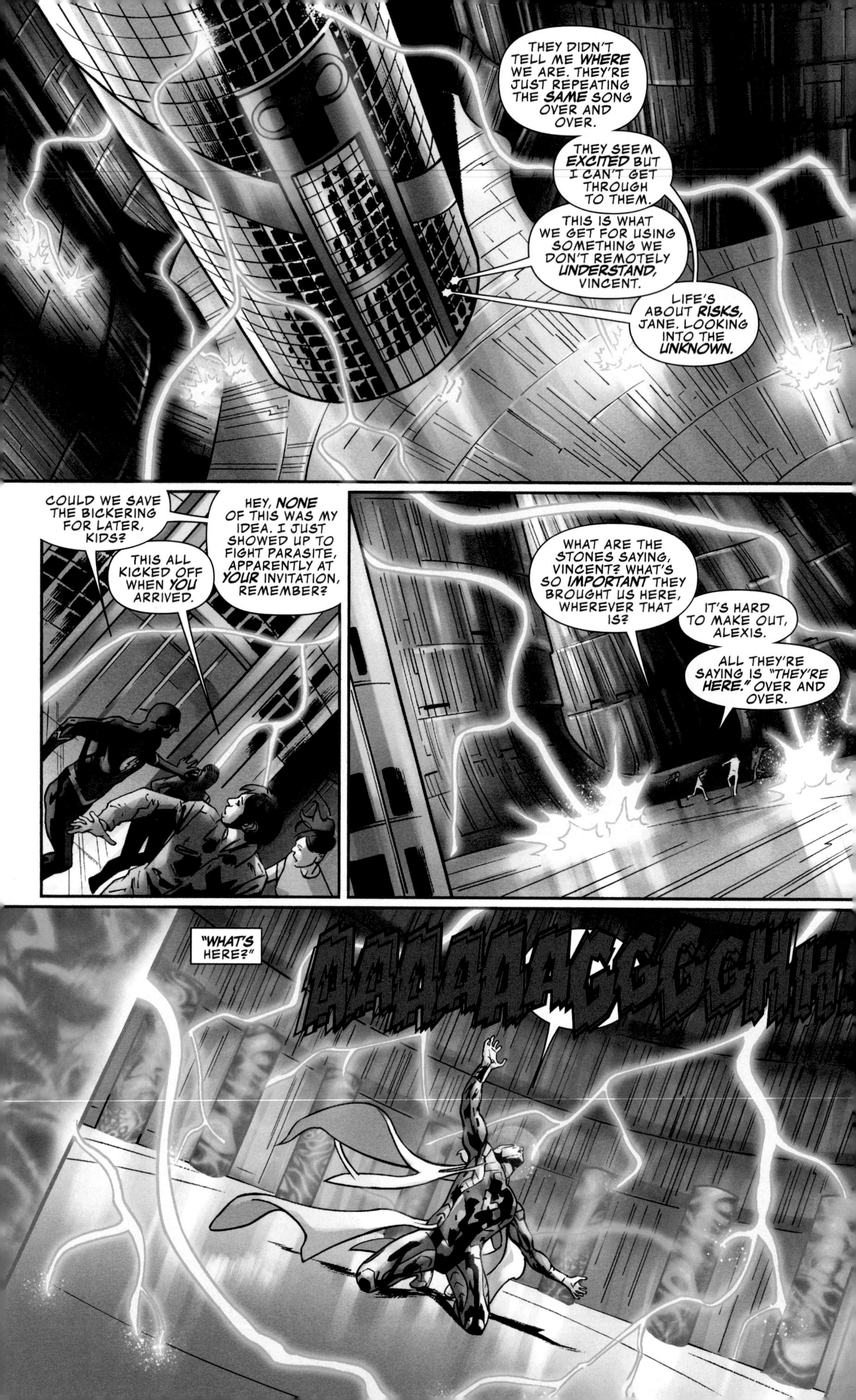
THEY DIDN'T TELL ME WHERE WE ARE. THEY'RE JUST REPEATING THE SAME SONG OVER AND OVER.
THEY SEEM EXCITED BUT I CAN'T GET THROUGH TO THEM.
THIS IS WHAT WE GET FOR USING SOMETHING WE DON'T REMOTELY UNDERSTAND, VINCENT.
LIFE'S ABOUT RISKS, JANE. LOOKING INTO THE UNKNOWN.
COULD WE SAVE THE BICKERING FOR LATER, KIDS?
THIS ALL KICKED OFF WHEN YOU ARRIVED.
HEY, NONE OF THIS WAS MY IDEA. I JUST SHOWED UP TO FIGHT PARASITE, APPARENTLY AT YOUR INVITATION, REMEMBER?
WHAT ARE THE STONES SAYING, VINCENT? WHAT'S SO IMPORTANT THEY BROUGHT US HERE, WHEREVER THAT IS?
IT'S HARD TO MAKE OUT, ALEXIS.
ALL THEY'RE SAYING IS "THEY'RE HERE." OVER AND OVER.
"WHAT'S HERE?"
AAAAAAAGGGHH

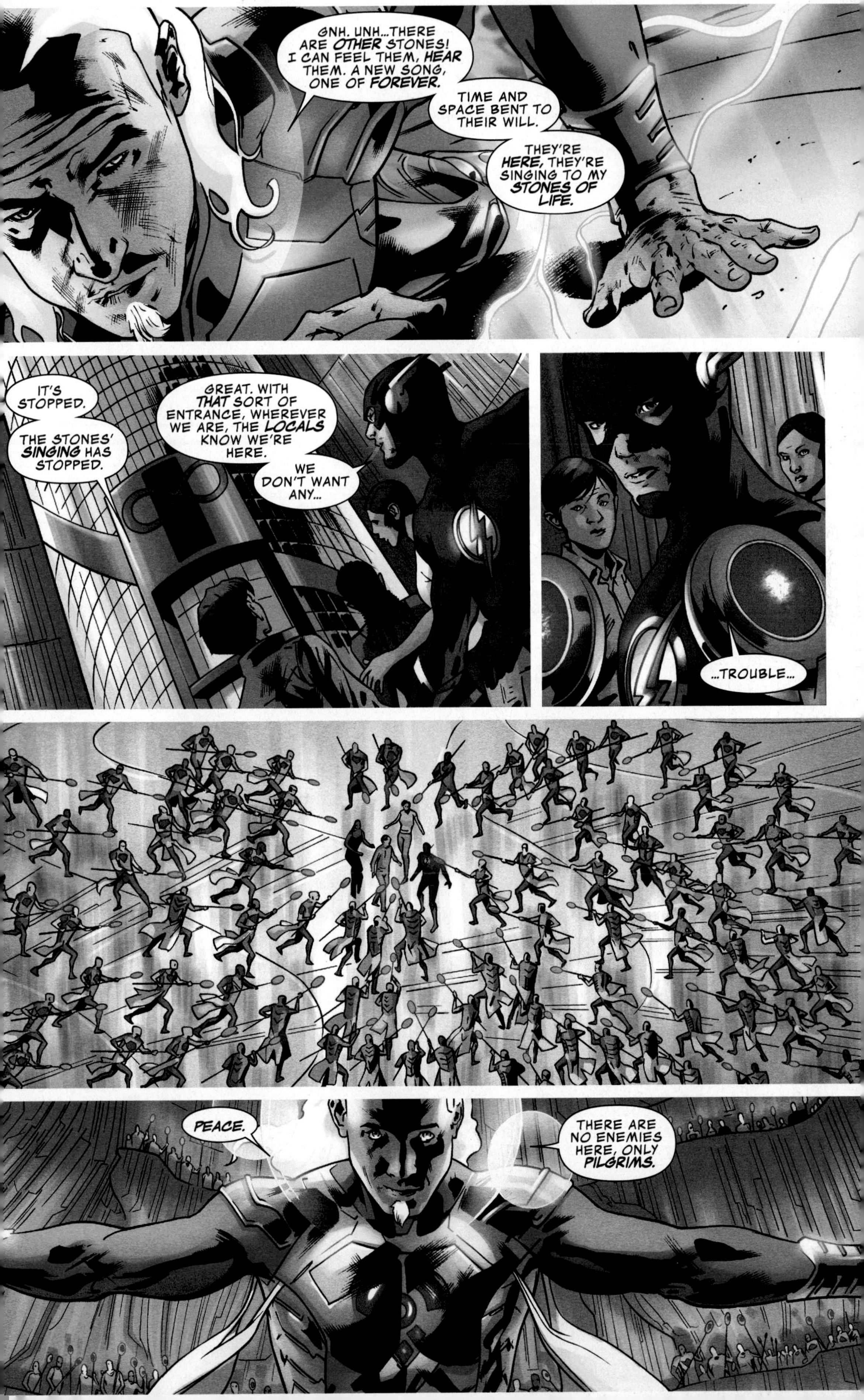
GNH. UNH...THERE ARE OTHER STONES! I CAN FEEL THEM, HEAR THEM. A NEW SONG, ONE OF FOREVER.
TIME AND SPACE BENT TO THEIR WILL.
THEY'RE HERE, THEY'RE SINGING TO MY STONES OF LIFE.
IT'S STOPPED.
THE STONES' SINGING HAS STOPPED.
GREAT. WITH THAT SORT OF ENTRANCE, WHEREVER WE ARE, THE LOCALS KNOW WE'RE HERE.
WE DON'T WANT ANY...
...TROUBLE...
PEACE.
THERE ARE NO ENEMIES HERE, ONLY PILGRIMS.

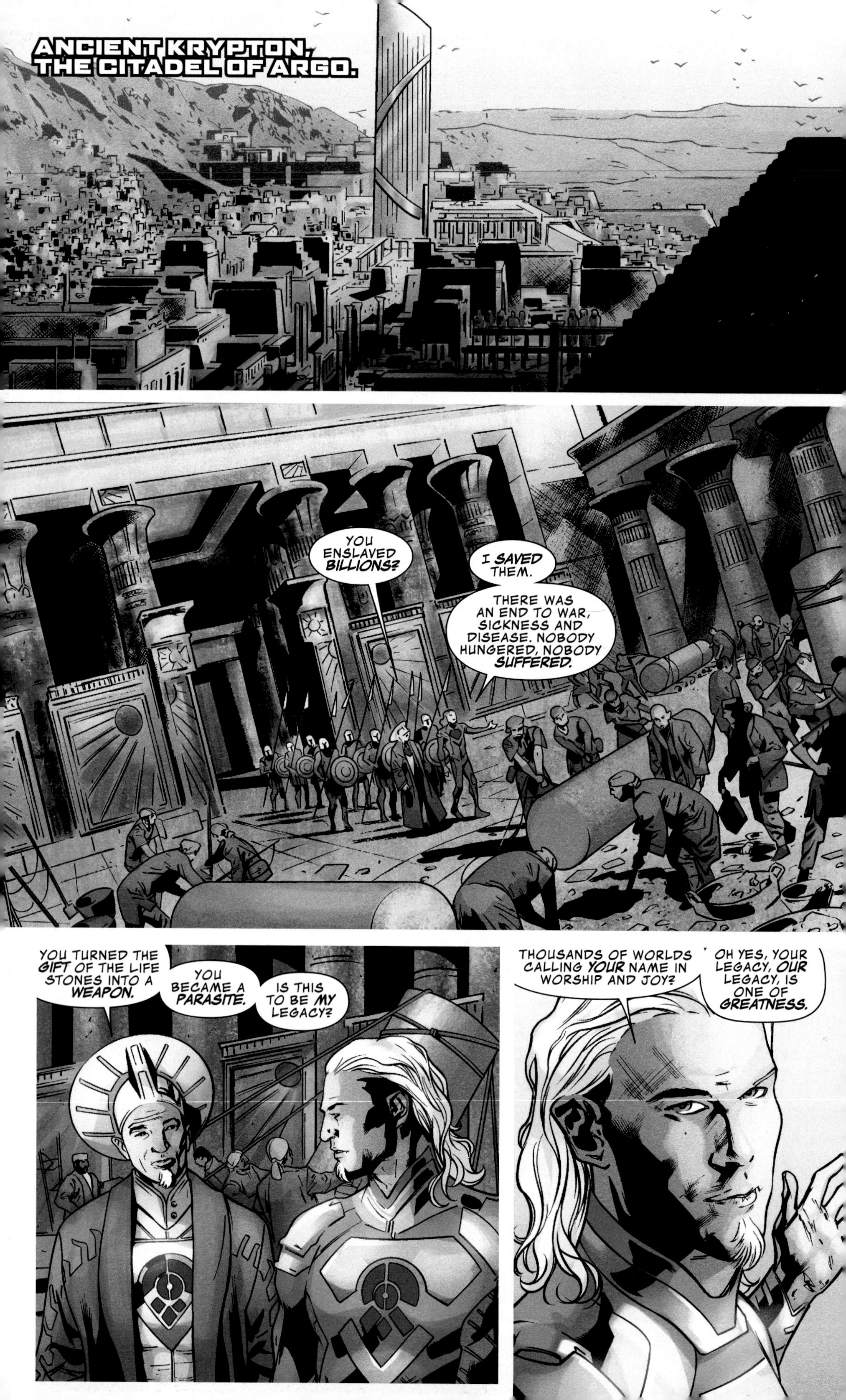
ANCIENT KRYPTON, THE CITADEL OF ARGO.
YOU ENSLAVED BILLIONS?
I SAVED THEM.
THERE WAS AN END TO WAR, SICKNESS AND DISEASE. NOBODY HUNGERED, NOBODY SUFFERED.
YOU TURNED THE GIFT OF THE LIFE STONES INTO A WEAPON.
YOU BECAME A PARASITE.
IS THIS TO BE MY LEGACY?
THOUSANDS OF WORLDS CALLING YOUR NAME IN WORSHIP AND JOY?
OH YES, YOUR LEGACY, OUR LEGACY, IS ONE OF GREATNESS.

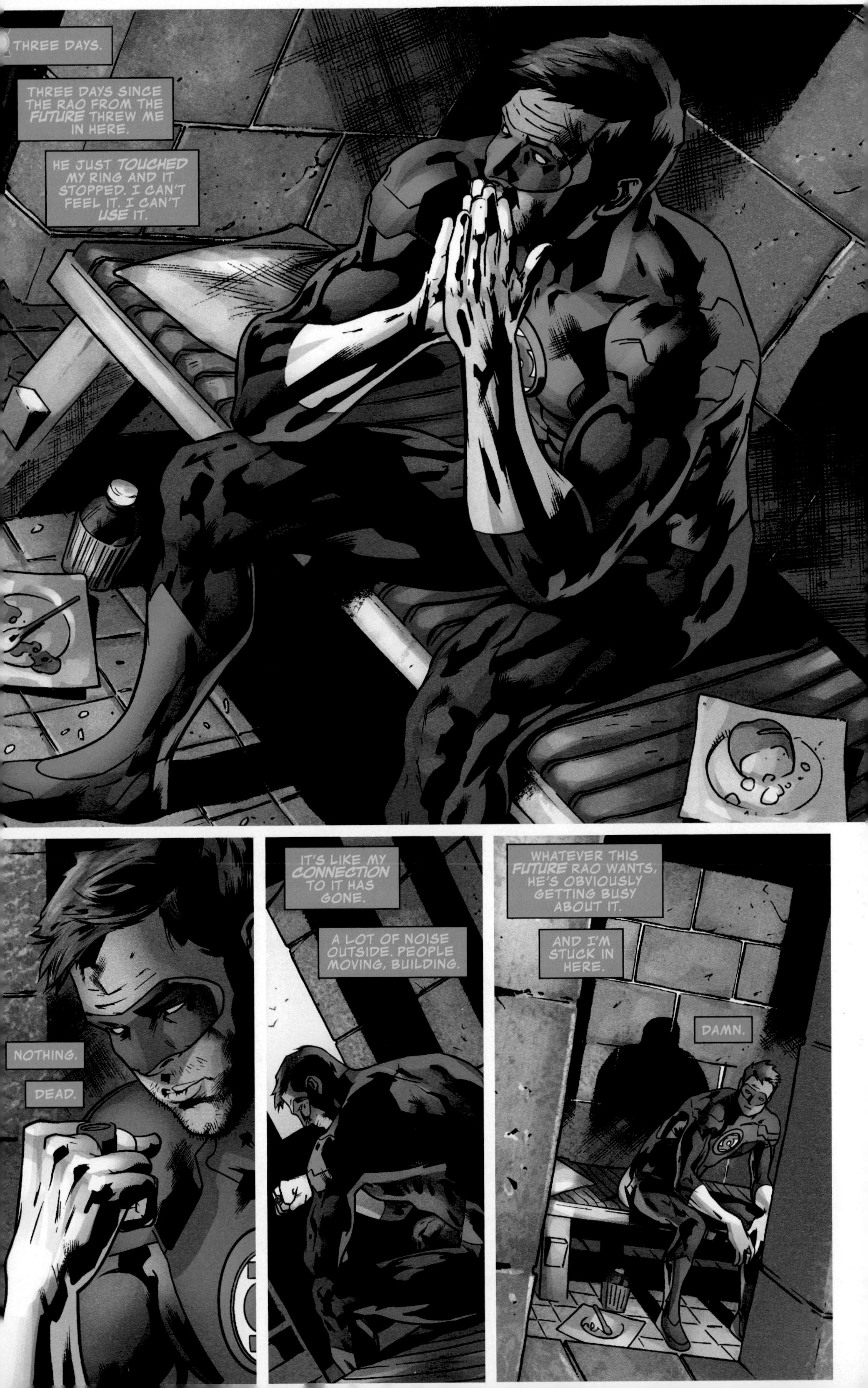
THREE DAYS.
THREE DAYS SINCE THE RAO FROM THE FUTURE THREW ME IN HERE.
HE JUST TOUCHED MY RING AND IT STOPPED. I CAN'T FEEL IT. I CAN'T USE IT.
NOTHING.
DEAD.
IT'S LIKE MY CONNECTION TO IT HAS GONE.
A LOT OF NOISE OUTSIDE. PEOPLE MOVING, BUILDING.
WHATEVER THIS FUTURE RAO WANTS, HE'S OBVIOUSLY GETTING BUSY ABOUT IT.
AND I'M STUCK IN HERE.
DAMN.

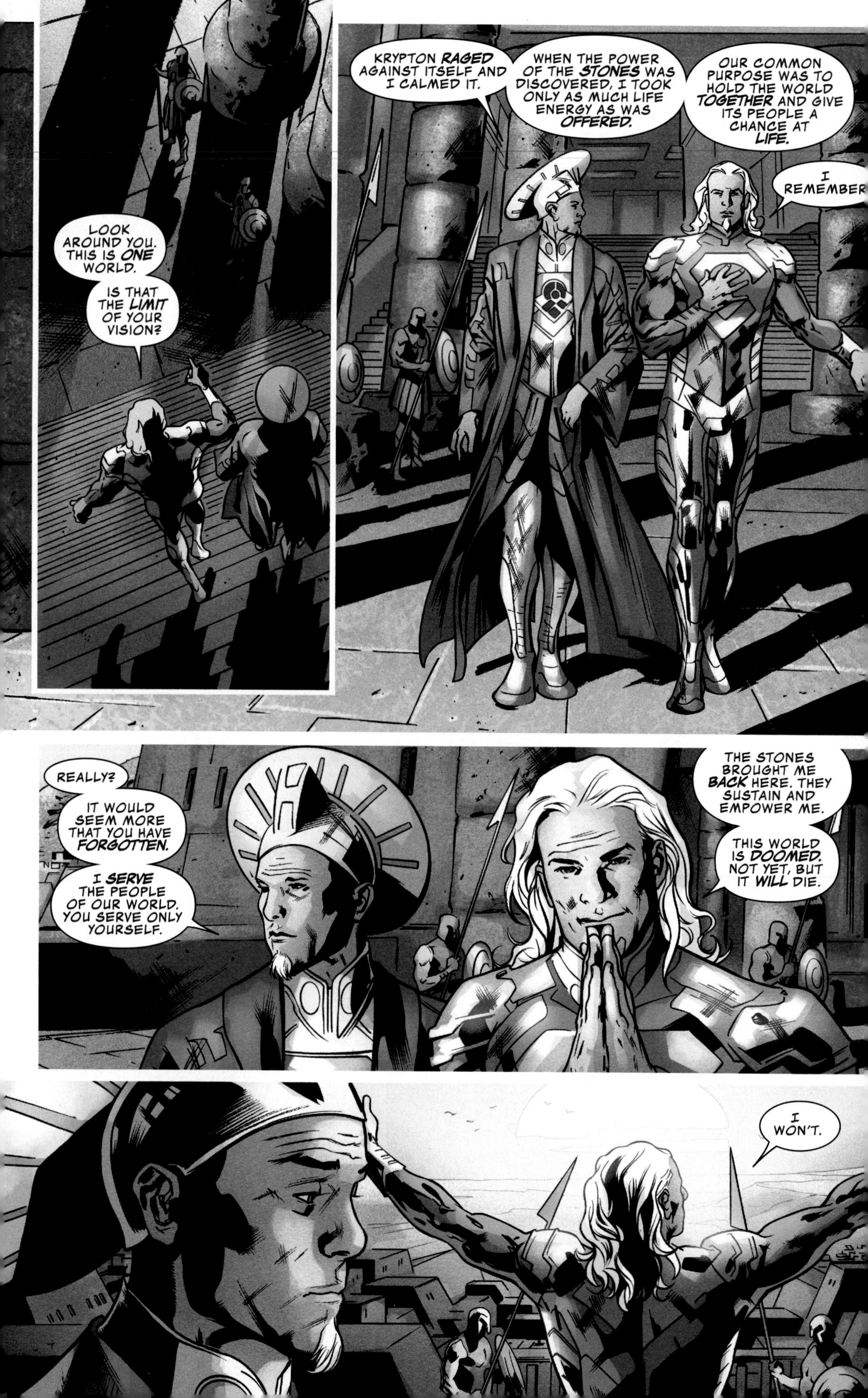
LOOK AROUND YOU. THIS IS ONE WORLD.
IS THAT THE LIMIT OF YOUR VISION?
KRYPTON RAGED AGAINST ITSELF AND I CALMED IT.
WHEN THE POWER OF THE STONES WAS DISCOVERED, I TOOK ONLY AS MUCH LIFE ENERGY AS WAS OFFERED.
OUR COMMON PURPOSE WAS TO HOLD THE WORLD TOGETHER AND GIVE ITS PEOPLE A CHANCE AT LIFE.
I REMEMBER
REALLY?
IT WOULD SEEM MORE THAT YOU HAVE FORGOTTEN.
I SERVE THE PEOPLE OF OUR WORLD. YOU SERVE ONLY YOURSELF.
THE STONES BROUGHT ME BACK HERE. THEY SUSTAIN AND EMPOWER ME.
THIS WORLD IS DOOMED. NOT YET, BUT IT WILL DIE.
I WON'T.

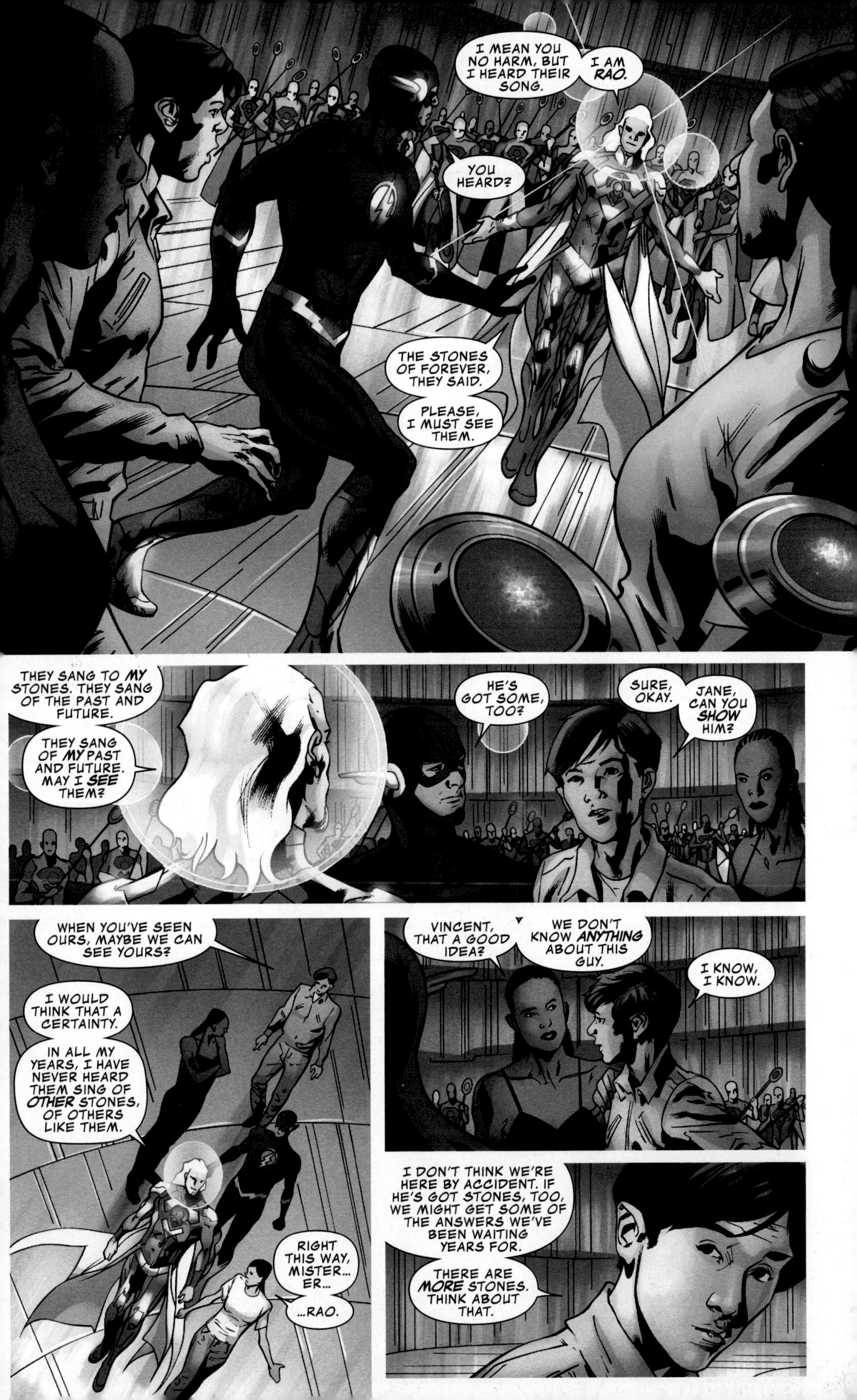
I MEAN YOU NO HARM, BUT I HEARD THEIR SONG.
I AM RAO.
YOU HEARD?
THE STONES OF FOREVER, THEY SAID.
PLEASE, I MUST SEE THEM.
THEY SANG TO MY STONES. THEY SANG OF THE PAST AND FUTURE.
THEY SANG OF MY PAST AND FUTURE. MAY I SEE THEM?
HE'S GOT SOME, TOO?
SURE, OKAY.
JANE, CAN YOU SHOW HIM?
WHEN YOU'VE SEEN OURS, MAYBE WE CAN SEE YOURS?
I WOULD THINK THAT A CERTAINTY.
IN ALL MY YEARS, I HAVE NEVER HEARD THEM SING OF OTHER STONES, OF OTHERS LIKE THEM.
RIGHT THIS WAY, MISTER... ER...
...RAO.
VINCENT, THAT A GOOD IDEA?
WE DON'T KNOW ANYTHING ABOUT THIS GUY.
I KNOW, I KNOW.
I DON'T THINK WE'RE HERE BY ACCIDENT. IF HE'S GOT STONES, TOO, WE MIGHT GET SOME OF THE ANSWERS WE'VE BEEN WAITING YEARS FOR.
THERE ARE MORE STONES. THINK ABOUT THAT.

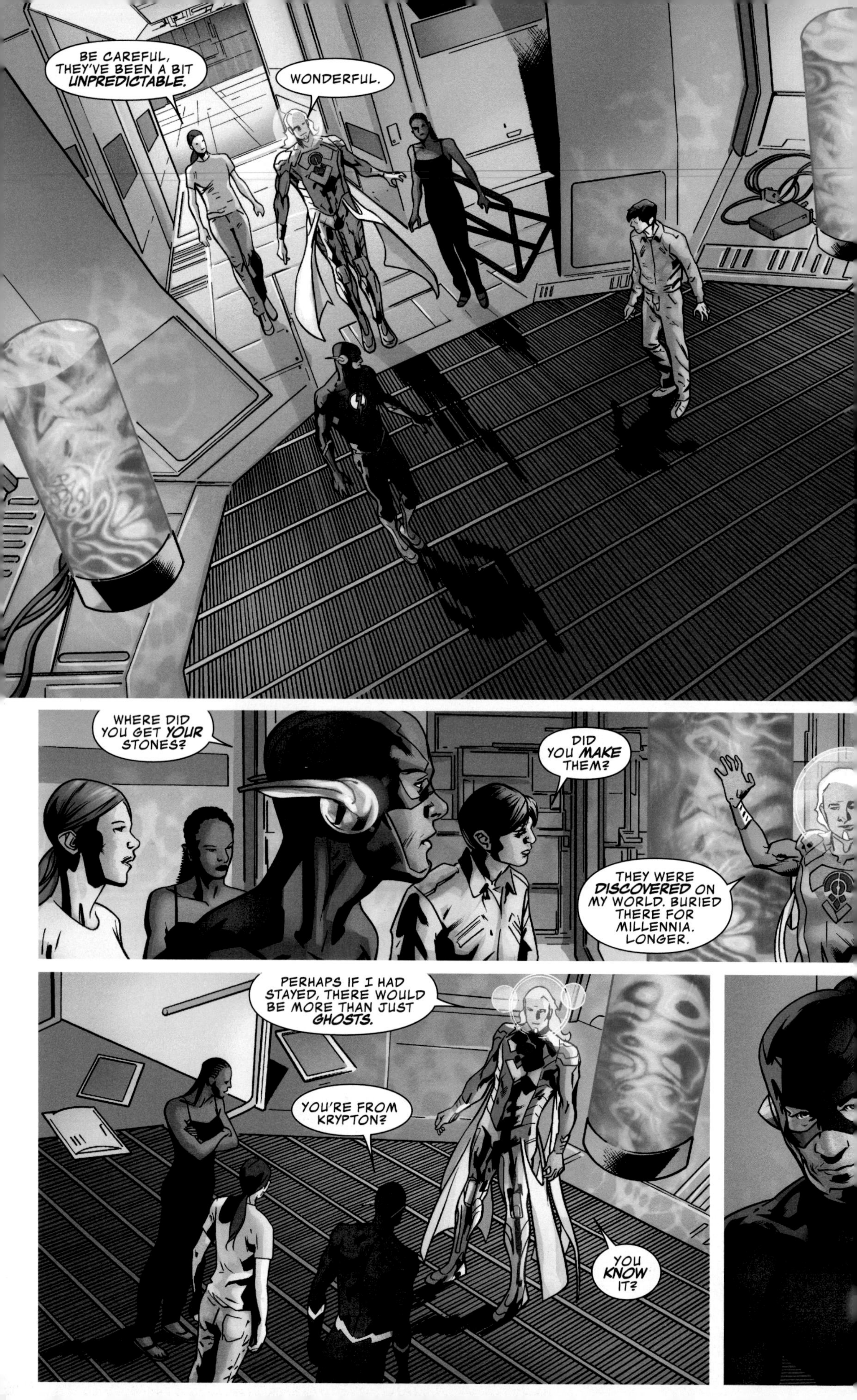
BE CAREFUL, THEY'VE BEEN A BIT UNPREDICTABLE.
WONDERFUL.
WHERE DID YOU GET YOUR STONES?
DID YOU MAKE THEM?
THEY WERE DISCOVERED ON MY WORLD. BURIED THERE FOR MILLENNIA. LONGER.
PERHAPS IF I HAD STAYED, THERE WOULD BE MORE THAN JUST GHOSTS.
YOU'RE FROM KRYPTON?
YOU KNOW IT?

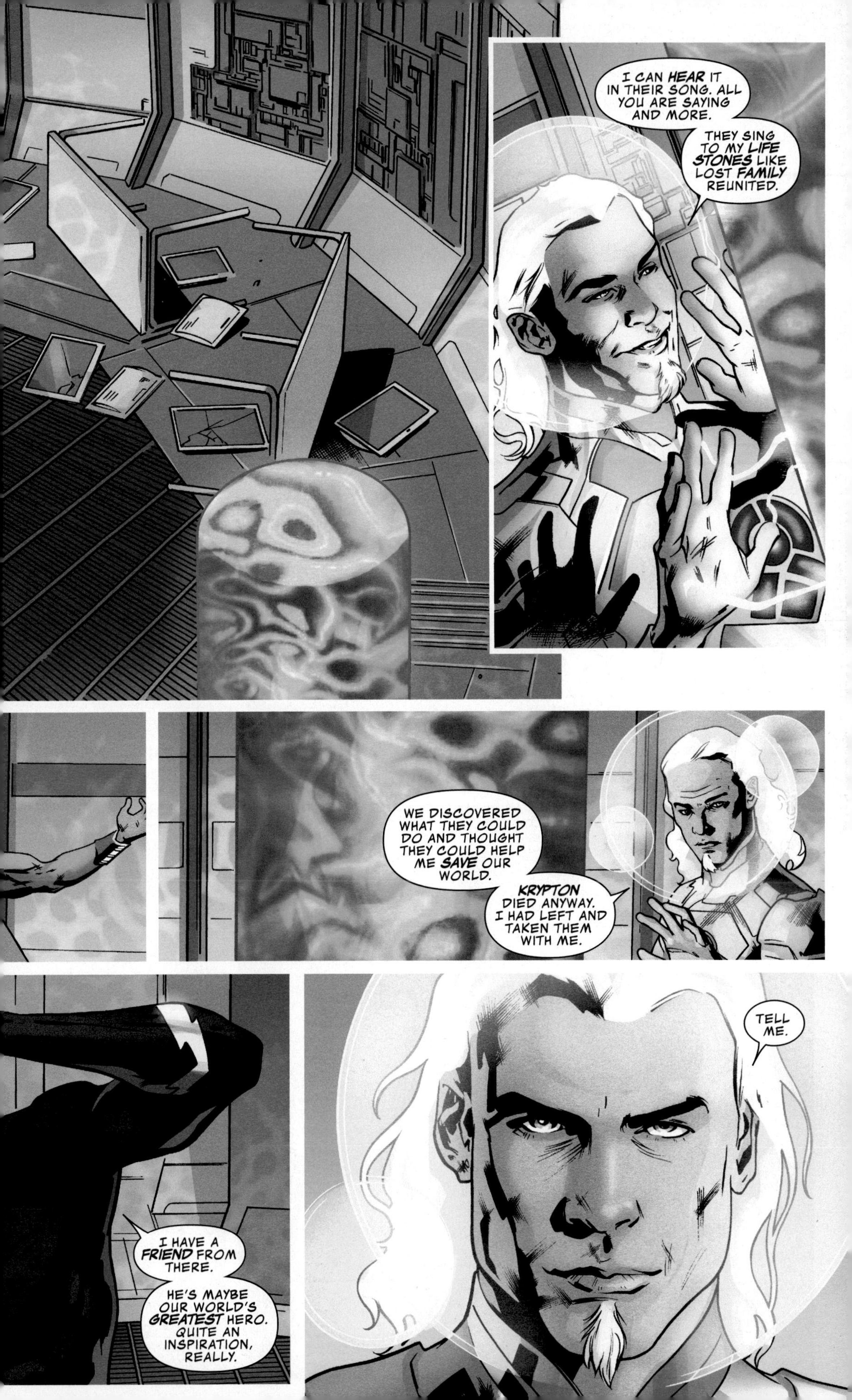
I CAN HEAR IT IN THEIR SONG. ALL YOU ARE SAYING AND MORE.
THEY SING TO MY LIFE STONES LIKE LOST FAMILY REUNITED.
WE DISCOVERED WHAT THEY COULD DO AND THOUGHT THEY COULD HELP ME SAVE OUR WORLD.
KRYPTON DIED ANYWAY. I HAD LEFT AND TAKEN THEM WITH ME.
I HAVE A FRIEND FROM THERE.
HE'S MAYBE OUR WORLD'S GREATEST HERO. QUITE AN INSPIRATION, REALLY.
TELL ME.

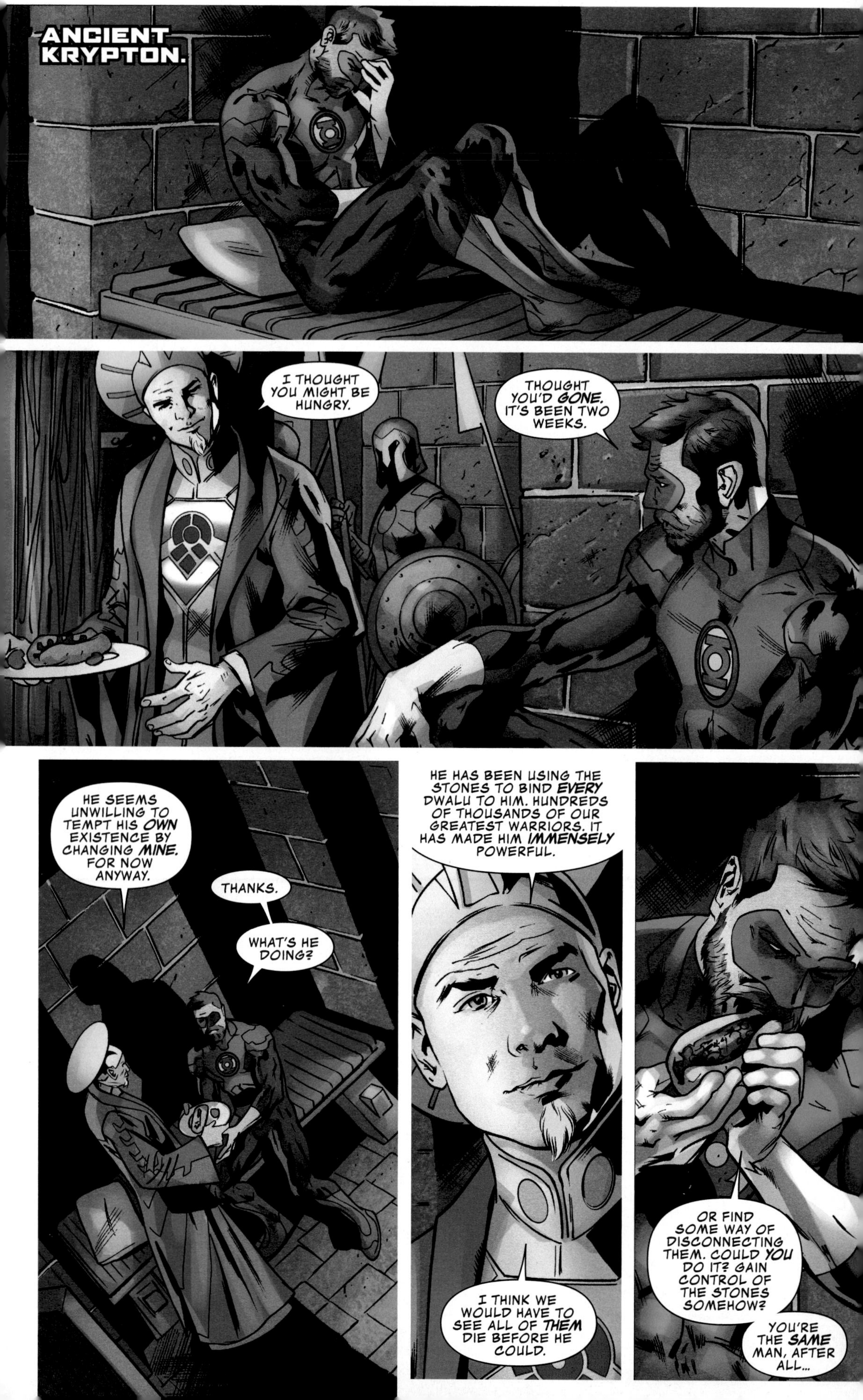
ANCIENT KRYPTON.
I THOUGHT YOU MIGHT BE HUNGRY.
THOUGHT YOU'D GONE. IT'S BEEN TWO WEEKS.
HE SEEMS UNWILLING TO TEMPT HIS OWN EXISTENCE BY CHANGING MINE. FOR NOW ANYWAY.
THANKS.
WHAT'S HE DOING?
HE HAS BEEN USING THE STONES TO BIND EVERY DWALU TO HIM. HUNDREDS OF THOUSANDS OF OUR GREATEST WARRIORS. IT HAS MADE HIM IMMENSELY POWERFUL.
I THINK WE WOULD HAVE TO SEE ALL OF THEM DIE BEFORE HE COULD.
OR FIND SOME WAY OF DISCONNECTING THEM. COULD YOU DO IT? GAIN CONTROL OF THE STONES SOMEHOW?
YOU'RE THE SAME MAN, AFTER ALL...

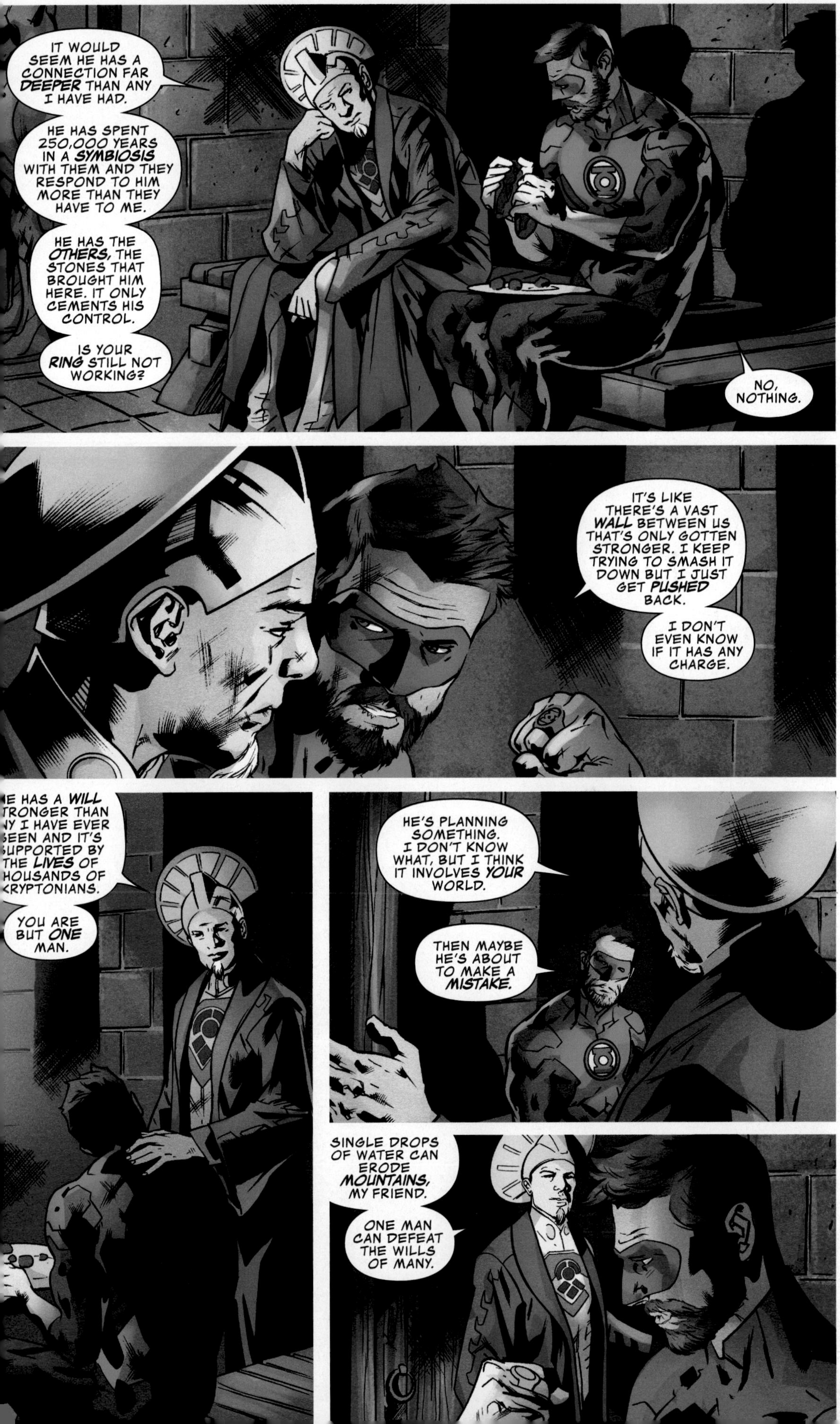
IT WOULD SEEM HE HAS A CONNECTION FAR DEEPER THAN ANY I HAVE HAD.
HE HAS SPENT 250,000 YEARS IN A SYMBIOSIS WITH THEM AND THEY RESPOND TO HIM MORE THAN THEY HAVE TO ME.
HE HAS THE OTHERS, THE STONES THAT BROUGHT HIM HERE. IT ONLY CEMENTS HIS CONTROL.
IS YOUR RING STILL NOT WORKING?
NO, NOTHING.
IT'S LIKE THERE'S A VAST WALL BETWEEN US THAT'S ONLY GOTTEN STRONGER. I KEEP TRYING TO SMASH IT DOWN BUT I JUST GET PUSHED BACK.
I DON'T EVEN KNOW IF IT HAS ANY CHARGE.
E HAS A WILL TRONGER THAN NY I HAVE EVER SEEN AND IT'S UPPORTED BY THE LIVES OF HOUSANDS OF KRYPTONIANS.
YOU ARE BUT ONE MAN.
HE'S PLANNING SOMETHING. I DON'T KNOW WHAT, BUT I THINK IT INVOLVES YOUR WORLD.
THEN MAYBE HE'S ABOUT TO MAKE A MISTAKE.
SINGLE DROPS OF WATER CAN ERODE MOUNTAINS, MY FRIEND.
ONE MAN CAN DEFEAT THE WILLS OF MANY.

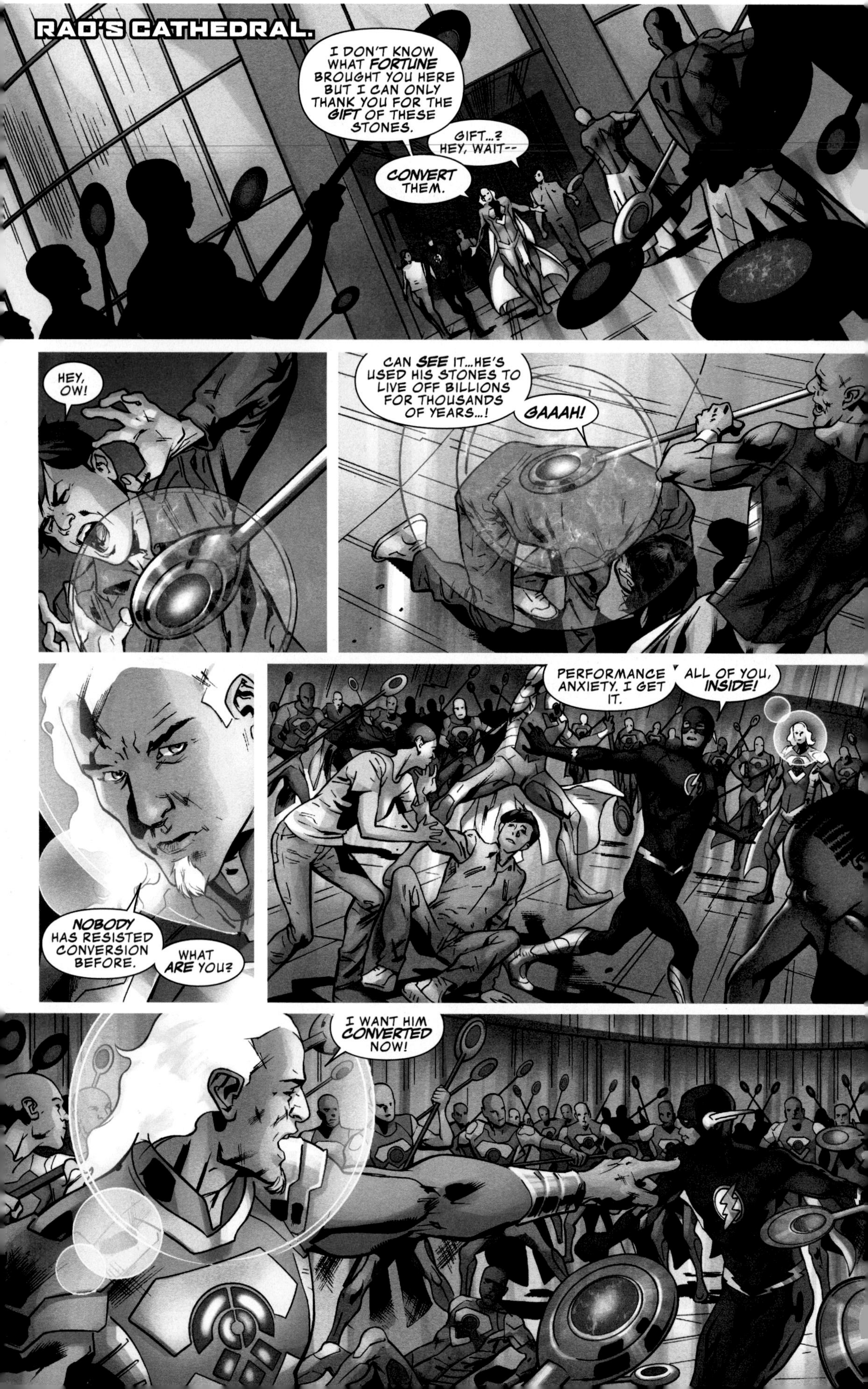
RAO'S CATHEDRAL.
I DON'T KNOW WHAT FORTUNE BROUGHT YOU HERE BUT I CAN ONLY THANK YOU FOR THE GIFT OF THESE STONES.
GIFT...? HEY, WAIT--
CONVERT THEM.
HEY, OW!
CAN SEE IT...HE'S USED HIS STONES TO LIVE OFF BILLIONS FOR THOUSANDS OF YEARS...!
GAAAH!
NOBODY HAS RESISTED CONVERSION BEFORE.
WHAT ARE YOU?
PERFORMANCE ANXIETY. I GET IT.
ALL OF YOU, INSIDE!
I WANT HIM CONVERTED NOW!

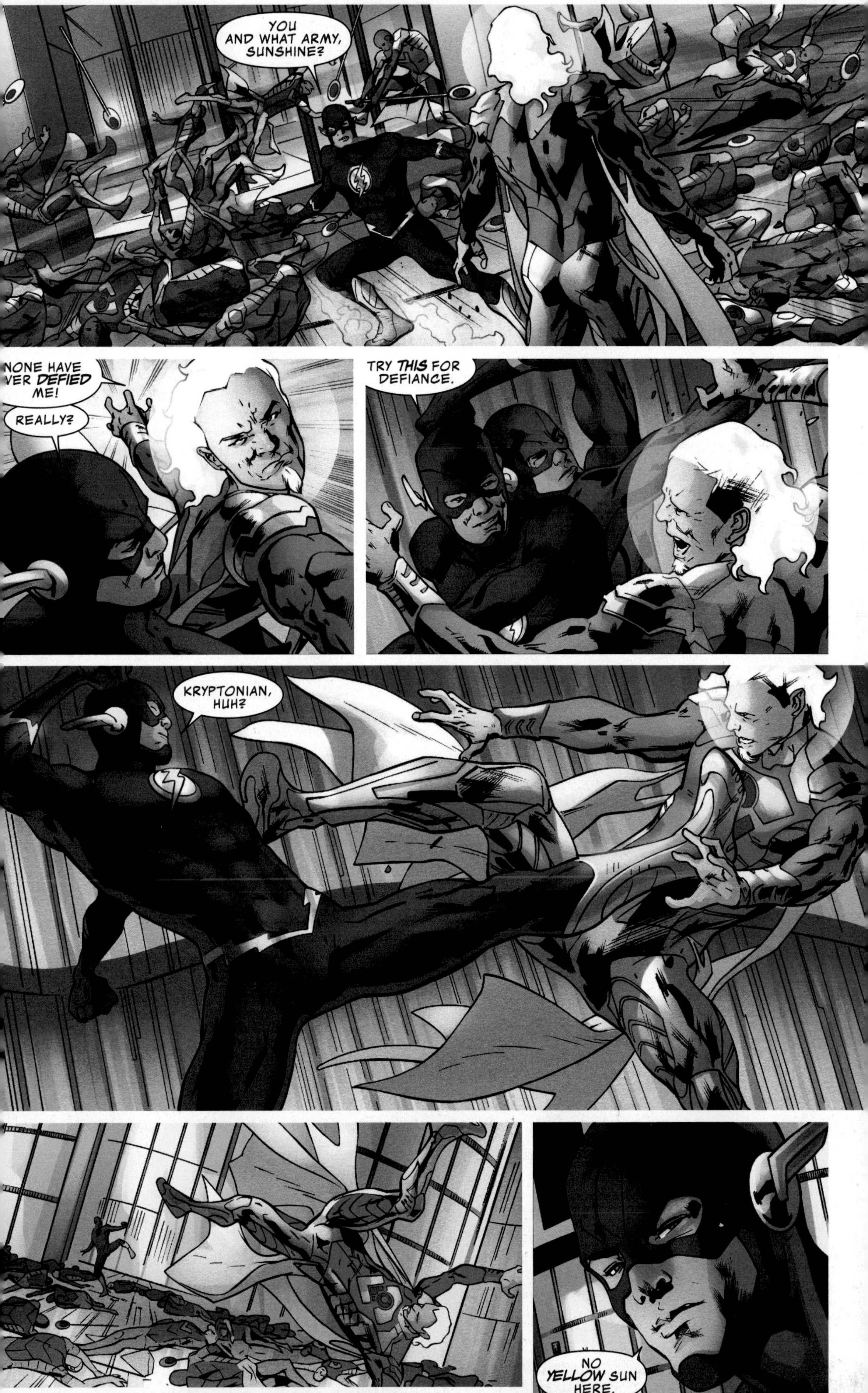
YOU AND WHAT ARMY, SUNSHINE?
NONE HAVE EVER DEFIED ME!
REALLY?
TRY THIS FOR DEFIANCE.
KRYPTONIAN, HUH?
NO YELLOW SUN HERE.

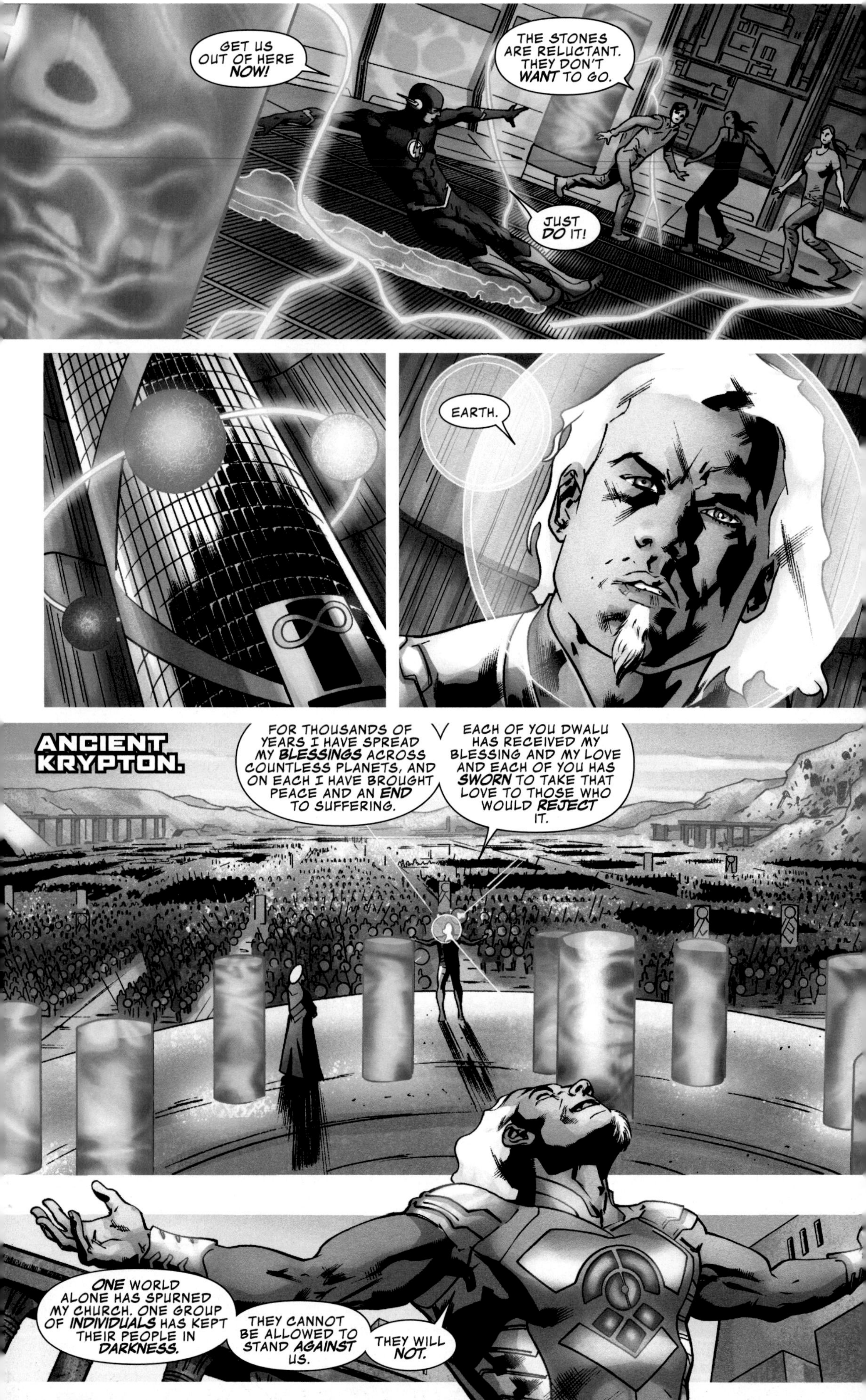

GET US OUT OF HERE NOW!
THE STONES ARE RELUCTANT. THEY DON'T WANT TO GO.
JUST DO IT!
EARTH.
ANCIENT KRYPTON.
FOR THOUSANDS OF YEARS I HAVE SPREAD MY BLESSINGS ACROSS COUNTLESS PLANETS, AND ON EACH I HAVE BROUGHT PEACE AND AN END TO SUFFERING.
EACH OF YOU DWALU HAS RECEIVED MY BLESSING AND MY LOVE AND EACH OF YOU HAS SWORN TO TAKE THAT LOVE TO THOSE WHO WOULD REJECT IT.
ONE WORLD ALONE HAS SPURNED MY CHURCH. ONE GROUP OF INDIVIDUALS HAS KEPT THEIR PEOPLE IN DARKNESS.
THEY CANNOT BE ALLOWED TO STAND AGAINST US.
THEY WILL NOT.

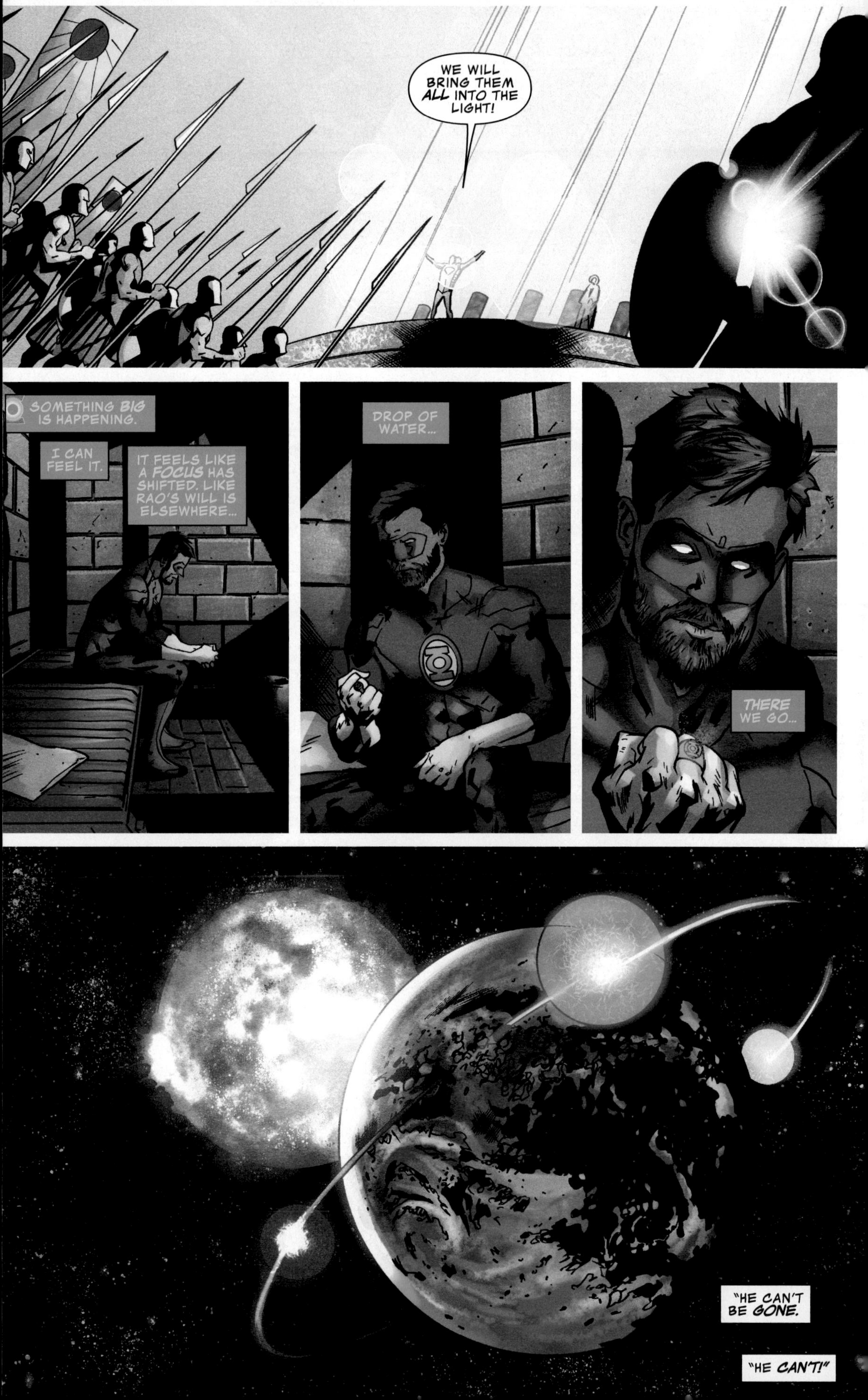
WE WILL BRING THEM ALL INTO THE LIGHT!
SOMETHING BIG IS HAPPENING.
I CAN FEEL IT.
IT FEELS LIKE A FOCUS HAS SHIFTED. LIKE RAO'S WILL IS ELSEWHERE...
DROP OF WATER...
THERE WE GO...
"HE CAN'T BE GONE.
"HE CAN'T!"

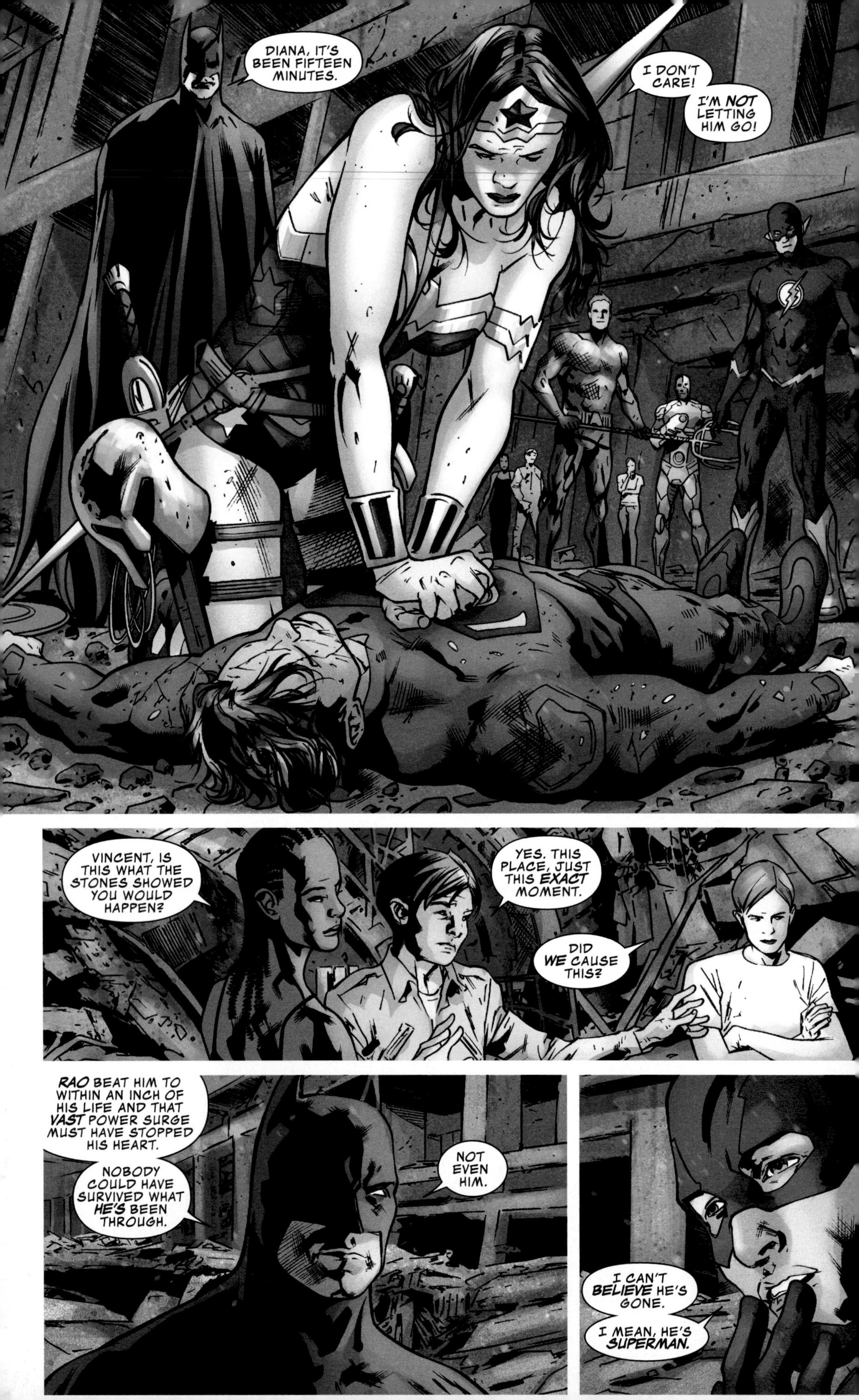
DIANA, IT'S BEEN FIFTEEN MINUTES.
I DON'T CARE!
I'M NOT LETTING HIM GO!
VINCENT, IS THIS WHAT THE STONES SHOWED YOU WOULD HAPPEN?
YES. THIS PLACE, JUST THIS EXACT MOMENT.
DID WE CAUSE THIS?
RAO BEAT HIM TO WITHIN AN INCH OF HIS LIFE AND THAT VAST POWER SURGE MUST HAVE STOPPED HIS HEART.
NOBODY COULD HAVE SURVIVED WHAT HE'S BEEN THROUGH.
NOT EVEN HIM.
I CAN'T BELIEVE HE'S GONE.
I MEAN, HE'S SUPERMAN.

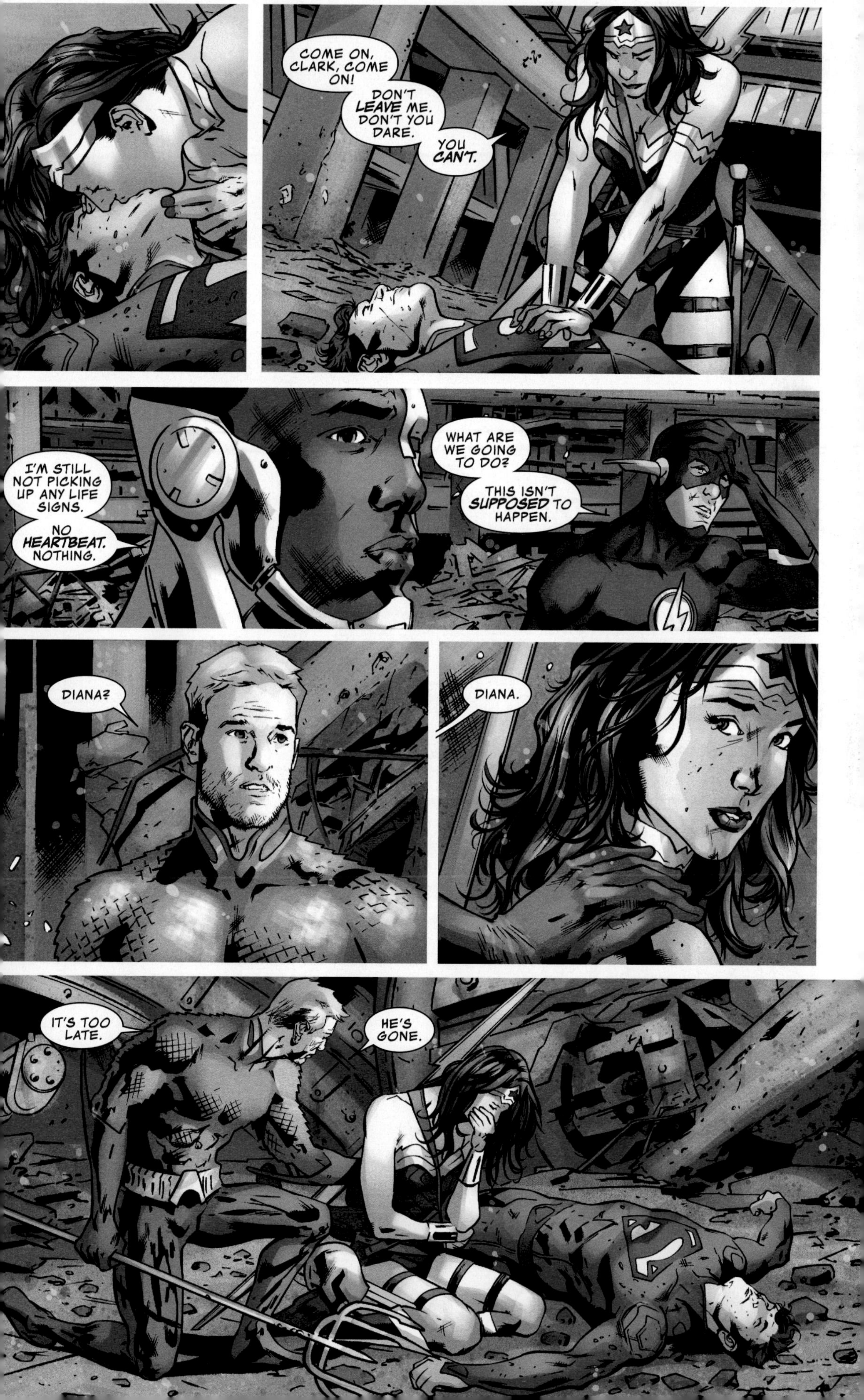
COME ON, CLARK, COME ON!
DON'T LEAVE ME. DON'T YOU DARE.
YOU CAN'T.
I'M STILL NOT PICKING UP ANY LIFE SIGNS.
NO HEARTBEAT. NOTHING.
WHAT ARE WE GOING TO DO?
THIS ISN'T SUPPOSED TO HAPPEN.
DIANA?
DIANA.
IT'S TOO LATE.
HE'S GONE.

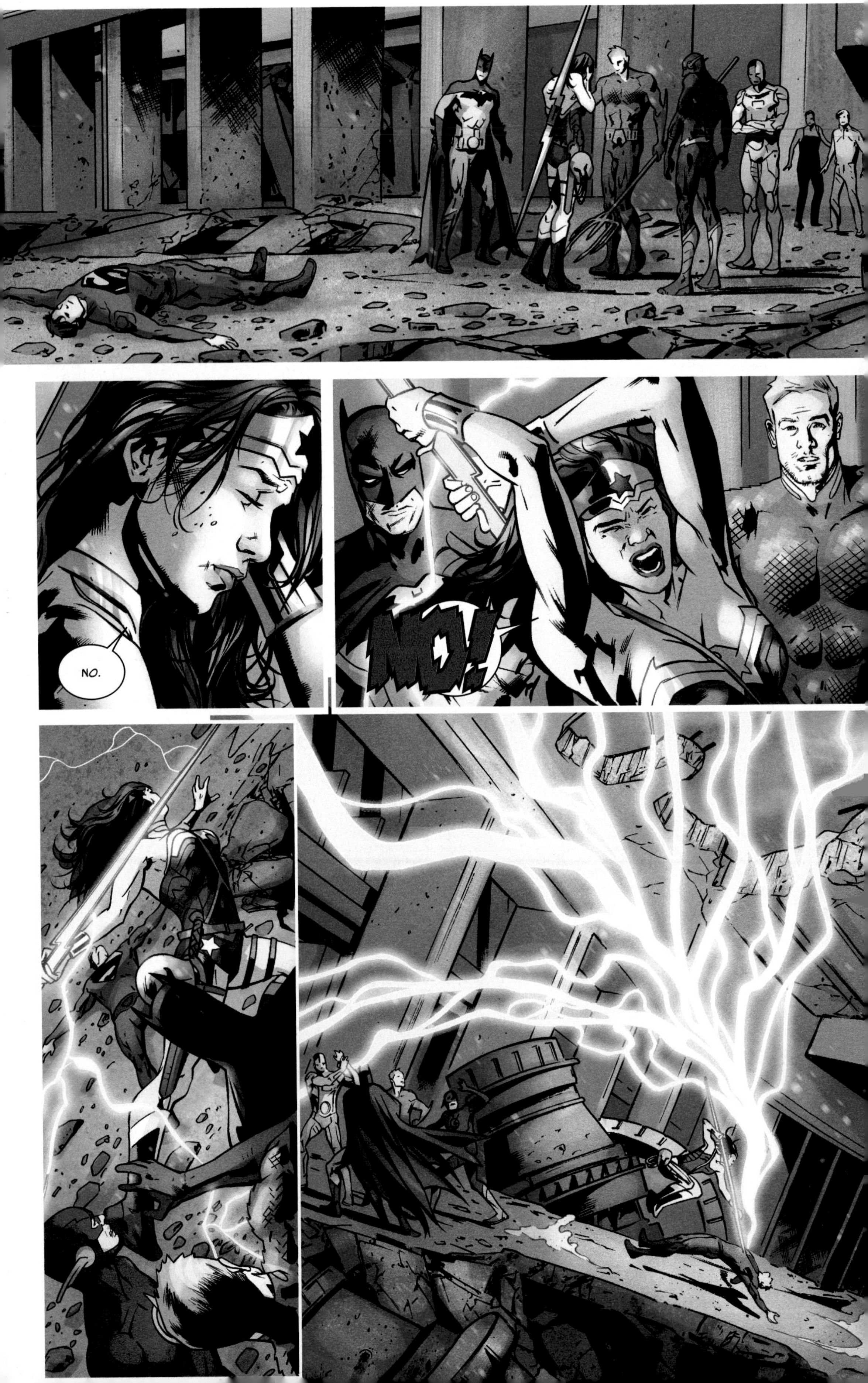
NO.
NO!

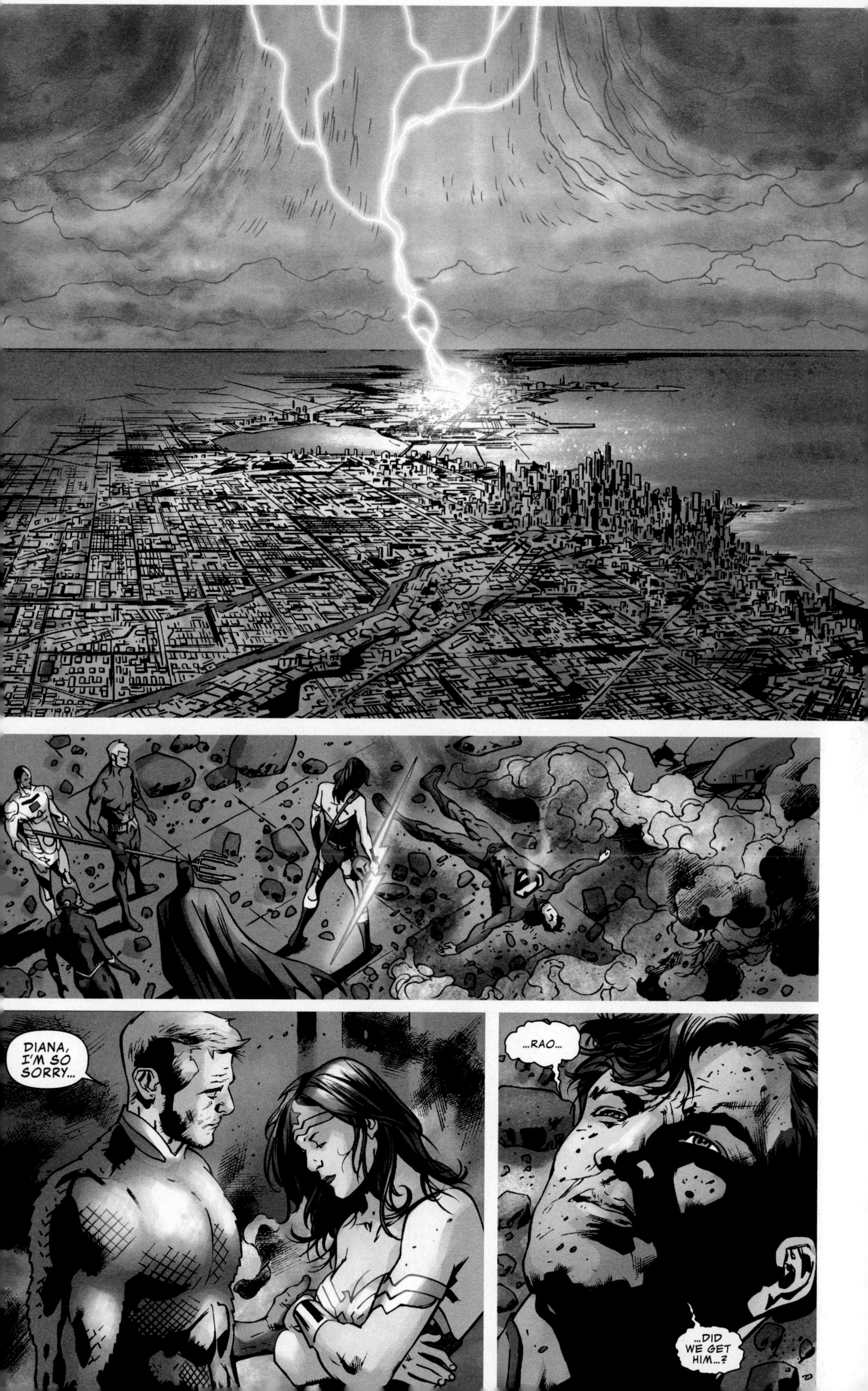
DIANA, I'M SO SORRY...
...RAO...
...DID WE GET HIM...?

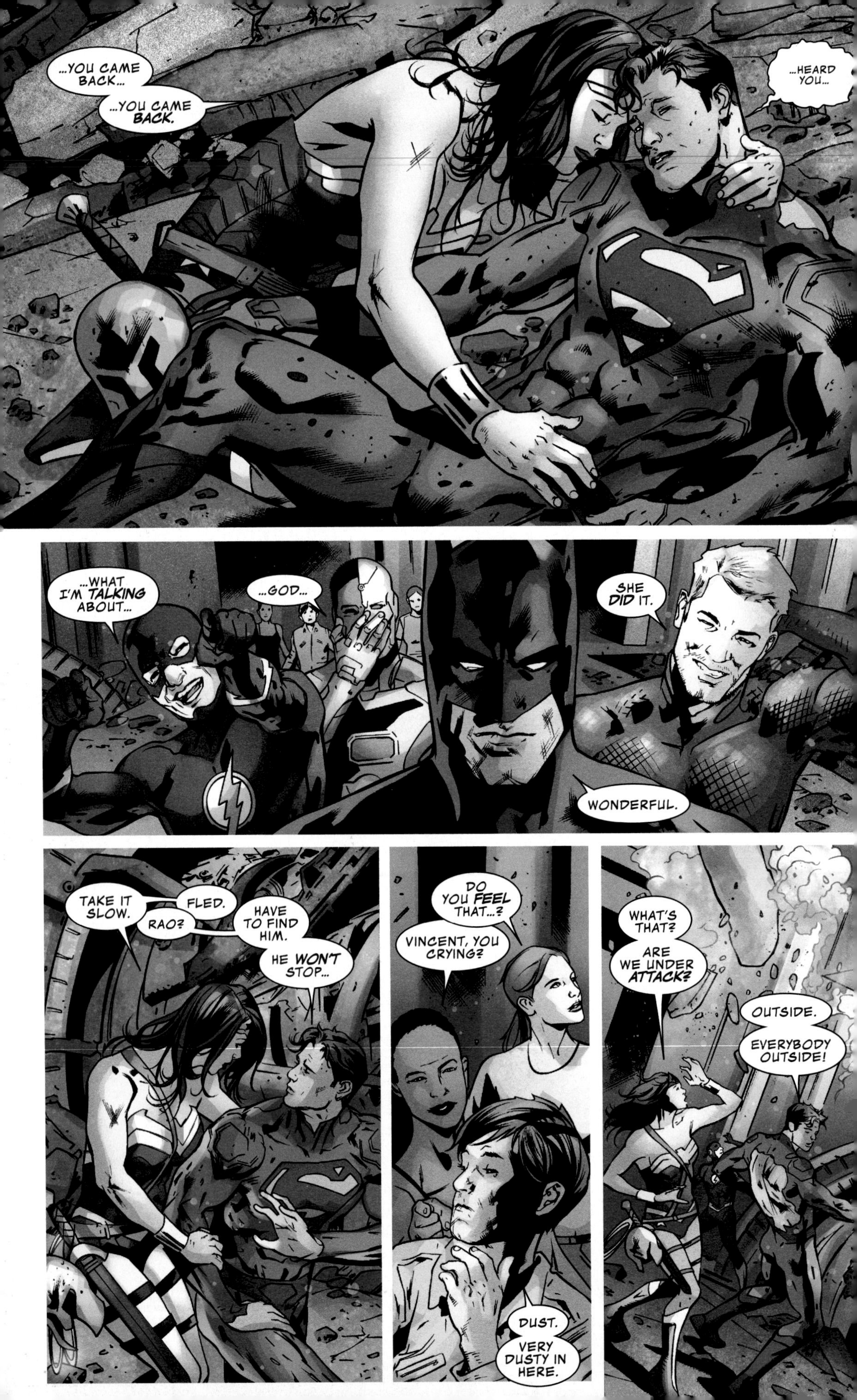

...YOU CAME BACK...
...YOU CAME BACK.
...HEARD YOU...
...WHAT I'M TALKING ABOUT...
...GOD...
SHE DID IT.
WONDERFUL.
TAKE IT SLOW.
FLED.
RAO?
HAVE TO FIND HIM.
HE WON'T STOP...
DO YOU FEEL THAT...?
VINCENT, YOU CRYING?
DUST.
VERY DUSTY IN HERE.
WHAT'S THAT?
ARE WE UNDER ATTACK?
OUTSIDE.
EVERYBODY OUTSIDE!

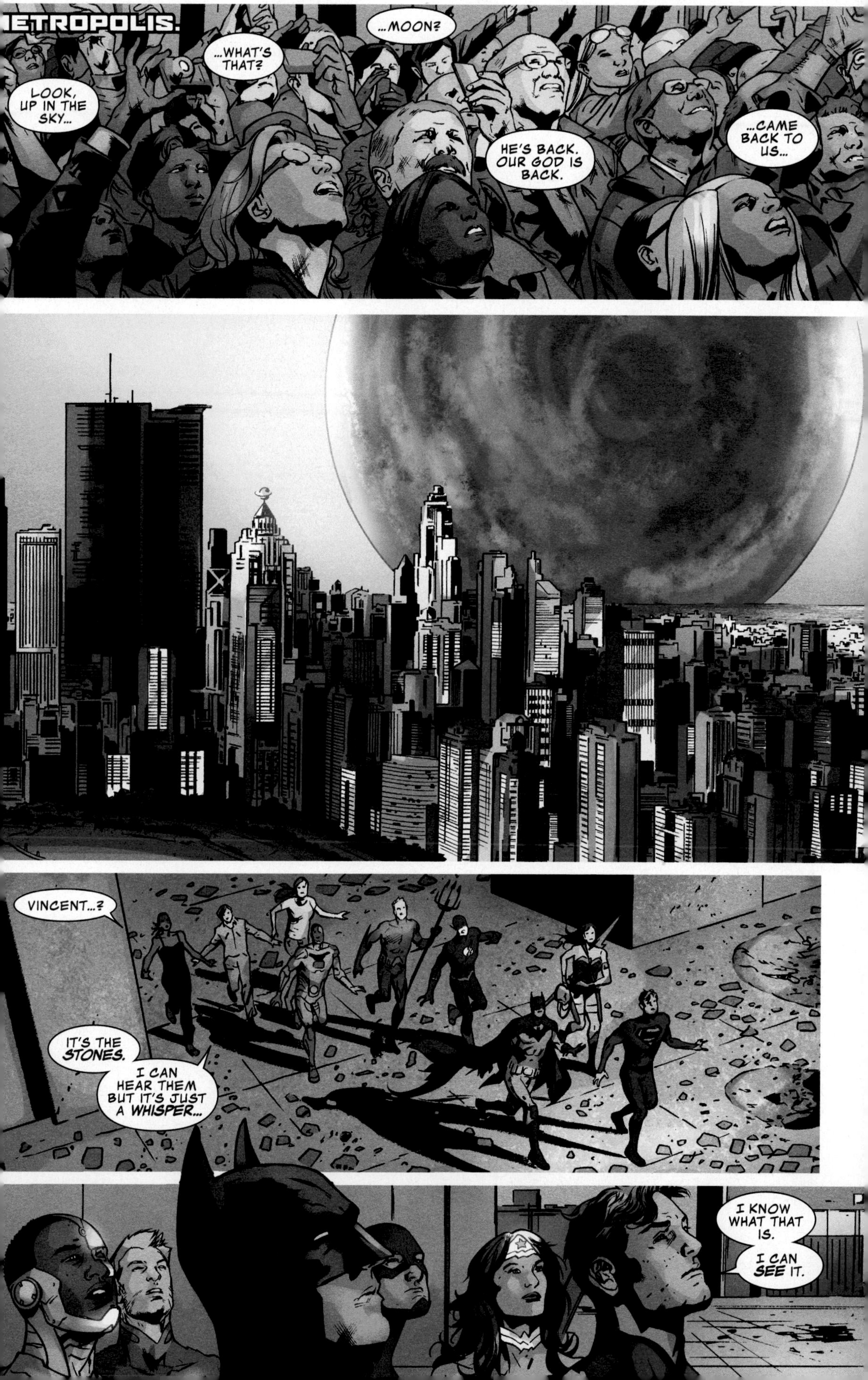
METROPOLIS.
LOOK, UP IN THE SKY...
...WHAT'S THAT?
...MOON?
HE'S BACK. OUR GOD IS BACK.
...CAME BACK TO US...
VINCENT...?
IT'S THE STONES.
I CAN HEAR THEM BUT IT'S JUST A WHISPER...
I KNOW WHAT THAT IS.
I CAN SEE IT.

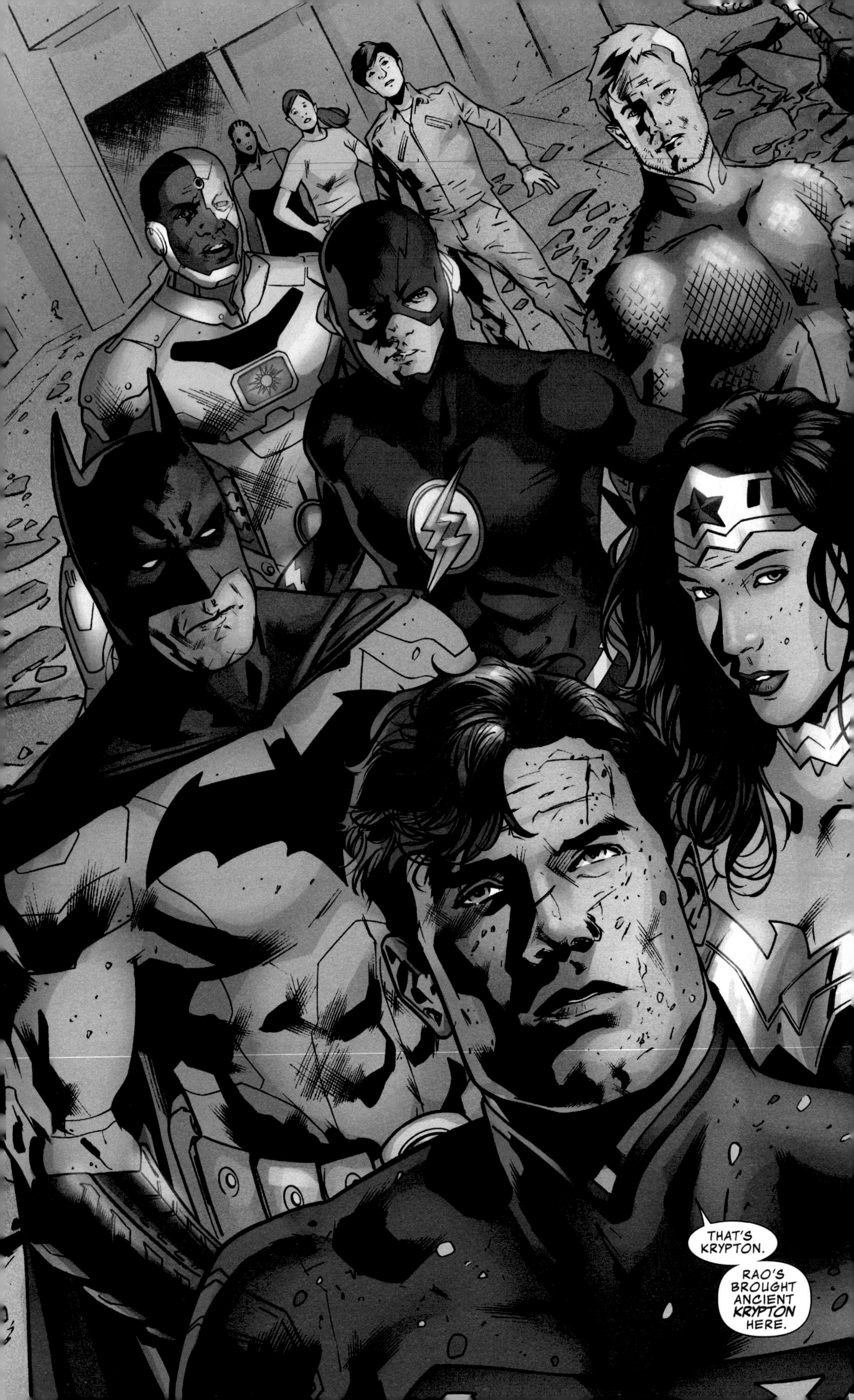
THAT'S KRYPTON.
RAO'S BROUGHT ANCIENT KRYPTON HERE.

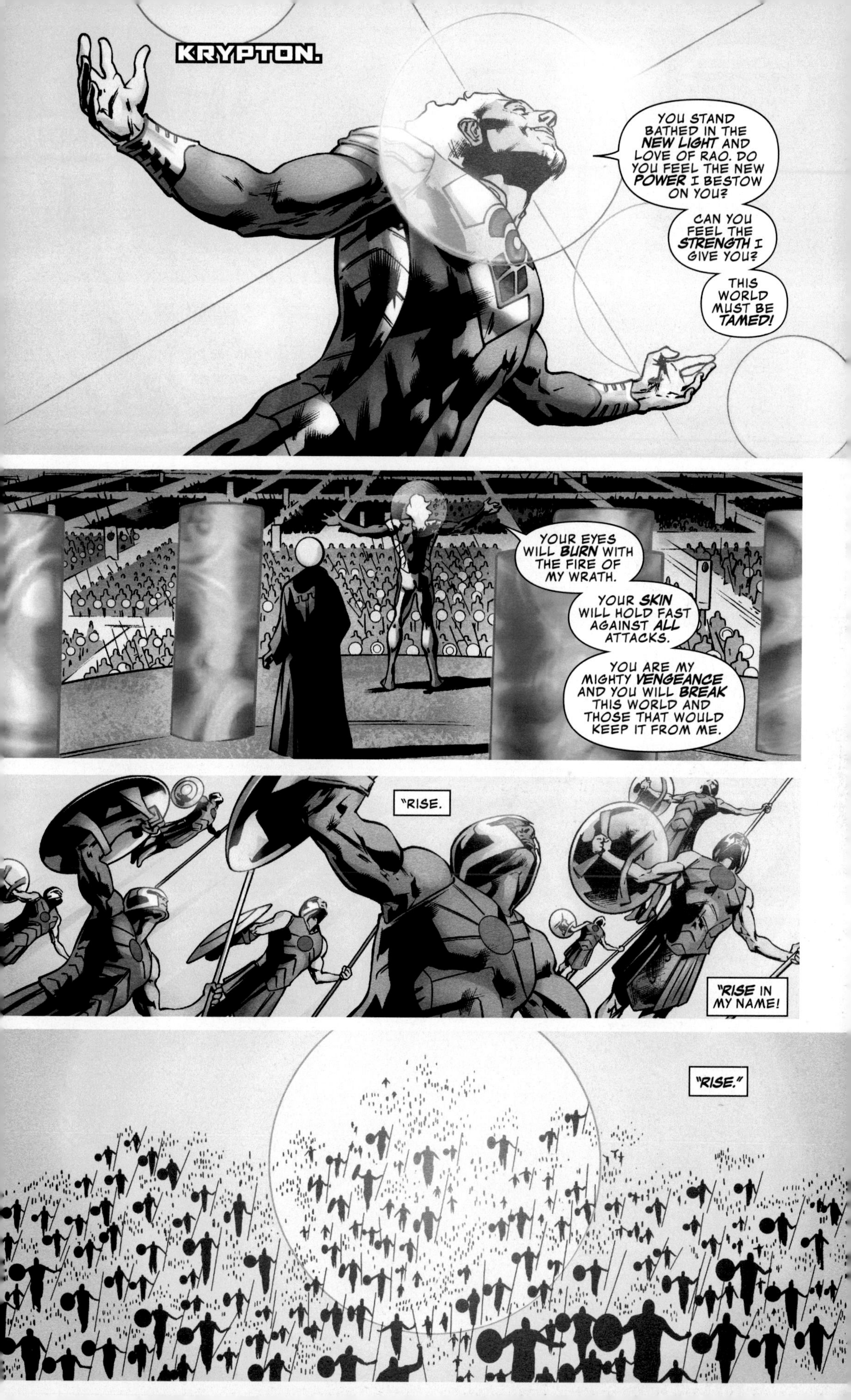
KRYPTON.
YOU STAND BATHED IN THE NEW LIGHT AND LOVE OF RAO. DO YOU FEEL THE NEW POWER I BESTOW ON YOU?
CAN YOU FEEL THE STRENGTH I GIVE YOU?
THIS WORLD MUST BE TAMED!
YOUR EYES WILL BURN WITH THE FIRE OF MY WRATH.
YOUR SKIN WILL HOLD FAST AGAINST ALL ATTACKS.
YOU ARE MY MIGHTY VENGEANCE AND YOU WILL BREAK THIS WORLD AND THOSE THAT WOULD KEEP IT FROM ME.
"RISE.
"RISE IN MY NAME!
"RISE."

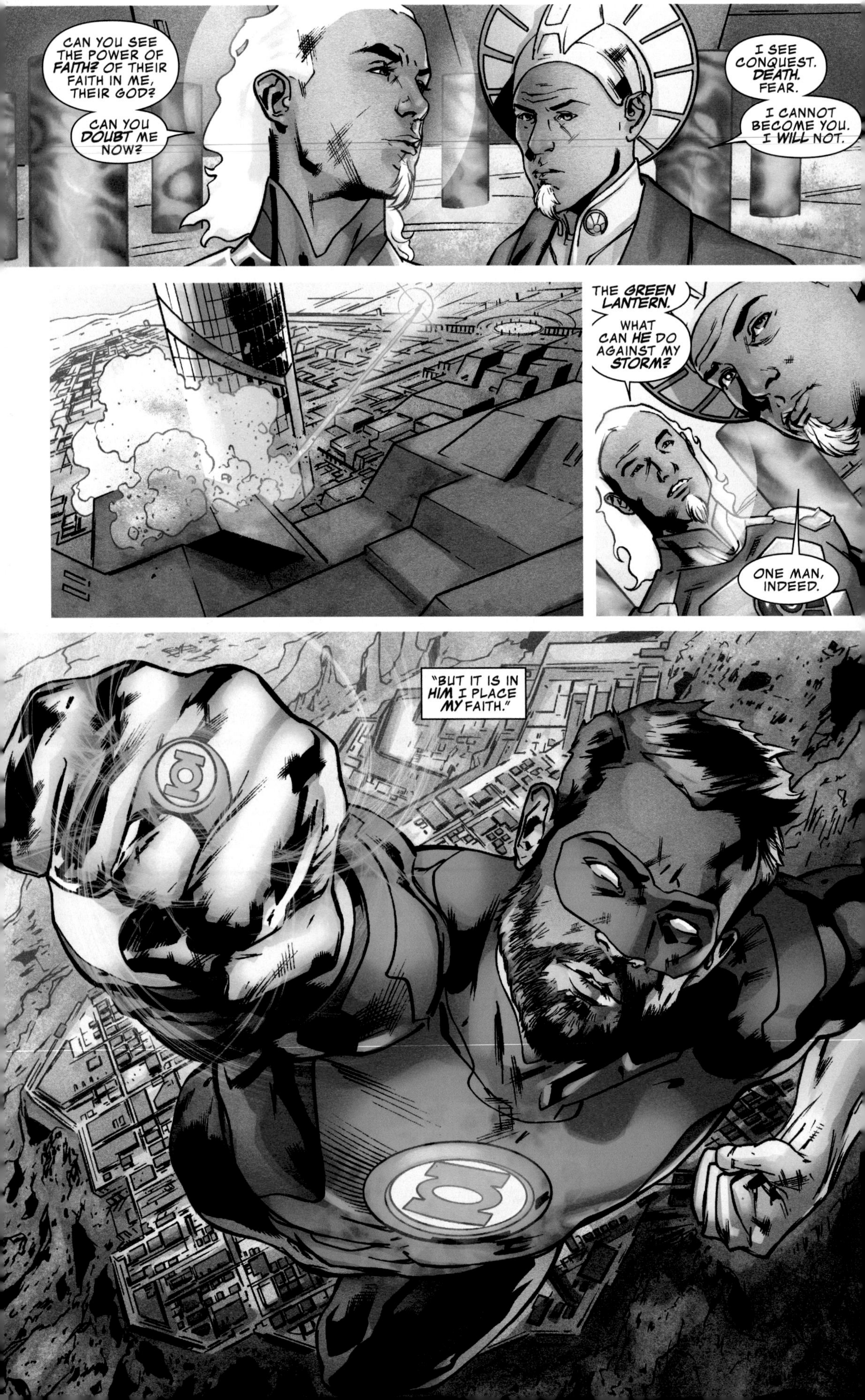
CAN YOU SEE THE POWER OF FAITH? OF THEIR FAITH IN ME, THEIR GOD?
CAN YOU DOUBT ME NOW?
I SEE CONQUEST. DEATH. FEAR.
I CANNOT BECOME YOU. I WILL NOT.
THE GREEN LANTERN.
WHAT CAN HE DO AGAINST MY STORM?
ONE MAN, INDEED.
"BUT IT IS IN HIM I PLACE MY FAITH."

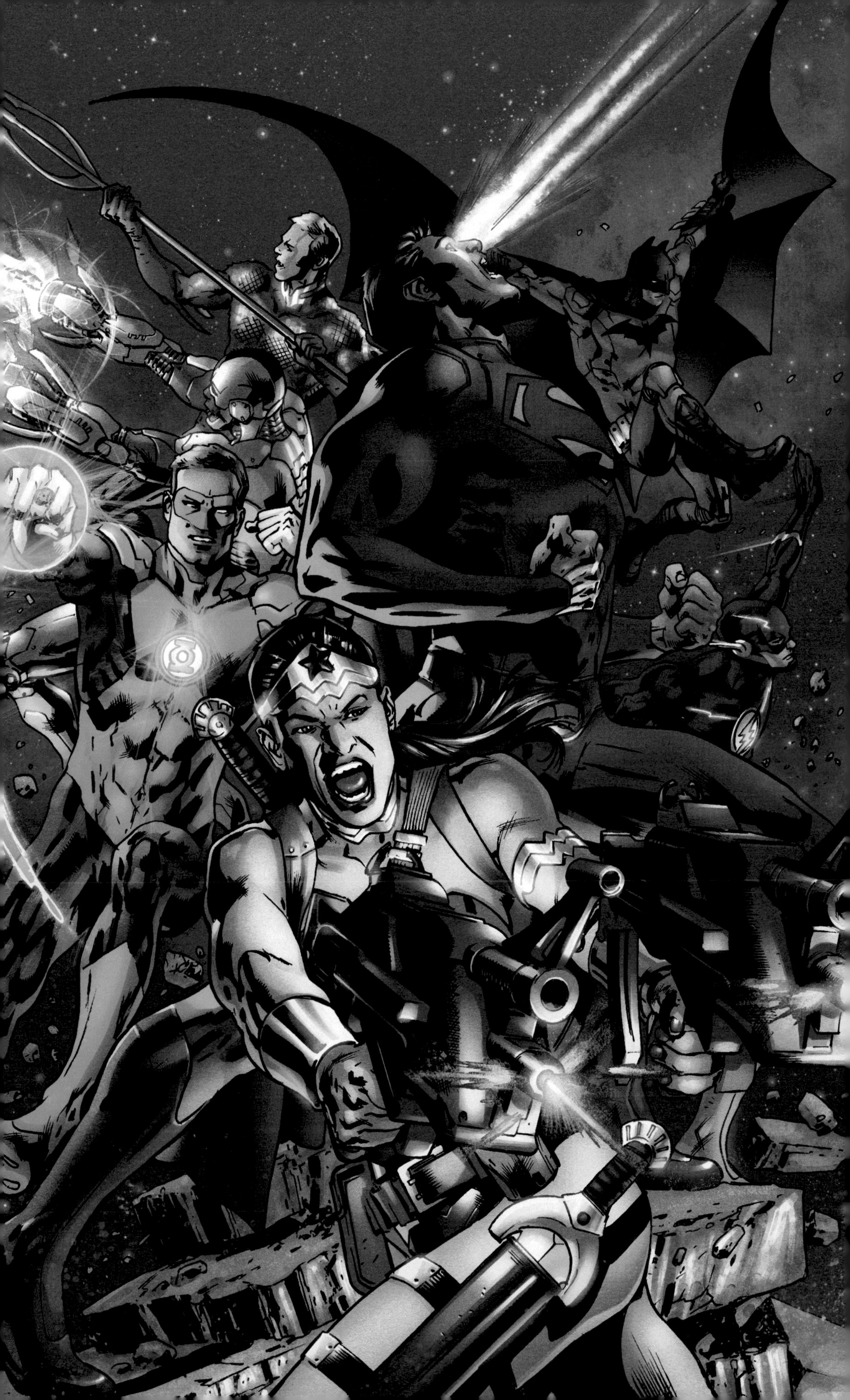

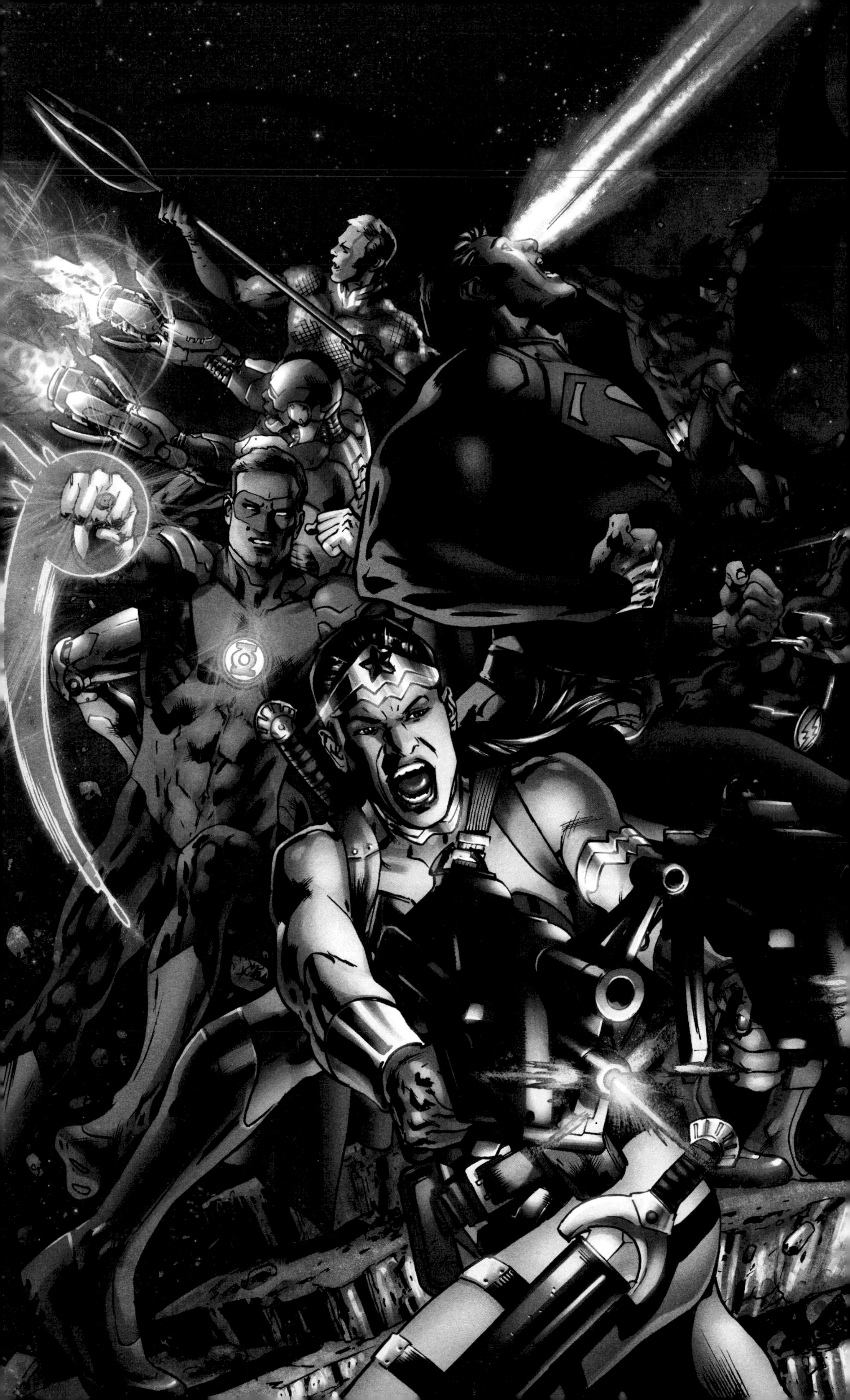

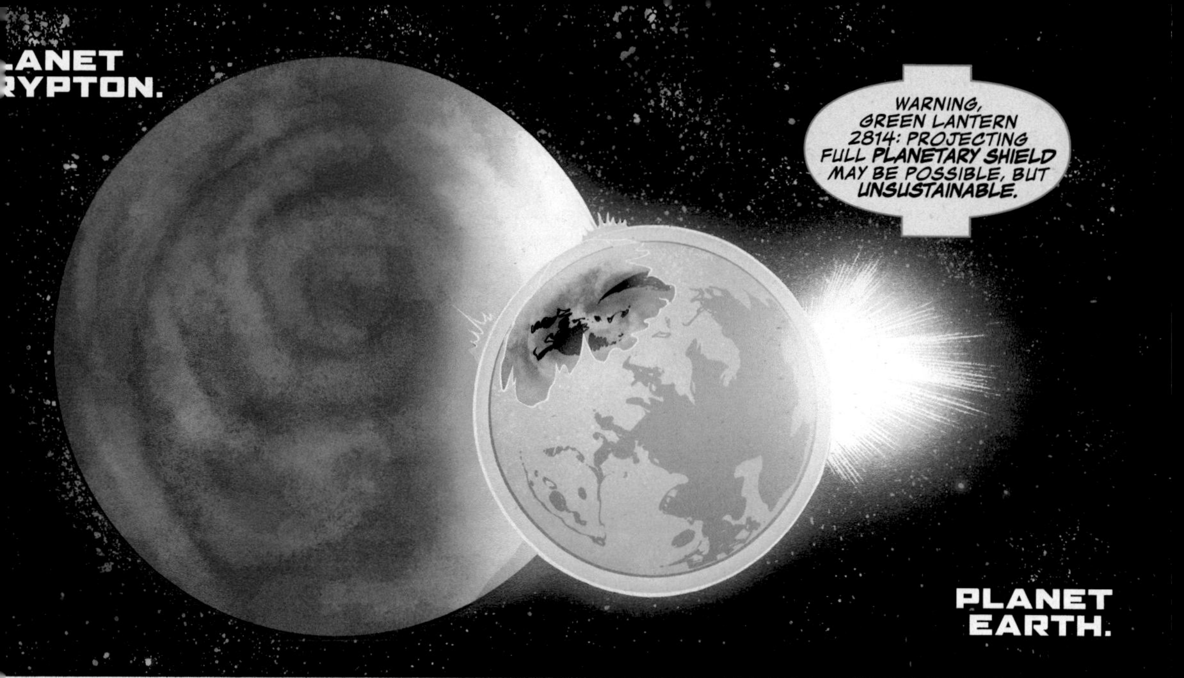
LANET
RYPTON.
WARNING, GREEN LANTERN 2814: PROJECTING FULL PLANETARY SHIELD MAY BE POSSIBLE, BUT UNSUSTAINABLE.
PLANET EARTH.

DC COMICS PRESENTS

THE JUSTICE LEAGUE OF AMERICA POWER AND GLORY

PART NINE

RYAN HITCH — PLOT
TONY BEDARD — SCRIPT
TOM DERENICK — PENCILLER

NIEL HENRIQUES
SCOTT HANNA — INKERS
JEREMIAH SKIPPER — COLORIST
CLAYTON COWLES — LETTERER
AMEDEO TURTURRO & DIEGO LOPEZ — ASSISTANT EDITORS
BRIAN CUNNINGHAM — EDITOR

COVER BY BRYAN HITCH AND ALEX SINCLAIR

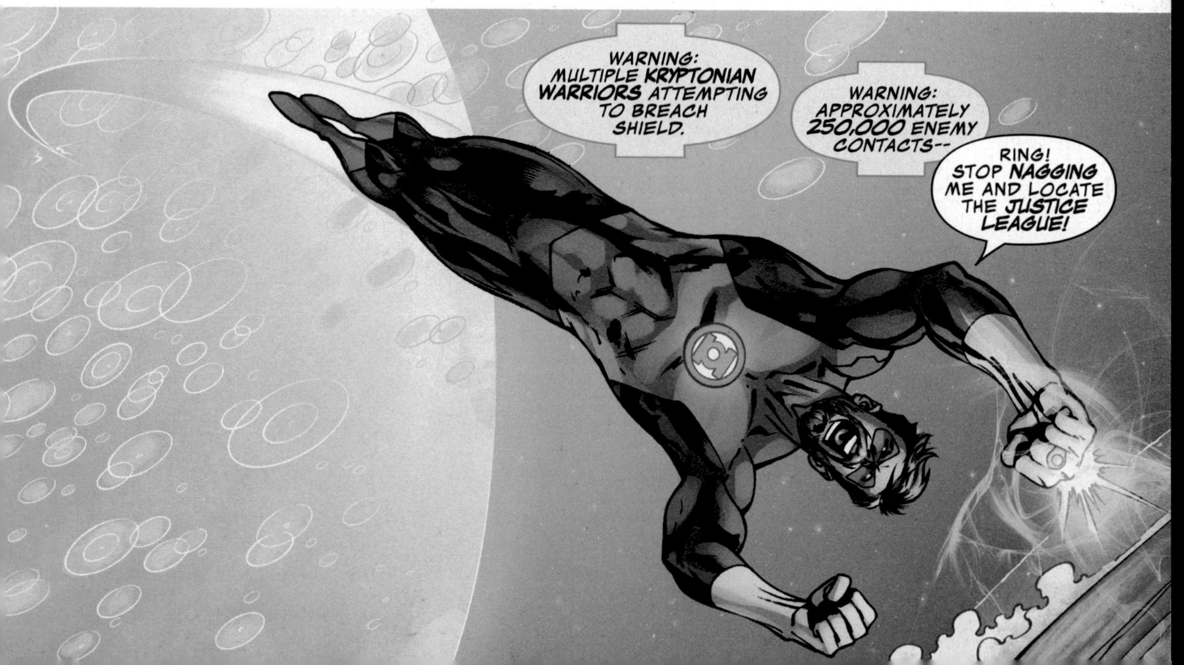
WARNING: MULTIPLE KRYPTONIAN WARRIORS ATTEMPTING TO BREACH SHIELD.
WARNING: APPROXIMATELY 250,000 ENEMY CONTACTS--
RING! STOP NAGGING ME AND LOCATE THE JUSTICE LEAGUE!

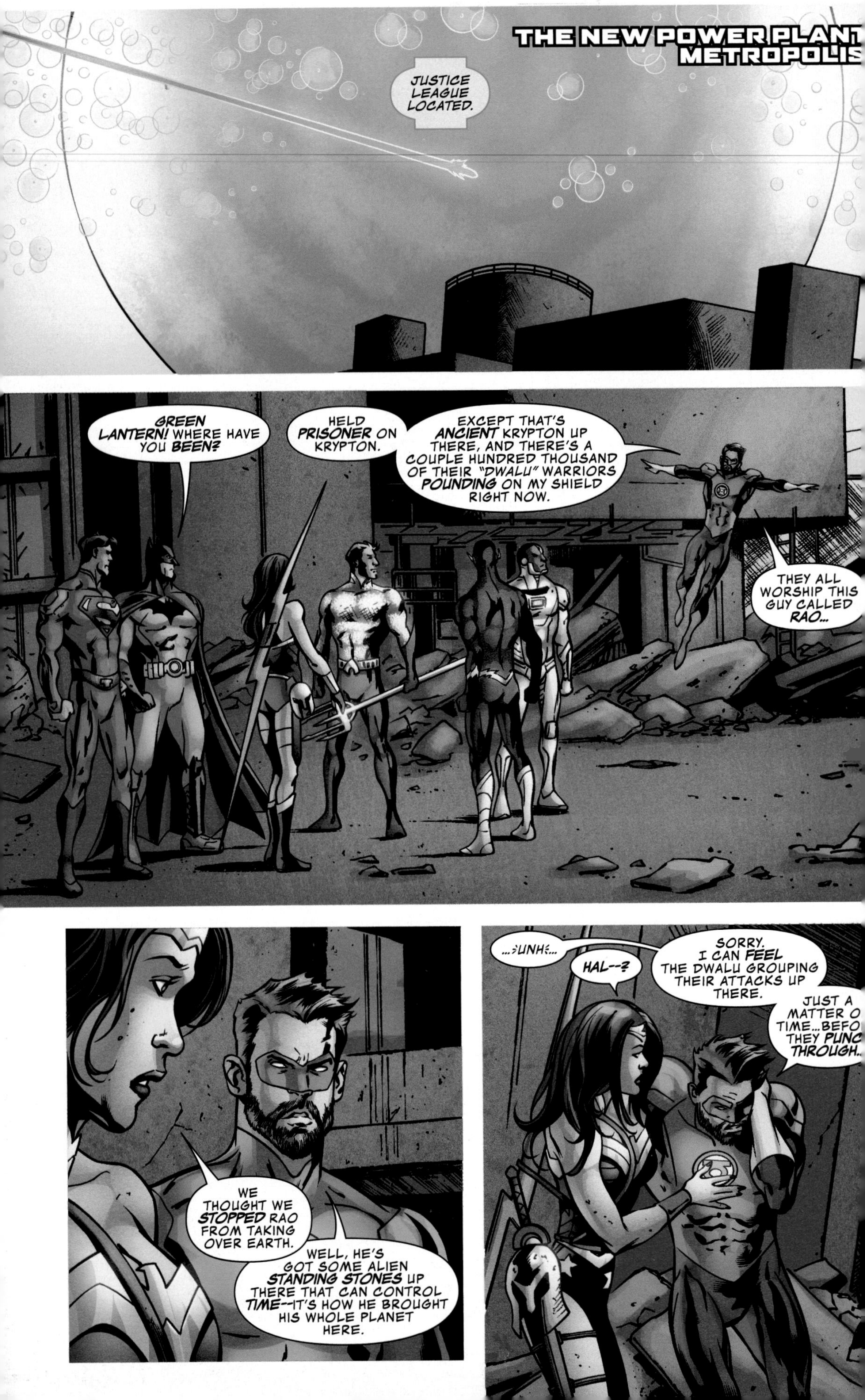
THE NEW POWER PLANT
METROPOLIS
JUSTICE LEAGUE LOCATED.
GREEN LANTERN! WHERE HAVE YOU BEEN?
HELD PRISONER ON KRYPTON.
EXCEPT THAT'S ANCIENT KRYPTON UP THERE, AND THERE'S A COUPLE HUNDRED THOUSAND OF THEIR "DWALU" WARRIORS POUNDING ON MY SHIELD RIGHT NOW.
THEY ALL WORSHIP THIS GUY CALLED RAO...
WE THOUGHT WE STOPPED RAO FROM TAKING OVER EARTH.
WELL, HE'S GOT SOME ALIEN STANDING STONES UP THERE THAT CAN CONTROL TIME--IT'S HOW HE BROUGHT HIS WHOLE PLANET HERE.
...UNH...
HAL--?
SORRY. I CAN FEEL THE DWALU GROUPING THEIR ATTACKS UP THERE.

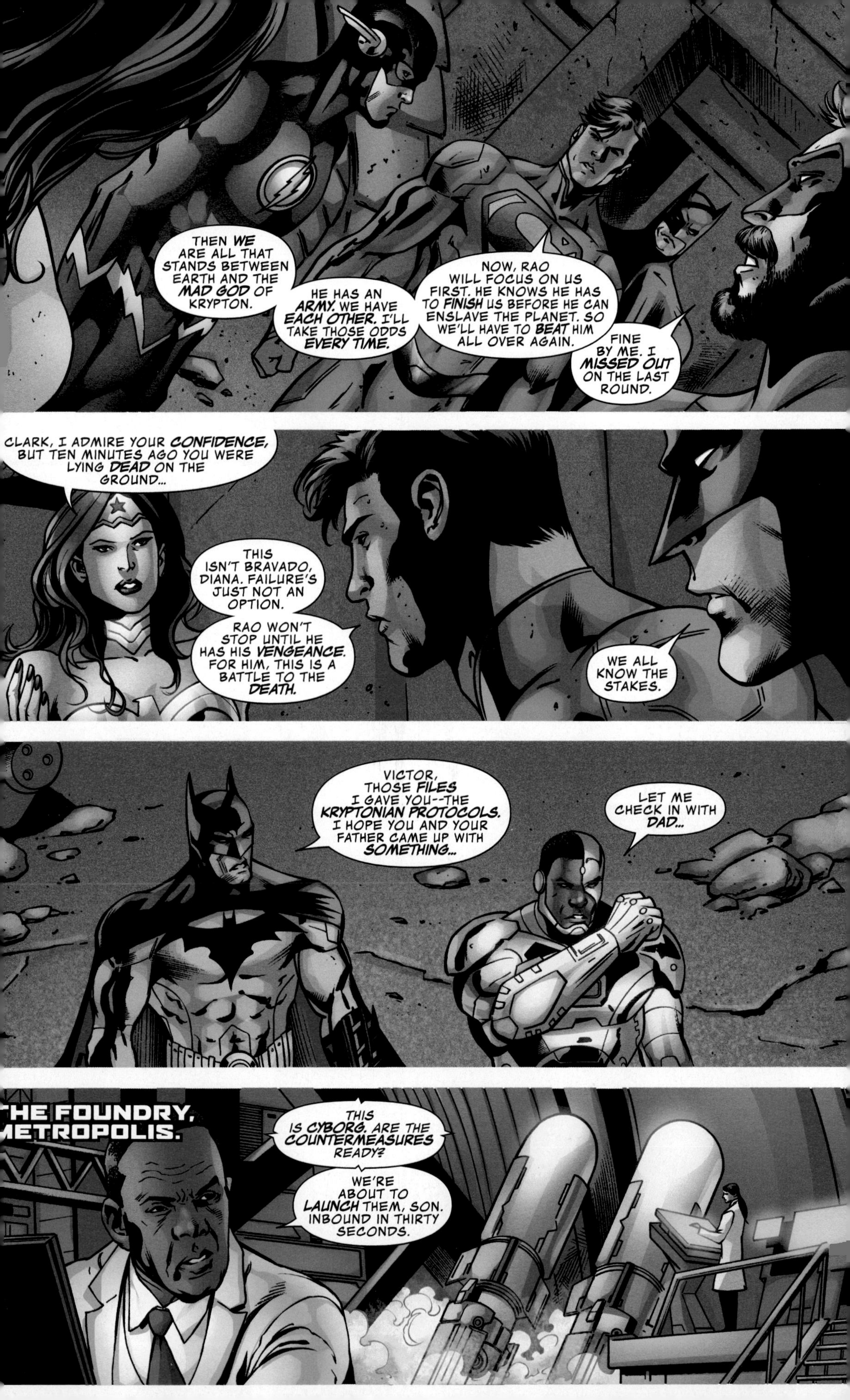

THEN WE ARE ALL THAT STANDS BETWEEN EARTH AND THE MAD GOD OF KRYPTON.
HE HAS AN ARMY. WE HAVE EACH OTHER. I'LL TAKE THOSE ODDS EVERY TIME.
NOW, RAO WILL FOCUS ON US FIRST. HE KNOWS HE HAS TO FINISH US BEFORE HE CAN ENSLAVE THE PLANET. SO WE'LL HAVE TO BEAT HIM ALL OVER AGAIN.
FINE BY ME. I MISSED OUT ON THE LAST ROUND.
CLARK, I ADMIRE YOUR CONFIDENCE, BUT TEN MINUTES AGO YOU WERE LYING DEAD ON THE GROUND...
THIS ISN'T BRAVADO, DIANA. FAILURE'S JUST NOT AN OPTION.
RAO WON'T STOP UNTIL HE HAS HIS VENGEANCE. FOR HIM, THIS IS A BATTLE TO THE DEATH.
WE ALL KNOW THE STAKES.
VICTOR, THOSE FILES I GAVE YOU--THE KRYPTONIAN PROTOCOLS. I HOPE YOU AND YOUR FATHER CAME UP WITH SOMETHING...
LET ME CHECK IN WITH DAD...
THE FOUNDRY, METROPOLIS.
THIS IS CYBORG. ARE THE COUNTERMEASURES READY?
WE'RE ABOUT TO LAUNCH THEM, SON. INBOUND IN THIRTY SECONDS.

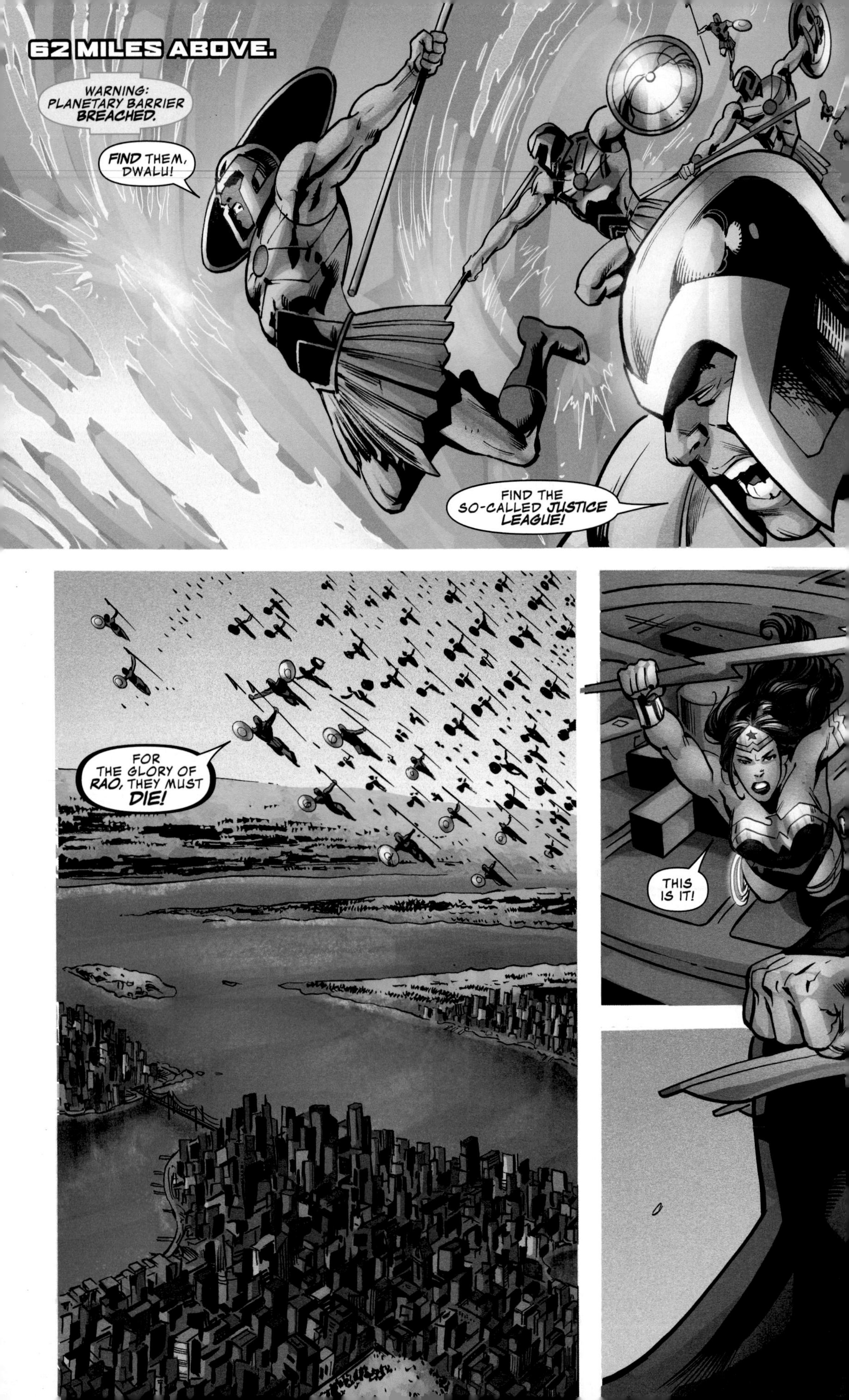
62 MILES ABOVE.
WARNING: PLANETARY BARRIER BREACHED.
FIND THEM, DWALU!
FIND THE SO-CALLED JUSTICE LEAGUE!
FOR THE GLORY OF RAO, THEY MUST DIE!
THIS IS IT!

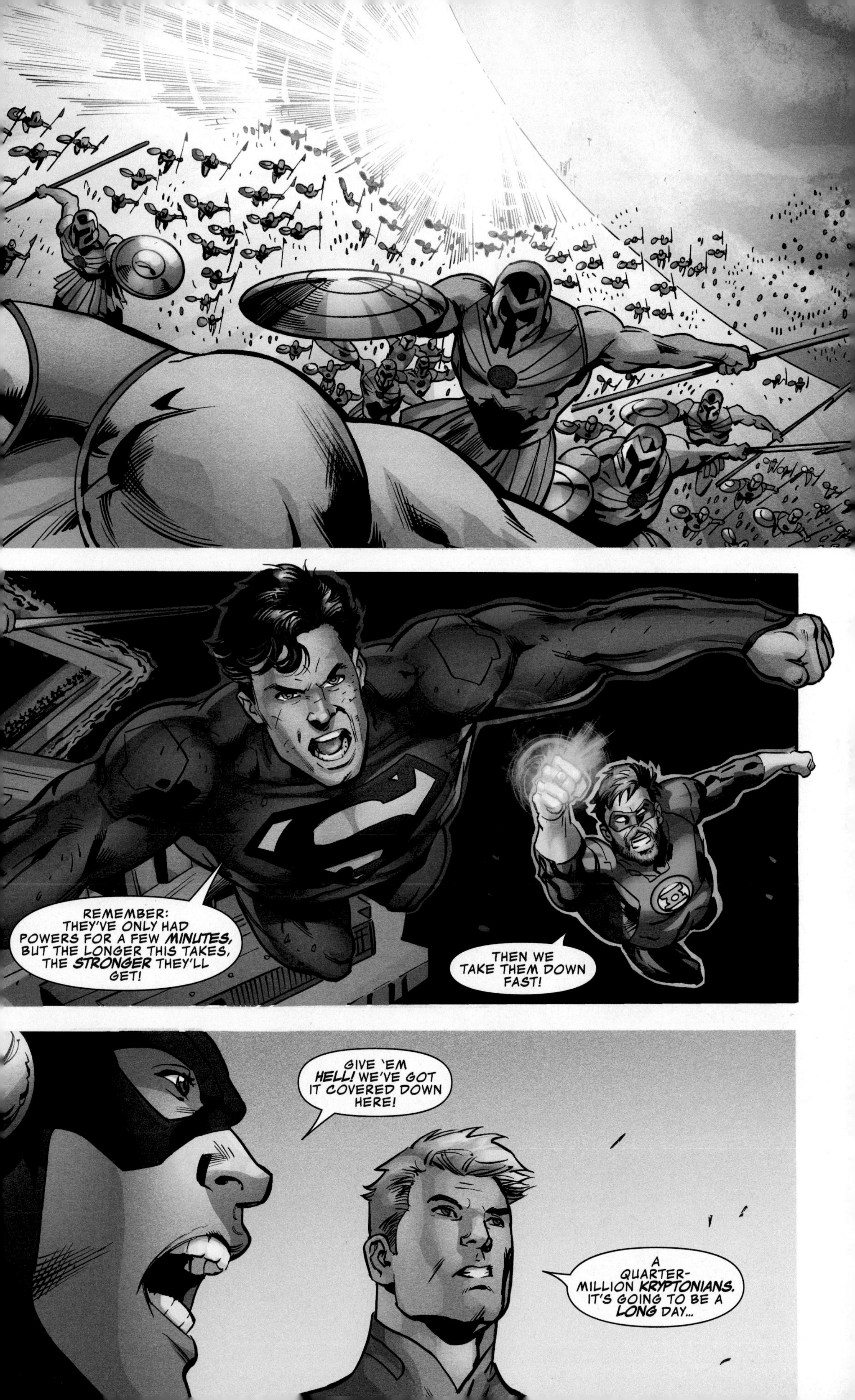
REMEMBER: THEY'VE ONLY HAD POWERS FOR A FEW MINUTES, BUT THE LONGER THIS TAKES, THE STRONGER THEY'LL GET!
THEN WE TAKE THEM DOWN FAST!
GIVE 'EM HELL! WE'VE GOT IT COVERED DOWN HERE!
A QUARTER-MILLION KRYPTONIANS. IT'S GOING TO BE A LONG DAY...

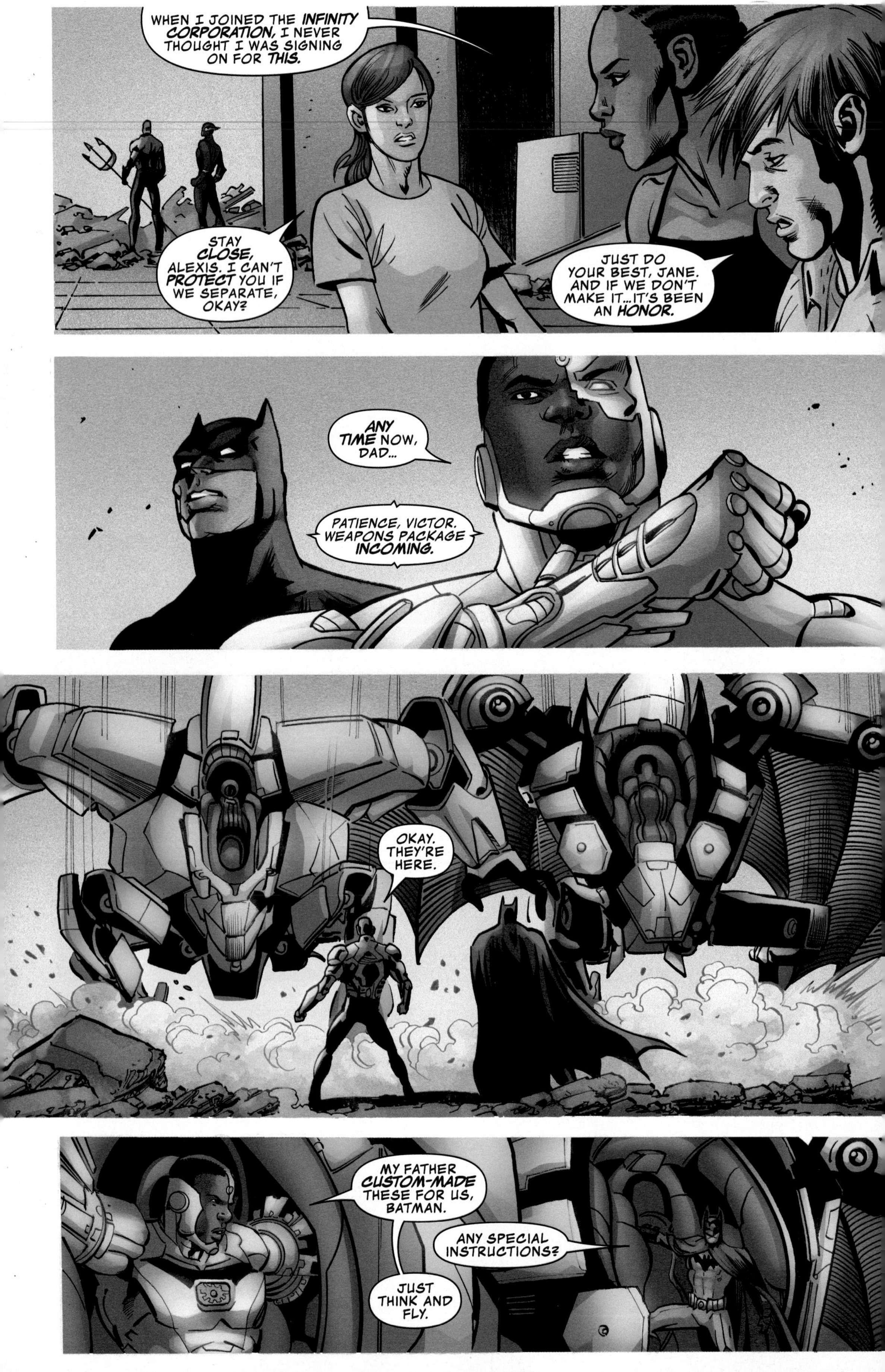
WHEN I JOINED THE INFINITY CORPORATION, I NEVER THOUGHT I WAS SIGNING ON FOR THIS.
STAY CLOSE, ALEXIS. I CAN'T PROTECT YOU IF WE SEPARATE, OKAY?
JUST DO YOUR BEST, JANE. AND IF WE DON'T MAKE IT...IT'S BEEN AN HONOR.
ANY TIME NOW, DAD...
PATIENCE, VICTOR. WEAPONS PACKAGE INCOMING.
OKAY. THEY'RE HERE.
MY FATHER CUSTOM-MADE THESE FOR US, BATMAN.
ANY SPECIAL INSTRUCTIONS?
JUST THINK AND FLY.

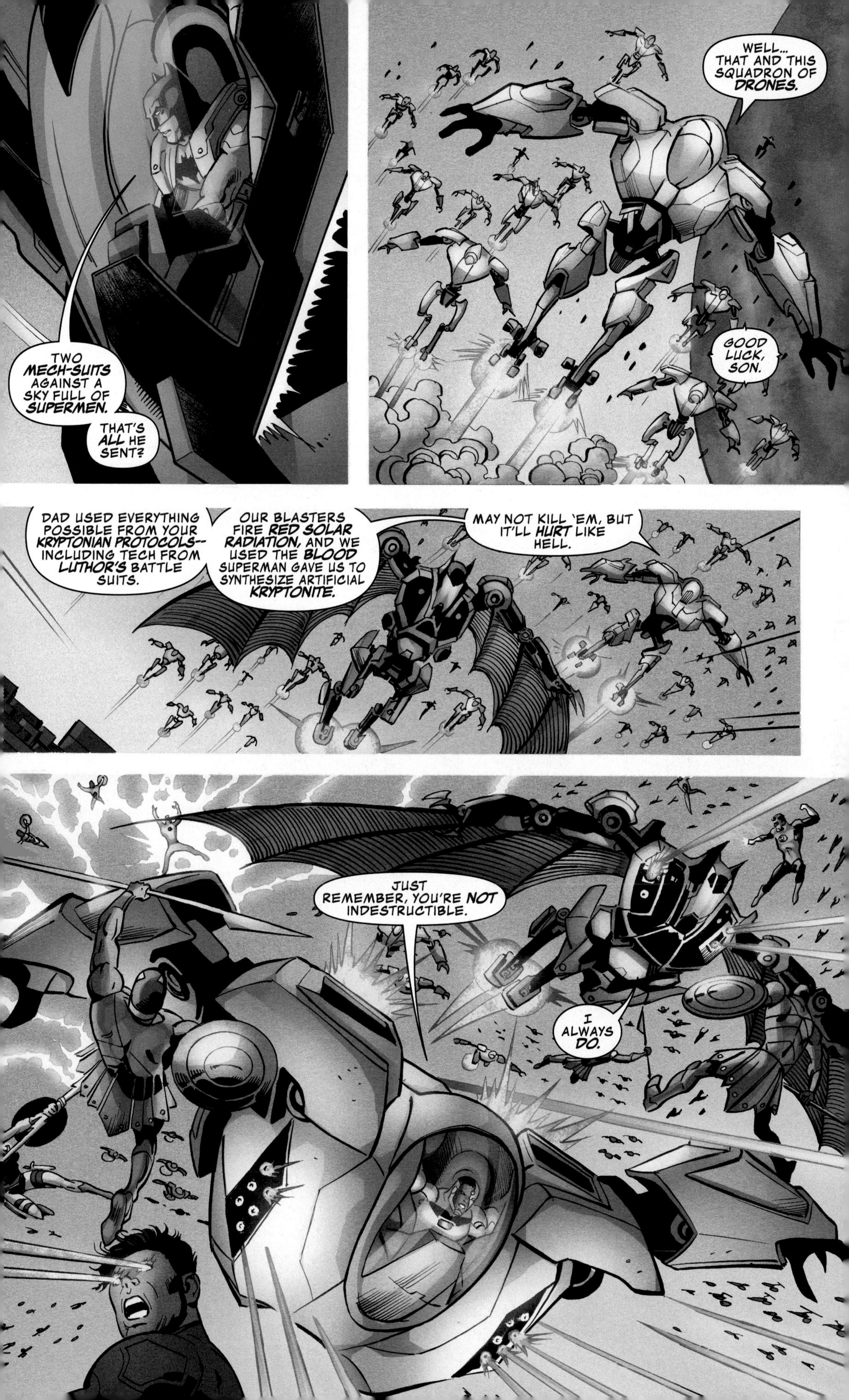
TWO MECH-SUITS AGAINST A SKY FULL OF SUPERMEN.
THAT'S ALL HE SENT?
WELL... THAT AND THIS SQUADRON OF DRONES.
GOOD LUCK, SON.
DAD USED EVERYTHING POSSIBLE FROM YOUR KRYPTONIAN PROTOCOLS-- INCLUDING TECH FROM LUTHOR'S BATTLE SUITS.
OUR BLASTERS FIRE RED SOLAR RADIATION, AND WE USED THE BLOOD SUPERMAN GAVE US TO SYNTHESIZE ARTIFICIAL KRYPTONITE.
MAY NOT KILL 'EM, BUT IT'LL HURT LIKE HELL.
JUST REMEMBER, YOU'RE NOT INDESTRUCTIBLE.
I ALWAYS DO.

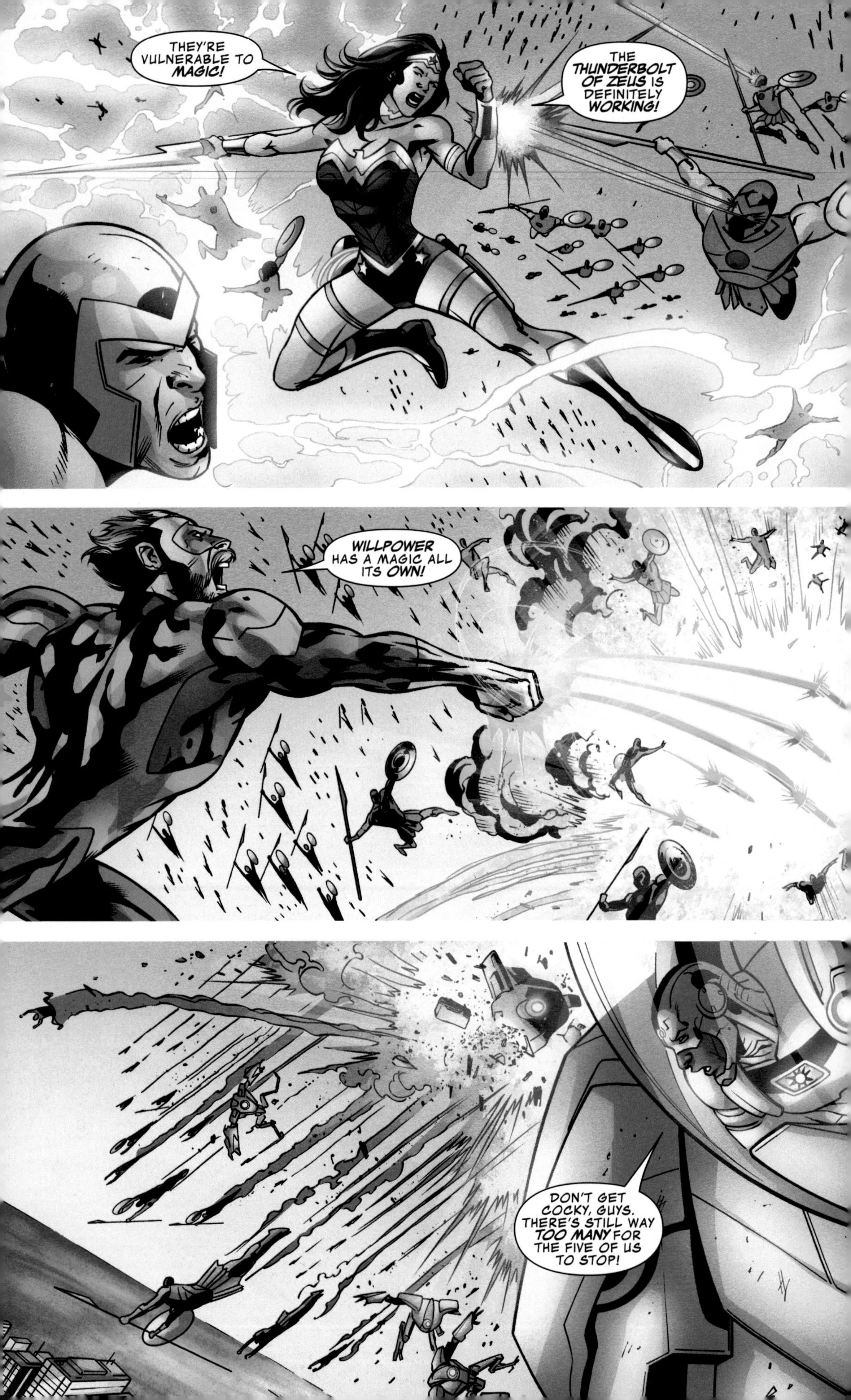
THEY'RE VULNERABLE TO *MAGIC!*
THE *THUNDERBOLT OF ZEUS* IS DEFINITELY *WORKING!*
WILLPOWER HAS A MAGIC ALL ITS *OWN!*
DON'T GET COCKY, GUYS. THERE'S STILL WAY *TOO MANY* FOR THE FIVE OF US TO STOP!

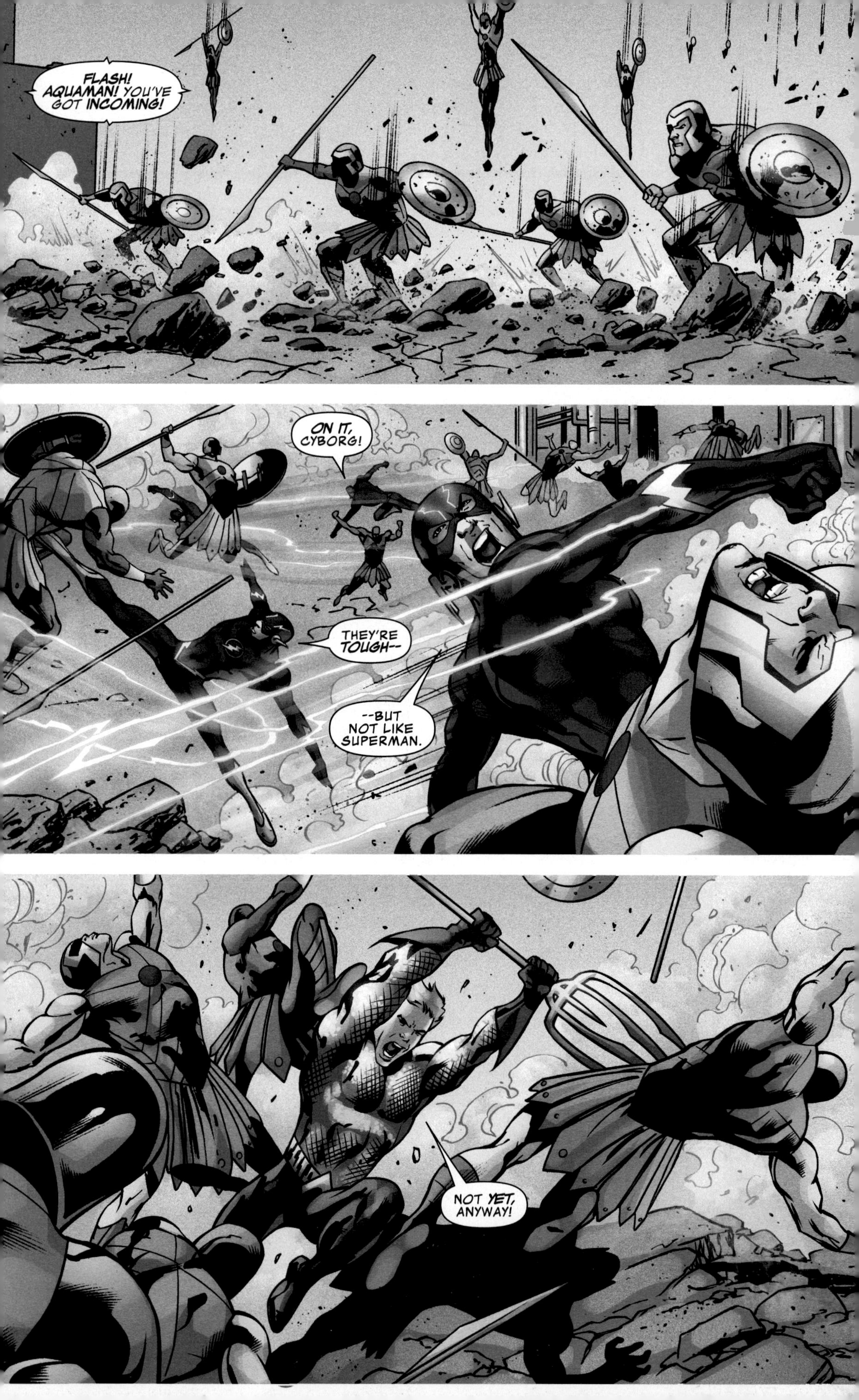
FLASH! AQUAMAN! YOU'VE GOT INCOMING!
ON IT, CYBORG!
THEY'RE TOUGH--
--BUT NOT LIKE SUPERMAN.
NOT YET, ANYWAY!

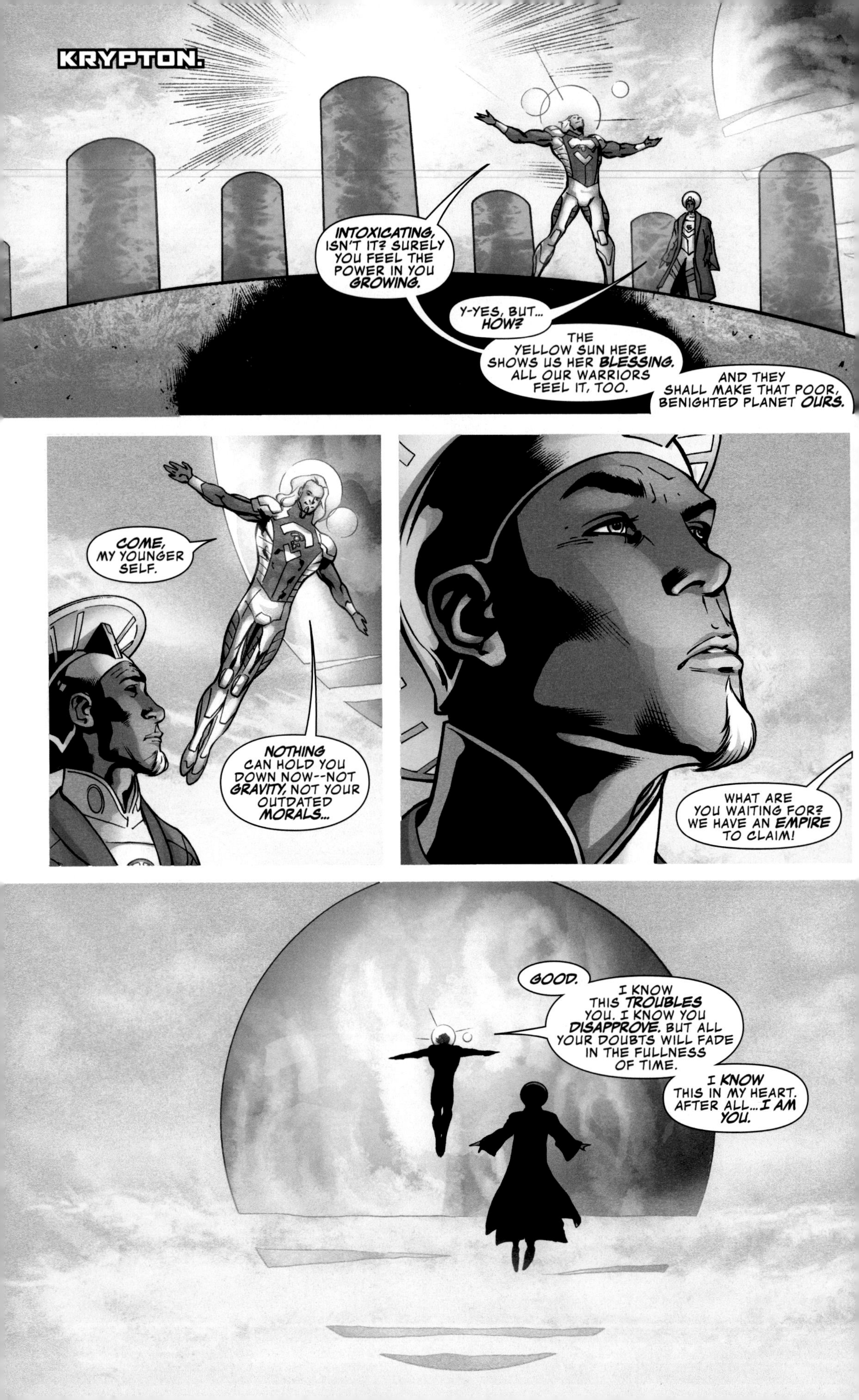
KRYPTON.
INTOXICATING, ISN'T IT? SURELY YOU FEEL THE POWER IN YOU GROWING.
Y-YES, BUT... HOW?
THE YELLOW SUN HERE SHOWS US HER BLESSING. ALL OUR WARRIORS FEEL IT, TOO.
AND THEY SHALL MAKE THAT POOR, BENIGHTED PLANET OURS.
COME, MY YOUNGER SELF.
NOTHING CAN HOLD YOU DOWN NOW--NOT GRAVITY, NOT YOUR OUTDATED MORALS...
WHAT ARE YOU WAITING FOR? WE HAVE AN EMPIRE TO CLAIM!
GOOD.
I KNOW THIS TROUBLES YOU. I KNOW YOU DISAPPROVE. BUT ALL YOUR DOUBTS WILL FADE IN THE FULLNESS OF TIME.
I KNOW THIS IN MY HEART. AFTER ALL...I AM YOU.

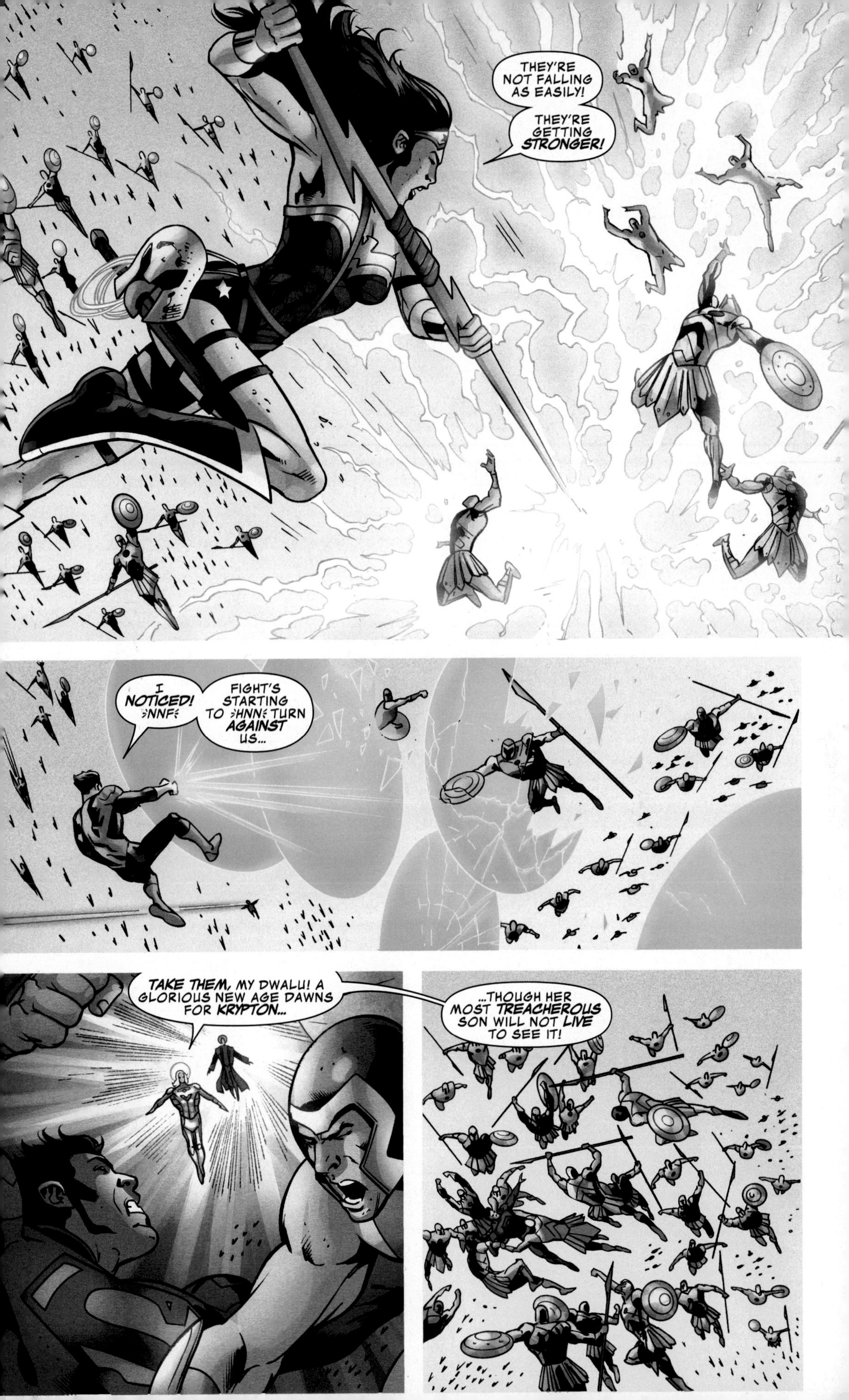
THEY'RE NOT FALLING AS EASILY!
THEY'RE GETTING STRONGER!
I NOTICED! NNF
FIGHT'S STARTING TO HNN TURN AGAINST US...
TAKE THEM, MY DWALU! A GLORIOUS NEW AGE DAWNS FOR KRYPTON...
...THOUGH HER MOST TREACHEROUS SON WILL NOT LIVE TO SEE IT!

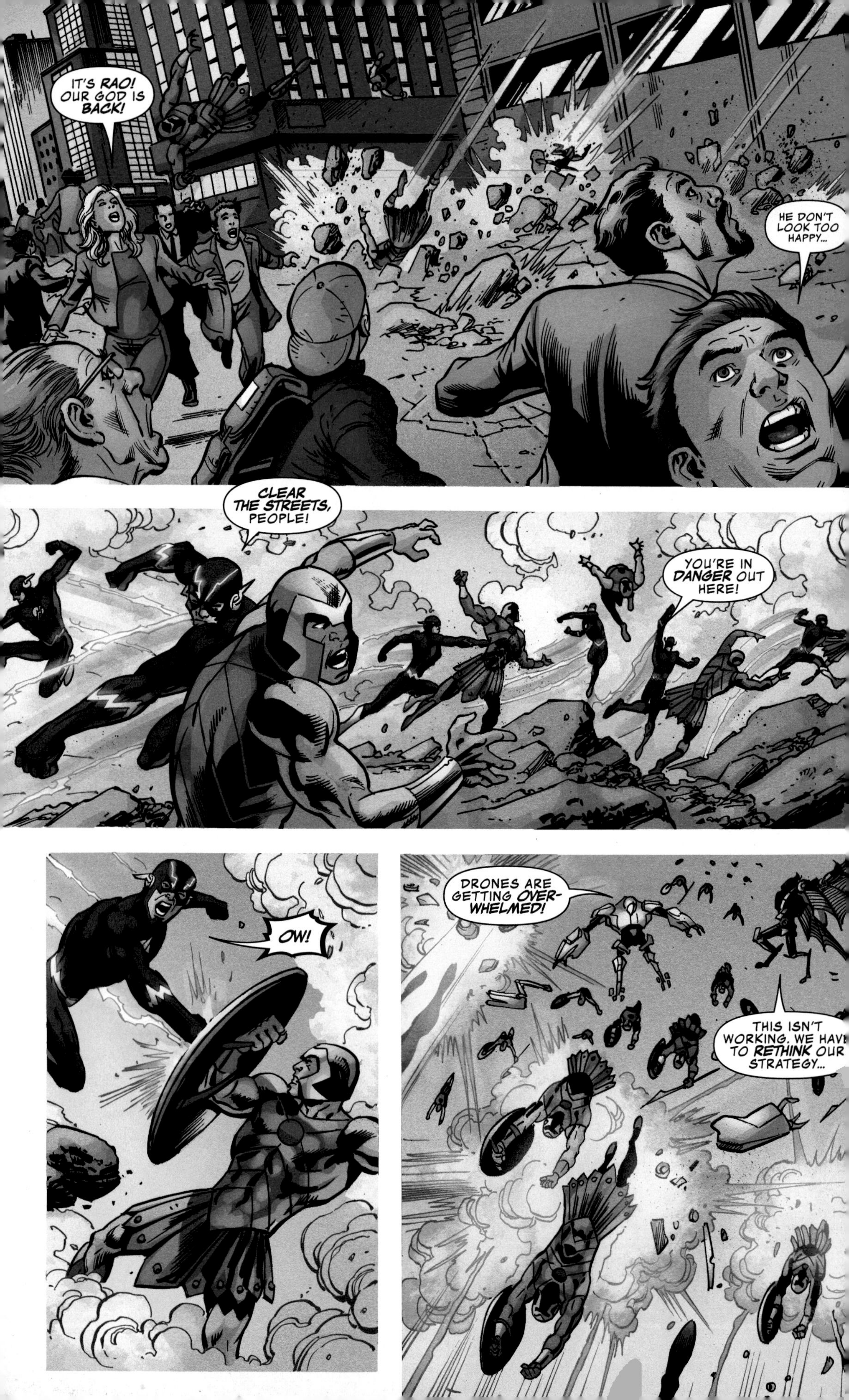
IT'S RAO! OUR GOD IS BACK!
HE DON'T LOOK TOO HAPPY...
CLEAR THE STREETS, PEOPLE!
YOU'RE IN DANGER OUT HERE!
OW!
DRONES ARE GETTING OVER-WHELMED!
THIS ISN'T WORKING. WE HAVE TO RETHINK OUR STRATEGY...

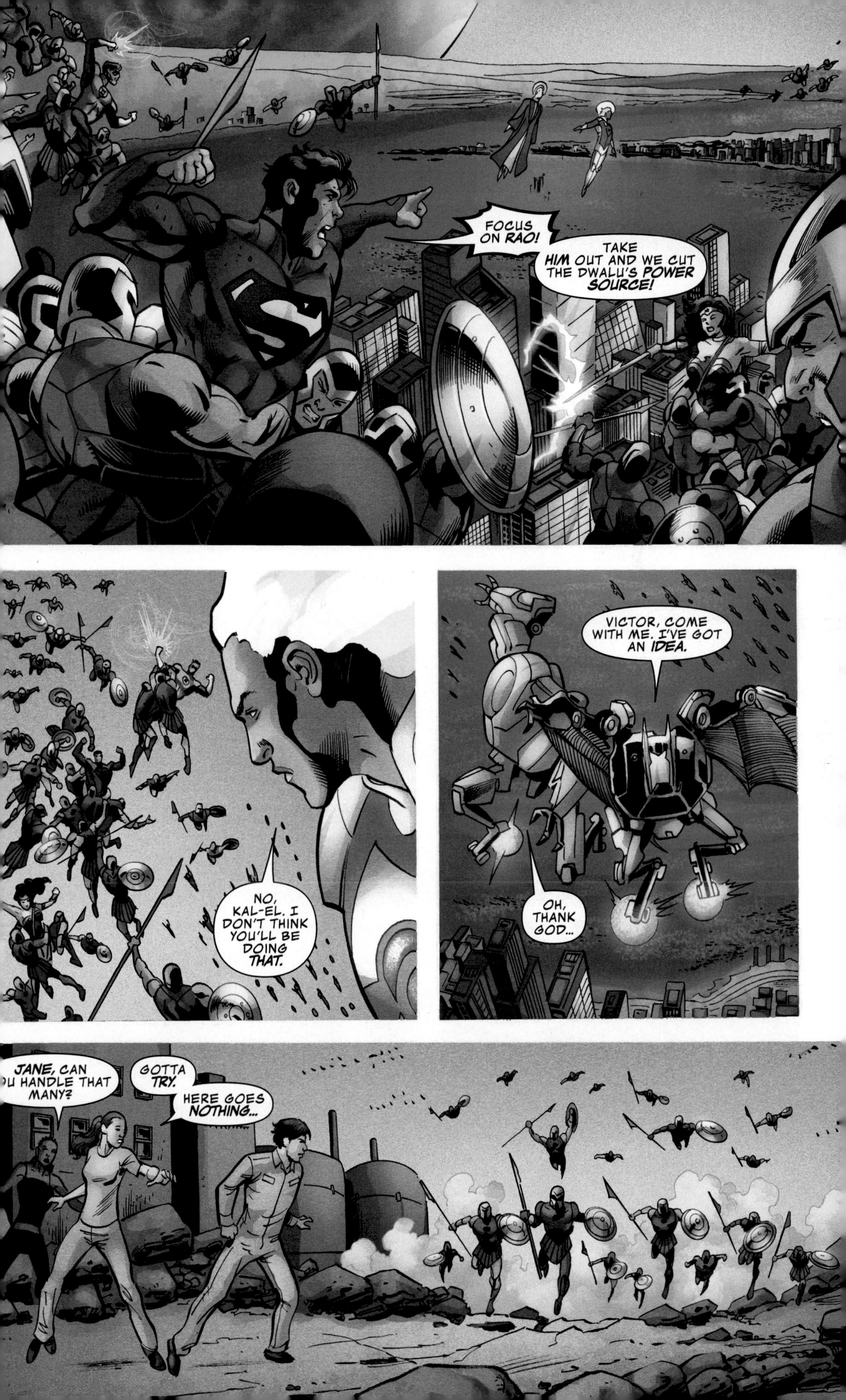
FOCUS ON RAO!
TAKE HIM OUT AND WE CUT THE DWALU'S POWER SOURCE!
NO, KAL-EL. I DON'T THINK YOU'LL BE DOING THAT.
VICTOR, COME WITH ME. I'VE GOT AN IDEA.
OH, THANK GOD...
JANE, CAN U HANDLE THAT MANY?
GOTTA TRY.
HERE GOES NOTHING...

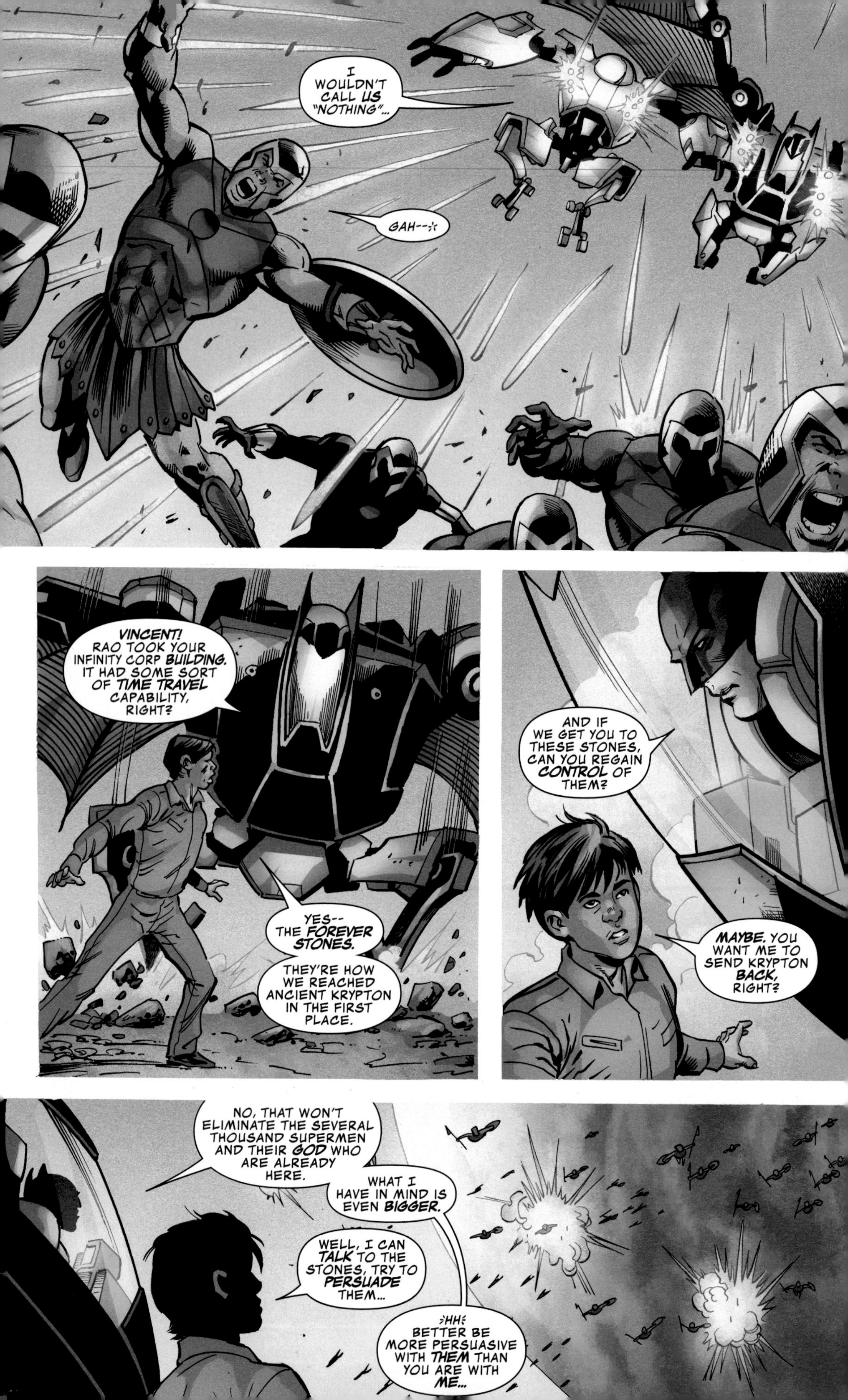
I WOULDN'T CALL US "NOTHING"...
GAH--!
VINCENT! RAO TOOK YOUR INFINITY CORP BUILDING. IT HAD SOME SORT OF TIME TRAVEL CAPABILITY, RIGHT?
YES-- THE FOREVER STONES.
THEY'RE HOW WE REACHED ANCIENT KRYPTON IN THE FIRST PLACE.
AND IF WE GET YOU TO THESE STONES, CAN YOU REGAIN CONTROL OF THEM?
MAYBE. YOU WANT ME TO SEND KRYPTON BACK, RIGHT?
NO, THAT WON'T ELIMINATE THE SEVERAL THOUSAND SUPERMEN AND THEIR GOD WHO ARE ALREADY HERE.
WHAT I HAVE IN MIND IS EVEN BIGGER.
WELL, I CAN TALK TO THE STONES, TRY TO PERSUADE THEM...
HH BETTER BE MORE PERSUASIVE WITH THEM THAN YOU ARE WITH ME...

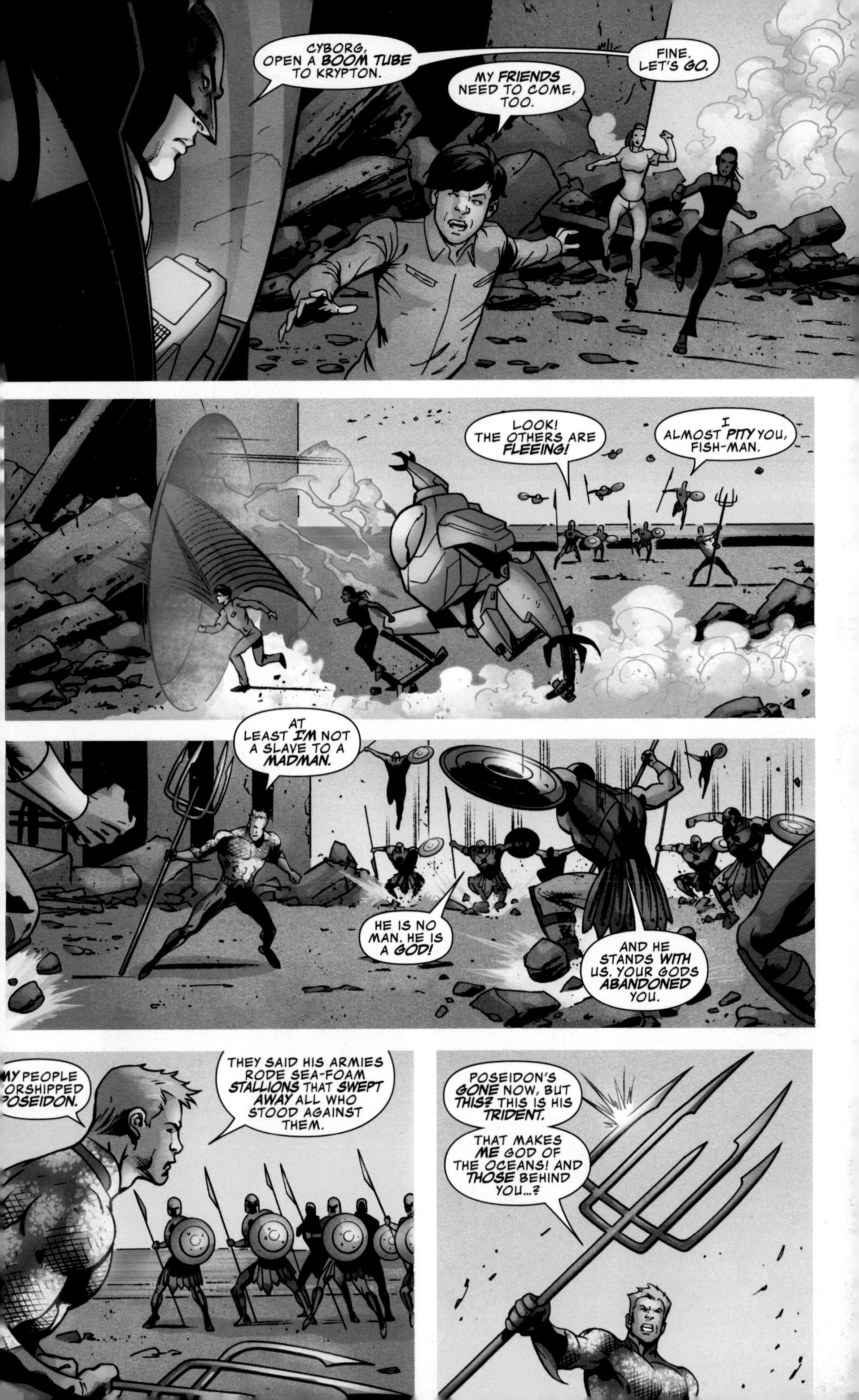
CYBORG, OPEN A BOOM TUBE TO KRYPTON.
FINE. LET'S GO.
MY FRIENDS NEED TO COME, TOO.
LOOK! THE OTHERS ARE FLEEING!
I ALMOST PITY YOU, FISH-MAN.
AT LEAST I'M NOT A SLAVE TO A MADMAN.
HE IS NO MAN. HE IS A GOD!
AND HE STANDS WITH US. YOUR GODS ABANDONED YOU.
MY PEOPLE ORSHIPPED OSEIDON.
THEY SAID HIS ARMIES RODE SEA-FOAM STALLIONS THAT SWEPT AWAY ALL WHO STOOD AGAINST THEM.
POSEIDON'S GONE NOW, BUT THIS? THIS IS HIS TRIDENT.
THAT MAKES ME GOD OF THE OCEANS! AND THOSE BEHIND YOU...?

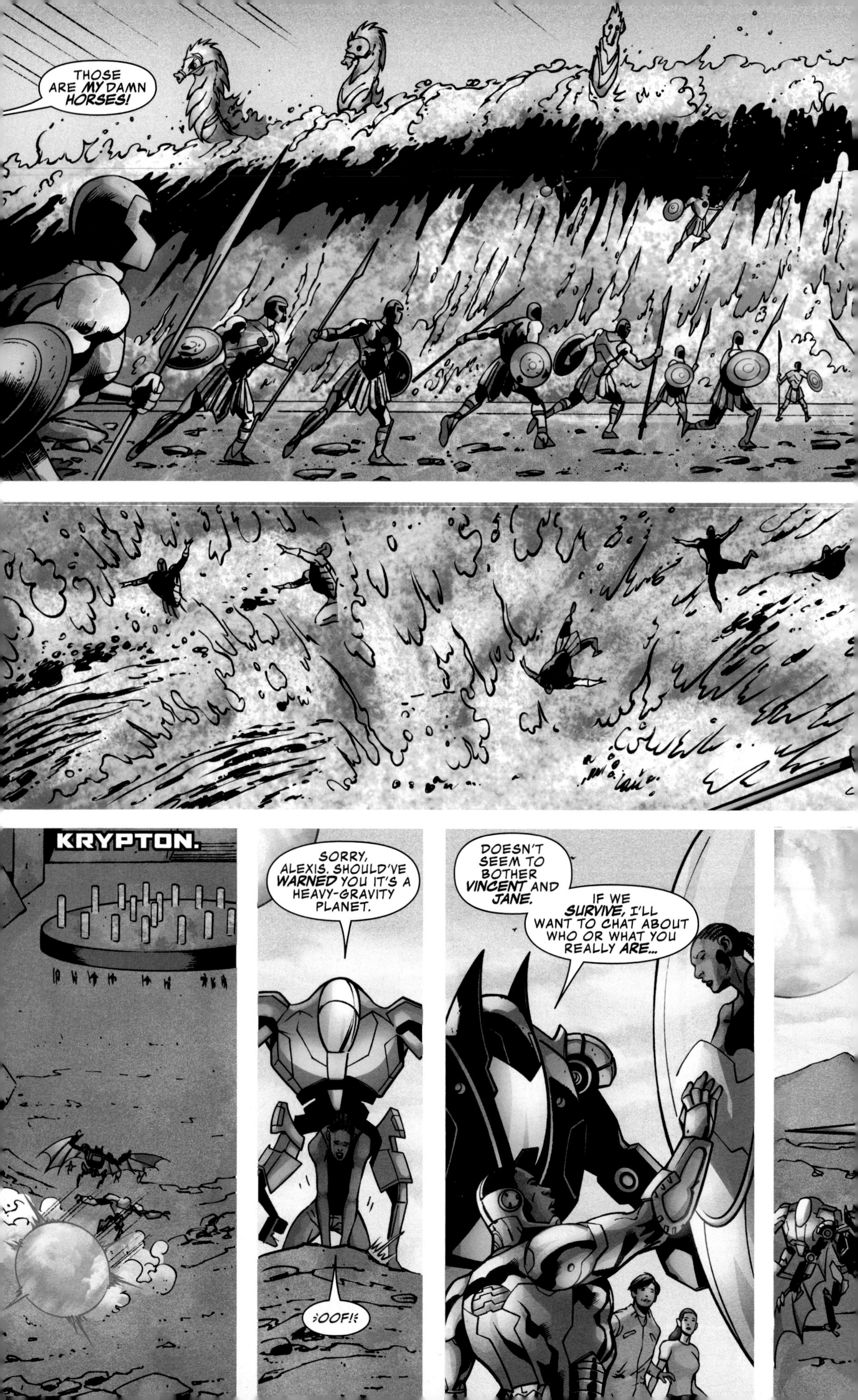
THOSE ARE MY DAMN HORSES!
KRYPTON.
SORRY, ALEXIS. SHOULD'VE WARNED YOU IT'S A HEAVY-GRAVITY PLANET.
OOF!
DOESN'T SEEM TO BOTHER VINCENT AND JANE.
IF WE SURVIVE, I'LL WANT TO CHAT ABOUT WHO OR WHAT YOU REALLY ARE...

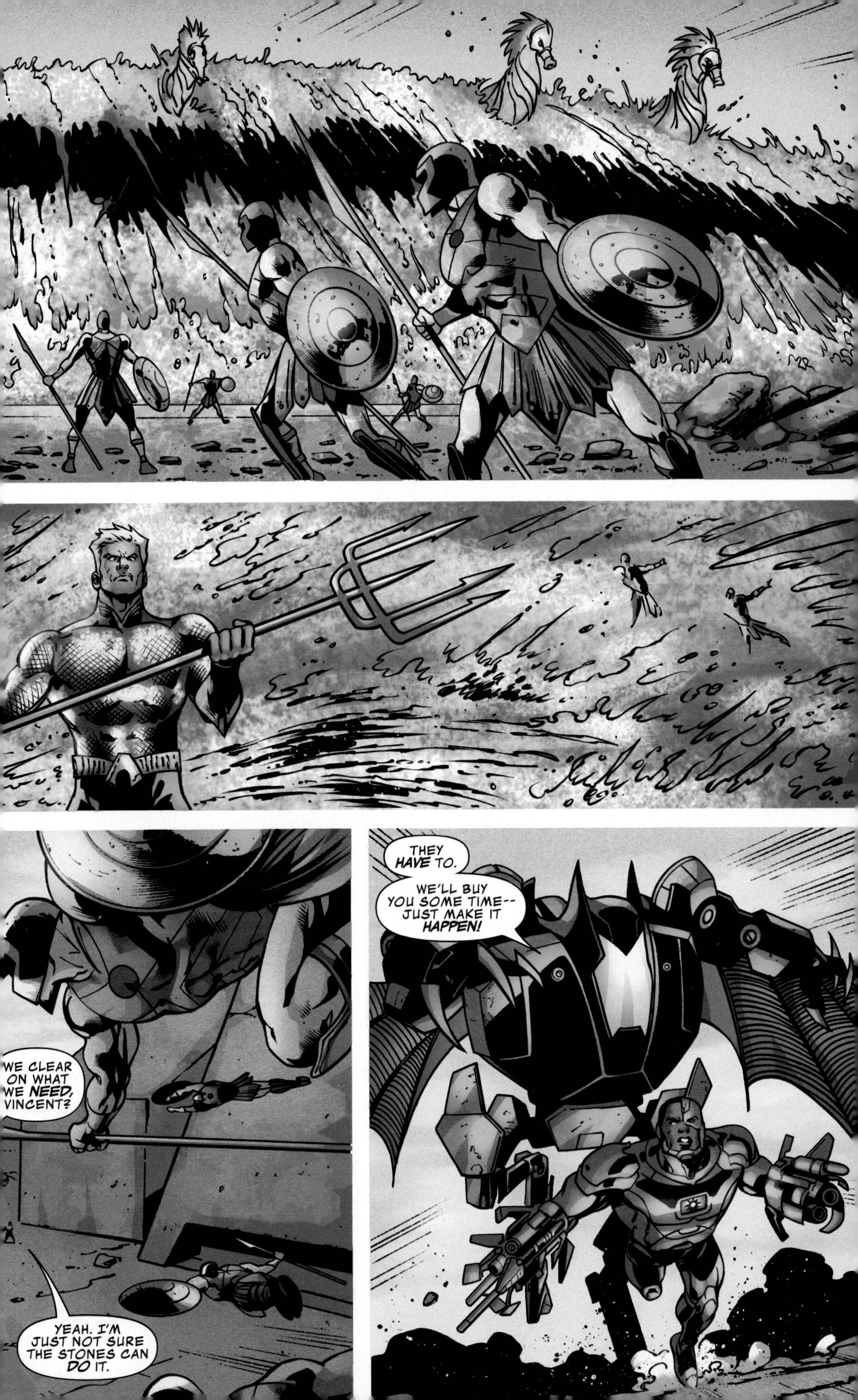
WE CLEAR ON WHAT WE NEED, VINCENT?
YEAH. I'M JUST NOT SURE THE STONES CAN DO IT.
THEY HAVE TO.
WE'LL BUY YOU SOME TIME-- JUST MAKE IT HAPPEN!

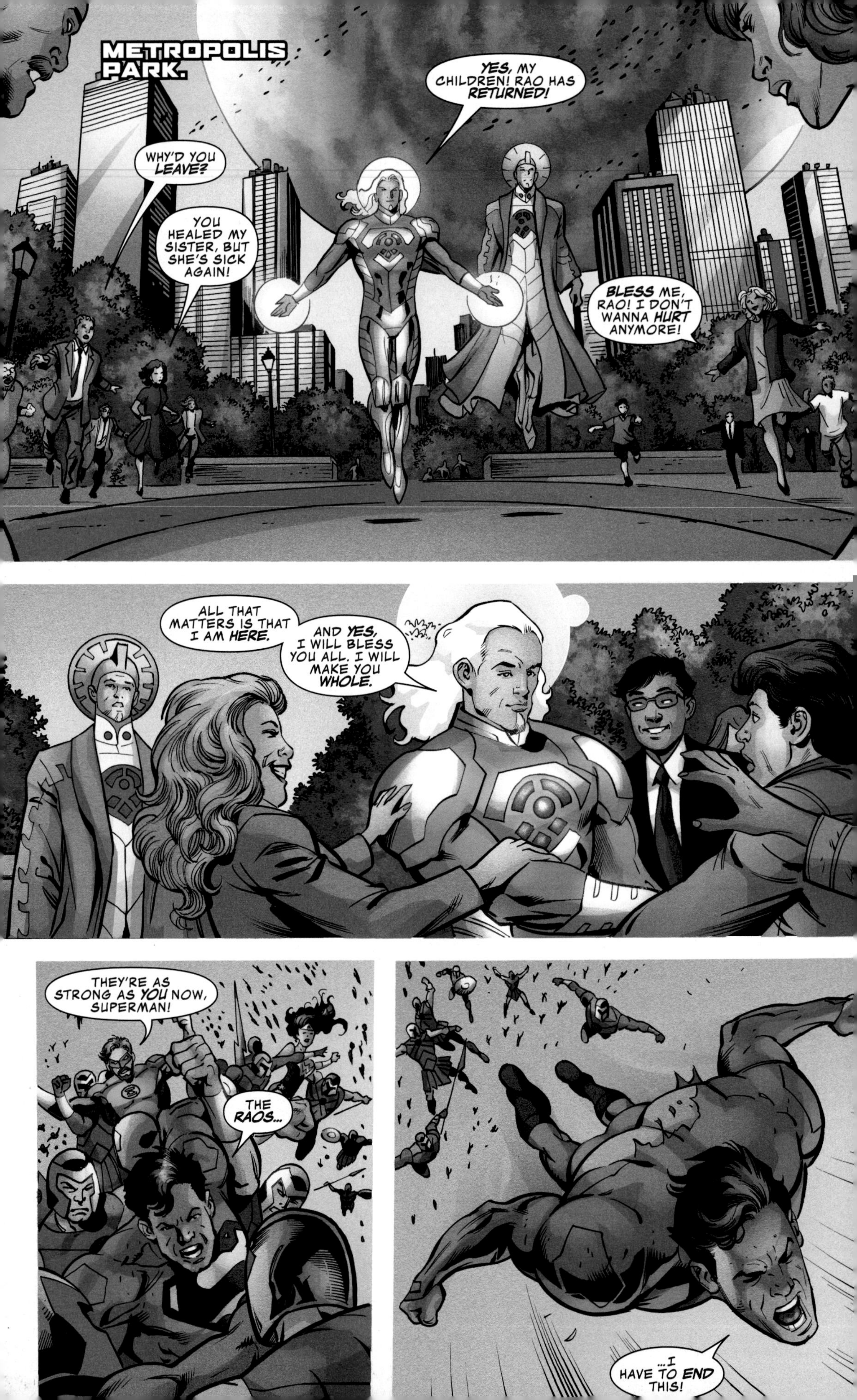
METROPOLIS PARK.
YES, MY CHILDREN! RAO HAS RETURNED!
WHY'D YOU LEAVE?
YOU HEALED MY SISTER, BUT SHE'S SICK AGAIN!
BLESS ME, RAO! I DON'T WANNA HURT ANYMORE!
ALL THAT MATTERS IS THAT I AM HERE.
AND YES, I WILL BLESS YOU ALL. I WILL MAKE YOU WHOLE.
THEY'RE AS STRONG AS YOU NOW, SUPERMAN!
THE RAOS...
...I HAVE TO END THIS!

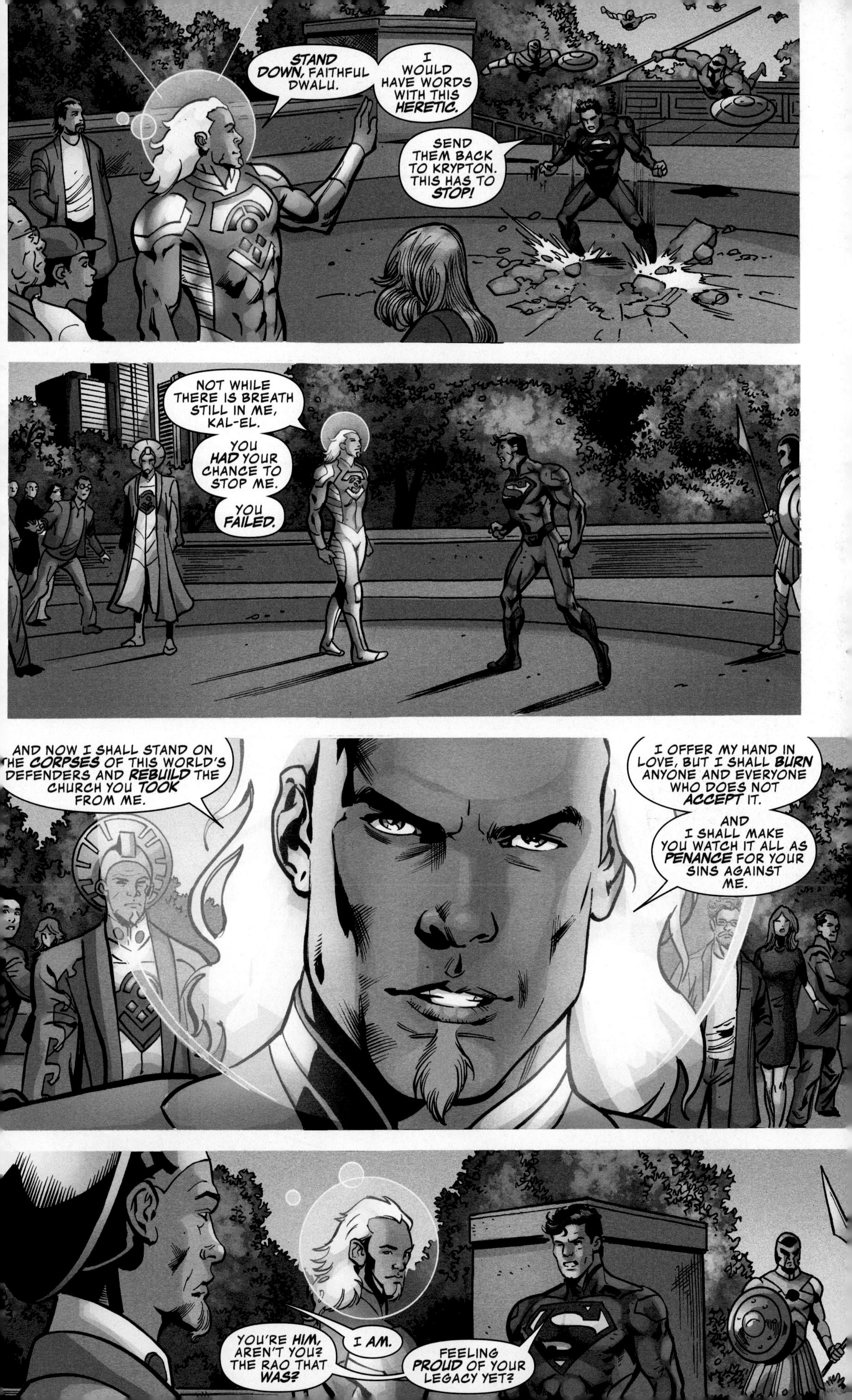
STAND DOWN, FAITHFUL DWALU.
I WOULD HAVE WORDS WITH THIS HERETIC.
SEND THEM BACK TO KRYPTON. THIS HAS TO STOP!
NOT WHILE THERE IS BREATH STILL IN ME, KAL-EL.
YOU HAD YOUR CHANCE TO STOP ME.
YOU FAILED.
AND NOW I SHALL STAND ON THE CORPSES OF THIS WORLD'S DEFENDERS AND REBUILD THE CHURCH YOU TOOK FROM ME.
I OFFER MY HAND IN LOVE, BUT I SHALL BURN ANYONE AND EVERYONE WHO DOES NOT ACCEPT IT.
AND I SHALL MAKE YOU WATCH IT ALL AS PENANCE FOR YOUR SINS AGAINST ME.
YOU'RE HIM, AREN'T YOU? THE RAO THAT WAS?
I AM.
FEELING PROUD OF YOUR LEGACY YET?

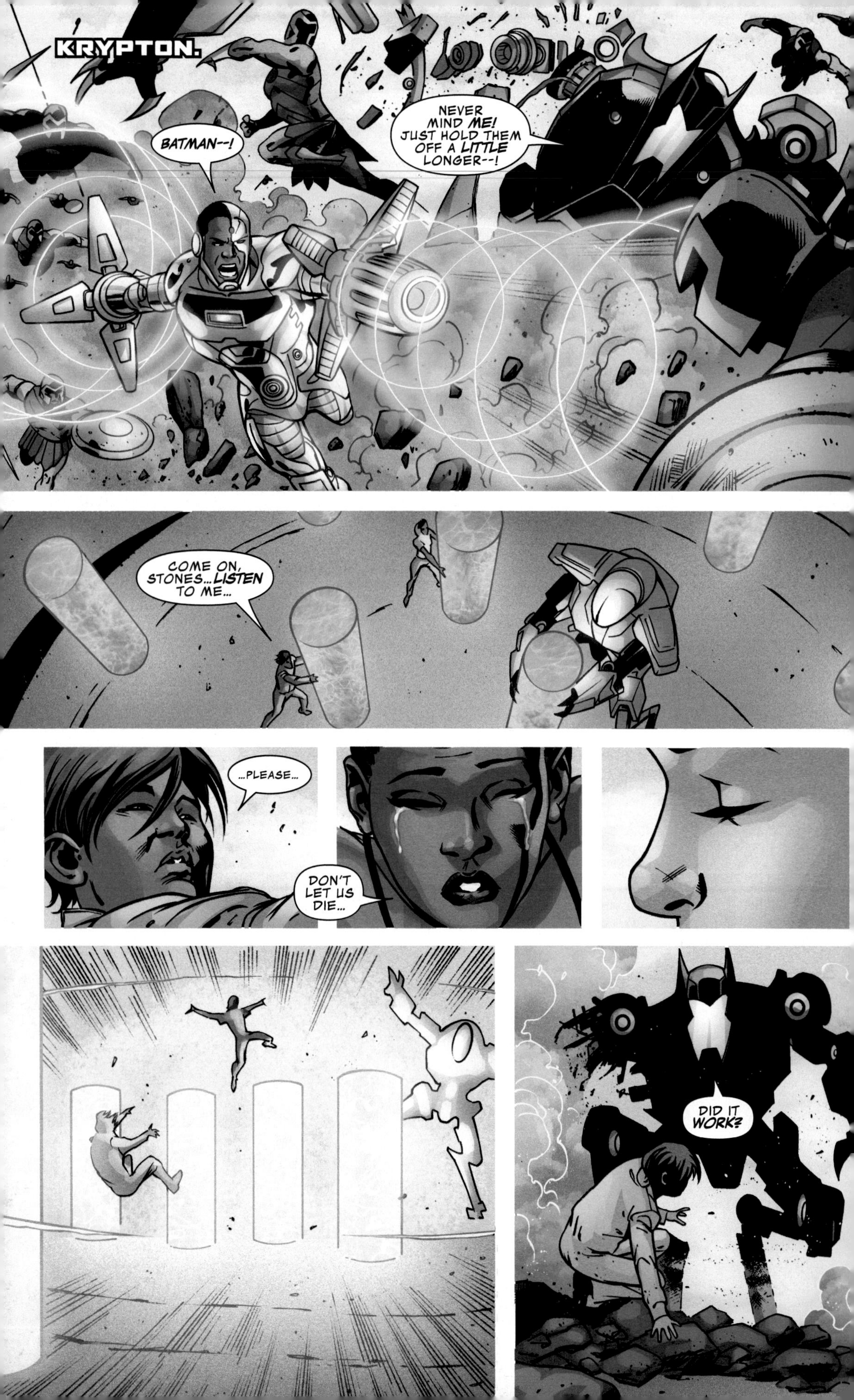
KRYPTON.
BATMAN--!
NEVER MIND ME! JUST HOLD THEM OFF A LITTLE LONGER--!
COME ON, STONES... LISTEN TO ME...
...PLEASE...
DON'T LET US DIE...
DID IT WORK?

SEE FOR YOURSELF.

METROPOLIS.

THE SUN--!

HOW CAN THIS BE?

WHAT'S HAPPENING? WHAT IS THIS?!

FOR YOU, RAO...?

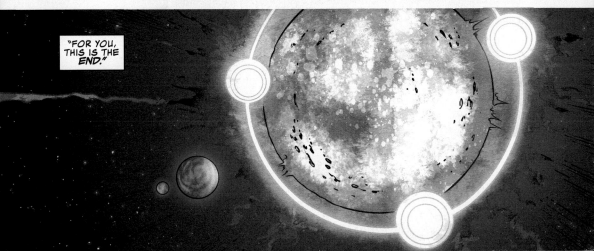

"FOR YOU, THIS IS THE END."

YOUR DAYS OF CONQUEST-- OF *LEECHING* THE LIFE FORCE OF YOUR FOLLOWERS--ARE FINALLY *OVER.*

WHUH--?

SUIT: *BROADCAST* ON ALL JUSTICE LEAGUE *COMM LINKS...*

THIS IS BATMAN. THE INFINITY CORPORATION *COMMANDEERED* THE FUTURE STONES.

AS YOU'VE NO DOUBT *NOTICED,* THEY ACCELERATED SPACE-TIME AROUND THE SUN, *AGING* IT INTO A RED GIANT.

NO! WHAT HAVE YOU *DONE?!*

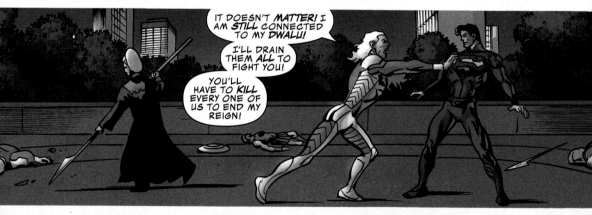

IT DOESN'T *MATTER!* I AM *STILL* CONNECTED TO MY *DWALU!*

I'LL DRAIN THEM *ALL* TO FIGHT YOU!

YOU'LL HAVE TO *KILL* EVERY ONE OF US TO END MY REIGN!

AND I *KNOW* YOU, KAL-EL. YOU JUST DON'T HAVE THAT IN YOU!

THIS WORLD'S *SUN* MADE YOU STRONG, BUT ITS *VALUES* MADE YOU WEAK!

YOU'RE AN *EMBARRASSMENT* TO KRYPTON!

YOU ARE THE *LAST* PERSON WHO COULD EVER TRULY *STOP* ME!

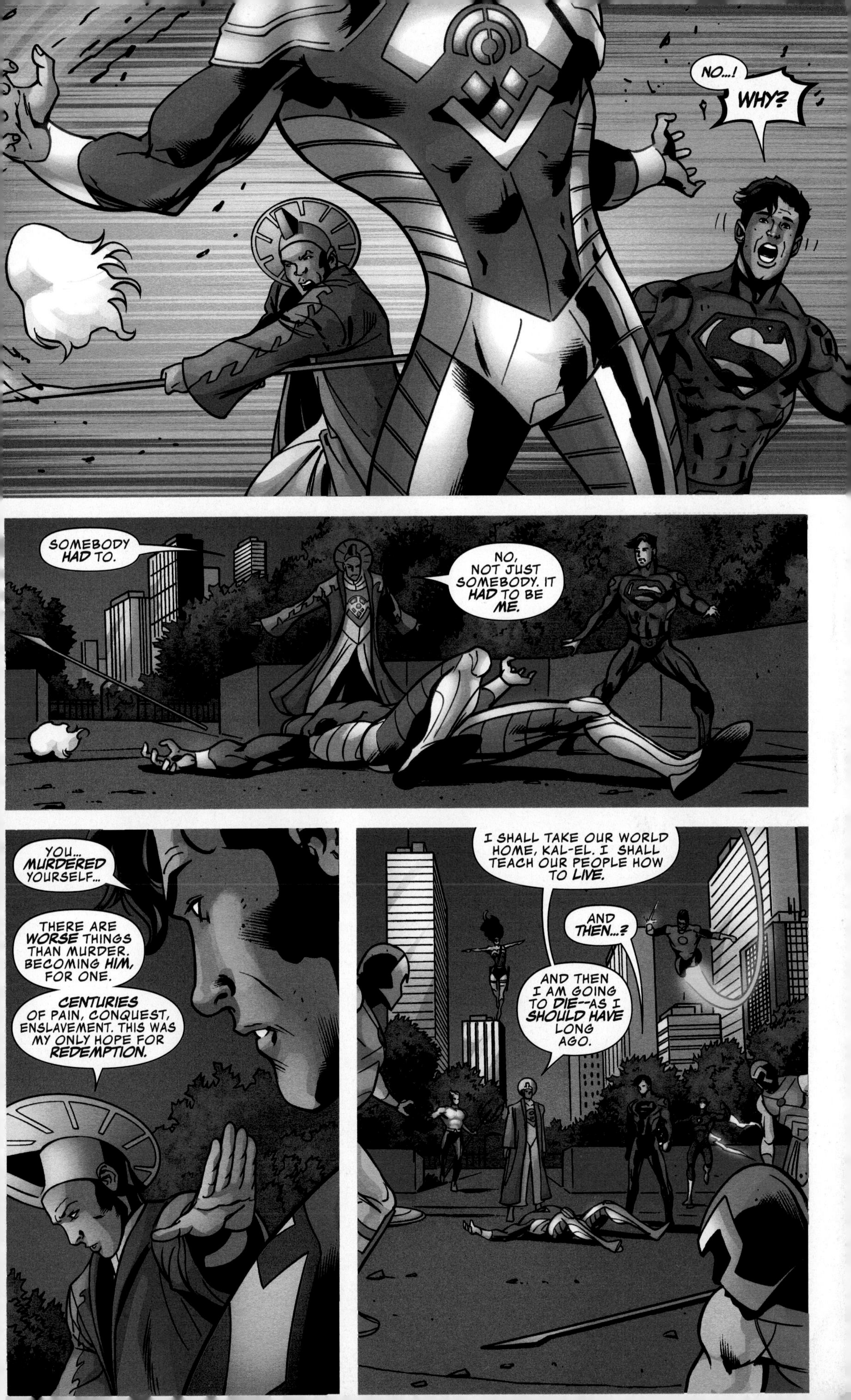

NO...!
WHY?
SOMEBODY HAD TO.
NO, NOT JUST SOMEBODY. IT HAD TO BE ME.
YOU... MURDERED YOURSELF...
THERE ARE WORSE THINGS THAN MURDER. BECOMING HIM, FOR ONE.
CENTURIES OF PAIN, CONQUEST, ENSLAVEMENT. THIS WAS MY ONLY HOPE FOR REDEMPTION.
I SHALL TAKE OUR WORLD HOME, KAL-EL. I SHALL TEACH OUR PEOPLE HOW TO LIVE.
AND THEN...?
AND THEN I AM GOING TO DIE--AS I SHOULD HAVE LONG AGO.

KRYPTON.

SO, VINCENT... WERE YOU *WRONG* ABOUT WHAT THE *FOREVER STONES* SHOWED YOU?

I MEAN, SUPERMAN *DIDN'T* DIE, THE WORLD DIDN'T *END.*

I DON'T KNOW...

I THINK MAYBE THIS WAS THEIR *AGENDA* ALL ALONG-- TO CONNECT WITH THE *LIFE STONES,* THE ONES RAO ALREADY HAD.

THEY'RE *BUILDING* TOWARDS SOMETHING...AND I DON'T KNOW WHAT THAT *IS.*

"SUPERMAN *DID* DIE, THOUGH. WE *ALL* SAW IT.

"BUT WHEN THEY AGED THE SUN, THE STONES SHOWED ME *ANOTHER* FUTURE...

"HE REALLY *IS* GOING TO DIE. BUT THEN COMES *ANOTHER* SUPERMAN...

"...AND SOME SORT OF AWAKENING-- A NEW *CRISIS* IS ON THE WAY."

JLA
JUSTICE LEAGUE OF AMERICA

VARIANT COVER GALLERY

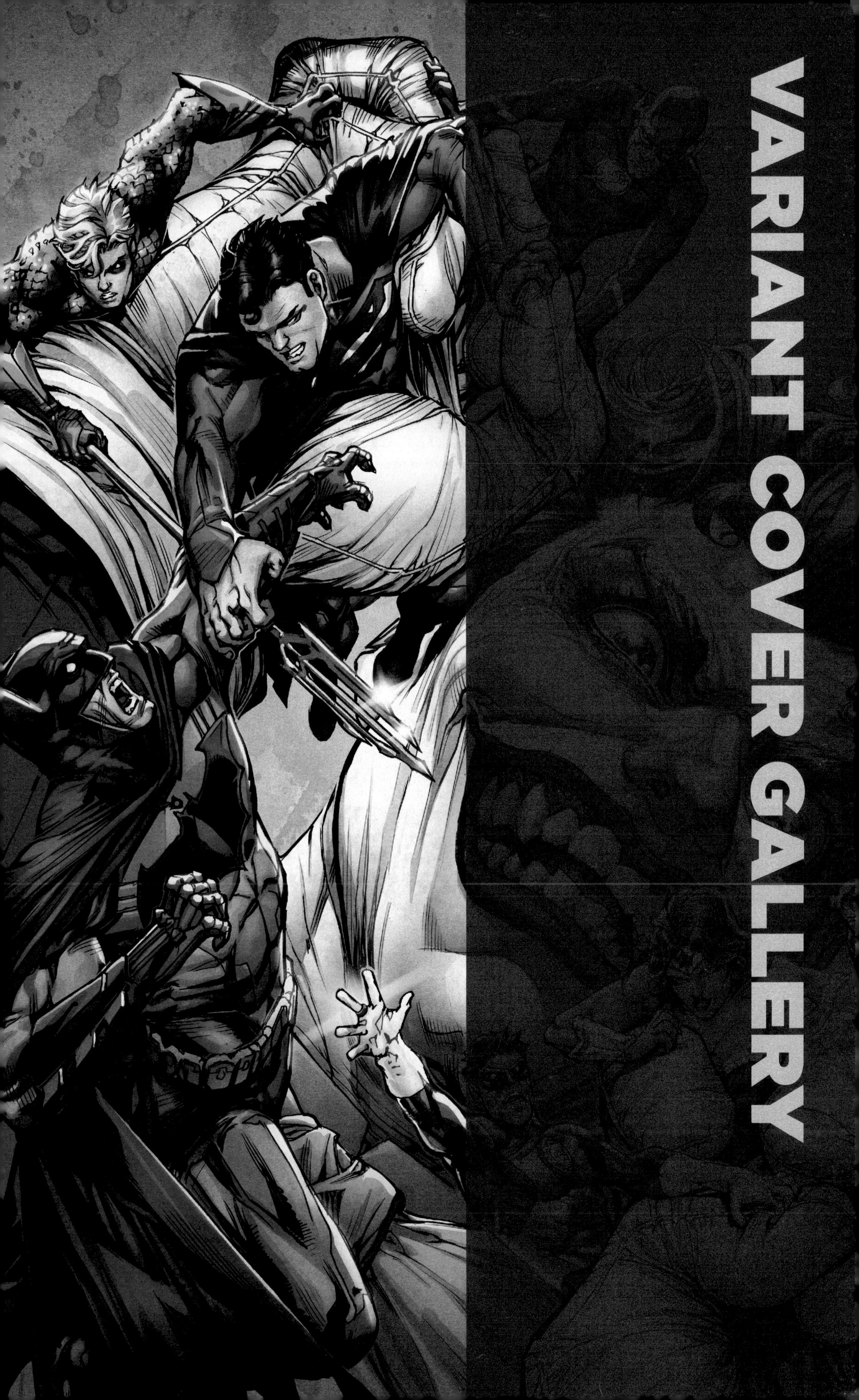

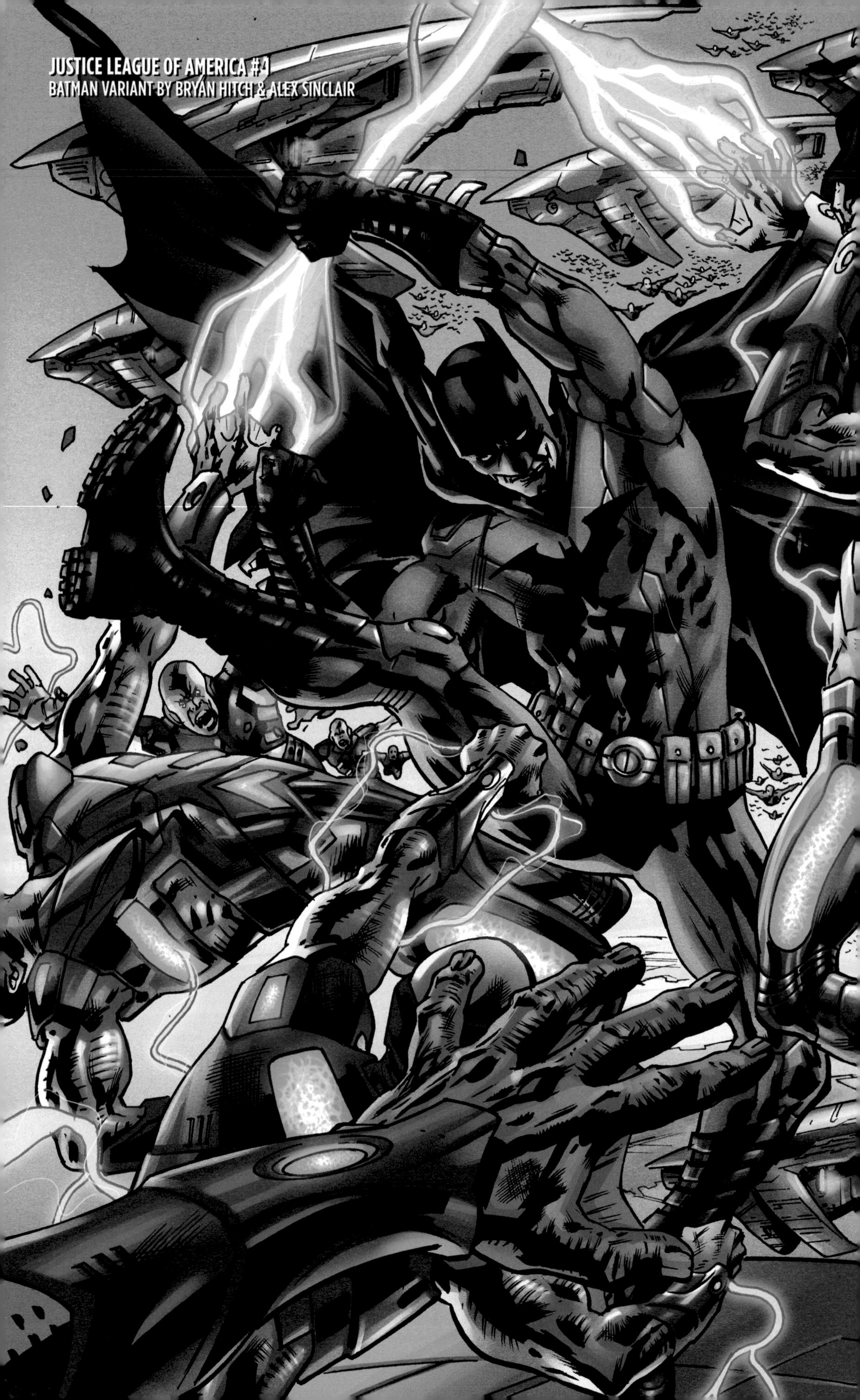

JUSTICE LEAGUE OF AMERICA #4
BATMAN VARIANT BY BRYAN HITCH & ALEX SINCLAIR

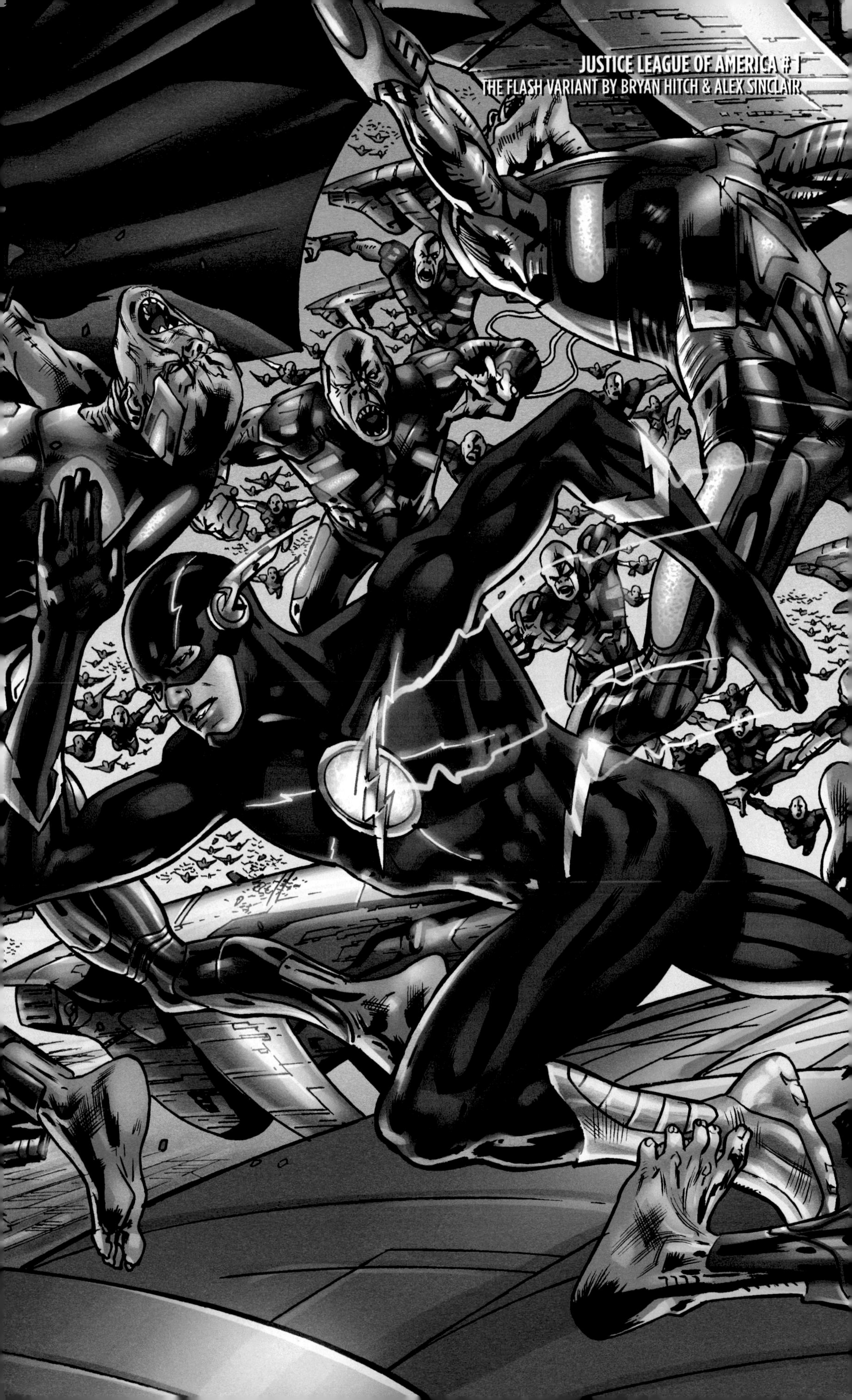

JUSTICE LEAGUE OF AMERICA #1
THE FLASH VARIANT BY BRYAN HITCH & ALEX SINCLAIR

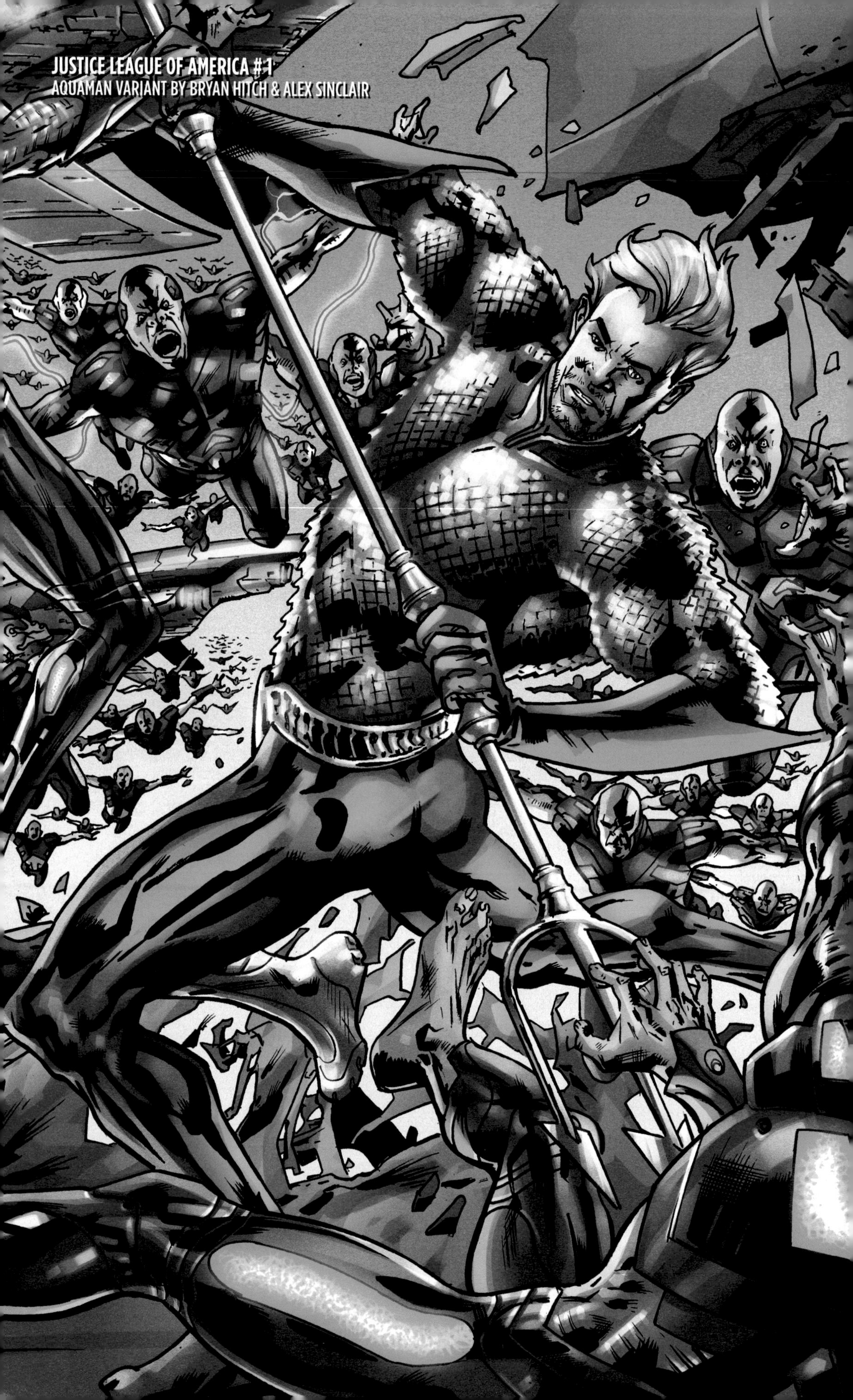
JUSTICE LEAGUE OF AMERICA #1
AQUAMAN VARIANT BY BRYAN HITCH & ALEX SINCLAIR

JUSTICE LEAGUE OF AMERICA # 1
SUPERMAN VARIANT BY BRYAN HITCH & ALEX SINCLAIR

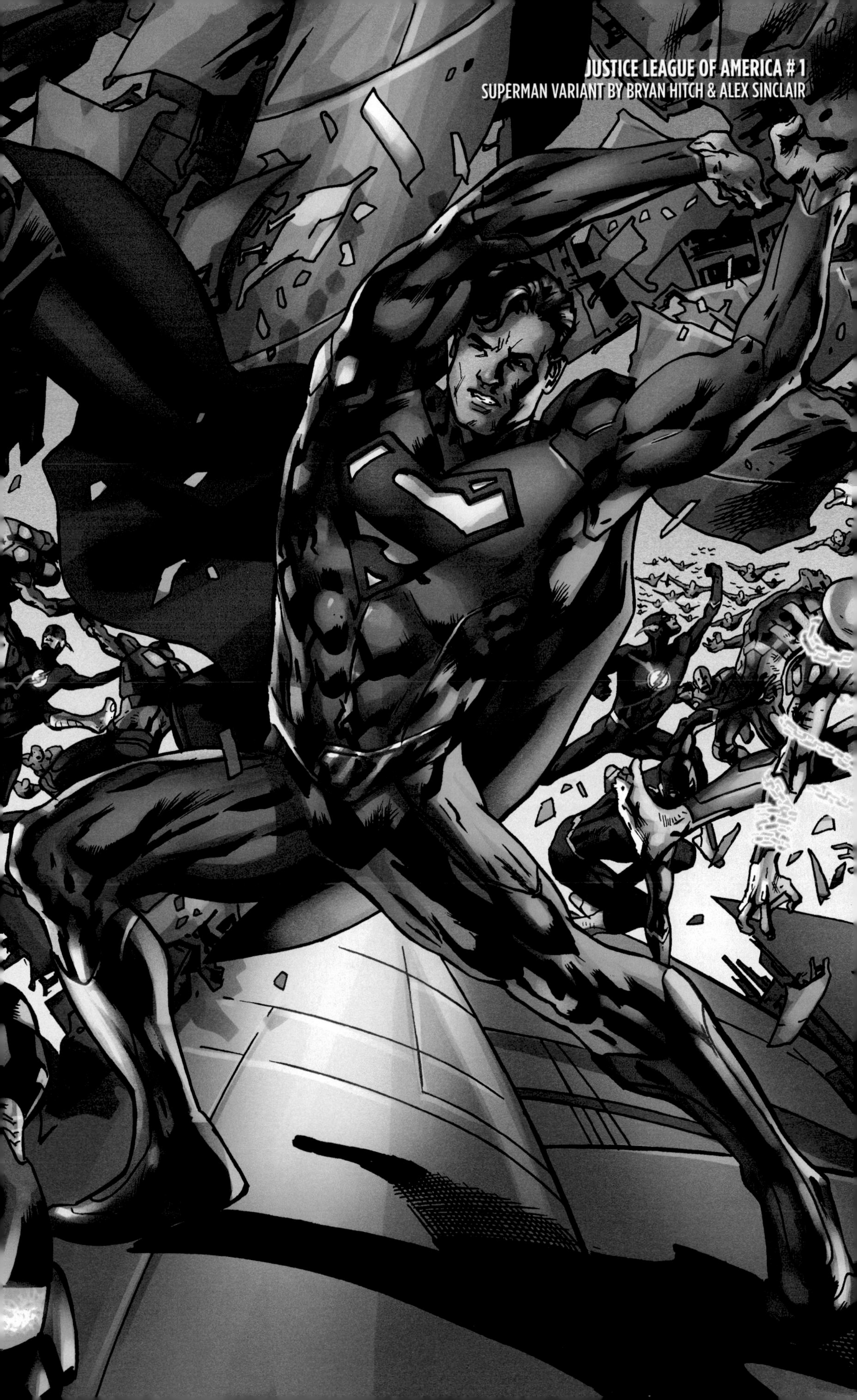

JUSTICE LEAGUE OF AMERICA # 1

GREEN LANTERN VARIANT BY BRYAN HITCH & ALEX SINCLAIR

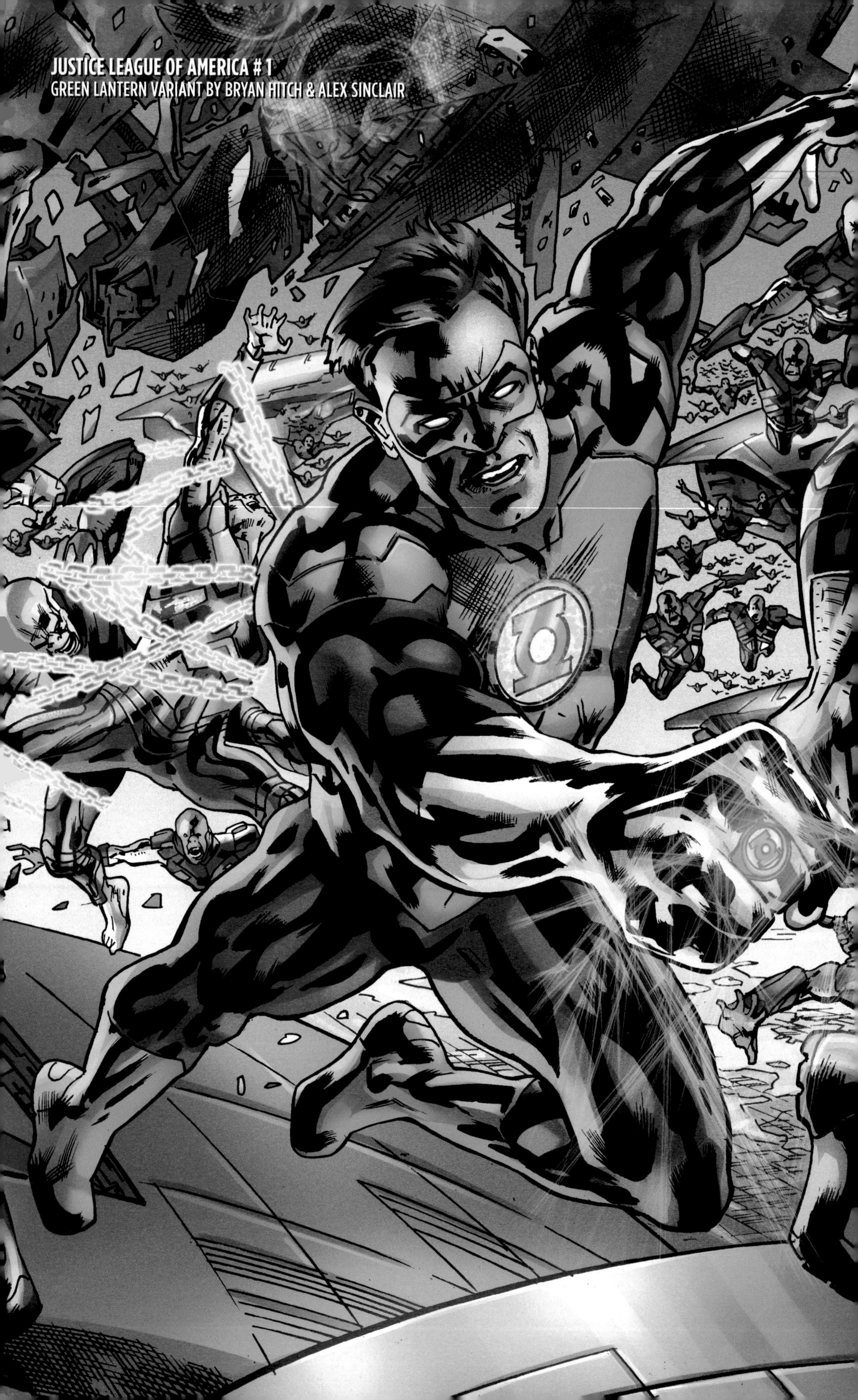

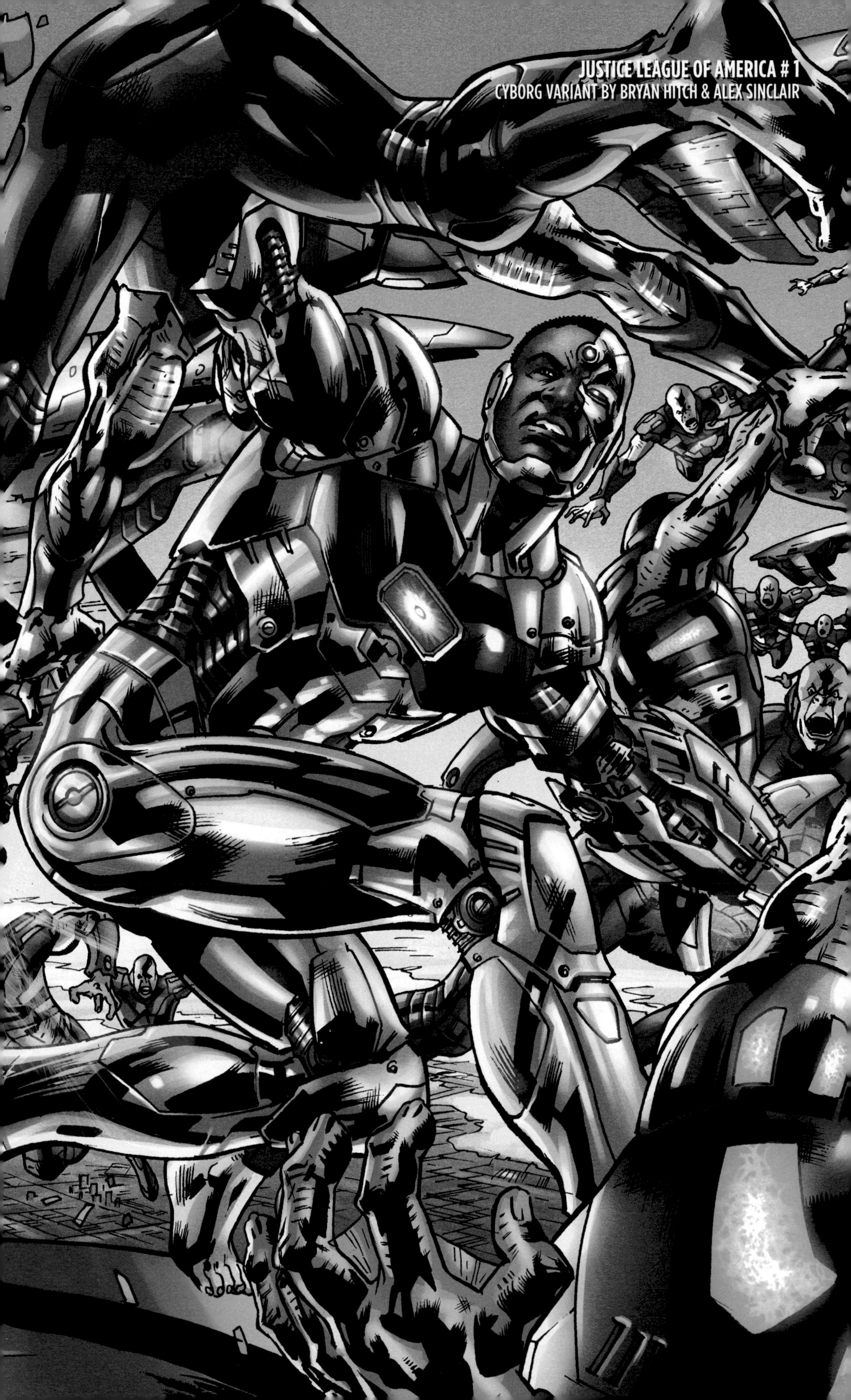

JUSTICE LEAGUE OF AMERICA # 1
CYBORG VARIANT BY BRYAN HITCH & ALEX SINCLAIR

JUSTICE LEAGUE OF AMERICA # 1
WONDER WOMAN VARIANT BY BRYAN HITCH & ALEX SINCLAIR

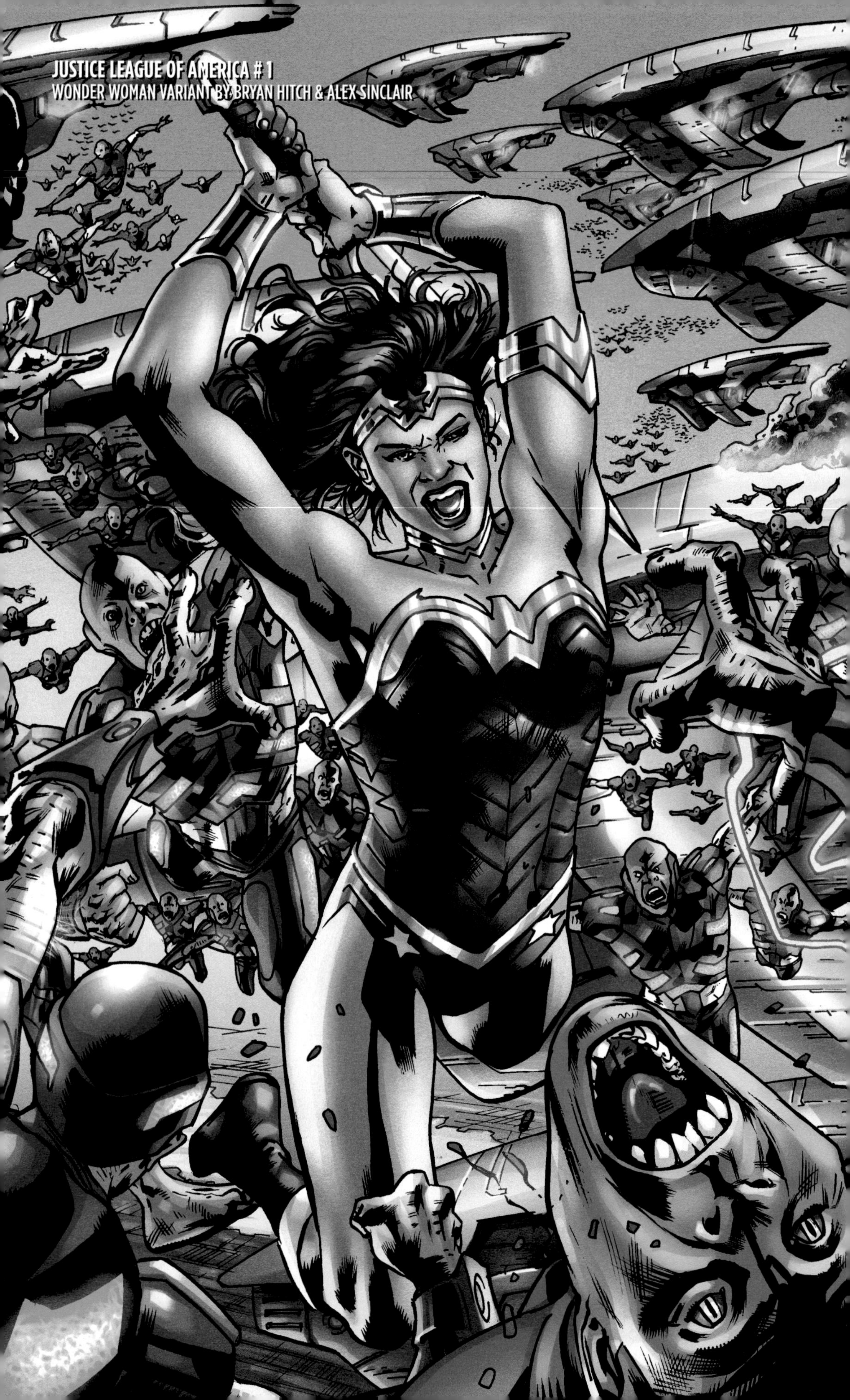

JUSTICE LEAGUE OF AMERICA #1
JOKER 75TH ANNIVERSARY VARIANT BY HOWARD PORTER & HI-FI

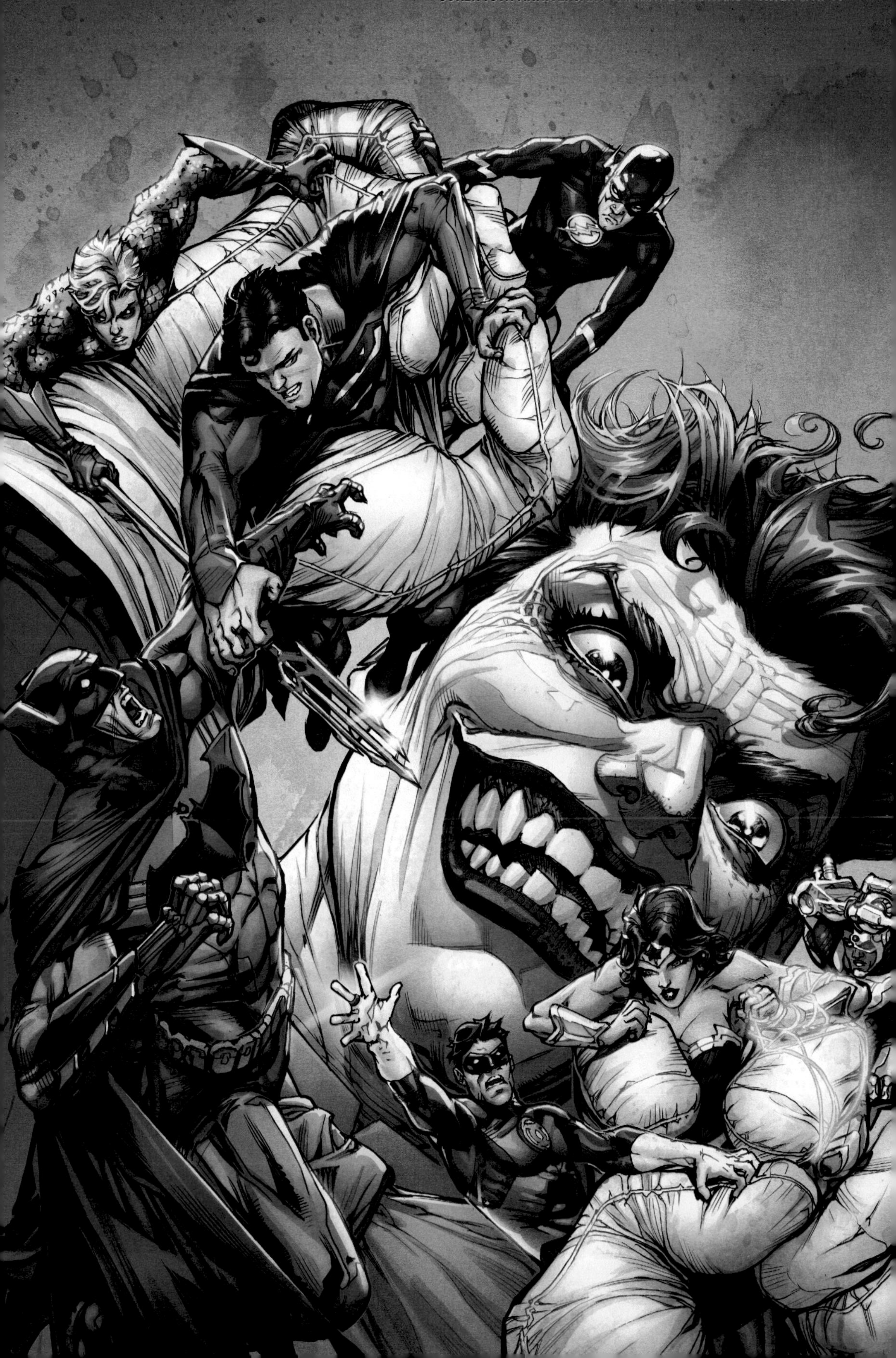

JUSTICE LEAGUE OF AMERICA #2
TEEN TITANS GO! VARIANT COVER BY CRAIG ROUSSEAU

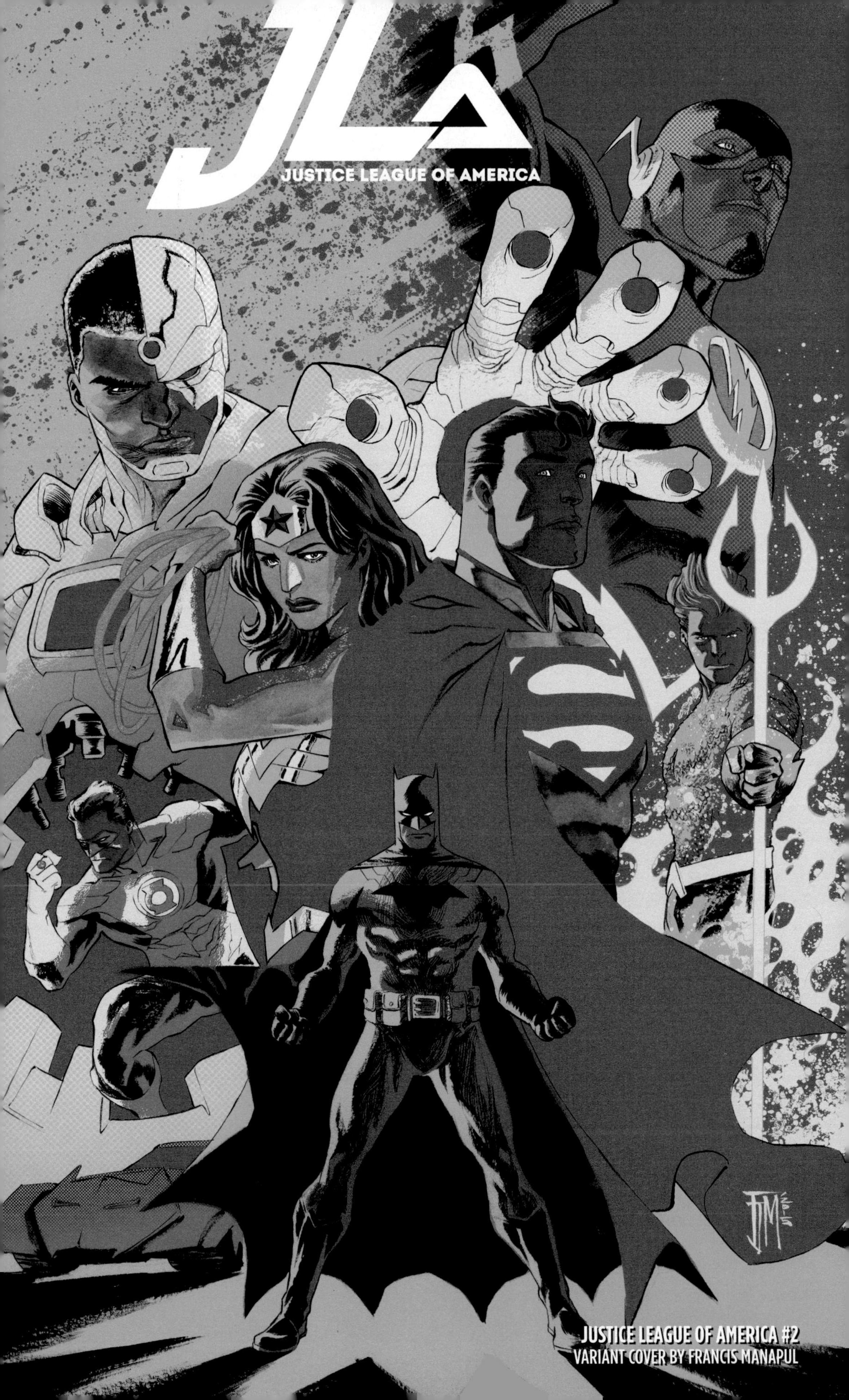
JLA
JUSTICE LEAGUE OF AMERICA

JUSTICE LEAGUE OF AMERICA #2
VARIANT COVER BY FRANCIS MANAPUL

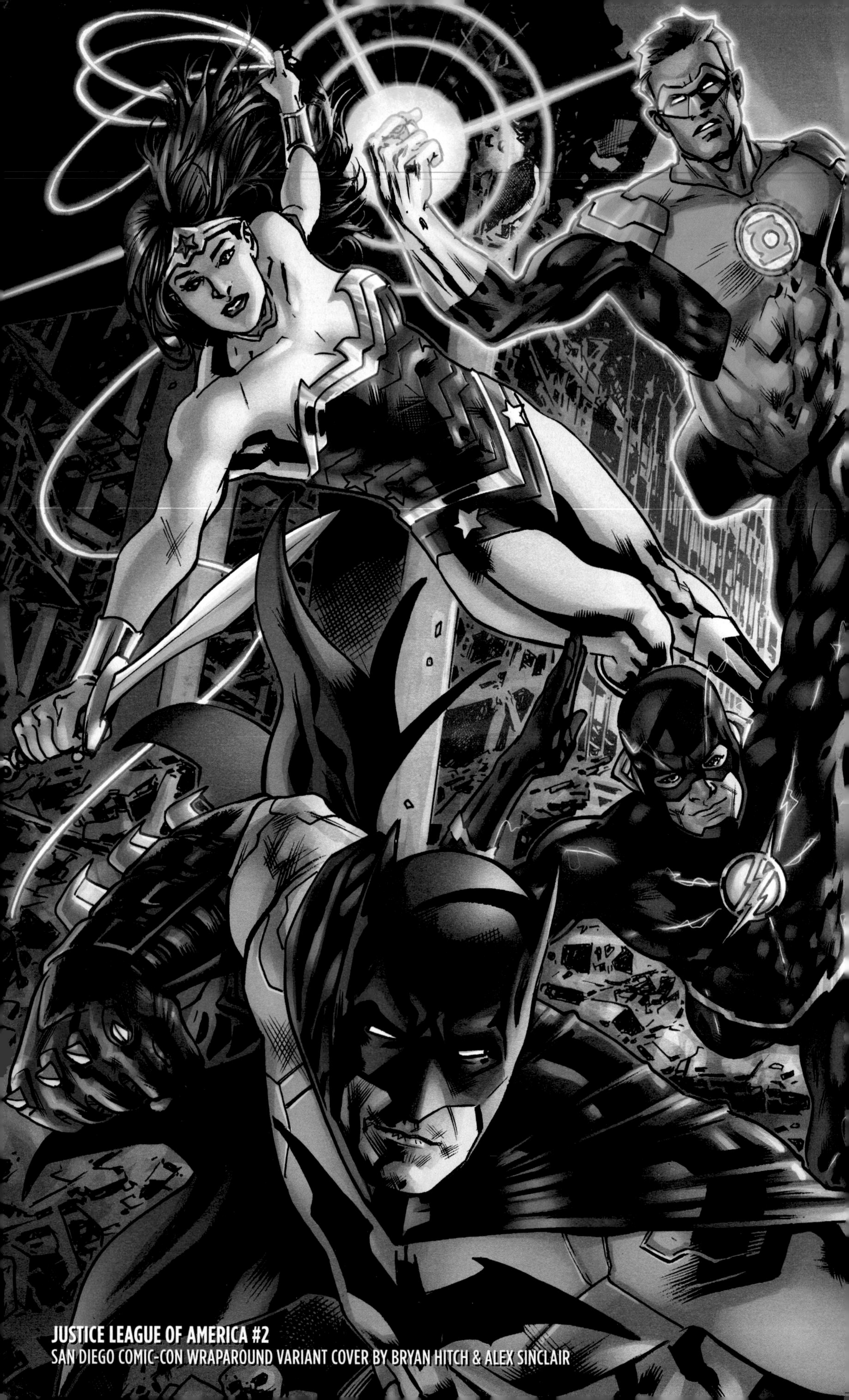

JUSTICE LEAGUE OF AMERICA #2
SAN DIEGO COMIC-CON WRAPAROUND VARIANT COVER BY BRYAN HITCH & ALEX SINCLAIR

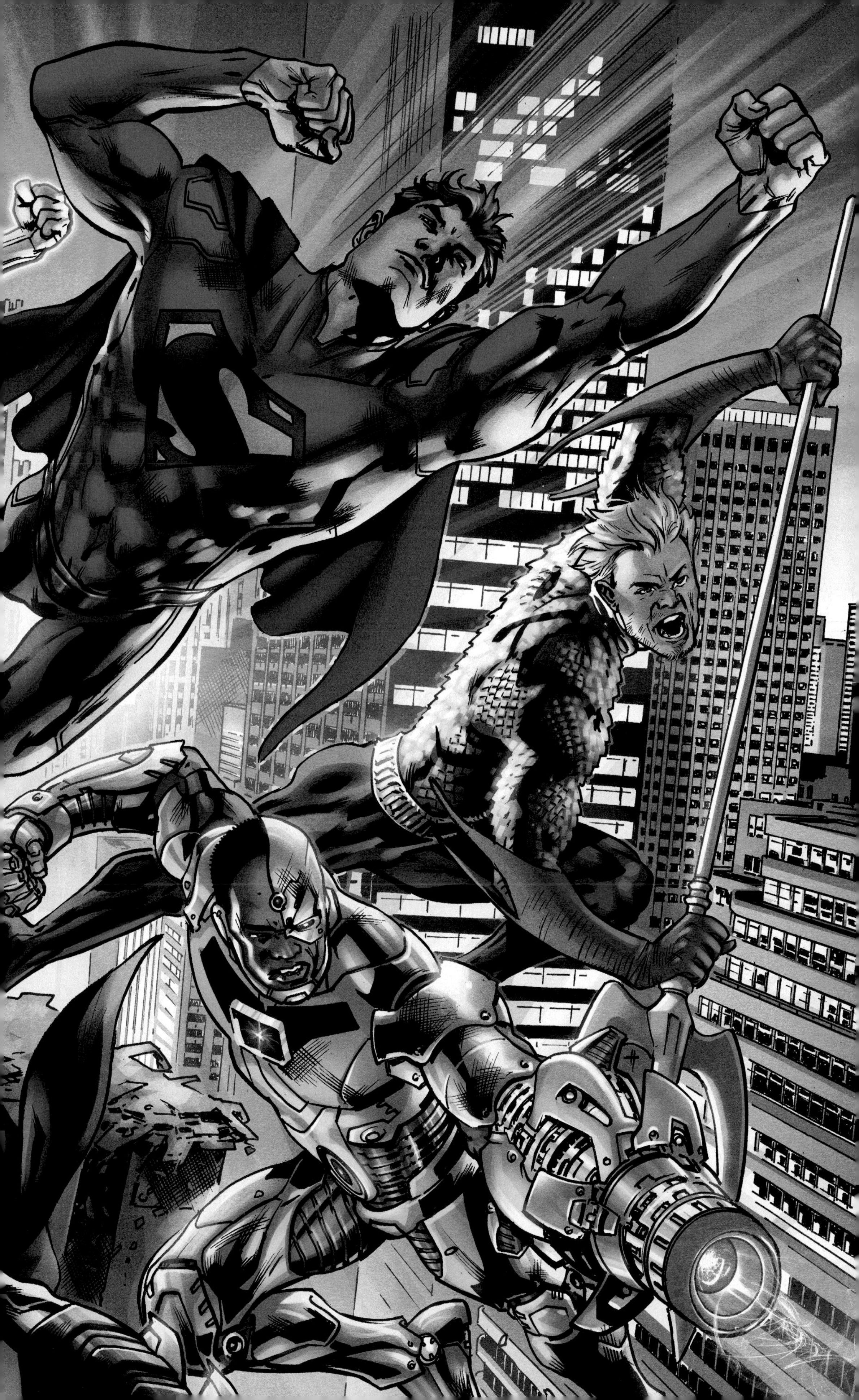

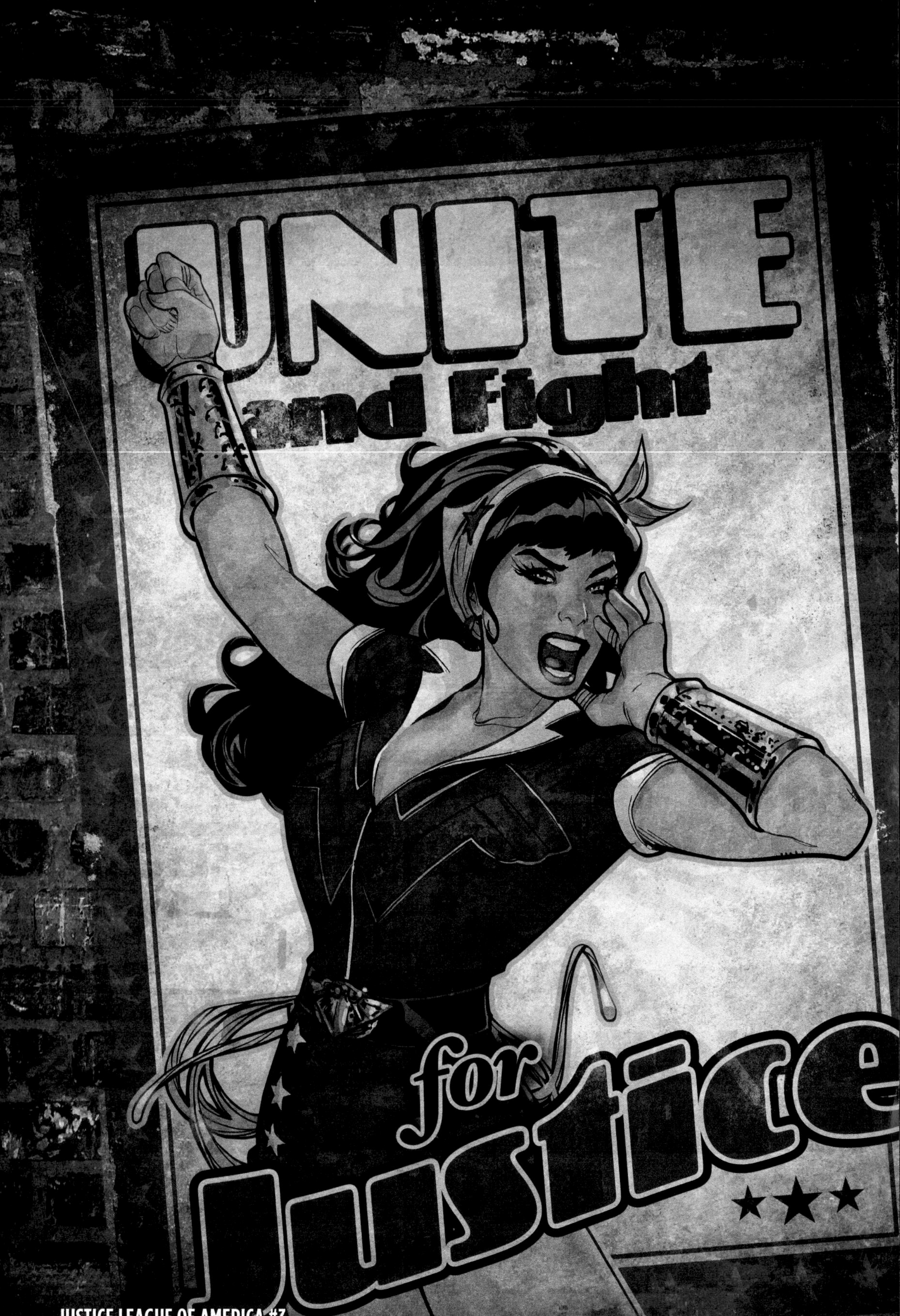
UNITE
and Fight
for
Justice

JUSTICE LEAGUE OF AMERICA #3
DC BOMBSHELLS VARIANT COVER BY TERRY & RACHEL DODSON

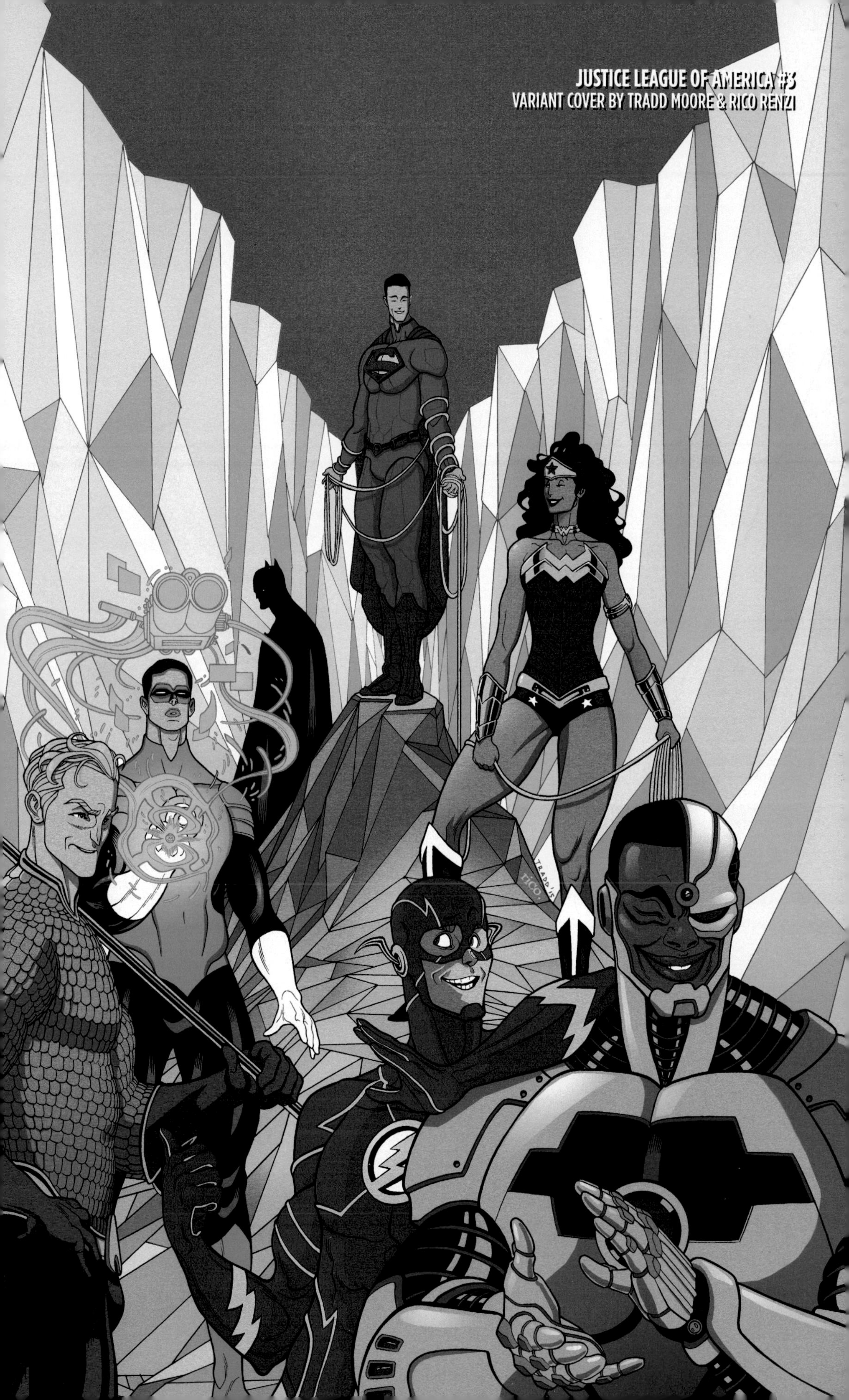

JUSTICE LEAGUE OF AMERICA #3
VARIANT COVER BY TRADD MOORE & RICO RENZI

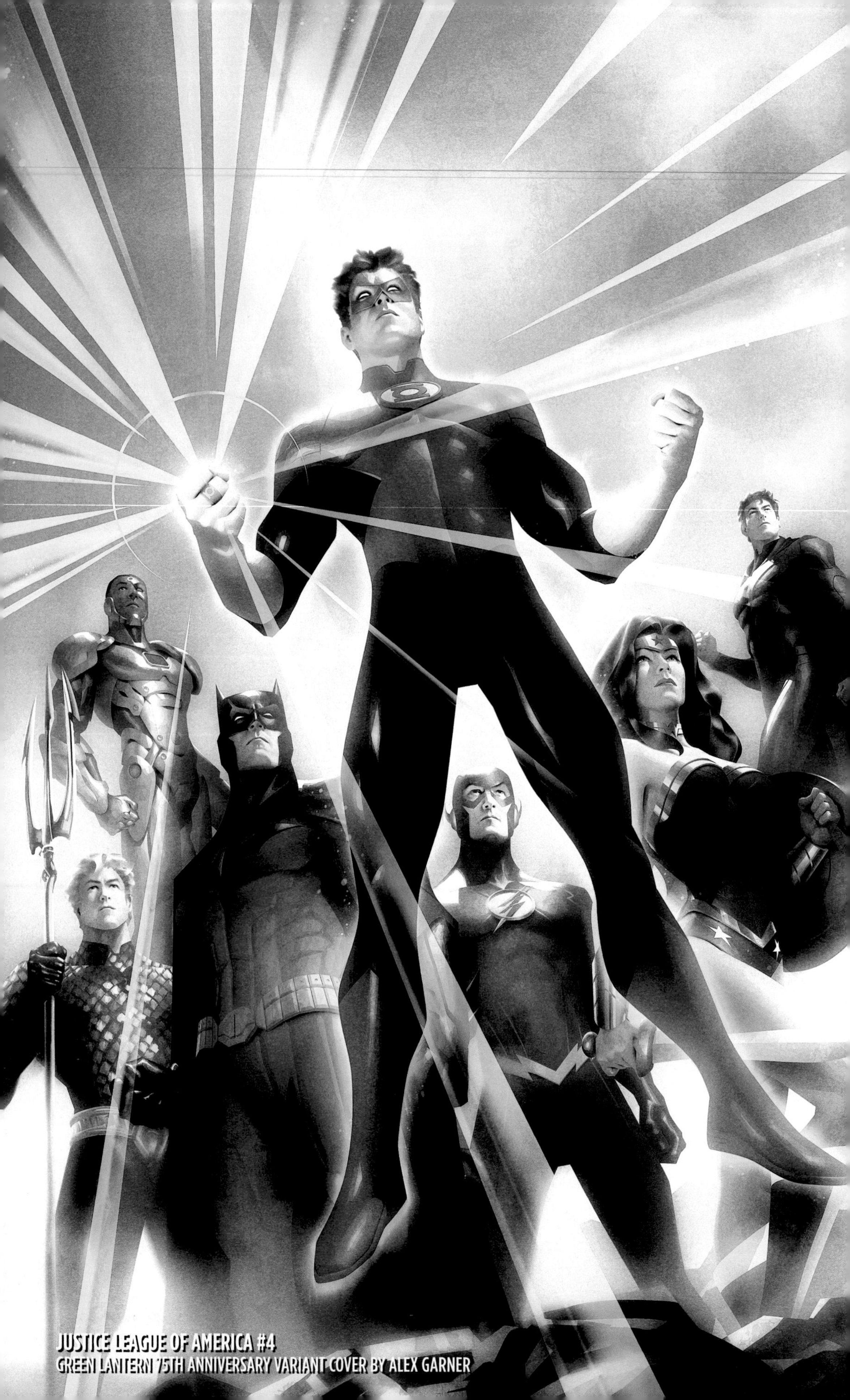

JUSTICE LEAGUE OF AMERICA #4
GREEN LANTERN 75TH ANNIVERSARY VARIANT COVER BY ALEX GARNER

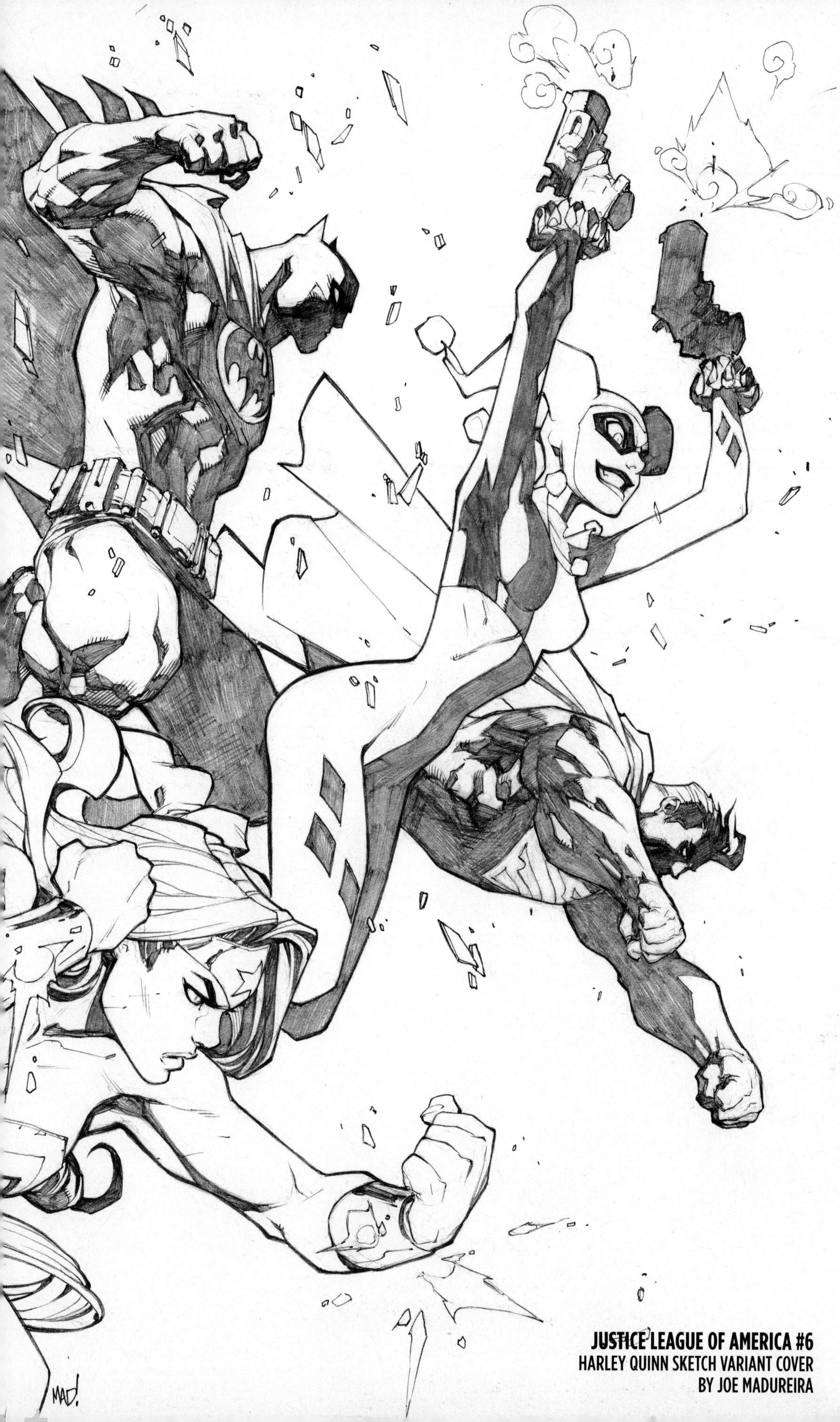

JUSTICE LEAGUE OF AMERICA #6
HARLEY QUINN SKETCH VARIANT COVER
BY JOE MADUREIRA

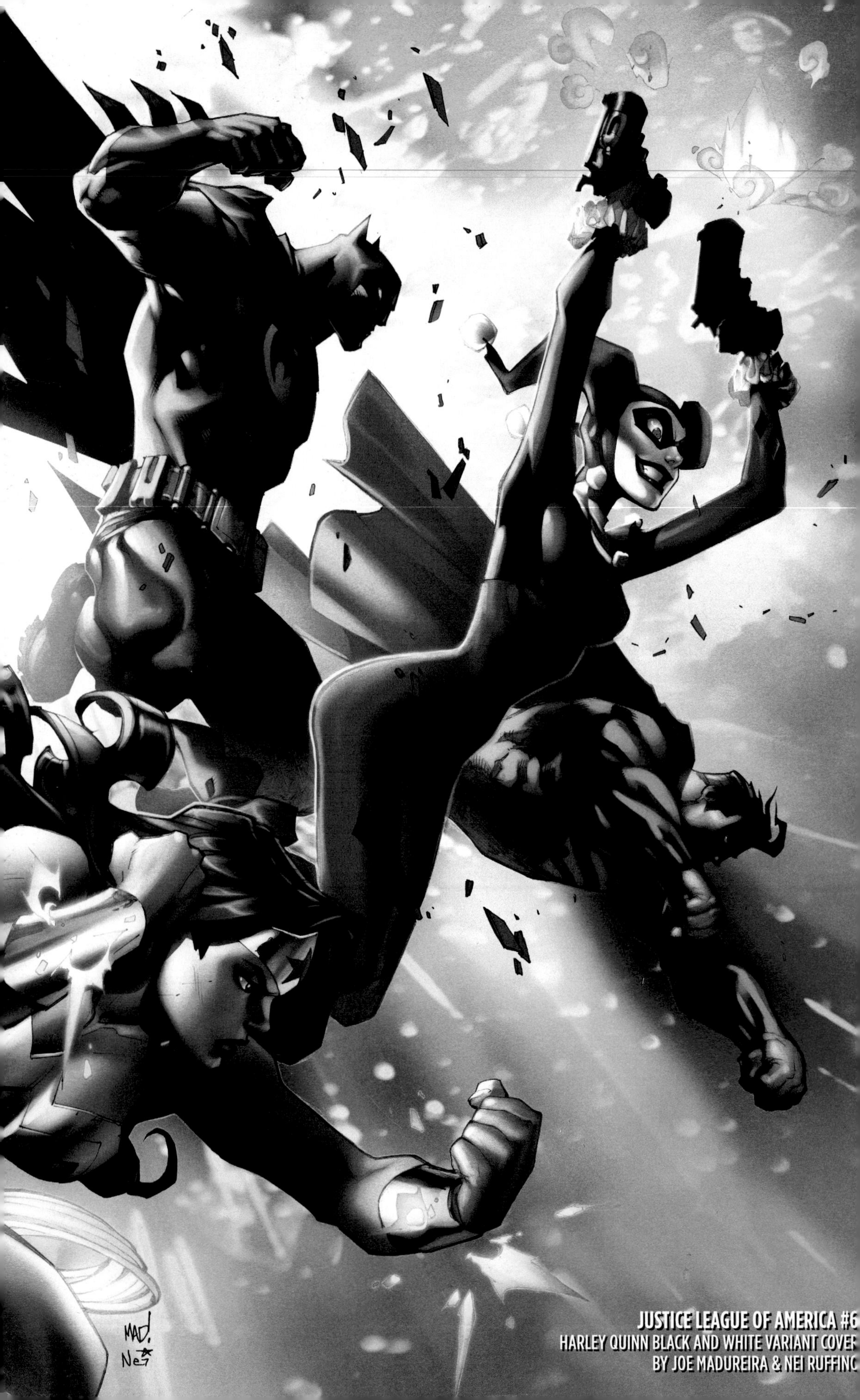

JUSTICE LEAGUE OF AMERICA #6
HARLEY QUINN BLACK AND WHITE VARIANT COVER
BY JOE MADUREIRA & NEI RUFFINO

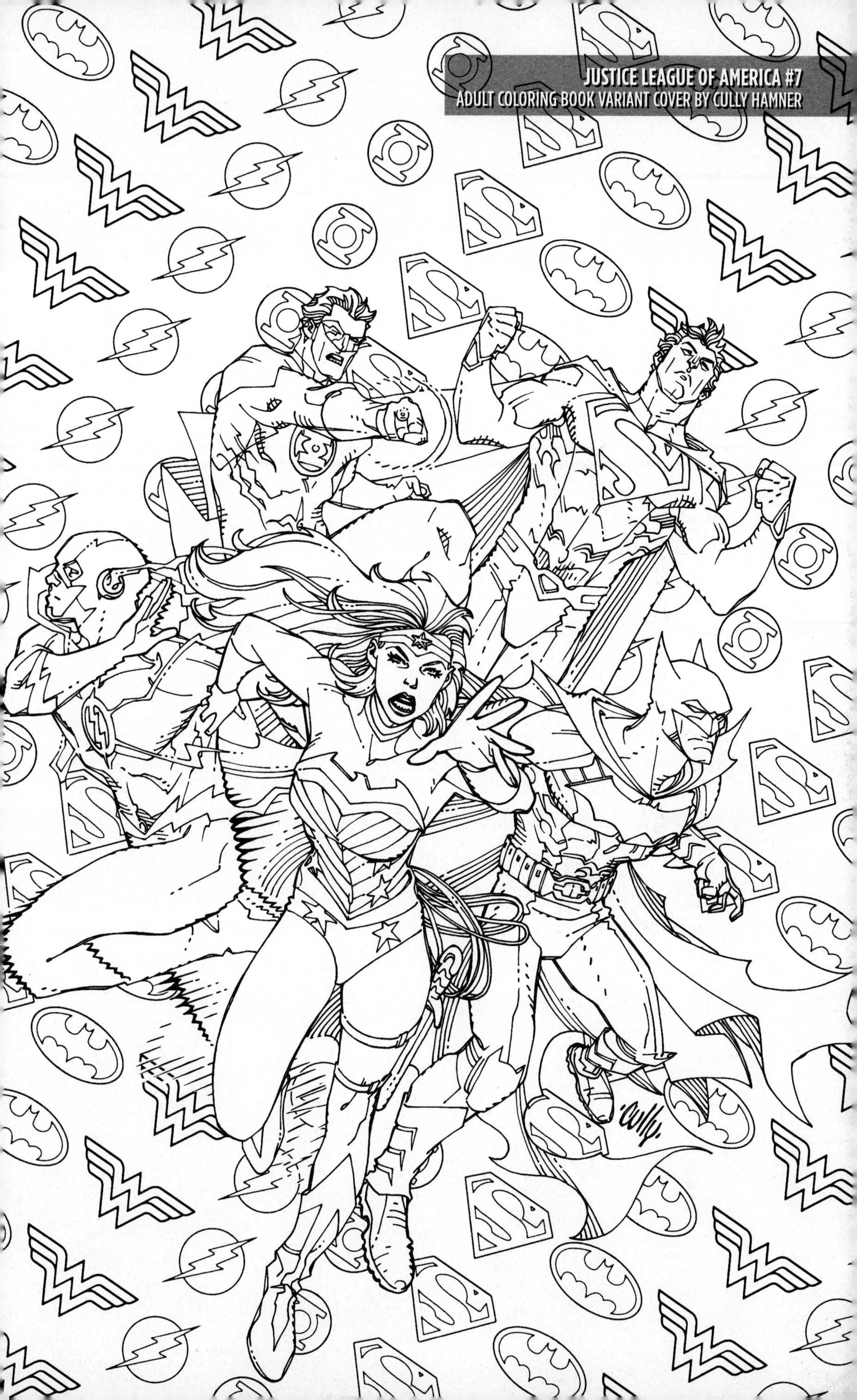

JUSTICE LEAGUE OF AMERICA #7
ADULT COLORING BOOK VARIANT COVER BY CULLY HAMNER

JUSTICE LEAGUE OF AMERICA #8
VARIANT COVER BY NEAL ADAMS, BILL SIENKIEWICZ & ALEX SINCLAIR

JUSTICE LEAGUE OF AMERICA #9
BATMAN V SUPERMAN VARIANT COVER BY JIM LEE & ALEX SINCLAIR

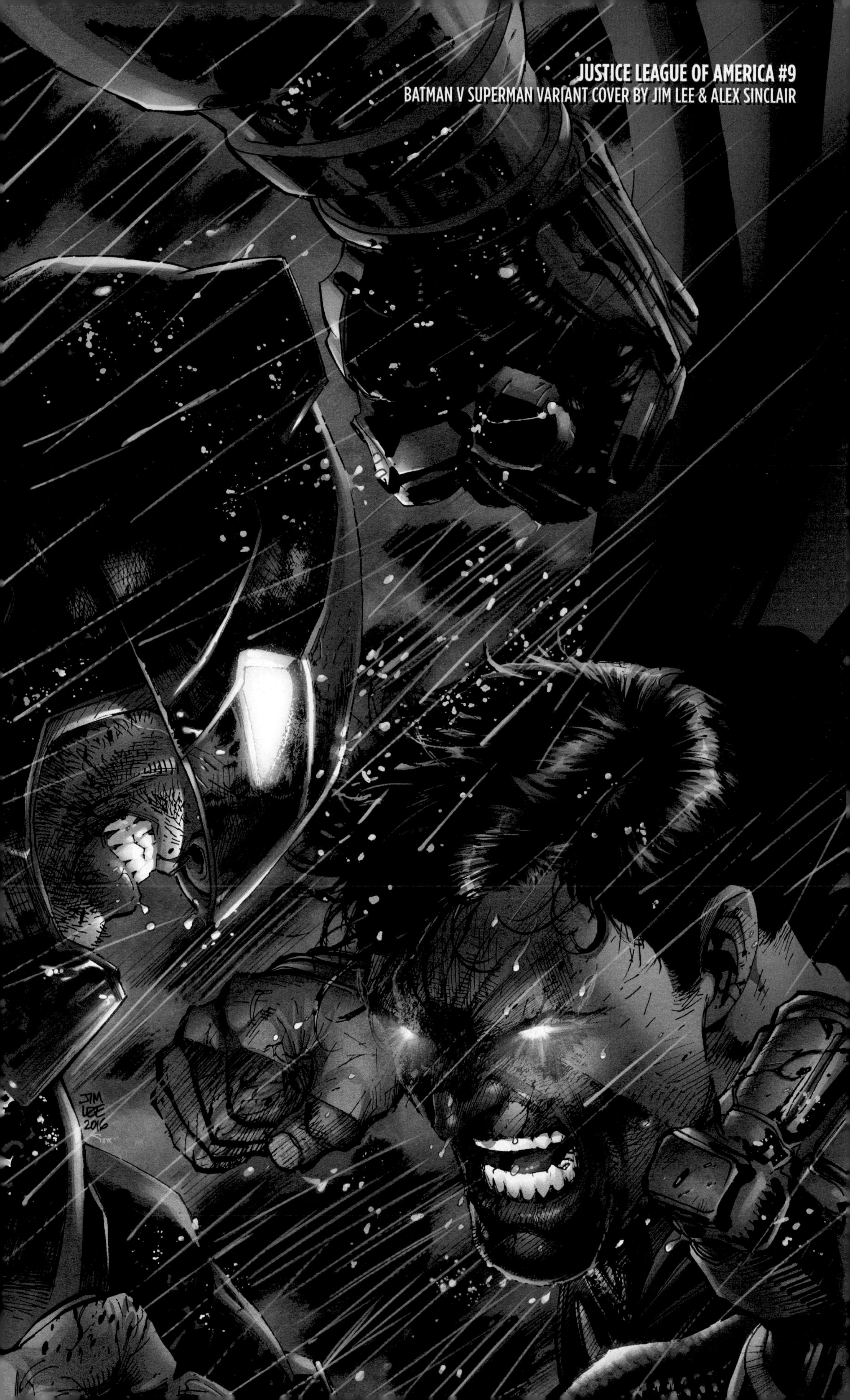
JIM LEE 2016

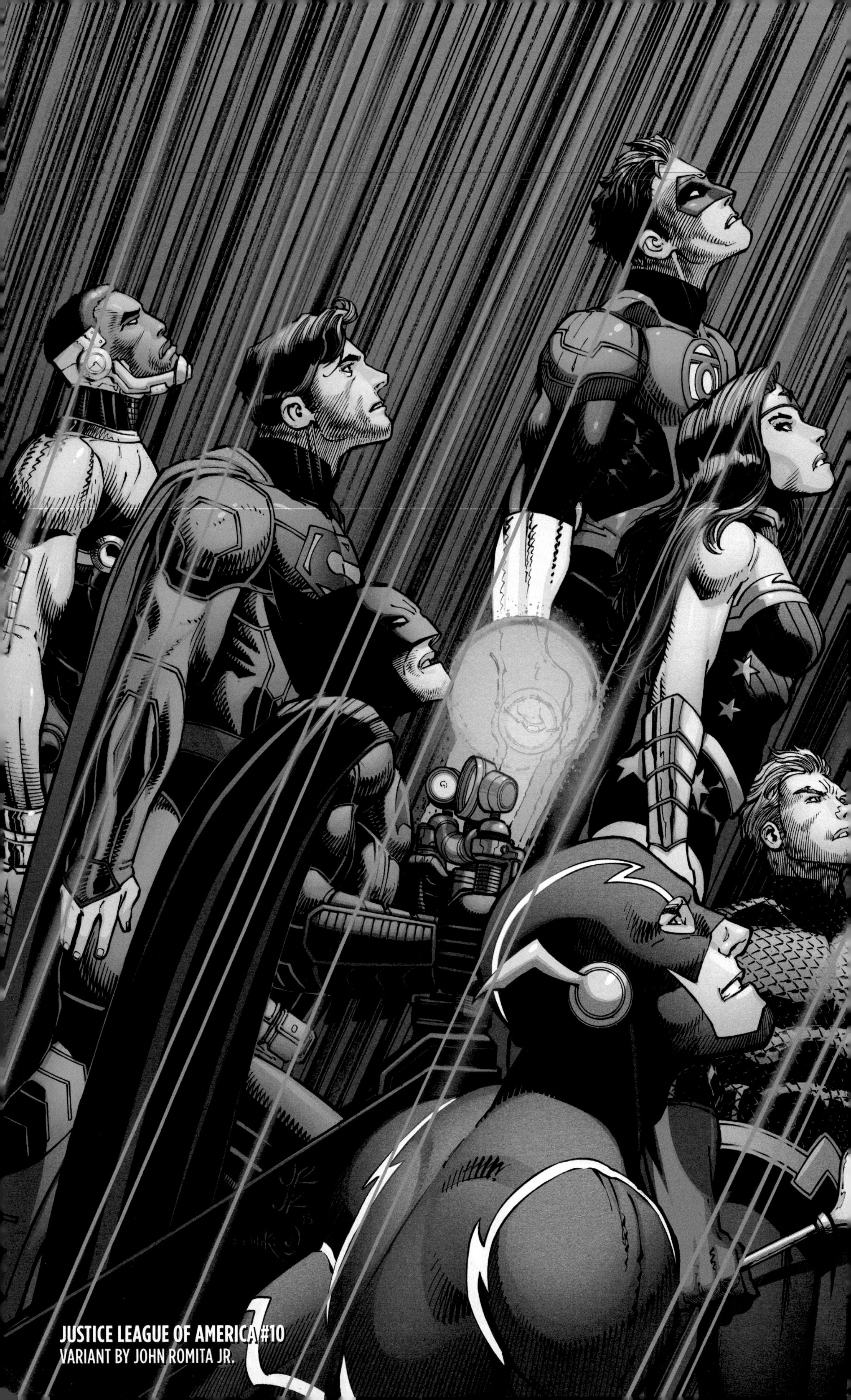

JUSTICE LEAGUE OF AMERICA #10
VARIANT BY JOHN ROMITA JR.

"Some really thrilling artwork that establishes incredible scope and danger."
—IGN

DC UNIVERSE REBIRTH
JUSTICE LEAGUE
VOL. 1: The Extinction Machines
BRYAN HITCH
with TONY S. DANIEL

VOL.1 THE EXTINCTION MACHINES
BRYAN HITCH • TONY S. DANIEL • SANDU FLOREA • TOMEU MOREY

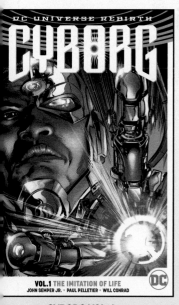

VOL.1 THE IMITATION OF LIFE
JOHN SEMPER JR. • PAUL PELLETIER • WILL CONRAD

CYBORG VOL. 1:
THE IMITATION OF LIFE

VOL.1 RAGE PLANET
SAM HUMPHRIES • ROBSON ROCHA • ETHAN VAN SCIVER • ED BENES

GREEN LANTERNS VOL. 1:
RAGE PLANET

VOL.1 THE DROWNING
DAN ABNETT • PHILIPPE BRIONES • SCOT EATON • BRAD WALKER

AQUAMAN VOL. 1:
THE DROWNING

THE NEW YORK TIMES BESTSELLER

DC THE NEW 52!

JUSTICE LEAGUE

VOLUME 1 ORIGIN

"WRITTEN BY GEOFF JOHNS, WITH ART BY THE GODLY JIM LEE, JUSTICE LEAGUE IS A MUST READ."
— COMPLEX MAGAZINE

GEOFF **JOHNS** JIM **LEE** SCOTT **WILLIAMS**

"Welcoming to new fans looking to get into superhero comics for the first time and old fans who gave up on the funny-books long ago."
– SCRIPPS HOWARD NEWS SERVICE

JUSTICE LEAGUE

VOL. 1: ORIGIN
GEOFF JOHNS
and JIM LEE

JUSTICE LEAGUE
VOL. 2: THE VILLAIN'S JOURNEY

JUSTICE LEAGUE
VOL. 3: THRONE OF ATLANTIS

READ THE ENTIRE EPI

JUSTICE LEAGUE VOL
THE G

JUSTICE LEAGUE VOL
FOREVER HERO

JUSTICE LEAGUE VOL
INJUSTICE LEAG

JUSTICE LEAGUE VOL
DARKSEID WAR PA

JUSTICE LEAGUE VOL
DARKSEID WAR PA

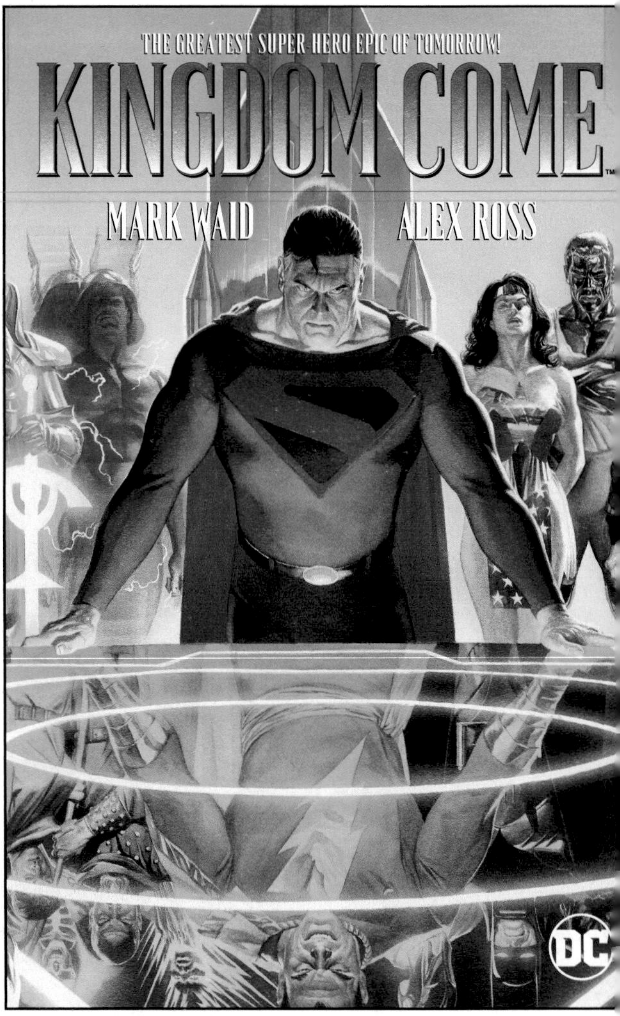
THE GREATEST SUPER HERO EPIC OF TOMORROW!
KINGDOM COME
MARK WAID
ALEX ROSS

"One of the best comic stories ever told."
– WASHINGTON EXAMINER

"Waid's charged dialogue and Ross' stunning visual realism expose the genius, pride, fears and foibles of DC's heroes and villains."
– WASHINGTON POST

MARK WAID
with ALEX ROSS

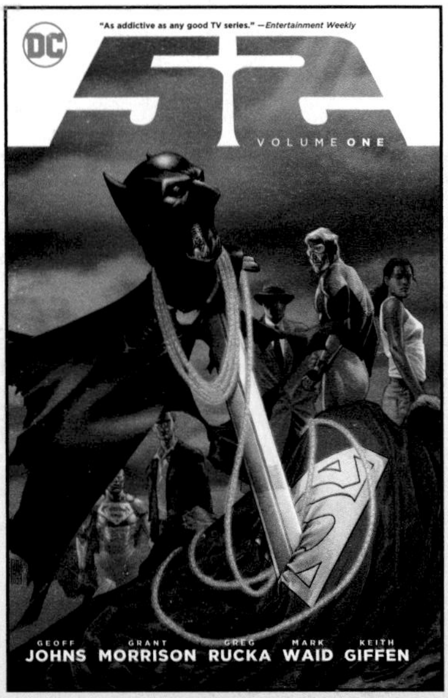
"As addictive as any good TV series." —Entertainment Weekly
52
VOLUME ONE
GEOFF JOHNS GRANT MORRISON GREG RUCKA MARK WAID KEITH GIFFEN

52 Volume One

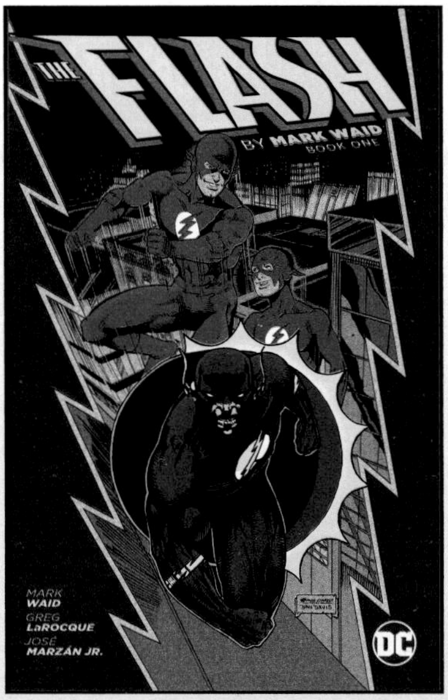
THE FLASH
BY MARK WAID
BOOK ONE
MARK WAID
GREG LaROCQUE
JOSÉ MARZÁN JR.

THE FLASH BY MARK WAID

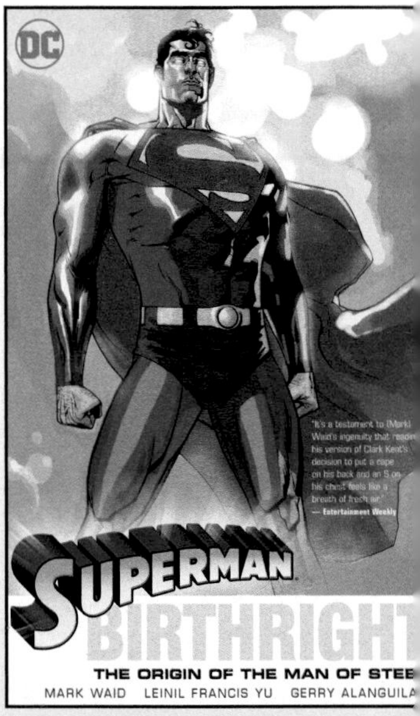
SUPERMAN
BIRTHRIGHT
MARK WAID LEINIL FRANCIS YU

SUPERMAN: BIRTHRIGHT

Get more DC graphic novels wherever comics and books are sold!